INTERNATIONAL ENCYCLOPEDIA of WOMEN and SPORTS

EDITORIAL BOARD

ANNE BOLIN
Elon College, North Carolina

JOAN CHANDLER
University of Texas, Dallas

BARBARA DRINKWATER
Pacific Medical Center, Seattle

JENNIFER HARGREAVES
Roehampton Institute, UK

FAN HONG
DeMontfort University, UK

DARLENE KLUKA
Grambling State University, Louisiana

DAVID LEVINSON
Berkshire Reference Works

VICTORIA PARASCHAK
University of Windsor, Canada

ROBERTA J. PARK
University of California, Berkeley

CHRISTINE SHELTON
Smith College, Massachusetts

MARJORIE SNYDER
Women's Sports Foundation (USA)

PATRICIA VERTINSKY
University of British Columbia

ANITA WHITE
International Working Group on Women & Sport, UK

WAYNE WILSON
Amateur Athletic Foundation, Los Angeles

INTERNATIONAL ENCYCLOPEDIA of WOMEN and SPORTS

VOLUME 3

Edited by

KAREN CHRISTENSEN

ALLEN GUTTMANN

GERTRUD PFISTER

Macmillan Reference USA

an imprint of the Gale Group

New York • Detroit • San Francisco • London • Boston • Woodbridge, CT

AUGUSTANA UNIVERSITY COLLEGE
LIBRARY

Copyright © 2001 by Macmillan Reference USA, an imprint of the Gale Group

All rights reserved. No part of this book may be reproduced in any form or by any means, electronic or mechanical, including photocopying, recording, or by any information storage and retrieval system, without permission in writing from the Publisher.

Macmillan Reference USA
1633 Broadway
New York, NY 10019

The Gale Group
27500 Drake Rd.
Farmington Hills, MI 48331

ISBN 0-02-864954-0 (set)
ISBN 0-02-864951-6 (vol. 1)
ISBN 0-02-864952-4 (vol. 2)
ISBN 0-02-864953-2 (vol. 3)

Printed in the United States of America

1 2 3 4 5 6 7 8 9 10

Library of Congress Cataloging-in-Publication Data

International encyclopedia of women and sports / edited by Karen Christensen, Allen Guttman, Gertrud Pfister.
p. cm.
Includes bibliographical references and index.
1. Sports for women—Encyclopedias. 2. Women athletes—Encyclopedias. I. Christensen, Karen, 1957– II. Guttmann, Allen. III. Pfister, Gertrud, 1945–

GV709.I58 2000
796′.082—dc21 00-062518

S

SABATINI, GABRIELA

(1970–)

ARGENTINEAN TENNIS PLAYER

Although she won only one Grand Slam event and was generally seen by experts as never having lived up to her potential to be the best women's tennis player of the 1990s, Gabriela Sabatini was one the best-known and most popular women of professional tennis in the late 1980s and early 1990s. Her appeal and celebrity status were due to a combination of her ability on the court, her good looks, and her elegant style of play.

Gabriela Sabatini was born on 16 May 1970 in Buenos Aires, Argentina. Buenos Aires is the tennis capital of South America, and when she indicated an interest in the sport, her parents enrolled her in a junior program and then arranged for her to train for a professional career in Boca Raton, Florida. In 1983 she joined the world junior tour of tennis and became the youngest player ever to win the prestigious Orange Bowl Girls 18 singles tournament at the age of thirteen years, seven months, and one week. After winning a total of six junior titles, she was ranked number one on the International Tennis Federation world junior list for 1984. With little left to accomplish at the junior level, she turned professional in January 1985.

Sabatini made a splash on the women's tour her first year when she made the French Open semifinals (the youngest women to have done so at the time) before falling to Chris Evert. She finished the year ranked number eleven after starting the year ranked number seventy-four. Her success continued in 1986 as she entered the top ten and remained there for ten straight years. By this time, many experts were beginning to see her as the future of women's tennis, a status she never achieved. From 1985 to 1995 she stayed near but never reached the top. She appeared in at least one Grand Slam (U.S. Open, French Open, Wimbledon, Australian Open) semifinal each year and won at least one tournament on the tour in each year with the exception of 1993. Some of her highlights were winning the 1990 U.S. Open, being a finalist at Wimbledon in 1991, and winning a total of twenty-seven tournaments in her twelve-year career. Nonetheless, it was Steffi Graf and Monica Seles who became the top women's tennis players of their generation.

Gabriela Sabatini delivers a serve during the 1987 French Open. (TempSport/Corbis)

In 1992 a fiery orange-red rose was named the "Gabriela Sabatini Rose" in her honor, making her the first tennis player to receive such a tribute. After sustaining various injuries in 1996, she announced her retirement at the age of twenty-six. In her career she amassed over $8 million in prize money and earned millions more in endorsements, including being the first women to sign a multimillion dollar contract with Pepsi Cola Corp. in 1991. After her career ended, she remained active in sports and was selected as one of the athlete representatives to the International Olympic Committee (IOC).

Jonathan Cornwell

Bibliography

West, Karen. (1996) "Farewell Gaby." <www.dpo.uab.edu/~yangzw/gaby1.html>. 1996.

SAILBOARDING *see* Windsurfing

SAILING

Sailing as a sport developed from a form of transportation that uses the action of the wind on sails to drive a vessel across the water. Superstition and folklore have long held that to have a woman on board ship is to court disaster. When this attitude is added to the usual arguments against women participating in sports of any type, it is perhaps not surprising that women have faced difficulty gaining acceptance in some branches of the sport, notably among the larger racing yachts. They have nevertheless long participated in sailing.

Sailing is a sport of great contrasts. Officially called "yachting" by the International Olympic Committee (IOC), sailing is one of very few sports in which men and women can and do compete together; yet despite having documented their abilities, women's sailing has generated various controversies. Club sailboat races often have children competing with adults and able-bodied sailors alongside those with disabilities, yet true elite competition indeed involves a restricted group. On light days, sailing can be very relaxing, providing one is not trying to race, and yet on stormy days, especially under racing conditions, the sport can provide an extremely tough physical challenge. Unlike most other sports, one can truly enjoy sailing without being competitive by taking pleasure in being outside and enjoying the beautiful nature of the sport and its surroundings. In competition, however, sailing can be deadly earnest. The sport can be a cooperative team activity, with a crew working together, or it can provide the ultimate individual challenge, as lone sailors take on huge expanses of water.

HISTORY

The first sailboat was probably a raft-like structure with a simple mast and single sail hanging from it. Such a boat could sail adequately with the wind, but neither across nor at an acute angle to it. Most societies living near water developed their own craft, using local materials. The peoples of the ancient Middle East built reed boats around 3500 BCE, and later built dhows; the Greeks and Romans developed galleys, using sails and slave-powered oars, around 1000 BCE. The Chinese had the distinctive junk rig from approximately 300 BCE, and the Vikings probably used their rigged longboats to reach what is today called North America around 700 CE.

The sport of sailing, as distinct from the form of transportation, probably began in the Netherlands in the seventeenth century. Because the large early racing boats were so costly to buy and maintain, sailing was initially a sport only for the wealthy. In the 1660s, a race was held in London between King Charles II's boat and one owned by the Duke of York. The first regatta was organized by the Water Club of Cork, Ireland, in 1720. Until the late nineteenth century, when small boats began to be produced, the sport of sailing remained the province of the rich. Before they were mass-produced, each sailboat was distinctive enough to require that it be rated by a complex formula to permit meaningful racing against dissimilar vessels. Various formulas were used, but the rating system gave rise to the names of some of the early classes such as a "half rater" which is a "6-meter" or "12-meter."

Two women race a 470 sailboat in the Caribbean in 1992. (Neil Rabinowitz/Corbis)

In the last hundred years the sport has developed several branches: racing (both in small, relatively inexpensive, dinghies and large keelboats), speed trialing, and cruising. Sailing became an Olympic sport in the second Olympic Games of 1900. While some boats remain at sea for months or even years at a time, most boats are sailed within sight of land and are launched each time they sail.

Ocean racing, in which the larger boats compete offshore, began in 1866 when three boats raced across the Atlantic. *Henrietta* beat *Vesta* and *Fleetwing* in a close race. The crews of the time were professional seamen. In the 1920s, amateur sailors took over, and because the sport was contested in the open sea, often hundreds of miles offshore, it was considered to be dangerous. Virtually no women were involved in offshore racing at that time. To encourage women in the United States, in 1924 the Mrs. Charles Francis Adams trophy was donated for women in keelboat racing, and this trophy is still raced for today.

THE FIRST WOMEN SAILORS

Among the first women known to have sailed were a few female pirates. Alvilda, a Goth pirate from southern Sweden, went to sea to escape an arranged marriage and took with her an all-female crew. In the seventeenth century, due to the relative inefficiency of sailing rigs (their mast and sail configuration), boats of all sizes often had to be rowed, making the exclusively female nature of the crew all the more remarkable. Around the same time, off the southwest coast of England, it is known that when the men of the villages were press-ganged into King Henry VIII's navy, the women took over their fishing smacks and continued to make a living for their families.

During the eighteenth century, several women disguised themselves as men and ran away to sea for a variety of reasons. The most famous female pirates also date from this time. Anne Bonney, the daughter of a wealthy Irish lawyer who had immigrated to what was then known as Carolina, married a man of whom her father disapproved and was disinherited by him. She and her husband fled to try to make a living in the Bahamas. Following a divorce in 1719, Anne married John Rackham and the pair led a pirate life. On board one of the ships they captured was another woman, Mary Read, who joined Anne and John Rackham in piracy. They were briefly successful but in 1720 their own boat was boarded, and Anne and Mary were taken prisoner, tried, and sentenced to death for piracy.

WOMEN SAILORS IN THE AMERICA'S CUP

Female sailors who received great publicity at the time were those assembled by the America^3 Foundation to try out for an all-women crew in the America's Cup of 1995. They were not the first women to participate in this event, however. The America's Cup, which began as the Hundred Guinea Cup because that is what it cost to make in 1851, was first raced around the Isle of Wight, off the coast of southern England. All except one of the competing yachts were British; the exception was the schooner *America.* After an all-day race, *America* won the race and the trophy that later came to bear her name. No women were part of any of these crews, and it was not until 1895 that the first woman participated in an America's Cup race. Her name was Hope Goddard Iselin, and she acted as timekeeper then and also in 1899 and 1903; the American defender boat was successful in each of these races.

In 1934 and 1937, there was a woman on board both the defender and challenger yachts. Phyllis Brodie Gordon Sopwith and Gertrude Vanderbilt were both timekeepers for their respective husbands. During these years, the position of timekeeper was especially crucial because the boats were then so large (around 40 meters [131.2 feet] compared to today's boats, which measure around 20 meters [65.6 feet]) that it could take around 40 seconds to jibe a boat. In 1934 Sis Morrs Hovey also was a timekeeper on one of the boats in the trials.

Christy Crawford was backup navigator on Dennis Conner's boats in 1980 and 1983, and Dory Vogel was backup navigator in Conner's 1987–1988 campaign. In 1992 Dawn Riley was pitman (sail packer below decks) aboard *America*^{3}. By this time, the America's Cup format had become what it remains today: a defender series in which any number of boats from the previously victorious country compete in trials for the right to defend the Cup, and a challenger series in which boats from any other country compete for the right to challenge the defender. Both series are sailed as match races, with only two boats in any race, in a round-robin format.

Following Bill Koch's success in winning the America's Cup in 1992 in *America*^{3}, he announced that he would put together an all-women crew to race for the right to defend the Cup in 1995. His reasoning was that women had traditionally not been given a fair chance to show what they could achieve in big boat racing and he hoped that when an all-women's crew did well, their accomplishment might help to change that thinking.

DAWN RILEY AND THE AMERICA'S CUP

The only woman to lead an effort to capture the America's Cup is Dawn Riley of the United States. The 35-year-old Riley began sailing with her family in Michigan at age thirteen and has competed in numerous international events, including two America's Cups (1992, 1995) and the Whitbread around-the-globe endurance race. As head of her own non-profit organization for the America's Cup 2000 she must raise $28 million from sponsors to support the effort, design and build the *America True*, and recruit and train a crew. At the close of 1999 her crew was in training in Australia and the *America True* was under construction.

Some people immediately wrote off the idea and the crew as having no hope because they believed women lacked sufficient strength. They certainly lacked Cup experience, exactly what Koch was trying to reverse. The tryouts attracted nearly 700 women, however, most of whom either had a background in sailing or were either Olympic-level rowers or endurance athletes. From this group, twenty-eight women were selected as the pool to sail aboard *Mighty Mary.*

One of the most notable was Jennifer "J.J." Isler (1965–), 1992 women's 470-class Olympic bronze medal winner and former Rolex Yachtswoman of the Year. As well as being the first woman to skipper on the international match racing circuit, she had also formerly been the first woman captain of the Yale University sailing team. Dawn Riley (1965–) had been a member of the 1989–1990 all-women's team in the Whitbread Round the World Race, skippered the all-women's team in the 1993–1994 race, and was the only woman to have had previous America's Cup experience. Debbie (1970–) and Katie (1973–) Pettibone, sisters, grew up sailing on the Great Lakes, where their mother and grandmother had also sailed and raced. Annie Nelson (1960–) held fifteen national and international sailing titles. She also directed national racing clinics and windsurfed 70 miles (112.7 kilometers) in one day to cross Peru's Lake Titicaca. Linda Lindquist (1963–) had been a member of the first all-women's crew to compete in the Newport–Bermuda race in 1992. Following nine months of 12-hour-a-day, six-day-a-week training, this crew (with the last-minute addition, after much soul searching, of Dave Dellenbaugh as tactician—ironically, the one position where strength is not a necessity) did well in the defender trials, eventually and somewhat controversially just losing out to Dennis Conner's boat for the right to defend the Cup against New Zealand.

WOMEN IN LONG-DISTANCE SAILING

There are many notable long-distance sailing firsts. The first woman to sail across the Atlantic single-handed was Anne Davison of Great Britain, who left Plymouth, England, in May 1952 in her 7-meter (23-foot) sloop *Felicity Ann.* Women sailed singled-handed around the world for the first time in 1977, when three women made successful individual efforts: Krystyna Chojnowska-Liskiewwicz of Poland sailed her 9.5-meter (31-foot) *Mazurek* westward around the world via the Panama Canal from Las Palmas; Naomi James (1949–), a British resident originally from New Zealand, sailed from Dartmouth, England, in her 16-meter (52-foot) *Express Crusader* around all five southern capes (to the south of New Zealand's South Cape, Australia's South East Cape and Cape Leeuwin, South Africa's Cape of Good Hope, and South America's Cape Horn); and Brigitte Oudry of France circumnavigated via three capes in her 10.5-meter (35-foot) boat, *Gea.* (Joshua Slocum [1844–1909], born in Nova Scotia, had been the first man to do so in 1895 aboard his 11.2-meter [36-foot] *Spray.* His counterclockwise voyage, using the prevailing winds, took three years and was the subject of the famous book, *Sailing Alone Around the World.*)

The first woman to sail alone around the world without stopping was Kay Cottee of Australia in her 11.5-meter (38-foot) *Blackmore's First Lady,* taking 189 days in 1988. (The nonstop feat had first been accomplished in 1969 by Robin Knox-Johnson, who took 313 days.) In 1990, Florence Arthaud, in a 18-meter (59-foot) trimaran, *Pierre Premier,* set a single-handed west-to-east transatlantic record.

In offshore racing, Clare Francis (1946–) wrote of her adventures in *Woman Alone: Sailing Solo Across the Atlantic.* In 1976 she had been the first British woman to complete the Observer Single-handed Transatlantic Race. The race started on 6 June and she finished on 4 July. Prior to this, she had completed the Round Britain Race in 1974, finishing third, and in 1977–1978 she was the first woman skipper of a boat in the Whitbread Round the World Race.

In blue-water cruising, as contrasted with racing or record setting, numerous women have helped to popularize the sport. In 1955, Susan and Eric Hiscock of Great Britain completed a three-year round-the-world voyage in their 9-meter (30-foot) *Wanderer III,* and they later repeated the circumnavigation two more times. Lin and Larry Pardy of Canada have cruised around the world in their 7-meter (23-foot) boat *Seraffyn.* Between 1968 and 1980 they completed an eastward circumnavigation that they wrote about in *Cruising in* Seraffyn.

Isabelle Autissier, French competitive sailor. (APP/Corbis)

OLYMPIC COMPETITION

Sailing was first an event of the Olympic Summer Games in France in 1900. No women participated that year, and the event was not held in St. Louis in 1904. In 1908, however, Frances Rivett-Carnac of Great Britain took part in the only 7-meter (23-foot) class entry with her husband. While most of the Olympic events took place in London, the yachting was divided between Ryde, on the Isle of Wight (site of the first America's Cup race in 1851), and the Clyde Estuary in Scotland. She thus became the first Olympic yachtswoman. No other woman participated until 1928, when Virginie Heriot of France won gold in the 8-meter (26-foot) class among a field of eight boats. She was therefore the first woman to win a gold medal in contested Olympic competition. Several women have competed in the open sailing classes since then. For example, in the 1984 Tornado class event, Paul Elvstrom of Denmark made an unprecedented seventh appearance in the Olympic Games. This time, at age fifty-six, he entered with his daughter, Trine, and came fourth. In 1988 they also participated but did not win a medal.

In 1988 the first women-only class competed at the Games. This was in the 470-dinghy class, a two-person boat. The event was won by Allison Jolly and Lynn Jewell of the United States, with M. Soderstrom and B. Bengtsson of Sweden in the silver medal position, and L. Moskalenko and I. Tchounikhovskaia of the Soviet Union winning the bronze medal. In 1992 a women's class was added to the board sailing event, and a single-handed class for women only, the Europe, was also added. The 470 winners were Theresa Zabell and Patricia Guerra of Spain, followed by Leslie Egnot and Janet Shearer of New Zealand in second place and J.J. Isler and Pamela Healy of the United states in third place. The Europe class was won by Linda Andersen of Norway, with Natalia via Dufresne of Spain and Julia Trotman of the United States taking second and third, respectively. In 1996 the total Olympic sailing events were the Europe (single-handed women), Finn (single-handed men), Laser (open), 470 (women), 470 (men), sailboard (women), sailboard (men), Soling (open keelboat), Star (open keelboat), and Tornado catamaran (open). Thus there were three events specifically for women, three specifically for men, and four that were open to both men and women, although the Laser tended to favor people who were taller and heavier than most women. In 1996, in the 470 class, gold went to Theresa Zabell (1965–) and Begona via Dufresne (1971–) of Spain, silver to Yumiko Shige (1965–) and Alicia Kinoshita (1967–) of Japan, and bronze to Ruslana Taran (1970–) and Olena Pakholchik (1964–) of Ukraine. The Europe class was won by Kristine Roug (1975–) of Denmark, with Margriet Matthijsse (1977–) of the Netherlands second and Courtenay Becker-Dey (1965–) of the United States third.

WOMEN-ONLY EVENTS

A controversial point that women sailors debate is whether the increase in the number of sailing events specifically for women helps to encourage women in the sport. Until 1988 all Olympic sailing was open to either gender. In general terms, with most men tending to be taller and heavier than most women, this gave an advantage in some classes to men. In the Laser class, for example, the advantage goes to the sailor who weighs around 165 pounds and is tall enough to exert the leverage needed to keep the boat upright in windy conditions. In the Finn class, even taller and heavier sailors predominate. It was for these reasons that women-only classes were introduced. In 1988 the 470 class (a two-person centerboard dinghy) was split into a men's and a women's event. In 1992 a women's single-hander, the Europe, was introduced alongside the men's single-hander, the Finn. The ideal weight for Europe sailors is between 100 and 170 pounds.

The different men's and women's and combined events listed above for 1996 remained in effect in 2000, except that the 49er, a high-performance (open) dinghy class replaced the Star. Discussions were held about adding a women's match racing event in which only two boats compete together (similar to the America's Cup format) rather than fleet racing, but this idea was tabled for the 2000 Games. Clearly, however, the trend at the highest level is toward more races segregated by gender.

On one side, segregation ensures that the number of female competitors will grow in comparison to the number of male competitors. The fact that greater numbers of women see that there are chances for them in the sport has given women's sailing a boost. And all-women crews, such as that of the *Mighty Mary* in the America's Cup, have shown that women are just as capable as men at mounting formidable challenges to male teams. The fact that so few women had been involved in this race before indicates that *Mighty Mary* probably did give women greater opportunities to excel and that there will likely be a trickle-down effect to all keelboat racing as the old prejudices against women are discounted.

On the other hand, there is a danger that women may begin to evaluate themselves only against other women, not in open competition. If this happens, instead of raising the level of women's sailing, if women are content to race only among themselves, then they are not likely to continue to challenge men for the very highest achievements in sailing. Furthermore, in some cases it makes more sense to mix male and female crews. For example, the ideal size for the person steering in the 470 class is between 5′5″ and 5′10″ and 125 to 140 pounds, and for the crew it is between 5′10″ and 6′2″ and 135 to 150 pounds. Ironically, this was the first class to be segregated by gender at the Olympic Games.

In a 1992 survey conducted by *Sailing World* magazine, 79 percent of the women respondents indicated they wanted more women-only events. Regarding how women are treated on board, 61 percent of the women said they thought women are treated differently than men, while 59 percent of the men said they thought women are treated equally.

OTHER ACCOMPLISHMENTS

Another branch of sailing is the setting of speed records. In 1988, at Les Saintes Maries in France, Bridgette Gimenez of France set the women's speed record of 37.26 kilometers per hour (kph) (23.15 miles per hour [mph]) at a time when the men's speed record was 40.33 kph (25.06 mph).

Other sailing-related ventures in which women have excelled include founding and managing sailing schools and becoming top-class photographers of sailing events. Examples include Patience Wales, the editor of *Sail* magazine, one of North America's major sailing periodicals, and Elizabeth Meyer, who, in 1989, completed a $10-million repair of *Endeavour,* a J class ex-America's Cup boat, raced by "Tommie" and Phyllis Sopwith in the 1934 event. Women have also been involved in the design of boats for many years. For example, the oldest centerboard boat in the world that is still racing is the 4-meter (13-foot) clinker/lapstrake (overlapping plank construction) Water Wag class from Ireland, which was redesigned in 1900 by Mamie Doyle, the daughter of the original designer.

RULES AND PLAY

Most boats today have a single mast, with one or more jib sails in front, and a mainsail. Some of the most popular dinghies in the world today are the child's Optimist (7.5 feet/2.3 meters), the Mirror, Sunfish, 420, 5-0-5 (all monohulls), and the various sizes of Hobiecat catamaran, or twin-hulled boat. Each of these latter boats are between 3 and 4.9 meters (10 and 16 feet) long and is either trailed to the beach or left on it overnight.

Sailboat races are unlike most other races in that all competitors—that is, the boats—are moving about before the start. There is a countdown and all boats vie for the most favorable position at the start, maneuvering to be exactly on the line, going as fast as possible when the starting gun sounds. Thereafter, they race around a predetermined course that usually involves sailing on all the different points of sailing relative to the wind direction. In most club-level races, there is no referee on the water. All boats are expected to keep to the rules, and if one thinks another has not done so, either inadvertently or otherwise, the only remedy is to protest (indicated by flying a small flag on board). Where once boats were only able to sail with the wind blowing in the same direction as they wished to go, sailboats may now go effectively anywhere relative to the wind. Thus they may start on a beat, or close-hauled course, when their sails are pulled in tight to the line of the boat and the wind is at approximately 45 degrees to their heading. By the action of the wind's forces on the sails, and by using the underwater keel or centerboard fin to counteract sideways thrust, a boat is able to make progress upwind by tacking, or zigzagging, back and forth. This is the point of sailing that requires the most skill to do well, because the wind is always changing both its direction and its speed.

Because these zigzags take boats on many different courses to a marker buoy, it is very difficult to watch sailboat racing and know who is leading. This may be one reason that the professional sailing circuit gets relatively little coverage on television, although with the use of microcameras high up the mast, exciting action shots have become possible. When the wind blows across the boat's heading, she (boats are always referred to as being female) is said to be on a reach and the sails are about halfway out. When the boat sails with the wind, she is said to be running; the sails are all the way out to catch the maximum amount of wind and often a colorful extra sail, a spinnaker, is set at the front, or bow, to make the boat go faster.

Boats may turn in one of two directions. If, during the course of the turn, the bow heads into the wind, the boat has tacked or come about; if at some point in the turn the back, or stern of the boat points into the wind, the boat is said to have gybed (jibed), or "worn ship" in the old days. A boat is steered by either a wheel or a tiller that is attached to a fin called a rudder that projects into the water from the stern. To stop, a boat must either be headed into the wind so that the sails no longer contain the wind's power but flap like a flag, or the sails may be let out to achieve the same result of flapping, or luffing, sails.

There are many rules that govern racing, but the three most fundamental are: (1) a boat with the wind blowing over her left or port side, said to be on port tack, must give way to a boat with the wind blowing over her starboard or right side; (2) when boats are on the same tack, the one behind must give way to the one ahead; and (3) when boats are on the same tack, a boat that is to windward, or closer to the source of the wind, must give way to a boat that is to leeward, or downwind, of her. Any boat that hits a buoy on the course must do one 360-degree turn to absolve herself; a boat that acknowledges being in the wrong and hits another boat must do two 360-degree turns before continuing in the race.

CONCLUSION

The days when women were believed to bring bad luck with them when they boarded a vessel are long gone. Sailing is one of very few Olympic sports (the others being equestrian and various shooting events) in which men and women can and do compete in open competition. Unlike many other sports, in some classes of sailing it is realistic to have men and women compete together. On the other hand, many women enjoy women-only events, and they have demonstrated that women-only teams can compete against all-male teams and win.

Shirley H. M. Reekie

Bibliography

Doherty, John S. (1985) *The Boats They Sailed In*. New York: Norton.

Francis, Clare. (1977) *Woman Alone: Sailing Solo Across the Atlantic*. New York: McKay.

Isler, Jennifer ("J.J."). (1993) "Looking Through the Glass Ceiling." *Sailing World* (February): 24–26.

Johnson, Peter. (1989) *The Sail Magazine Book of Sailing*. New York: Knopf.

McClintock, Kristan. (1992) "Survey Results." *Sailing World* (November): 28–30.

Pardy, Lin, and Larry Pardy. (1976) *Cruising in* Seraffyn. New York: Seven Seas.

Slocum, Joshua. (1901) *Sailing Alone Around the World*. New York: Century.

Thrower, Rayner. (1980) *The Pirate Picture*. London: Phillimore.

SALISBURY, THE MARCHIONESS OF

(1750–1835)

ENGLISH PEER AND SPORTSWOMAN

Like many of her English contemporaries, Edith Stewart, the Marchioness of Salisbury, was an accomplished archer, but she preferred the hound and the horn to the bow and arrow. She was probably the most avid and certainly the most renowned huntress of her age. *The Sporting Magazine* described her as "an elegant and accomplished horsewoman" who "rode with as much intrepidity as judgment." The journal noted that "a friend who sits at our elbow assures us that he was a constant attendant of [Hatfield] Hunt for eighteen successive years, during which she was seldom absent a day." Riding sidesaddle, wearing sky-blue hunting attire, she cleared fences, splashed through streams, and stayed with the hounds until they had cornered and killed the fox. At the conclusion of the hunt, she entertained her guests at Hatfield House, "remarkable for its character of hospitality." After her husband's death, in 1775, she became the Master of the Hatfield Hunt, a post that she held until 1819. In her seventies, her eyesight failed her, but she continued to ride to the hounds. When she approached a fence, her groom was said to shout, "Damn you, my lady, jump!"

The Marchioness of Salisbury riding sidesaddle and leading the chase. (Allen Guttmann)

She remained "hale and vigorous" into her eighty-sixth year. Her death came not from the usual debilities of old age but rather by accident. After she had retired to her dressing room to write a note, flames from a candle set her dress on fire. As her obituary observed, "the venerable Lady found a tomb amid the moldering ruins of the palace over which she had presided for more than half a century."

Allen Guttmann

Bibliography

The Sporting Magazine. (1836) 87 (January): 258–261.

SCHNEIDER, VRENI

(1964–)

SWISS ALPINE SKIER

Born in Elm, Switzerland, on 26 November 1964, Vreni Schneider competed in Alpine skiing at the international level from 1983 to 1995. Despite frequent injuries—above all a ruptured disc, which tormented the last years of her career—she established a remarkable record. She won fifty-five World Cup races, six slalom and five giant slalom World Cup titles, and three overall World Cup titles, in 1989, 1994, and 1995. In the Olympics, she won giant slalom and slalom at Calgary in 1988, and she repeated her slalom triumph at Lillehammer in 1994. She was the first woman skier to win three gold medals, and, counting her silver in combined events and bronze on giant slalom in Lillehammer, the first woman skier to win five Olympic medals.

Swiss skier Vreni Schneider competes in the giant slalom event at the 1992 Winter Olympics. (S. Carmona/Corbis)

Normally reserved and easygoing, on the slopes she displayed a surprisingly aggressive will to win. It was often said that Schneider skied as a man, with round shoulders and very close to the posts that marked the slalom course. Schneider's fluency only in her native German-Swiss language limited her ability to exploit her triumphs commercially.

Gherardo Bonini

Bibliography

Matthews, Peter, Ian Buchanan, and Bill Mallon. (1993) *The Guinness International Who's Who of Sport*. London: Guinness Publishing.

"Schneider dà l'addio alle gare." (1995) *La Nazione*, March 21, p. 14.

Umminger, Walter, ed. (1992) *Die Chronik des Sports*. Munich: Chronik Verlag.

SCHOOL ACHIEVEMENT

Since about 1980, there has been increased interest, in the popular and academic press in the United States, in the relationship between athletic participation and academic achievement. Initially, the majority of this attention was focused on men competing in revenue-producing sports at Division I colleges or universities, and subsequently on boys participating at the middle school (ages 11 to 15, approximately) and high school (ages 15 to 18, approximately) levels.

But, beginning in the early 1990s, a growing number of reports have examined the relationship between athletic participation and academic achievement among women competing in intercollegiate sport as well as among girls competing at the high school level. This increased interest is not surprising given the post–Title IX increases in the number of girls and women participating in sport at all levels, the elevated status of women's sport, and the improved opportunities for women to make a living from their sport-related talents. Initial reports indicate that girls and boys achieve at similarly high academic levels during high school and that women athletes achieve at higher levels academically than their male counterparts at the college level. It has been suggested, however, that the adoption of a sport model resembling that of men may cause a decrease in the academic achievement levels among girls and women who participate in organized sport.

The purpose of this article is to examine the relationship between sport participation on the one hand, and academic achievement levels and educational aspirations of girls and women participating at the high school and college levels on the other. The anecdotal and empirical evidence cited in this entry originates from studies of athletes participating in U.S.-based sport programs—an important clarification, most organized sport participation in the United States is tied to academic institutions, whereas in other cultures sports are associated with nonacademic clubs and are often perceived as just another extracurricular activity. Although foreign-born athletes are participating in U.S. intercollegiate athletics programs at increasing rates, no research as of 1999 delineated the academic achievement levels of foreign versus domestic athletes.

ACADEMIC ACHIEVEMENT AT THE HIGH SCHOOL LEVEL

Most girls are introduced to organized sport during their grade school years (ages 5 to 12, approximately). Little if any research has been conducted, however, to examine the relationship between athletic and academic achievement among youngsters at the grade school and middle school levels. Since research on future identity (i.e., how children would like to be remembered by classmates) reports that girls prefer to be remembered as outstanding students and as popular with peers, it is possible to assume that empirical evidence may point toward a positive relationship between sport participation and academic achievement at those early levels. Conjecture is not necessary at the high school level, as data exist to document the relationship at this particular stage. The availability of this information is important, since data from the National Federation of State High School Associations indicate that girls are participating in high school athletics at the highest rate ever—more than 2.2 million girls each year.

Data contained in a report from the 1997 President's Council on Physical Fitness suggest that girls who participate in high school athletics have higher grades than those who do not, with additional evidence suggesting that achievement may vary across geographic and ethnic lines. Specifically, research indicates that Hispanic athletes living in rural areas achieve higher grade point averages (GPAs) than their nonathlete peers. No relationship was found to exist between athletic participation and academic achievement for African-American or white athletes, or those living in nonrural areas. Moving beyond symbolic representations of achievement, additional evidence suggests that young women who participate in high school sport have higher educational goals or aspirations than their nonathlete counterparts and that sport participants are more likely to remain enrolled in school. Specific ethnic and geographic analyses indicate that rural Hispanic athletes as well as rural and suburban white athletes have lower school attrition rates than their nonathlete peers.

In addition to lower dropout rates, girls who participate in high school sport have higher educational goals than those who do not participate. Although these aspirations may not necessarily include the traditional four-year college experience, evidence suggests that white athletes, including those from lower socioeconomic backgrounds, have a greater likelihood than their nonathlete peers of attending and remaining enrolled in a post–high school academic institution. For individuals considering a traditional post–high school educational experience, extent of involvement in interscholastic athletics (along with socioeconomic status) is a better predictor of admission-dependent standardized test scores (i.e., ACT, SAT) than participation in other extracurricular activities. Research suggests a positive relationship between high school athletic participation and college progress for white and Hispanic girls from rural areas, but no relationship or in some instances a negative relationship for African-American girls from rural schools.

Former high school athletes who proceed directly into the work force face a more uncertain future than their college-bound peers, since no positive relationship has been observed between involvement in high school sport and occupational aspirations or success for girls from any ethnic group or geographic locale. In fact, when compared to their nonathlete peers, African-American athletes from urban areas tend to have

RELATIONSHIP BETWEEN SPORTS AND ACADEMICS REMAINS UNCLEAR

The enactment of Title IX in 1972 opened the door to females in high school and collegiate sports in the United States. As more girls and young women participated in organized sports, educators began to study the relationship between sports participation and academic achievement. A new topic of study (much research exists on sports and school achievement among males), it is not yet clear if and how sports participation and school achievement are related and if differences exist across ethnic and socioeconomic groups.

lower occupational aspirations and to work in lower-status occupations than their nonathlete peers. It appears that the time spent on sport-related activities detracts from the athletes' abilities to develop the job skills and gain the work experience necessary to compete for entry-level positions and subsequent advancements. Though it has been determined that young women who participate in athletics at the high school level have higher educational aspirations and are more likely to attend college than their nonathletic peers, little attention has been devoted to quantifying academic achievement at the pre-college levels.

ACADEMIC ACHIEVEMENT AT THE COLLEGE LEVEL

At the college level, however, much more is known about the academic achievement of female athletes. Although they have historically obtained the highest GPAs of all college students, their grades have been declining steadily throughout the 1990s. This trend is somewhat evident in the results of a 1992 study in which women athletes obtained grades similar to a control group of nonathletes matched on ethnicity, standardized test scores, and residency status, but significantly lower than those of a randomly selected unmatched control group of nonathletes. Examination of performance in particular content areas or on specific educational skills reveals a positive relationship between athletic participation and critical thinking or broad analytical skills, but significantly smaller gains in comparison to nonathlete peers on reading comprehension.

When examining another quantitative measure of academic achievement, graduation rate, data indicate that women athletes graduate at higher rates than all other categorized subgroups. Data from 307 NCAA Division I institutions indicate that 70 percent of white and 56 percent of African-American women athletes who entered college during the 1991–1992 academic year had graduated within six years. This is compared to 57 percent of all student-athletes and 56 percent of all students. The only sport discussed specifically in this data was basketball, where 66 percent of the women and 41 percent of the men graduated within six years. Among women basketball players the highest graduation rates were recorded by American Indians (75 percent), while the lowest graduation rates were recorded by Hispanics (47 percent).

The inherent limitations (e.g., varying number of credits per semester, academic major, etc.) of using quantitative measures such as GPA and graduation rate to assess academic achievement and make intra- and intergroup comparisons have prompted some researchers to use alternative methods. These include participant-observations and interviews to assess the experiences and perceptions associated with academic achievement and the processes through which academic progress is made. These data suggest that, unlike their male counterparts, the educational aspirations and academic achievement levels of women student-athletes become increasingly more important as they progress through college. By sacrificing a social life and operating within an athletic subculture that supports academic achievement, women are able to focus on academics and obtaining a college degree.

CONCLUSIONS

Research examining the impact of athletic participation on academic achievement suggests that for most girls, participation in interscholastic sports has few if any detrimental effects and in certain populations actually helps women achieve a higher GPA. Research on educational aspirations and academic progress is relatively optimistic, revealing that girls who participate in high school sport have lower attrition rates, higher educational goals, and a greater likelihood of attending and completing college than their nonathlete peers. This is particularly true for Hispanic and white girls from rural areas (though data fail to demonstrate a corresponding improvement in occupational status and, in fact, point toward a negative relationship for African-American girls participating in high school sport). The positive trends in academic achievement and progress continue at the college level, where women who participate in intercollegiate athletics obtain higher GPAs and graduation rates than subgroups of their athlete and nonathlete peers. Unfortunately, little if any research has explored the occupational achievement level or status of women who participate in college sport.

One of the primary reasons that girls and women who participate in organized sport may report better academic achievement levels and greater educational aspirations than boys and men is due in large part to the fact that, from grade school and beyond, boys appear to have more of their identity tied up in the athlete role and athletic participation than females. Girls are socialized at an early age to realize that their chances of playing professional sport or earning a living from sport-related careers are slim and that therefore they should direct their efforts toward obtaining a good education and pursuing realistic career goals. Reports also suggest that the sport-related social status and mobility gains enjoyed by boys and men are not equivalent for girls and women, forcing them to rely on their academic achievements and classroom accomplishments (as opposed to athletic status and name or team recognition) to obtain employment opportunities and workplace advancements.

Anecdotal evidence and early empirical data suggest that the trend of higher academic achievement and greater educational aspirations among women athletes might be changing as women's sport becomes more commercialized and as opportunities arise for them to compete at the professional level and to make a living from sport-related careers. Girls and women must be cautioned against identifying too closely with the male sport model and reminded that a well-balanced student-athlete experience is the key to success in their educational and occupational pursuits.

Barbara B. Meyer

See also Race and Ethnicity; Socialization; Youth Sports

Bibliography

Coakley, Jay J. (1998) *Sport in Society: Issues and Controversies*, 6th ed. Boston: Irwin McGraw-Hill.

Feltz, Deborah L., and Maureen R. Weiss. (1984) "The Impact of Girls' Interscholastic Sport Participation on Academic Orientation." *Research Quarterly for Exercise and Sport* 55: 332–339.

Goldberg, Alan D., and Timothy J. L. Chandler. (1992) "Academics and Athletics in the Social World of Junior High School Athletics." *The School Counselor* 40: 40–45.

Haworth, Karla. (1998) "Graduation Rates for Athletes." *The Chronicle of Higher Education* (20 November): A41–A44.

Hood, Albert B., Andrew F. Craig, and Bruce W. Ferguson. (1992) "The Impact of Athletics, Part-Time Employment, and Other Activities on Academic Achievement." *Journal of College Student Development September* 33: 447–453.

Meyer, Barbara B. (1990) "From Idealism to Actualization: The Academic Performance of Female College Athletes." *Sociology of Sport Journal 7*, 1: 44–57.

Picou, J. Steven, and Sean Hwang. (1982) "Educational Aspirations of Academically-Disadvantaged Athletes." *Journal of Sport Behavior* 5: 59–76.

The President's Council on Physical Fitness and Sports. (1997) *Physical Activity and Sport in the Lives of Girls*. Minneapolis: University of Minnesota, Center for Research on Girls and Women in Sport.

Sabo, Donald, Merrill J. Melnick, and Beth E. Vanfossen. (1993) "High School Athletic Participation and Postsecondary Educational and Occupational Mobility: A Focus on Race and Gender." *Sociology of Sport Journal* 10, 1: 44–56.

Weiler, Jeanne. (1998) *The Athletic Experiences of Ethnically Diverse Girls*. New York: Institute for Urban and Minority Education.

Wells, Richard H., and J. Steven Picou. (1980) "Interscholastic Athletes and Socialization for Educational Achievement." *Journal of Sport Behavior* 3: 119–128.

Winter, David, David McClelland, and Abigail Stewart. (1981) *A New Case for the Liberal Arts: Assessing Institutional Goals and Student Development*. San Francisco: Jossey-Bass.

SCHOTT, MARGE

(1928–)

U.S. BASEBALL TEAM OWNER

Marge (Margaret) Schott was the first female owner of the Cincinnati Reds baseball team and also one of the most controversial owners of a professional sports team in the history of sports.

Born on 18 August 1928, Schott was the second oldest of five daughters born to Edward and Charlotte Unnewehr. For much of her early life she was the son her father did not have. In 1952 she married Charles "Charlie" Schott, from a prominent Cincinnati family. Without children,

Marge Schott celebrates a Reds victory with Pete Rose in September 1985. (Bettmann/Corbis)

Schott filled her time with volunteer work, hobbies, and her St. Bernard dogs. When her husband died in 1968, Schott assumed a hands-on approach to business, applying skills gleaned from her father (whose company made cigar boxes), her husband, and her father-in-law (whose businesses included car dealerships, construction, and real estate).

In 1980 she became a limited partner in the Cincinnati Reds baseball team and in 1985 bought two general partner shares, which gave her control of day-to-day operations. Schott was convinced that if she had not raised the millions necessary to "save" the Reds, the team would have moved away from Cincinnati, a point that is disputed by others. Undisputed is the pioneering role of the Reds in the history of major league baseball. The Reds trace their origins back to the Cincinnati Red Stockings, a team that created baseball history in 1869 as the first professional baseball club; in 1975 and 1976, the Cincinnati Reds, nicknamed the Big Red Machine, won back-to-back World Series titles.

Schott's contribution to Reds history as the first female owner was marked by controversy. The business skills she learned in the 1950s from her male mentors made her tough but were completely inappropriate for managing a baseball team in the 1990s. She showed sincere compassion when ill health struck the families of her staff, but she also displayed undisguised contempt for her employees and for the hierarchy of major league baseball. In 1993, the other team owners suspended her for twelve months after she was found guilty of making racial and ethnic slurs. The National League also required her to attend special sensitivity-training courses, but changes in her behavior were imperceptible. A further suspension occurred in 1997 when she was implicated in improper dealings at one of her car dealerships. This led to pressure from the league to sell her shares in the Cincinnati Reds and relinquish her management role. In defense of her behavior, she cited her sense of humor and her belief that she faced particular difficulties because she was a woman in a man's world and had not been a part of the old boys' network.

Despite the dissonance off-field, the players maintained the Cincinnati Reds' reputation with four consecutive second-place finishes from 1985 to 1988 and a World Series victory in 1990. Initially, Schott endeared herself to the fans, whom she considered her extended family, by keeping admission and food prices the lowest in the National League. Though she delighted in joining the fans in the stands and signing autographs, public support waned in the late 1990s. Her clashes with the league's administrators had lost her some local support. On 15 September 1999, her management role with the Reds ended when she sold her controlling interest (36.7 percent of the team's shares) in the team for $67 million to her limited partners, in a deal approved by the owners of the other teams.

Lynn Embrey

Bibliography

Bass, Mike. (1993) *Marge Schott: Unleashed.* Champaign, IL: Sagamore.

Gorn, Elliott J., and Warren Goldstein. (1993) *A Brief History of American Sports.* New York: Hill and Wang.

Reilly, Rick. (1996) "Heaven Help Marge Schott." *Sports Illustrated* 84, 20: 72–87.

SCOTLAND *see* United Kingdom

SCOTT, BARBARA ANN

(1928–)

CANADIAN FIGURE SKATER

Barbara Ann Scott is the most successful female singles figure skater produced by Canada, and she was the first internationally dominant champion after World War II. Scott was born on 9 May 1928 in Ottawa, Ontario, and began skating at age seven when she joined the Ottawa Minto Skating Club. By age ten she had completed all preliminary stages of training and was ready for national competition, the youngest Canadian ever to do so. In 1939, at age eleven, she became Canadian junior singles champion. She repeated that title in 1940 and tried to win the senior championship in 1941 and 1942, but was runner-up both years to Mary Rose Thacker. These achievements came despite her father's death in 1941, which left her mother with little money for her daughter's training. Fortunately for the young skater, family friends supported her career.

The Canadian championships were not held in 1943, but Scott won her first of five straight Canadian senior championships in 1944. In 1945 and 1947 Scott won the now-defunct North American championships. When international competition resumed after World War II in 1947, Scott entered the world and European championships—in that era, the European championships were not restricted to natives of Europe. Thus, in 1947, within six weeks, she held the concurrent titles of Canada, North America, Europe, and the world. Although she was a proficient free skater, her victories were often won because of her dominance in the school figures (required technical elements), for which her practice habits were legendary. Scott trained year-round. In the winter, she continued to train at the Ottawa Minto Skating Club, while in the summer months, she trained in the northern Ontario town of Schumacher.

Her triumphs in 1947 brought her fame at home; a huge welcome was arranged and Ottawa's children were given half a day off from school so they could watch the parade. The citizens of Ottawa also pitched in to present her with a new yellow convertible. But future International Olympic Committee president Avery Brundage protested this gift, demanding that Scott return the car or risk losing her amateur status. Scott returned the car and was allowed to compete at the 1948 Olympic Winter Games. She dominated the competition at St. Moritz and easily won the gold medal, defeating Austria's Ewa Pawlik, who took the silver medal.

Barbara Ann Scott performs a jump before spectators at the St. Moritz Olympic Games in 1948. She went on to take the championship title. (Hulton-Deutsch/Corbis)

After the 1948 Olympics, Scott turned professional and was a huge success. She skated with the Ice Capades, starred in a London theatrical ice show based on the musical *Rose Marie,* and finished her career while starring in the Hollywood Ice Revue. Scott retired from skating in 1955 to marry American publicist and businessman Thomas V. King, whom she had met while traveling with the ice shows. They settled in Chicago, where Scott began a second sporting career of training and showing horses.

Bill Mallon

Bibliography

Ferguson, Bob. (1985) *Who's Who in Canadian Sport.* Toronto: Summerhill Press.

Wise, S. F., and Douglas Fisher. (1974) *Canada's Sporting Heroes.* Don Mills, Ontario: General Publishing Company.

SEARS, ELEONORA

(1881–1968)

U.S. SPORTSWOMAN

Eleonora Sears was an avid sportswoman, a leader in society, a controversial figure because of her independent ways, and an anonymous supporter of numerous potential champions and struggling sport organizations.

Eleonora Randolph Sears, daughter of a wealthy Boston upper-crust family, was born on 28 September 1881. She was extremely proud of her heritage, which included being the great-great-granddaughter of Thomas Jefferson and the granddaughter of the U.S. Minister to France in 1892–1893, Thomas Jefferson Coolidge. She was also a niece of the first United States tennis champion, Richard Sears. From the time she was a small child, she devoted her energies to sports. She was unlike many of her female counterparts of the day, who demurely watched sporting contests without a thought of participation. Known as "Eleo," she was constantly excited by the thought of trying and doing activities whether they were then labeled "men's sports" or "women's sports."

Affluence enabled her to act on her interests. She participated in all sorts of sports, from tennis, squash, riding, sailing, and swimming to polo, trapshooting, and hiking. She was serious enough about these sports to win some 240 trophies during her sporting career. In addition to being one of the first society women to play polo (while riding her horse astride), she was also national women's squash champion and one of the first American women to fly in an airplane and to drive a car. Horses were her most enduring passion, and at one time she owned the best breeds in the United States.

Her tennis achievements deserve special mention. She was national doubles champion in 1911, 1915, 1916, and 1917 and was runner-up for the singles title in 1912. She was also on the championship mixed-doubles team in 1916. After official national rankings were introduced in 1913, she was ranked sixth in 1914, tenth in 1915, and ninth in 1916. She was inducted into the International Tennis Hall of Fame in 1968.

By the time of her death on 26 March 1968, at the age of 86, Sears was a legendary figure. Her years had been exciting ones and she deserved the obituary title given to her by the *New York Times:* Pioneer in Women's Sports.

Joanna Davenport

SELES, MONICA

(1973–)

U.S. TENNIS PLAYER

Monica Seles and her German rival, Steffi Graf, were the dominant women tennis players of the early 1990s. Seles's career was interrupted for two years after she was stabbed in the back by a Graf fan at a tournament in Germany in 1993. Although she returned to the tour in 1995 and has been ranked since then in the top five, she did not return to the level of dominance she had achieved prior to the assault.

Monica Seles was born on 2 December 1973, in Novi Sad, Yugoslavia. She began playing tennis at age six and was only nine years old when she won the Yugoslav 12-and-under championship. She won the 12-and-under European championship the following year. In 1985, as an 11-year-old, she kept the European championship and was named Yugoslavia's Sportswoman of the

Year. She turned professional in February 1989 at the age of fifteen. Her family moved to the United States, and in 1994 Seles became a U.S. citizen.

In her second tournament as a professional, the 1989 Houston Open, Seles defeated top-seeded Chris Evert. Her career skyrocketed the following year. Seles won the Italian Open, the German Open, and her first Grand Slam title, the 1990 French Open. She surpassed the million-dollar mark in career earnings at the 1990 Wimbledon tournament. She moved to the top in the world rankings on 11 March 1991, at age seventeen years, three months, and nine days, the youngest tennis player (male or female) to reach the number one ranking. She was known for her two-handed forehands and backhands and ability to control the court with power and ball control from the baseline. She was also easily recognizable to fans by the loud grunts that accompanied her shot-making.

From October 1990 to March 1992, Seles reached the finals of twenty-one straight tournaments. She won three consecutive French Opens (1991–1993), two Australian Opens (1991–1992), and two U.S. Opens (1991–1992). At Wimbledon, the only Grand Slam title she never won, she was a quarter-finalist in 1990 and finalist in 1992. By winning $2.457 million in 1991, Seles set a record for single-season earnings, a record she broke in 1992 with $2.622 million. She was named the Women's Tennis Association Player of the Year in 1991 and 1992; the Associated Press Female Athlete of the Year in 1991 and 1992; and the UPI International Athlete of the Year in 1991 and 1992.

On 30 April 1993, during a changeover while competing in a quarter-final match against Magdalena Maleeva in Hamburg, Germany, Seles was stabbed in the back, just below the left shoulder blade, by a crazed fan of her rival, Steffi Graf of Germany. Seles was ranked number one at the time of the attack. Her recovery from the injury took more than two years, as she had to overcome the physical injury and emotional distress before she could return to the tour.

Seles won the 1995 Canadian Open, her first event back on the women's professional tennis tour after an absence of more than two years. Continuing her comeback, Seles won the 1996 Australian Open, her ninth Grand Slam title, and won tournaments in Tokyo and Sydney and on the grass at Eastbourne (England). In 1997 and 1998 she did well in several tournaments but failed to win any of the Grand Slam events, losing in the semifinals of the 1997 French Open and the finals of the 1998 French Open as well. Nonetheless, she was successful enough to be ranked number four in the world in 1998 and number three in 1999.

Monica Seles competing at the 1990 French Open. (TempSport/Corbis)

Since becoming a U.S. citizen, Seles has been a regular member of the U.S. Federation Cup team (which plays teams from other nations).

Janet Woolum

Bibliography

Corel WTA Tour Player Guide. (1998).

Layden, Joe. (1996) *Return of a Champion: The Monica Seles Story.* New York: St. Martin's Press.

Seles, Monica, with Nancy Richardson. (1996) *Monica: From Fear to Victory.* New York: HarperCollins.

SELF-DEFENSE

Women's self-defense refers to practices that help a woman protect herself from harm. Should she be threatened with physical harm, a woman with self-defense skills, both physical and verbal, will probably be better able to escape the situation. Self-defense programs are debated, though it is generally accepted that girls and women should be trained in self-defense and training must include deciding when and how these skills should be used. Self-defense training may give women a sense of strength and control. These characteristics may translate into an air of confidence that makes them less likely targets of attack.

HISTORY

Throughout history, the ability to defend oneself physically has been considered an important survival skill for males, particularly those in law enforcement and the military. This generally has not been the case for females except in civilizations in which women have trained for combat (for example, ancient Sparta, medieval Japan, modern Israel). Self-defense training is deemed more acceptable for women today than in the past, and many more self-defense programs designed for them are available. This is the case, however, primarily in countries where violence against women is an acknowledged problem and where society accepts a woman's right to use her bodily powers to defend herself. Consequently, the majority of contemporary women are still neither encouraged to develop self-defense skills, nor offered opportunities to do so.

Two instructors show how a woman can defend herself against a would-be attacker during a public demonstration on Hampstead Heath, c. 1950. (Hulton-Deutsch Collection/Corbis)

Despite such limitations, much progress has been made in making the public more aware that girls and women need self-defense skills. Some feminists argued that violence against women could not be eradicated by educating men that such acts are wrong or by focusing solely on the mental empowerment of women; women would have to be strong of body, as well as mind, and be able to defend themselves physically when necessary. To accomplish this goal, self-defense instruction was clearly needed.

Not all feminists shared this positive attitude toward self-defense for women. Some, in fact, viewed it as promoting traditional male characteristics, particularly aggression. Ironically, this group found themselves aligned with nonfeminist women and men who argued that women's use of physical force would cause them to reject female virtues such as pacifism, altruism, and self-sacrifice. Such thinking was counterbalanced by that of other feminists, particularly those whose work in battered women's shelters and rape crisis centers allowed them direct contact with physically and sexually abused women. They saw the initial devastation, as well as the positive changes that often occurred among those who learned to defend themselves. During the early 1980s, when this group began to organize a challenge against the rising tide of sentiment coming from individuals who opposed females protecting themselves on the grounds that it was unfeminine, the women's self-defense movement in the United States was born.

The efforts of these American feminists and those from other countries have led to changes in public perceptions. For example, people today are more likely to view sexual battery as a serious social problem and women, in particular, recognize that while they may be capable of penetrating the barriers to male-dominated professions and trades, they are still vulnerable to physical and sexual assault. Responding to this transformation in consciousness, law enforcement officials (police, lawyers, and judges) more readily perceive battery and rape as criminally actionable offences, and federal and state governments provide more publicly funded solutions (such as shelters providing safety from spousal violence and offering lessons in self-defense). Even media personnel have responded: today, we see far more images on television and in film of women who choose to fight back rather than play passive, helpless victims.

An instructor teaches residents of Blackheath, England, how to fend off attack in the wake of a local crime wave in 1950. (Hulton-Deutsch Collection/Corbis)

MODERN SELF-DEFENSE

Keeping pace with these changes, self-defense training for women has also advanced. Instead of educating women to comply with their attacker's wishes or to rely solely on mace, pepper sprays, whistles, personal alarms, and cellular phones, which was common in the past, today's instructors emphasize using one's body to overcome an attacker. Moreover, modern training is more likely to be integrative—merging observation, judgment, communication, physical self-defense, and occasionally feminist insights into one comprehensive program—and to come in a variety of packages. For example, Model Mugging involves aggressive unarmed self-defense against padded male attackers. Chimera provides an all-female environment and female attackers. Martial arts training at mixed-sex and women-only dojos serves to educate women in specific self-defense techniques. Finally, cardio-combat and boxing have seen increasing popularity in health clubs. An ideal program helps women gain a deeper understanding of the nature and prevalence of violence against them. It also teaches them how to evaluate risk and vulnerability quickly and realistically in diverse circumstances; examine their attitudes and behaviors and how they influence their victim potential; use verbal and nonverbal skills to de-escalate a potentially volatile situation; and use physical techniques against an attacker when necessary.

Studies of women who have taken self-defense training indicate profound and lasting changes in physical ability to defend oneself and self-perception. Such changes seem to be even more pronounced when they are acquired in women-only spaces (female students and teachers), particularly those infused with feminist spirit and ethics. Regardless of setting, however, findings indicate that women derive an array of benefits. These include empowerment of the mind and body; enhanced body image and self-esteem; enhanced perceptions of other women and the female body; and healthier relations with men at work and in social arenas. Findings also suggest that healing from incest, rape, and other psychosexual traumas is often enhanced by self-defense training and that healing occurs in ways that are qualitatively different from traditional psychological therapy.

Feminists, particularly those who have learned and taught self-defense, have long understood the benefits of such training for women and, thus, have emphasized self-defense as a critical skill. Others extensive research on rape survivors and avoiders have found that women who participate in sports, particularly contact sports, have a far better chance of avoiding physical assaults than those who are nonathletic.

CONCLUSION

Based on all of the evidence, it is reasonable to conclude that if females experienced self-defense training, particularly at young ages, there would be significant improvements in the way they perceive themselves and their physical capabilities and fewer men who target women because they view them as physically and psychologically vulnerable.

Sharon R. Guthrie

Bibliography

Bart, Pauline, and Patricia O'Brien. (1993). *Stopping Rape: Successful Survival Strategies.* New York: Teachers College Press.

Castelnuovo, Shirley, and Sharon Guthrie. (1998) *Feminism and the Female Body: Liberating the Amazon Within.* Boulder, CO: Lynne Rienner Publishers.

Guthrie, Sharon. (1997) Defending the Self: Martial Arts and Women's Self-Esteem. *Women in Sport & Physical Activity Journal*, 6, 1: 1–28.

McCaughey, Martha. (1997) *Real Knockouts: The Physical Feminism of Women's Self-Defense.* New York: New York University Press.

Nelson, Joan. (1991) *Self-Defense: Steps to Success.* Champaign, IL: Leisure Press.

SELF-ESTEEM

Value judgments and evaluations pertaining to the self are among the most fundamental choices humans make. They are often accompanied by an emotional component typically labeled pride, esteem, shame, or guilt. Using these judgments, evaluations, and emotions, human beings develop a general sense of self-worth, a sense of confidence about meeting life's challenges, and a general assertiveness about their personal right to happiness, achievement, and success. This is self-esteem.

Self-esteem has the potential to improve with achievement and diminish with failure, with achievement and failure constantly being defined by the individual. Self-esteem depends on our experiences in life, particularly those experiences we deem most important. If a girl or woman places great emphasis on sport, her self-esteem could be determined by the nature of her athletic experiences.

Research suggests females have a greater risk of low self-esteem than males. Girls' self-esteem diminishes as they grow older, with the severest drop occurring in the middle school years. Sport participation appears to offer a positive effect. Studies show that female athletes generally have higher self-esteem than female nonathletes.

EFFECTS OF SELF-ESTEEM

Self-esteem is fundamental to human growth and development. High self-esteem relates positively to an impressive array of variables: life satisfaction, motivation, persistence, overall success, healthy behaviors, friendliness, ability to express oneself, level of activity, self-trust, trust of others, a positive response to professional help when mentally ill, lower probability of relapse in recovery from alcoholism, and reduced negative stress and illness symptoms.

In contrast, negative self-evaluations, self-dislike, or low self-esteem relate positively to depression, anxiety, stress symptoms, psychosomatic illness, hostility, dislike and distrust of others, competitiveness, spouse and child abuse, entering into abusive/unhappy relationships, alcohol and drug abuse, eating disorders and unhealthy dieting, poor communication (nonassertive, aggressive, defensive, critical, or sarcastic styles), promiscuity, dependency, sensitivity to criticism, tendency to put on a false front to impress others, social difficulties and social withdrawal, loneliness, poor scholastic performance, preoccupation with problems, and unreasonable social status concern.

THE DEVELOPMENT OF SELF-ESTEEM FOR GIRLS AND WOMEN IN SPORT

Self-esteem takes root in early childhood experiences and develops over time into a relatively stable but flexible aspect of self-concept. A person must have a sense of her own value or worth if she is to develop self-esteem. Yet most world societies socialize girls and women into roles subordinate to those of boys and men. Studies classifying such traits as aggressiveness and competitiveness as "masculine," show that adolescent females who perceive themselves as having these traits have higher self-esteem. Sport develops skills and abilities commonly associated with masculinity. This relationship helps to explain the positive relationship between sport participation and self-esteem in girls and women. Research has shown that female athletes display higher scores in masculinity, overall self-concept, and in self-concept of physical ability, but did not differ from non-athletes in femininity and in other areas of self-concept. Investigators suggest that female athletes can be more masculine, hence the more favorable self-concept and higher self-esteem, without considering themselves to be less feminine.

For males and females, a major source of self-esteem is a sense of competence and efficacy. Studies in human development show that competence and efficacy develop when children have the freedom to explore, play, and handle objects, not just observe them. In most cultures, boys are more carefully socialized to be independent and achievement-oriented. They are expected and encouraged to move out and away from the parent and are given more freedom to explore and roam outside the home. Parents encourage their boys to play with "boys'" toys, (transportation and building toys). Girls, however, are more often encouraged to stay close. They receive more social interaction and play indoors more often with soft toys like dolls and stuffed animals. They also engage in cooperative versus competitive activity more often than boys. According to Jay Coakley, a leading sport sociologist, young girls are still more likely than boys to be protected, taken care of, and encouraged to be nurturing individuals. Through different kinds of play during these same developmental years, boys learn how to strive toward a goal, accept mistakes and defeat, to cooperate, and to handle competition within a hierarchy similar to the military or a large corporation.

NEGATIVE PERCEPTIONS

Throughout history women have worked to change the negative view of women in sport as they insist on becoming more involved in physical activities. Unfortunately, as women have taken advantage of greater opportunity and continually redefined their capabilities in sport, they have often become the target of criticism. Nineteenth and early twentieth-century critics claimed that sport participation "masculinizes" women, causing muscular development and reproductive damage. As late as the 1950s and 1960s, girls and women were likely to be told that vigorous physical activity causes damage to the uterus and subsequent birth problems. It was sometimes asserted that most women athletes are lesbians or that muscular development makes a woman unattractive to men. More recently, homophobic reactions have reduced sponsorship of female

THE SIX PILLARS OF SELF-ESTEEM

Nathaniel Branden, a leading theorist on the concept of self-esteem, states that true self-esteem cannot be enhanced directly. He suggests that it can be enhanced most effectively through the construction and reinforcement of the "Six Pillars of Self-Esteem."

1. *The Practice of Living Consciously*
   Being honestly aware of the world around me and living accordingly
2. *The Practice of Self-Acceptance*
   Refusing to be in an adversarial relationship to myself
3. *The Practice of Self-Responsibility*
   Taking my life in my hands, my goals, my happiness
4. *The Practice of Self-Assertiveness*
   Standing up for myself; being willing to be who I am openly
5. *The Practice of Living Purposefully*
   Living and acting with intent; using my powers to obtain my goals
6. *The Practice of Personal Integrity*
   Behaving in a way that is congruent with my values, morals, and convictions

professional athletes. Moreover, girls and women in sport continue to receive less media attention than boys and men.

CONCLUSION

Encouraged by the impact of feminism and the growing number of positive role models in the media, more girls and women have begun to experience the fundamental relationship between physical competence, efficacy, and the way they feel about their bodies and themselves. In the United States and other countries around the world, what was once primarily relegated to men has become more available to women. Women have more opportunity than ever before to participate in sport and experience the self-esteem associated with accomplishment within the sport arena.

Barbara T. Waite

Bibliography

American Association of University Women. (1992) *Shortchanging Girls, Shortchanging America.* Washington, DC: American Association of University Women.

Battle, J. (1982) *Enhancing Self-Esteem and Achievement: A Handbook for Professionals.* Seattle: Special Child Publications.

Beal, Carole R. (1994) *Boys and Girls: The Development of Gender Roles.* New York: McGraw-Hill.

Branden, Nathaniel. (1969) *The Psychology of Self-Esteem.* Toronto: Bantam.

———. (1994) *The Six Pillars of Self-Esteem.* New York: Bantam.

Cate, Rodney, and Alan Sugawara. (1986) "Sex Role Orientation and Dimensions of Self-Esteem among Middle Adolescents." *Sex Roles* 15, 3/4: 145–158.

Coakley, Jay J. (1994) *Sport and Society: Issues and Controversies.* 5th ed. St. Louis, MO: Mosby.

Colton and Gore. (1991) "Risk, Resiliency, and Resistance: Current Research on Adolescent Girls." Ms. Foundation.

Coopersmith, Stanley. (1967) *The Antecedents of Self-Esteem.* San Francisco: W. H. Freeman.

Dyreson, Mark. (1998) *Making the American Team: Sport, Culture, and the Olympic Experience.* Urbana, IL: University of Illinois Press.

Fitzgerald, Hiram, and Michael Walraven, eds. (1986) *Human Development 86/87.* New York: Plenum.

Foley, Denise, and Eileen Nechas. (1993) *Women's Encyclopedia of Health and Emotional Healing.* Emmaus, PA: Rodale Press.

Hall, Evelyn, Beverly Durborow, and Janice Progen. (1986) "Self-Esteem of Female Athletes and Nonathletes Relative to Sex Role Type and Sport Type." *Sex Roles* 15, 7/8: 379–390.

Harter, Susan. (1983) "Developmental Perspective on the Self-System." In *Handbook of Child Psychology,* vol. 4, 4th ed., edited by E. M. Hetherington. New York: John Wiley & Sons, 275–376.

Kane, M. (1988) "The Female Athletic Role as a Status Determinant within the Social Systems of High School Adolescents." *Adolescence* 23: 253–264.

Liittschwager, Jean, and Lisa Wilson. (1998) *Personal Communication.* Redwood Shores, CA: Cheskin Research.

Marsh, Herbert, and Susan Jackson. (1986) "Multidimensional Self-Concepts, Masculinity, and Femininity as a Function of Women's Involvement in Athletics." *Sex Roles* 15, 7/8: 391–416.

McKay, Matthew, and Patrick Fanning. (1987) *Self-Esteem: A Proven Program of Cognitive Techniques for Assessing, Improving, and Maintaining Your Self-Esteem.* Oakland, CA: New Harbinger.

Melpomene Institute. (1993) *Melpomene Journal* 12, 3. St. Paul, MN: Melpomene Institute.

Orenstein, Peggy. (1994) *School Girls: Young Women, Self-Esteem, and the Confidence Gap.* New York: Doubleday.

Schiraldi, Glenn R. (1993) *Building Self-Esteem: A 125 Day Program.* Dubuque, IA: Kendall/Hunt.

Sonstroem, Robert J. (1984) "Exercise and Self-Esteem." In *Exercise and Sport Sciences Reviews,* vol. 12, edited by R. Terjung. New York: Macmillan.

Weinberg, Robert S., and Daniel Gould, eds. (1995) *Foundations of Sport And Exercise Psychology.* Champaign, IL: Human Kinetics.

SENEGAL

Senegal is a nation in West Africa with a population of approximately 7.8 million. The region became a French colony in 1840, was a bridgehead for the conquest of the territories that made up French West Africa (AOF) from 1895, and had a pioneering role in the French colonial system. This explains why many of the first female African athletes were of Senegalese origin. Senegal officially has continued to champion sports for women, but many cultural barriers remain and many girls do not participate in sports after they leave school.

HISTORY

Beginning in 1938, military instructors gave physical education classes at native girls' schools in the District of Dakar and Dependencies. The French administration was very proud of this initiative and noted that the dragging gait of young Muslim girls had become supple and their bearing jauntier. Though memories of this are growing faint, the recollections of these pioneers indicate that they paved the way for the development of Senegalese women's sports after World War II.

Following the example of the Vichy government (1940–1943 in the AOF), which encouraged French women's sports at the instigation of Marie-Thérèse Eyquem, the colonial authorities promoted the participation of women in public sports. Thus, in 1943, the pupils of Van Vollenhoven College, joined by those from several primary and Catholic schools of Dakar and Rufisque, gathered in Dakar for the girls' track and field championships. After the war, the range of sport activities available to Senegalese women expanded to include basketball and volleyball. From 1955 on, young women played in regular basketball championships in Dakar and Saint-Louis. Over time, physical activities further diversified, and women began competing in judo, handball, and even wrestling.

After Senegal became independent in 1960, women were further encouraged by an atmosphere of emancipation. President Léopold Sédar Senghor energetically intervened and encouraged young women to participate in sports and competitions because he believed that sports would liberate young African women by improving their health and their physical appearance. As Senegalese women became more involved in the sports movement, they accepted administrative responsibilities. Marie-Thérèse Campbell, a basketball player, became vice president of Jeanne d'Arc, one of Dakar's most prestigious clubs, and Albertine Gonçalvès took on the presidency of the national cycling federation in 1984.

ELITE COMPETITION

In the 1970s, Senegalese women became involved in regional competitions and saw some success. The national handball team won a silver medal at the first West African Games, held in Lagos, Nigeria, in 1977. In 1984, Constance Senghor broke the African high-jump record. In 1998, Marie-Nicole Diedhiou won the African wrestling championship. But the most striking achievement is that of the basketball players known as the Senegalese Lionesses. After pocketing a bronze medal at the Friendship Games in Dakar in 1963, they successfully went for the gold at the African Games three times: in Lagos in 1973, in Algiers in 1978, and Harare in 1995. They struck gold again six more times in the African championships and yet again at the Jeux de la Francophonie in 1997. Some outstanding players have since joined American clubs (Mame Maty Mbengue and Mariama Camara) or French teams (Aïda Ndong and Khady Ndoye).

These continental successes do not mean that women's sports in Senegal are at world-class levels. As of 1999, no Senegalese female athlete had ever won a medal in the Olympic Games and the basketball team had not yet made it through the Olympic selection process. As for the few athletes who competed in the sprinting and high-jump competitions (Julie Marie Gomis and Ndew Niang in the 1968 Mexico City Games, Marème Mboye in the 1980 Moscow Games, Constance Senghor in the 1984 Los Angeles Games, Aïssatou Tandian in the 1988 Seoul Games, and Ndèye Bineta Dia in the 1992 Barcelona Games), they often finished far behind the winners.

From the very beginning, supporters of women's sport encountered numerous cultural and religious preconceptions. In the interval between the two world wars, even the most advanced segment of the Senegalese population displayed outright hostility toward activities played in clothing deemed degrading for a woman (shorts were the main target of their resentment). This mind-set continued to be common after World War II, and young women from traditional families were often reluctant to take up sports. Often they participated in sports only because they were compelled to do so in secondary schools or Catholic associations. Today most female athletes in Senegal come from upper-class backgrounds. Constance Berthe Agbogba, for example, the first Senegalese woman to have earned a black belt in judo (in 1972), was a student at medical school at the time of her success. But the vast majority of Senegalese women are still not involved in sports.

Bernadette Deville-Danthu

Bibliography

Deville-Danthu, Bernadette. (1997) *Le sport en noir et blanc, du sport colonial au sport africain dans les anciens territoires français d'Afrique occidentale (1920–1965).* Paris: L'Harmattan.

SENIOR SPORTS

Among the largest multisport events held in the last quarter of the twentieth century are those dedicated to adults over the age of thirty-five. Titled variously as Senior, Masters, or Veterans Games, these Olympic-style events can draw 25,000 competitors at a time. Such senior sports events are being held on an almost continuous basis somewhere in the world. From local meets with a hundred or so competitors to international events with tens of thousands, sport for seniors has been a growing trend. In most of these events, 15 to 30 percent of the contestants are women. From the beginnings of senior sports in the 1960s and 1970s, women have been considered equal partners in most senior sports venues.

SENIORS AND SPORT

The participation of women in sport knows no age limit. Toward the end of the twentieth century there was an upsurge in physical activity for older females. One emerging aspect of the "fitness boom" has been competitive athletics for middle-aged and older women. There is no question that physical activity is beneficial to older women. Aerobic activities have been shown to increase the function of the cardiovascular system. Women who exercise vigorously have a lower risk of heart disease than those who do not. Weight-bearing exercise and strength training contribute to bone and muscle strength and may help to prevent the onset of osteoporosis and other musculoskeletal afflictions. Physical activity is positively linked not only to increased life span but also to an improvement in the quality of life. In one study it was reported that the oxygen transport systems in older female athletes increased to the levels expected in sedentary twenty-five-year-olds. Age has been found to be no barrier to physical activity in women.

Physical activity for older women, however beneficial it may be, has not traditionally been the norm. Society has had fairly strict ideas about what is appropriate behavior for older women, approving of sports such as tennis and golf (in Europe and the Americas) and "Mama-san" volleyball (in Japan) but showing dismay at participation in power lifting or the pole vault everywhere. The advent of competitive sport for seniors has provided women with an acceptable avenue to pursue some level of physical activity throughout life. In fact, many senior female sports participants did not begin to pursue active sports until after the age of fifty.

In a survey of competitors at a Senior Olympics, Fontane and Hurd (1992) found that women often started their competitive career late in life. Only 23.5 percent of the women surveyed had competed in college sports, while 42 percent had not participated in sports in either high school or college. For most of these women, the primary reasons for becoming involved in sport were for the enhancement of health and for recreation. Other key reasons for sport involvement were social aspects and the opportunity for competition.

SENIOR GAMES

One of the earliest senior sport events began in California in 1969. Warren Blaney began a program to give senior citizens an opportunity to compete in a variety of sports. In the first Senior Olympics in 1970, contests were held in swimming, diving, and track and field events. That first event attracted two hundred athletes over fifty-five years of age. The Senior Games have grown considerably since their inception. The U.S. National Senior Sports Organization was formed in 1985 and by 1998 included a network of more than 240 sanctioned Senior Games at the local, state, and regional level. Senior Games take place in forty-eight states, the District of Columbia, and Canada. Each of these feeds into the biennial National Senior Sports Classic. With a total yearly participation of more than 250,000 people, this is

Swimmers prepare for the start in the women's division of the Senior Olympics swim competition in Ojai, California. (ChromoSohm/Corbis)

one of the largest multisport competitions for seniors in the world.

The Senior Games are open to anyone over the age of fifty. This age standard was modified to fifty-five in 1996. There is no upper age limit. Local, state, and regional competitions serve as qualifying rounds for the National Senior Sports Classic. Sports that are offered for competition can be as varied as the locales at which events are held. The Senior Sports Classic hosts competition in the following sports: archery, badminton, basketball, bowling, cycling, golf, horseshoes, race walk, racquetball, road race, shuffleboard, softball, swimming, table tennis, tennis, track and field, triathlon, and volleyball. In each of these sports men and women compete by basically the same rules, although not against each other. Women are not restricted or barred from any competition.

In the smaller, more local Senior Games, other events are added to the competitive format as interest demands. Local games might include a competition in dance or art, bridge or chess, boating or skiing, or some other activity of interest to the participants in the area. In general, the emphasis is not on sports that require a large team effort, but rather on those in which pairs or individuals may participate. In the basketball competition, for example, rarely is the typical full-court game played. Instead, three-on-three contests, tests of shooting skill or dribbling, and one-on-one competition are the norm. This allows seniors to practice and compete without the necessity of organizing a large group of people to form an ongoing team.

Senior Games were developed to encourage seniors to participate actively in their lives. This philosophical base has remained constant as the program has developed. The addition of the qualifying festivals provided opportunities for larger numbers of participants while keeping each event a manageable size. As the Games have grown, the participation of women has kept pace. In the second Senior Olympics, held in 1989, women made up 38 percent of the competitive field.

MASTERS AND VETERANS SPORTS

Governing organizations in a number of sports began to offer masters-level competition in the late 1960s and early 1970s. In 1966, as an example, David Pain convinced track and field promoters to start including a "masters mile" in several track meets. Based on the success of this venture, Pain decided to organize the first masters national track and field championships, held in San Diego in 1968. In this first all-masters meet the minimum age was set at forty. No events for women were included. A number of women in the San Diego Track Club pressured Pain to include women's events. In the second national meet, three events were added, open only to family members of competing males. Women did not gain a permanent place in masters track and field in the United States until 1972. During that same year Pain took a group of masters athletes to Europe for a series of meets (no women were included). Talks held during this tour led to the introduction of the first international masters championships, to be held biennially.

The spread of senior sports in Europe made it possible to stage the first World Masters Track and Field Championships in 1975 in Toronto, Canada. At this inaugural meet there were six events open to women. Eighty women signed up to compete, comprising six percent of the total competitors. At the same time, women's participation in the U.S. national meet was as at only three percent. During the second World Masters Championships, the World Association of Veteran Athletes (WAVA) was formed. A request went out for women to submit their best performances to be included in the new WAVA record books. At this point, only about 30 women were competing in the United States and only 300 worldwide.

In the WAVA constitution, written in large part by lawyer Robert Fine, the only mention of gender difference was to establish thirty-five as the minimum age for women and forty as the minimum age for men. In the rest of the document there is no mention of gender. Fine intentionally left mention of women out of the document to ensure that there would be complete equality in treatment of the sexes. The effect has been to produce an athletic format in which women and men compete in the same events with modifications made strictly to compensate for size and strength. This did not mean that all events were offered for women immediately, however. The inclusion of a number of events for women took a period of years and pressure from women. In the World Veterans Games in 1995, 31.5 percent of all competitors were women. Women had the opportunity to compete in all track and field events, including the triple jump, pole vault, weight throw, and steeplechase, events usually reserved for male competitors.

Masters swimming followed a similar pattern of development beginning in 1971. From the start there was inclusion of women in swimming competition. By 1998 U.S. Masters Swimming counted 30,000 members.

Similar efforts at providing masters competition were taking place in many other sports as well. In some sport structures, masters athletes

PRISCILLA WELSH—LATE BLOOMING MASTER ROAD RUNNER

Master road runner Priscilla Welsh became one of the most successful older athletes, at various times holding the United States Masters records in the 8K, 10K, 15K, 10-mile, half-marathon and marathon races. Welsh's entrance into sports and road racing was different than that of most older athletes. She started running at age 34 to lose the weight she had gained after she quit smoking. At age 39 she made the British Olympic team as a marathoner. At age 48 she was found to have breast cancer and became a supporter of the Race for the Cure race series.

had always been included by simply expanding the number of age categories used for competition. In other sports, specific efforts were made to meet the needs of senior athletes by starting new divisions for masters.

In 1985 the first World Masters Games were held in Toronto, Canada. These games were patterned after the Olympics, being multisport in nature. Athletes in twenty-five sports came from all over the world to compete. At the 1994 Games in Australia more than 24,000 competitors registered. The Games are open to anyone of masters age, with no qualifying standards. Athletes participate in the games representing themselves as individuals or as part of a team. No scores are kept by country or nationality.

While women in 1998 made up less than one-half of the competitors in the Games in Portland, Oregon, opportunities for women were present there. Most sports included divisions in five-year age groups for men and women. The only notable exception was water polo, which had no women's division. Women were free to compete in track and field, badminton, basketball, baseball, bowling, canoe/kayak, cycling, diving, fencing, soccer (association football), golf, orienteering, rowing, rugby, sailing, shooting, softball, squash, swimming, table tennis, tennis, triathlon, volleyball, weightlifting, and windsurfing.

The women of Oakland, California's Oakland Women's Rowing Club, c. 1963. (Ted Streshinski/Corbis)

Masters and veterans sports tend to be highly competitive, often featuring athletes who are ex-Olympians. Age-group records are kept by the governing bodies of each sport. In fact, records set by senior athletes in a number of events would have been medal-winning performances in earlier Olympic Games. In general an examination of the age-group records in masters competition indicates that losses in speed, strength, and endurance are not as great as might be expected with age. Women's performances in track and field, swimming, cycling, weightlifting, and possibly rowing remain at 60 percent or more of the capabilities of younger female athletes. The records for women well into their eighties show that women retain around 50 percent of their younger performance levels.

While some women competing at the masters level have trained for many years, as with the senior games, a large number of those competing in the latter part of the twentieth century did not begin to participate until after the age of fifty. Many of the women competing in masters games at this time were in school before the adoption of Title IX in the United States. Few women of this period had been exposed to highly competitive athletics while in high school or college. Many began to compete late in life for the fitness aspects of sport. Upon finding that they could compete successfully, many masters women began training seriously at a mature age.

As the first women to compete under Title IX moved into the age group for masters competition, the number of women in the younger age groups began to climb. The initial level of performance also increased. As more women who had trained all of their lives continued that training into old age, it was expected that records in all areas of senior sport would continue to improve. Also expected in the beginning of the twenty-first century was an upsurge in women's participation in senior sports that reflected the increased participation of women in sports at all levels.

Nancy Hamilton

See also Aging; Osteoporosis

Bibliography

Fontane, Patrick E., and Peter D. Hurd. (1992) "Self-Perceptions of National Senior Olympians." *Behavior, Health and Aging* 2, 2: 101–111.

Kavanagh, Terence, and Roy J. Shepard. (1990) "Can Regular Sports Participation Slow the Aging Process? Data on Masters Athletes." *The Physician and Sports Medicine* 18, 6: 94–102.

Law, James. (1994) "Senior Games as a Model for Health Care Reform." *Proceedings: Health Promotion and Disease Prevention with Older Adults.* <http://garnet.berkeley.edu/~aging/>.

Spirduso, Waneen Wyrick. (1995) *Physical Dimensions of Aging.* Champaign, IL: Human Kinetics.

Wallace, Linda. (1997) "Oral History: Women in Masters Track and Field." Unpublished master's thesis, Central Washington University. <http://members.aol.com/eslchris/thesis.html>.

SEPAKTAKRAW

Sepaktakraw is a Southeast Asian sport that, like many sports around the world, had its origins in a traditional folk game. The sport is similar to volleyball or badminton in that it requires passing a ball back and forth over a net, but is also like soccer in that the competitors cannot hit the ball with their arms or hands. As women's sport participation in Southeast Asian nations was quite limited in the past, sepaktakraw remains mainly a sport played by men. However, women have played recreationally for some years and in the late 1990s, women's teams have competed in regional sports festivals.

HISTORY

Sepaktakraw is derived from a traditional Asian circle game that was first played about 500 years ago. In the circle game, players stood in a circle and tried to keep a woven ball in the air as long as possible without using their hands or arms. The circle game had no set rules, required very little space—which was important in the jungles of Southeast Asia—and the ball was woven out of rattan, which was abundant. The circle game provided villagers of all ages with fun, recreation, and a sense of shared community.

The circle game is still a popular form of takraw, played recreationally throughout Southeast Asia, and it has taken hold in other countries as a form of recreational sport. The circle game has more recently evolved into a competitive sport in its own right. The original version was first developed in Thailand as *takraw lawd huang,* or hoop takraw. Players hung a hoop 5.8 meters (19 ft.) above the center of a circle and tried to kick the ball into the hoop with their feet. The more difficult the style of kick used to put the ball through the hoop, the more points were awarded for the successful kick. A new variation of hoop takraw was approved during the International Sepak Takraw Federation (ISTAF) biennial congress in November 1996. Known as round circle takraw, the game is played with five players who stand in a circle and receive different levels of points for each passing kick. The more difficult the passing kick, the more points awarded the team. Round circle takraw was included as a medal event in the 1998 Bangkok Asian Games.

In the early 1900s takraw enthusiasts in Southeast Asia decided to add a net and a set of rules similar to volleyball to make the game more challenging and competitive. In 1945 an exhibition match was held in Penang, Malaysia, where it received a tremendous response and spread quickly throughout the Malaysian Peninsula and Southeast Asia. In 1960, representatives of various Southeast Asian countries met in Kuala Lumpur, Malaysia, to establish a standard set of rules and regulations for the game.

In 1965 two developments occurred that were to change the course of the sport. First, on 19 December 1965, the sport was officially named *sepaktakraw* after heated discussions among delegates from Malaysia, Singapore, Indonesia, Thailand, and Laos at the Southeast Asian Peninsula (SEAP) Games Federation meeting. A compromise was reached whereby the word *sepak* (the term used in Malaysia, Singapore, and Indonesia that translates as "kick") and the word *takraw* (the term used in Thailand that means "woven ball") were combined for the official name of the net game. Second, the sport became international when it was introduced at the SEAP Games (now known as Southeast Asian Games) as an official medal event.

In 1984 high technology came to sepaktakraw when a Thai inventor revolutionized the sport with the introduction of a new synthetic sepaktakraw ball. While the traditional rattan ball worked well, quality control problems, lack of standardization, and decreasing supplies of rattan threatened the growth of the game. With the introduction of the new high tech synthetic balls, the sport received a needed boost and the stage was set for sepaktakraw to spread around the world. Almost all players around the world began using synthetic takraw balls.

In 1988 the Asian Sepak Takraw Federation (ASTAF) officially formed the International Sepak Takraw Federation (ISTAF) as the global governing body for the sport. Since that time, many new countries outside Asia have taken up the sport, including the United States, Australia, Finland, Canada, Great Britain, Germany, and Egypt. In Western nations, the sport is played mainly at the recreational level in schools and colleges, and there is less interest in forming elite teams for international competition. In the United States, it is especially popular in California. ISTAF has established a global promotional campaign to help popularize the sport throughout the world. It is ISTAF's goal to have sepaktakraw become the first team sport from Asia to achieve Olympic status.

Since the 1980s, sepaktakraw has continued to spread internationally, becoming a medal event for the first time in 1990 Asian Games and again at the 1994 Asian Games. In 1997 a women's division was added for the thirteenth King's Cup sepaktakraw world championships, and in the same year women competed for the first time at the Southeast Asian Games. At the 1998 Bangkok Asian Games, sepaktakraw included men's and women's events as well as the new round circle discipline, providing six medal events for men and five for women.

RULES AND PLAY

One of the features of sepaktakraw, and a reason for its growing popularity, is its simplicity. It is a team game involving three players per side. The object is to volley the ball over the net into the opponents' court, using any part of the body except the hands or arms. Each team is allowed three contacts with the ball to get it over the net. Unlike volleyball, in takraw one player may contact the ball more than one time consecutively. Points are scored by the serving team when the receiving team fails to return the ball over the net. Matches are won by winning two out of three sets, with a set being fifteen points. In 1996 ISTAF changed the rule so that no extra margin or extra points are played—the set is played straight and the first team to reach fifteen points wins the set. The third set, if necessary, is played to only six points and is referred to as a "tiebreaker." A *regu* (single team or squad) consists of four players, but only three may be on the court at one time. Each regu must have an appointed captain. A team consists of three regus for a total of twelve players.

All sepaktakraw courts are standard in size and are about equal in size to badminton courts. Sepaktakraw may be played indoors or out, although most major tournaments outside the United States are played indoors. The key piece of sepaktakraw equipment is the takraw ball. Originally woven from rattan, takraw balls range in weight from 140 grams to 200 grams. Normally, younger and beginner players begin with lighter balls and move up in weight. For advanced players, the optimal weight for advanced sepaktakraw balls is 175 grams. The tightness of the weave of takraw balls determines the spring, bounce, and speed. The other important piece of equipment is the athlete's footwear. Most players prefer to kick in court shoes. They are popular mainly because of their support and flat surface at the instep, unlike the flared sole of a running shoe.

The equipment for the women's game differs from that for the men's game in two ways. First, the net is lower for women (1.45 m) than for men (1.55 m). Second, the ball is smaller, with a weight of from 150 to 160 grams compared to 170 to 180 grams for men. The manner of play for women is also different; the women's game features longer rallies. Women players, at least thus far, cannot spike the ball into their opponents' court with the same power as the men; this enables the defensive players to "dig" the ball more easily and to keep it in play. Therefore, the women's game features longer rallies and is considered by many spectators to be more exciting than the men's game, which has short rallies ended by a powerful and unreturnable spike.

The Editors

Bibliography

International Sepak Takraw Federation. (1999) <http://www.sepaktakraw.com>.

SERBIA AND MONTENEGRO

***see* Yugoslavia**

SEXUAL HARASSMENT

Sexual harassment is generally defined as unsolicited and unwanted sexual attention that a person in a position of power pays to someone in a subordinate position. The most frequent scenario involves powerful men and less powerful women, but same-gender harassment also occurs, as does harassment of subordinate men by women. In terms of women athletes, sexual harassment would most likely involve such attention from a male coach or other man who might affect a woman's career.

HISTORY

The behaviors that constitute sexual harassment have existed as long as have men and women, but only in recent decades have such unbalanced relationships been characterized as harassment. For much of history, this kind of behavior was viewed as normal, natural, and, in some situations, part of the social order. Women kept silent about it, fearing retribution.

In the 1970s, with that decade's wave of feminism, women began to assert their right to be free of such attention and, presumably, the term "sexual harassment" was coined. Media coverage helped to bring sexual harassment to the public's attention, and two social phenomena helped bring sexual harassment to the forefront. The first was that women entered the work force in record numbers. A second influence was the movement for equal rights for women, which contributed to a shift in the way both women and sexuality were viewed.

Sexual harassment and sexual abuse (also referred to as gender violence) are not new phenomena, yet discussions and research on this topic in the context of sport are still scarce. Allegations of sexual harassment by athletes against coaches have become more prevalent since the mid-1980s, however, and an ever-increasing number of romantic/sexual relationships between coaches and athletes have come to light. This has made the ethical behavior of coaches a prominent concern for sports administrators. In scientific literature, investigations into the relationship between sport and gender violence are frequently reported; this research—mainly conducted in North America and Europe—has been stimulated by feminist work in sports on sexual harassment and gender relations. Research has focused primarily on professional standards, legal status, social order on college campuses, and sexual violence in the locker room.

Very few major national-level surveys of sexual harassment and abuse have been conducted. One study gathered data about the incidence, experience, perceived fears, and safety levels (i.e. how safe they felt) among Canadian Olympians. In the Netherlands, the national Olympic committee sponsored a qualitative investigation about harassment and abuse experienced by young male and female athletes. In England, Celia Brackenridge has been leading studies on sexual harassment and abuse at various levels, including top-level sports. In Germany, Birgit Palzkill and Michael Klein have conducted research for the German Sport Foundation. And in the United States, Carol Ogelsby and Dan Sabo have been working on this issue in conjunction with the Women's Sport Foundation. Also, Karin Volkwein and associates in 1997 carried out a survey on perceptions and experiences of sexual harassment among female college students. Mariah Burton Nelson, former elite athlete and now a journalist, has published two books on women and sport that address the need for athlete/child protection. Other countries currently engaging in research into gender violence in sport include Israel, Norway, Denmark, and Australia.

DEFINING SEXUAL HARASSMENT AND SEXUAL ABUSE

Sexual harassment and sexual abuse are two different, though related, phenomena. The WomenSport International task force defines both. Sexual harassment is "unwanted, often persistent, sexual attention. It may include: written or verbal abuses or threats; sexually oriented comments; jokes, lewd comments or sexual innuendoes; taunts about body, dress, marital status, or sexuality; shouting and/or bullying; ridiculing or undermining of performance or self-respect; sexual or homophobic graffiti; practical jokes based on sex; intimidating sexual remarks, invitations or familiarity; domination of meetings, training sessions or equipment; condescending or patronizing behavior; physical contact, fondling, pinching or kissing; sex-related vandalism; offensive phone calls or photos; bullying on the basis of sex."

Sexual abuse, according to the foundation, occurs "after careful grooming of the athlete until she believes that sexual involvement with her abuser is acceptable, unavoidable, or a normal part of training or everyday behavior. It may include: exchange of rewards or privileges for sexual favors, groping, indecent exposure, rape, anal or vaginal penetration by penis, fingers, or objects, forced sexual activity, sexual assault, physical or sexual violence, and incest."

Similarly, the Women's Sport Foundation defines sexual harassment as "the unwanted imposition of sexual advances in the context of relationship of unequal power. It impairs one's access to educational resources and one's right to enjoy a healthy athletic experience."

There are parallels between sexual harassment and sexual abuse; both are discriminatory and display an abuse of unequal power between the harasser and the harassed on a personal level, as well as within the social structure or hierarchy of power. Sexual harassment "is an abuse of power in which its user relegates women to vulnerable, inferior workplace positions through sexual coercion and/or unwelcome sexual advances and innuendoes. Generally, the harasser occupies a position of power and authority and then abuses that power by sexually harassing the employee." In fact, only a minority of about 25 percent of cases of sexual harassment are botched seductions in which the harasser is trying to get someone to engage in sex, and even fewer cases, about 5 percent, involve a bribe or threat. Instead, the real underlying motive of sexual harassment seems to be men's assertion of their power.

RISK FACTORS

Sexual harassment is extremely widespread. It is said to touch the lives of 40 to 60 percent of working women and similar proportions of female students in colleges and universities. Sexual harassment and abuse can occur between male and female, female and male, male and male, and female and female. However, reports of gender violence are highest between male (as the harasser)

FEMALE REPORTERS AND SEXUAL HARASSMENT IN LOCKER ROOMS

Sexual harassment of female sports reporters who cover men's sports remains a problem in the sports world. The problem was little discussed in public until 1990 when *Boston Herald* sports reporter Lisa Olson, who covered the New England Patriots football team, reported that one player had exposed himself and made sexually suggestive remarks to her in the locker room and was cheered on by other players. Olson's reporting led to similar reports by other female reporters who had come to accept such harassment as "part of the job" and to efforts by professional teams to make locker rooms more hospitable to female reporters.

and female (as the harassed), although same-gender harassment is becoming more frequent. National figures on sexual harassment in the United States reveal that one out of four women will be sexually harassed at some point during her academic or working life. And 35 percent of female students say they experience some form of gender harassment from their instructors or professors. Official complaints of sexual harassment and sexual assault underestimate incidences of sexual violence; the National Victim's Center reported for 1992 that 84 percent of all rapes go unreported. Despite the large amounts of evidence of sexual harassment, students seem to pursue few complaints through official grievance procedures.

Many factors may contribute to this silence, including the individual's vulnerability, lack of assertiveness, and lack of awareness of or refusal to recognize blatant instances of sexual harassment. In some cases, the silence might be due to the failure of institutions, such as university campuses or sport clubs, to publicize complaint mechanisms adequately, their reluctance to regulate private lives and personal relationships, and gender bias inherent in their policies and procedures. Therefore, any sample based on official reports does not accurately represent the number of incidents of sexual harassment and sexual assaults.

In sports, risk of sexual harassment or abuse arises from a complex interplay of factors. These include weak organizational controls within sport clubs, dominating and controlling behaviors by coaches, and vulnerability, low self-esteem, and high ambition among athletes. Athletes are particularly vulnerable when they become emotionally reliant on or obsessed with their coaches, who are not subject to independent monitoring.

EFFECTS OF SEXUAL HARASSMENT

Sexual harassment can devastate a person's physiological health, physical well-being, and vocational development. Women who have been harassed often change their jobs, careers, job assignments, educational programs, or academic majors; female athletes who have been harassed often leave their sport. In addition, women have reported psychological and physical reactions to being harassed that are similar to those induced by other forms of stress. The American Psychological Association (APA) lists the following psychological reactions: depression, anxiety, shock, denial, anger, fear, frustration, irritability, insecurity, embarrassment, feelings of betrayal, confusion, feelings of being powerless, shame, self-consciousness, low self-esteem, guilt, self-blame, and isolation. Physiological reactions include headaches, lethargy, skin reactions, weight fluctuations, sleep disturbances, nightmares, phobias, panic reactions, and sexual problems. Career-related effects listed are decreased satisfaction in the sport, unfavorable performance evaluations, absenteeism, and withdrawal from sports.

Sexual harassment by coaches has significant effects on athletes, as it does on the institution or coach involved. The Women's Sport Foundation points out that "sexual harassment claims can result in large monetary damages against the harasser and/or educational institution where the harassment took place. Accusations of harassment adversely affect the image of the institution or team and the coach's career. The potential loss of employment is great whenever sexual harassment is brought forward or when accusations are handled poorly by administrators."

SEXUAL HARASSMENT, SPORTS, AND THE IMBALANCE OF POWER

Sexual harassment in sport might be more difficult to detect than in other life situations. The demanding schedule associated with sports puts coaches and athletes in constant contact with each other. Researchers note that a coach's primary goals are to display the sport for the fans and to promote positive institutional relations. The relationship between a coach and an athlete is critical for the success of the team. Coaches often try to reduce the psychological distance between themselves and their athletes in order to control them. Young and adolescent athletes might tolerate harassment by the coach more than they would put up with such behavior in other social spheres. Young athletes accept the coach as an authority figure who gives orders that extend into the private sphere of their lives, including: "the choice of doctor, nutritional matters, weight gain or loss, hours of training, playing when injured, curfew, use of alcohol and cigarettes, sexual activity, [and] social activity." Individual rights in sport usually take a back seat to the notion of winning and the good of the team. Several studies demonstrate that even the most assertive and independent women rarely question the coach's authority, nor do they challenge coaches' psychologically manipulative or abusive behavior. They may fear that a rejection of their coaches' sexual advances could end their athletic career.

Furthermore, many sports involve a lot of hands-on instruction. For example, both gymnastics and wrestling require close physical contact during practice between the coach and the athlete. Touching the athlete is part of the sporting experience; however, not every touch may be appropriate. Hence, athletic situations provide an easy means for the coach to come physically close to the athletes. This leaves open the possibility for abuse or taking advantage of this situation. The physical, technical, and social power that the coach has over the athlete provides further grounds for trespassing and possibly abusing this power. The question is whether these various interactions the coach has with the athlete can be construed as a form of sexual harassment. Many people believe that judgment about the culpability of the coach's behavior ought to be based solely on the recipient's perception. Hence, the Woman's Sport Foundation notes, "whether the harasser's behavior is deliberate and purposeful or simply has the effect of creating an offensive atmosphere does not matter. Only the outcome counts." Others believe that this standard can be unfair to the coach.

Substantial amounts of research have concluded that sexually aggressive behaviors (sexual harassment and sexual assault) are usually a form of violence, not a form of sexuality, and are due to a mixture of social and psychological factors, with sociological elements also playing a major role. Particularly in sports and athletics, social factors such as masculine hostility toward women and the imbalance in power based on status and gender are evident. It has been well documented that sexual harassment is more prevalent in institutions based on hierarchical principles with unequal distribution of power.

Comparative anthropological research by Peggy Sanday spells out other social factors that contribute to the prevalence of sexual misconduct in societies. She found that cultures that display a high level of tolerance for violence, male dominance, and sex segregation had the highest frequency of rape, both individual and gang rape. Thus, sexual assault and sexual harassment are likely to occur in a group environment that binds men emotionally to one another and contributes to their seeing sex relations from a position of power and status, such as in the environments of the military and sports.

In the context of sports, the coach holds power over the athletes in regard to money, playing time, and even team membership. Sexual harassment is more frequently perpetrated by males against females. This situation seems to be the case because men hold physical power over women, and the social structure also puts them in a superior position. Based on the ratio of men to women employed in sports, as a workplace, it appears women are prime targets for sexual harassment.

Once people understand what constitutes sexual harassment, complaints over incidents of harassment occur more frequently. Currently very few sports institutions around the world have educational programs about sexual harassment in place.

BODY EROTICS AND THE MEDIA

The increasing perception of the female athlete as an erotic object is an additional problem related to gender violence in sport. This image has been hyped by the media in recent years. In top-level sport, where female athletes are becoming more dependent on managers than on coaches, marketing one's fit body has become a focus. Professional sport has become entertainment, and viewing a female body as an erotic image often becomes more important than the actual athletic performance.

Where sport has become a business, the primary focus becomes satisfying the interests of the sport consumers. Recent research points out that this has led to further degradation of female athletes. In many cases, young women are dropping out of sport because of the erotically charged atmosphere, although they might not have experienced personal pressure. When women leave sport, it again becomes a male domain, where men continue to reproduce their "male superiority" and dominance over women—the breeding ground for gender violence in the first place.

Karin A. E. Volkwein
Gopal Sankaran
Dale R. Bonsall

Bibliography

American Medical Association. (1998) "Diagnostic and Treatment Guidelines for the Mental Health Effects of Family Violence." <http://www.ama-assn .org>.

American Medical Association. (1998) "Strategies for the Treatment and Prevention of Sexual Assault." <http://www.ama-assn.org>.

American Psychological Association. (1998) "Public Communications—Sexual Harassment: Myths and Realities." <http://www.apa.org>.

Benedict, Jeffrey, and Alan Klein. (1997) "Arrest and Conviction Rates for Athletes Accused of Sexual Assault." *Sociology of Sport Journal* 14: 86–94.

Bohmer, C., and A. Parrot. (1993) *Sexual Assault on Campus: The Problem and the Solution.* Lexington, MA: Lexington.

Brackenridge, Celia. (1991) "Zwischengeschlechtliche Trainerbeziehungen: Mythos, Drama oder Krise?" *Coaching Focus* (Nationale Trainerstiftung, Leeds) 16: 12–14.

———. (1994) "Fair Play or Fair Game? Child Sexual Abuse in Sport Organizations." *International Review for the Sociology of Sport* 29: 287–299.

———. (1995) "Das kann hier doch gar nicht passieren. Sexuelle Belaestigung und Missbrauch im Sport." In *Fair Play—fuer Maedchen und Frauen im Sport?*, edited by Fair Play Initiative des deutschen Sports unter Federfuehrung der Deutschen Olympischen Gesellschaft & Bundesausschuss Frauen im Sport des DSB. Frankfurt/Main, Germany: DSB, 32–39.

———. (1996) "Healthy Sport for Healthy Girls? The Role of Parents in Preventing Sexual Abuse in Sport." Paper presented at the Pre-Olympic Scientific Congress, Dallas, TX.

———. (1996) *The Stronger Women Get, the More Men Love Football: Sexism and the American Culture of Sports.* New York: Harcourt Brace.

———. (1998) *Child Protection in British Sport—A Position Statement.* Chelterham, UK: Chelterham and Gloucester College.

Cleary, J., C. Schmieler, L. Parascenzo, and N. Ambrosio. (1994) "Sexual Harassment of College Students: Implications for the Campus Health Promotion." *Journal of American College Health* 43: 3–10.

Crosset, Todd, Jeffrey Benedict, and Mark McDonald. (1995) "Male Student-Athletes Reported for Sexual Assault: A Survey of Campus Police Departments and Judicial Affairs Offices." *Journal of Sport and Social Issues* 19, 2: 126–140.

Figone, A. (1994) "Teacher-Coach Role Conflict: Its Impact on Students and Student-Athletes." *Physical Educator* 51: 29–34.

Hall, Anne. (1996) *Feminism and the Sporting Bodies: Essays on Theory and Practice.* Champaign, IL: Human Kinetics.

Kane, Mary Jo, and Lisa Disch. (1993) "Sexual Violence and the Reproduction of Male Power in the Locker Room: The 'Lisa Olson Incident.' " *Sociology of Sport Journal* 10: 331–352.

Kirby, S., and L. Greaves. (1996) "Foul Play: Sexual Harassment and Abuse in Sport." Paper presented at the Commonwealth Games Conference, Victoria, BC, Canada.

Klein, Michael, and Birgit Palzkill. (1997) "Gewalt gegen Frauen und Maedchen im Sport." Praesentation von Ergebnissen der Studie, Vortrag auf der Tagung des Ministeriums fuer die Gleichstellung von Frau und Mann in NRW Gewalt gegen Frauen und Maedchen im Sport, Essen, Germany.

Lenskyj, Helen. (1992) "Unsafe at Home Base: Women's Experience of Sexual Harassment in University Sport and Physical Education." *Women in Sport and Physical Activity Journal* 1: 19–33.

Masteralexis, Lisa. (1995) "Sexual Harassment and Athletics: Legal and Policy Implications for Athletic Departments." *Journal of Sport and Social Issues* 19, 2: 141–156.

Messner, Michael, and Don Sabo. (1994) *Sex, Violence, and Power in Sports: Rethinking Masculinity.* Freedom, CA: Crossing.

National Victim's Center. (1992) *Rape in America: Report to the Nation.* Arlington, VA.

Nelson, Mariah Burton. (1996) *Are We Winning Yet? How Women Are Changing Sports and Sports Are Changing Women.* New York: Random House.

Palzkill, Birgit. (1993) "Kœrper- und Bewegunsentwicklung in Gewaltverhæltnissen—Was hat Sport mit sexueller Gewalt zu tun?" In *Frauen und Sport in Europa*, edited by Petra Giess-Stueber and Ilse Hartmann-Tews. Sankt Augustin, Germany: Academia.

Sanday, Peggy. (1981) "The Socio-Cultural Context of Rape: A Cross-Cultural Study." *Journal of Social Issues* 37: 5–27.

———. (1990) *Fraternity Gang Rapes: Sex, Brotherhood, and Privilege on Campus.* New York: New York University Press.

Sexual Assault/Sexual Harassment: Resource and Policy Guide. (1992) Temple University, Philadelphia.

Volkwein, Karin, Franke Schnell, Dennis Sherwood, and Anne Livezey. (1997) "Sexual Harassment in Sports: Perception and Experiences of Female Student-Athletes." *International Review of the Sociology of Sport* 32, 3: 283–296.

Women's Sport Foundation. (1994) *An Educational Resource Kit for Athletic Administrators: Prevention of Sexual Harassment in Athletic Settings.* East Meadow, NY.

WomenSport International. (1998) *Sexual Harassment and Abuse in Sport.* Chelterham, UK: Cheltenham and Gloucester College.

SEXUALITY

Three basic issues in women's sports involve questions of sexuality. The first is the old question of whether women, as women, should be involved in sporting activities at all. As recently as the 1970s, scientists, physicians, and physical educators wondered whether women would weaken or lose their reproductive ability if they participated intensively in sports.

The second question is whether women should be displaying their bodies before men. In other words, some social critics have argued that women should not appear before men attired in sports costumes if those costumes might tend to inflame men's erotic imaginations.

The third question, ironically, asks whether a woman's desire to engage in sports at all reflects her lack of femininity or deviant sexual desires. Traditionally, these three issues and concerns have limited and restricted women's involvement in sports. And none of the three has completely been resolved in any society to the extent that a young girl's or woman's interest in sports is value-neutral.

SHOULD WOMEN PLAY SPORTS?

At the end of the nineteenth century, most Western physicians believed that women were by their very natures less healthy than men. Women's reproductive organs and their monthly cycles were viewed as so debilitating as to render women unfit for many physical activities—at least so long as the women were not working-class. Therefore, at the end of that century, when women began demanding the right to participate in sports, enormous energy was focused on determining whether they could do so safely.

One response by physical educators worried about female athletes' physical stamina was to modify the rules of certain sports to make them less strenuous. This was done to basketball; various physical educators—women—devised alternate rules that limited the amount of running any individual player would do. Similarly, in 1928, after several women collapsed while running the 800-meter race at the Olympics, Olympic officials decided that in the future they would not allow women to compete at any distance greater than 400 meters, presumably to protect the competitors' health.

Because of this widespread belief that too much exercise might harm women, generations of schoolgirls in the United States and Western Europe faced constricted and limited programs of sports—where they were available at all. As late as the early 1970s girls were commonly excused from any physical education while they were menstruating. Not until the late 1970s did this fear that women would lose their health and fertility if they exercised too much finally begin to disappear. Women such as the marathoners Grete Waitz and Joan Benoit demonstrated vividly that women could indeed run great distances, remain well, and eventually give birth. Recent research suggests that women may in fact be better suited to running and swimming greater distances than men.

SHOULD WOMEN DISPLAY THEIR BODIES?

As the sport historian Allen Guttmann has argued, eros must be understood and accepted as part of the pleasure of sporting activities. Whether the athlete achieves pleasure through the physical activity or the audience derives pleasure from observing the finely muscled body in motion, the erotic draws us to athletic display. Since girls and women first began to compete in games dedicated to Hera in ancient Greece, the question of whether they should be doing so to gain erotic pleasure has been publicly debated. Similarly, the question of whether men should be present to observe females in athletic competition has been answered in a variety of ways.

Manon Rheaume, the first female goalie in the National Hockey League, holds a hockey stick while posing for publicity photos. Such public displays of sexuality are a matter of considerable controversy in the women's sports movement. (Neal Preston/Corbis)

Although respectable married women in classical Greece were expected to avoid the public spotlight, girls and women from Sparta to Athens did come together to honor the gods and goddesses, with such gatherings occasionally including athletic competition. In Sparta, the scantily clothed, or naked, bodies of young women were displayed in foot races and were intended to reveal which among them was most likely to be the mother of a strong, healthy child. Because the Greeks were less likely to see the body as corrupt, they were less likely to fear or despise the presentation of female bodies in this way. But by the Middle Ages, with the Christian emphasis on the dangers of the body and sexuality, women's ability to appear in public in athletic activities was severely limited, although an aristocratic woman like Mary, Queen of Scots, is remembered as a golfer, and other women were known in their day because of their skill with the bow.

In the non-Western world, Islamic society places the greatest restrictions on viewing the female body. Depending on the interpretation of Muslim law, all or part of the body must be covered in the presence of unrelated men. This has effectively barred most Muslim women from competitive sport, although some countries have arranged competition so that women may indeed participate.

During the nineteenth century, the sexual component of sports was once again acknowledged, especially as working-class girls and women competed as walkers, runners, and dancers for men to see and admire. The experience of respectable women, however, was quite different. Sporting women in the United States and Western Europe were expected to disguise their bodies to avoid exciting male attentions. Indeed, athletic competitions among women were often closed to all but a carefully chosen man or group of men, as was the case when Senda Berenson introduced basketball to students at Smith College.

The twentieth century saw a struggle by female athletes to find appropriate clothing in which to compete, against a countervailing force requiring them to deny that their physical display might arouse the passions of the participants and spectators. This struggle began in the swimming pool. Early swimming costumes of heavy wool weighed down and constricted swimmers' ability to perform. In response, athletic women began to demand—and get—lighter and more skin-tight costumes. As they did so, female swimmers and divers became identified in the public mind as especially beautiful and desirable women. Indeed, swimmers like Esther Williams and skaters like Sonja Henie parlayed their skill in the pool and on the ice into Hollywood careers. Whether they turned their wearers into stars or not, the suits did permit faster swimming. Athletes in other sports have faced similar problems in getting manufacturers to produce appropriate clothing.

By the 1960s female swimmers were insisting that they could go faster if their swimsuits did not limit the range of motion in their arms—as was the case with men's swimsuits. Accordingly, the Australian Olympic champion, Dawn Fraser, arranged a private race in which she appeared topless to prove her point that her times would come down if her swimsuit would only let her—her time did indeed come down. Following this, East German athletes incited quite a bit of comment when they first began appearing in swimsuits that, when wet, clearly revealed their breasts.

Finally, to prevent the further sexualization of swimming, FINA, the international swimming federation, banned the two-piece suit for women from formal competition. Other organizations place similar restrictions. Figure skaters, for example, were required to wear skirts instead of all-revealing unitards. The width of the crotch in a gymnast's leotard has been an issue, as has the length, color, and tightness of the tennis dress. And in 1998 a high school relay team in Colorado was even disqualified because the competitors were not wearing bras of the same color. Clearly, then, costume matters.

That the young women on the high school relay team were disqualified for the color of their bras is unusual in that women involved in track and field have not traditionally been defined as sexually desirable beings, especially in the white community. Because these women tend to be more obviously muscled and because they tend to sweat, they have generally been regarded as less female and hence less attractive. However, the late Florence Griffith-Joyner consciously challenged those attitudes when she appeared at the 1988 Olympic trials in an explicitly provocative one-legged track suit. Her obvious beauty and attention to her appearance reminded the world that athletic women, even though muscled and sweaty, can be objects of sexual desire.

Finally, the connection among beauty, grace, and athleticism appeared first in the twentieth century in the person of the figure skater Sonja Henie. The three-time Olympic champion parlayed her skill on the ice into a movie career that made her one of the most famous women of the world in the years before World War II. After the war, the woman on ice held a special but non-threatening fascination. Further making this connection between beauty and athleticism was figure skater Katarina Witt, the 1984 and 1988 Olympic champion, long noted for her skimpy costumes, who was featured in a nude photo spread in *Playboy* magazine in 1998.

IS SPORT FEMININE?

Women's physicality has been closely related, in people's minds, with sex and reproduction. Men's physicality, on the other hand, is connected with physical labor, physical competition, and military prowess as well as sexuality. In the 1990s, the World Wide Web added a new dimension to what some see as a connection between women's sports and women's sexuality. Internet searches for women's wrestling or Asian women's sports produce suggested links to sex sites offering photographs of women, rather than any information about women's sport.

To compete at the Olympic Games women must submit to a gender verification test, designed to determine whether they are, in fact,

DISCRIMINATORY DRESS CODE?

In November, 1998 the International Volleyball Federation, which governs international play, passed a new dress code requiring female players to wear short and tight outfits. At the world championships, five teams were fined for failing to conform to the code, and the Cuban team, which wore tight, short, form-fitting outfits was awarded a prize of $10,000 as "the most fashionable team." The new dress code was an attempt to follow the example of beach volleyball and use the physical attractiveness of the players to attract more fans.

genetically female. This procedure is not required of male athletes, and it has forced young girls and women to prove their right to compete in a way not demanded of men.

When the modern Olympic Games opened up athletic possibilities for women, officials did not address the issue of whether the athletes who said they were female in fact were female. But by the 1932 Olympic Games, charges began to appear that certain participants were taking advantage by competing as women when they were actually men. At the same time, athletes who were authentically female had their victories credited to their more masculine traits. The athletic success of the three-time medalist Babe Didrikson, for example, was ascribed to her "boyish" body, which some newspaper reporters used as an innuendo to question whether she was like other women.

Because human beings may have a variety of genetic diseases that require sex assignment, officials determined that women must be officially proven to be women. As the case of Stella Walsh (revealed during her autopsy to have male sex characteristics) seemed to establish, prudence required such proof. Then, after World War II, as athletes from the Soviet bloc began to appear on the international scene, a number of those women, such as the famous Press sisters, were put on the spot. Accusations flew that the Soviet Union and other Eastern bloc nations were sending women who were not really female to athletic competitions. Once the authorities announced that there would be gender verification, the Press sisters quit competing, adding further fuel to the fires of accusation and counteraccusation.

Whether sports are appropriate for girls and women because of fears that they might excite their own eroticism was also at issue in the twentieth century. For example, with the bicycle craze at the dawn of this century, social critics worried that women would use the bicycle seat to masturbate. However, by the 1990s doubters in the United States discovered something surprising. Statistics revealed that young women involved in sports tended not to become pregnant until they chose to do so, usually after their high school athletic career was over. It seemed, therefore, that athletic women were at the very least refraining from at least some forms of sexual gratification.

The most constant focus of discussion about women's participation in sport in the twentieth century was the alleged overrepresentation of lesbians in competition. Once lesbianism was deemed a problem, the popular belief took hold that strong, muscular, coordinated athletes are so because they are lesbian. This common supposition traditionally tended to limit athletic participation in the white community, where girls and women who might otherwise have been interested in athletic competition chose not do so to avoid being labeled deviant. Further, jealous men made it more difficult for heterosexual women to participate in sports when they charged that competitive women were reserving their erotic energies for the members of their team. Some critics even went so far as to suggest that female coaches were only interested in coaching to have sexual access to their players. Finally, some sportscasters, as late as the 1990s, still were willing to argue that women's sports would never be popular so long as there were so many lesbian participants.

CONCLUSION

These issues are certainly less controversial than in earlier years. It is generally acknowledged that women athletes will retain their reproductive capacity. Lesbianism remains problematic, and overtly lesbian athletes may lose commercial opportunities. Nevertheless, girls and women continue to demand equal access to the gymnasium and the playing field.

Wanda Ellen Wakefield

See also Body Image; Fashion; Griffith-Joyner, Florence; Henie, Sonja; Islamic Countries' Women's Sports Solidarity Council and Games; Lesbianism; Reproduction; Witt, Katarina

Bibliography

Cahn, Susan K. (1994) *Coming On Strong: Gender and Sexuality in Twentieth Century Women's Sport.* New York: Free Press.

Guttmann, Allen. (1991) *Women's Sports: A History.* New York: Columbia University Press.

———. (1997) *The Erotic in Sports.* New York: Columbia University Press.

SHINTY

Shinty is a stick-and-ball sport played by teams with a curved stick or caman (usually now made of laminated hickory or ash, formerly of natural woods such as willow, hazel, oak, elm, or birch) and a small spherical leather-covered ball, in the past made of fungus, wood, cork, or hair. Shinty has always been an almost exclusively male sport, although efforts by women to form women's teams date from the 1890s. In 1998 tournament play for women began in Scotland.

HISTORY

Shinty is the game of the Gael—the characteristic sport of the Highland area of Scotland, with its roots deep in the Celtic culture that spread from Ireland with Christian missionaries around the time of St. Columba (521–597 CE). The English name is believed to derive from *sinnteag* (leaping); from *caman* comes the Gaelic name of the sport, *camanachd* (the game of shinty), but there are many other historical and regional variants on the name of the sport, such as *iomain* (driving), *shinnie, cammack, cammag,* and *cnapan* (the Welsh equivalent). From *cam* (crooked) is also derived *camogie,* the English name given to the game of women's hurling in Ireland. The old English game bandy and the Welsh bando were similar. The former was common across England but seems to have died out by the eighteenth century; the latter was popular in Wales, especially Glamorgan, in the nineteenth century but was never developed into an organized sport and seems to have been displaced by rugby and football.

Apart from the myths and legends about Cu Chulainn, the earliest record of the sport is a reference to a caman in an Irish document dating from the twelfth century. In Scotland there are written references to the common game in the early seventeenth century, and the eighteenth-century Statistical Account of Scotland evidences the wide spread of the game across much of rural Scotland from Caithness in the north to the Borders in the south. The traditional playing time was the winter months, with the Christmas/New Year festivals the most common occasion for local matches. Toward the end of the eighteenth century the game was declining, even in the Highlands, as that area emptied of people by assisted or sometimes forced emigration to towns and cities of Lowland Scotland and abroad. The game went with the emigrants further afield to Canada (where there are clear links with the origins of ice hockey in Ontario, as well as shinty itself in the Maritime Provinces); in Australia and South America there are also records of shinty playing. From a Scotland-wide game, it receded to Skye, Badenoch, and Argyllshire, the latter area possessing a strong local tradition right through beyond the 1860s.

With the growing interest in Gaelic matters in the later nineteenth century, the sport saw a resurgence. The Shinty Association of clubs in the southern half of the country constituted themselves in 1877 and agreed on a set of rules that was widely circulated. In 1880 Captain Alexander Macra Chisholm of Strathglass (1825–1897) devised a set of rules to which the northern clubs played until, in October 1893, a conference of thirty-three recognized shinty clubs met to constitute the Camanachd Association and formalize national rules.

RULES AND PLAY

Shinty is played by two teams of twelve, normally with three substitutes permitted over a game, which consists of two periods of 45 minutes. The field of play must be between 128 and 155 meters long (140–170 yards) and 64 to 73 meters wide (70–80 yards). The goals are 3.66 meters (4 yards) wide and 3.05 meters (10 feet) high; there is a penalty area 9 meters (10 yards) from the center of the goal, 3.66 meters (4 yards) broad with quarter circle extensions to the bye-line. An attacking player within this area ahead of the ball is off-side. A defending player who commits an infringement inside this area concedes a penalty against the defending team. This is struck from a point at midfield 18 meters (20 yards) from the goal line.

Only the goalkeeper is allowed to handle the ball and that only within the 9-meter area, by slapping or stopping it with his open hand. Players may not head or kick the ball, but may stop it with one foot, provided it is at rest on the ground

A CONTEST FOR FAMILY HONOR

In his *Journal of a Tour of the Hebrides* (1785), James Boswell, the famous biographer of Dr. Samuel Johnson, reported women watching a game similar to shinty. This report from 1821 also shows the early involvement of women when the Campbells challenged their rivals the Macleans to a match on Calgary Sands in Mull, Argyllshire. While women did not participate in this match, they were active promoters and avid spectators of the sport, showing an enthusiasm that later led to women's participation as players:

"Everything was done on both sides to get their men to turn out on the day appointed, and so great was the feeling and excitement that Colonel Campbell of Knock, whose farm was nearly twenty miles from the Calgary Sands, ordered his men to appear at Calgary and take part in the contest for honours. Mrs. Clephane of Torloisk sent word round all her tenants and crofters to be sure and attend the match to assist her cousin (Hector Maclean). The day was all that could be desired, and the number that turned out was much beyond the expectations of either party. At the appointed time the Shinty was tossed for sides. Then the wooden ball, as was then customary, was deposited in a hole in the sand, when a struggle took place to unearth it. Whoever was fortunate enough to get it out made off at full speed towards the goal, driving it before him, this being considered the feat of the day if well done. The playing was furious and determined. The Torloisk estate players placed their best men in reserve; they lay hidden in the brushwood to the west of the Sands, whence they watched the play. From time to time a fresh man would dash out upon the Sands and enter into the fray. Ultimately they were one and all upon the field. The contest grew hot and furious. Hail after hail was scored by the Macleans, until the Campbells were compelled to give in and leave the field, vanquished and crestfallen."

Rev. Ninian MacDonald
(1932) Shinty : a Short History. *Inverness, Scotland: Robt Carruthers & Sons 79–80.*

at the moment of contact. A strike can be blocked by the swing of a caman that is within playing distance of the ball. There is no restriction in the height or direction of hitting with the caman, apart from striking an opponent or swinging overhead in a dangerous manner when close to other players. The caman itself must have a head (triangular in shape) capable of passing through a ring 6.3 centimeters (2.5 inches) in diameter and may have no plates, screws, or metal in any form attached to or forming part of it. The former condition is the one that most distinguishes the shinty caman from the Irish hurley.

The referee starts a match, and restarts after a goal and at half-time, by throwing the ball up over a height of 4 meters (12 feet) between the opposing center players, who stand with their camans crossed above their heads ready to play the ball as it comes down. There are also two goal judges to assist the referee, and linesmen to identify where a ball has gone out of play over the sidelines. A player of the opposing team takes a hit-in by throwing the ball up directly overhead and hitting it as it comes down but is still directly overhead. If the ball is hit across the bye-line by an attacking player, a goal-hit is taken; if by a defender, a hit-in is taken from the corner. Fouls outside the penalty area incur a free-hit with all other players more than 5 meters (16 feet) distant when it is taken. A goal may not be scored directly from a free-hit.

A set of composite rules, adjusted to provide no advantage to either game, has been developed for international Scotland/Ireland shinty/hurling matches. Similarly, rules have been amended for First Shinty, a game developed under the auspices of the Team Sport Scotland initiative of the Scottish Sports Council to encourage development of the game, played indoors in a safe manner, among primary school children of both sexes.

SHINTY AND WOMEN

Traditionally shinty was a man's game. The comment by the Reverend Ninian MacDonald, in his history of shinty, that all men are equal under the turf and on the turf conveys the taken-for-granted gender mind-set of a society that distinguished physically demanding sport from those recreations permitted to women. Society viewed women's role as one of observers and supporters—forming an audience for the events and participating sometimes in the post-match dancing (although more frequently it was only the male participants who danced the reels). Elizabeth Grant (1797–1885), the Highland Lady of memoir fame, records watching shinty about 1815 on Speyside. As late as 1876, the famous Skye poet Mrs. Mary MacPherson (1821–1898), known as Mairi Mhor nan Orain, wrote of her contribution to the New Year shinty match by baking bannocks for the Hogmanay lads, and writing a poem afterward. Yet some evidence dating from 1897 suggests that the ladies of Inverness played shinty. Twentieth-century social changes doubtless altered women's perceptions, if not men's, and the lack of written evidence of women's participation in playing may not represent what was actually taking place. The author Marion Campbell has recorded that during the New Year shinty matches of her childhood in the 1920s, there were occasional efforts to get either a juniors' or women's game going, indicating that the idea of women playing shinty was not inconceivable. The contribution of women on the administrative side was acknowledged by the Camanachd Association in 1933 when a woman became a vice president, but the fine print of rules still indicates the assumption of male officials and players of the sport. An early search of the Web site of the Camanachd Association, launched in June 1998, found no mention of women anywhere on its pages, although the association's forthcoming development plan does give support to the women's game.

THE 1990s

Following the example of Scottish women playing football and rugby, the perception of shinty as a male sport no longer holds true, and the women's game is beginning to develop. The North district's first women's shinty tournament, held in May 1998 at Fort William, had four teams (Kingussie, Glenurquhart, Kincraig, and St. Andrew's University) competing in a nine-a-side newcomers' league, while the longer-established Oban Dunadd (along with Oban Camancheroes one of the earliest Argyllshire clubs), Glengarry, and Strathglass competed for the Johnston Trophy. A tournament in Oban in July 1998 attracted eight clubs. Competitions now exist for national indoor primary clubs, and there is an under-fourteen spring league for girls. Given this growth in the traditional heartlands of shinty in Badenoch and Argyll, the future of women's shinty seems assured.

Lorna Jackson

Bibliography

Campbell, John Francis. (1861) *Popular Tales of the West Highlands*. Edinburgh, Scotland: Edmonston and Douglas.

Campbell, Marion. (1977) *Argyll: The Enduring Heartland*. London: Turnstone Press.

Hunter, James. (1994) *A Dance Called America*. Edinburgh, Scotland: Mainstream Publishing.

Hutchinson, Roger. (1989) *Camanachd! The Story of Shinty*. Edinburgh, Scotland: Mainstream Publishing.

Jarvie, Grant. (1999) *Sport in the Making of Celtic Cultures*. London: Cassells.

MacDonald, Rev. Ninian, OSB. (1932). *Shinty: A Short History*. Inverness, Scotland: Robt Carruthers & Sons.

MacLagan, Robert. (1901) *The Games and Diversions of Argyleshire*. London: Folklore Society.

MacLennan, Hugh Dan. (1993) *Shinty!* Nairn, Scotland: Balnain Press.

———. (1995) *Not an Orchid*. Inverness, Scotland: Kessock Communications.

———. (1998) Shinty's Place and Space in World Sport. In *The Sport Historian* 18 (1 May): 1–23.

O'Maolfaibheal, Art. (1973) *Caman: Two Thousand Years of Hurling in Ireland. Dundalk, Scotland: Tempest Press.*

Shinty Yearbook. (1971–) Inverness, Scotland: Camanachd Association.

Sinclair, Sir John. (1983) *The Statistical Account of Scotland 1791–1799*, Wakefield, England: EP.

Strutt, Joseph. (1801; new edition 1969) *Sports and Pastimes of the People of England*. Bath, England: Firecrest.

Thomson, Derek. (1994) *The Companion to Gaelic Scotland.* Glasgow, Scotland: Gairm.

SHOOTING

Shooting is a collection of sports that, at the Olympic level for women, encompasses shooting with pistol, air pistol, air rifle, small-bore rifle, and shotgun. In a more general sense, the sport includes clay target shooting with three divisions—trapshooting, skeet shooting, and sporting clays; pistol shooting; rifle shooting; and single-shot shooting with four categories—German *schuetzen*, shooting in the standing position; prone long-range shooting; American bench rest shooting; and silhouette shooting at steel targets. Although shooting was primarily a male activity and sport, women shooters were present at the early development of the sport and women around the world have been active participants since the 1950s.

HISTORY

Shooting as a sport rather than as a hunting or military activity probably began in the fifteenth century, when rifle barrels were refined to the point where shooters could control the direction of the projectile with some degree of precision. For the first several centuries, few women were involved in shooting because shooting was associated with the male activities of hunting and warfare.

In the middle and late nineteenth century, when shooting competitions became more common in Europe and elsewhere, women were still denied opportunities to participate, though they attended matches as spectators. While the impact of American shooter and entertainer Annie Oakley needs to be stressed, there is little doubt that many unheralded outdoorswomen, country ladies, pioneer settlers, and independent types found themselves in settings where shooting was a necessary, appropriate, and accepted "work sport." For example, in Victorian New Zealand a diary by Helen Wilson, a young housewife, reveals a woman who found recreational participation helpful in breaking down the prejudices that categorized women as servers and home providers. In the early 1890s she gave a marvelous account of a duck shoot where she shot the birds and her husband stripped and dived into the river to recover them. Again within the New Zealand context, there is evidence that, in the 1840s, 1850s, and 1860s, female settlers emigrating from Great Britain took part in shipboard shooting competitions, mostly of a trapshooting variety.

In 1860 the British National Rifle Association (BNRA) was founded. Their first official shooting range was sited at Wimbledon Common, Surrey, and Queen Victoria fired the first shot at the inaugural Wimbledon Common shoot. The BNRA later in the century relocated to Bisley Common, Surrey, where the first Bisley Imperial Prize Meeting was held in 1890. Bisley Camp is home to full-bore target shooting, the British Sporting Rifle Association, and the British Pistol Club.

Following the setting up of the BNRA in 1860, organized target shooting grew rapidly and spread to the colonies. America did not lag behind, and the National Rifle Association (NRA) of America was formed in 1871. In 1906 Elizabeth (Plinky) Topperwein of San Antonio, Texas, was the first woman in history to compete in a NRA match. While this was seen as unusual, NRA rules did not bar her from competition and she was awarded a medal. Topperwein broke nearly all of Annie Oakley's records for shotgun and rifle shooting at thrown targets.

In the early twentieth century, trapshooting grew in popularity in the United States; while most shooters were men, women did participate. A *New York Times* article on 31 December 1916 contains a quote from John Philip Sousa, the composer and bandmaster, who observed:

> Women are finding trapshooting even more enjoyable than golf, tennis, and the other games they now play. In the shotgun game she is not classified as a woman. She is not segregated from the man. She meets men, shooting on an equal footing. Indeed women have so far advanced in trapshooting that they are permitted to enter the Grand American [competition]. Shooting makes a woman agile and alert. I have shot at the traps with many women and never have I seen an ungraceful one who used a shotgun well.

One of the first female shooters to score well in open competition against men was Marjorie

Foster of England. The thirty-three-year-old Women's Legion World War I motor driver defeated ninety-nine male marksmen and won the King's Prize trophy at Bisley—and £1,250—with her very last shot, becoming the first woman ever to win the trophy in the seventy years it had been awarded.

The contest description vividly chronicles a titanic encounter in which Foster eventually had a shot-by-shot duel with a Lieutenant Eccles of the Seaforth Highlanders. Dressed in a khaki coat and shorts with a battered felt hat over "shingled hair," Foster found that everything came down to her last shot. When she hit a bull's-eye, at a distance of 1000 yards, there was a "pandemonium of cheers and shouts on the historic Bisley rifle range." Princess Helena Louise, the king's cousin, spoke to her and acknowledged her "marvelous performance." King George sent her the following telegram:

> I most heartily congratulate Miss Foster on winning my prize. That she should have done so is a wonderful achievement in the history of rifle shooting and as such will be universally acclaimed.

By the mid-1930s skeet shooting had become widely popular in the United States and was thought by some to be especially attractive to women because the weapons were quieter, lighter, of smaller gauge, and with less kick/recoil. Maribel Y. Vinson (1936), in an article entitled "Women in Sports," supported the thesis that skeet shooting was an ideal sport for athletic women. She also noted that the sport's popularity was resulting in designers of women's fashion creating a special ladies' shooting attire.

> The right costume is important to a good score. A free-swinging pleated skirt, oxfords for a good stance, and jackets that have big pockets or a belt for cartridges and a reinforcement of soft doeskin on the right shoulder are essential. There must be no lapel or breast pocket to catch the gun as it comes up from rest position for the actual shot.

Twenty years later, in 1956, the National Skeet Shooting Association (of America) released statistics showing that a Mrs. Leon (Carola) Mandel broke three open (men and women) world records, thus becoming the first woman in the history of skeet shooting or trapshooting to lead all competitors, both men and women, in the annual competitive averages.

Women practice shooting at the first Women's Rifle Club in 1908 at Carisbrook on the Isle of Wight in England. (Hulton-Deutsch Collection/Corbis)

In 1963 the annual Amateur Championships of America trapshooting jamboree—an open competition with men and women—saw twenty-seven-year-old Sheila Egan of Mount Vernon winning the competition at Pelham Manor, New York. It was the first triumph by a woman in this event, which was first held in 1936. Nevertheless, the 13 May 1965 *New York Times* account of her victory—at least from a revisionist historical perspective—smacks of an excess of patronizing condescension. The tenor of the piece is uncomfortably sexist. For example, the headline reads "Model Defeats Men," and in the piece Egan is described as a "blue-eyed model" who "can handle a shotgun, skillet or fashion assignment with equal skill." During the competition itself Egan was praised for her coolness under pressure—"as cool as a model taking a plunge at Jones Beach."

International women's shooting competitions really took off in the early 1950s. The Randle Trophy, a women's team match, began in 1952 with teams of ten members firing on national ranges. Twenty shots are fired at distances of 45.7 and 91.4 meters (150 and 300 feet). The dominating presence has been the United States. Another, more short-lived, competition for women was the Northern Sea Cup Match. Eight northern European nations took part in the series, which ran from 1964 to 1969. In 1970 Britain organized and promoted a similar competition for all members of the International Shooting Union (ISU).

While Marjorie Foster's success at Bisley in 1930 marked the first major breakthrough for women shooters, her competition was restricted to personnel with a military link or association in the British Empire. The first female to establish herself on the global stage of open shooting competition was Margaret L. Thompson (nee Murdock, born 25 August 1942 in Topeka, Kansas). Murdock shot a score of 391 to win a gold medal in the small-bore rifle competition at the 1967 Pan-American Games. Not only was her score a world record, it was the very first time that a female had bettered a man's record in any sport.

RULES AND PLAY

Modern shooting—organized competition with standard rules and relatively uniform equipment—began in 1907 when eight countries formed the International Shooting Union. Women, however, did not begin participating in major international shooting events until after World War II. The Bisley competitions in Great Britain were exceptions in that women took part beginning in the 1920s.

The first world championship for women took place in 1966. Olympic open shooting (men and women together) began at the 1968 Mexico Olympics. At the 1984 Los Angeles Olympics some shooting events (pistol, small-bore rifle, and air rifle) were made all-male or all-female. The 1996 Olympics in Atlanta saw all shooting events compartmentalized along gender lines, with 130 women competing in five events: 25-meter pistol, 10-meter air pistol, 10-meter air rifle, 50-meter three-position small-bore rifle, and double trap. Men compete in ten events. The nationalities of the women winners—China, Russia, Poland, Yugoslavia, and the United States—indicate how international the sport has become since the 1950s. Since 1984 Olympic women's shooting has been dominated by East European countries and occasional American success. Russia has been the most dominating presence in terms of winning Olympic medals, having accumulated nine in the 1988, 1992, and 1996 Games. Bulgaria and Yugoslavia hold second place in the medal count, each having won six medals in 1988, 1992, and 1996. Both the United States and Germany have six shooting medals to their credit, and China has won four since 1984. Other countries whose women have won medals are Poland (3), Australia (2), and Canada, Italy, Japan, Mongolia, and South Korea (1 each).

One of the problems for women shooters is financial support. Unlike (beach) volleyball or basketball or track and field, the sport does not have a lucrative professional or quasi-professional league or circuit. Deena Wigger, who finished ninth in the rifle event at the 1988 Seoul Olympics and won gold medals at the Pan-American Games of 1983 and 1995, has commented, "You're

SHOOTING AS AN INTERNATIONAL SPORT

Like many sports, shooting first became an organized sport in Great Britain, then became popular in the United States, and later became an international sport, with athletes from other nations dominating the sport. The results of the 1996 Olympics support this conclusion:

25m	pistol	Li Duihong	China
10m	air pistol	Olga Klochneva	Russia
10m	air rifle	Renata Mauer	Poland
50m	small-bore rifle	Alexandra Ivosev	Yugoslavia
	double trap	Kim Rhode	United States

almost stagnant for those years when you're training for the Olympics. It's like you're not making progress in other areas of your life." Compounding this economic hardship are the demands of a sport that can be all-consuming.

The 1992 Olympics were the final competition in which men and women competed together. Launi Mieli (1996:28), writing in the *American Rifleman,* observed that Shan Zang of China, en route to winning a gold in skeet, dominated the field by shooting a perfect 200/200 in the preliminaries. Her Olympic record-setting performance "spoke volumes about the ability of women to shoot on an equal level with men".

The National Rifle Association of the United States continued to introduce shooting to women in the 1990s. *The NRA Women's Shooting Event Handbook* provides step-by-step guidelines to help NRA clubs set up an enjoyable half-day introductory shooting event for women. It is not generally known that the National Riflemen's Association changed its name to the National Rifle Association in recognition of the increasing number of women members. Several women have won open NRA national championships, including Mary Stidworthy of the U.S. Army, who defeated some 500 contestants in the 1997 small-bore prone rifle championship.

Some women display a number of physical, physiological, and psychological characteristics that work to their advantage in the sport of shooting. According to 1992 standard rifle gold medalist Launi Mieli, women have several advantages. First, women's lower center of gravity improves shooting stability, balance, and equilibrium. Second, women frequently enter the various shooting disciplines with fewer predetermined expectations. Third, women, in the sphere of shooting, seem very receptive to implementing advice from others to improve their technique. Finally, women demonstrate the patience and readiness to wait, and wait, and wait to take the optimum shot.

Scott Crawford

See also Hunting

Bibliography

Antal, Laslo. (1983) *Competitive Pistol Shooting.* East Ardsley, UK: EP Publishing.

Arlott, John, ed. (1975) *The Oxford Companion to World Sports and Games.* London: Oxford University Press.

Crawford, Scott A. G. M. (1986) "Recreation at Sea—Leisure Pursuits on the Otago (New Zealand) Bound Emigrant Ships, 1847–1869." *Mariners Mirror: The International Journal of the Society for Nautical Research* 73, 3 (August): 319–328.

Elkins, F. (1936) "Skeet Fad is Gaining." *New York Times* (19 July).

Hickok, Ralph. (1992) *The Encyclopedia of North American Sports History.* New York: Facts-on-File, 325–326.

Howard, S. (1998) "In Search of Remarkable Women." *American Rifleman* 146, 1 (January): 28.

Mieli, Launi. (1996) "NRA Woman's Voice." *American Rifleman* 144, 11 (November/December): 28.

The NRA Women's Shooting Event Handbook.

Parish, David, and John Anthony. (1981) *Target Rifle Shooting.* East Ardsley, UK: EP Publishing.

Thompson, E. (1996) "Women's Voice." *American Rifleman* 144, 4 (April): 24.

Vinson, Maribel Y. (1936) "Women in Sports." *New York Times* (13 September) p. 10, Sports Section.

Wilson, H. (1951) *My First Eighty Years.* Hamilton, New Zealand: Paul's Book Arcade, 137.

Wilson, R. L., and G. Martin. (1998) "Little Miss Sure Shot." *American Rifleman* 146, 10 (October): 46–49, 58–60.

SHOUAA, GHADA

(1973–)

SYRIAN HEPTATHLETE

Ghada Shouaa is the only Syrian athlete (male or female), as of 1999, to have won a gold medal in the Olympics and also the first Middle East athlete to win a medal in the world track and field championships. The victories made her a national hero in Syria and a symbol of the possibility of international sports success.

Shouaa was born in Mahada, about 200 miles from Damascus, into a Christian Arab family. Her father was a petroleum engineer. At 5 feet, 10 inches, Shouaa was first attracted to basketball and played for the national team in 1989–1990

Ghada Shouaa of Syria celebrates after winning the 800-meter running event at the World Track and Field Championships in 1995 in Barcelona, Spain. (Diether Endlicher/AP Photos)

while working part-time in an electronics factory. She then switched to track and field and began to practice for the heptathlon on an old track in Mahada. She placed twenty-fourth at the 1991 world championships and twenty-fifth at the 1992 Olympics, and then withdrew from the 1993 world championships. In 1994 she came to the attention of the international sports community when she finished first in the Asian Games at Hiroshima with a world-class score of 6,360 points.

Her success also made the Syrian government and sports federation take notice of her potential. The federation retained the former Soviet field coach Kim Bokhantsov to train her, and the government provided financial support so that she could train in Egypt, Italy, and Australia, although Syria remained her training base. The support and training paid off; she won the gold in the prestigious Gotzis, Austria, championship in 1995 and later that year won the world championship in Sweden. In 1996 her victories continued with a repeat of the victory at Gotzis and then a gold at the Atlanta Olympic Games, where she defeated Natalya Sazanovich of Belarus and Denise Lewis of Great Britain.

The Asian, world, and Olympic victories made Shouaa a celebrity in Syria. President al-Assad awarded her a new house and an automobile as rewards, television and radio broadcasters hailed her Olympic victory as "glorious and marvelous," and people were reported to be greeting each other the day after her victory with the salutation "mabruk," meaning congratulations. In 1997 she injured her back, delaying her quest to break the world record for the heptathlon.

Despite her success, Shouaa is not without her critics. Purists criticize her technique and argue that her success is due to sheer physical strength rather than correct and smooth technique. Others have suggested that her victories in the Olympics and other world events came when the three leading heptathletes of the early 1990s—Jackie Joyner-Kersee of the United States and Heike Drechsler and Sabine Braun of Germany—competed with or had to withdraw because of injuries. Her supporters point out that her scores in the these events were all world class and that perhaps she is the leader of a new generation of heptathletes. Shouaa herself has indicated that she regrets not being able to compete against the now-retired Joyner-Kersee and that she hopes her success will encourage more Syrian women to participate in sports.

David Levinson

Bibliography

Hendershott, Jon. (1996) "Shouaa Too Stong." *Track and Field News* (October):73.

"It's Shouaa Enough." *Track and Field News*. (1995) December, p. 49.

Powell, David. (1995) "Syria Celebrates Shouaa Gold." *The Times of London* (11 August).

SILAT

Silat is the indigenous martial art of Indonesia and Malaysia. Its prominent features are weapon training, ground combat, kicks, strikes, and grappling techniques, as well as locks, pins, and holds.

It is a graceful martial art, with circular and fluid as well as rapid movements that are often accompanied by music.

Silat was initially an all-male activity, and it is still predominantly male due to cultural and religious factors. Since the early 1970s, as these countries have modernized, women have begun to participate more in silat. Their visibility has also increased because of silat's popularity in the West, where women began to take part earlier.

HISTORY

The early development of silat is closely linked to the Minangkabau, an ethnic group on the island of Sumatra. Anthropologists believe that these people created the basis of what is now known as *pencak silat* throughout the Indonesian archipelago. From Sumatra, silat spread to many islands of Indonesia and became intermingled with other martial arts from China, Southeast Asia, and India. Today more than 800 different styles of silat are recognized throughout Indonesia.

Silat's tradition as an all-male activity arose from its culture of origin. The Minangkabau, as a matrilineal society, had separate living quarters for women and men. Young unmarried men lived in the *surau*, or men's house, where they developed the art of silat as a means of self-defense and self-discipline. Silat was closely linked to life in the surau and to the practice of Islam, which was introduced into Sumatra around the sixteenth century. Religious practices, too, centered around the surau. *Surau* is a specific Minangkabau term and custom, although other similar customs exist in other ethnic groups throughout Indonesia, under different names. Given these Islamic influences, silat remained an almost exclusively male activity to which women had little access. Mixed training of male and female students was generally discouraged, and since silat was traditionally practiced at night and outdoors, women were excluded from the training. Forms of nightly entertainment available to women usually took place indoors and included storytelling and folk singing.

Indonesia became independent in 1949, and the new government began efforts to modernize the nation. Since that time, silat schools have detached themselves from the surau, and since the early 1970s have opened their doors to women.

Silat is taught in public schools as part of physical education programs established by the government and also in private clubs. Female pupils are encouraged to participate in the training. Since silat has become a sport, the number of female practitioners has increased dramatically. Javanese, Balinese, Sundanese, and other ethnic groups in Indonesia have their own distinct silat forms. Typically, silat taught as a sport in schools is a standardized version of one of these distinct local variants of silat.

RULES AND PLAY

Since the middle of the twentieth century, many styles of silat have developed, including a new branch that is a competitive sport. Others have remained almost exclusively focused on self-defense and are often taught in private to a few select students.

The type of silat that is taught as a sport has added a ranking system, something not used in the traditional silat training as a martial art. Students of sport silat must pass tests and are awarded colored belts that reflect their rank. Participation in local tournaments is also based on the ranking system, and participants of equal rank compete against each other. Tournaments on the international level admit only contestants of the higher ranks.

Indonesia alone has more than 1,000 official silat schools (*perguruan*). The latest data from PERSILAT headquarters (the sport's international association) in Jakarta suggest that between 20 percent and 25 percent of silat practitioners in Indonesia are female. This percentage varies with the region, style, and age group, with urban areas having more female participants than rural areas. Generally, many more females under fifteen practice silat than do older women. Females typically stop practicing silat once they are married, while male practitioners generally continue. Female teachers can be found in many of these schools, but they are a definite minority.

The national organization of silat in Indonesia is IPSI (Ikatan Pencak Silat Indonesia, established in 1947), based in Jakarta; it is the lead organization of PERSILAT (Persekutan Pencak Silat Antarabangsa—International Pencak Silat Federation), the international umbrella organization for silat. PERSILAT has branches elsewhere in Asia and in Europe, the Middle East, Australia, and North and South America.

In nations around the world there are silat schools where silat is taught as martial art, a sport, or both. In other countries, too, women have taken up the practice. Schools that emphasize the sport aspect of silat support competitions and host regional and national tournaments. PERSILAT organizations hold national qualifying competitions and send national champions to higher-level international tournaments in Indonesia and Malaysia. European countries also hold European silat championships.

ELITE COMPETITION

World championships and other international tournaments are held in Indonesia and Malaysia every few years. As of 1999, the most recent World Pencak Silat Championships had been held in 1987, 1992, and 1997. Another important international competition is the Nusantra, or World Invitational, which is held every two years. Borneo was the site of the 1999 Nusantra competition. The Southeast Asia Games also include silat as a competitive sport.

Women have participated in all international tournaments since their inception, although their competitions are separate from those of men. The percentage of female participants in competitions varies, but on average they constitute between 10 and 20 percent of all participants. That is a lower percentage than in tournaments on the national level, where they constitute about 20 percent to 25 percent. Indonesia and Malaysia have the strongest pool of female silat athletes. Within Europe, the Netherlands and Spain have had the most consistent, strongest, and largest contingent of female silat competitors. The United States and Australia have increasingly stronger female teams as well. Women participate as referees and jurors

RANDAI FOLK THEATER

West Sumatra (Indonesia) is the birthplace of a popular folk theater form that developed out of the local martial arts called silek (the local name for silat). Called Randai, this theater genre is the main performing art form of the Minangkabau ethnic group, one of the last remaining matrilineal societies in the world.

Randai is a composite art form consisting of martial arts, dance, instrumental music, song, and acting. Just like silek, Randai was originally an all-male tradition, but over the past thirty years female performers have made their way into Randai. Theatre troupes today are mixed and feature both female and male performers. Only very few all-male groups remain active today while just thirty years ago all Randai troupes had young boys playing female roles. The girls and women performing in Randai have to be trained in silek.

Randai evolved at about 1900 and its development was greatly influenced by the silek. The indigenous martial arts form continues to be featured prominently in Randai today. Randai employs a circular formation in its martial arts dance called galombang that is derived from a circular formation employed in the regular martial arts practice. The movement repertoire employed in this dance and in fighting scenes is taken from techniques of the various regional silek styles. Costumes for male actors and for galombang dancers are derived from those traditionally worn in silek. Certain musical elements, mainly the percussive sequences, have evolved from specific clapping techniques found in silek. Randai texts are derived from Minangkabau stories and often feature silek thematically. Conflicts in the stories often culminate in fighting scenes acted out with silek techniques. Silek in Randai is used dramatically to highlight climactic points in the story and to enhance the visual beauty of scenes.

As more and more female performers participate in Randai a shift in focus to female heroes is perceptible—especially to female protagonists who are proficient in silek. In this sense, Randai, firmly rooted in silek and Minangkabau tradition, is a mirror of continuity and changes in the Minangkabau culture.

on all levels of tournaments for the female competitions.

The tournaments feature combat (*olahraga*) and form (*kembangan*) competitions. In the combat competitions, the athletes are judged on a point system based on executed techniques and hits. Like most combative sports, silat combat competitions are divided into weight divisions.

The form competitions are divided into solo forms (1.5 minutes in length) and group forms (5 minutes in length). Both of these are further subdivided into sequences with and without weapons. In both forms the athlete's performance is judged based on difficulty and variety of the executed techniques (*wiraga*), on expression, on proper etiquette and grace (*wirasa*), and on precision, rhythm, and timing with the music (*wirama*).

CONCLUSION

Women compete in all categories but have historically excelled especially in the form competition. Although still hampered by cultural factors in some parts of the world, women seem likely to continue to increase their participation in this practice.

Kirstin Pauka

Bibliography

Draeger, Donn F. (1972) *Weapons and Fighting Arts of the Indonesian Archipelago.* Rutland, VT: Tuttle.

Orlando, Bob. (1996) *Indonesian Fighting Fundamentals.* Boulder, CO: Paladin Press.

Wahab, Anuar Adb. (1989) *Silat Olahraga: The Art, Technique, and Regulation.* Kuala Lumpur: Dewan Bahasa dan Pustaka, Kementerian Pendidikan Malaysia.

SINGAPORE

Singapore is a small nation with a population of just under 4 million, located in Southeast Asia between Malaysia and Indonesia. Singapore became an independent island state in 1965 when it separated from Malaysia, but the country continued to follow a sport system that is strongly associated with the legacy of British colonial rule of the region. The colonial inheritance, which had hindered participation by women, established only a weak platform for widespread participation. A Sport for All policy began in 1973 with the founding of the Singapore Sports Council. Sport for All promotes exercise, recreation, and a healthy lifestyle. There has also been a complementary thrust toward sports excellence.

Initially the policy focused on male fitness and the need for rugged armed forces recruits and healthy workers. Great emphasis was placed on voluntary involvement in health and fitness activity programs for women. Nevertheless, women's participation rates remained low for many years. By 1980, only 20 to 30 percent of all participants were female. By 1992, the figure had apparently risen to 37.6 percent, and five years later to 42 percent.

The traditional games for women in Singapore are characteristic of many British Commonwealth countries: swimming, netball, tennis, hockey, badminton, yachting, table tennis, and track and field. Newer additions, which have proved popular, include ten-pin bowling, volleyball, and basketball. The Asian martial arts such as taekwondo, judo, and wushu are still played in schools and clubs, and competitively at a regional level.

The years that immediately followed World War II mark the beginning of international representation in sports for Singaporean women. At the first Asian Games (New Delhi, 1951), Lorenza Dowdeswell became the first woman to win a medal for Singapore at any major games, taking silver for the 200-meter sprint and the 80-meter hurdles. Tang Pei Wah became the first Singaporean woman to compete in the Olympic Games in 1952, in the 80-meter hurdles. Janet Elizabeth Jesudason and Mary Klass participated at the Melbourne Games in 1956 in the 100-meter sprint and the 200-meter sprint.

In swimming, Singapore achieved its first international successes after independence. At the first Southeast Asia Peninsula Games, eleven-year-old Patricia Chan won the first of the thirty-nine gold medals she was to achieve between 1965 and 1973. Water sports were, and remain, the sports in which Singapore has had the most success.

The most popular and successful of the team games are hockey and netball. However, individual games provide the best illustration of the potential of Singaporean women at the international level. Adeline Wee won the ten-pin bowling title at the World Games held in London in 1985, and Mah Li Lian was Asian squash champion between 1988 and 1994. At the biennial Southeast Asia Games, the most successful sport has been swimming. Multiple medal winners have included Junie Sng (in 1977 and 1979) and Joscelin Yeo (in 1993 and 1995). In the Asian Games, success has come in the sports of yachting, bowling, and squash.

Female Olympic representation has been sporadic. Between 1948, when Singaporeans first participated, and 1996, only thirteen women represented Singapore at the Olympics, compared to ninety-one men. The following participated under the Singaporean flag: Tang Pei Wah (1952), Janet E. Jesudason (1956), Mary Klass (1956), Patricia Chan (1972), Tay Chin Joo (1972), Chee Swee Lee (1976), Surattee Khatijah (1988), Zarinah Abdullah (1992, 1996), Joscelin Yeo (1992, 1996), May Ooi (1992), Yvonne Danson (1996), Jing Jun Hong (1996), and Tracey Tan (1996). In the sports administration, Annabel Ess, an executive member of the International Hockey Federation, received an International Olympic Committee award for her contribution to Olympism in 1990.

The vision of the Singapore Sports Council is to instil in Singaporeans a lifelong appreciation of sports as a means to help people enjoy a better life. The Sports for Life program focuses on potential participants and aims to make it easier for all Singaporeans to enjoy the benefits and fun of playing sports and keeping fit. The focus on working adults, housewives, senior citizens, and family participation indicates the importance of the role assumed by women. The institution of a National Women's Sport Carnival in 1997 was an important initiative to encourage housewives and senior citizens to participate.

Nicholas G. Aplin
Teoh Chin Sim

Bibliography

Aplin, Nicholas G. (1998) "Values and the Pursuit of Sports Excellence: The Case of Singapore." Unpublished doctoral dissertation.

Singapore Sports Council. (1997a) "National Sports Participation Survey."

Singapore Sports Council. (1997b) "Annual Report."

SKATEBOARDING

Skateboarding is a recreational and competitive sport in which the skateboarder rides the wheeled board as a surfer rides a wave. As a so-called new sport, skateboarding has something of an anti-establishment image. The participants have overwhelmingly been male, and although several societal factors have discouraged female participation, girls and women were making an inroad into the sport in the late 1990s.

First popular in the 1960s, the sport has gone through several periods of change since then. In each period, the style of skateboarding changed in a way that often reflected the dominant values of some element of the United States youth culture of the time. For example, skateboarders were associated with surfboarders in the 1960s, with punks in the late 1970s and early 1980s, and with the grunge movement during the 1990s. Although skateboarding often conveys this counterculture ethos, the sport also has a significant mainstream component.

HISTORY

Although no exact date can be established for the origins of the sport, it is a twentieth-century invention. It is believed that the first skateboards were created by connecting roller-skate wheels to a board. Although some publicly and privately funded skateboard parks have been established, the majority of skateboarding takes place on the streets. The beginning of its popularity can be located in the 1960s in the United States with the mass marketing of skateboards. The subsequent rise of skateboarding led to many injuries that prompted medical associations to warn people of the inherent dangers of the sport. These concerns, as well as the concerns of property owners, led to a ban on skateboarding in public areas in many communities. These issues as well as design limitations led skateboarding to decline in popularity in the late 1960s and early 1970s.

Skateboarding's appeal rebounded in the early 1980s when a new design, using polyurethane wheels and a wider board, made the sport more exciting for young men because they could now launch themselves off the ground and performs twists and turns in the air. Previously, skateboards were long and thin and the style of the sport was like slalom skiing. The basic jumping skill is called an ollie. With this skill skateboarders are able to jump and then slide their boards on variety of obstacles they find on the streets. Since the early 1980s the boards have become shorter and wider, and the street or trick style of skateboarding has been very popular. This trend is similar to the change in downhill skiing from slalom to the inclusion of so-called hot-dog skiing. Other styles of skateboarding have recently emerged, including all-terrain boards that have oversized wheels and are used to travel on unpaved ground.

Although the vast majority of skateboarders have been young men, males and females who participate share similar reasons for becoming involved in the sport. These include the individualistic nature of the sport, the freedom to participate without competing, and the absence of a bureaucratic structure that makes it possible for others to control the conditions of their participation. Skateboarders have acknowledged their anti-establishment stance as a desire to participate in a sport in which they can practice a physical activity without strict regulations and without adult control.

LIMITS ON FEMALE PARTICIPATION

One of the key social factors that has discouraged participation by girls and women has been traditional gender expectations, especially the link between sports participation and being masculine. Although skateboarding has been an alternative for young people who do not fit into or accept mainstream types of sport, it remains an especially important means to confirm young males' masculinity. One way to prove masculinity is to demonstrate that one is not feminine. To uphold the masculine status of skateboarding, many males have not actively encouraged female participation, relying on gender stereotypes to explain the lack of female participation. For example, many young male skateboarders believe that girls did not want to participate in a sport where they may injure or bruise themselves because it would not look right for a female to flaunt bruises. When females have tried to skate with these males, they have often been labeled in a derogatory fashion, one that did not give females credit for being skateboarders. A common label was Skate Betty. These were females who were described as girls who wanted to meet cute guys, not to skateboard seriously. Occasionally, young male skaters claimed that females were not naturally suited to such a risk-taking sport.

Skateboarding is not just a sport for the young, as this elderly woman demonstrates. (Richard Hamilton Smith/Corbis)

Another factor affecting females is the social world of the skateboarding industry. The majority of skateboarding companies are run by former skateboarders, mainly men from the United States. Consequently, very few companies sponsor female skateboarders, and the advertising of skateboard companies rarely portrays females as legitimate skateboarders. For example, of the several hundred professional skateboarders in the 1990s, only a few have been female. One of the top skateboarders is Cara-Beth Burnside, a woman who was also a member of the 1998 U.S. Olympic snowboarding team.

THE FEMALE RESPONSE

Female skateboarders often acknowledge that the social expectations for females constrain their opportunities to be seen as legitimate skateboarders. They feel that males do not take them seriously and that to be accepted they need to be better than most of the males. Other females note that their male friends who are supportive tend to be patronizing, which indicates that they are not being treated as equals. Many of the younger females try to fit in by being one of the guys.

The skateboarding industry is changing in ways that encourage female participation. Some companies are now owned by women, and others are more open than before to sponsoring females. Another factor influencing the greater acceptance of females is the economic reality involved in the marketing of alternative sports in the 1990s. During that decade, commercialization of these sports became a profitable venture, with the Extreme Games, a festival of alternative and high-risk sports, televised on the all-sports television network, ESPN. In addition, a major skateboarding company helped sponsor another ESPN promotion of skateboarding, the All Girls Skate Jam. Thus, while skateboarding is neither a mainstream sport nor a sport popular with girls and women in 1999, it continues to grow in popularity and some women continue to compete.

Becky Beal

See also Extreme Sports

Bibliography

Beal, Becky. (1995) "Disqualifying the Official: An Exploration of Social Resistance in the Subculture of Skateboarding." *Sociology of Sport Journal* 12: 252–267.

———. (1996) "Alternative Masculinity and Its Effects on Gender Relations in the Subculture of Skateboarding." *Journal of Sport Behavior* 19, 3: 204–220.

Davidson, Ben. (1976) *The Skateboard Book.* New York: Gosset & Dunlap.

Davidson, Judith. (1985) "Sport and Modern Technology: The Rise of Skateboarding, 1963–1978." *Journal of Popular Culture* 18, 4: 145–157.

Egan, J. (1998) "Athlete: Girl Over Board." *Conde Nast Sports for Women* 166 (April): 133–135.

Maeda, Karen. (1991) "Rights for Skateboarders." [Letter to the editor] *Windsor Beacon* (October): 17.

SKATING, ICE FIGURE

Figure skating combines gymnastics and dance on ice and adds to this its own unique form of athletic movement. In Europe and North America figure skating reigns as the quintessential girls' sport. For much of the twentieth century, figure skating was one of only a handful of sports viewed as compatible with the physical and moral standards of femininity. Today the sport is so closely identified with girls and women that boys who figure skate are often ridiculed by their peers. Indeed, some amateur figure skating associations have designed seminars and other programs to encourage boys to stick with the sport—an ironic development given that in its earliest days figure skating was an almost exclusively male pastime.

HISTORY

The history of figure skating is a history of social and technological change. Archaeological evidence in Northern Europe and North America suggests that humans were using bone runners as a form of winter transport several thousand years ago. Skating historians invariably refer to the wearers of such primitive skates as men, but there is no way of knowing from the bone remnants themselves whether males or females wore them. Eventually bone was replaced by wood and then, sometime during the Middle Ages, iron replaced wood. Fixed to the bottom of a block of wood, an iron runner permitted a skater to push harder and move faster across the ice.

Although ice skating is mentioned in Icelandic stories dating back to the second century, the first recorded eyewitness report was published in England, in Latin, in 1180. In his *Description of London,* William Fitz-Stephen described how groups of young men, some with bones tied to their feet, "do slide as swiftlie as a bird flyeth in the aire." The oldest existing picture of skating shows what may have been the aftereffect of such speed; it is also the first evidence that women did skate. A Dutch woodcut from 1498 shows a young girl, Lidwina (1380–1433), lying on the ice after a fall, two female friends at her side. Skating historians seem most interested in Lidwina's curved iron skates and in a man in the background of the image. The man is gliding with his free leg (the leg that is not on the ice) raised to the side, a pose that suggests that he is using edged blades and performing a Dutch roll, the height of skating technique at the time (now called an outside edge). More important, the woodcut suggests that skating was an acceptable pastime for males and females in the late 1300s. Lidwina never fully recovered from her injuries and lived in great pain for the rest of her life. Her heroic suffering led, in 1890, to her canonization by the Roman Catholic Church. She is now known as the patron saint of skaters. The people of Schiedam in the Netherlands, where Lidwina's bones are interred, say that it was her protection that saved the town from bombing during World War II.

In the Netherlands, skating was recreation and a way of getting easily from place to place. A painting by Pieter de Hoogh (1629–c. 1677) shows two women skating with baskets on their heads, most likely en route to market. Other prints show men and women from all classes, even the aristocracy, skating together on crowded canals. In a letter to Louis XIV, the French ambassador to the Netherlands wrote: "Twas a very extraordinary thing to see the Princess of Orange clad in petticoats shorter than are generally worn by ladies so strictly decorous, these tucked up half-way to her waist, and with iron pattens on her feet learning to slide sometime poised on one leg sometime on another." In shortening her petticoats and tucking up her skirt, the Princess of Orange discovered a fine solution to one of the difficulties that early women skaters faced—heavy skirts that impeded their ability to move on the ice.

As with many other sports, it was the aristocracy who had the time and the resources to develop skating beyond the basics. In Holland, it was the ladies of the Dutch court who taught the exiled Stuarts of England to skate. Home from exile in the 1660s, the Stuarts—the family of the future Charles II—brought iron skates and the Dutch roll. Several decades of unusually cold weather gave the English the opportunity to perfect their newfound skating skills. By 1742 the world had its first skating club, established in Edinburgh. But despite the example of the Princess of Orange and other noblewomen a century earlier, only upper-class men were permitted to join the club, and even they had to demonstrate that they could skate a circle on each foot and jump over three hats laid out on the ice.

In 1772 British lieutenant Robert Jones wrote the first textbook on skating. In it he lamented the absence of ladies on the ice, perhaps more for the sake of the men than that of the ladies themselves: "No motion can be more happily imagined for setting off an elegant figure to advantage, nor does the minuet itself afford half the opportunity [that skating does] of displaying a pretty foot," he observed. Later clubs, like the Skating Club of London, established in 1830, eventually devised a set of scaled-down entrance requirements specifically for ladies. There was, however, no similar loosening of the restrictions regarding class background. It was not until the twentieth century that organized figure skating ceased to be the preserve of the wealthy.

The tendency to assume women less capable or less willing than men to perform the edges and turns of the nineteenth-century skating repertoire is best represented by the safety frame. This wooden device, shaped like the railing on a small balcony, supported the skater as she pushed it along the ice in front of her. The frame was meant to free Victorian women of the fear of falling and the possibility that they might expose their underclothes. Of course, helpful male skaters were available to serve the same purpose. Combination skating—when a group of skaters performed patterns together on the ice—and hand-in-hand skating were promoted as a means of ensuring women's safety. During an era when interactions between well-to-do women and men were carefully scrutinized, a pleasant side effect of these precursors to pairs and ice dancing was that they made it possible for men and women to meet each other and even to touch in public without fear of social scandal.

During the last half of the nineteenth century, technical developments made skating easier and more accessible. The institutionalization of figure skating as a sport accelerated. Steel skates were developed in Philadelphia in 1848. The first covered rink was built in Quebec City in 1858, complete with gaslights for safe skating at night. Artificial ice was invented in London in 1876. In this context, clubs grew up in Europe and North America. In England, the National Skating Association was founded in 1879 and merit tests were developed shortly thereafter. Other national skating associations followed, and the International Skating Union (ISU) was formed in 1892 as a means of standardizing rules for competitions.

Throughout this growth period, competitions were organized for women and men on the local and the international levels in figure and free skating. In most competitions men and women competed against each other. Nevertheless, only men skated at the first world championship, held in St. Petersburg in 1896, and at subsequent championships until 1902. Never imagining that a woman might be bold enough to compete against men, skating officials had written no rule to prohibit women's participation. So when English skater Madge Syers (1881–1917) entered the world championship in London in 1902, officials had no legitimate reason to keep her from skating. Syers went on to win the silver medal, behind the great Swedish skater Ulrich Salchow (1877–1949). But many observers, including Salchow himself, thought she should have won. The next year, the ISU changed the rules of the competition to prohibit women from competing, arguing that the length of women's skirts prevented judges from seeing their feet. It was not until 1906 that a women's competition was finally included, and Madge Syers became the first women's world champion. She repeated her win in 1907 and also in 1908, when figure skating made its Olympic debut at the Summer Games in London, one of the first sports to allow women to participate. In Britain, women and men continued to challenge each other at the national championships until the 1930s. Women were not permitted to judge international skating events until 1947.

In the era of the first international competitions, competitors were adults. Male competitors were often professional men who fit their skating around their careers. Female competitors were often, like Madge Syers, married women of high social standing. In competition the emphasis was on school figures and somewhat formal free skating routines. But while men experimented with a growing repertoire of jumps and spins, women were expected to maintain an elegant, nonathletic demeanor. Not until the 1920 Olympics did a woman, bronze medalist Theresa Weld (1893–1978) of the United States, perform a single-revolution jump—a salchow—in competition. For doing so she was chastised by the judges for her unfeminine behavior. Some say the jump cost Weld the gold medal. But her daring opened the door for further change.

SONJA HENIE AND THE MODERN ERA

In 1924, at the Winter Olympics in Chamonix, an eleven-year-old girl from Norway stunned the crowd and the judges with her youth, her combination of athleticism and artistry, and the shortness of her skirt. Sonja Henie (1912–1969), who was to become the most popular figure skater ever, finished last in this first international appearance, before going on to win ten world championships and three Olympic gold medals. It is an understatement to say that she changed the face of figure skating. As a child in what had previously been an adult sport, Henie introduced an athleticism that had not yet been seen in women's skating. Because of her youth, she broke no rules of decorum by wearing the short skirts that allowed her to do the jumps and spins usually performed by men. She was also among the first skaters to choreograph a skating program as if it were a ballet solo. Before this innovation, free skating routines relied heavily on the turns and edges used in school figures, linked up by a few special tricks. Henie's programs told a story with jumps and spins worked into a seamless whole.

Huge crowds greeted Sonja Henie at competitions and exhibitions. At the 1936 Olympics, rumors that a young British skater named Cecilia Colledge (1920–) had a good chance of dethroning the longstanding champion brought 200,000 people out to watch Henie's (barely successful) struggle to retain her crown. Retiring from competition after the 1936 season, Henie toured with her own skating show before heading for Hollywood. There she rented a rink and gave a performance that helped to launch her career with Twentieth Century-Fox. The first of Henie's eleven movies, *One in a Million,* was produced that same year.

As an Olympic champion, an exhibition skater, and a movie star, Henie was almost single-handedly responsible for bringing figure skating into popular culture. Her visibility in movie theaters and in newspaper and magazine advertising helped to transform skating from an upper-class to a middle-class sport and to create a glamorous image for women's skating. Idolized by thousands of young girls, Henie was the first ice princess. At the same time, she was said to be a ruthless businesswoman and she was one of the most financially successful female professional athletes ever.

THE RISE OF ARTISTIC SKATING

In her career as a show skater, Henie was following a tradition that had started in the mid-1800s with American-born skater Jackson Haines (1845–1879). In skating histories Haines is widely acknowledged as the founder of artistic skating. While European and North American skaters were pursuing a mechanical, scientific style, Haines drew on his dance training to introduce arm movements, adapt ballroom dances, and experiment with ballet positions on skates. Haines's international style was rejected as too ornamental in North America, so he left his wife and children and traveled to Europe. There his exhibitions received a much warmer reception, and Haines became a star.

Skating shows sprang up across Europe in his wake. One of their first female stars was Charlotte Oelschlagel (1896–1984), who began skating professionally in Berlin at the age of ten. In 1915 she moved to New York to skate at the Hippodrome—twice a day before an audience of 6,000 people. She also appeared in advertisements—one for a type of hair fastener—and in the first skating movie, *The Frozen Warning* (1915), a World War I spy story. Oeschlagel was the first woman to perform an axel jump, she invented the death spiral, and she performed as the dying swan from *Swan Lake* (on skates) alongside famed ballerina Anna Pavlova (en pointe). That her $5,000-per-week contract lasted for three years was concrete evidence of the appeal of the ice show as a modern form of entertainment. Oeschlagel was the necessary background to Sonja Henie's success. Even today, skating remains one of the few sports where professional opportunities for women are equal to—and sometimes surpass—those available to men.

French figure skater Surya Bonaly. (Neal Preston/Corbis)

After Henie, women's figure skating continued to advance technically, closing the gap between male and female skaters. Colledge, world champion in 1937, was the first woman to land a double jump, a salchow, in competition. Canadian Petra Burka (1946–) landed the first triple jump when she won the world championship in 1965. But it took another decade for triple jumps to become an expected part of women's programs. American skater Linda Fratianne (1960–), 1977 and 1979 world champion, was the first woman to land two different triples in her program, but what also set her apart was that she landed them easily and confidently. Just a few years later, another American, sixteen-year-old Elaine Zayak (1965–), won the world championship with six triple jumps in her program—four triple toe-loops and two triple salchows. The ISU responded to Zayak's groundbreaking feat with a rule that now prohibits skaters from performing any jump more than once in the long program, unless the second attempt is part of a combination jump. Concerned that the emphasis on triple jumps was removing the grace and elegance from women's (but not men's) skating, the ISU also instituted a rule requiring women's long programs to include a spiral. Skating's version of the arabesque, the spiral is a move in which the skater glides on one foot with her free leg elevated behind her.

Despite the ISU's nervousness about women's technical development, women now routinely land everything that men land except the triple axel and the quadruple toe-loop. But even this gap may close in the future. Two women have successfully landed the triple axel in competition: Midori Ito (1968–) of Japan in 1989, the year she became world champion, followed by Tonya Harding (1970–) of the United States, world silver medalist in 1991. American Michelle Kwan (1980–), the 1996 and 1998 world champion, is just one of a number of female skaters said to be working on the triple axel. Surya Bonaly (1974–) of France, world silver medalist from 1993 to 1995, has attempted—but never landed—quadruple toe-loops in competition.

One of the consequences of the increasing level of difficulty in women's programs is that elite skaters are becoming younger: 1994 Olympic gold medalist Oksana Baiul (1977–) of Ukraine was sixteen; Michelle Kwan won her first world championship at the age of fifteen; Tara Lipinski (1983–), 1997 world champion at fourteen, won the gold medal at the 1998 Olympics at the age of fifteen. An excellent jumper, Lipinski is 4 feet 11 inches tall, weighs 81 pounds, and still has the body of a child. The physics of jumping means it is generally easier for girls to learn triples before they reach puberty, as narrow-hipped, flat-chested bodies turn more easily in the air. Some observers worry that the huge emphasis placed on jumping ability may turn skating into an ice-bound version of gymnastics—a sport restricted to tiny girls at the expense of the maturity and artistry that come with experience.

In part, the tremendous technical achievements of recent free skaters are a result of improved coaching and better facilities. They are also a result of the now commonplace tendency for elite athletes to train full time in their sports. But more importantly, free skating has benefited immensely from the elimination of school figures from competition. Where figures once counted for 60 percent of a skater's score, in 1968 they were reduced to 50 percent. In 1973 the ISU introduced the short program to singles and pairs events. The organization was responding to public outcry following the win of Austria's Beatrix Schuba (1951–) in the 1972 world championships. Schuba, unmatched in her ability to trace school figures, placed ninth in the free skating portion of the competition—the only part of the competition seen by television viewers, who could not understand why such a lackluster skater was on the top of the podium. With the introduction of the short program, figures fell to 30 percent of the total mark. They were finally phased out altogether in 1990.

The short program is skating's pressure cooker. A fall or an error on one of its required elements can cost a skater a chance at a medal. While the rules—and the name—for the short program have changed over the years, they have always reflected the ISU's understanding of the difference between male and female skaters. Until recently, women were permitted to perform only two triple jumps in the program while men had the opportunity to do three if they executed a triple-triple combination. Both men and women must do three different spins. However, women are required to make one of these a layback spin, where the skater arches her back, sometimes until it is parallel with the ice—a position that suggests an extreme vulnerability—as she spins. The spin, which men rarely perform, requires flexibility and is thought to be one of skating's most feminine moves. Women, unlike men, are also required to perform a spiral sequence.

MALE SKATERS, FEMALE SKATERS

Despite the fact that the technical gap between male and female skaters is narrowing—or perhaps because of it—regulations and traditions in skating work to augment differences between the sexes. Some of these are based on everyday stereotypes of masculinity and femininity, while others hark back to skating's early days as a sport for the wealthy, for example, the tradition of calling female skaters "ladies" rather than women. While in some sports the tendency is to treat men and women more alike, in skating they continue to be distinguished from each other. For instance, the rules require women's long programs to be half a minute shorter than men's; they also require women's costumes to have skirts—a simple body suit and tights or a unitard are considered to present too athletic an image. Judges are known to reward women for making their jumps look effortless, while they reward men for showing off their strength and power. In skating, success for female athletes depends on the ability to appear feminine while expending the same energy required of a player in a 60-minute hockey game.

The importance of aesthetics in figure skating is reflected in the practice of awarding technical and presentation marks for each performance. In theory, presentation is meant to be a combination of musicality, expressiveness, and style; in fact, it often has much to do with appearance. Anecdotal evidence suggests that female skaters go to great lengths to achieve the right look—cosmetic surgery, breast reductions, extensive dental work, constant dieting—often with the encouragement of coaches, parents, judges, and other skating officials. In some skating schools and in many skating shows, skaters are required to submit to regular weigh-ins, a practice that is increasingly frowned upon as research shows that female skaters are at increased risk for eating disorders. As in other areas of popular culture, the ideal body type in skating has become considerably leaner over the past quarter-century.

A narrowly defined esthetic also means that for much of this century, the quintessential "ice princess"—the idolized female skater—has been conventionally pretty, unquestionably feminine, and white. While the majority of skaters are still pretty and white, it is no longer rare to see a person of color competing at the Olympics or world championships. Since 1985 eighteen of thirty-nine medalists in women's singles at the world championships have been women of color. In all the years before 1985, only one medalist was not white. This recent increasing diversity on the podium is slowly translating into a new image of the ice princess, expanding the range of preferred looks in the sport. For instance, after winning the Olympic silver medal in 1998, the elegant Chinese-American skater Michelle Kwan has had more success with endorsements and appearances than gold medalist Tara Lipinsky, who is white. In 1992 Japanese American Kristi Yamaguchi (1971–) was not so fortunate. After she won the Olympic gold medal, it was widely reported that her success in attracting endorsement contracts in the United States was surpassed by that of bronze medalist Nancy Kerrigan (1969–), whose white skin fit easily with the ice princess ideal. Even Japan's Midori Ito, the most technically advanced women's skater ever, has talked about her unhappiness with her look, with the shape of her small, muscular body—a shape that made it possible for her to land a triple axel—and about how she prefers the taller, leaner bodies of the European and North American skaters, who tend to be white.

In the 1990s, figure skating grew tremendously popular. Some say that the rapid growth of the skating business is an offshoot of the furor over the Kerrigan–Harding incident. At the 1994 U.S. Nationals, gold medal favorite Nancy Kerrigan was attacked on the knee by a pipe-wielding male assailant who was hired by the husband of Kerrigan's main rival, Tonya Harding. Harding went on to win the nationals when Kerrigan was forced to withdraw. The scandal made public the cut-throat side of skating and led to massive media interest in the women's event at the 1994

FIGURE SKATING GETS STAR BILLING ON TELEVISION

Of all women's sports, the most popular with television viewers in the United States (the majority of whom are women) is figure skating. Amateur and professional figure skating competitions, some designed especially for television, are shown regularly on network television and sport networks. Women's figure skating is so popular as televised entertainment that, according to Nielsen Media Research, the sixth highest rated American television show of all time is the women's figure skating competition on 23 February during the 1994 Winter Olympics. The competition two days later ranks #32 on the list. The only sporting events rated higher than the competition on the 23rd are Super Bowls XVI in 1982 and XVII in 1983. The only television shows rated above these sports events are episodes of *M*A*S*H*, *Dallas*, and *Roots*.

Olympic Games—it was to be the first time that the newly healthy Kerrigan would compete against Harding. Kerrigan weathered extensive physiotherapy and the media storm to place second and has since gone on to a successful professional career. Harding finished eighth. She was later stripped of her national title and banned from participating in officially sanctioned skating events. The sport of skating has not looked back. For competitive skaters there are more so-called amateur competitions offering prize money. For professional skaters there are more tours, more shows, more televised specials. There are also more agents involved in the sport, more promoters, more writers publishing books. And in all of these ventures, women play a major role.

THE BUSINESS OF SKATING

It is the business side of skating that most sets it off from other women's sports. In skating the women are as visible as the men—in some countries, especially the United States, they are more visible. For an elite few, this visibility can translate into a lucrative professional career supported primarily by female spectators. Indeed, without women fans, the skating industry would collapse. This makes skating events particularly attractive to television sports programmers and to advertisers, who usually find it hard to attract significant numbers of women viewers.

CONCLUSION

Figure skating is a mixed blessing for women. Where once women were not even allowed to join figure skating clubs, they are now the majority in the sport and the majority in its audience. Skating provides women unique athletic opportunities, but these come with a cost. Like Sonja Henie, skating's toughest athletes and most successful businesswomen are still expected to look and behave like princesses—too many go to dangerous lengths to do so. As the age of skaters drops, it is unlikely that this contradiction will be resolved any time soon.

Mary Louise Adams

See also Henie, Sonja; Kerrigan, Nancy

Bibliography

Baughman, Cynthia. (1995) *Women on Ice: Feminist Essays on the Tonya Harding/Nancy Kerrigan Spectacle.* New York: Routledge.

Brown, Nigel. (1959) *Ice-Skating: A History.* London: Nicholas Kaye.

Goodfellow, Arthur. (1977) *Wonderful World of Skates: Seventeen Centuries of Skating.* Mountainburg, AR: A & T Goodfellow.

Henie, Sonja. (1940) *Wings on My Feet.* New York: Prentice-Hall.

Milton, Steve. (1996) *Skate: 100 Years of Figure Skating.* Toronto: Key Porter.

Ryan, Joan. (1995) *Little Girls in Pretty Boxes: The Making and Breaking of Elite Gymnasts and Figure Skaters.* New York: Doubleday.

Smith, Beverley. (1994) *Figure Skating: A Celebration.* Toronto: McClelland and Stewart.

Whedon, Julia. (1988) *The Fine Art of Figure Skating: An Illustrated History and Portfolio of Stars.* New York: Harry N. Abrams.

Wilkes, Debbi, with Greg Cable. (1994) *Ice Time: A Portrait of Figure Skating.* Scarborough, Ontario: Prentice-Hall.

SKATING, ICE SPEED

Speed ice skaters skate as fast as possible against competitors. Women have always skated, and although many women participated in recreational skating, it was a considerable time before women could enjoy speed skating as one of their own organized sports.

HISTORY

The precise origins of ice skating are unknown. The oldest pair of skates found in Europe is reputed to be more than 4,000 years old, so skating can certainly be traced to the pre-Christian era. Skating was born out of a need for rapid movement in the winter climates of the Northern Hemisphere. The Netherlands was the home of modern ice skating. During winter in Amsterdam, the market was supplied by goods moved along frozen canals, including eggs carried in baskets on women's heads. In the same way that cycling or running had their roots in practical use, ice skating was often the only way that people were able to travel quickly and even conduct business during the long winter. Most Dutch children learned to skate at an early age, holding themselves upright by pushing a chair in front of them. Probably due to its usefulness, ice speed skating was about a hundred years ahead of figure skating in its development. Whereas figure skating tended to be the preserve of the town dwellers and the wealthy in the sixteenth and seventeenth centuries, speed skating was the sport favored by the less wealthy classes. These lower classes took part in touring races and town-to-town competitions, in which participants raced to see which person could get to the next town the fastest.

Skating was imported to Britain in the eighteenth century by Frieslanders who came to help build canals in the eastern part of England. The first speed skating competition is thought to have been held on the fens in eastern England in 1763. Skating was a popular pastime not only in England but also in Scotland, where the first club was set up in 1742. Many ice skating competitions were held in Britain through the latter part of the nineteenth century, and almost every town in the north and east of England had its own champion. Like boxing and horse racing, skating involved a great deal of betting. These British races seem to have been the preserve of men. However, at the same time in the Netherlands, women were taking part in touring speed skating races. In 1805, in Leeuwarden, a race was held in which 130 women took part. The town-to-town races and touring races were open to women as separate events; they did not compete against men. Women's competitions became increasingly peripheral as the nineteenth century wore on and the sport became increasingly organized by men. Participation in speed skating was considered unsuitable and immodest for women. Women continued to participate, however, and the first official world record was eventually set in Poland in January 1929. Their male counterparts had been setting world records since 1893 and competing internationally since 1885. Women had to wait until 1936 to have their own world championships recognized. The race for Olympic recognition was even slower. Women's speed skating was a demonstration sport in the 1932 Olympics in Lake Placid, but it did not become a full event until the 1960 Games at Squaw Valley. In contrast, men's speed skating had been part of the Winter Olympics since Chamonix in 1924. Speed skating has lagged far behind figure skating in terms of recognition as an Olympic-level sport for women. Figure skating adhered to the norms of femininity and was therefore acceptable, whereas speed skating has elements of strength and endurance that were regarded as less suitable for women, a factor that delayed its development as an Olympic sport.

Isabelle Charest, Canadian speed skater, competing in the women's 500-meter short track event at the 1994 Winter Olympics. (TempSport/Corbis)

Short-track speed skating has a much shorter history, and in this particular aspect of the sport the participation of men and women in organized competition has developed at the same pace. Although the precise date of short-track speed skating's origins have not been documented, it is said to have had its beginnings in indoor skating halls. Interest in indoor skating peaked in the 1920s and 1930s. Events at these early competitions consisted of unorganized circuit races. The first official meet was in Ayr, Scotland, in 1948, but it was not until 1967 that the International Skating Union (ISU) recognized short-track speed skating. The first ISU-recognized meet in which men and women were almost equally represented was held in 1978 in Solihull, England. At that event, skaters from eight different nations took part. Both men's and women's short-track speed skating made their debut at the same Olympics. They appeared as a demonstration sport at the 1988

AUGUSTANA UNIVERSITY COLLEGE
LIBRARY

Calgary Olympics and as part of the official program at Albertville in 1992.

RULES AND PLAY

All the different distances that figure in the race competition program in international events are spread over two days. Since most speed skaters compete in several events involving different distances, the number of races in which they take part in the course of 48 hours is quite a feat, considering the physical nature of the sport and the high levels of speed and endurance required. It would be like asking a runner to compete in the 100-, 200-, 800-, and 1500-meter races within the space of two days.

Long-track speed skating consists of two skaters racing on a two-lane 400-meter track, but they are racing against the clock, not each other. Pairs are drawn by ballot. During the race, the skaters must skate in both lanes; otherwise one would have an unfair advantage over the other. Lanes are changed at a point of the track called the crossing line. The rules for the sport were developed with the men's sport in mind and were later adopted for the women's competitions. The only difference between the men's and women's events is the length of the races. Women participate in the 500-, 1000-, 3000-, and 5000-meter races, whereas men compete at an additional distance of 10,000 meters and have no 3000-meter event.

It is sometimes assumed that short- and long-track speed skating differ only in that short track takes place indoors and long track outdoors, but this is not always the case. Short track is skated on a much smaller track, only 111 meters long. The skaters wear more protective equipment than long-track skaters; because these are peloton races

CLAP SKATES

Technology is a constantly increasing influence in sport, and ice speed skating is no exception. The latest advance is the clap skate or Klapschaats (in Dutch). The clap skate gets its name from the clap sound that is made as the blade snaps back into the pivot holding the blade.

Instead of the skate being attached to the boot in two places as with standard style skates, the blade attachment at the front is hinged, and the rear is slotted into a pivot which allows the skater to lift her heel in the air and extend her calf muscles fully. Thus the full length of the blade is on the ice a little longer with each stroke. In effect, the speed skater gets a longer push. The front of the skate blade does not dig into the ice as with a standard long track speed skate, so there is less friction on the ice with each stroke. Gerrit Jan Van Ingen Schenau at the Vrie University in Amsterdam studied long track speed skaters and discovered that speed skaters suppress an urge to extend their ankle during a stroke. In order to adapt to the new clap skates, long track speed skaters had to undergo a period of extensive retraining.

Clap skates have reduced race times. The following table compares 1997, when the traditional skate was used, and 1998 in which competitors predominantly used clap skates.

Women	500m	1000m	1500m	3000m	5000m
1997	38.69	1:17.65	1:59.30	4:09.32	7:03.26
1998	37.51	1:15.43	1:57.58	4:07.13	6:59.61
Decrease in lap time (sec.)	0.94	0.89	0.46	0.18	0.15
Decrease in finish time (sec.)	3.0	2.9	1.4	0.9	0.9

Thus far, the clap skates have only been used in the long track speed skating events, but manufacturers have been designing short track clap skates, so it will not be long before spectators hear the sound of the clap skates during short track events.

(a pack of skaters racing on the same track), there is more chance of collision or injury. The events at the 1992 Albertville Olympics included a 500-meter individual race and a 3000-meter relay. A 1000-meter race was added at Lillehammer in 1994. Spectators find the pack start and the sharply angled turns of the short-track skaters more thrilling to watch than long track. The possibility of a collision or fall is more likely in short track, which also adds to its excitement. Short-track speed skating has proved popular in countries whose climate would ordinarily not allow residents to participate in winter sports. For example, South Korea, a country not known for its success in the long-track event, won the Olympic gold in the women's short-track relay at Lillehammer.

Although speed skating is a sport that is often associated with the Dutch, it was not until 1968 that Carolina Geijessen, a twenty-one-year-old Dutch secretary, won Olympic gold in the 1000 meters. During Amsterdam winters Geijessen skated to work each day, a mirror of the seventeenth-century women carrying their eggs to market. The Soviet Union, East Germany, and the United States had long dominated the long-track sport, and all (the first two now as Russia and Germany) continue to do well. Lydia Skoblikova of the Soviet Union won two gold medals in the 1960 Squaw Valley Olympics and gold in all four events at the next Olympics in 1964 at Innsbruck. Bonnie Blair was the most successful U.S. Winter Olympian, with six medals. Although she has the same number as Skoblikova, Blair won her medals over a greater number of Olympic Games. Blair dominated the 500- and 1000-meter races. Like runners, speed skaters must concentrate on their particular talents, and multidistance champions such as Skoblikova are a rarity.

Women have influenced the men's events as well. Eric Heiden, the gold medal winner of all the men's speed skating events at Lake Placid in 1980, was coached by Dianne Holum, who had won silver and bronze medals at the 1968 Grenoble Olympics and gold and silver at the 1972 Games in Sapporo. Women continue to play a key role in the coaching, administration, and promotion of men's and women's speed skating.

Ice speed skating is a demanding and at times dangerous sport that is never likely to attract enormous numbers of participants. Women, however, after starting late, have done an impressive job of catching up to men in all aspects of the sport.

J.P. Anderson

Bibliography

Dyer, K.F. (1982) *Catching Up the Men: Women in Sport.* London: Junction Books.

Pratty, John. (1998) "Hinged Blades Skate Through Records." *Sports Technology* 1: 5–9.

Wallechinsky, David. (1992) *The Complete Book of the Olympics.* London: Aurum Press.

SKATING, IN-LINE

In-line skating is a variant of roller skating using a skate that employs a series of wheels, generally four or five, set in a straight line to mimic the ice skate. Since the sport took off in 1984, women and men have participated on equal terms. Released from the necessity of a frozen surface, the modern in-line skate sacrifices the precise control of the dual-axle roller skate for greater speed and adaptability to a wider range of surfaces.

HISTORY

In-line skating saw explosive growth in the late 1980s and early 1990s. The in-line skate itself, however, is more than 200 years old. Joseph Merlin separated skating from the winter ice with his introduction of an in-line roller skate at a London reception in 1760. Roller skates eventually developed into a cushioned, dual-axle device permitting superior maneuverability. The initial concept survived only as an off-season training aid to skiers and ice skaters. In 1979 Scott Olson, a nineteen-year-old American semiprofessional hockey player, modified an in-line skate for hockey use. Five years later, in 1984, Olson sold the patent rights to a private investor. Rollerblade, the resulting company, launched a major marketing campaign that popularized in-line skating and made the company's name synonymous with in-line skates and the sport of in-line skating.

Rollerblading has become a popular form of exercise in recent years. Here, a woman rollerblades on a road in Sun Valley, Idaho. (Karl Weatherly/Corbis)

Since that time, in-line skating has enjoyed a virtually even split between male and female participation. Several elements may have contributed to that situation. Certainly ice and roller skating, with their large numbers of female enthusiasts, fueled the early growth of in-line skating in North America and Europe. That in-line skating emerged in the 1980s, an era of generally rising female participation in sports and growing interest in physical fitness, may also have contributed to the apparent equality of participation that marks in-line skating. Finally, the wide range of activities in and the social nature of in-line skating contributed to its general appeal.

RULES AND PLAY

In addition to purely recreational involvement, in-line skaters may participate in competitions in speed and stunt skating. The latter, often termed "aggressive skating," consists of various maneuvers that bear a close resemblance to those found in skateboarding. Speed skating assumes a number of forms ranging from informal local events to those governed by the rules of the Federation Internationale de Roller-Skating, which accepts in-line skates in all categories of roller skating competition and has speed and hockey divisions reserved for in-line skaters. The superior speed of in-line skates has virtually eliminated dual-axle roller skates from speed competitions.

Roller hockey, the sport for which in-line skates assumed their modern form, became the first roller sport in the Olympics with its exhibition appearance in the 1992 Barcelona Games. Based on ice hockey, in-line roller hockey has professional leagues. As with other types of in-line skating, female and mixed-gender leagues may be found; however, the association with ice hockey appears to have rendered roller hockey the most male-dominated of the in-line activities.

Jefferey Charlston

Bibliography

Italia, Bob. (1991) *In-Line Skating.* Minneapolis: Rockbottom.

Joyner, Stephen. (1993) *The Complete Guide and Resource to In-Line Skating.* Cincinnati, OH: Betterway Books.

Rappelfeld, Joel. (1992) *The Complete Blader.* New York: St. Martin's Press.

SKATING, ROLLER

Roller skating is skating removed from the need for ice. A roller skate features a series of wheels attached to a plate, itself mounted on a boot or clamped onto the skater's shoe, to reproduce the abilities of the ice skate on virtually any smooth surface. Roller skates employ two different designs toward that end. In-line skates mount wheels along a single blade in direct imitation of the ice skate. The in-line design, although adaptable to many surfaces and quite fast, does not offer precise control. To meet that need, the dual-axle roller skate evolved. Mounting pairs of wheels on axles supported by cushioned suspensions permits the skilled roller skater to maneuver with a subtlety impossible on either ice or in-line skates. The smaller, wider wheels and greater friction of that configuration also make the dual-axle roller skate slower and more dependent on a smooth surface than the earlier in-line design. Women's participation is mostly in artistic competitions, while men are more often found in speed and hockey events. The introduction of in-line skates has brought more women into the sport, although mainly at the recreational level.

A woman competes in a roller skating race. (David Reed/Corbis)

HISTORY

Roller skating as an athletic activity may be traced back to Joseph Merlin, a member of the Dutch Royal Academy of Sciences and maker of musical instruments. Merlin invented the in-line skate as a warm-weather alternative to ice skating and introduced it to the public at a London reception in 1760. While playing the violin and rolling about for the crowd's entertainment, Merlin, with his violin and a large mirror, discovered that it was not possible to turn or brake on the new invention. Merlin survived the discovery. The violin and mirror did not.

Further experimentation eventually produced the dual-axle design, also known as the quad skate because of its consistent use of four wheels per foot as opposed to the various numbers used on in-line skates. Promotion of that design by sporting goods manufacturers and exercise advocates in the late nineteenth century in the United States and Europe led to roller skating's great boom period, which lasted from roughly the 1880s through the 1920s.

The final two decades of the nineteenth century brought about many social changes, not the least of which was the widespread use of electric lights and the subsequent expansion of indoor evening entertainment. In that climate, roller skating became one of the few sporting activities in which men and women could participate together without offending Victorian social mores. Skating rinks, featuring wooden floors and live music, appeared in large cities. Within, singles and couples could socialize in pleasant surroundings while exercising. Few entertainments at that time combined the health benefits of such exercise with music and socializing between the sexes. Of these activities, roller skating was one of the least objectionable to conservative sentiment.

From the origin, the modern sport of roller skating developed. Over the next decades, changes in materials and construction improved the dual-axle skate considerably. The next boom in roller skating, however, did not use the dual-axle skate but the in-line design, and occurred in the late 1980s. In addition to purely recreational indoor and outdoor use, roller skating emerged as a competitive sport under the auspices of the Federation Internationale de Roller-Skating (FIRS) and various national governing organizations recognized by the International Olympic Committee. As either recreation or competitive sport, roller skating may be found throughout the world, with its greatest popularity in Western cultures.

RULES AND PLAY

Competitive roller skating is broken down into three categories: hockey, artistic, and speed. Roller hockey is a virtual duplicate of ice hockey. Played with a small rubber ball rather than a hardened puck, it is a fast game of team competition. In 1992 roller hockey became the first roller sport in the Olympics with its exhibition appearance in Barcelona. Speed skating, in unregulated contests and in those sanctioned by FIRS and the various national organizations, is divided into single and relay events of various distances, again much like its counterpart on ice. Each of these types of roller skating has witnessed considerable change since the later 1980s as modern in-line skates, with their superior speed, have replaced traditional dual-axle designs.

Artistic roller skating is more distinct from its ice skating cousin, and it remains the province of dual-axle skates despite recent attempts to modify in-line skates to improve their maneuverability. Internationally sanctioned competitions divide artistic skating into several different disciplines, each requiring precise control and artistry in the execution of various maneuvers.

Roller figure skating consists of various turns and edges executed on a series of three linked circles, 6 meters (19.7 feet) in diameter, marked on the skating surface. At more advanced levels, a similar set of 2-meter (6.6-foot) circles featuring loops are added. Skaters are judged on their ability to trace, or follow, the circle while executing required maneuvers in their proper locations and maintaining proper posture.

Freestyle skating features jumps and spins executed to instrumental music, as does pairs skating. The latter involves a male–female team, while the former, as in figure skating, separates the genders in all but the introductory skill levels.

Dance skating, however, may permit the sexes to compete against each other in single events or to combine for team competitions. Roller dance features the performance of a set sequence of steps to traditional instrumental music, reminiscent of ballroom dancing. The final discipline in artistic roller skating, free dance, combines the execution of such dances with the performance of an original routine that may include spins and simple jumps, set to instrumental music.

WOMEN'S PARTICIPATION

Women's participation in artistic skating has traditionally surpassed that of men, while in speed skating and roller hockey that situation has been reversed. Following the introduction of in-line skates into competitions, probably because in-line skating has always appealed to both genders, the latter two disciplines have seen a slight increase in female participation. As a whole, however, the sport is clearly divided along gender lines.

Analysis of membership information from the United States Amateur Confederation/Roller Skating, the organization governing FIRS-sanctioned competitions in the United States, reveals a sharp split. In the years 1994–1997, total participation in artistic, speed, and roller hockey competitions remained virtually equal between the sexes. By event, however, the division is clear: 70 percent of experienced artistic skaters are female, 40 percent of speed skaters, and from 10 percent to 13 percent of hockey players.

This gender division is not apparent among beginners. At the entry level for artistic skating, where skaters learn basic skills, participation is evenly divided between males and females. If they continue to practice the sport, skaters progress from that level into competition, but apparently few males pursue the sport long enough to rise into the experienced categories. They may, instead, elect to pursue one of the other types of skating.

This split between males and females may have multiple explanations, but traditional stereotyping clearly plays a major role. Male participation as a percentage peaks with the team sport of hockey; declines through speed skating, with its small team and individual participation in racing; and reaches its lowest levels in the artistic divisions. Female participation is the mirror image, highest in artistic skating, with its emphasis on artistry, subjective performance, music, and costumes. The artistic female skater is celebrated as graceful and feminine, while the hockey player is praised for mastery of traditionally masculine forms of competition.

This division does not contradict the figures of skating equipment manufacturers, which suggest that total participation is largely gender-neutral. It simply indicates the persistence of gender stereotypes in the selection of activities at the level of organized national, and by implication international, competition. This, in turn, must be attributed to larger cultural forces that encourage women to participate in artistic recreations emphasizing skill while pushing men toward more overtly physical and team sports that demand strength and stamina.

CONCLUSION

Roller skating is a sport in transition, still adapting to the reintroduction of in-line skates and to resultant changes in demographics and skaters' interests. Although divided by gender at the competitive level, recreational participation is more evenly balanced between the sexes. There is, therefore, reason to believe that participation in the highest levels of roller skating may eventually become gender-neutral.

Jefferey Charlston

Bibliography

Joyner, Stephen. (1993) *Complete Guide and Resources to In-Line Skating.* Minneapolis: Rockbottom.

National Museum of Roller Skating. (1983) *First Fifty Years: American Roller Skates 1860–1910.* Lincoln, NE: Author.

Phillips, Anne-Victoria. (1979) *Complete Book of Roller Skating.* New York: Workman.

Stoll, Sharon Kay. (1983) *Roller Skating; Fundamentals and Techniques.* New York: Leisure Press.

SKIING, ALPINE

A female skier negotiates the terrain on a steep mountain slope at the Arapahoe Basin Area. (Bob Winsett/Corbis)

Alpine skiing is the more daring version of cross-country skiing. Instead of gliding smoothly across flat or gently rolling terrain, Alpine skiers speed down mountain slopes, accommodating their movements to the bumps and rises, and swerving around obstacles. Women Alpine skiers in the early years of the sport were either local or wealthy. Although Alpine skiing remains a fairly expensive sport, women skiers today come from a broad range of backgrounds. Some ski for recreation; others compete exactly as do their male counterparts.

HISTORY

Following 4,000 to 5,000 years of skiing across the countryside by men and women in northern China, Siberia, and Scandinavia, skiing as a sport appeared in the Alps of Europe in the late nineteenth century. Speeding down wooded mountain slopes required different techniques for a safe descent, and the new Alpine method, known as the Arlberg technique, was named after the Austrian region where Hannes Schneider (1890–1955) developed his systematic way of teaching. This spawned the varieties of skiing in the 1920s known today as downhill and slalom. They had their genesis in winter mountaineering. Following the conquest of a peak or col (or saddle, that is, a ridge between two peaks), an accomplished skier cut a straight track down the mountain. These runs were possible above the tree line, and up to the end of the 1920s, races were often called straight races. But once a skier reached the trees, straight running became impossible. Out of the problem of tree running, modern slalom emerged, a run requiring turning around obstacles.

The men—and very few women—who took to climbing mountains, crossing cols, and speeding down hills in the European Alps were from the educated elite, generally brought up to consider their female counterparts if not angels in the house, at least refined and delicate persons who needed physical, moral, and economic protection. The history of women's Alpine skiing until the 1930s is bound up with the concern for women's health, with the demands that a physical sport makes on fashion, with the acceptance of a sport as a social mixer, with aspects of competition, and with money.

Apart from some locals, women who skied in the Alps in the first forty years of the twentieth century came from wealthy backgrounds. They journeyed to ski resorts from Great Britain, Germany, France, Switzerland, Austria, and northern Italy. They came, too, from other industrialized countries of the world—from the United States and Canada, and even a few from South America.

Although local girls, along with boys, took to the skiing, few became experts. Alpine skiing up to World War II basically remained a male preserve. Those women who became good skiers—and in the 1930s men hoped they would—usually took to racing. In the Olympic arena, women's Alpine events were first staged in 1936 at Garmisch-Partenkirchen, Germany.

In the Cold War period, communist governments poured money into training athletes to ensure that their performances would reflect well on the nations. Women were included, and the communist bloc turned in a series of remarkable placings in the Winter Olympic Games, especially in Nordic cross-country, often seen as a folk sport. They were less successful in Alpine skiing events, which were too intertwined with bourgeois capitalism. Even in countries such as the United States, whose women have won medals, the interest, such as it has been, still lies mostly with the men's events.

ALPINE SKIING BEFORE WORLD WAR II

Curiously, it was the British, coming from a country with few skiing opportunities, who had a major influence on the development of Alpine skiing. In the early part of the twentieth century, the wealthy of England took to winter sporting. In 1913, *The Sphere*, an English glossy weekly, had a centerpage drawing of men and women cavorting on skis, ski-joring (skiing—being pulled along behind a horse), and obviously having a grand old time in the mountains. "All England is in Switzerland," read the caption. All England was not, of course, in Switzerland, but the English upper classes had taken to skiing. Of 5,432 members of the Public Schools Alpine Ski Club, 1,341 were women, 31 held university degrees, 89 were titled, and 793—about 60 percent—were classified as "Miss." Skiing undoubtedly provided a venue where an eligible Miss might meet an available Captain: officers constituted 847 of the club's membership.

Alpine skiing for those women was not like it is today. It was an outdoor party: off to the mountains for a bracing climb up in good company, and then came the thrilling run down. In the 1920s, this downhill "schuss" became increasingly attractive, and speed, "the cry of the moment," was the great desire. Women, however, were caught in a bind; they were expected to be partners in this jolly outdoor sport, but at the same time they should remain retiring and beautiful and give an aesthetically pleasing performance.

Speed and dash did away with the long dress and large-brimmed hat of the day. Dress prior to 1914 was much associated with beauty and health. The first article of clothing to go was the corset, even though a specially designed ski corset was available in 1911; it allowed the lungs to function slightly more normally, but the possibility of real exertion was still questionable. The long dress, which made such a marvelous impression at the turn of the century, was really "too much sail" for women's competition only fifteen years later. When corsets were removed, when dresses were shortened, when trousers replaced skirts, it was not merely a change in women's fashion; it was a revolution in gender relationships. The old guard took it hard. In France there were rules against photographing women in masculine clothes; in Germany a 1920 police order barred women in trousers in Annenberg. Yet ten years later advertisements illustrated "a really smart little suit . . . Man-Tailored in Navy or Oxford Grey."

Up to the turn of the century, skiing had been considered a manly sport. With the increasing intensity of nationalism across Europe, women, as part of the state, were to be included. Norway, when freeing itself from Sweden in 1905, gave clear indication that skiing played a role in its national regeneration and strength. This new attitude came to the fore most clearly in France, where, after the defeat by Prussia in the 1870–1871 war, the Germans appeared to be preparing to do it all over again. What France needed was not only "combatants but the mothers of combatants," as politicians and others fretted over the declining numbers of births. Skiing could help provide fitness for motherhood. Most energy was directed toward finding recruits for the *chasseurs alpins* (mountain soldiers) and training them in skiing, but voices were heard advocating ski training for girls and women to provide a healthy body in which a future front-line soldier could get an advantageous start. "Come on ladies, let's work for France," implored one postcard. Skiing would give the nation "solid men and women, as well balanced physically as in moral terms . . . which will contribute to the betterment of the race."

One woman who answered her country's call was Marie Marvingt, who dominated French women's skiing in the period prior to World War I, went on to rally the troops on the Dolomite front, and in the 1920s founded the first ski school for Arabs in Morocco. This "fiancée du danger" was also an accomplished aviatrix, and in the early years of the twentieth-century flying and skiing were often associated in their derring-do.

Marie Marvingt was the only woman to have established a ski school in the 1920s and about the same time, the first ski instruction book by a woman was published in Vienna. It was artistic in the sense that the woodcuts were colored and each part of the instruction was accompanied by a verse. But Emma Borman's *Brieflicher Lehrgang des Skilaufens* was hardly noted. Although women had led excursions into the mountains on skis (for American troops immediately after the armistice) and had been involved in starting clubs (Ski Club Arlberg), there was slow acceptance for women as ski instructors. Instruction was bound up with training for the testing of body and soul against the high mountains. "Trainers," as early instructors in the United States were called, imparted a disciplined approach, and discipline was thought to be the realm of men, not women. In Germany, the Deutsche Ski-Verein listed 4 women instructors for the 1930–1931 season; the next year there were 9, along with 122 men.

WOMEN'S RACING

When women's racing was first seriously discussed on an international level in 1928, a Polish delegate suggested special rules. Others proposed an event to be judged on "elegance." The majority were against competition because of the possibility of injury. Only very gradually, as the standard of women's skiing improved, did women take up racing. In the 1929 Arlberg-Kandahar, the most prestigious Alpine event, twenty-two women entered; by 1937 the number had increased only to thirty-one. These figures are typical and show how slowly attitudes—and the expertise of women—changed.

The caliber of women's racing in the 1930s was mixed. In New Zealand, the authorities set three flags far apart in a slalom to ensure a nonfalling winner. Only a stick-rider finished the gradual downhill without falling. In Europe, Paula Weisinger won a major championship, partially because her husband-to-be skied ahead of

1999 WORLD CHAMPIONS

Women's World Cup
Downhill: Renate Goetschl, Austria
Slalom: Sabine Egger, Austria
Giant Slalom: Alexandra Meissnitzer, Austria
Super-G: Alexandra Meissnitzer, Austria
Overall: Alexandra Meissnitzer, Austria
Nations Cup: Austria

World Championships
Slalom: Zali Stegall, Austria
Combined: Pernilla Wiberg, Sweden
Downhill: Renate Goetschl, Austria
Super-G: Alexandra Meissnitzer, Austria

her, warning of the tricky spots. There were only mild objections. Betty Wolsey, one of the up-and-coming Americans, related how she was chosen for the team "more by good luck than ability." This apathetic attitude was reflected in the lack of spectator interest in women's skiing. Nowhere is this clearer than at the 1931 Fédération Internationale de Ski (FIS) championship held in Cortina, Italy. Forty-three men competed before the thirty-one women. Once the men's race was over, the spectators moved off down the wood path that was the women's course, not bothering to stay for the race; indeed, some competitors fell because of the spectators on the course.

By 1936 some women had become well known: the Norwegian all-rounder, Laila Schou-Nilsen; Audrey Sale-Barker and Doreen Elliot from Britain; the Lantschner sisters, Inge and Hadwig, from Austria; and Roesli Streiff and Paula Weisinger from Switzerland and Italy, respectively. None compare with Belgian-born, Swiss citizen turned German, Christl Cranz. She snatched the gold at the 1936 Olympics from the surprising winner of the downhill, sixteen-year-old Laila Schou-Nilsen, with a near-perfect slalom, seven full seconds ahead of the second-place woman. Schou-Nilsen was fifth. In the combined total (for which medals were awarded), the German women obtained gold and silver, exactly matching the medals of the German men. In 1936 the British humor magazine *Punch* ran a cartoon comparing the different reactions to women in the snow. In 1886 the fallen lady is surrounded by gallant gentlemen helping her up. In 1936, when a woman has taken a header into the snow, there are only grins on the faces of the other skiers, men and women, as they whiz by.

ALPINE SKIING AFTER WORLD WAR II

Europe, the Soviet Union, and Japan all lay in tatters at the end of World War II. The one country whose land was untouched and whose finances were not in ruins was the United States. However, many women had taken men's jobs during the war, and not a few had become ski instructors and excellent ski racers. At the time it was judged an extraordinary feat when Gretchen Frazer won her gold medal in the 1948 Winter Olympic Games at St. Moritz, yet women had been skiing at this level for years: the records showed that Clarita Heath had already come in fourth in the FIS championship in France in 1938. Still, U.S. women's skiing was coming of age. At St. Moritz, Andrea Mead Lawrence, then only sixteen years old, came in twenty-eighth in the downhill and seventeenth in the slalom. Four years later, she won golds in downhill and giant slalom. To this day, American women have had greater Olympic success than the men.

But for America, skiing is not of national concern as it is for Austria and France. In those countries it is the men (Toni Sailer, Franz Klammer, Jean-Claude Killy, and more recently the Italian Alberto Tomba) who are remembered, even revered, much more so than such great competitors as Germany's Rosi Mittermaier or the Goitschel sisters from France. Ski racing is still very much a man's world.

For the recreational woman skier, the first major change after the war came in the world of fashion. Maria Bogner's stretch pants appeared on the market in 1948, and in the early 1950s, they were the identifying mark of women who skied. They not only contributed to the continuation of the male eye-pleasing ideal but also enabled women to ski faster—or at least look fast.

In the 1960s and 1970s, there was an increasing female clientele for skiing. As more middle-class women moved into the service workplace, they had more disposable income, and many chose to spend winter vacations in snow country. Ski magazines wrote articles to appeal particularly to the single woman, and in the mid-1970s, the first of the women-only ski weeks was held in Squaw Valley, California.

At the same time, the ski resorts prompted a further increase in the number of women skiing. They had sponsored children's ski classes since before World War II, but now they began to provide day-care centers. Today the staff will take even toddlers out on skis for a little while, so mothers are free to enjoy the slopes.

The female skier was wooed by the ski manufacturers, too. In 1983, the Hart Ski Company began marketing a ski designed by a woman (ex-U.S. Olympian Suzy Chaffee) for women. A little later, boot manufacturers began outfitting women with boots of different height, weight, and flex.

Marielle Goitschel of France clears a gate in the slalom event at the 1968 Winter Olympics in Grenoble. (International Olympic Museum)

In recent times, there has been a direct approach to women as skiers in their own right. Paralleling the feminist movement, some women skiers attempted to be treated as men's equals. This trend was epitomized by some of the top female racers just before the 1994 Lillehammer Olympics, when they not only refused their last training run but insisted on a press conference to protest that their course on the Hafjell was not a real downhill in comparison to the men's course on the Kvitfjell.

RULES AND PLAY

Olympic races—like all other major world competitions—are governed by FIS rules. There are minor differences between course requirements for men and women. For example, men's downhill has to have between an 800- and 1100-meter (875- and 1203-yard) vertical drop, whereas the women's course is defined by a 500- to 800-meter (547- to 875-yard) vertical drop. The women's slalom, with forty-five to sixty-five gates, is designed on slopes with a 140- to 200-meter (153- to 219-yard) height difference. The men's course requires a 180- to 220-meter (197- to 241-yard) drop in height and is contested through fifty-five to seventy-five gates. The differences are even less in the giant slalom and super-G. In parallel skiing—made for television—the courses for men and women are exactly the same.

The FIS lays out regulations very minutely for equipment. Skis, boots, poles, bindings, ski stoppers, helmets, gloves, suits, and back protectors all have detailed requirements. Regardless of whether the skier is male or female, the minimum height of the shovel—the tip—of the slalom and giant slalom ski is 50 millimeters (2 inches) and for the downhill and super-G it is 30 millimeters (1.2 inches). Even underwear is regulated; it "may not be plasticised or treated by any chemical means (gaseous, liquid, or solid)," according to the regulations. Racers may use back protectors, but the top edge must not be "above the seventh cervical vertebrae." In fact, the only difference in FIS rules for women is that the minimum length of ski for downhill and super-G must be 180 centimeters (70 inches) for women and 10 centimeters (4 inches) longer for men. There are no limitations for slalom or giant slalom.

These specifications indicate just how carefully competition is regulated on a world scale. The Olympics is one major event; another is the World Cup competition that runs through the entire season. It is this competition that is draining on the racers as they move from week to week from Sapporo to Sestrière, from Vail to Val d'Isère on a continuous circuit.

It is not surprising, then, that modern ski racing (and modern Alpine skiing) techniques are alike for men and women. Thus, in downhills (viewed mostly on television because comparatively few people actually watch ski events, though more do so in Europe than in North America) both men and women pre-jump and hold similar tuck positions. In slaloms, women smack the break-away poles with a fierceness equal to any man's.

There are no major female coaches in the world for Alpine skiing, even though some effort has been made to invite the best ex-racers to coach in the United States. However, women continue to close the gap in timing records with men. For example, in the kilomètre lancé (the flying kilometer), a test of pure speed, Melissa Dimino of the United States got over the 200-kph mark in 1984, and, as of 1999, Carolyn Curl had a top speed of 231.660 kph (143.947 mph), only 12 kph (7.5 mph) slower than the men's record.

As attitudes change and women demonstrate their skills, rules and events reflect those changes. The swiftness with which mogul skiing was incorporated in the Olympic program is an example. Ballet skiing—perhaps just because of its association with femaleness—has all but disappeared after its ten years or so of faddish popularity. Now being called "acroski" and involving such maneuvers as the gut flip, it is trying to shed its feminine image.

The huge majority of women skiers, however, are not those who race, go "bump" skiing, or otherwise ski at the extreme edge of their own expertise; most women recreationally. This sort of skiing is indistinguishable from what is available to men, so one can generalize that in modern recreational Alpine skiing, women find an equality of conditions and treatment that is more elusive in the competitive sphere.

E. John B. Allen

Bibliography

Allen, E. John B. (1990) "Sierra 'Ladies' on Skis in Gold Rush California." *Journal of Sport History* 17, 3: 347–353.

Altschul, Craig. (1971) *A Bunny's Guide to Skiing*. Hollywood: Creative Sports.

Carbone, Claudia. (1996) *Women Ski*. Hamstead, NH: World Leisure.

Lighthall, Nancy, et al. (1979) *Skiing for Women*. Palm Springs, CA: ETC Publications.

Marvingt, Marie. (1911) "Les femmes et le ski." In *Les Sports d'Hiver,* edited by Louis Magnus and Renaud de la Fregeolière. Paris: Lafitte, 178–181.

Mauritsch-Bein, Barbara. (1991) "Die Anfänge des Frauensports in der Steiermark." *Sport: Sinn & Wahn*. March Supplement, 131–132, 216–221.

Pfister, Gertrud. (1994) "Gracefully and Elegantly Downhill: Women and the Sport of Skiing in Germany, 1890–1914." In *Winter Games Warm Traditions,* edited by Matti Goksøyr et al. Lillehammer, Norway: Ishpes, 223–239.

Roth, Elsa. (1955) "Querschnitt durch die Entwicklung des schweizerischen Damen Skisportes." *Schweizerischer Skiverband,* Annual, 4–31.

Slanger, Elisa, and Dinah B. Witchel. (1979) *Ski Women's Way*. New York: Summit Books.

SKIING, CROSS-COUNTRY

Cross-country skiing and ski jumping are the two activities that form the sport of Nordic skiing. Until 1956 cross-country skiing, and especially the ski federations and organizations that sponsored competitions, was dominated by the views of Norwegian, Swedish, and Finnish middle-class men. Some of these nations included female athletes early on in competitions; others did not. After 1956 women from the Soviet Union and Scandinavian female winners of the Olympic Games helped to change this orientation.

HISTORY

Skiing in the Nordic countries and Estonia can be traced back to the early Stone Age. Girls and women who had to ski on a daily basis in the rural areas of Finland, Sweden, Norway, Russia, and Estonia were often accomplished skiers. According to Olaus Magnus in "Historia de gentibus septentrionalibus," Nordic women made long ski trips during the winter to baptize their babies in churches. In the 1800s, women skied with babies on their backs to get to Christmas and other winter gatherings. Roads were often impassable during the winter, so special winter routes were taken that often crossed frozen lakes and ponds.

Cross-country skiing was not only found in Europe. By 1852 in California, following the Gold Rush, camps had been established above the snowline. By the end of the 1850s, sources indicate that even "ladies" traveled on skis. The *Sacramento Daily Union* reported in 1860 that some of these ladies even surpassed men in skiing over the mountains. According to the paper, a mother and her sixteen-year-old daughter skied thirty-nine miles across the Sierra range. Snow could be up to 3 meters (9.9 feet) deep in these camps.

EARLY COMPETITIONS

Attitudes toward women and skiing seem to have differed depending on whether it was a necessary part of daily life and recreation or whether it was for competition. The first skiing competitions in Norway in the 1860s often consisted of the same three events that are practiced in modern Nordic skiing—cross-country, downhill, and jumping. The first newspaper account of these races comes from Trysil in 1862:

> The race started on a long hill with approximately a 35° angle, ran down to an open area, and then up a hill again, where the spectators and officials were placed. There was a jump, constructed of snow, placed at the bottom of the downhill run. This significantly increased a race that nature had already made difficult enough. The challenge was simply to get down the hill without falling. This required both agility and balance.
>
> (*Morgenbladet*, 2 February 1862)

As skiing became more specialized, jumps were often singled out as one event, cross-country as another, and, sometimes, downhill as a third. Competition in Nordic skiing consisted of ski jumping and cross-country, while skiers in Central Europe developed downhill and slalom, or Alpine, skiing. Competition in American women's skiing concentrated mostly on slalom and downhill, not on cross-country. It seems that ski competitions increased during the 1890s in the Nordic countries, Russia, and in Estonia. According to Finnish sources, ski competitions came to Estonia via Finland.

Several women's ski clubs were formed in Norway beginning in 1887. In 1889 a club in Steinkjer, called "Skade," after the Nordic goddess who was an excellent skier and huntress, wanted to give priority to women's skiing. The club arranged competitions and trips for women to the forests and mountains. Eva Nansen, the wife of the famous Norwegian scientist and polar explorer Fritjof Nansen, promoted women's skiing by introducing more practical clothing for women skiers: no corsets, and long skirts with warm pants underneath. She used this outfit on her honeymoon in 1890 when she traveled from Oslo to Norefjell.

Women ski up a slight hill in a 15- kilometer freestyle cross-country ski race during the World Cup Ski Races in 1989. (Scott T. Smith/Corbis)

Newspapers supported women's cross-country skiing as long as women did not compete. When cross-country skiing was seen in light of the women's movement from the 1880s onward, it received heavy criticism in the leading national newspaper. The main argument was over whether it was too masculine for women to ski near towns or in the mountains while wearing pants—whether those pants were hidden by skirts or not.

Resistance to women's cross-country competitions seemed to grow as the sporting aspect of skiing grew in Norway, where cross-country skiing was defined as a man's sport. For middle-class women to participate purely for fun, instead of taking care of their house, husband, and children, was incomprehensible and unacceptable to men. Finnish and Swedish men were more tolerant, for some reason, and Finnish and Swedish women were able to compete in national championships before the end of World War I. Norwegian women had to wait until 1954.

As late as 1949, competitions that emphasized style were arranged to preserve "femininity" and reduce the skiers' speed. Starting in 1882, the Swedish skiing organization promoted 2-kilometer (1.24-mile) cross-country skiing competitions for girls under the age of fifteen. Swedish and Finnish ski federations sent women to compete in cross-country competitions in the Nordic *Skispelen* (ski games), but Norway only sent women in 1917. They came in far behind their Nordic sisters.

Descriptions of women participating in these events often focused on their sweat, breathlessness, messy hair, or unfeminine clothing to keep women away from competitions. The Worker's Athletic Federation in Norway and Finland, however, arranged competitions for women starting in the 1920s.

The Féderation International du Ski (FIS) put pressure on the Norwegian Ski Federation to include women's cross-country skiing for the first time in the Olympic Games in Oslo in 1952. Eighteen women from Czechoslovakia, Yugoslavia, Italy, France, Germany, Finland, Sweden, and Norway participated in the 10-kilometer (6.2-mile) race. Lydia Widman of Finland was the first winner of a women's cross-country ski competition in the Olympic Games, and Finland won the gold, silver, and bronze medals. Athletes from Nordic countries held the first twelve places in the competition. Women from the Soviet Union, and later from Russia, have dominated since 1956.

THE DOMINANCE OF SOVIET AND RUSSIAN WOMEN

Following the Revolution of 1917, Lenin wanted to develop a socialist society with a well-trained and physically healthy population. The official ban on bourgeois ideology also included banning certain ideas about femininity. Sports were seen as a means of personal liberation for men and women, and they came under national governmental control in 1925. They were regulated by a national Committee on Physical Culture and Sport, an umbrella organization that included workers' unions, schools, and organizations from the fields of science, medicine, and top-level sports. Following World War II, the focus of the committee was on producing top-level athletes who could demonstrate Soviet superiority on the international stage.

Soviet policies concerning rights for women in sports were far more liberal than those of other nations. The Soviet Union participated in cross-country skiing for the first time in the Winter Olympics at Cortina in 1956. They took the gold and silver medals in the 10-kilometer race as well as fourth and fifth place, while Sweden took the bronze and the Finnish skier finished sixth. They also took the silver in the 4 × 5-kilometer relay, with Finland first and Sweden third. At the games in 1960 in Squaw Valley, Soviet women swept the first four places in the 10-kilometer event but again finished second in the relay. Due to Soviet influence, from then on women from most Eastern European countries also competed in cross-country skiing.

Women from the Soviet Union have continued to dominate. However, when the 5-kilometer race was introduced at the games in 1968, Toini Gustavsson of Sweden defeated the Soviet women in the 5-kilometer and 10-kilometer races. But Soviet dominance was quickly restored when Galina Kulakowa dominated the women's events in the 1972 Games. Women from Finland and the Soviet Union were at the top of the sport until the 1980 Olympics, when Barbara Petzold of East

1999 WORLD CHAMPIONS

10k freestyle: Stefania Belmondo, Italy
15k freestyle: Stefania Belmondo, Italy
5k classic: Bente Martinsen, Norway
30k classic: Larissa Lazhutina, Russia
Overall: Bente Martinsen, Norway
4x5k relay mixed: Russia

Germany won the 10-kilometer event and a Norwegian team won the relay. After the collapse of the Soviet Union in 1991, women who before had represented the Soviet Union started to represent their own countries. Ljubow Jegerova of Russia won the 10-kilometer event and a new event called the 15-kilometer classic in 1994.

The new freestyle races were first won by skiers from non-Nordic countries, in part because of resistance to change by the Nordic skiing organizations. In freestyle, skiers use skating movements to propel themselves forward. The technique and event were developed and managed by Bill Cock, an American. An Italian, Stefania Belmondo, won the 30-kilometer freestyle in 1992. Manuela Di Centa won the same event in 1994. She also won the 15-kilometer classic, extending Italy's dominance over two consecutive Olympic Games. In 1998, however, Russian women won all four women's distances (5, 10, 15, and 30 kilometers), in addition to the relay.

FUTURE OF WOMEN'S CROSS-COUNTRY SKIING

There are declining numbers of men and women in cross-country skiing in the Nordic countries. Polish-English sociologist Zygmunt Bauman explains this in terms of Western culture's focus on the pursuit of pleasure. Pleasure is defined more on an individual basis than a collective basis. Young people seem to choose snowboarding and other fun sports that focus on creativity, individual taste, joy, and communication with their peers, instead of sports requiring stamina and long, lonely training sessions. For cross-country skiing to develop into the twenty-first century, new events must be added and new countries must develop elite skiers. If not, many young skiers will most likely choose other sports.

Gerd von der Lippe

Bibliography

Bauman, Zygmunt. (1997) *Intimations of Postmodernity.* New York: Routledge.

Haarstad, Kjell. (1993) *Skisportens oppkomst i Norge* [*Roots of Skiing in Norway*]. Trondheim, Norway: Tapir.

Magnus, Olaus. (1976) "Historia de gentibus septentriornalibus." In *Historia om de nordiska folken* [*History of the Nordic People*] edited by John Granlund. Stockholm, Sweden: Gidlund.

Mo, Kristen. (1994) "The Development of Skiing as a Competitive Sport. Morgedal: The Cradle of Skiing: Fact or Fiction?" In *Winter Games Warm Traditions* (Selected papers from the second international ISHPES seminar, Lillhammer, 1994). Oslo, Norway: Norwegian Society of Sports History and the International Society for the History of Physical Education and Sport (ISHPES), 182–191.

SKIING, FREESTYLE

Freestyle skiing is a winter snow sport that emerged in the 1970s as a recreational alternative to Alpine and Nordic skiing. Since then it has evolved into one of the most popular Olympic sports among spectators and has seen a large increase in participation by women. Freestyle skiing consists of the mogul, aerial, and acro (formerly "ballet") events. Mogul events involve skiing down bumpy hills with fast times and specified jumps. Aerials are jumps, spins, and flips into the air from ramps. Acro is acrobatic (gymnastic-like) skiing down a groomed path.

HISTORY

Stories of Norwegian peasants taking part in jumping competitions for money date back to the late 1700s, but there is no record of whether the competitions included women. German figure skater and doctor Fritz Reuel came up with the concept of freestyle skiing as a sport. In 1928 he wrote *New Possibilities in Skiing,* a work that pioneered the concept of dancing on skis. Following Reuel's writings, Norwegian Stein Eriksen and his brother translated them into action. Forced to stay in his yard during the German occupation of Norway in World War II, he and his brother transferred their gymnastic skills to their skis and performed flips off jumps at their home. In 1953 the sport gained momentum and notice when Eriksen began performing flips for the crowds at the ski areas he visited on his travels.

Only since the late 1960s have people sought a formal way of pushing the boundaries of what they do on skis, and during this time freestyle ski-

American skier Jan Bucher in the ballet event at the 1991 Kingdom Classic World Cup. (Bob Winsett)

ing has become widely popular. For skiers, it represents a way to add freedom, fun, and challenge to their sport. Peter Miller wrote in *Peter Miller's Ski Almanac* (1979), "Freestyle skiing was born in defiance of the organized racing structure, of the style-conscious instructor world, of all laws including gravity." Less flattering descriptions of the inception of the sport do exist; Raymond Flower suggests that so-called hotdogging (a derogatory synonym for freestyle skiing) was an offshoot of the pop and drug scene. In general, skiers were looking for ways of getting away from the perfect parallel turn, which was the goal of ski instructors in the 1950s and 1960s.

Referring to what was happening on the slopes at this time and the growing popularity of freestyle skiing, *Ski* magazine in 1966 referred to the "demonstration of free-style skiing"—perhaps the first official record of the new name of the sport. In the early 1970s the sport was known by both names, freestyle and hotdogging, but as it gained structure in the late 1970s, the term "hotdogger" became derogatory.

While freestyle began in Europe, it first became popular in North America, where most of the early formal competitions first took place. In 1966 one of the first organized competitions, the Masters Tour, was held at ski areas in Vermont to show off the different tricks and routines that were being developed.

The first National Pro Am Championships of Freestyle Skiing, held in March 1971 on the True Grit run at Waterville Valley, New Hampshire, is the first record of a competition that included a woman: Suzy Chaffee of Rutland, Vermont. Shortly after the Waterville Valley competition, an independent competition was held in Aspen, Colorado: the K2 Hot Dog Contest.

The first competition in Waterville Valley consisted of a long run that included sections of mogul skiing followed by jumps. In the late 1960s and early 1970s it was common for skiers to ski down an entire run and be required to do all three events of what became freestyle. Skiers were required to hit jumps and ski through mogul runs, with points being awarded for spectacular recoveries (backward skiing, rolls, and the like). The K2 Hot Dog Contest in Colorado was the first to break the events into aerials, moguls, and ballet (known as "acro" after 1995). Many successful female mogul skiers of the early 1970s moved from being successful Alpine racing athletes to being freestyle daredevils.

In 1973 athletes competing on the professional tours formed the International Freestyle Skiers Association (IFSA) to help identify rules and standards, primarily to ensure their safety. Even with the rules, the daredevil antics of the freestyle skiers caused problems. In 1976 insurance became a larger obstacle for athletes than the competitions themselves. In the mid-1970s, two skiers were severely injured in two separate accidents, leaving them paralyzed. The threat of lawsuits from the injuries of such accidents created fear and left the event organizers, the insurance companies, and the ski resorts afraid to host events.

The liability concerns notwithstanding, sponsors put money into more competitions between 1973 and 1976, and freestyle skiing took off. These tours became largely professional because there was no need to consider amateur status. Freestyle skiing athletes did not need to qualify for the Olympics at that time, and they could accept money for winning competitions without jeopardizing their eligibility in any other event. Amateur at that time referred to more of a junior (developing) athlete, while the professional skiers were the top athletes who could win money on the "professional circuit." The Colgate Women's Freestyle Skiing tour started in 1974 and by 1975 boasted $90,000 in prize money, money that was exclusively for women athletes. Observers suggested that a woman could earn $15,000 for just a few short months of skiing. In 1973 Chaffee was the first woman to win money in freestyle. Chaffee was also the first competitor to ask that music be played during her ballet run. Chaffee faced ridicule, but she proved to be a pioneer; by 1974, all ballet runs were performed to music. Marion Post is recognized as being the first woman to perform a back flip in competition. She went on to win $29,000 and the women's overall title in 1976.

Chaffee broke ground in competition, especially ballet, and again as the only woman on a demonstration team (a group of skiers who perform in movies). The team performed in movies such as *Moebius Flip,* a film about the new moves being performed by freestylers, including the back flip with a full twist—the "moebius."

In 1979 the Federation International du Ski (FIS) began sanctioning freestyle skiing events. In 1980 the first FIS World Cup competition was held in the Poconos, a mountainous region in the eastern United States, which consisted of two competitions (three events each plus combined) for women and men. Jan Bucher of the United States (1957–) dominated this event and every level of freestyle skiing for the next ten years with her technical tricks and artistic movements. Five nations competed in this first World Cup event: France, West Germany, Great Britain, Canada, and the United States. There were four World Cup venues in four countries in 1980; as of 1999, the sport had grown to include fourteen events per season. The 1998 season saw women from twenty-four countries competing on the World Cup tour.

PROFESSIONAL TO AMATEUR

The transition to amateur competition was a major turning point in the organization of freestyle competitions. While there were some professional shows for acro and aerials (professional or pseudo-professional events still exist for male aerialists), the professional organizers began to host events strictly for moguls. These still occur, especially in the United States, where events made for TV audiences remain popular. Sponsorship money is now directed toward individual World Cup competition, individual athletes, and teams rather than focused on individual athletes, as in the 1970s.

Freestyle skiing took its next step toward achieving Olympic status by holding world championships in Tignes, France, in 1986. Bucher again took the spotlight in the ballet event while an emerging rival, Connie Kissling (1961–) of Switzerland, took the combined title. World championships have been held every two years since that time.

OLYMPIC FREESTYLE

Freestyle's Olympic debut as a demonstration sport did not disappoint the crowd at the 1988 Calgary Winter Olympics. In fact, ballet was one of the first events at the Calgary Games to sell out, and although Bucher was second in the event, the competition between her and Christine Rossi of France drove the artistic side of the sport to new levels.

Moguls were recognized at the 1992 Albertville Olympic Games, where Donna Weinbrecht of the United States (1965–) became the first female gold medalist in the sport. Ballet and aerial were again demonstration events. Two years later in Lillehammer, Norway, aerials were added to the Olympic program, but this time ballet skiing was left out. Lina Tcherjazova of Uzbekistan (1968–) was the first woman to win Olympic gold in aerials. The freestyle community remains hopeful that acro will gain Olympic status.

While Canada and the United States dominated the early years of the sport, this is changing. Countries such as China are starting to push the limits in women's aerials, and the Scandanavians and Japanese are setting new standards in women's moguls. The Russians brought skiers with gymnastics training into freestyle and completely dominated women's acro in the late 1990s.

RULES AND PLAY

Freestyle skiing consists of three events: moguls, aerials, and acro. Rapidly developing is the additional event of dual moguls, where skiers ski side-by-side down two separate courses in a race to the bottom. There are a few different judging formats, but all take into account speed, air (height of jumps), and turns. This event was held at the world championships for the first time ever (men and women) in March 1999 at Meiringen-Hasliberg, Switzerland. Before 1997 athletes had the option of competing in one event, multiple events, or all three—the combined event that was formally ended in 1997.

Mogul skiing consists of rapid turns on steep, bumpy terrain. The courses range from 200 to 280 meters (219 to 306 yards) in length and are usually considered advanced runs. The moguls (bumps of snow) on the run are formed in one of two ways: by the natural movement of snow that occurs as many skiers take the same path down a slope or by a snow-grooming machine. Man-made moguls are gaining popularity at international competitions as well as at ski areas with extremely hard snow. At competitions, man-made moguls make all paths down the course similar, a development that purists argue has made competitions less exciting as skiers have fewer decisions to make during their run.

Many sports are complementary to the three events of freestyle skiing. A mogul skier needs strong legs and a relatively fearless attitude. An ability to carve a ski—using the design of the ski to efficiently and effectively turn (or divert the direction) of the ski and the skiier—is also sought. Often skiers move from Alpine skiing (ski racing) into mogul skiing, since Alpine skiers have to deal with high speeds on treacherous courses and are able to carve a ski efficiently through a turn. Skills and experience such as these make any woman wishing to ski moguls more likely to achieve early success.

The top five women mogul skiers averaged 33.01 seconds to ski the Izuna Kogen 1998 Olympic Mogul course. While this is slightly slower than the rates at which men ski, the gap is closing as the level of competition continues to rise. Skiers receive points based on the quality of their turns, air, and speed; the maximum score attainable is 30 points. The moguls on the course are roughly 1 meter (3.28 feet) tall and are relatively symmetrical in their occurrence down the course. Making her way through fifty to seventy turns, the skier is required to perform two different upright aerial maneuvers off prepared jumps. These jumps are placed approximately one-third and two-thirds of the way down the hill. While the rules state that jumps are to be no larger than the moguls around them, in practice they are often much larger and are always shaped more abruptly to assist the athlete in getting higher in the air, a quality that is rewarded by the judges. Many top-level events now require the snow in the landing area of the jumps to be softened by shovel to reduce the force of the impact on the athletes.

In the dual-mogul event, women ski head-to-head in a round-robin type event in which the top women are seeded, as in tennis. The terrain and the course selection can give a great advantage (or pose a challenge) as the winner of each dual continues to the next round. While the courses are supposed to be very similar, often one will change during training and will become more difficult or slower because of unique course development. Skiers in a dual format are judged basically by the same method that is used in the single-mogul event.

As with mogul skiers, a woman aerialist needs to be relatively fearless and must have acrobatic experience. Aerialists often come from one of two different backgrounds: skiing or acrobatics. A woman who has experience as a diver, trampolinist, or gymnast has a distinct advantage over someone without the same flipping and twisting skills. The other stream of athletes entering aerials is made up of combined skiers—often younger women who have skied in club programs and have expanded their skill set to include aerials.

An aerial site consists of a smooth in-run (intermediate slope), a flat "table" where the jumps (kickers) are placed, a steep landing, and a flat stopping area. The landing area is one of the most intimidating parts of the aerial site. At 38 degrees, it is steeper than most runs at a ski area. Skiers start with single flips, skiing at about 45 kilometers per hour (kph) (28 miles per hour [mph]) off a hand-shaped jump that is 2 meters (6.6 feet) high. They are launched into the air, where they perform the skill before landing on the steep but well-groomed landing hill. More difficult moves require more air to perform, which skiers obtain by gaining more speed (about 54 kph [33.6 mph] for doubles, 60 kph [37.3 mph] for triples) and jumping off larger kickers. A double kicker is approximately 3 meters (9.8 feet) high while many triple kickers are 3.5 meters (11.5 feet) high.

Ideally, a woman learning aerials would start on a small jump, where she would perform upright aerials, gaining the valuable skills of landing and knowing where she is in the air. From the upright jump, a woman would spend time on either a trampoline or diving board before moving to a "water ramp."

Water ramps are plastic ski slopes that mimic the in-run and jump of an "on-snow" aerial site. A skier skis down the in-run, jumps off the jump, and lands in water. This allows a skier to safely learn the motor skills required to flip and twist her body. While basic water ramps have been in place since 1972, many larger and better sites are being constructed all over the world. The greater the improvement and skill of a skier, the greater the need to use a larger water ramp.

Skiers perform single, double, and triple flips, with or without twists, off water ramps, with more and more women taking these moves to the snow sites. In competition, Jacquie Cooper (1973–), of Australia, and other women have performed up to two twists in three flips.

Although different women have performed triple flips in each of the Olympic Winter Games (either in training or in competition), the 1998 season marked the first in which the top women were expected to do triple flips. When women competed as combined skiers, their training time was divided between the three disciplines. In addition, late site preparation at many competitions and limited training centers prevented the level of women's aerials from being up to the technical standards that they had set in the other disciplines. Specialization of women has seen the sport reach new heights as women's technical abilities improve.

In contrast to the other types of freestyle skiing, women who perform acro do not need the same propensity toward risk. Acro draws dancers, gymnasts, figure skaters, and other skiers—disciplines in which artistic acrobatic skills are required. In the 1990s, women from Russia, such as Natalia Razumovskaya (1975–), Elena Batalova (1964–), and Oksana Kushenko (1972–), have entered acro from the sport of gymnastics; they dominated the international competitive scene as they set new standards for creativity and technical skills.

While there have been different scoring formats for acro, they have all rewarded athletes who performed a balance of spins, steps, jumps, and flips while showing artistic creativity that relates to their chosen music. Female athletes receive 50 percent of their score from six technical tricks (jumps and flips) and 50 percent from the balance of their performance. Acro courses are groomed runs, 160 meters (175 yards) long and approximately 37.5 meters (41 yards) wide, which are usually as steep as a low-end intermediate run.

CONCLUSION

Freestyle skiing has grown swiftly and undergone several transformations—recreational to profes-

SKIERS—ONE FOR ALL AND ALL FOR ACRO

Lisa Downing of Canada (1961–) was proud to talk about her experiences and what they meant to her. "Back in the early 1980s through to 1986 . . . Support wasn't great from the event organizers, but the support women received from each other was phenomenal—the majority of them still keep in touch once or twice a year and try to get together whenever possible."

When she attempted to convince the international decision-making bodies to include acro in the Winter Games, former competitor Julia Snell of Great Britain (1963–) witnessed the same spirit as she lobbied the athletes to band together to support this move. Snell has continued to be a leader in the sport, initiating such changes as the name of the discipline from ballet to acro in 1995. The athletes realized that they needed to make a more objective and concise package to move away from the subjective image of figure skating in international competition. Changing the name to acro highlighted the athletic demands of the sport and made it better recognized and represented. People such as Snell are still working towards gaining Olympic status for acro.

sional to amateur. As in most sports, freestyle skiing officials have conducted a strength/weakness analysis in an effort to make the sport more marketable and give the audience—television viewers, spectators, and sponsors—a better product. As with other ski events, men dominate, but women are a growing presence with increasing technical skill and flair.

Todd Allison

Bibliography

Athans, Greg (1978) *Ski Free*. Toronto, Ontario: Clarke, Irwin & Company.

Beaudry, M. (1996) *Leapin' Wizards: Flying Through the Air with the Greatest of Skis, Canada's Thrilling Aerialists Set their Horizons on Topping the World.* Camden-East, Ontario: Equinox.

Broze, M. C. (1978) *Freestyle Skiing*. New York: Arco.

Bryden, W., P. Lougheed, and B. Mulroney. (1987) *Canada at the Olympic Winter Games: The Official Sports History and Record Book.* Edmonton, Alberta: Hurtig Publishers.

Canadian Freestyle Web site: (1998) <http://infoweb.magi .com/freestyl/index.html>.

Canadian Ski Association, Freestyle Discipline. (1978) *Freestyle Yearbook/Recueil Annuel '78/79.* Vanier, Ontario: Canadian Ski Association/Association Canadienne de ski.

Claridge, Marit, and Cheryl Evans. (1987) *An Usborne Guide: Skiing and Other Winter Sports.* EDC Publications.

CTV. (1988) *CTV Host Broadcaster Venue Handbook: Demonstration Sports. Max Bell and COP.*

FIS Freestyle Archives: (1998) <www.zip.com.au/~birdman/>.

Flower, Raymond. (1976) *The History of Skiing and Other Winter Sports.* Angincourt, Ontario: Methuen.

Gamma, Karl. (1973) *The Handbook of Skiing*. New York: Alfred A. Knopf.

Johnston, John. (1990) *Water Ramp Jumping: A Sport Within A Sport* (Bulletin). Berne, Switzerland: F.I.S.

———. (1991) *Building a Sport—Phase 2* (Bulletin). Berne, Switzerland: F.I.S.

Johnston, John, Michel Daigle, and D. Bowie. (1974) *Freestyle Skiing Technique Manual.* Vancouver, British Columbia: Winter Habit Productions.

Kalacis, Eric. (1982) "Freestyle Skiing: Flip First: On a Water Ramp." *Coaching Review* 5 (November/December).

Miller, Peter. (1979) *Peter Miller's Ski Almanac.* Garden City, NY: Nick Lyons Books.

Stathoplos, D. (1988) "Cutting the Mustard: Jan Bucher and Ballet Skiing, a Demonstration Event, Have Been Battling Their Hot-Dog Reputations for a Long Time." *Time* (Toronto), (1 February).

Wieman, Randy. (1979) *Freestyle Skiing*. Rexdale, Ontario: Hunter Rose Co.

Winter Sport Web site: (1998) <www.wintersports.org/freestyle>.

Additional information provided by Bernard Weichsel, Walt Hiltner, Julia Snell, Frank Bare, Bob C. Young, Bob Howard, Chuck Martin, Lisa Downing, John Johnston, Peter Judge, and Joseph T. Fitzgerald.

SKIING, NORDIC *see* Skiing, Cross-Country; Ski Jumping

1999 WORLD CHAMPIONS

World Cup
Moguls: Ann Battelle, United States
Dual Moguls: Michelle Roark, United States
Aerials: Jacqui Cooper, Australia
Overall: Jacqui Cooper, Australia

World Freestyle Championships
Acro: Natalia Ragumovslesya, Russia
Aerials: Jacqui Cooper, Australia
Dual Moguls: Sandra Schmitt, United States

SKIING, WATER

Water skiing is a sport of strength and nerve in which participants hang on to a rope and allow themselves to be pulled through the water by a speeding powerboat. It is very popular as a recreational activity and is also a competitive sport. Participants range from the graceful trick skier, who slides across the well-formed wakes of water to perform incredible acts, to the adrenaline-seeking speed skier and everyone in between. Women participate in all water skiing events, although only about 25 percent of skiers are women.

HISTORY

Although its actual origins are unknown, the beginnings of water skiing can be traced back to the early 1900s. One version is that it came into being during a swim on a fishing trip. A fisherman did not want to get back into the boat, and the captain did not want to wait around for him. The captain then attached a rope to a wide board, threw it overboard, and informed the swimmer that if he did not want to get back onto the boat, he would have to hold on and be towed back. Soon afterward the swimmer was standing on the board and calling for another rope to hold on to. Thus, perhaps, water skiing began.

Since its inception, whatever that may have been, water skiing has developed in all dimensions. Initially, the sport's main limitation was speed, with boats managing a top speed of 20 kilometers per hour (kph) (12.5 miles per hour [mph]). After several years the board on which the skier stood, called an aquaplane, was split in two, creating two skis and increasing the skier's ability to maneuver. The skiers were attached to the skis by rubber bands, and skegs (like nails, punched into the skis to hold the rubber bands in place) were fitted to the underneath of the skis to provide direction. Soon afterward, the rope attached to the skis was removed and the skiers were linked to the boat only by the rope that they held in their hands.

The first documented water skier was Ralph Samuelson, who in 1922 used a pair of skis 2.4 meters long (8 feet) and 22.9 centimeters (9 inches) wide to ski across a lake in Minnesota. In 1925 Fred Waller developed Akwa-Skees, which were smaller, more streamlined skis; they were easier to ski on, and his invention would change water skiing forever. As boats became more powerful, more people in the United States began to ski.

Interest in water skiing grew, and the phenomenon spread to Europe. The French were particularly enthusiastic, as evidenced when Count Maximilian Pulaski brought water skiing exhibitions to the French Riveria in 1929. Count Pulaski retained his interest and later invented the foot binding of the water ski.

PROFESSIONAL DEVELOPMENT AND PARTICIPATION

In 1939 the American Water Ski Association (AWSA) was established by Dan Hains, a New Yorker, and soon afterward the association sponsored the first national championships at Jones Beach State Park on Long Island. Three events were contested: slalom, tricks, and jump. These events are still contested today, and their format has not changed. Under AWSA auspices, the American national championships have been contested biennially since then, except during World War II.

With men and women taking part in all events, women have retained a significant place in all facets of water skiing. In 1935 two French women, Madame Savard and Madame Langlois performed demonstration runs at the Paris exhibition. Later in 1939, Savard and Madame de Meylen gave daily exhibitions of the new sport at the New York World's Fair, further promoting women in water skiing. In 1935 the Water Skiing Federation was formed in Paris by Mrs. Frank Jay Gould, an American who at the time was president of the Juan-les-Pins Water Skiing Club (France). The main aim of the club was to encourage the practice and development of the sport of water skiing by all possible means, particularly by organizing meetings, sporting occasions, competitions and so forth that might assist its aim.

Water skiing took on an international flavor in 1946 when France, Belgium, and Switzerland created the International Water Ski Union (IWSU). In 1947 Madame Savard established the French Water Skiing Federation, which consisted of five

Women's world champion slalom water skier Jennifer Leachman. (Rick Doyle/Corbis)

clubs. In that same year, the first European water skiing championships were held. Two years later the first world championships were held in Juanles-Pins, France. The United States, Belgium, Switzerland, Italy, and Denmark all sent competitors. On this occasion, the United States was victorious.

Australia sent its first team to the 1952 world championships in Toronto, Canada, and while their contenders, Betty Leighton and John Kumn, did not win any medals, they took back a wealth of knowledge about skiing techniques and judging methods that helped the fledging Australian Waterskiing Association make some remarkable progress. Australia would go on to produce several world champions, including Sharon Dodgson, who won the 1998 world barefoot championships.

Water skiing competitions are contested not only by scoring points for certain tricks or distances covered, but also for artistry. In 1974 the first National Show Ski Tournament, hosted by the Rock Aqua Jays Ski Club, was held in Janesville, Wisconsin. Here athletes were required to display the art of skiing, much as synchronized swimming displays the art of aquatic movement. Barefoot competitions are also very popular; the first national and world barefoot championships were held in 1978 in the United States, and they have been contested annually since then.

Water skiing became an exhibition sport at the 1972 Olympics, but as of 1999 it is still not an official sport of the Olympics. More than 350 water skiing tournaments are held each year, and the number of participants is constantly growing.

RULES AND PLAY

Tournament skiing is split into three categories—slalom, tricks, and jump. All skiers compete in each event, and a combination of the three scores indicates the overall winner. Slalom is sometimes referred to as monoskiing because skiers use one ski, instead of the usual two. The ski has two foot bindings, one in front of the other. The front binding is sealed to prevent the skier's foot from slipping off the ski. The back binding can also be sealed, although some skiers prefer to have the back binding open to allow more freedom of movement. By having the back binding open the skier can start skiing with one foot in the water to help with balance, then place her foot into the binding after she has achieved a standing position.

Slalom involves negotiating a predetermined course. Throughout the course, water buoys are spaced 41 meters (135 feet) apart and 11.5 meters (37.9 feet) out from the center line, in an alternating manner. As their skiing ability increases, skiers take on more challenging slaloms by using shorter tow ropes. All competitors start with ropes that are 23 meters (76 feet); once they have successfully negotiated the entire course, the tow rope is shortened to 18.25 meters (60 feet), then 16, 14.25, 13, 12, 11.25, and finally 10.75 meters (from 59 to 35.5 feet). Those skiers reaching the 11.25- and 10.75-meter shortenings are skiing on a rope that is shorter than the distance from the boat to the turn buoy. They must make up the difference entirely by reach.

Trick skiing is usually competed on one ski, although beginners generally start learning on two trick skis. A trick ski differs from a normal ski in that it does not have a fin. This allows the skier to complete tricks that require 180-degree turns. The ski rope that is used is also different. The handle is shorter and has a toe-hold incorporated into its design. The skier uses the toe-hold to complete tricks in which she is holding the handle not with her hands but rather with her feet.

In ski jumping, skiers are required to jump as far as they can, using a ramp that is 1.8 meters (6 feet) off the water. The speed is set at a constant 56 kph (35 mph) for all open divisions. The skis used are much larger than those used for normal skiing; they are longer and wider and are specially designed to be aerodynamic. Skiers are required to wear helmets to protect themselves in case of an accident.

Another variant is barefooting, which has the same three components as tournament skiing, differing only in that there are no buoys to reach in the slalom event. Instead, the skiers gain points by crossing the wake as many times as possible in the allotted 15 seconds. More points are given if the wake crossing is achieved on one foot, with the greatest number of points achieved for crossing the wake backward on one foot. The trick events are also the same, with skiers completing similar tricks, skiing forward and backward. The jump event is also identical, the only difference being the height of the ramp, which is set at 45.7 centimeters (18 inches). Initially barefooters who tried to jump did so in a seated position; that is, after leaving the edge of the ramp, they maintained a sitting position in anticipation of the landing. Today the jumping style has become more flamboyant and dangerous, with skiers attaining an almost vertical position during midflight. They then have to manuever their bodies back into a sitting position before landing. The result is a spectacular sight, but only professional skiers are encouraged to try this. Equipment required for barefooting is somewhat different from that required for tournament skiing. Most important are the helmet and a special wetsuit that protect skiers when they fall at high speeds. The final requirement is a speed boat that is capable of achieving speeds up to 80–90 kph (50–55 mph).

Martha Mitchell, Florida champ, and Katy Turner, former national title holder practice for the Water Skiing Championships in 1950. (Bettmann/Corbis)

WOMEN'S PARTICIPATION

The proportion of registered women water skiers in the United States is quite low. Skiers have to be registered to ski in a competition; this is for the purpose of recording numbers as well as insurance. Surveys of sports participation indicate that there are 13 million to 16 million water skiers, with approximately 1.7 million new participants taking up the sport each year. The AWSA reports that only 25 percent of its members are female. Why this percentage is disproportionately low remains unknown. Social factors seem an unlikely explanation, as the essence of the sport focuses on glamour and artistry, which might tend to appeal to rather than deter many women. The only exception to this is the jumping component; ramp jumping by nature is dangerous, and it is recommended only for athletes who have attained a relatively high degree of mastery, not casual skiers.

Gavin Freeman

Bibliography

Favret, Brett, and Daniel Benzel. (1997) *Complete Guide to Water Skiing*. Champaign, IL: Human Kinetics.

Kistler, Bruce. (1988) *Hit It! Your Complete Guide to Water Skiing*. Champaign IL: Leisure Press.

Wansey, Martin. (1990) *In Search of Gold*. Canberra, Australia: Australian Sports Commission.

West, John. (1990) *Water Skiing: The Skills of the Game*. Marlborough, UK: Crowood Press.

SKI JUMPING

Ski jumping has traditionally been regarded as *the* sport for males in those nations where it is popular. It is a sport that "makes boys into men." In most countries, ski jumping is regarded as unsuitable for women because it is too dangerous for "the weaker sex." As of 1998, women's ski jumping was still excluded from the world championships and the Winter Olympic Games. Nonetheless, attitudes toward women and ski jumping in Le Féderation International de Ski (FIS), Sweden, and the United States are slowly changing, and some people recognize that the sport may be especially suitable for women.

HISTORY

Ingrid Olavsdottir Vestby is the first woman known to have taken part in a ski-jumping competition—in Trysil, Norway, in 1862:

> She pushed off, and raced down the jump, took off, and flew till she landed, firmly planted on her skis, far past the point where many a brave lad had lost his balance earlier in the competition. The spectators roared their approval—the first "bravos" of the day. Their relief was great for they had never before seen a girl jump on skis and they had been more than a little anxious as she flew over their heads.
>
> *(Bø 1992, 107–108) (translated by author)*

The skis that she wore were quite different from those of today, made of long pieces of wood without heel bindings. The jumps were much smaller, too. The winning jump at the Trysil competition was only 11.5 meters (12.5 yards).

Girls and women in the rural areas of Finland, Sweden, Norway, and Russia who had to use skis on a daily basis were often accomplished skiers. But it was first and foremost men and boys who used skis for recreation and participated in the ski-jumping competitions that began at the end of the nineteenth century. According to Norwegian sources, ski jumping as a competitive sport started in Norway.

Women in Norway seemed to participate more actively in local ski-jumping competitions before 1900, when national rules and official referees began to dominate the sport. Sports organizations referred to medical opinion when they needed to justify the push for regular training, and medical opinion often discouraged participation by women. Focusing on upper-middle-class women, "especially married women who have given birth, and whose reproductive organs have been through a process which all too often reduces them to a morbid state," some doctors warned against participation in ski jumping:

> Therefore especially jumping, and ski jumping should, from a medical perspective, be discouraged for women. . . . The very training called for—standing upright during a jump—is far more strenuous than realized. Not only are many muscles under continuous strain, but the heart, as well as the rest of the nervous system is under great strain. One must concentrate one's full attention on the run down to the take off and maintain this concentration during the flight. All of one's muscles, one's very will are put to the test. This state of mind is very strenuous both physically and mentally for more or less weak, nervous and untrained women.
>
> *(Døderlein 1896–97, 73)*

Although the negative attitude toward women's participation in sports gradually changed, male leaders in ski federations around the world continued to believe that ski jumping was too dangerous for women.

The most famous female ski jumpers in Sweden and Norway in the 1930s were the Nor-

Two female skiers jump from a ridge during a descent holding hands and somersaulting. (Ales Fevzer/Corbis)

wegian teenagers Johanne Kolstad and Hilda Braskerud. According to *Sports Manden* (*The Sportsman*) in 1931, Kolstad set a world record for women when she jumped 45 meters (49 yards) in a competition in Nordre Land, south of Lillehammer in the east of Norway. Despite appeals from some local clubs, organized competitions in Norway still excluded women from participating in ski jumping. Because of this, Kolstad started competing in Sweden, Finland, the United States, and Canada, in addition to appearing in circuses in England. She set a new world record in 1938 in New Hampshire (United States), jumping 72 meters (79 yards).

This record stood until 1972, when Anita Wold of Norway jumped 80 meters (87.5 yards). The following year Wold jumped 94 meters (103 yards) in Czechoslovakia. Her longest jump, 97.5 meters (106.6 yards), was in Japan. In 1999 Eva Ganster from Kitzbühel, Austria, held the record with a jump of 167 meters (182.6 yards).

A CHANGE OF ATTITUDE

According to the Swedish ski-jumping expert Bengt Nybelius, in 1999 only the United States and Sweden had ski-jumping rules that allowed girls and women to compete with athletes of their own sex and not simply as an add-on to men's events or together with boys. Understandably, these rules created the possibility of developing ski jumping into a sport that includes girls and women, and both these countries have national championships for female ski jumpers.

It may be that ski jumping needs women and girls if it is to survive in the future, especially with the introduction of new ski sports such as snowboarding. In Scandinavian countries the number of boys and men who participated in ski jumping declined drastically in the early 1990s. In 1996 there were more ski jumps in Norway than there were ski jumpers in the Norwegian ski federation. An FIS committee on ski jumping decided in May 1998 to include women in the sport, asking for the cooperation of the different ski federations in participating countries in this endeavor. The goal was to arrange a world championship for women at the junior class level in the year 2000.

Changes in ski jumping have enhanced its suitability for women. Skiers using a V-style jumping technique have their ski tips pointing away from each other. It is easier to achieve longer jumps this way, and skiers are not as likely to hit their faces with their skis as they were when they held their skis parallel to each other. Important qualities for a ski jumper to have are a slight build, a flexible body, good balance, a low center of gravity, and the ability to focus—all qualities that seem to characterize female bodies and minds. Thus, some experts see ski jumping as a new growth sport for women, although it is also clear that the old ideology of ski jumping being a sport that "makes boys into men" must change if women are to become full participants.

Gerd von der Lippe

Bibliography

Bø, Olav. (1992) *På ski gjennom historia.* Oslo, Norway: Samlaget.

Døderlein, Christian. (1896–97) "Skiløbning." In *Yearbook for the Centralforeningen for udbredelse af idræt.* Kristiania (Oslo, Norway): Brøggers trykkeri.

Mo, Kristen. (1989) "Norwegian Resistance Against the Winter Olympic Games in 1928." In *Yearbook of the Norwegian Association for Sport History,* edited by M. Goksøyr and K. Mo. Oslo, Norway:

Information was also provided by Bengt Nybelius (Committee of Women's Jumping).

SLEDDING—SKELETON (CRESTA RUN) TOBOGGANING

Tobogganing is a popular, traditional winter recreational pastime in many countries, especially where there is plenty of snow and winter is long. In skeleton or Cresta Run tobogganing, a single rider assumes a head first, prone position upon the "skeleton" toboggan.

HISTORY

The origin of the toboggan is ascribed to the Native American people who inhabited the snow-covered northern forests of present-day Canada. Native Americans fashioned a simple yet highly functional sledge or sled from long thin strips of birchwood poles or slats with turned-up ends, fastened together with deer-leather thongs. In modern times, the toboggan has become popular as it has been transformed from its original practical use of transporting goods into a craft designed for winter recreational pastimes and competitive sport. In Europe, the use of toboggans for winter recreational purposes has been recorded in documents as far back as the sixteenth century. As a sport, tobogganing was introduced by English and American visitors at the Alpine recuperative centers in Davos and St. Moritz, Switzerland, in the last half of the nineteenth century, and the sport soon became popular among tourists in the snow-covered Swiss Alps region during the winter. Tobogganing was considered to be an excellent form of recreation for people with disabilities, since it could be performed while sitting in an upright position.

Much experimentation in the design of both toboggans and runs took place during this period, and in 1879 two toboggan runs were designed and constructed at Davos, Switzerland. In 1881 national toboggan competitions began on a course located on a road between the hamlets of Davos and Klosters in Switzerland. In the latter part of that decade, tobogganing became popular in Canada, Switzerland, Germany, Austria, the United States, and Russia, with toboggan runs built in each of these countries.

During the 1880s, as its popularity increased, tobogganing evolved and branched off into three main forms: skeleton or Cresta tobogganing, luging (which developed from the one-person toboggan), and bobsleighing or bobsledding (dubbed the "bob-sleigh" because the early riders leaned back and then "bobbed" forward to increase speed on the straightaway sections). The skeleton or Cresta toboggan is the original sport from which the luge (which is a French and a Swiss-French word for "toboggan" or "sled") and bobsleigh vehicles and events were developed. In 1964 luge became an Olympic event and replaced skeleton or Cresta tobogganing as a competitive sport. At this juncture, luge tobogganing emerged from the shadow of bobsledding events, which had already attained Olympic status in 1924.

Skeleton or Cresta tobogganing began in 1884 in St. Moritz, Switzerland, when an Englishman, Major W. H. Bulpetts, designed a toboggan run in the Cresta Valley as an alternative to the Klosters Road near Davos. On 18 February 1885, the Grand National, the first major competition on this newly created course, was held between a team from Davos and a team from St. Moritz. Tobogganists in this race assumed a face-forward, sitting position on the toboggan, and used their hands and feet to brake the craft. The team from Davos won. Shortly thereafter, the St. Moritz Tobogganing Club was formed in 1887, and this led to further development and improvement of the Cresta toboggan run. Major Bulpetts was one of the founding members of the club. The St. Moritz Tobogganing Club had a rather exclusive membership and fee schedule, with numerous members from Great Britain, Switzerland, and the United States.

Women had been club participants from its early days, including riding the races at the Cresta Run. Most early female tobogganists wore skirts and had to use an elastic strap around their legs to keep their skirts from flapping in the wind and getting caught in the sled runners. If women tobogganists "dared" to wear breeches or pants in this early era, they did so at the risk of being derogatorily referred to as "fast" women. Regarding women riders, a Mrs. J. M. Baguley drew attention in 1919 when she placed among the last eight competitors of the Curzon Cup (see below). She finished ahead of her husband by one-eighth of a second combined time in a race over three heats. In the early 1920s, she put in a very respectable performance on the famed Swiss Cresta Run course: 48.9 seconds from junction (start) to finish. Her record time in 1921 would have been good enough to place in the top ten toboggan runs in the 1948 Olympics, but by then women were banned from toboggan competition. Some women tobogganists had had bad spills on the toboggan runs of that period, and a debate about women's safety followed, which resulted in limited access to competition for many years.

Aside from the Grand National toboggan competition, the Ashbourne Cup (now known as the Curzon Cup) was inaugurated in 1910. The Cresta Run was included in the 1928 and 1948 Olympic Games, but thereafter tobogganing faded from the forefront of popular winter sports. A series of World Cup skeleton toboggan races were reinitiated in 1985. More than twenty countries had skeleton sliding teams that competed in World Cup and world championship events annually through the 1990s.

In this revival of skeleton tobogganing, women competed in the same (or similar) type of race events as men but against other women's teams for the national and world team positions. May Bieri (Switzerland), Steffi Hanslik (Germany), Susan Speiran (Canada), Ursi Walliser (Switzerland), Alexandra Hamilton (Great Britain), Juleigh Walker (United States), Astrid Ebner (Austria), Aya Shibata (Japan), Melissa Hollingsworth (Canada), and Diana Sartor (Germany) are among the top ten ranked women skeleton tobogganists.

RULES AND PLAY

The Cresta Run is composed of packed snow upon which water is sprayed to form a smooth ice surface. At a length of 1.2 kilometers (three-quarters of a mile), the Cresta course descends 156.7 meters (514 feet) from start to finish and covers a varied snowscape wherein no two curves or slopes are alike, nor is there a straightaway section; several of the curves are configured almost as right angles with high banks.

Four women on a toboggan, ready for some winter fun in the 1920s. (Bettmann/Corbis)

In the 1990s, the Cresta Run was an extremely winding and challenging course with steep banks rebuilt each year by the St. Moritz Toboggan Club. In contrast to luge or bobsledding competitions, in which the size and weight of the craft are regulated, toboggans used in the Cresta run can be any size, shape, or weight, with speed and stability being the guiding design factors. The type of toboggan preferred on the Cresta course is known as the "steel skeleton." Its basic design, according to the U.S. Bobsled and Skeleton Federation, measures 0.9 meters (3 feet) in length and 40.6 centimeters (16 inches) in width; it weighs between 32 and 52 kilograms (70 and 115 pounds) depending upon the tobogganist's weight. A critical selection factor for competitors is that the toboggan dimensions be a "good fit" for the user in terms of length, width, height, and weight. Mechanical brakes and steering components, however, are not allowed on the toboggan.

"Raking" equipment, composed of steel-spiked toe pieces screwed into the racer's boots, is applied in the run for steering and braking purposes. Cresta Run safety equipment is similar to that used in luge events: an approved-design crash helmet with goggles, a face shield or visor, and a chin guard; padded gloves with an outer covering of studs or gauntlets (metal knuckles) to prevent "Cresta hand" (scraping one's knuckles on the ice); leather elbow pads; and leather kneepads.

Good judgment gained through experience is necessary both to select the most appropriate toboggan and to determine the strategies and techniques to use in running down the course. A good run down the Cresta course may be made in under seventy-five seconds. Skilled tobogganists achieve speeds of eighty kilometers (50 miles) per hour near the top of the run and accelerate to nearly 145 kilometers (90 miles) per hour at the finish area.

At the close of the 1990s, skeleton tobogganing remained a minor sport, although it continues to appeal to a small number of men and women who are attracted to its challenges.

Katharine A. Pawelko

Bibliography

"Fifty and one hundred years ago: Toboggan slide." (1988) *Scientific American* 259, 1: 12.

Arlott, John, ed. (1975) *The Oxford Companion to World Sports and Games.* New York: Oxford University Press, 1034–1039.

Bass, Howard. (1968) *Winter Sports.* South Brunswick, NJ: A. S. Barnes.

Bernstein, Jeremy. (1988) "Raking (Cresta Run in St. Moritz)." *The New Yorker* 64 (28 March): 88–90, 93–98.

Brabazon of Tara, Lord. (1966) "Tobogganing." *Winter Sports.* London: Lonsdale Library.

Caskey, George B., and David G. Wright. (1966) "Coasting and Tobogganing Facilities: A Manual and Survey on Construction and Operations." *Management Aids Bulletin No. 62.* Wheeling, WV: National Recreation and Park Association.

Conover, Garrett, and Alexandra Conover. (1995) *A Snow Walker's Companion: Winter Skills from the Far North.* Camden, ME: Ragged Mountain Press.

Cook, T. A. (1894) *Notes on Tobogganing at St. Moritz.* New York: Scribner.

Cross, Gary. (1990) *A Social History of Leisure Since 1600.* State College, PA: Venture Publishing.

Federation Internationale de Bobsleigh et Tobogganing (FIBT). (1997) "History of the Federation Internationale de Bobsleigh et Tobogganing, The International Bobsleigh and Skeleton Federation," <http://bobsleigh.com/history.html>.

Seth-Smith, Michael. (1976) *The Cresta Run: History of the St. Moritz Tobogganing Club.* New York: Foulsham.

St. Moritz Toboggan Club. (n.d.) *Cresta Magazine.*

Turner, Al. (1995) "The Big Freeze." *Leisure Management* (August): 58–59.

Wright, Graeme. (1978) "Snow Vehicles." In *Rand McNally Illustrated Dictionary of Sports.* New York and Chicago: Rand McNally.

SLED DOG RACING

Sled dog racing developed rapidly as an international competitive and professional sport during the second half of the twentieth century. However, as it is dependent on snow and ice, it is restricted to North America, Scandinavia, and Central Europe. Until recently sled dog racing had developed separately in each of these regions because of the cost of transportation and quarantine regulations meant to prevent the spread of dog-related diseases.

CHARACTERISTICS AND VARIETIES OF DOG SLEDDING

The basis of all different styles of dog sledding is that dogs are running and pulling because they enjoy it and want to please their human drivers. The dogs are directed by spoken commands, and the psychological relationship between dogs and musher has to be intimate. The leader dog must understand everything that is said to it and guide the others accordingly. In Alaskan-style racing, drivers use from three to twenty male and female dogs to pull their sled, usually tied in sets of two with one or two lead dogs. The driver stands on the runners of the dogsled, steers the sled by giving commands to the dogs and by shifting her weight, twisting the handlebar, and using a brake and snow hook to stop the dog team. She can help the team somewhat by running behind the sled or by kicking with one foot, but the dogs, mostly of the polar type, do the bulk of the work.

Competitive mushing is a way of life; to train and raise a dog team is an all-consuming activity and a year-round practice. During the off-season, the dog teams are trained for speed, strength, and endurance, and the dogs have to be fed and looked after every day. A professional driver needs to run a kennel of up to 100 dogs and develop a scientific and planned breeding program to be able to get good leader dogs or dogs with either sprint or endurance traits. Dog food, equipment, and veterinary bills for a relatively large number of dogs all add up to large expenses, and drivers need to pay attention to their sponsors all year long.

The Alaskan-style dog mushing is the best known of several varieties of racing because of the Iditarod Sled Dog Race across the rough winter landscape of Alaska—1800 kilometers (1120 miles) from Anchorage to Nome. Since the beginning of the 1970s, the race has developed from a local cultural event into a global and commercial sport, media, and tourist event. The popularity of the Alaskan style is embedded in the American dream of individualistic male pioneers who had the courage to go into the wilderness and conquer the new land and in people's imagination of being a modern adventurer.

The Nordic style combines the traditional Scandinavian way of cross-country skiing and dog driving; one to three dogs pull a smaller sled, called a *pulk,* while the skier on cross-country skis is tied to the *pulk* and skis actively. The stronger the skier is, the more she can help the dogs. She is not allowed actually to help the dog pull the *pulk,* however. The Nordic style—also known as the Pulka style—was first used in ambulance transportation when skiing developed as mass recreation. Nordic-style competitions have been organized on a regular basis since the 1930s, and since

THE LAST GREAT RACE ON EARTH: THE IDITAROD SLED DOG RACE

The first white hunters, trappers, and explorers in the Arctic learned the art of traveling by dogsled from the natives for whom dog teams were a necessary means of survival. When the settlers came to Alaska following the gold strike in the late nineteenth century, the only way of traveling over land in the wintertime was by dog teams. They followed what is today known as the Iditarod Trail, which has become a National Historic Trail designated by the United States Congress. In 1908 the first dog sled competition, the All-Alaska Sweepstakes (650 kilometers), was organized among the male settlers in Nome in order to decide who was the best driver and who could run the best team. When gold mining began to slack off, most people returned to their homes. Subsequently, the use of airplanes in the late 1920s and the development of the snowmobile meant the beginning of the end for the dog team as a standard mode of transportation.

Modern Alaskan dog mushing race was reinvented in the late 1960s by Dorothy G. Page who organized a spectacular dog race, although much shorter, to wake up the Alaskans to what mushers and their dogs had done for Alaska and to celebrate the 100th anniversary of America's purchase of Alaska from Russia. It was Joe Redding-ton Sr., however, who organized the first race across Alaska, from coast to coast in 1973.

Each team spends from ten to seventeen days in blizzards and extremely low temperatures, but they also face the silence and the beauty of the wild Arctic winter landscape. The driver needs to combine endurance, stamina, good judgement, strategy, as well as a distinct spirit of adventure. In the early years of the race, native mushers had the knowledge and the skills required, and its official purpose was to promote the breeding of sled dogs in Alaska.

From being a diffuse celebration of Alaska's past, the Iditarod later became explicitly connected to an event in 1925 when a relay team of mail carriers drove by dog teams to take serum to the diphtheria-stricken village of Nome and saved the population. The celebration of the modern race as a historic tradition excludes the natives from relating their traditional lifestyles to the race, and they no longer dominate it. It takes about two million dollars and thousands of hard working volunteers to run the Iditarod, which involves about seventy teams and one thousand dogs. First prize in 1999 was $54,000.

Four-time Iditarod champion Susan Butcher and her dogsled team train on the packed ice near Koyuk, Alaska, in 1991. (Paul A. Souders/Corbis)

the 1950s international competitions have been held every year in the Scandinavian countries. In the 1970s the sport was exported to other European countries, and in mid-1980s to North America. Shorthaired German pointers are most commonly used.

More recently, another style—skijoring—which combines the principles of cross-country skiing and dog mushing, has developed. A dog in harness tows a skier by a line 2.13 to 3.7 meters (7 to 12 feet) long. The line is either hand-held or attached to a special belt worn by the skier. Cross-country skis are most commonly used, as the skier can then help the dogs by striding or skating. Most skijorers limit their dog power to one or two dogs, with three dogs as the maximum. A skijoring team can travel surprisingly long distances, depending on the type of dog(s) and the skier's ability. In the mid-1980s skijoring began to catch people's attention all over North America and developed as a competitive sport. In Europe this kind of dog driving without the *pulk* is predominantly viewed as a training technique for Nordic-style mushing. Skijoring allows the skier to experience the speed and pleasure of dog mushing on a smaller, more economical scale. However, all styles can be used for competition, recreational touring, rescue work, and transportation of disabled people.

HISTORY

Traveling with dogs on ice and snow originated among the native peoples of the Arctic in Siberia, North America, and Greenland. Dogs have always been humans' hunters, companions, guardians, workers, and guides, and they have proved to be adaptable to almost anything humans wish them to be. The Alaskan-style dog mushing evolved from the native style, which used several dogs tied in a fan in front of the sled.

It was polar explorers in the late nineteenth century who brought the knowledge and skills of dog driving to Europe. In the dramatic fight between hardy men crossing Antarctica, Norwegian Roald Amundsen and his dog teams had proved to be superior compared to the snowmobiles used by the British explorer Robert F. Scott. In the 1920s these events inspired the evolution of the Nordic style of dog mushing in Scandinavia. The sport evolved separately elsewhere in Europe because of different cultural and topographical conditions.

When the "Last Great Race on Earth," the Iditarod, was first organized in 1973, thirty-four men signed up to participate. No rules prohibited women from participation, however, and in 1974 two women, Mary Shields and Lolly Medley, entered and completed the race. Most of the men that the two women passed on their way to Nome quit the race; only two men chose to finish behind them. Every year since then a handful of women have participated, but in the beginning it was not clear to the women that they were accepted. Susan Butcher (1954–) made the real breakthrough for women when she was the first woman to finish among the top ten in 1979.

Butcher created a climate in which it was expected that a woman could beat the men and even win in this challenge of the North. She came in second in 1982 and 1984, and was leading the race in 1985 when a moose killed two and injured thirteen of her dogs. Thus it was another woman, Libby Riddles, who in 1985 became the first woman to win the Iditarod. Because of extremely bad weather conditions, it was the slowest race ever, and it was questioned whether her victory was a real achievement. The following three years Butcher won the race, and she was even able to set a trail record in 1986 and 1987. In 1990 she triumphed for the fourth time, becoming one of the most winning drivers ever and helping to explode the lingering myth of women as the weaker sex. Butcher was selected the Outstanding Female Athlete of the World by the International Academy of Sports in 1989.

The second half of the 1980s became critical years for the male image of the Iditarod; the race could no longer be conceptualized as male competitors fighting against one another, the wilderness, and Alaska's often brutal winter weather. It was reconceptualized as a contest in which women and men compete as equals.

Sprint racer Roxy Wright-Champaine (c. 1950–) was the first woman to win the North American championship, the Anchorage Fur Rendezvous world championship in Alaska, and the Alpirod in Europe. She was a very skillful and knowledgeable driver and won many other sprint races in North America.

Nordic-style competitive dog sledding was originally conceptualized as a man's sport, one that creates men out of boys and keeps the boys alive in men. The Norwegian Ebba Winge (1912–) began to compete in the early 1950s, and for years she was the only woman competing. Formerly an Olympic cross-country skier, she was thrilled by the new style of dog racing once she was introduced to it. Although she was forty when she started, she became Scandinavian champion several times.

Norwegians Anita Andreassen (1960–) and Lena Boysen (1969–) were pioneers when the Pulka style became popular outside Scandinavia. From 1988 to 1998 they won five world and eight European championships in the Nordic style. As a world competitor also in bicycling, Andreassen was honored as the Outstanding Norwegian Athlete of the Year in 1996; Boysen was the only dog driver to become world and European champion and to win the World Cup in Alaskan and Nordic styles. Her success, she said, was due to her love for the dogs, which made them perform with the extra edge that was needed.

In the Finnmark Race—a long-distance Alaskan-style event—a few women have participated every year, but as of 1999 they have not been able to challenge the men. However, many women are involved as handlers or helpers and do a lot of the everyday work of feeding, caring for, and training dogs.

In 1987 Monica Kristensen (1950–) of Norway organized a successful Norwegian–British scientific sled dog expedition to the South Pole. The expedition followed the same route as the polar explorers had seventy-five years earlier.

As a response to male dominance of the sport, a group of women—mostly friends, lovers, and spouses of male drivers—created a women-only dogsled race in northern Norway in 1994. The race has become a noncompetitive, annual event, attracting up to 35 participating teams with 150 dogs. This Alaskan-style race, known as *Asgardsreien,* is an alternative to the time- and resource-consuming long-distance race; it focuses instead on recreation, friendship and social togetherness, the dogs, and the wilderness. In North America, women-only wilderness organizations and female professional dog drivers have for years offered dogsled programs just for recreation and adventure.

MODERN INTERNATIONAL DOGSLEDDING COMPETITIONS

Since the late 1970s dogsled racing has become a fast-growing sport. The Alaskan-style dog mushing, which is the national sport in Alaska, spread to Scandinavia, then to Central Europe. During the 1990s the interest in the sport increased also in Japan and the Southern Hemisphere. There are several associations that organized local, national, and international competitions in both styles of dogsledding, but the Alaskan style has dominated worldwide. In North America there were about 300 Alaskan-style competitions every year, and there are about 100 official competitions around Europe. The best-known Alaskan-style race in Europe was the Alpirod; run between 1988 and 1995, it was a series of sprints from town to town through Italy, Germany, France, and Switzerland.

The Alaskan-style Finnmark Race, far north of the Arctic Circle in Norway, has since 1992 been the longest race (in either Alaskan or Nordic style) in Europe: 1000 kilometers (621 miles) through uninhabited Arctic wilderness. Unlike the Iditarod, the Finnmark lacks a mythical and unifying imagination related to the race, perhaps because the traditional way of transportation across frozen northern Scandinavia was cross-country skiing and reindeer pulling *pulks*. Due to the fact that the Nordic style is a relatively new sport outside Scandinavia, the sport is dominated by Scandinavians.

The International Sled Dog Racing Association (ISDRA), founded in 1966, was for years the central governing body of sled dog competitions, while the European Sled Dog Racing Association (ESDRA) was founded in 1983. ESDRA functions as an umbrella organization for the national associations in Europe and is responsible for the arrangement of the European championship, which has been offered since 1984. ISDRA and ESDRA cofounded the International Federation of Sleddog Sport (IFSS) in 1985. Today IFSS is the overall coalition of national federations to promote international dogsled competitions. It became a member of the General Association of International Sports Federations in 1986. While the Alaskan Sled Dog and Racing Association has organized what they call women's and open world championship races in North America, since 1990 it was IFSS that organized the official world championship and since 1996 has promoted a World Cup series. IFSS is working to gain entrance in the Olympic Winter Games, and dogsled races have been a demonstration sport several times: Alaskan style in 1932 (Lake Placid) and Nordic style in 1952 (Oslo). In 1996 IFSS organized more than 20,000 mushers, 1,000 events, and about 45,000 teams of dogs. These numbers are high because each driver competes in different classes—four, six, or eight dogs in Alaskan-style (sprint) classes, and one, two, or four dogs in the Nordic style. Very few of these mushers or dogs are professionals. All the associations work to promote the health and welfare of sled dogs, and in all competitions veterinarians supervise the dogs' health. On the organizational level, IFSS cooperates closely with the International Sled Dog Veterinary Medical Association.

RULES AND PLAY

Most races in the Alaskan and Nordic styles fall into two categories: sprint races and distance races. Sprint races are usually from 5 to 50 kilometers (3.1 to 31 miles) and are often organized in heats; the same trail is run two or three days in a row. Middle-distance races are less than 500 kilometers (310.7 miles), while long-distance races are longer than that. The latter contain several checkpoints and mandatory rest stops. In Alaskan style there are limited classes of four to ten dogs and an unlimited class with no limit to the maximum number of dogs per team. In long-distance races the drivers have to bring the equipment needed for whatever situation and weather might occur. They have to sign in at all the checkpoints along the trail and complete all mandatory stops. All dogs must be maintained in good condition, and no dogs may be added during the race. In the Alaskan style there are actually many more sprint races than distance races, but the long races get the most media attention. In the Nordic style there are one-dog and unlimited classes (two to four dogs), as well as relays. A specified weight is carried in the *pulk*.

In the Alaskan style, women and men compete on equal footing, though some men think women have advantages because they are generally not as heavy, which makes it easier for the dogs. However, the race's tremendous demands on strength, endurance, and stamina tend to even out any advantages due to the weight of the individual musher. Nordic style and skijoring, however, are always separated into men's and women's classes in all distances and in relays. Given equally capable dogs, these races are more like footraces and are divided into men's and women's classes for the same reasons.

Kirsti Pedersen

Bibliography

Cellura, Dominique. (1990) *Travelers of the Cold: Sled Dogs of the Far North.* Anchorage, AK: Alaska Northwest Books.

Dolan, Ellen M. (1993) *Susan Butcher and the Iditarod Trail.* New York: Walker and Co.

Freedman, Lew, and DeeDee Jonrowe. (1994) *Iditarod Dreams: A Year in the Life of Alaskan Sled Dog Racer DeeDee Jonrowe.* Seattle, WA: Epicenter Press.

Høe-Raitto, Mari, and Carol Kaynor. (1991) *Skijor with Your Dog.* Fairbanks, AK: OK Publishing.

International Federation of Sleddog Sport. (1999) <http://www.worldsport.com/worldsport/sports/sleddog/home>.

Kardell, Iben. (1997) *The Last Great Race and Its Contestants: An Anthropological Account.* Oslo, Norway: University of Oslo.

Kristensen, Monica. (1987) *Mot 90° syd.* Oslo, Norway: Grøndahl.

Norges Hundekjørerforbund. (1976) *Norges Hundekjørerforbund 25 år.* Oslo, Norway: Norwegian Sled Dog Racing Association.

SLOVENIA *see* Yugoslavia

SMETANINA, RAISA PETROVNA

(1952–)

RUSSIAN CROSS-COUNTRY SKIER

Over a long career that encompassed five Olympics, Raisa Smetanina compiled one of the greatest records of any female cross-country skier. Smetanina was born on 29 February 1952 in Mokhcha, Komi, in the Soviet Union, a region near the Ural Mountains, where she learned to ski in the frigid winters. She grew up as an only child and remained single throughout her long career, focusing almost exclusively on her skiing. She began competitive skiing in 1967 and was first named to the Soviet national team in 1972.

Raisa Smetanina (left) celebrates with her Russian relay teammates at the 1992 Winter Olympics. (Allsport/International Olympic Museum Collection)

Smetanina first came to international attention at the 1974 world championships, where she helped the Soviet Union relay team to the championship. This led to her greatest Olympic performance at Innsbruck in 1976. She competed in three events, medaling in all three, with a silver in the 5-kilometer and golds in the 10-kilometer and the team relay. Smetanina went on to compete at the Olympic Winter Games in 1980, 1984, 1988, and 1992, retiring after the Albertville Olympics. During that time, she won ten Olympic medals, including four golds. To the two gold medals in 1976, she added another individual gold in the 1980 5-kilometer race and she helped the Soviet women's relay team to a gold medal at the 1992 Olympics. Her gold medal in the relay came only twelve days before she turned forty years old, making her, at her retirement, the oldest female gold medalist in Winter Olympic history.

Smetanina also won thirteen medals at the world championships. Of these, three were gold medals, including relay titles with the Soviet Union team in 1974 and 1985. Her only individual world title came in the 20-kilometer race in 1982. In addition to her international triumphs, Smetanina won twenty-one Soviet Union championships and was named an Emeritus Master of Sport of the Soviet Union. Smetanina grew up skiing in the classic Nordic style, and she never adjusted well to the gliding skating technique that was popularized in the early 1980s. She stubbornly refused to learn the skating style and thereafter her competition was confined to the shorter classic-style races.

Bill Mallon

Bibliography

Matthews, Peter. (1998) *Whitaker's Almanack. International Sports Records and Results.* London: The Stationery Office.

SMITH, ROBYN C.

(1944–)

U.S. JOCKEY

Robyn C. Smith was one of the first American female jockeys to be granted a license and to break into the previously male-dominated profession of thoroughbred horse racing. She faced many obstacles, such as size, gender bias, and a late beginning in the profession, but she was able to pave the way for other riders to fulfill their dreams of riding at prestigious tracks, having the opportunity to ride quality mounts, and visiting the winner's circle at tracks all over the country.

Jockey Robyn Smith in 1972. (Jerry Cooke/Corbis)

Most jockeys begin riding as small children, but Smith developed her interest in her early twenties. While studying acting, she began riding each morning, setting herself the goal of becoming an expert rider. In 1968 she began racing and by 1969 she had convinced officials at Golden Gate Park in San Francisco that a female jockey could attract media attention and spark interest in the declining sport of thoroughbred racing. (That same year, Diane Crump became the first female jockey to compete against men on a major U.S. flat track, at Hialeah in Florida.) Later that year, Smith moved to New York, in hopes of getting a better chance at a good mount. At Aqueduct racetrack, on 5 December 1969, Smith rode Exotic Bird to a fourth-place finish (losing third place and a high-stakes money finish by only a nose), thus proving herself capable of handling a horse in strong competition with male jockeys. In 1970 Smith became the first female to race at Saratoga, and in 1973 she became the first female jockey to win a major stakes race, the Paumanauk Handicap at Aqueduct.

Smith stands 5 feet, 7 inches (1 m, 67.5 cm) tall, whereas most jockeys measure in about 5 feet to 5 feet, 2 inches (1 m, 50 cm–1 m, 55 cm). She had to fight her weight constantly, which detracted from strength needed to control a horse. Losing weight without sacrificing strength is a major concern for jockeys, and it was a reason given by many trainers for not choosing Smith to ride their horses. In her career, she rode fewer than 100 mounts per year, compared to the 1,000 or more per year usually ridden by experienced jockeys. Despite the small number of races she entered, between 1970 and 1974 she won 18 to 20 percent of her races and the admiration of several top owners around the circuit, including Alfred G. Vanderbilt. By 1975 Smith was a regular rider for Vanderbilt's stables at prestigious venues throughout the United States, helping pave the way for other women.

Smith retired from racing after only ten years and married Fred Astaire. Smith helped with the training of his champion horses and continued to advocate, break barriers, and open doors for women jockeys.

Debra Ann Ballinger

Bibliography

Bernikow, Louise, ed. (1997) *The American Women's Almanac: An Inspiring and Irreverent Women's History*. New York: Berkeley Reference Works.

Boutilier, Mary A., and Lucinda SanGiovanni. (1983) *The Sporting Woman*. Champaign, IL: Human Kinetics.

Heinemann, Sue. (1996) *The Timelines of American Women's History*. New York: Berkeley Publication Group.

Stambler, Irwin. (1975) *Women in Sports*. Garden City, NY: Doubleday.

Kim Stacey from the United States balances as she flies to win the halfpipe event of the Snowboarding World Championships in Germany. (AFP/Corbis)

SNOWBOARDING

Snowboarding is a new sport that in slightly more than thirty years has gone from being a barely acceptable recreational sport to an Olympic sport. As the name suggests, snowboarding involves moving across the surface of the snow while standing on a board without the benefit of poles, as in skiing. Competition involves races downhill for speed and jumps with aerial maneuvers.

Women have been involved since the early years of the sport in the 1960s, although the majority of snowboarders are men. Snowboarding is closely tied to youth culture, and initially many skiers and ski establishments did not accept it because it was viewed as too dangerous and its enthusiasts too uninhibited. As it became more and more popular and spread to Europe and Asia, however, ski centers created slopes dedicated to the sport.

HISTORY

Snowboarding developed slowly from a variety of sources. Some trace its origins to 1963, when Tom Sims (now a major manufacturer of snowboards) formed a crude snowboard in his eighth-grade shop class. Others think that the ancestor of the modern snowboard was the mid-1960s toy designed by Sherman Poppen called the Snurfer (a combination of "snow" and "surfer"). This board was made to stand on, but it had no bindings and was steered not by stainless-steel edges but by a rope tied to the front. By the early 1970s, these prototypes—or at least ancestors—had developed into a modern snowboard.

Although women's participation in snowboarding remained low for more than a decade, some women defied what had quickly become a traditionally male-dominated sport by becoming early snowboard aficionados. As interest and popularity grew in the late 1980s, more women discovered snowboarding, building their numbers from a fraction of the total group of participants to more than 25 percent at the end of the 1990s. Although they have much smaller pools from which to draw high-level competitors, women enjoy approximately equal numbers of contests and events as men.

In the winter of 1981–1982, the first loosely organized snowboard championships were held in Colorado. The same winter Burton Snowboards sponsored the first championships, which eventually evolved into the U.S. Open Snowboarding Championships. A year later, in the winter of 1982–1983, Lake Tahoe hosted the world championships. To unify fragmented competitions and to showcase snowboarders in 1988, the North American and European Snowboard Associations scheduled the first World Cup of snowboarding. This contest consisted of four competitions of four events each: the giant slalom (one racer against the clock, weaving between widely spaced gates, following the contours of the mountain); the dual slalom (two racers weaving between narrowly spaced gates, racing each other and the clock); moguls (participants weave through wave-like bumps on the snow, competing for time and style points); and the halfpipe (judged on points only). This first World Cup was dominated in the women's division by Petra Mussig of West Germany.

As the number of participants and spectators increased, the International Olympic Committee (IOC) decided to include snowboarding as an exhibition sport in the 1998 Olympic Games in Nagano, Japan, featuring two events the halfpipe and the giant slalom. Though Americans were heavily favored in the halfpipe event, European riders won most of the medals in both events. Karine Ruby of France, Heidi Renoth of Germany, and Brigitte Koeck of Austria won the first three places in the women's giant slalom event, and Nicola Thost of Germany, Stine Brun Kjeldaas of Norway, and Shannon Dunn of the United States won the first three spots in the halfpipe event. In non-Olympic years, snowboard riders can compete on the professional circuit that begins in British Columbia in November and travels all year through the Rocky Mountains, the Alps, Alaska, Sweden, and New Zealand, ending in Chile in September.

RULES AND PLAY

The two basic kinds of snowboarding mirror their counterparts in skiing: Alpine and freestyle. Alpine snowboarders compete in timed competitions similar to Alpine ski racing, focusing on speed and quick turns. Freestyle snowboarders usually compete in halfpipe (a trench-like structure with facing arched ramps 3.4 meters [11.2 feet] high) competitions, focusing on airborne tricks and maneuvers similar to those in skateboarding. In halfpipe competitions, points are awarded for the difficulty of each maneuver, the number of airborne rotations, and the ability to land in control of one's body.

A snowboard consists of a board constructed of layers of lightweight balsa wood strips and foam, covered in polyurethane on the top and a material called Petex on the bottom (the same material used on the bottom of skis). Stainless-steel edges give the board strength and allow it to cut into the snow. Alpine and freestyle snowboarders each have boards modified for their particular event. Alpine snowboards are stiffer, longer (about 180 centimeters [72 inches]), and have a region near the middle of the board that allows sharper turns than freestyle boards. Freestyle boards are shorter (155–165 centimeters [62–66 inches]), have less sidecut, and have upward-turned ends, called rises, to allow for safer landings in the halfpipe.

To secure the rider's feet to the snowboard, special boots and bindings are necessary. Alpine snowboarders usually wear rigid, ski-type boots with plate bindings; these are designed for maximum control of the board when carving (making fast, tight turns). Freestyle snowboarders usually wear soft boots. These boots require a different type of binding, with a rigid plastic support on the heel side of the binding and clamp-like straps to hold the boots to the board. This system allows freestyle snowboarders more comfort and flexibility when performing acrobatic stunts.

To maximize speed and safety during competition, Alpine snowboarders wear downhill skiing–type speed suits and helmets. Freestyle snowboarders are usually seen in oversized waterproof jackets and pants to allow freedom of motion. To protect their hands when grabbing the sharp, stainless-steel edges of their snowboards during tricks, freestyle snowboarders often wear Kevlar-palmed gloves (the same material as in bulletproof jackets) as a final piece of specialized equipment.

WOMEN AND FREESTYLE ATTITUDE

Though women's snowboarding has been slow in gaining participants, female snowboarders make up for their small numbers with their very distinctive style. Freestyle snowboarders in particular set out to make eye-popping fashion statements, including tattoos, sexually suggestive stickers, marijuana paraphernalia, body piercings, and such scant and strange clothing combinations as polyester pants and a bra.

Although most Alpine snowboarders welcome the challenge and attention brought by increased competition and team activities, freestyle snowboarders do not necessarily feel the same way. Many top-level female freestyle snowboarders are friendly with each other but prefer to "board alone." American contenders proved to be an individualistic lot when Circe Wallace and Cara-Beth Burnside objected to the halfpipe exhibition at the 1998 Nagano Olympic Games because they would be forced to train and travel as a team and wear uniforms. Even less formal competitions such as ESPN's X-Games provoke wariness and a resistance to following the rules of structured competition. Athena, Barrett Christy, and Morgan LaFonte, all top halfpipe riders, boycotted the games because they placed too much emphasis on competition and not enough on fun.

CONCLUSION

The popularity of snowboarding coupled with the number of participants worldwide has led to the sport's becoming an official Olympic sport. At the end of the 1990s only two snowboarding events were considered Olympic disciplines: halfpipe and giant slalom. As an increasing number of both male and female snowboarders take to the slopes, it seems likely that more snowboarding events will attain Olympic recognition in the future.

Kristi Lowenthal

Bibliography

Gutman, Bill. (1997) *Snowboarding: To the Extreme!* New York: Tom Doherty Associates.

White, Dana. (1988) "Shredheads Go Mainstream." *Skiing* 1, 41 (September): 82.

SNOWSHOE RACING

Snowshoe racing is a winter sport with a long history that receives relatively little attention in the modern sports world, getting lost among the myriad of winter sports. Nonetheless, snowshoe racing was one of the fastest growing of the snow sports in the 1990s, and it continues to offer excellent competition opportunities to men and women of all ages and abilities.

One appealing feature of snowshoe racing is that it is open to participation by many people. Here, women compete in the 50-meter race at the 1999 Special Olympics. (AP Photos)

HISTORY

Archaeologists suggest that snowshoes were developed in central Asia more than 6,000 years ago. People made the journey from Asia to North America on snowshoes before the Bering Strait opened between the continents. Native Americans perfected snowshoe designs, which they based on the familiar paw prints of animals that they hunted in the snow. Working with the materials available, the early designers developed hundreds of varieties of snowshoes for walking on different kinds of snow and terrain. Some snowshoes reached up to 2.1 meters (7 feet) in length, but by the end of the nineteenth century most styles were about .92 meter (3 feet) long.

As traders, hunters, explorers, and surveyors moved into the western regions of North America, they depended on snowshoes to get around in the snowy Rocky Mountains and the frozen and remote reaches of Canada. For early mountaineers and gold miners in Alaska and the Yukon, snowshoes were a necessity. As with many outdoor activities, competitive races began taking place as soon as a few early snowshoers decided to find out who was the fastest.

As early as the eighteenth century, residents of Quebec formed snowshoe clubs and held hikes, races, and banquets. The first snowshoe races were organized by the these clubs, with race distances ranging from 100 yards (91.4 meters) to 6 miles (9.7 kilometers). The first commercial, large-scale production of snowshoes began in Maine in 1862. The recreational use of snowshoes began to blossom with the formation of more clubs throughout the United States and Canada in the twentieth century. In the 1920s, outing clubs in New England organized "tramps" for experienced and novice snowshoers through the Green and White Mountains of Vermont and New Hampshire. Snowshoe fever continued unabated until it was eclipsed by skiing in the 1930s.

The proven design and materials (mainly wood and hide materials) of the traditional snowshoe remained the standard until the early 1970s, when metal alloy frames and fabric decks were introduced. The lighter, more maneuverable shoes meant athletes could get an excellent low-impact aerobic workout regardless of their skill level, and with the fitness boom of the late 1980s, the sport took off once again. A resurgence of organized snowshoe events such as hikes, races, and guided tours helped fuel the expansion of community trails and parks for increased snowshoe access. The sport has even managed to expand beyond seasons. In 1996 the Extreme Heat races were held in the Great Sand Dunes in south-central Colorado.

MODERN SNOWSHOEING

According to the National Sporting Goods Association, the number of people participating in snowshoeing increased from 640,000 in 1995 to nearly a million in 1996. The numbers of participants is expected to continue to increase for several reasons. First, snowshoeing can provide an excellent cardiovascular workout. Second, since people of all ages can snowshoe, it is a great way for families to enjoy the beauties of winter together. Third, it is a very easy to learn, since it is essentially a form of walking, and it is inexpensive compared to many other winter sports. Shoes range in price from $50 for children's shoes to $350 for high-tech gear, and they can be used with a variety of boots.

Snowshoeing has evolved into three distinct forms: recreational hiking, advanced mountaineering, and racing or sport. Different types of snowshoes are available to meet the specific needs of each form. Recreational and sport shoes are generally lighter and have less complicated bindings than snowshoes for hiking or climbing on more rugged terrain. Racing snowshoes also provide less traction, since races are held on groomed trails. Racing snowshoes are generally about 22 inches (55.9 centimeters) long and 8 inches (20.3 centimeters) wide, and weigh a little over 3 pounds per pair. Snowshoes for deep powder or heavy snowshoes are larger, about 33 by 10 inches (83.8 by 25.4 centimeters), and weigh slightly more.

Participants wear shoes or boots suitable to the discipline that fit into the snowshoe's bindings. Running shoes can be worn for running on dry snow, while hiking boots are recommended for hiking or slushy snow. As the sport has grown, many manufacturers have developed and marketed sport-specific shoes and boots.

The technique of snowshoeing is the virtually the same as walking or running. The boot fits into a hinged binding that permits ankle flexibility. A rolling motion from heel to toe offers the best efficiency, comfort, and traction. More leg lift is required, especially in hiking or recreational snowshoeing in deep snow, since the shoe will sink into the snow.

RULES AND PLAY

In terms of racing, the motion is very similar to cross-country skiing without the glide. In most competitions, racers use poles not only for added propulsion but also for stability. This provides some exercise for the upper body, as well as spreading weight over a wider area to minimize sinking.

Racing events are offered in most of the same distances and configurations as track events. Sprints can be 100, 200, or 400 meters (328, 656, or 1312 feet). Cross-country and distance events can be 5, 8, or 10 kilometers (3.1, 5, or 6.2 miles). Relay races are also available. Most races of any given distance have women's divisions as well as men's.

Snowshoe racing is increasing in popularity and offers competition to men and women of all abilities. It is growing because it is easy to learn, fun to do, and relatively inexpensive to enjoy. It is also expanding into a warm-weather sport contested in sandy desert climates, which will generate more interest and likely new technology. As the sport continues to grow, more opportunities will be available for women and men as well.

Jim Hunstein

Bibliography

Adventure Corps Web site. (1999) <http://www.adventurecorps.com>.

Snowlink Media Center Web site. (1999) <http://www.snowlink.com>.

Yubashoe Sport Snowshoe Company Web site. (1999) <http://yubashoes.com>.

SOARING *see* Gliding; Hang Gliding

SOCCER

Association football (or soccer, as it is called in the United States and Canada) is the most popular participatory and spectator sport in the world. Soccer is still a sport dominated by men, but in the twentieth century the number of women participating in soccer grew tremendously, both in recreational play and elite competition.

EARLY HISTORY

England was the birthplace of soccer, where the Football Association (FA), the game's governing body, was founded in 1863 and the first professional league (with twelve teams) was established in 1888. Soccer rapidly developed as the favorite participant and spectator sport of working-class males. In the early 1900s crowds of 100,000 or more attended the national cup finals and matches at Manchester United's Old Trafford and Chelsea's Stamford Bridge stadiums. In 1923 the first FA Cup Final at Wembley, the national stadium, attracted about 200,000 spectators.

A goalkeeper goes in to take the ball from an attacking forward in a football match between female munitions workers during World War II. (Hulton-Deutsch Collection/Corbis)

The first recorded organized game of women's soccer took place on 23 March 1895 at Crouch End in London, between a team from the north of England and one from the south. The match was set up by the aptly named Nettie Honeyball, who became the first secretary of the English Ladies' Football Team. The team from the north won.

During World War I, women's soccer grew dramatically. Women took over in factories for the men who went to war, and they also spontaneously took over the traditional male pastimes, such as soccer. The most famous of these teams was Dick, Kerr Ladies from Preston, founded in 1917. They disbanded in 1965, having played 828 games (758 wins, 46 draws, and 24 losses). By 1957 they had raised £150,000 for charity.

Although women's soccer became successful as a spectator and participant sport during the war, the male establishment resented this; in 1921 the FA stated that the game of soccer was unsuitable for women and banned them from all FA-

MEN'S SUPPORT FOR BANNED WOMEN'S SOCCER

Even the professional players, who previously helped train the women or refereed matches, had to be careful of associating with the women's teams, lest they themselves fall foul of the [Football Association]. Over the next four decades there were several incidences of referees, trainers, and clubs being suspended for being involved in women's football. The legendary Preston and England international, Tom Finney, explained how it was after the ban: "I remember being invited to referee at several of their [Dick, Kerr Ladies'] matches and being presented to the girls. There wasn't much women's football in those days and to actually see them play was quite remarkable. Some of them were very good players, and they always had big crowds. I know the FA did not look very kindly on them, and it was thought that we professional players should not encourage them. I personally couldn't see that they were doing any harm, especially when they were helping so many people by raising such a lot of money for charity."

GAIL NEWSHAM

(1997) In a League of Their Own. *London: Scarlet Press.*

affiliated pitches. This ban sent women's soccer into a swift decline and lasted for seventy years.

Despite FA opposition and a ban on using the same grounds as FA-affiliated men's teams, a women's team called the Manchester Corinthians became famous for playing charity matches abroad in the 1950s, thereby avoiding the hostile atmosphere in Britain. They participated in what was probably the first international women's tournament in 1957 when they went to Berlin to play against teams representing Germany, Austria, and the Netherlands. Over approximately twenty years, until they disbanded in the early 1970s, the team played 287 matches and raised thousands of dollars.

Women's soccer in Germany and the Netherlands followed a similar course. Matches were planned in the early 1950s in Hamburg, but Deutscher Fussball-Bund (DFB) imposed a ban similar to the one the FA had imposed in England. Nevertheless, a group of businessmen organized an unofficial West German team that played the Netherlands in 1956, subsequently organizing more matches around West Germany and then staging the European championship in Berlin in 1957. In the Netherlands, attempts to establish women's soccer in the 1890s and 1920s were thwarted by the KNVB (the Dutch counterpart of the FA). When a Dutch Ladies Soccer Association was founded in 1955, the KNVB banned them from using affiliated pitches (fields). Not until the Union of European Football Associations (UEFA) requested that national governing bodies take control of women's soccer did the KNVB accept the women's game.

POST–WORLD WAR II DEVELOPMENT

In England the modern era began with the 1966 men's Fédération Internationale de Football Association (FIFA) World Cup, which England won. The victory inspired huge interest in the game and encouraged women to take it up. Most significantly, it spawned women's leagues, the first of which was started in Southampton in 1966. The best players joined Southampton Women's Football Club, and in 1967 they, along with other leading English clubs, played in the first international tournament to be organized in England in Deal, Kent. The tournament was staged for the next four years, attracting teams from Britain, Czechoslovakia, the Netherlands, and Germany.

In 1969 the Women's Football Association (WFA) was established in England, and in the 1971–1972 season the FA finally rescinded their 1921 ban. At the start of this season, there were almost 100 WFA-affiliated clubs playing in local leagues, a national cup competition was started, and an official international team was selected. England played its first official international match against Scotland, also playing its first official international match.

By 1976 the WFA included 300 clubs and twenty-five leagues, but by 1991 that figure had changed little, because the association still lacked the support of the FA and a sound structure, resources, and financial backing. In 1991–1992, England formed a national league of thirty teams. The FA took charge of the game in 1993, dissolving the WFA, and formulated a women's soccer strategy to provide a development structure to the game for the first time. This was the first opportunity for schoolgirls to take part, and the FA also rescinded its ban on girls under age eleven playing mixed-gender soccer.

INTERNATIONAL DEVELOPMENT IN THE EARLY 1970s

In 1969 Italian businessmen hosted the first major international tournament since the Berlin tournament of 1957. The four-nation event was held in Turin, with Italy beating Denmark in the final. Denmark went on to win several unofficial world cup competitions, and in 1972 the Danish men's soccer association took control of women's soccer and the women played their first "official" international match in 1974, against Sweden.

Italy formed a federation in 1969 and established a national league and a national team a year later, with some top players from other countries recruited to the league. Up until the mid-1980s, this league attracted the top foreign players. Italy dominated women's soccer in the 1970s and 1980s, hosting several unofficial European cups and what were termed "little world cups." These matches were not officially sanctioned by FIFA, the world governing body, and involved only a small number of countries. Italy was something of a haven for women's soccer at this time, with many supporters and strong backing, even though fans of men's soccer remained lukewarm.

FIFA AND UEFA TAKE THE LEAD

The commercially led growth of European women's competitions expanded to Mexico, where a "little world cup" was played in 1971 by teams from Germany, Austria, Mexico, and Argentina, as well as those who had played in Turin two years before. The Union of European Football Associations (UEFA) reacted to the growth of women's soccer by voting to put the sport under the control of the national governing bodies.

The UEFA organized the first official European championship in 1982–1984. The competition had its seventh final in 1997, with Germany gaining a fourth championship. FIFA organized an unofficial women's world tournament in Guangzhou, China, in 1988, won by Norway. This paved the way for an official FIFA world championship in 1991, again in China, with the U.S. team victorious. The competition, known as the Women's World Cup, is played every four years, with the 1999 event held in and won by the United States (defeating China in the final). The 1996 Olympics featured an inaugural women's tournament, with the United States winning. This also marked the first time that a woman, Bente Skogvang of Norway, refereed an Olympic soccer final.

INTERNATIONAL EXPANSION IN THE 1980s

The 1980s saw the rise of Germany, Norway, and Sweden as well as the United States, with Italy remaining strong and England and Denmark having less success. Italy has never won a European championship, despite appearing in two finals, in 1997 and 1993, and achieving third place twice and fourth place once. The United States has shown the most phenomenal development, coming from nowhere to win the 1991 Women's World Cup. At the end of the 1990s, the United States, Norway, Germany, and China dominated the game, with Sweden and Italy trying hard to maintain their top status, Denmark making a resurgence, and Brazil leading the advance of nations "new" to the women's games.

RULES AND PLAY

Soccer is played by teams of eleven players on a pitch (field) whose maximum size 130 yards (119 meters) long and 120 yards (110 meters) wide. The aim is to pass the ball among team members who use the feet or other parts of the body—except the hands and arms—to propel it into the opposing team's goal. The goals are 8 feet (2.4

meters) high and 8 yards (7.3 meters) wide, spanned by a crossbar and fitted with a net to receive the ball once it has crossed the goal line. Each team has a goalkeeper, the only player allowed to use her hands, who covers the entire penalty area of the field. Four defenders are responsible for preventing the other team from scoring and are grouped across the first third of the field in front of their goalkeeper. In front of the defenders are three or four midfield players; the number and placement of these players is decided on by coaches and managers. Midfielders are chosen for their ability to pass the ball upfield to their attackers while still defending their end of the field. The three or two attackers are primarily there to score goals.

A drawn match can be decided by penalty kicks from a point 12 yards (11 meters) away from the center of the goal by "golden goals"—a type of "sudden death" overtime. Infringements of the rules within the penalty area result in penalty kicks which are direct free kicks at the goal from the penalty spot. Free kicks are given when infringements occur in other parts of the pitch, and they take place where the infringement occurred. When the ball goes out of bounds, the game is restarted with a throw-in from the sides or by a goal-kick (when the attacking team has shot wide of the goal). If the defending team sends the ball past their own goal-line, then the attacking team takes a corner kick from the corner of the pitch. Most of the rules (laws) are simple with the exception of Law 11, which states that a player is offside if he or she is nearer to the opponents' goal line than both the ball and the second-last opponent. Breach of this rule results in a free kick. The rules of the game are upheld by a referee and two assistants. Games last ninety minutes. The teams switch ends of the field after the first half.

WOMEN'S WORLD CUP

The Women's World Cup is the international championship tournament for women's soccer. The first tournament was played in 1991 in China (although it was not yet called the World Cup), the second was played in Sweden in 1995, and the third in the United States in 1999. The United won in 1991 and 1999, and Norway won in 1995. In its current form the World Cup involves teams from sixteen nations who play a round-robin tournament with the eight finalists then playing a single-elimination round. The 1999 event was arranged by the Women's World Cup 1999 Organizing Committee, Inc. under the direction of the Fédération Internationale de Football Association (FIFA).

The 1999 World Cup was the most successful women's sports event in history. It attracted several major corporate sponsors, over 600,000 spectators at stadiums in the United States and hundreds of millions of television viewers around the world. All of the games were broadcast on television. The sixteen teams were from Asia (Korea DPR, Japan, China, Australia), Europe (Denmark, Germany, Italy, Norway, Russia, Sweden), Africa (Nigeria, Ghana) and the Americas (Canada, United States, Mexico). The United States defeated China for the gold medal by a score of 5-4 on penalty kicks following 120 minutes of scoreless play.

Some women's sports advocates saw the 1999 World Cup as one of three most important events in recent women's sport history, along with the passage of Title IX in 1972 and the Billie Jean King-Bobbie Riggs "battle of the sexes" tennis match in 1973. They cite the large audiences and television viewership as signs that women's professional sports can be a viable enterprise. They also see the success of the World Cup as the first step in organizing a women's professional soccer league in the United States, which will follow the 2000 Olympics where women's soccer is expected to be a popular event. There are others, however, who argue that problems remain for forming a professional women's league in the United States, including the generally low level of interest in soccer, the need to maintain a very high quality of play, and the limits soccer poses as a television sport, given its lack of scoring and the absence of time-outs.

THE NEXT STAGE: MAJOR WORLD TEAMS

Two "sleeping giants" finally asserted themselves in the major world competitions in the mid-1990s. China placed fourth in the 1995 Women's World Cup and was the runner-up in the 1996 Olympics and the 1999 Women's World Cup; Brazil reached fourth place in the 1996 Olympics and made it to the round of eight (quarter-finals) in the 1999 Women's World Cup. China can credit its success to government targeting of top players. While Brazil has been among the top two or three World Cup teams in men's soccer for many years, the country's enthusiasm for soccer has only recently spilled over to the women's game. Brazil was, however, the first South American country to respond positively to FIFA's directive to organize official women's leagues by 1985.

The major turning point for Brazilian women's soccer was the government's decision to fund the team's preparation for the 1996 Olympics. Pele, perhaps one of the best-known soccer players in history, was key in encouraging women's soccer when he was the country's sports minister.

The other top nations are characterized by their general support for equal opportunity for women. Sweden and Norway in particular discourage gender stereotyping, and this is reflected in their attitude toward women's soccer. Soccer is the most popular women's game in both countries. It is not only on the field of play that women in these two nations have been successful; several women are involved in the areas of administration, coaching, and refereeing. Sweden became the first country to have a female national coach when Gunilla Paijkull took charge of the 1988 world championship team; another woman, Marika Domanski Lyfors, held the post in the late 1990s. Paijkull serves on FIFA's technical committee. Ingrid Johnsson of Sweden became the first woman to referee a FIFA final and is very actively involved in setting up special courses and training programs for women referees. Sweden's most famous woman player was Pia Sundhage, who retired after the 1996 Olympics, after playing in 146 international matches, and is employed by the Swedish national association as full-time coach for the under-sixteen national team. The Swedish semiprofessional league clubs attract foreign players, who are found jobs and accommodations. In Thorsten Frennstedt, Sweden has one of the top women's soccer journalists in the world.

Nevertheless, Norway has overtaken Sweden as a world force in women's soccer. The game has been developed along lines parallel to the men's game. The country's top woman player is Heidi Store, who held the world record of having played in 151 international matches when she retired from international soccer in 1998 (the record has since been broken by Kristine Lilley of the United States). Linda Medalen was a regular on the Norwegian team throughout most of their successes. She played for Norway in the 1988 unofficial World Cup in China and played a major part in every other World and European Championship, finishing her career in the 1999 World Cup in the United States. Medalen played for Nikko in the professional Japanese league for two seasons, but returned to Norway in 1997.

The other most successful European nation, West Germany, imposed a ban on women's soccer in 1955 but rescinded it in 1970. The Deutscher Fussball-Bund (DFB) officially took charge of the game in 1977 when Hannelore Ratzeburg was appointed to represent women's soccer on the DFB's governing committee. She was also appointed as a member of both UEFA's and FIFA's women's committees. In 1975 an official German women's team was organized, and in 1982 a top male DFB coach took charge of it but spent his final years mentoring a female coach, Tina Theune Meyer, to become his successor in 1996. The men's association has always been very supportive of women's soccer. Continuity is considered an important part of the successful German men's and women's soccer system, and Meyer is mentoring her assistant, former team captain Sylvia Neid, thereby ensuring continuity at the top. Funding from television money and sponsorship has been made available to develop the women's game, and with excellent participation figures (over half a million in 1995) and a new national league formed in 1997–1998, Germany qualified for the 1999–2001 European championship to seek a record fifth victory.

UNITED STATES

Women's soccer in the United States represents the most successful development in any country in recent years. Participation rates in women's soccer are 39 percent of the total, nationally. By 1996 an estimated 9 million girls and women were participating. It is not surprising that the United States won the inaugural FIFA Women's World Cup in 1991; although the U.S. women only reached third place in the next event in 1995, they returned to a dominant world position in 1996 by winning the inaugural Olympic tournament and in 1999 by again winning the Women's World Cup.

The 1999 Women's World Cup, hosted by the United States, was by far the largest and most successful women's sports event ever. Several multinational companies sponsored the series of matches, and all thirty-two games were on national television, the majority of them live. The United States Soccer Federation (USSF) saw the event as an important milestone toward creating the first women's professional league in the United States.

Cultural acceptance of the sport in the United States came about extremely quickly, as evidenced by the extraordinary participation figures and the national team's Women's World Cup victories in 1991 and 1999 and Olympic victory in 1996. Unlike some European nations, the United States has not had to overcome years of tradition that defined soccer as unsuitable for women. Furthermore, Title IX of the Educational Amendments of 1972, which attempts to ensure that women's athletics receive equal funding with men's in colleges and other institutions, has helped the college system become a vehicle for the growth and development of the game. A total of seventy-five universities and colleges started new women's soccer teams between 1992 and 1995. The college system is fed by volunteer-led recreational soccer, which often involves mixed-gender teams of grade- and middle-school-aged children.

As with the other top nations, the United States has provided the world of women's soccer with some outstanding leaders, such as Anson Dorrance, who successfully developed players at the University of North Carolina and was head coach of the national team that won the 1991 Women's World Cup. Tony DiCicco, who had been Dorrance's assistant coach, became head coach of the 1999 World Cup team, with Lauren Gregg as assistant head coach and former national team captain April Heinrichs in charge of the under-sixteen squad. Players such as Michelle Akers and Mia Hamm have received endorsement contracts from several advertisers. The United States also boasts Kristine Lilley, who at the end of the twentieth century held the world record of having played in almost 200 international matches.

OTHER NATIONS CATCH UP

By 1991 more than 100 nations were affiliated with FIFA and had registered organized women's competitions in their countries, and UEFA registered a record thirty-four out of a possible fifty-one national teams for the 1998–1999 championships. FIFA also enlarged the 1999 Women's World Cup to include sixteen teams instead of twelve, as in past competitions. FIFA general secretary Joseph S. Blatter was so impressed with the 1995 Women's World Cup that he stated: "The future of football is feminine."

United Kingdom

Participation in women's soccer is undoubtedly growing, although some countries are still trying to break through prejudice and hostility. Others

WHO SHOULD COACH THE WOMEN'S SOCCER TEAM?

On 18 January 2000, the United States Soccer Federation announced that it had selected April Heinrichs to coach the U.S. Women's Soccer team, the first woman to coach the U.S. national team. Heinrichs was a member of the 1991 U.S. team which won the first World Cup and had served as the coach of the University of Virginia women's team. The selection of Heinrichs was not without controversy as the Federation passed over the team's assistant coach, Lauren Gregg, who had been recommended by former coach Tony DiCicco.

have problems finding the money to develop the game. Development opportunities in England in the late 1990s were excellent, but it took almost a century for this to happen. The prejudices and barriers that women in England had to overcome over the course of many years are still being fought in other countries. One of the main problems in England has been tradition. Women who played the game seriously challenged the sanctity of the traditionally masculine domain of soccer. Of course, unequal gender structures and practices are not unique to women's soccer. Since the FA took complete responsibility for women's soccer in England, the participation rate has grown rapidly, with about 25,000 girls and 17,000 women playing in 1999, compared to 2,000 and 10,000, respectively in 1993. Great strides have been made at the youth level, with 51 percent of girls playing soccer in school and the establishment of more than sixty new youth leagues in a mere four years. However, England has been hampered by the relatively late acquisition of the support and development structures that the Scandinavian countries, Germany, and the United States have had in place for years. At the international level, England is playing catch-up. Bias exists elsewhere as well; in other parts of the world women have struggled to overcome barriers to playing soccer.

South America

South America is dominated by Brazil in both men's and women's soccer. In the male-dominated culture that prevails on that continent, there are signs of optimism, particularly in Argentina. The president of the Argentine soccer association, Julio Grondona, used his influence to start a domestic championship for women in 1991 that had grown to include fourteen teams by 1997. The two top women's teams are affiliated with the two most popular men's professional teams, River Plate and Boca Juniors. Some of the clubs pay their players a small amount of money for transportation and food expenses in addition to providing soccer gear, the stadium, and training facilities.

Argentina has made considerable progress at the international level, given that they only began competing in 1994, with a 3–2 victory over Chile. They lost 7–1 to Brazil in the qualifying rounds of the Confederation of North and Central America and Caribbean Federations (CONCACAF) group for the 1999 Women's World Cup; in the second qualifying playoff they lost 3–2 to Mexico, giving the Mexicans CONCACAF's second qualifying place—following Brazil—in the Women's World Cup. (Mexico thus became the first Spanish-speaking country to qualify for a Women's World Cup.) Argentina easily beat the other South American teams, although they had a close game with Peru. The national team's involvement in the Women's World Cup has increased their television exposure and revenue. The top domestic games are televised weekly, with teams receiving 1,000 pesos each month for the transmissions. Former Argentinean star player Sergio Goycochea provides the commentary, which adds to the credibility.

Other South American nations have made less progress both in success on the field of play and in becoming more egalitarian toward women's soccer. Typical of the less successful South American nations is Bolivia, where discrimination against women has held back their national team. Only La Paz and Santa Cruz have organized women's teams; and the current national team reflects this reality, with twenty of the twenty-two players coming from Santa Cruz. Women's soccer only became an official sport in South America in 1982 after FIFA recommended that each South American association take responsibility for the game. Like most Latin American women's teams, the Bolivian players have had to overcome a series of discouraging obstacles.

Oceania

In Oceania, Australia and New Zealand battle for supremacy over the smaller nations of Papua New Guinea, Tahiti, Tonga, and Western Samoa. Australia has had little success in Women's World Cup competition so far; although they qualified in 1995, they lost all their games. They also qualified for the 1999 Women's World Cup. As with some other nations, the 2000 Olympics proved the catalyst for a development program. They put an ambitious plan in place to try to win the Olympic gold medal. The Australian Sports Commission increased the funding of the Australian Women's Soccer Association with the aim of improving all aspects of the game, including encouraging the national men's league teams to support women's teams and funding coaching for state women's teams in a national summer league. The national team has a development program, and players are paid to play for it. For the Olympics, they attempted to replicate the preparation system of the United States by inviting the top twenty players to a residential camp.

Africa

African teams have special difficulties with traveling to matches because the continent is so large and some countries are not very stable politically. Nigeria was the continent's representative at the 1991 Women's World Cup, having qualified without much difficulty by beating Ghana, Guinea, and Cameroon, but in the championship they did not win a single game. In 1995 they showed some improvement, narrowly losing to England 3–2 and then drawing 3–3 with Canada. They qualified for the 1999 championship by overcoming stiff challenges from Ghana and South Africa.

As well as traveling distance, South Africa has been uniquely handicapped by the twenty-year isolation it experienced due to its apartheid policy, which ended in 1991. In 1997 Fran Hilton-Smith was appointed to take charge of a newly formed national team and to improve the women's game with coaching clinics. Although the culture is dominated by men, Hilton-Smith is making progress, with sponsorship from sportswear companies and the South African Football Association.

OVERCOMING ANTI-FEMALE PREJUDICE

The struggle to overcome men's prejudice has been hard even in Europe. Thirty-four European nations competed for the eighth European championship and qualification for the 1999 Women's World Cup, but there is a vast difference in opportunities between leading nations and some of the smaller countries that are not as well prepared or experienced. Greece, for instance, is still fighting for better support for women's soccer, which received a boost by the International Olympic Committee's decision to hold the 2004 Olympic Games there. This decision will likely help increase support for women's soccer. Xanthi Konstadinidou is the driving force behind Greek women's soccer. She began to promote her country as a serious women's soccer nation by staging an international club tournament in Greece in the summer of 1998.

Even in the United Kingdom, the five member nations have been slow to develop women's soccer. In 1994 the Republic of Ireland became the first to implement a comprehensive development plan, which concentrated on establishing a quality domestic and international youth program. This included an under-sixteen and under-twenty team. Scotland and Wales have established similar programs; only Northern Ireland lacks such a development plan.

One of the major events that led to the removal of barriers to women's soccer in England involved the Sex Discrimination Act and a schoolgirl named Theresa Bennett. In 1978 the twelve-year-old Bennett was banned by the FA from playing soccer with boys in a local league. The FA's decision was initially overturned in court on the grounds that it had failed to provide her with recreation facilities, but the FA won a reversal on appeal under Section 44 of the Sex Discrimination Act (1975). Although Bennett lost her case, the affair elicited considerable sympathy from the media for her and many other girls who were enthusiastic about playing soccer. Eventually the problem was overcome; in 1991 the ban on girls under eleven years of age playing mixed competitive soccer was rescinded and the English Schools Football Association (ESFA) was charged with the responsibility of developing girls' as well as boys' soccer in schools. When the FA took over responsibility for running girls' and women's soccer in 1993, one of their key initiatives was the development of small-sided leagues for girls, between four and six players per side, as depending on the age group; this action, combined with the ESFA's initiatives in schools, at last gave girls structured opportunities to participate in the same way as boys.

Women's soccer in England had been hampered not only by the fact that girls could not play soccer at the critical early skill-learning stage of junior school; in addition, once they moved to secondary school at the age of eleven, girls were and still are generally channeled into the traditional schoolgirl games of netball and field hockey. The only way most young women could play soccer was to join a women's team, which, at least in the early days, could entail lengthy and expensive travel. Another drawback has been the fact the primary school teachers receive very little training in physical education. The vast majority of these teachers are female, and they have little experience with soccer.

In July 1998 the FA named Hope Powell as the first full-time national women's coach. She was also the first woman to coach the national women's team. Powell was a player with Croydon and England, a Premier League team, and a FA-UEFA "B" coach. The previous male incumbent, FA "A" coach Ted Copeland, resigned after five years in the post. The FA started two national female youth teams: under-eighteen and under-sixteen teams in 1987 and 1998, respectively. England was the host and winning team in their group in the second UEFA under-eighteen championship.

SPECTATORS

Women's soccer was not considered a spectator sport until the upsurge in unofficial international championships in the 1970s and the official events in the 1980s and 1990s. It is only in recent years that the presence of women spectators at men's matches has been properly recognized in England; previously, their attendance had been valued largely for its civilizing influence on male spectators, well known for their sometimes vehement expression of support. Major international men's and women's soccer events have become more and more popular, and they have increasingly attracted more and more women spectators. For example, when England's men's team won the 1966 World Cup, it is estimated that only 1 percent of the 93,000 spectators at Wembley were women. The *Daily Telegraph* quoted figures from the British Market Research Bureau showing that between 1989 and 1994 the number of women who paid to watch at least one soccer game had risen by 25 percent to 1.04 million in 1994. England's dramatic semifinal defeat by Germany in the 1990 World Cup was watched by 25 million viewers in Britain alone, and 48 percent were women.

The first two Women's World Cup competitions attracted attendances of 510,000 (in China in 1991) and 112,213 (in Sweden in 1995) for the twenty-six matches. The U.S. team has achieved the largest regular following (around 6,000 for a top game), often selling out. The 1999 Women's World Cup attracted more than 600,000 spectators, with a crowd of more than 90,000 at the Rose Bowl in Pasadena, California, for the China–U.S. final. The Olympic final between the United States and China in 1996 broke the record for a women's match, with a crowd of 76,489 at Sanford Stadium in Athens, Georgia. In Germany, national team games attract around 3,000 to 4,000 spectators, and a crowd of 22,000 watched Germany defeat Norway in the European championship final in Osnabruck in July 1989. Important international matches in Scandinavia and Italy attract around 10,000. There were 8,500 watching Norway win the European championship against Sweden in Oslo in 1987; 8,000 saw them defeat Italy in the 1993 final in Cesena. However, in the 1997 European championship final in Oslo only 2,200 spectators saw Germany defeat Italy.

In Britain, the attendance of 53,000 at Goodison Park, Liverpool, to watch Dick, Kerr Ladies

THE 1999 WOMEN'S WORLD CUP ALL-STAR TEAM AS SELECTED BY FIFA

Goalkeeper	Gao Hong, China	Midfield	Sissi, Brazil
	Briana Scurry, United States		Zhao Lihong, China
Defense	Wang Liping, China		Liu Ailing, China
	Wen Lirong, China		Bettina Wiegmann, Germany
	Doris Fitschen, Germany		Michelle Akers, United States
	Carla Overbeck, United States	Forward	Jin Yan, China
	Brandi Chastain, United States		Sun Wen, China
			Ann Kristin Aarones, Norway
			Mia Hamm, United States

versus St. Helens on Boxing Day 1920, is still by far the largest crowd ever assembled for a women's soccer match in Britain. Approximately 2,000 to 3,000 fans now attend women's FA cup finals and international matches. The November 1978 England versus Belgium friendly match attracted 5,471 spectators to Southampton FC's Dell ground, and it was the modern record for the largest crowd at a women's soccer match not part of another event, until the 1999 Women's Cup Final.

Today, there is great potential to attract women to men's matches and both men and women to women's matches. The FA Premier League National Fan Survey 1996–1997 found that females constituted around one in eight of all spectators.

MEDIA INFLUENCE

The print media in England have played an important role in how the women's game is perceived, with coverage fluctuating between positive straight reporting and negative, biased stories. As far back as 1922, the *New York Times* and *Washington Post* printed serious reports about Dick, Kerr Ladies' matches against men's teams in the United States, but in England the emphasis was on information peripheral to the game; the reporting tended to be rather patronizing and condescending. There would, for example, be the obligatory reassurance that the team consisted of normal, married women who were only playing soccer as a means to an end—raising money for charity. News stories would state how much was raised, the names of VIPs, and information about the venue and the crowd; little was usually said about the players' soccer ability.

In the 1970s the English press vacillated between serious reporting and a concentration on the trivial, sometimes bordering on the rude. For example, Brian Glanville, one of the best soccer reporters in England, expressed his doubts about women's soccer in a report in the 24 June 1973 *Sunday Times* on England's third international match, headlined, "Goals and gals don't really mix." He made blatantly chauvinistic comments about the players' technical inadequacies and appearance. In contrast, several national daily newspapers gave very positive reports of England's 1–0 defeat of Italy in 1977, and the *Daily Express* journalist was so surprised at the skills he witnessed from both teams that he wrote his article in the form of an apology, explaining that as a result of watching this match, he was no longer prejudiced toward women's soccer.

Part of the problem in Britain is that the media is dominated by men's soccer and the journalists are predominantly male. The era of women sports journalists did not start until the late 1980s, when Julie Welch started writing about sports, soccer in particular, for the *Sunday Times.* By the early 1990s, the *Sunday Telegraph, Independent,* and *Observer* had women sports journalists; by 1998 the *Daily Express* had a woman soccer reporter writing a weekly women's soccer column. But even the gender of the writer cannot compensate for the lack of a body of accurate knowledge that has led to inaccurate reporting and a tendency to trivialize women's soccer and treat it as a novelty. In 1997 the first women's soccer magazine, *On the Ball,* appeared in England.

Television, though slow to pick up on women's soccer, has been, on the whole, favorable in its coverage. In England, the national television channel, the BBC, was the first to report on women's soccer matches in 1971, announcing the early national cup final results on Sunday evening news reports. A few years later, the BBC televized highlights of the 1976 national cup final. This breakthrough was not sustained in the ensuing years, and it wasn't until 1989 that Channel 4, a minority-interest commercial station, provided regular and excellent coverage of women's soccer, presented by Hazel Irvine, one of the first television reporters of men's football in Scotland. Sadly, Channel 4 pulled out from covering the 1992–1993 season; Sky TV, the satellite channel, has taken up where Channel 4 left off.

The Italian press in the 1970s, and particularly *Corriere dello Sport,* carried regular reports on the women's national league matches, the international team, and general articles about women's soccer issues.

When the Swedish team came to England for the second leg of the inaugural UEFA European championship final in 1984, they amazed everyone at the Luton Town ground when they arrived with a television crew and thirty-six press representatives. For the first leg in Stockholm, the game had been televized live. Local newspapers in Sweden cover their teams' progress well at the national level, and the 1995 Women's World Cup received a lot of media exposure. Sweden is one of the few nations that has its own women's soccer magazine, called *Nya Mal,* founded in 1986.

Germany, too, has a women's soccer magazine, called *Dieda,* which started in 1993. In general, the German regional media promote women's soccer, but the national sports papers cover only women's national league results and special events such as the European, world, and Olympic championships. The 1995 Women's World Cup group matches were given between thirty and forty-five minutes of television coverage. From the quarterfinals onward, all matches were shown live. The final between Germany and Norway attracted more than 5 million viewers, 14 percent of all households, which was 27.5 percent of the television market.

Media coverage of women's soccer in the United States, compared to that of some European countries, is very good. The newspaper *USA Today* usually carries news of the national team's matches and developments in the women's game, and in 1997 the first edition of *Women's Soccer World,* which provides comprehensive coverage of women's soccer from around the world, appeared.

But television exposure in the United States has not been as great as might have been expected. In the United States soccer has to compete for viewing time with traditional American male games such as American football, baseball, and basketball, and women's golf, tennis, and basketball receive greater coverage than women's soccer. A few of the top collegiate soccer matches, including the National Collegiate Athletic Association (NCAA) championship, have been shown on television in recent years, and the national team has received coverage during important competitions. However, even the victory in the 1996 Olympics did not receive nationwide television coverage, although the 1999 Women's World Cup received sixty-four hours of television coverage by ABC and ESPN. Of the thirty-two games, twenty-seven were broadcast live, with the remaining contests shown on the same day. And for weeks after the U.S. victory, players were shown on television—in parades and ceremonies in their honor, on news shows, and on entertainment talk shows.

CONCLUSION

There are many reasons to believe that women's soccer will mirror the men's game in its growth and development, meaning that it has the potential to become the most popular women's sport around the world. That this has not happened yet seems to be due to cultural barriers in many nations in which soccer is viewed as a male sport and in which full participation in sports is viewed as inappropriate for women. Many advocates argue that continued growth and spread of the sport will result only if these nations follow the example of nations where women's participation in sports is encouraged and supported.

Sue Lopez

Bibliography

Lopez, Sue. (1997) *Women on the Ball: A Guide to Women's Football.* London: Scarlet Press.

Newsham, Gail. (1997) *In a League of Their Own!* London: Scarlet Press.

Sir Norman Chester Centre for Football Research. (1997) *FA Premier League National Fan Survey 1996–97: Summary.* Leicester, UK: University of Leicester.

SOCIALIZATION

Socialization is a lifelong process through which individuals develop and shape their social identities, sense of self, and ability to participate in social roles and relationships. It is a complex social and psychological process that every member of every society experiences. In the course of this lifelong process, people learn and adapt to the culture's standards for normal behavior (norms), its attitudes, values, beliefs, and practices. In doing so, they also help maintain and reshape these same elements. They learn to create their own identities and senses of self so that they can participate successfully in social roles and relationships. Traditional feminine behavior is a prime example of this.

Socialization is not only important to the individual. Through this process, societies maintain stability and order. At the same time, by socializing people in particular ways, societies also

One of the most important socialization functions of team sports is to encourage sociability, teamwork, and mutual support. Here, softball teammates greet and cheer one another before the game. (Geoffrey Bluh)

maintain the established structures of power, privilege, and prestige. The outcome of this process, however, depends on the individual. Gender, race, ethnicity, social class, age, physical ability/disability, education, religion, where one lives, the historical period in which one lives, and the immediate people with whom one shares one's life all play a role.

Increasingly, researchers are realizing that traits and forms of behavior once believed natural, or innate, are in fact products of socialization. This is particularly true for women in general and athletes in particular. When society taught women that they were weak and delicate, they believed themselves incapable of strenuous activities. Now taught the opposite, at least in Western societies, they display their strength enthusiastically.

VIEWS OF SOCIALIZATION

Investigators have studied socialization from different perspectives. From the point of view of the behaviorist, children imitate the values, beliefs, and practices of people important to them, who in turn reinforce, praise, reward, and support this behavior. The child then incorporates these values, beliefs, and practices into her own developing way of looking at the world.

This perspective implies that socialization is essentially a one-way process in which new members of society have little to do with their socialization and are made to be social by the significant people around them. More recently, sociologists have recognized that socialization is an interactive or reciprocal process, of which internalization is only one aspect. The interactive perspective assumes that new members of society help to construct their own socialization. They are viewed as actively engaged in evoking, interpreting, organizing, and using information from the social environment to shape their own role in the society. For example, children interact and negotiate within groups of other children, and this allows them to come to understand such social concepts as gender. They learn what is considered appropriate and inappropriate physical activity for girls and for boys and then decide how they will incorporate such social expectations within their own lives and senses of themselves. Some children will decide to conform to such expectations, while others will choose essentially to ignore them and engage in physical activity generally deemed inappropriate for their gender.

SPORT-SPECIFIC SOCIALIZATION

Socialization as it relates specifically to sports, although more limited in focus than general socialization, is a very broad area that sport sociologists in North America have studied extensively. As a result, much of what we know about sport-specific socialization is limited to Germany, the United States, and Canada.

Sport socialization has customarily been divided into specific areas, including sport socialization, or socialization into sport, and sport as socialization, or socialization through sport. In the first area, sport socialization, the primary question is how and why people do or do not become involved in competitive sport and other forms of physical activity. In the second, sport as socialization, the fundamental question is how and how much sport participation influences social attitudes, values, beliefs, and practices. Related to these is the topic of sport desocialization. Here the fundamental question is how and why athletes withdraw from or leave sports.

SPORT SOCIALIZATION

Sport socialization does not occur by chance. Rather, it depends on and is shaped by several major factors that interact with one another. These include the personal characteristics of the individual (physical, sociological, and psychological) and those around her (parents, siblings, peers, teachers, coaches). They also include broader aspects of society (the family, mass media, religion, community, education); geographic and climatic region (city, farm, mountains, desert); the way the culture views behaviors, values, and beliefs related to sports; and historical context. For example, a young girl from a poor Muslim family in Jordan is far less likely to become an elite field hockey player than a young girl growing up in a middle-income Protestant family in England.

An individual's personal characteristics—physical, sociological, and psychological—play important roles in determining who will and will not become active in sports. One important factor is physical ability or disability. While people with disabilities now have more and more opportunities to take part in sports, it remains true that relatively few become serious participants. At the same time, innate physical ability or the lack of it does not guarantee that someone will or will not take part in sports, that is, experience sport socialization.

Gender ranks among the most important characteristics that influence sport socialization. Worldwide, disproportionately fewer female than male children become involved in sports. In many cultures, sport and physicality are strongly associated with masculinity and strongly disassociated with femininity. Males are expected to be masculine; to establish and maintain their masculinity, they must demonstrate physical strength and skill. Young males are expected to develop sports skills and to participate in sports. In contrast, females are expected to be feminine, and many cultures view the demonstration of superior physical strength and skill as unfeminine. Girls and women who do become part of the sporting world may be steered—socialized—toward sports viewed as more appropriate or feminine, such as gymnastics, swimming, and figure skating, rather than toward less conventionally feminine sports, such as basketball, football, wrestling, and baseball.

The people who are part of a person's daily life, the significant others, also influence whether someone becomes involved in sports. For infants, children, and adolescents such people usually include parents, siblings, other relatives, peers, coaches, and teachers. For girls, early, strong, and positive influence from mothers and fathers is one of the most important and critical factors associated with their involvement in sports. Parents may influence children in many ways, including encouraging infants to be physically active and taking part in physical play with young girls. Parents may also provide them with toys that require and help in the development of gross motor skills, teach them physical skills, offer them sports equipment and opportunities to play, and themselves take part in sports.

Siblings generally are not as influential as parents. Although older sisters and brothers actively involved in sport may serve as models and thus affect their younger sisters, this influence ranks relatively low. Peers, in contrast, rank high in the amount of influence they exert on girls playing sports. As young girls grow older and reach adolescence, they tend to spend less time with their parents and more time with peers. Female athletes indicate that the most important peers in their lives—their friends—tend most often to be fellow athletes. Coaches, while generally not very important in the early stages of sports involvement, matter to a female athlete's continued participation in sports. In countries where physical education is part of the school curriculum, physical education teachers may also play a significant role in girls' decisions to join or not join in sports; they serve as models, provide encouragement, and teach athletic skills.

Social agents—such as the family, mass media, religion, the community, and education—may also foster or discourage sport socialization. One's immediate family is typically the most influential agent during infancy and childhood. The family's values and beliefs about girls and sports help determine what opportunities female infants and children have to develop interest, ability, and skill in sports and physical activities. In families that do not value girls' involvement in sports, female children will likely also devalue and avoid sports, develop low levels of physical skill, and ultimately not become socialized into the world of sport. In families that value and encourage involvement in sports, female children are more likely to develop interest and skills in sports.

The mass media have become a major source of information about sports. What we read, watch, and hear about sport via newspapers, magazines, books, radio, television, movies, video games, and the Internet helps to shape what we know, feel, and believe about sports. Although media coverage of girls' and women's sports is improving, it still tends to portray male athletes as superior to female athletes, women's sports as less important and interesting than men's sports, and participation in sports as more appropriate for boys and men than for girls and women. These media messages are important determinants in whether girls involve themselves in sports because they help to maintain and reinforce societal views of sport as more or less important for females. Such messages help to shape young girls' developing beliefs about sports and their relative importance in their lives.

Religion, too, is a consideration in girls' and women's involvement in sports. In some areas of the world, the dominant religion views girls and women as subordinate members of society and their involvement in active sports as inappropriate. In many other areas of the world, however, sports and religious beliefs are no longer directly linked, although they may still be related. For example, in North America, most churches have abandoned their earlier opposition to sports, and many religious organizations, such as the Young Men's Christian Association (YMCA), the Young Women's Christian Association (YWCA), the Catholic Youth Organization (CYO), and Athletes in Action (AIA), embrace and promote participation in sports, especially among young people.

Communities throughout the world provide sporting opportunities to their members. Girls

TAKE YOUR DAUGHTER TO THE SLOPES

The Snow Sports Association for Women (SSAW) sponsors an annual Take Your Daughter to the Slopes Day at winter snow sports centers in North America. The program, called D-Day, is meant to encourage parents and their daughters to spend a day together cross-country or downhill skiing, snowboarding, or snowshoeing. Ski centers offer discounts of lift tickets, free lessons, door prizes, and other incentives to attract families to the slopes. The purpose of the program is to get more girls and women involved in snow sports and to attract more women to ski resorts.

and women living in communities that sponsor sports clubs and/or youth sports programs may have more opportunity to become involved in sports. In North America, where sports are linked to the educational system, schools are also important agents in sport socialization. Elementary, middle, and secondary schools, as well as colleges and universities, instruct students in sports through physical education courses and offer competitive sports opportunities through well-developed intramural and interscholastic athletic programs.

The process of sport socialization, or involvement, is also powerfully influenced by geography and climate; a culture or ethnic group's view of what constitutes normal sports behavior, values, and beliefs; and historical context. Where a girl grows up, and in what kind of climate, probably affects her chances of learning a specific type of sport and being encouraged to take part in athletics. For example, girls growing up in a well-developed urban area with a mild climate may have greater opportunities to learn and play outdoor sports such as tennis or golf than they would if they lived in a rural, remote, cold-weather region of the world. In addition, culture and ethnicity have powerful effects on women's sports participation. In many Asian cultures, for example, women's participation in sports is neither favored nor encouraged. Finally, historical context is important. Before the 1970s, girls and young women in the United States had little opportunity to participate in organized sports. Since then, however, public attitudes have changed to the point that today such participation is generally viewed favorably.

SPORT AS SOCIALIZATION

Different cultures hold different beliefs about the effects of sports participation, but at the same time many also believe that taking part in sports itself develops social attitudes, values, beliefs, and practices. Although some studies suggest that men and boys learn negative attitudes toward women through sports participation, the most common belief is that sports build character, develop leaders who can compete successfully, improve people's self-image, and instill desirable personality characteristics. Since the 1950s, many studies have looked at socialization through sport, examining the various possible effects. They found no consistent or conclusive support for these beliefs. Often such research compares athletes to nonathletes, finds that the athletes differ in positive ways, and concludes that their sports involvement has produced these effects. The flaw in these conclusions is that they fail to consider that certain types of people with particular social and psychological characteristics may be attracted to and remain involved in sport. This means that the differences between athletes and nonathletes may be due to other factors entirely. As a result of these studies, socialization through sport, a phrase which implies that participation in sports causes the athlete to change in psychological or social ways, has been replaced with the phrase sport as socialization, which depicts more accurately the effects of sports participation.

Sports, like education, religion, or the family, provide a context in which experiences may occur that can change a person's life. Sports participation in and of itself, however, is not the source of these experiences. Rather, they are the product of the social relationships that go along with sports. No universal or unique set of socialization experiences is associated with sports. Such experiences vary tremendously in nature and significance depending on many factors. These may include how a particular sport is structured and organized, what relationships develop among the participants, and how each interprets or finds meaning in the experience. For example, in highly competitive sports most female athletes learn to play with and through pain and injury and accept it as a normal part of being an athlete. In contrast, in less competitively structured sports, such as a youth sports program or jogging club, athletes may be encouraged to learn to take care of their bodies and avoid playing with pain or injury.

LEAVING SPORTS: SPORT DESOCIALIZATION

Sport desocialization is a complex process that differs with the circumstances of each person's life. The process ranges from a gradual, well-planned, positive experience to an abrupt, unplanned, and traumatic process of ending one's active involvement in sports. Some people experience it more than once in a lifetime; for others, the first departure may mark a lifelong break with all sports or just one sport. Athletes may opt out of sports when they end a long, successful playing career in a highly competitive sport or terminate leisurely participation in a youth sports program. Some who leave one sport may take up another, stay with the same one in a different capacity, or shift to teaching, coaching, or administrative work. Typically, a person's departure from sports coincides with some other life change, such as graduation, employment, marriage, or parenthood.

Negative experiences may cause young girls to drop out of youth sports programs. They might be bored and not having fun, or they may not like an overemphasis on competition and winning. They may find the physical training excessive, be unsuccessful, perceive themselves as physically incompetent, or feel too much pressure from their parents to take part and to succeed. Alternatively, they may like the sport but find they do not have enough opportunity to play in games, or they may have a punitive coach. If a girl leaves sports for negative reasons, she usually reaches this decision over a period of time. In these circumstances, the desocialization, or opting out, is a welcome experience. Young girls who have enjoyed sports may nevertheless drop out, sometimes to spend more time with their friends who are not athletes, or to become involved in other activities.

Adolescent girls may drop out of sport programs for the same reasons as younger girls, but their age and maturity level may cause them to experience the process of desocialization differently. Many adolescent girls who were involved in competitive sports as children drop out because they are not selected for older groups and more competitive teams. In these cases, they may find the desocialization abrupt and difficult, particularly if they had identified strongly with their earlier participation. Many adolescent girls also decide to drop out of sports because they want to spend more time in other social situations. In North America, many girls who participate in high school athletics choose not to continue in college or have that choice made for them when they are not selected for teams. European girls often drop out of sports clubs when they reach their middle or late teens.

Elite-level athletes who have spent their lives playing competitive sports can experience the process of leaving in quite different ways. How they respond to the end of their involvement may depend on whether they leave voluntarily, whether they have identities beyond their sport, and whether they have the social and material means to change careers and ways of life. Athletes who leave their careers because of injury are essentially forced to stop, and they often find their departure abrupt and traumatic. In contrast, athletes have a more positive experience if they have planned their retirement from active sporting careers, have the money and education to shift to other careers, and do not define themselves solely as athletes.

CONCLUSION

A society's attitude toward women's participation in sports affects how girls are socialized, and those who do take part in sport may in turn adopt different values and beliefs. Parents and educators must consider this interaction as they seek to produce strong women.

Cynthia A. Hasbrook

See also Gender Equity; Puberty; Youth Sports

Bibliography

Bandura, Albert. (1969) "Social Learning of Identificatory Processes." In *Handbook of Socialization Theory and Research,* edited by D. A. Goslin. Chicago: Rand McNally.

Coakley, Jay J. (1998) *Sport in Society,* 6th ed. Boston: McGraw-Hill.

Eitzen, D. Stanley, and George H. Sage. (1997) *Sociology of North American Sport,* 6th ed. Madison, WI: Brown & Benchmark.

Greendorfer, Susan L. (1983) "Shaping the Female Athlete: The Influence of the Family." In *The Sporting Woman,* edited by M. A. Boutilier and L. SanGiovanni. Champaign, IL: Human Kinetics.

Guttmann, Allen. (1978) *From Ritual to Record: The Nature of Modern Sports.* New York: Columbia University Press.

Hargreaves, Jennifer. (1994) *Sporting Females: Critical Issues in the History and Sociology of Women's Sports.* London: Routledge.

Lindesmith, Alfred R., Anselm L. Strauss, and Norman K. Denzin. (1991) *Social Psychology,* 7th ed. Englewood Cliffs, NJ: Prentice-Hall.

McPherson, Barry D., James E. Curtis, and John W. Loy. (1989) *The Social Significance of Sport.* Champaign, IL: Human Kinetics.

Messner, Michael A. (1992) *Power at Play: Sports and the Problem of Masculinity.* Boston: Beacon Press.

Nixon, Howard L., and James H. Frey. (1996) *A Sociology of Sport.* Belmont, CA: Wadsworth.

Pfister, Gertrud. (1983) *Geschlechtsspezifische Sozialisation und Koedukation im Sport.* Berlin: Bartels J. Wernitz.

SOFTBALL

Softball is an outgrowth of men's baseball that uses a different type of ball and modified rules. It began as a men's sport but caught on quickly with women after World War II. Today it is played by women's, men's, and mixed groups.

Softball traveled to the far corners of the earth as a recreational activity for American soldiers during World War II. By 1996 softball was played in more than 100 countries. Estimates suggest that more than 45 million people play softball worldwide, of whom 60 percent are women. Multiple versions of the game exist, with the two main ones being fast pitch and slow pitch. The fast-pitch version reached its ultimate international competition as an Olympic event for women in Atlanta in 1996. At the elite level, the evolution of women's fast-pitch softball has been consistently aided and encouraged by mostly male administrators and coaches.

Xu Jian, Chinese softball player. (Wally McNamee/Corbis)

HISTORY

George Hancock, the inventor of softball, was celebrating the results of a football game when he was inspired to formalize the rules of what had begun as horseplay while a group of young men settled wagers on the football score. The young men were waiting patiently at the Farragut Boat Shed in Chicago as the telegraph wire spat out the results. As they celebrated, someone fashioned a boxing glove into a ball and the group began tossing it around. One young man grabbed a pole and used the pole as a defense. Very soon they were engaged in "indoor baseball." Hancock refined the rules as the new game spread throughout Chicago, meeting the need for a sport that could be played indoors, out of the bitterly cold northern winters, between the traditional football and baseball seasons. Hancock also realized its potential as an outdoor sport, and in the spring of 1888 he adapted it to a diamond smaller than that of regulation baseball and modified its name to "indoor–outdoor."

However, indoor–outdoor came under increasing pressure from another infant indoor sport, basketball, which James Naismith had developed as part of a class assignment at Springfield College, Massachusetts, in 1891, also to provide a good winter game. Indoor–outdoor held its own against basketball, however, and in ten years had spread to sixteen states in the United States. The game's organizers then took the first tentative international step with the establishment of a league in Toronto, Canada. Meanwhile, in 1895 in Minneapolis, fire officer Lewis Rober, Sr., had created a game for his men to play on the vacant lot next door to the fire station. Whether or not Rober knew of Hancock's game has not been determined. Rober's game served a similar purpose of providing meaningful activity in a restricted space. In honor of Rober's team, the Kittens, the sport was recognized as Kitten League Ball in 1900, then shortened to Kitten Ball, and eventually renamed "diamond ball" in 1922.

Walter C. Hakanson, director of the Denver Young Men's Christian Association (YMCA), recommended the name "softball" in 1926 at a meeting in Colorado called to standardize the rules in that state. "Soft" was intended to designate the difference between the larger, lighter ball and the small, hard baseball. Different versions of the game appeared across the United States under various names, including playground ball, recreation ball, big ball, twilight ball, army ball, mush ball, sissy ball, and dainty drawers. Even today multiple versions of the game can be found, including the most popular slow pitch; the fast pitch (the version played at the Olympics); modified pitch, which has elements of both of the former; 16-inch ball in Chicago; and over-the-line ball on the sandy beach flats of San Diego, California. The first national organization, the Amateur Softball Association of America (ASA), was formed in 1933 after a successful promotion at the Chicago World's Fair. Softball sustained its growth to earn a strong reputation as a participatory sport, with more than 42 million Americans (women and men) playing a version of the game by 1991. It had not, however, received comparable media attention until the 1996 Olympics.

From its beginnings in the harsh northern winter, softball has thrived in times of adversity. President Franklin D. Roosevelt implemented his New Deal package in 1933 to jump-start American recovery from the Great Depression. He emphasized public works to provide employment, and recreation facilities were central to his plan. More than 3,000 athletic fields were constructed between 1935 and 1940, with at least one softball diamond in each.

The international dispersion of softball was a by-product of World War II, according to Arthur T. Noren, who wrote in 1947, "In every corner of the globe, wherever there was a lull in the action, men brought out bats and softballs, staked off a diamond and the game was on. England, Germany, Alaska, Iceland, and the far-flung islands of the Pacific all resounded to the cry of 'Batter Up!' and most of the time it was for softball." Whether or not softball survived the war and grew in every corner of the globe depended on the extent to which the local community had played alongside the troops, the popularity of existing local sports, and the enthusiasm of ex-service personnel who chose to stay rather than return to the United States and other expatriates. In Australia, for example, the game grew and prospered as a women's sport with support from North American men. In the state of New South Wales (NSW), a Canadian, Gordon Young, was placed in charge of physical education in the state education system. On the outbreak of war in 1939, he was also given responsibility for the National Fitness Council. Young was passionate about softball (presumably from his undergraduate studies at Springfield College, Massachusetts) and vigorously promoted it as a game for primary (elementary) schools with minimal playing space. His wife, Pat, took charge of NSW women's softball in 1946.

In the state of Victoria, softball was introduced in 1942 by Sergeant du Vernet of the United States Special Services, who was responsible for organizing recreational activities for the troops and nurses. While attempting to arrange matches for the nurses, he contacted organizations with women's baseball teams. The feminine qualities of softball (smaller playing area, shorter matches, a larger ball, and a smaller bat), which were not considered likely to develop "unsightly muscles," quickly converted the women, who went on not only to establish a strong softball association in Australia but also to take the lead in conducting the first world championship in Melbourne in 1965.

The state of Queensland benefited from the presence of a former American semiprofessional baseball player, Mack Gilley, who was invited to help the women reestablish baseball after the war. Gilley appraised their skills and recommended they try softball. Gilley's drive led to the playing of the first interstate competition in 1947. Across the Tasman Sea in New Zealand, softball had been played by both men and women since 1937, when W. H. Wilson of the Ford Motor Company imported a few bats and balls so his staff could keep

A SPECIAL RIVALRY: AUSTRALIA VERSUS THE UNITED STATES

Australia first played the United States at the inaugural Women's World Championship in Melbourne in 1965. In lobbying to host the championships an Australian delegation had argued to the Amateur Softball Association of America (ASA) that participating teams should be comprised of the best players in a nation, rather than the winning team of the national tournament. Australia selected its team at the national championships in 1964, but in an ironic twist eight players were from the same club team, Rebels, which played in the Victorian state association. The United States was represented by Raybestos Brakettes which had won four ASA World Series since 1958.

The Brakettes were employed by the Raybestos company which made car brake components. In an era when the telephone was neither a common nor reliable means of international communication and mail took months to reach Australia, the teams knew very little about each other but each had a point to prove, the Americans as the originators of the sport, the Australians as the instigators of the World Championship. The Australians having the advantage of receiving *Balls and Strikes,* the official publication of the ASA, had learned that Bertha Tickey, a forty-two-year-old grandmother, was the undisputed queen of pitching. In nineteen years she had notched up 147 no-hit games. In their first encounter Tickey held Australia scoreless until the fourth inning when Marjorie 'Midge' Nelson slammed a home run to give Australia a 1-0 lead. America tied the match in the seventh inning, but Nelson again batted Australia out of trouble. Not only did Australia win 2-1 but for the first time in her career Tickey was called for illegal pitching. America won their second encounter 7-0, setting the scene for a tense semi-final. Then, Australia won 7-0 and went on to their fourth match in the grand final with the psychological edge. The injured Tickey did not play. Donna Lopiano took the pitching plate for America. At the bottom of the sixth inning with no score registered, Australian batter, Elinor McKenzie, hit a double to center field. The next batter was out. Facing the third Australian batter, Lopiano let go a wild pitch that flew clear over the head of her catcher. Such was McKenzie's speed that she sprinted from second to home, avoided the tag and gave Australia a 1-0 lead which they held to win the Diamond Trophy as first world champions.

A special rivalry had developed between these two nations but it was to be another thirty years before Australia again briefly gained the ascendancy. With a win-loss record of 115-1 the Americans were the clear favorites at the Olympics in Atlanta in 1996. A home run by Dani Tyler in the fourth inning appeared to give them a 1-0 lead but ever-alert Australian first-base player, Kerry Dienelt, had noticed Tyler had not touched home base as she crossed it. Dienelt threw to Australian catcher, Joyce Lester, who played the base and appealed. Tyler's run was not allowed. The scores were level again at 0-0. America scored in the top of the tenth inning. In a do-or-die effort with a runner apparently stranded on second base, two batters already out and two strikes on her Australian batter, Joanne Brown hit a home run off American pitching legend, Lisa Fernandez. Brown had been a teammate of Fernandez when they each held athletic scholarships at the University of California-Los Angeles. When it looked like America would be undefeated in its first push for the first Olympic medal for softball and Fernandez would pitch a perfect tournament, Australia stole the limelight with a 2-1 victory gaining front page cover in *USA Today,* and softball's international magazine, *World Softball.* The American team regrouped and won the gold medal play-off against China. Thus Australia and America share international softball honors: one the first world champion, the other the first Olympic champion.

physically fit. Both Australia and New Zealand embraced the fast-pitch version, and only in the 1990s did these countries begin to play slow pitch.

Softball was established as a women's sport in the Union of South Africa (now the Republic of South Africa) and Rhodesia (now Zimbabwe) in 1947, preceding its introduction as a men's sport by two years. Here it was strongly influenced by British servicemen who had played softball in North Africa and Italy. In England before 1980,

American expatriates, often associated with the film industry, were the major slow-pitch softball players. Since the mid-1980s, the sport has taken hold among both women and men, with 90 percent participating in mixed slow-pitch teams and the remainder equally divided between single-sex and fast-pitch teams.

The International Softball Federation (ISF) was formed in 1950, with the ASA, the Canadian Softball Association, and Confederation Deportica Mexicana (Mexico) as charter members. Australia affiliated with the fledgling ISF in 1953 and played a pivotal role in the establishment of international competitions. Three test series were played between Australia and New Zealand beginning in Melbourne in 1949. Australia won that series and two more played in 1951 and 1954. Australia hosted South Africa in 1960. That year, during discussions with the South African manager, Jan Crafford, about the future of the sport, representatives of the two countries conceived a plan for a truly international championship. The Diamond Trophy commissioned for this series was intended to become for softball what the Davis Cup had become for tennis. In 1962 three Australian women—Esther Deason, Marj Dwyer, and Merle Short—visited the world series conducted in Stratford, Connecticut, by the ASA. Although a guest team from Japan and a Canadian team registered with the ASA both played, Deason, Dwyer, and Short viewed the world series as a domestic American competition. It seemed to the Australians that the men overseeing the ASA and ISF had a limited understanding of the international appeal of the sport. With support from the Japanese team manager, Jiro Iwano, the Australian women lobbied the American men until they agreed that Australia could host an international venture, provided the country took full responsibility. Using the list in the ASA rule book of nations affiliated with the ISF, Australia invited twenty-two nations to the first women's world championship, held in Melbourne in 1965. Five nations took part: New Zealand, the United States, Japan, Papua New Guinea, and Australia. The first men's international championship was held in Mexico in 1966. After some delay, the second women's championship was held in Japan in 1970 and was played thereafter every four years. The host nations, Australia and Japan, won the first two women's championships. The United States as host also won at Stratford, Connecticut, in 1974. This marked the first of many U.S. international victories, with only one loss, to New Zealand in 1982. Championships for under-nineteen women and men were inaugurated in 1981 in Edmonton, Canada. Initially the championships were played at the same venue, but since 1987 different venues and dates have been used.

From the outset the ISF harbored a vision of softball as an Olympic sport and as early as 1952 planned for its inclusion in the Summer Games. Led by Don Porter—executive director of the ASA (1963–1998) and secretary-treasurer (1965–1987) then president (1987–present) of the ISF—softball proponents mounted determined campaigns, only to be continually frustrated. Optimism ran high in 1984 when it appeared likely that softball would be accepted for the Los Angeles Games to provide a women's counterpart for baseball, but this did not occur. The International Olympic Committee (IOC) officially made softball an Olympic sport in June 1991, raising the hopes that it would be included as a demonstration sport in Barcelona in 1992. The IOC quashed the plan because it felt resources were stretched to the limit. Fittingly, then, when softball was finally accepted, it was played on American soil in Atlanta in 1996. Eight teams contested for the first Olympic medal: the United States, China, Australia, Japan, Canada, the Netherlands, Taiwan, and Puerto Rico.

While waiting in the wings of the Olympic stage, softball developed alternative competitions. Australia inaugurated the mini–world series in Brisbane in 1981. This series became the South Pacific Classic in 1985, which is contested between world championships with Australia and New Zealand alternating as hosts. Softball is part of the Pan-American Games and the Asian Games, and top national teams increasingly tour regularly to maintain their competitiveness.

RULES AND PLAY

The playing area and rules of fast pitch and slow pitch have many common elements. The sport is played on a diamond-shaped area with white canvas bases in each corner and the pitching base in approximately the center. These distances varied until they were finally set by the ISF at 18.29 meters (60 feet) between bases, and 12.19 meters (40 feet) for women and 14.02 meters (46 feet) for men from the pitching point to home plate. The playing area is divided into fair and foul territory. Fair territory is inside the lines extending from home base out through first and third bases respectively.

Team size has varied over time, with current rules allowing nine players on the field in the fast-pitch version. They are pitcher, catcher (like back-stop in rounders or wicket keeper in cricket), first base, second base, third base, shortstop (approximately halfway between second and third base but free to move according to knowledge of the strengths and weaknesses of the batter), left field, center field, and right field. In elite fast-pitch competition, both fielding and batting positions have become increasingly specialized and often the pitcher, who dominates the game, will not bat. Instead, a designated batter will be used, effectively increasing the team to ten. Slow pitch is characterized by long hits, so there is an additional outfielder.

The pitcher must release the ball underarm from either a forward and back underarm swing, the slingshot, or a full arm circle, the windmill pitch. In fast pitch the ball travels directly from pitcher to catcher at approximately hip height, and in elite competition it may travel at speeds in excess of 100 kilometers (60 miles) per hour. Slow pitch derives its name from the requirement that the ball travel in an arc above the shoulder height of the pitcher and catcher. The slower pace allows the batter plenty of time to view the ball, resulting in more and longer hits. The bat is similar to a baseball bat but smaller in diameter and made of aluminum. Despite the name "softball," the ball is anything but soft. It is made of leather and is 12 inches (30.5 centimeters) in circumference. To accommodate the increasing numbers of female participants, modern helmets include an opening for a ponytail. The game is controlled by a central or plate umpire positioned behind the catcher and assisted by at least one but preferably two base umpires stationed in the field near first and third bases.

Chinese pitcher at the 1996 Atlanta Olympics. (Wally McNamee/Corbis)

WOMEN'S PARTICIPATION

Indoor baseball preceded basketball for men, but the reverse is true for women, and basketball is credited with creating a more conducive climate for physical activity for women late in the nineteenth century. Baseball made minor inroads into women's schools in the United States, but by and large physical educators rejected it because it was perceived as masculine. Indoor baseball was far more acceptable for women, but it almost lost out to basketball's popularity until it was relocated outdoors. Early in the twentieth century the National Playground Association lobbied for more access to school playgrounds during out-of-school time for both girls and boys. The adult game blossomed in the leagues sponsored by industry. The result was that women's softball was characterized as a working-class sport, an image that still persists in Western countries and stands in marked contrast to its origins with upper-class men. The most significant development for women, however, appears to have been in 1929, when Gladys Palmer of Ohio State University prescribed rules on behalf of the National Committee on Women's Athletics of the American

Physical Education Association. The rules addressed both indoor and outdoor versions but essentially determined the key features of the sport as it is played today.

Palmer recommended that the players wear a short-sleeved white blouse with a black tie, black bloomers, a white belt, black stockings, and ankle-high tennis shoes. Such a uniform was eminently suitable for young ladies in educational institutions, but in the flourishing industrial leagues, satin shorts generated more sex appeal, although they totally disregarded the practicalities of the base runner sliding into bases or the fielder hurling herself at full stretch across the ground to stop a ball. With the advent of international competition in the 1960s practical considerations prevailed, and most teams opted to wear trousers like those worn by baseball players. They later shifted to shorts with sliding pants underneath to give additional protection to the thighs. Shorts, it is argued, are more suitable for the warm weather in which softball is played.

Softball was included in physical education classes, but unlike other sports for U.S. women, the game was played in industrial leagues, taking advantage of summer evenings lengthened by daylight saving time and summer vacations. Prior to the establishment of the ASA in 1933, various leagues and parks and recreation departments held control of the game. Between the world wars, women physical educators who emphasized cooperation and participation over competition did not control the game. Because of this, eight teams were able to take part in the tournament held in conjunction with the Chicago World's Fair in 1933.

World War II sent most women out of the home to offices, factories, and playing fields. Philip K. Wrigley, a major chewing-gum manufacturer and owner of the Chicago Cubs baseball club, saw the potential for women to fill the void in professional baseball when many star male players enlisted. The All-American Girls' Professional Baseball League (AAGPBL), as depicted in the 1992 movie *A League of Their Own,* began playing by softball rules when it was established in 1943, but to increase its public appeal the league gradually moved to regulation baseball until its demise in 1954, when it fell victim to the postwar move that pushed women back into the home. All the AAGPBL players were white. They maintained their feminine appearance—and perceived womanly character—through their compulsory attendance at beauty classes and the wearing of skirts, which were even more impractical than shorts. Several attempts to establish a professional softball league for women floundered during the 1970s and 1980s, but the Women's Professional Fastpitch (WPF), set up in 1997, appears as of 1999 to have adequate financial sponsorship.

Title IX affected softball for women significantly. The 1972 law, which prohibits discrimination on the basis of sex in American educational institutions that receive federal grants, gave a tremendous boost to women's intercollegiate athletic programs. Under Title IX, scholarships that had been granted only to males gradually opened up to females, and by 1982 women's fast-pitch softball had become a serious college sport. As competition in college fast pitch became more intense, talent scouts began to include the under-nineteen international championships and the women's open on their recruit-

A DIRE LACK OF PUBLICITY

A major problem facing the Women's Professional Softball League (six teams in the Midwest and east) is a lack of interest by the media. Although softball is played by over 40 million people in the United States and 3 million more girls and young women play softball than soccer, soccer, basketball, ice skating, volleyball, and gymnastics get far more media coverage. The league recognizes the need to build media coverage if women's professional softball is to survive, and perhaps a breakthrough took place during the 1999 season when several games drew good audiences on the ESPN and ESPN2 networks.

ing agendas. As a result, a considerable number of women from other countries have attended U.S. universities on scholarships to play softball. One-third of the members of the Australian team that competed in the Atlanta Olympics had considerable experience in the U.S. college system, and some had won major awards in pitching and batting. With the acceptance of softball into the Olympics, Australian players have been eligible since 1993 for scholarships from the Australian Institute of Sport. The scholarships do not provide permanent financial security, but they do ease players' financial burdens and give them some indication of what they might expect in a professional league.

Cultural differences engender different sports philosophies. In Japan softball has benefited from the close association of sports teams with major corporations. For part of the day the women work for their corporations, and for the remainder they train for the company team. The Japanese, too, are now recruiting internationally, with non-Japanese players not obliged to be otherwise employed in factories or offices.

While scholarships and professional leagues have confirmed fast pitch as a women's sport, they have not resulted in comparable growth for women in coaching, officiating, or administrative positions. Throughout the growth of women's softball worldwide, men have dominated these supporting roles. Of the twelve-member ISF executive committee, only one was female in 1999, Rosemary Adey (vice president, South Pacific). Male coaches and umpires were highly visible in the Atlanta Games.

CONCLUSION

Since its inception as a men's recreational game, softball has become a serious, competitive sport for men and women, although it also remains a major form of recreation. Although at the elite level softball is primarily a women's game, the administration of the sport remains with men.

Lynn Embrey

Bibliography

Babb, Ron, and the Amateur Softball Association. (1997) *Etched in Gold: The Story of America's First Ever Olympic Gold Medal Winning Softball Team.* Indianapolis, IN: Masters Press.

Balls & Strikes. The Official Publication of the Amateur Softball Association of America. (1999) Oklahoma City: Amateur Softball Association of America.

Dickson, Paul. (1994) *The Worth Book of Softball.* New York: Facts on File.

Embrey, Lynn. (1995) *Batter Up! The History of Softball in Australia.* Bayswater, Victoria: Australian Softball Federation.

———. (1997) " 'Great hit, Jo-Jo': Leveling the International Softball Scoreboard." *Sporting Traditions: Journal of the Australian Society for Sports History* 14, 1: 55–78.

Fidler, Merrie A. (1982) "The Establishment of Softball as a Sport for American Women, 1900–1940." In *Herstory in Sport: A Historic Anthology of Women in Sports,* edited by Reet Howell. West Point, NY: Leisure Press, 527–540.

Fromer, Bob. (n.d.) *Softball in the U.K.*

Kennedy, Kostya. (1997) "On an Idyllic Opening Night, a Women's Pro Softball League Made a Historic Pitch." *Sports Illustrated* 86, 23: 31.

Noren, Arthur T. (1947) *Softball* (The Barnes Sports Library). New York: A.S. Barnes.

Seymour, Harold. (1990) *Baseball. The People's Game.* Oxford: Oxford University Press.

SOKOL MOVEMENT

The Sokol (falcon) movement emerged in nineteenth-century Eastern Europe as a response to *Turnen* (German gymnastics). The Slavic peoples of the time were, with the exception of the Russians, ethnic nations without states. The Slavic peoples of Eastern Europe consist of the Eastern Slavs (Ukrainians, Belarussians, Russians); Western Slavs (Poles, Czechs, Slovaks); and Southern Slavs (Bulgarians, Serbs, Croats, Macedonian Slavs, and Slovenes). The Sokol movement, founded on liberal-democratic principles, was a substitute for institutions, such as schools and the army, which the Slavic people of Eastern Europe lacked. Accordingly, the movement never restricted itself merely to physical education. The Sokol clubs provided paramilitary training and staged marches, parades, and mass demonstrations that were seen as the "embodiment of the nation."

The first Sokol club was founded in Prague in 1862 by Miroslav Tyrs and Jindrich Fügner. The social composition of the Sokol movement in Austrian-ruled Bohemia mirrored the social composition of the Czech movement for national independence. The members were primarily small businessmen and middle-class professionals or intellectuals.

The physical education promoted by the movement was a blend of German *Turnen* and modern sports. There were also elements borrowed from Greek antiquity and paramilitary exercises. The Sokol movement's distinguishing characteristic was its emphasis on mass displays of a political and cultural nature. It was not unusual for 40,000 or more participants to gather for these demonstrations.

Long before the outbreak of World War I—the war that led, indirectly, to Slavic freedom from foreign domination—the Czech combination of physical education and nationalism had become a model for other Slavic people. Sokol clubs and federations were founded in Poland, in the Ukraine, in parts of Russia, and throughout the Balkans. In 1908 the various national federations united to form a single multinational Sokol organization.

Almost from the beginning, the Sokol clubs included women among their members. Since the emphasis was on demonstrations of national and cultural solidarity rather than on competition, there were fewer barriers to women's participation. Women were, however, more prominent in the Czech than in the Balkan Sokol clubs.

Diethelm Blecking

See also Czechoslovakia, Czech Republic, Slovakian Republic; Poland; Yugoslavia

Bibliography

Beranova, Jitka. (1998) "The Sokol." In *Cultural and Educational Activities of Czech Physical Education Organizations*, edited by Jitka Beranova and Marek Waic. Prague: Narodni Muzeum, 95–120.

Blecking, Diethelm, ed. (1991) *Die slawische Sokolbewegung*. Dortmund: University of Dortmund.

SOUTH AFRICA

The Republic of South Africa is a large nation with a population of more than 40 million people from several different ethnic groups. In 1948, the political policy of apartheid, or racial segregation, was established, legitimizing harsh forms of discrimination against the nonwhite majority. Women of all races also experienced discrimination, but black African women were placed in the most restricted position of all. These inequalities were reflected sharply in the world of sport.

After years of struggle, bloodshed, and resistance, and the growth of national and international protest movements, beginning in 1989 reforms were instituted toward ending apartheid, and in April 1994, the first multiracial elections were held in South Africa. With these elections, the country changed radically. Apartheid was replaced by the putative nonracial, nonsexist Republic of South Africa. Understandably, change has been difficult because the political and cultural practices of apartheid were enforced and inscribed in social practice for nearly half a century. Everyone in South Africa today lives with the legacy of apartheid.

SPORT IN APARTHEID SOUTH AFRICA

During the period of apartheid (1948–1994), there was a mandatory division of the nation into four racial categories—whites, coloreds (mixed race), Indians, and natives or Bantus ("black" applies to all people of color). By means of the government's racist philosophy and practice of "separate but equal" development, the white minority (12.5 percent of the population) maintained a particularly violent and repressive form of control, which, for the huge majority of South Africans, meant a denial of human rights and fundamental freedoms in political, economic, social, and cultural areas of life. Inequalities of gender were also intrinsic to the racial relations of apartheid.

The world of sports mirrored these relations, which reflected the extraordinary power and privilege of white men. Sports were also sites of inequalities between men and women in all social and racial groups. White communities had multiple facilities and money for different sports, with priority for men's cricket and rugby; Indian and colored areas had far fewer resources, most of which were used by men; for Africans, facilities in the townships were sparse, and mostly only for men's soccer (association football). In rural areas, facilities were virtually nonexistent for both sexes. Sports were irrelevant for the vast majority of African women, who were struggling for survival and had to contend with traditional forms of male domination at the same time.

Black schools had virtually no facilities or programs for sports, reflecting the generally huge differences between white and African schools. In 1984, for example, the government spent 9.84 rand on sports resources for every white schoolchild but only 0.41 rand for every African child. The absence of facilities for girls in African schools, combined with poverty, travel problems, and male controls, made participation in sports impossible for the majority of African girls.

Racial divisions were also enforced in sport. Because of the government's segregated sports policy and the wide range of apartheid laws and regulations, freedom of travel was impossible. Black people were barred from using the facilities that were in white areas.

Nevertheless, there existed throughout the period of apartheid, a surprisingly active nonracial (antiracist) sports movement in which women were involved, although in fewer numbers than men. The main representative body for black sport was the South African Council on Sport (SACOS), and although the organization was male-dominated, women worked with great determination, and in the face of tremendous difficulties, to keep female sport alive in the black communities. The SACOS slogan was "No normal sport in an abnormal society."

The most active SACOS members were colored women with professional backgrounds—mostly teachers. Lacking resources—facilities, sponsorship, skilled coaching, and regular competition—these women used ingenuity and their own transport and money, as well as great determination and dedication, enabling events and competitions to continue in such sports as field hockey, softball, netball, and track and field. There were nonracial local leagues and interprovincial competitions, and there were SACOS sports festivals known as the Olympics of the Oppressed, first held in 1982, where the best of the nonracial athletics took place.

Because of its apartheid policy, and as a result of the efforts of the South African Non-Racial Olympic Committee (SANROC), following the 1960 Olympics South Africa was banned from the Olympics, the Commonwealth Games, and the All-Africa Games. The predominantly male character of South African sports up until that time meant that very few South African women had been members of the national team; at the 1960 Olympics the national team had consisted of fifty-six men and two women.

Two South African women compete at table tennis. (Hulton-Deutsch Collection/Corbis)

SPORTS IN POST-APARTHEID SOUTH AFRICA

In contrast to the apartheid ideas and practices of separateness and inequality, post-apartheid South Africa has a humane philosophy of unity and tolerance, symbolized in the motto, "One Nation—Many Cultures: Together We Become." Nevertheless, it has been extraordinarily difficult to change longstanding structures of inequality based on race and gender and to alleviate the extremes of poverty and wealth that create massive problems for sports development. The population is estimated to be approximately 42.5 million: Africans comprise 77.4 percent; whites, 12.5 percent; coloreds, 7.7 percent; and Indians, 2.4 percent. African women comprise 72 percent of all women over eighteen years of age.

The new policies notwithstanding, change began very slowly. Between 40 percent and 50 percent of adult South Africans are unemployed; 50 percent of the population still live in poverty; 10 million live in areas without electricity; and 42 percent of deaths result from chronic diseases.

Elana Meyer of South Africa (right) running with Derartu Tulu of Ethiopia in the 10,000-meter event at the 1992 Summer Olympics. Meyer finished second, Tulu first. (AP Photo)

Squatter camps are increasing in size because Africans are moving in large numbers into the towns from the rural areas and the previous homelands. As of 1999, 48.3 percent of the population was urban and 51.7 percent (predominantly African), nonurban. African women and children living in rural areas and in squatter camps are the most severely deprived groups in the population, enduring appalling living and health conditions. South Africa also has the highest rate of violence and rape against women in the world.

Under these conditions, sheer survival is the priority for huge numbers of women. Nevertheless, sports programs can improve the quality of life for others who are less seriously deprived. Overall, less than 21 percent of South African women participate in organized sports. Estimated figures show that of these, 51 percent are white, 35 percent are colored or Indian, and 14 percent are African. Figures for men from all ethnic groups are much higher; it is estimated that 40 percent of African men participate in some sport.

In 1994, the democratically elected government of national unity put in place a reconstruction and development program (RDP) directed at black communities to eradicate the inequities of the past. The RDP made the provision of sports for disadvantaged communities a priority. The Department of Sport and Recreation (DSR), working with the government-funded National Sports Council (NSC—the umbrella organization for sport in South Africa) and the National Olympic Committee of South Africa (NOCSA), aimed to implement radical changes. The NSC launched an initiative known as Protea Sport, intended to introduce sports into deprived areas. Recognizing the problems of unequal gender divisions, the NSC targeted girls and women as especially needy groups, especially in communities that had historically been on the margins of the society. Such a strategy was essential, because, as Cheryl Roberts points out, contemporary South African sports are gender-biased, male-dominated, and sexist. The Women's Sports Foundation, originally established as an autonomous body in 1994, became a standing committee of the NSC (Women's Sports Committee) responsible for monitoring gender affairs, and many sports federations developed programs to include women, some of which put quota systems in place.

Here, too, change began slowly. In spite of the official philosophy of gender equality, men held the vast majority of leadership positions at national, regional, and local levels. Although the women's sports movement has developed momentum, and more women are now involved, men continue to dominate sports organizations. There are four women out of ten members on the NOCSA executive committee; two women out of eight elected members of the NSC; four women out of eight members of the NSC Sports Development Committee; one woman out of nine provincial ministers with responsibility for sports. In addition, there are two female members of parliament who are concerned with the promotion of sports; and out of 140 sports federations, only 65 have Women's Desks (sections).

The NSC works with the national and provincial departments of sport and recreation to promote gender equity. There are NSC women's desks in each of the provinces; there is an elected Women in Sport South Africa (WASSA) initiative in each province, coordinated by a WASSA national committee, with its own steering committee (with representatives from all nine provinces). Facilitated by the DSR, the WASSA structures take responsibility for policy development and program implementation. The Western Cape (the province whose capital is Cape Town) has been proactive in formulating a gender-equity policy for the province. Nationally WASSA has a strategy whose mission is to develop a culture in which women and girls will have equal opportunities, equal access, and equal support in sports and recreation at all levels and in all capacities as decision makers, administrators, coaches, technical officials, and participants. The DSR has begun a series of capacity-building workshops, and there are similar projects at the provincial level. There are also plans for launching a Girls in Sport campaign and a database for women in sports.

ELITE SPORTS

An elite sports program, Operation Excellence, was inaugurated to help South African women make an impact as they return to international competition. Black women represented South Africa for the first time at the 1992 Olympics (Rencia Nasson, fencing; Cheryl Roberts, table tennis; Marcel Winkler, track), then also at the 1994 Commonwealth Games and the 1995 sixth All-Africa Games. However, national sports teams are still predominantly male. South Africa sent sixty-two men and twenty-five women to the 1992 Olympics; eighty men and thirty-two women to the 1994 Commonwealth Games; 259 men and seventy women to the 1995 All-Africa Games; seventy men and eighteen women to the 1996 Olympics; and 130 men and eighty-two women to the 1998 Commonwealth Games.

Black women still face the greatest hurdles at the local level. The legacy of apartheid has deprived township women of sports infrastructures, and they remain seriously underprivileged and lacking in resources. Even so, they are active agents in the creation of sports practices, and they work to secure better opportunities, to break down traditional myths and stereotypes, and to nurture previously untapped talent in their communities.

CONCLUSION

One of the most hopeful signs is the strong endeavor by women from very diverse race, class, and cultural backgrounds to work together to challenge patterns of oppression and domination in sports participation and administration and to organize courses, seminars, training, and coaching sessions. For example, programs are in place for women from Indian communities, where cultural and religious factors are significant, and for disabled women, who in the past have been virtually excluded from sports. Sportswomen in South Africa—characterized as the new "Rainbow Republic"—understand the need to create unity from diversity.

Jennifer Hargreaves
Denise Jones

Bibliography

Archer, Robert. (1987) "An Exceptional Case: Politics and Sport in South Africa's Townships." In *Sport in Africa: Essays in Social History,* edited by William F. Baker and James. A. Mangan. New York: Africana Publishing Company, 199–249.

Cammack, Paul, David Pool, and William Tordoff. (1993) *Third World Politics.* London: Macmillan.

Haffajee, Ferial. (1995) "The Sisterly Republic." *New Internationalist* 265: 11–13.

Hain, Peter. (1982) "The Politics of Sport Apartheid." In *Sport, Culture and Ideology,* edited by Jennifer Hargreaves. London: Routledge and Kegan Paul, 161–182.

Hargreaves, Jennifer. (1997) "Women's Sport, Development, and Cultural Diversity: The South African Experience." *Women's Studies International Forum* 20, 2: 191–209.

Jones, Denise E. M. (1995) "The Emergence of a Non-Alternative Physical Education for Females in South Africa." In *Sport as Symbols, Symbols as Sport,* edited by F. J. van der Merwe. Berlin: International Society for the History of Physical Education and Sport.

Lessing, Margaret, ed. (1994) *South African Women Today.* Cape Town: Maskew Miller Longman.

Ramsamy, Sam. (1982) *Apartheid: The Real Hurdle.* London: International Defence and Aid Fund.

Roberts, Cheryl. (1993) "Black Women, Recreation and Organised Sport," *Agenda* 17: 8–17.

———. (1993) *Against the Grain: Women in Sport in South Africa*. Cape Town: Township Publishing Co-operative.

———. (1995) *Sportswoman*. Cape Town: Township Publishing Co-operative.

SOUTH KOREA

Se Ri Pak defends her title at the 1999 U.S. Women's Open in Mississippi. (AFP/Corbis)

Korea is located in the peninsula that extends southward from the northeastern corner of the Asian continent. The country was divided at the thirty-eighth parallel into North and South Korea at the end of World War II. South Korea is known as the Republic of Korea (ROK). North Korea, under a communist government, is the Democratic People's Republic of Korea. South Korea has a population of about 44 million. For a variety of cultural reasons, women and girls did not participate in sport or physical activity until the start of the twentieth century, but since that time they have made considerable progress at all levels of competition, including the Olympic Games.

CULTURAL RESTRAINTS

For many centuries, tradition and culture combined to exclude women from sporting activities. South Korea borders China, and its society and culture have been heavily influenced by Chinese philosophy, literature, art, science, and technology. From the fifteenth to the nineteenth century, Confucian philosophy dominated. South Koreans used the ideology and disciplines of Confucianism to guide them in their social ethics, culture, politics, and education. Confucianism, however, places intellect above all, and during this time, only intellectual activity was valued. Physical activity and sports had no place in this scheme of things. In-

SE RI PAK

The best-known international South Korean athlete is golfer Se Ri Pak. In 1998, at the age of 21, she won four tournaments on the LPGA tour including two majors (LPGA Championship and U.S. Women's Open) and was voted Rookie of the Year. She was trained by her father, a construction company executive, and is sponsored by Samsung. While rewarding professionally, her first year on the tour was difficult personally as she spoke little English, had few friends, and was closely watched by her sponsors. In the fall she returned to South Korea and was hospitalized for exhaustion. She returned to the tour for 1999 and performed well again although not as spectacularly as in the previous year.

deed, physical education and sports were prohibited by the schools because Confucian influence.

South Korea's class system also figured into the avoidance of physical activities. In general, the upper classes had a distaste for physical exertion and work, believing that such activities were suitable only for members of the lower classes. Thus only middle- and lower-class South Koreans took part in folk games and recreational activities through the nineteenth century. These factors combined effectively prevented the development of any tradition of sports or physical activity in South Korea.

For girls and women, the situation was even more restrictive. The male-dominated social system placed little value on women and small children and emphasized the father–son relationship. However, at the beginning of the twentieth century, as contact with the Western world became more intensive and South Korea began to enter the modern age, sports began to develop. Since that time, three principal activity areas have emerged: physical education, elite sports, and lifelong sports.

PHYSICAL EDUCATION

At the end of the nineteenth century, schools in South Korea began to include physical education and sports in their curricula. For women and girls, gymnastics was offered first, followed by basketball and tennis in 1911. Sinsil Kim, who was called the mother of Korean education, contributed to the development and promotion of women's sports, and taught badminton and folk dance at the Women's University in 1930. In 1945, she founded the College of Physical Education as part of the scientific and professional education system, and in 1954 she founded the Korean Women's Physical Education and Sport Association.

The 1970s brought a major shift in emphasis in the schools. Up to that time, education focused on a core academic curriculum of language, mathematics, and science as students prepared for various entrance exams. Schools were still heavily influenced by Confucian philosophy, and intellectual ability was paramount. Physical education was essentially ignored. The government, however, became concerned about the physical fitness of Korea's young people, and the curriculum was revised, with students required to take physical fitness tests as part of their entrance exams at all levels of school.

The 1990s brought further change as the Ministry of Education sought to create the "new" education. For the twenty-first century, the government has a master plan to revamp the country's educational system. In this new system, entrance exams will be abolished and schooling will balance education in the intellectual, emotional, and physical domains, developing all three simultaneously.

According to this plan, in the primary schools, first- and second-grade will use play as physical education. Play satisfies children's basic needs and at the same time develops their physical strength. By the third and fourth grades, students will be introduced to gymnastics, expressive movement, and health education. Fifth- and sixth-graders will add to these track and field, swimming, and dance. Junior high school and the first year of high school will involve all of the above activities, plus individual and team sports as well as the theory of physical education and sports. After tenth grade, through the eleventh and twelfth grades, physical education becomes an elective subject. Students who choose to continue will take part in individual and team sports, fitness activities, dance, movement therapy, and health education.

In reality, however, not all schools adhere strictly to this plan, and some still ignore sports and physical education to some degree. Girls' physical education has lagged behind that for boys, since physical education is sometimes taught only to boys. Similarly, sports for girls in schools are also limited compared to those for boys.

Further hampering the development of physical education were single-sex schools. Until the 1980s, most of South Korea's schools were not coeducational. The government is continuing its efforts to make schools coeducational, and in doing so, trying also to coordinate girls' and boys' physical activities and sports.

ELITE SPORTS FOR WOMEN

Until 1960, women's participation in elite sports was restricted by the societal and cultural factors discussed above. Since then, however, elite women athletes have played a highly visible role in national and international sporting events. South Korean women took first place in an international tournament for the first time at the 1973 table tennis world championships in Sarajevo, Yugoslavia. More significant and meaningful, however, was their first Olympic medal—the bronze, won by the women's volleyball team at the Montreal Olympics in 1976. At the 1984 Los Angeles Olympics, women won the gold medal in archery, and two silver medals, one in basketball and another in handball. Four years later, at the 1988 Seoul Olympics, South Korean women won four gold medals, two silver medals, and one bronze medal. At the 1992 Olympics, women captured six gold medals in archery, handball, badminton, shooting, and judo, one silver in archery, and three bronze in badminton and table tennis. One well-known South Korean female athlete is 21-year old professional golfer Se Ri Pak. In 1988, in her first year on the women's tour, she won four tournaments, including two major championships, and was voted Ladies Professional Golf Association Rookie of the Year. She drew much attention from the media in South Korea and became a national celebrity as well as a role model to countless South Korean children.

These achievements reflect the substantial progress South Korean women have made in competitive sports at the international level. Elite sports are closely linked to political, economic, and sociocultural factors, and successful performances are important indicators of national competitive power and prestige. In elite competition, women's sports have become more significant than men's as women have won more gold medals in Olympic competition, and they have contributed more to the promotion of national prestige. Until recently, however, women took part in only a limited number of sports at this level, including swimming, table tennis, gymnastics, volleyball, basketball, field hockey, track and field, archery, badminton, and shooting. Recently, they have been allowed to participate in events once thought suitable only for men, such as weightlifting, judo, and wrestling.

Women's sports are supported by various organizations. These include the Korean Amateur Athletic Association (KAAA); the Sport Association; the Korean Alliance for Health, Physical Education, Recreation, and Dance (KAHPERD); and the Korean Physical Education Association for Women (KWPEA).

THE SPORT FOR ALL MOVEMENT

Historically, woman's participation in life sports began officially in 1920, with the founding of the Chosun (the former name of Korea) Physical Education Association. Until the late 1950s, however, women's sports remained undeveloped. When South Korea was developing economically in the 1960s and 1970s, women had little opportunity to participate in sports. However, with South Korea's emergence as an industrial nation and the resulting increase in leisure time, South Koreans have developed a greater awareness of sports. In 1982, the Ministry of Sport was founded to prepare for the 1988 Seoul Olympic Games and to develop sports. At the same time, the Sports and Physical Education Promotion Law was enacted, making provisions for government support of life sports for the entire population.

THE FUTURE

With educational change, economic development, and changing political ideology have come changes in women's roles and in the way girls and women think about their futures. Most girls aspire to professional status, with specialized jobs, and, like boys, they also want to be involved in sports and other physical activities.

A national survey showed that between 1985 and 1995, the percentage of women participating in sport increased from 18.6 percent to 44.9 percent. The most popular sports are now swimming, aerobics, badminton, and bowling. The reasons women gave for their involvement in sports included an awareness of the need for physical activity, better management of leisure time, a desire for a positive and active way of life, and better health.

Young-Il Na
Chung-Hae Hahm

Bibliography

Committee of Reformation on Education. (1996) *A Plan for Establishment of New Education System.* Seoul, Korea.

Han, Yang-soon. (1989) "Woman and Sport." *Journal of Korean Physical Education Association for Women* 3: 3–22.

Jo, Mea-Hae. (1996) *A Research of the Curriculum for Classified by Level in PE.* The Seminar of the Association of Korea Sport Pedagogy.

Korea Sport Science Institute. (1997) *Sport Indicators of Korea*. Seoul, Korea.

SPAIN

Spain, located in southwestern Europe, has a population of about 40 million. The social and political changes that occurred in nineteenth- and twentieth-century Spain were often dramatic and of such importance that they influenced all areas of Spanish life, including sports, and all segments of the population. As for sports, we can identify three major periods. The first extends from the reign of Ferdinand VII (1808 to 1833) to the beginning of the Civil War (1936). The second corresponds to the Franco dictatorship (the end of the Civil War in 1939 to Francisco Franco's death in 1975). The third extends from 1975 to the present.

1808–1936

In the first period, women's physical education was highly conditioned by conceptions of womanhood. During the eighteenth and nineteenth centuries, women were expected to be wives and mothers, and their education was directed toward this end. Beliefs about femininity drew further limits around a woman's education. Women were thought to be delicate, sensitive, fragile, and unsuited for strenuous thought or strenuous physical activity. Prejudices of the medical community and the requirements of modesty also stifled the few attempts that were made to establish physical education for girls.

At its best, such education was no more than a simple project in the minds of the more progressive primary school and physical education teachers. Some voices were raised in support of physical education for girls, like those of Dr. Jose Fraguas, author of *Historia de la Gimnástica Higiénica y Médica* (A History of Hygenic and Medical Gymnastics) and *Tratado Racional de Gimnástica y de los Ejercicios y Juegos Corporales* (Rational Treatise of Corporal Exercises and Games), who called for development of women's physical education. For the most part, however, his call was ignored. In practice, Spanish girls' schools during the second half of the nineteenth century did not include exercise or athletic skills of any sort in their curricula; women's physical education was limited to instruction in hygiene.

In 1883, there was a small change in policy when the Central School of Theoretical and Practical Gymnastic Teachers was established at the University of Madrid. It opened in 1887 with students of both sexes (an unusual policy for the time). The short-lived school closed for financial reasons in 1892.

It was not until the end of the nineteenth and beginning of the twentieth century that urban middle-class women began to participate in gymnastics and sports. It was at this time that the first sports clubs were founded in Madrid, Barcelona, and other cities, and sports such as golf, skiing, skating, and lawn tennis began to attract upper-class and middle-class women.

However, the practice of sports by women was still limited to a privileged minority, and it was not until the 1920s and 1930s that women's participation became fairly widespread. The most outstanding among the sportswomen of the period was the tennis player Lily Alvarez, the first Spanish woman to participate in European and world competitions. In 1926 she took part in the Wimbledon tournament, was a finalist in the two following years, and won the French Open doubles final in 1929. She also skied (she was Spanish champion in 1941) and motored.

1939–1975

The second period in the development of women's sports coincided with Franco's regime (1939–1975) and was firmly marked by his personality. The dictator's essential characteristic was an obsession with stability. The freedom that had been characteristic of the previous period was replaced by a policy that made it necessary to obtain governmental authorization for practically all types of activity. The mass media and the educational system were used to inculcate the regime's conservative ideas and values. In order to suitably socialize the young, teaching about the importance of the (Roman Catholic) Church and the Falange (the Spanish Fascist party) was incorporated into the curriculum.

On 22 February 1941 Franco signed a decree creating the National Delegation of Sports of the

ARANTXA SANCHEZ VICARIO

The best known female Spanish athlete (and perhaps best known Spanish athlete around the world in the 1990s) is the tennis player Arantxa Sanchez Vicario. Born in Barcelona on 18 December 1971, Sanchez Vicario is a member of an international tennis family, with brothers Emilio and Javier playing on the men's professional tour. Sanchez Vicario has been the most successful of the three, winning four Grand Slam singles titles (French Open 1989, 1994, 1998; and U.S. Open 1994), nine Grand Slam doubles titles, and 28 tour singles titles. She has also represented Spain in the Federation Cup, Hopman Cup, and Olympics. In 1994 she was ranked the number-one woman tennis player in the world.

Traditionalist Falange and the Juntas of the National Syndicalist Offensive (JONS). The decree entrusted the "direction and promotion of Spanish sport" to the Falange. The Women's Section of the Falange pursued the attainment of the "ideal" woman and considered physical education to be a means of achieving this end. Approved physical activities were Swedish (Ling) gymnastics, folk dancing, and sports considered suitable for women—especially volleyball, basketball, and team handball. Swimming, tennis, skiing, mountaineering, and field hockey were also approved. Other sports such as boxing, cycling, and certain track and field events were prohibited because they were thought incompatible with a woman's role as wife and mother.

The Isabel la Católica Teacher Training Academy was established as the center for training female teachers to teach physical education to girls. The programs were deeply imbued with Falangist ideology. All schools in Spain had a teacher from the Women's Section, who, as well as physical education, taught home crafts and "formation of the national spirit." The approach was supported by physicians who provided "scientific" justification.

Tennis player Arantxa Sanchez Vicario in action at the French Open in 1995. (Ales Fevzer/Corbis)

1975–THE PRESENT

At the close of the 1960s, Spanish society began to change as modernization took hold and government control weakened, a process that culminated with the death of Franco. As part of decentralization, the Women's Section was closed and the sports institutions became responsible for both women's and men's sports. The Isabel la Católica Academy closed as well, and female physical education teachers were thereafter trained in the National Institutes of Physical Education, which are coeducational universities without any government-defined ideology. Primary and secondary schools adopted coeducation, which implied the beginning of the recognition of equal rights in education.

The most important event in this period was the Barcelona Olympics in 1992. The 1992 Olympic year had already begun in an important way for Spanish sportswomen, as Blanca Fernández Ochoa won a bronze medal in the slalom at the Winter Olympics in Albertville. To this medal were added those awarded in Barcelona: Miriam Blasco and Almudena Muñoz in judo; Teresa Zabell, Patricia Guerra, and Natalia Via Dufresne in yachting; the women's field hockey team; Carolina Pascual in rhythmic gymnastics; Arantxa Sánchez Vicario and Conchita Martínez in tennis; and Sánchez Vicario with her second medal, this time a bronze, also in tennis. In the 1990s, Arantxa Sánchez Vicario was Spain's best-known sportswoman and one of the best tennis players in the world. In 1996, ninety-four women on the Olympic team, though less than a quarter of the team, demonstrated that Spanish women were continuing to participate in competitive athletics.

Teresa González Aja

Bibliography

Amar y Borbón, Josefa. (1994) *Discurso sobre la educación física y moral de las mujeres.* Madrid: Cátedra.

Mujer y deporte. (1986) Madrid: Ministerio de Cultura.

Mujer y deporte. (1989) Madrid: Ayuntament de Barcelona.

Pajarón, Rocío. (1987) *La Educación Física en la Mujer en España.* Madrid: Universidad Autónoma.

SPECIAL OLYMPICS

The Special Olympics International (SOI) is a not-for-profit organization serving people with mental retardation. The SOI provides year-round sports, training, and competition for athletes all over the world, age eight or older, who are mentally retarded. Girls and women have always participated in the SOI.

HISTORY

The Special Olympics was founded by Eunice Kennedy Shriver in 1968 to give people with mental retardation opportunities to participate and compete in athletics. At the time, the common belief in American society was that these athletes could not master the physical and social skills needed for competition. Shriver believed otherwise and, with the help of the Kennedy Foundation and the Chicago Park District, organized the first International Special Olympics Games in Chicago, Illinois, during the summer of 1968. More than 1,000 athletes from twenty-six states and Canada competed in track and field, floor hockey, and aquatics during these historic games. The first international Winter Games got its start at Steamboat, Colorado, in 1977, with more than 500 athletes competing in skiing and skating events.

The SOI mission is "to provide year-around sports and athletic competition in a variety of Olympic-type sports for individuals with mental retardation by giving them continuing opportunities to develop physical fitness, demonstrate courage, experience joy and participate in the sharing of gifts, skills, and friendship with their families, other Special Olympics athletes and the community."

The SOI has grown in the years since its inauguration at Chicago's Soldier Field into a worldwide organization that serves over 1 million athletes with mental retardation in twenty-four different sports in Summer and Winter Games. Summer sports include aquatics, track and field, basketball, bowling, cycling, equestrian sports, golf, gymnastics, roller skating, sailing, soccer, softball, tennis, and volleyball. Winter sports include Alpine and cross-country skiing, figure skating, sailing, floor hockey, and speed skating. Badminton, bocce, powerlifting, table tennis, and team handball are included as demonstration sports. Each of the twenty-four sports is open for female participation. The Special Olympics ensures a level playing field among competitors by placing athletes in divisions based on their age, gender, and ability. The SOI World Games are held every two years (alternating Summer and Winter Games) in various countries. The 1999 SOI Summer World Games were based in North Carolina, in the United States. The International Olympic Committee (IOC) formally recognized the SOI in 1988 and, as it had not done for other international games for people with disabilities (for example, the Deaf Olympics and the Paralympics), granted permission to use the prestigious word "Olympic" in its name.

Shrivern developed the Special Olympics into one of the largest amateur athletic organizations in the world. Females with mental retardation have competed in the Special Olympics since its founding. More than 150 countries have SOI programs, with thousands of females volunteering as coaches, administrators, and officials. All sports are available for female athletes in these games. They compete at the local, state, regional, national and international levels. Loretta Claiborne of the United States, a track and field athlete, is one of the most outstanding athletes ever to compete in the Special Olympics. She has been inducted in the National Girls and Women in Sport Symposium Hall of Fame. Claiborne also serves on the SOI board of directors and is an accomplished public speaker.

Through the SOI, Shriver has been instrumental in developing programs that will increase opportunities in team sports for female athletes with mental retardation. For example, the SOI has established a grant program aimed at team development. Women and girls who compete in Special Olympic Games (worldwide) benefit from the grant money. The grants are given to state and national Special Olympic organizations, which implement the grant initiatives in partnership with local nonprofit organizations and/or sport federations. Officials at the SOI anticipate that the grant will lead to an increase in the number of women participating in team sports, particularly basketball, soccer, and volleyball. More recently, the SOI hosted the first all-female Special Olympics football (soccer) tournament in Mexico. Women and girls with mental retardation continue to participate in the SOI at all levels of competition. The SOI also encourages females to become involved as coaches, officials, administrators, and volunteers.

CONCLUSION

The Special Olympics International has filled a need that other sports programs have not addressed: to provide a chance at competitive athletics for people with mental retardation. The benefits, however, have spread beyond these individuals and influenced how many people view individuals with mental retardation.

Rebecca A. Clark

See also Deaf Olympics; Disability Sport; Goalball

Bibliography

DePauw, Karen P., and Susan J. Gavron. (1995) *Disability and Sport.* Champaign, IL: Human Kinetics.

Haskins, James. (1976) *A New Kind of Joy—The Story of the Special Olympics.* Garden City, NY: Doubleday.

Special Olympics International Fact Sheet. (1998) Washington, DC: Special Olympic International.

SPECTATORS

Anthropologists have documented the presence of women at the sports events of preliterate peoples in Africa and the Americas. Since women gathered to watch the Nuba wrestle in Sudan and to cheer the stickball players of the Creek and Cherokee tribes in North America, they probably behaved similarly at the dawn of Western civilization, but we know very little about female sports spectators before Greek and Roman antiquity.

Uncertainty remains, too, about the presence of women at the Greek athletic festivals celebrated at Olympia, Delphi, Corinth, and Nemea. From these sacred games, married women were barred, even as spectators. It is probable, but not certain, that unmarried women were also barred. (At Olympia, however, an exception was made for the priestess of the fertility goddess Demeter.) It is also probable that women attended the maidens' race at the games celebrated at Olympia in honor of the goddess Hera.

About Roman spectators we know a great deal, most of it unpleasant. Graffiti found in Pompeii and the satires of the second century CE poet Juvenal agree that girls and matrons not only admired but also fell madly in love with gladiators. The first-century poet Catullus urged women to "go and look at the [gladiatorial] games, where the sands are sprinkled with blood." Women did, indeed, throng to the arena to watch the deadly combats. Before the time of the emperor Augustus, men and women sat together, but he separated them and confined women to the back rows of the arena. At the chariot races that were the most popular sport of Roman and Byzantine civilization, the sexes were not segregated. Female fans of the two main competing chariot teams also joined the men in the bloody riots that frequently accompanied chariot races in Constantinople, Antioch, and Alexandria.

A WOMEN-ONLY CROWD (1896)

A description of the game between Stanford and Berkely, at which no male spectators were allowed

In this connection it should be set on record that there appeared to be no predominant type of woman among the spectators. There were old women, and young women, and short-haired women, and long-haired women, and pretty women, and plain women, and new women and—well, there may have been middle-aged women. But the really remarkable thing about them was the immense volume of noise they managed to create. It did one good to hear their cheers, and "bravos," and excited comments on the play. And as for the players themselves, they were simply vociferous. Their animal spirits would have been an object lesson to half the young men in San Francisco. Why, when the Stanford girls retired to their dressing-room after winning the game, nothing would content them but to turn handsprings on the floor—and fine, workmanlike handsprings they were.

The Examiner. *(1896). "Players Won by a Goal." San Francisco. April 5.11–20*

Women of a more peaceful sort were welcomed at medieval and Renaissance tournaments. Medieval romances by the poets Chrétien de Troyes, Wolfram von Eschenbach, and Sir Thomas Mallory mentioned women's presence at French, German, and English tournaments. An anonymous thirteenth-century poem, "The Key to Love," notes that young men flock to tournaments because they are places where "many a fancy wench abounds." There were ladies in abundance, too. According to the conventions of chivalry, it was for them that the knights jousted. Isabella and Joanna, the daughters of Edward III of England, made their first recorded public appearance at a tournament in Dunstaple in 1342. To make the princesses' gorgeously embroidered robes, eighteen workers were employed for nine days. The workers, who used eleven ounces of gold, were supervised by the king's armorer. It must have seemed, to medieval readers, only a small exaggeration when the French poet Eustache des Champs, writing of a tournament held in 1389, likened the female spectators to "angels of paradise." In the many medieval and Renaissance works of art that depict, in the foreground, knights at their violent play, women appear in the background in seats of honor. Two fine examples of this are a fifteenth-century painting by Domenico Morone and a sixteenth-century woodcut by Lucas Cranach.

Women were also present among the dead and injured when the wooden grandstands erected at tournament sites collapsed, which they did alarmingly often. John Stow's *Survey of London* records one such collapse in 1331; the ladies fell from above and injured "knights and such as were underneath." Ralph Holinshed's chronicles reported a similar accident at Westminster in 1581, in which "many of the beholders, men as well as women, were sore hurt, some maimed, and some killed."

Large numbers of women were also attracted by the colorful pageantry and exciting contests of the great archery tournaments that were the favorite sports spectacles of the nascent Renaissance bourgeoisie. Occasionally, especially in Flanders and Holland, the women were the archers as well as the spectators.

That the sports of the sixteenth and seventeenth centuries were often quite violent seemed not to bother the allegedly weaker sex. Elizabeth I of England, who was in her youth an accomplished hunter, delighted in bear-baits. In fact, her enthusiasm for these bloody combats between dogs and a chained bear was so great that she ordered London's theaters not to stage plays

Two women from Michigan watch the first U.S. National Senior Olympics, held in St. Louis, Missouri, in July 1987. (ChromoSohm/Corbis)

on Thursdays. The performances interfered with the bear-baits "which are maintained for her Majesty's pleasure." European visitors to Elizabethan London noted that ordinary Englishwomen shared their monarch's love of this pastime. A century later, John Houghton observed that a passion for bear-baits was still evident among aristocratic ladies as well as lower-class women. In 1670, when John Evelyn attended a bull-bait, "One of the bulls tossed a dog full into a lady's lap, as she sat in one of the boxes at a considerable height from the arena." Horse races also attracted huge numbers of spectators, male and female alike. During the period of Puritan rule, from 1649 to 1660, horse races were banned, but they achieved unprecedented popularity when Charles II was restored to the throne. The races that he sponsored at Newmarket, near London, attracted mostly male spectators, but women were strongly represented at the great races that were highlights of the eighteenth-century social season.

Although Charles Dickens and other observers noted a great deal of rowdy behavior and petty crime at nineteenth-century races, women seem not to have been deterred from attendance. There is every reason to believe that William Powell Frith's colorful painting, *Derby Day at Epsom* (1858), is a realistic rendering of an event that attracted hawkers, vendors, gypsy fortunetellers, acrobats, minstrels, gamblers, pickpockets, and all sorts of ordinary folk eager for a day at the races. If Frith was a reliable observer, girls were as much a presence as boys. We know from the accounts of Zacharias Conrad von Uffenbach and other European visitors to England that lower-class women were among the spectators at eighteenth-century boxing and wrestling matches. One of these hardened women told Uffenbach proudly that, two years earlier, wearing nothing but a shift, she had fought another woman in bare-knuckles combat. (Female pugilism was, in fact, quite common in eighteenth-century London.)

During the nineteenth century, as sports events became increasingly commercialized, entrepreneurs looked for ways to rid themselves of the numerous ruffians whose violence endangered property and frightened middle-class spectators. The problem was acute in the United States. Once baseball was established as the "national game," which occurred shortly before the Civil War, middle-class support weakened and the percentage of female spectators dropped sharply. The ironmongers and teamsters who left work early on Saturday to head directly for the ballpark were seldom accompanied by their wives or girlfriends. Realizing and lamenting the fact that half the population was staying away from the game, the owners of baseball franchises made major efforts to entice women through the turnstiles. That there were turnstiles was important: they enabled the entrepreneurs to control the crowds. The newly formed National League decided in 1877 to charge 50 cents for admission to the ballpark, an extra 10 cents for a seat in the bleachers, and an extra 25 cents for a seat in the grandstand, where ladies were assured of comfort and safety. When the directors of British soccer clubs constructed permanent stadiums early in the twentieth century, they adopted the same tactic. Until very recently, these grounds were divided between the covered stands, where middle-class men and women paid to sit, and the terraces, where working-class fans—most male—paid to stand and cheer. It is a sign of globalization that the Japanese adopted the same solution at almost the same time—not for ball games, but for sumo matches.

Another entrepreneurial tactic, especially popular among the owners of baseball teams, was the announcement of "Ladies' Day." Beginning in 1867, the Knickerbocker Base-Ball Club declared the last Thursday of each month to be a time when members of the club were to bring their wives, daughters, and girlfriends to the game. The ladies were admitted free if accompanied by a "gentleman" (defined as a paying male). The *New York Chronicle* greeted this innovation and opined that "the presence of an assemblage of ladies purifies the moral atmosphere" and represses "all the outburst of intemperate language which the excitement of the contest so frequently induces." Some journalists expressed fond hopes that the women whom the rowdies had once frightened away might yet become the means by which the rowdies were introduced to the code of quiet good sportsmanship. Such hopes may not have been utterly foolish. Between 1919 and 1939, when the number of female soccer spectators increased, the incidence of violence at British soccer matches decreased. Among the soccer hooligans that plagued British and European soccer in the 1970s and 1980s, there were very few young women.

On the whole, however, various efforts to attract female spectators to professional ball games have been only moderately successful. Numerous sociological studies indicate that women are still underrepresented as fans of baseball and the various "codes" of professional football (soccer, rugby, American football, etc.). Women are, on the other hand, likely to be present in large numbers at all sports—including American football—whose principal venue is the relatively protected environment of a college campus. The concern for protection was often extreme. At the first women's intercollegiate basketball game on 4 April 1896 (Stanford versus Berkeley), all the spectators were female because men were banned from the audience. Except for the college's aged president, male spectators were also prohibited from attending Smith College's intramural games. Well into the 1920s, female physical educators, fearful of "voyeurism," were adamant about excluding male spectators.

Women have always been attracted by the Oxford–Cambridge boat race, first contested in 1829. (The race was actually held at Henley on the Thames, but the crowd was overwhelmingly composed of "respectable" young people.) Harvard and Yale had their first regatta in 1852 at New Hampshire's Lake Winnepesaukee. Male and female spectators with connections to one or the other college came by rail from Boston and New Haven. Similarly, intercollegiate football weekends have always been coed social events as well as sports contests. Female spectators of college age no longer sport the raccoon coats and hip flasks of F. Scott Fitzgerald's day, but they continue to be an indispensable part of "the big game."

In the bleachers women get a suntan along with their bargain tickets at a 1945 baseball game. (Bettmann/Corbis)

Country clubs are another place where women have always felt free to watch as well as to participate in sports. The first such club was the Brookline Country Club, founded in 1882 to allow Boston's elite to amuse themselves without unwelcome intrusions by the mostly Irish American lower classes. The classic country club, however, was the All-England Croquet and Lawn-Tennis Club in suburban Wimbledon. There the code of spectatorship was perfected. While the tennis players, dressed in white to symbolize their distance from dirty work, served and volleyed, polite silence was to be broken only by applause for a well-played point. In actuality, the code was often violated. *Outing* magazine reported in 1885 that the female spectators were vociferous supporters of the handsome William Renshaw. Whenever he scored a point, they "clapped their hands loudly, stamped their feet and pounded on the floor with their parasols most vigorously."

At Spa, at Bad Homburg—wherever nineteenth-century European aristocrats spent their summers—tennis was the fashionable game for both sexes to play and for both sexes to watch. The spatial requirements of golf required too much movement for the game to become a popular spectator sport before the age of television (and it still lags far behind tennis among television audiences).

TELEVISED SPORTS

Although the Olympic Games of 1936 were the first televised sports event, television did not become a mass phenomenon until the postwar period. The medium transformed sports spectatorship. Women of all social classes were, in theory, able to follow sports that had previously been inaccessible. In fact, upper-class women seldom watched the boxing matches that were the mainstay of television sports in the 1950s. (They did, however, with suitable escorts, appear at ringside for highly publicized heavyweight championships.) Televised tennis matches, which became common in the 1970s, failed to interest lower-class women, who lacked the opportunity actually to play the game.

As a rule, women are less likely than men to be fans of televised sports, but the predominance of male viewers should not be exaggerated. Sociological studies done at various times and in various places throughout the modern world have found some 50 percent of all women (as compared to approximately 75 percent of all men) claim to be regular consumers of televised sports. Although the popular stereotype pictures husbands mesmerized by the World Series, the Super Bowl, or the World Cup while their resentful wives prepare dinner, women are a large percentage of the audience for men's sports. In the United States, roughly one-third of the fans of televised baseball are female; in Germany, soccer is "seen gladly" by 86 percent of the men and a surprising 52 percent of the women.

One reason that women are generally less likely than men to watch TV sports is that the events most frequently televised are those that appeal more to men than to women. When figure skaters and the gymnasts appear on screen instead of baseball and soccer players, female spectators comprise a majority of the audience. This sociological fact is frequently forgotten by the many psychologists who have studied the viewing habits of male and female sports fans. The psychologists have found that men pay closer attention to televised sports and are better informed about the players. This frequently reported finding is misleading because it is based on male and female responses to sports favored by men. It is likely that female viewers are more attentive to and more knowledgeable about the esthetic sports—like figure skating and diving—that most interest them. Women's enthusiasm for figure skating probably accounts for the fact that it is by a wide margin the most popular sport of the Winter Olympics.

Allen Guttmann

Bibliography

Guttmann, Allen. (1986) *Sports Spectators*. New York: Columbia University Press.

SPEEDBALL

Speedball is a sport that is part soccer, part football, and part basketball. It was designed to be free of physical contact and to emphasize the constant movement of the ball. The sport is not played much anymore, but when popular in the 1930s, it was played more by females than males—in all likelihood because it was one of the few sports open to women. Today it has almost disappeared, replaced by sports once played exclusively by men.

HISTORY

Speedball was invented in 1921 by Elmer D. Mitchell, the director of intramural sports at the University of Michigan. He meant it to serve as a fall sport for average students as well as more serious athletes and to fill the gap in the schedule between the winter sport of basketball and the spring sport of baseball. Sports historians do not agree about whether Mitchell intended the sport to be played by boys only or by boys and girls. By the 1930s, however, more females than males were playing speedball, probably because women in colleges and high schools had fewer sports opportunities than did men.

Speedball caught on because it was inexpensive, could be played on fields used for other sports such as soccer or field hockey, and was a safe form of exercise. It also required neither a great deal of athletic ability nor a great deal of instruction or practice. However, players had to develop a mix of skills, including kicking, catching, and passing, and early advocates of the sport thought that this mix of skills would make it appeal to a wide range of students.

The sport was widely adopted. Colleges and universities in the Midwest added it to their physical education programs and intramural sports, and it then spread across the United States. Outside the Midwest it was probably most popular in California, where high school students also played, and least popular in the East, where it failed to displace field hockey as the preferred sport for girls and young women. As a sport that required little in the way of special equipment or great athletic skill, it also was adopted by industrial and governmental recreation programs.

However, its appeal as a men's sport was short-lived. By the end of the 1930s speedball had been dropped as a recreational sport for men at many colleges, it disappeared as a high school sport in the 1940s, and by the 1950s it had disappeared altogether as a sport for men. By that time, soccer and flag football had joined basketball and baseball as the most popular recreational sports for boys and men.

From the mid-1930s on, and perhaps even earlier, speedball was probably more popular with girls and young women, and physical educators in high schools and colleges promoted it actively. Rules for women were codified in 1935 in the *Women's Soccer and Speedball Rulebook*, and that helped the sport spread from the Midwest across the nation. Speedball remained an important game for girls and women until the 1960s, when it was replaced by soccer. It has largely disappeared since then, although some college physical education programs still offer it as an elective.

RULES AND PLAY

Speedball is played with teams of from seven to eleven players each, who, through a combination of kicking, passing, and dribble-steps, try to advance the ball toward the goal line. They score points by kicking the ball into the goal or though the goalposts, catching it in the end zone, or kicking out of the end zone. The game is played in four periods of 10 minutes each at the college level and 8 minutes each at the high school level. The rules are slightly different for men and women, with women using a shorter field. Scoring also differs slightly, with women getting more points (2 to 1) for scoring touchdowns and men getting more points for most types of scores by kicks through or over the goalposts. The game also has some unique features: a player can pass or kick the ball to herself and can only play a grounded ball with her feet.

In the 1990s speedball for women has disappeared as females in high school and college across the United States now play soccer, basketball, softball, hockey, and other sports that were formerly reserved mostly for men.

The Editors

Bibliography

Mott, Jane A. (1972) *Soccer and Speedball for Women.* Dubuque, IA: C. Brown Co.

National Association for Girls and Women in Sport (NAGWS) Guide. (1980–1982) *Flag Football, Speedball, Speed-a-Way.* Reston, VA: American Alliance for Health, Physical Education, Recreation and Dance.

SPEEDBOATING

Speedboating is a varied sport that includes recreational and competitive activities in motorized watercraft. Competitive events range from local or regional meets to national and international championship competitions. The sport includes inland activities on lakes or rivers and offshore activities on the ocean and bays. Although men have been predominant in the sport, women also participate in speedboating on many levels, including female drivers who have gained championship status in mixed-gender competition.

Speedboating became a recognized sport following the invention of the internal combustion engine late in the nineteenth century. As the design of boats and engines became more diverse and sophisticated, the number of branches of the sport increased. Speedboating (also known as powerboating and other more specific designations) is divided into categories based on the type of activity and on specifications for the size and design of a boat's engine and body. Basic body categories include boats with angled V-shaped hulls, flatter-hulled hydroplanes, multihulled "cat" boats, and small personal watercraft such as jet-skis.

Among the most successful early woman powerboat racers was Marion ("Joe") Carstairs (1900–1993), an American-born heiress who raced internationally in the 1920s and early 1930s. She became well known for both her racing prowess and her colorful personality. During her career, she financed and supervised the construction of the hydroplanes she raced and as a driver won many races in competition with males, including the 1926 Royal Motor Yacht Club International. She also established a world speed record of the time for a 1.5-liter powerboat. Carstairs retired from active racing in the early 1930s and moved to an island in the British West Indies, where she lived until her death.

High-speed offshore powerboat racing (which had been eclipsed by inland races) experienced a resurgence in the 1960s, with the development of boats capable of maintaining both high speeds and more stability on choppy open water. Betty Cook, an American, was a significant figure in this aspect of the sport. She took up off-shore racing in the early 1970s, when she was in her fifties. Cook rose quickly as a competitive driver, setting many precedents for overall speed and accomplishments in offshore racing. Cook won numerous races and titles, including Union Internationale Motonautique (UIM) world championships in 1977 and 1979, and she was a three-time U.S. national champion between 1978 and 1982. Cook was also active in the technical side of the sport, helping to develop designs to improve the speed and efficiency of modern powerboats. Among other honors, she was inducted into the Motorsports Museum and Hall of Fame in Novi, Michigan. Cook died in 1990 at age sixty-seven.

In the 1970s, hydroplane driver Mary Rife established the official powerboat speed record for a woman, of 197 (317 kilometers) miles per hour, and she achieved faster unofficial speeds, according to the 1998 *Guinness Book of World Records.* As the technology has improved and the diversity of motorized watercraft has increased, new classes and forms of competition emerged over the later years of the twentieth century.

John Townes

Bibliography

Summerscale, Kate. (1998) *The Queen of Whale Cay.* New York: Viking.

SPONSORSHIP

Sponsorship is the term used to describe corporate support for a sporting event. Companies, many of which produce goods related to sports, fund the event in return for the positive publicity generated by having their name attached to it. They may also use sponsorship as a way to market to their target audience.

Some corporate sponsorship has been around for years. Avon was an early sponsor of women's running events at a time when women runners had few venues for competition. The Virginia Slims tennis tournament is another example. In tennis, Virginia Slims enabled the Women's Tennis Association (WTA) to provide a quality professional tournament unlike any before it. Yet the women's sport with the longest history of sponsorship is women's golf. In 1949 the Ladies Professional Golf Players Association (LPGPA) was created largely because of involvement by golf manufacturers. By 1950 the LPGPA had been renamed the Ladies Professional Golf Association (LPGA) and nine tournaments had been held. By the end of the 1950s, more than twenty tournaments were offered and prize money totaled $200,000. Over the years, the LPGA has grown phenomenally because of financial support from sponsors, both for tournaments and for individual players. By 1997, total prize money for the forty-three tournaments held was more than $30 million.

The most significant impact of corporate involvement on sports as of 1999 occurred with the 1984 Olympic Games. In an effort to finance the 1984 Games, the Los Angeles Olympic Organizing Committee looked to corporate America. Coca-Cola was reported to have paid $3 million for the privileged title of "official soft drink" of the Los Angeles Olympics. A transition in sponsorship had occurred between the 1976 Montreal Games and the 1984 Los Angeles Games. Montreal had incurred an enormous financial burden by hosting the games. Therefore, the Los Angeles Olympic Organizing Committee negotiated deals for corporate sponsorship of the Games, and this changed the course of sports. Some of the deals negotiated for the 1984 Olympics included: Anheuser-Busch ($11 million), Buick Motors ($5 million), Coca-Cola ($15 million), Levi-Strauss ($8 million), and McDonalds ($9 million plus a swim stadium). For the first time virtually everything was for sale, including television rights, commercials, product licensing, product exclusivity, training center support, product endorsements, and anything else a marketing person could devise.

Before Coca-Cola's revolutionary commitment to sports, corporations were having increasing difficulty developing marketing niches. During the 1980s they competed intensely in marketing and promotion, competition made necessary by the glut of information put before consumers. The Los Angeles Olympic Organizing Committee created opportunities for companies to exchange cash, goods, or services for use of the Olympics as a communication and marketing tool. Companies were quick to take advantage of the chance to advertise and promote their products via the Olympic platform. As a result, the 1984 Olympics generated a "profit" of $230 million and the 1984 Games became known as the "corporate Olympics."

The number of companies that became involved in sponsorship and the profit generated from the 1984 Olympics created a new problem of clutter in sport sponsorship. As a result of this overabundance of advertising and sponsorship, the International Olympic Committee (IOC) signed a contract in 1985 with the Lausanne-based agency, International Sport and Leisure (ISL). The result was The Olympic Programme (TOP). This system limited the number of sponsors, improved the benefits, and brought in much more money from sponsors. TOP proved successful in 1988, with research indicating "significant improvements in product image" for TOP members. The result for the IOC was more than $120 million from nine corporate sponsors. By 1992 the IOC had increased the number of allowed companies to twelve, and each sponsor was required to make a commitment of at least $10 million. For the 1996 Summer Games, Olympic officials asked for $40 million from each company, ten times what a 1984 sponsor contributed.

Due in part to the success of the highly publicized Olympic sponsorship programs, corporate sponsorship of sports flourished. Today sports marketing has become a major business. In 1987, sports was the twenty-third largest industry in the United States, totaling $50.2 billion a year. By 1990 corporate sponsorship had become the fastest-growing element of a $63.1 billion gross national sports product. As a result, corporations have been inundated with hundreds of sports sponsorship proposals annually. As the Olympic example has revealed, corporate support of sporting events has continued to grow at a phenomenal rate. Consequently, it has become essential for marketers to understand the process and unique opportunities available through sports sponsorship.

While this brief history has focused on sponsorship at the professional and international levels, it is important to note that sponsorship opportunities are increasing at all levels of sports. Businesses have supported nonprofit organizations through sponsorship of youth leagues, tournaments, and contests, as well as paying for signage on local ball fields and basketball courts. Organizations such as state athletic associations, school associations, school districts, and even individual school athletic programs are also looking to sponsorship as a solution to financial difficulties. Thus, sponsorship has truly become pervasive throughout sports.

RATIONALE FOR SPONSORSHIP

The many and varied corporations involved in sponsorship use equally varied rationales for their participation. Sports clearly have attributes that are attractive to corporate sponsors. For example, the image of products, services, or brands can be enhanced when a company aligns itself with the positive characteristics of a sporting event or successful athletes. Sports sponsorship is flexible, too, providing such opportunities as licensing, merchandising, cross-promotions, and dealer incentives, all of which have been developed and used. Sports sponsorship has also reached specific target markets in a more direct and cost-effective way than traditional forms of mass advertising. These factors, plus its usefulness in differentiating each company from the competition, has made sports sponsorship a unique vehicle.

TRENDS IN SPORTS SPONSORSHIP

Over time, companies have sponsored sport for various reasons. Typically, corporations have established well-documented criteria in their sponsorship plans. The most important of these include: affinity factor (image desired through association with a sport product), sanctioning organization, potential for merchandising, potential for press coverage, growth trend, timing, current sponsors, match between products and event, potential for important contacts, legal restrictions, and risks. In the 1990s, sponsors' primary objective was to increase their market share or sales.

MARKETING TO WOMEN THROUGH SPORT

Meeting a company's marketing objectives remains the primary reason sponsors are attracted to sports. Organizations selling a sports product are in the business of trying to attract a large audience/consumer base. Attracting more fans through major events has been an important goal of professional and college sports teams. As a result, companies have become involved in sports and/or event marketing because they expect the events to reach their desired audience through the fan base.

Traditionally, children were introduced to sports by parents. Marketers have acknowledged that children who watch and take part in sports often grow up to become sports spectators. Parents play a key role in children's interest in sports. As a result, companies have become more interested in addressing mothers through their marketing efforts.

Among the sports with a large female following, stock car racing, the Women's National Basketball Association (WNBA), and professional soccer have been especially successful in attracting sponsors and advertisers. Since the early 1980s, the number of knowledgeable female fans has increased significantly, due in part to improved opportunities for women in competitive sports. Consequently, corporations have begun to pay more attention to this market.

One of the difficulties corporations face in trying to develop this target audience is that the female audience is not a homogeneous one. Age, occupation, and family status are just three characteristics on which women vary. Typically, advertising and promotions have treated women as part of the family demographic. Thus, companies that sell grocery products and children's clothing, as well as car companies looking to promote their minivans, have used sponsorship of indoor soccer to reach the women who make such major decisions as what car to buy. In contrast, companies that want to sell products exclusively for women have been more interested in sports such as tennis or ice skating, whose audiences are close to 80 percent female.

Another example of women's sport marketing potential is female involvement in golf. Between 1980 and 1989, their participation increased from 30 percent to 37 percent, marking a trend that continued into the 1990s. From the companies' perspective, this is important because an increase in participants typically creates an increase in spectators and potential sponsors.

MARKET/MEDIA RELATIONSHIP WITH WOMEN'S SPORTS

Corporations have long realized that the media affects consumers' behavior. Therefore, marketing through events covered by the media adds value to their sponsorship. In the mid-1970s major corporations such as Colgate-Palmolive, Phillip Morris, L'eggs, Avon, and others decided to use women's sports as a vehicle for advertising their products. These sponsorships enabled specific women's tournaments to be covered on television. Initially, corporations were primarily willing to sponsor only socially acceptable women's sports, such as tennis, golf, figure skating, and gymnastics. Team and contact sports struggled for financial backing because of their nontraditional roles for women.

Intercollegiate basketball was the first amateur team sport to break through the stereotyping of television coverage. Previously, the National Collegiate Athletic Association (NCAA) Women's Basketball Final Four Championships received coverage on the same major network that covers the men's championships. However, in 1994 the cable network ESPN purchased the rights to cover the women's tournament, while the men's tournament was contracted with a separate network.

Improving the quality of women's sports, then, has resulted in better television coverage and more support from corporate sponsorship. Traditionally women were underrepresented in media coverage, and so corporations remained indifferent. However, as improvements in coverage have been made, spectators, consumers, and sponsors have also become more interested.

WOMEN'S PROFESSIONAL SPORTS

Compared to men, women have fewer sports in which to compete and the players generally earn less money. Many women professional athletes have depended on sponsorship or secondary careers to remain in competition. The most popular, and consequently the most successful, professional sports for women have been individual sports, particularly golf and tennis.

Gains have not come easily. Women have continually struggled to develop more professional opportunities for female athletes to pursue after college. Basketball has remained the most commonly offered sport in women's intercollegiate athletic programs. However, for most women the

CORPORATE SPONSORSHIP

Corporate sponsorship is the key ingredient in the commercialization and professionalization of sports. Men's sports draw far more sponsors because there are more male fans and athletes and also because the market of female fans is more heterogenous and more tied to specific sports than to sports in general. Nonetheless, for the past decade, more and more corporations have been sponsoring female sports through sponsorship of individual athletes; sponsorship of teams; financial support of facilities; sponsorship of events and annual tours; support of youth leagues and teams; marketing of events; provision of prize money; support of women's sport organizations; and support of their own women's sport programs.

opportunity to play professionally was limited until the late 1990s. In tandem with the success of the 1996 Women's Olympic team, two women's professional basketball leagues, the ABL (American Basketball League) and the WNBA, were formed. Each league completed successful seasons and was looking forward to continued support by corporate sponsors and fans. However, the ABL struggled to secure both television coverage and sufficient sponsorship; it ceased operations in December 1998. In contrast, the strength of the WNBA has been its excellent marketing and sponsorship record, influenced largely by its controlling interest, the National Basketball Association (NBA), which provides financial backing and marketing and management support.

Ice skating has long been a highly visible professional sport for women. The opportunities may be limited, but compensation has been very high for the featured skaters. Corporate sponsorship has also been more easily secured for figure skating because the skaters display socially acceptable female attributes—grace and beauty. Exceptional television ratings have added to figure skating's appeal to sponsors.

A variety of other, less visible professional sport opportunities also exist for women. Bowling, skiing, and beach volleyball have become possible avenues for a career in sports for a few female athletes. However, an athlete who takes part in them may spend more on sport-related expenses than she earns from the sport. Only those very highly skilled athletes with endorsements can earn a living as participants in these sports.

In addition to endorsing professional athletes, corporate sponsors provide prize money, tournament support, and assistance in the advertising of professional golf and tennis tournaments. Consistent television coverage is dependent upon sponsors buying advertising time. Otherwise, television coverage would most likely cease. The outlook for women considering a career in tennis or golf has been the most positive among all professional sports available to women. Both have been well established as professional sports for women and have received widespread public acceptance. Women's prize money has grown faster than men's, with increases of more than 3,000 percent recorded since the WTA was founded in 1973. In addition, television coverage of women's professional tennis and golf has been the most consistent of all women's sports covered.

Television coverage will be the next area in which women's professional sports will have to compete for equal standing. Television makes it possible for recreational participants to become spectators and, in turn, become consumers of sponsors' products. Today, television is a necessary ingredient for successful merchandising programs, as well as sales of corporate sponsorships. Television has become the primary source of revenue, earning governing bodies and event promoters hundreds of millions of dollars. Increasing interest and opportunity in women's sports has generated more market appeal, making marketing through women's sports a viable tool for many corporations. In addition, continuous increases in television coverage have created a market appeal that can only be expected to grow.

CORPORATE SPONSORSHIP OF INDIVIDUAL ATHLETES

High visibility remains the key to gaining a sponsor's interest. Companies have been less likely to spend money on women's sports because traditionally not enough people watched them. Companies support athletes who earn the public's respect and admiration by being top performers. In essence, companies try to "buy" that respect and link it with their image or product.

For a competitive athlete, corporate sponsorship and endorsement contracts have been the tangible payoffs for years of training. However, female athletes must have a combination of key elements to benefit from sponsorship. Being at the top of her sport does not insure financial support. Looks, personality, and intelligence need to be combined with high-visibility success for a female athlete to secure significant monetary reward. During 1992, Steffi Graf's $6 million package of sponsorship endorsements made her one of the most highly rewarded athletes in the world. Top golfers, such as Nancy Lopez, have also earned entry into the millionaire's club. Top performers in less popular sports like diving, rock climbing, and triathlon have been reported to make upward of $100,000 a year in endorsements from sponsors, although the number who do so is very low.

Every four years during the Olympic Games, women have their best opportunity in terms of endorsements. Mary Lou Retton set a high mark of over a million dollars following her 1984 gold medal performance in gymnastics. Earning potential has been impressive even for athletes in nontraditional sports during the Olympic Games. Bonnie Blair, despite the relative obscurity of speed skating, secured an estimated $100,000 in deals with Evian, Oakley, Xerox, Mizuno, Visa, Kraft, and Jeep/Chrysler before ever setting foot on the 1992 Olympic site. Nevertheless, an athlete who combines talent in a popular sport with extraordinary looks has a greater chance at more lucrative deals. The late Florence Griffith-Joyner amazed the world in 1988 with both her talent and her appearance. The result was post-Olympic endorsements estimated at several million dollars, uncommonly high for a track athlete.

CORPORATE SPONSORSHIP OF WOMEN'S SPORT

When event developers seek corporate sponsorship, physical appearance ceases to be an issue. Corporations that have become involved in sponsorship with groups such as the Women's Sports Foundation (WSF) have made substantial financial commitments based on common goals and access to potential consumers. Sudafed became the first national sponsor of the Women's Sports Foundation in 1993. They shared a commitment to supporting female athletes. Also in 1993, Reebok and the WSF became partners to create joint programs and services that would increase participation among women and girls in sports and fitness activities. Reebok became the second national sponsor of the WSF by supporting the foundation's mission through educational programs, grants, and recognition of athletic achievements.

UNIQUE ATTRIBUTES OF WOMEN'S SPORT SPONSORSHIP

For corporations, marketing to women via the athletic medium has become a valuable tool. As interest in women's sport continues to grow, marketing people must be prepared to establish women's sports properties and corporate packages to accommodate that interest. The growth and interest in women's sports has developed into a significant opportunity for corporate sponsorship. A corporate package may include tickets to the events, executive hospitality, privileged parking, scoreboard and public address announcements, and a variety of additional amenities.

In another example, Sara Lee committed $6 million to sponsor NCAA women's programs in 1990. Their stated goal was to provide better opportunities for women to pursue their academic and athletic aspirations. Even if sponsors are committed to promoting women, they still may not be interested in women's sport unless the proposal indicates that many women will be potential consumers of the company's products. Sponsors need to know specifics of how they will benefit from the sponsorship. Direct access to a certain number of potential buyers and users of their product, a position on the advisory board of the organization, premier seating or parking, free exhibit space, and other perquisites have been influential in sponsorship decisions.

CONCLUSION

With a sound mix of marketing and promotions, corporate sponsors have recognized a match of goals that creates a financially viable situation for both the sponsor and the women's sport. Nevertheless, marketing to women through women's sports has been considered cutting-edge strategy. Companies have started to cash in on the growing awareness and interest in women's athletics, and the vehicle has become more powerful and more recognizable.

Nancy L. Lough

Bibliography

Acosta, Vivian, and Linda Carpenter. (1994) *Women in Intercollegiate Sport, a Longitudinal Study—Seventeen Year Update.* Department of Physical Education, Brooklyn College, Brooklyn, NY.

Boutilier, Mary A., and Lucinda SanGiovanni. (1983) *The Sporting Woman.* Champaign, IL: Human Kinetics.

Brooks, Christine. (1990) "Sponsorship: Strictly Business." *Athletic Business* (October): 59–62.

Comte, E., and C. Stogel. (1990) "Sports: A $63.1 Billion Industry." *The Sporting News* (1 January): 60–61.

Ensor, Richard L. (1987) "The Corporate View of Sports Sponsorship." *Athletic Business* (September): 40–43.

Hofacre, Susan. (1994) "The Women's Audience in Professional Indoor Soccer." *Sports Marketing Quarterly* 3, 2: 25–27.

Hofacre, Susan, and Thomas Burman. (1992) "Demographic Changes in the U.S. into the Twenty-First

Century: Their Impact on Sport Marketing." *Sports Marketing Quarterly* 1, 1: 31–36.

Irwin, Richard L., and Linda Sutton. (1994) "Sport Sponsorship Objectives: An Analysis of Their Relative Importance for Major Corporate Sponsors." *European Journal for Sport Management* 1, 1: 93–101.

Junker, J. (1989) "Corporate Sponsorship of Special Events: A Case Study—The Sunkist Fiesta Bowl." *Leisure Industry Report* (August/September): 4–5.

Kuzma, John R., William L. Shanklin, and John F. McCally. (1993) "Number One Principle for Sporting Events Seeking Corporate Sponsors: Meet Benefactor's Objectives." *Sports Marketing Quarterly* 2, 3: 27–32.

Lehr, C.A., and M.A. Washington. (1987) "Beyond Women's Collegiate Athletics: Opportunities to Play for Pay." *Journal of Physical Education, Recreation and Dance* (March): 28–32.

Levin, S. (1992) "Spoils of Victory: Who Gets Big Money from Sponsors, and Why." *Women's Sports and Fitness* 14, 3: 63–69.

Meenaghan, Tony. (1991) "Sponsorship—Legitimizing the Medium." *European Journal of Advertising* 25, 11: 5–10.

Sandomir, R. (1988) "The $50 Billion Sports Industry." *Sports Inc.* (14 November): 11–23.

Shelton, Chris. (1991) "Funding Strategies for Women's Sports." *Journal of Physical Education, Recreation and Dance* (March): 51–54.

Stotlar, David K. (1989) *Successful Sport Marketing & Sponsorship Plans.* Dubuque, IA: Wm. C. Brown.

———. (1993) "Sponsorship and the Olympic Winter Games." *Sports Marketing Quarterly* 2, 1: 35–43.

Wilkinson, D. (1993) *Sponsorship Marketing: A Practical Reference Guide for Corporations in the 1990's.* Toronto: Wilkinson Group.

SPORT ASSOCIATION FOR ARAB WOMEN

The Sport Association for Arab Women was founded in Cairo, Egypt, in September 1996 under the auspices of the Arab League. The association was founded in recognition of the widely varying opportunities that women in Arab nations have to participate in sports. For example, in some nations, such as Egypt and Syria, women may take part in a variety of sports while in others, such as the United Arab Emirates, females may be active only as part of school physical education programs.

The mission of the association is to support the development of sports for Arab women by helping to establish a women's sports association in every Arab nation. The organization views participation in sport as beneficial to women and to society. The specific objectives include making women aware of sports and the value of sports, preparing women for leadership roles in sport organizations, developing recreational sports for women, training women as coaches and referees, organizing conferences, and facilitating cooperation among Arab nations.

The Editors

Additional information was provided by Nabila Ahmed Abdel Rahman.

SPORTSMANSHIP *see* Cooperation, Values and Ethics

SPORTSWEAR INDUSTRY

Clothing designed for sports is a modern phenomenon. While such clothing is closely associated with Western modernism, the development of sportswear and its spread have been closely associated with the rise and development of modern sports since the middle of the nineteenth century. While sportswear is now highly specialized, with different clothing for virtually every sport, sportswear has also generalized into a very popular form of clothing that is worn by many people in daily life.

Women dressed in fashionable ensembles for a dozen sports pose at the hour marks of a clock painted on a lawn in Miami, Florida, in the late 1920s. (Bettmann/Corbis)

HISTORY

In ancient times, it was unusual for special clothing to be donned for sports, and whenever this was the case, the clothing was inexpensive. Neither in ancient Egypt nor in the early civilizations of Middle and Latin America, where the practice of sports usually took the form of religious ritual and where it was almost always only men who participated, was there any reference to sports clothing. In ancient Greece, where, except for Sparta, sports were practiced for reasons of health and well-being, they were an essential part of life and they were usually restricted to men (who trained and competed in the nude). Sports for girls were limited to gymnastics and ritual footraces, like those at Olympia in honor of the goddess Hera. During the Roman and medieval period, few women participated in sports. Whenever women did participate, such as in a skating event or a footrace, they did so wearing their regular, everyday clothing. One exception to this rule can be seen in the mosaics of the Piazza Armerina in Sicily, where young female athletes are clothed in what look like bikinis. Horseback riding and falconry were also exceptions to the rule. For these pleasures, which were enjoyed by the nobility, aristocratic ladies wore specially sewn elaborate and expensive costumes. Their attire was meant to symbolize their status as members of the ruling class, but comfort during horseback riding was also important. At the other end of the social spectrum, working-class eighteenth-century English and Irish women took off their outer garments to engage in boxing matches.

THE MODERN ERA

In the course of the nineteenth century, sports such as gymnastics, hiking, swimming, and mountaineering became increasingly popular. By the end of the century, ball games, rowing, and track and field were widely practiced by men and even by a number of upper-class or upper-middle-class women. It was usually the men who first practiced the sport, but croquet and lawn tennis were sports that began with female as well as male participation. Around 1850 men began to wear special sports clothing, but sportswear for women was a rarity before 1890. For instance, late in the century, uniforms were uncommon for soccer (association football). It was only after World War I—when soccer became "the people's sport"—that the players began to wear short pants. Uniforms for American football and white flannels for cricket became common at approximately the same time. However, the vogue for sportswear was limited. Only the wealthy minority had the opportunity for regular sports participation. They had the time and the money. Furthermore, for many years there simply was no question of the use of special sports clothing for many sports.

Before one could begin to speak of specific sports clothing for women, additional changes had to occur. In the nineteenth century women were expected to conform to the required etiquette—in other words, to keep their bodies covered as much as possible. As long as women had to keep to these strict requirements for clothing, there was little room for specially adapted and comfortable sports clothing. Although social conventions slowed the development of sports clothing, the code was sometimes broken. A striking example of this was the case of the champion swimmer Annette Kellermann, who was arrested when she appeared in an "indecent" swimsuit. College girls and well-to-do ladies practiced sports in more comfortable clothing, but not where they could be seen by the general public. Although the American feminist Amelia Bloomer had tried in 1850 to introduce knickers into the world of fashion, "bloomers" were too extreme for all but the most emancipated women, although they did play a role in making sports more available to women in Japan when they were adopted there as the correct clothing for women gymnasts. When the "safety bicycle" conquered Europe and America at the end of the nineteenth century, progressive women adopted a version of bloomers because it was impossible to cycle in a corset and a long skirt, just as it was impossible to perform gymnastic exercises in a kimono.

Such resistance to sports clothing persisted until about 1920. Changes were finally stimulated by Jazz Age sensibilities, mainly in the sports of tennis and cycling (the latter not as a competitive sport but as a leisure activity). In the 1920s the French champion tennis player Suzanne Lenglen extended the mode of sports clothing. She daringly wore a light, comfortable, short-sleeved tennis costume made for her by the Paris fashion designer Patou. A colorful bandana topped off the costume.

THE MARKET FOR SPORTSWEAR

Sports clothing for men, which had until then been rather stiff, began to evolve. Tennis player René Lacoste, who was not satisfied with his outfit, borrowed the polo shirt and made it a household word. Athletes like Lenglen and Lacoste established a trend that with the years became more pronounced. With the increased participation of women in sport, sportswear became more acceptable, but not as everyday attire. The market for sports clothing remained rather limited. It was not until the 1960s that sports clothing became commercially important.

The creation of sports clothing as a major industry was made possible by the convergence of three trends. First, there was a massive increase in sports participation, which brought about an enormous demand for suitable clothing. Second,

WOMEN'S SPORTSWEAR

The sportswear industry was transformed in the 1990s by the rapidly growing number of female sports participants in North America, Europe, and Asia. Existing manufacturers expanded their lines to sell sportswear designed especially for women. New companies appeared in the marketplace with sportswear designed for women. Sizing down sportswear originally designed for men was no longer acceptable.

developments within sports themselves required changes and improvements in dress. Finally, the fashion world itself became involved in the design of sports clothing.

Sports clothing had to meet a number of functional requirements. Obviously, ease of movement as well as protection against cold or the intrinsic dangers of the particular sport were among these. In addition, clothes helped to identify the players and the sport. Uniforms or parts of the uniform, such as baseball caps, identified team members and their faithful fans. Developments in sports clothing were also driven by the desire to improve performance, which led to the adoption of materials to minimize water or air resistance. One example of this is the marketing in the late 1990s of swimsuits with less water resistance than that of bare skin. Another example is the aerodynamically designed helmets and sunglasses worn by cyclists. That esthetics also play a role can be seen in the carefully designed uniforms of women's gymnastics teams and the daring costumes of figure skaters. In these sports and in others, such as beach volleyball, one function of sportswear is to highlight the erotic appeal of the female athlete.

In the 1960s and 1970s, the same style of clothing, such as polo shirts and T-shirts, was often worn for any number of recreational sports. Since then, however, the trend has been to specialize, and many sports began to create their own look: wide-cut shirts and floppy shorts for basketball and tightly fitting knee-length pants for cycling are but two examples. The dazzling variety of modern sportswear is also a result of the increased number of sports open to women. For example, in the 1990s field hockey uniforms became "old hat," but women's rugby uniforms were new and trendy. In 1999, women's World Cup soccer shirts were the most popular item for girls, with many of those sold featuring the name and number of the U.S. star player, Mia Hamm.

Since the 1970s, sports have increasingly influenced fashion and fashion, in turn, has increasingly influenced sports clothing. If not eradicated, the boundary between daily clothing and sportswear has, at the least, been thoroughly blurred. In the 1980s and 1990s sports dress was no longer restricted to the playing field. It became noticeable as streetwear and was worn in classrooms, shops, restaurants, and even in corporate offices. It seemed that it was often more important to look athletic than actually to be so. Running shoes were worn in almost all circumstances, and sweatsuits were acceptable for relaxing at home if not for work.

Sports and fashion became interwoven. Major manufacturers of sports clothing (and other sports equipment), such as Adidas, Champion, Ellesse, Fila, K-Way, Nike, Patrick, Puma, Reebok, and Speedo, have expanded their market far beyond the sports sector. While sports manufacturers took over or became partners in companies producing regular clothing, companies specializing in sports clothing were taken over by competitors who had formerly restricted their output to "fashionable" women's wear.

SPORTSWEAR AS BUSINESS

In the 1990s, the world market for sports articles, even in the restricted sense limited to sportswear and clothing and sports equipment, was a multibillion dollar industry. The largest market was the United States, followed by Japan and then by the larger European nations. Nike of the United States was the largest company in this industry, followed by the German firm Adidas. Like other industries, the sportswear industry was dependent on market mechanisms and economic laws. To cut costs, firms frequently relocated their manufacturing operations to countries where labor costs were low. Sports clothing came mainly from nations such as Morocco, the Philippines, Tunisia, Malaysia, and Indonesia. Sports shoes were produced mainly in South Korea, Thailand, Indonesia, Taiwan, and China. In the continuous search for cheaper production, employee welfare was not of primary importance, and many companies were criticized for their labor practices by human rights and labor organizations. The industry made heavy investments in marketing. In particular, they offered huge sums of money for endorsements by prominent athletes such as Michael Jordan and Florence Griffith-Joyner. Many of these athletes, who already earned million-dollar salaries, made even more due to money paid them for these endorsements. Another way to increase a firm's market share was to act as the official supplier of athletic materials for national teams, college teams, or the Olympic Games.

Science and technology have contributed immensely to the development of the sportswear industry. Before the twentieth century, there were only natural textiles such as cotton, silk, and wool. Developments and improvements in synthetic textiles made it possible to produce new and better sports clothing. The 1945 invention of latex was quickly followed by additional synthetic fibers such as elastan, lycra, and nylon. Of primary interest has been the development and refinement of materials that are lightweight, moisture-proof, breathing, and, depending on the season, either warm or cool.

CONCLUSION

In the 1980s and 1990s sports became a big business and sports clothing became a major industry in which the laws of supply and demand governed competition that was as fierce as on the playing field. This situation is not likely to change in the future. Trends in the practice of sports showed a tendency toward individualization, innovation, and consumer orientation. But, after nearly two centuries of modern sports, the roles have been reversed. At first men (and a few women) participated in sports while wearing their everyday clothing; since the 1980s, sports clothes have been worn with increasing frequency by men and women as they go about their daily lives.

Erik De Vroede

See also Advertising; Fashion; Sexuality

Bibliography

Andreff, Wladimar, and Jean-François Nys. (1994) *Economie du sport (Que sais-je?)*. Paris: Presse Universitaire de France.

Borgers, Walter, et al. (1992) *Sportswear: Zur Geschichte und Entwicklung der Sportkleidung*. Krefeld: Van Acker.

De Vroede, Erik, ed. (1997) *Sport en mode*. Hasselt: Stedelijk Modemuseum.

Egger, Heike. (1992) " 'Sportswear': Zur Geschichte der Sportkleidung." *Stadion* 18: 127–157.

Gorris, Lothar. (1991) "Sport à la mode." *Zeitmagazine* 9: 41–48.

Gratton, Chris, and Peter Taylor. (1990) *Sport and Recreation: An Economic Analysis*. London: Spon.

Kamphorst, Teus J., and Kenneth Roberts. (1989) *Trends in Sports. A Multinational Perspective*. Culemborg, Netherlands: Giordano.

Simri, Uriel. (1983) *A Concise World History of Women's Sport*. Netanya, Israel: Wingate Institute for Physical Education and Sport.

SQUASH

Squash is an indoor racket sport, probably the fastest game inside four walls. There are 15 million squash players in the world, and they play on 50,000 courts in 130 countries. In terms of women's participation, squash has a unique history. Until 1986 the sport was run internationally by separate men's and women's associations, with far more resources devoted to the men's game. In 1985 the men's and women's units merged and despite predictions that involvement by women would disappear under male leadership, the opposite has taken place and women and men now share leadership of the sport.

HISTORY

Squash was invented at the Harrow school in England in about 1830 and from there spread to British colonies such as Australia, South Africa, Pakistan, Egypt, India, New Zealand, and Canada and in the 1880s to the United States. The U.S. version of the sport differed from the international version in that the court was narrower and the ball harder. In the 1980s the game was standardized in accord with the international form. The British Open championship, which served as the world championship until 1967, was first played in 1920. The Women's British Open was first played in 1922 and was dominated by British women until 1960, with Janet Morgan (1921–1990) winning the title ten times. Even more successful was the Australian Heather McKay, who won seventeen championships in a row, the last three from 1975 to 1977 after the sport entered the open era, with amateurs and professionals competing in the same tournament. In the United States, the first national championships were held in 1907, with the event dominated by men and women from Boston, Philadelphia, and Wilmington (Delaware).

Despite the women's championships, from the beginning squash was a men's sport and men players outnumbered women by more than ten to one, with some nations such as Egypt having no women players at all. Until 1985 squash was managed by separate men's and women's organizations. However, in 1985 they amalgamated under the banner of the International Squash Rackets Federation (ISRF). The constitution of this new body mandated that one of the two vice presidents must be a female. A Women's Committee, consisting only of females, was given responsibility for organizing the world championships for women and junior women, as well as advancing opportunities for women and girls in squash generally. This included the important task of identifying and encouraging women with appropriate skills for the various ISRF committees, such as coaching, rules and referees, medical, competitions, and technical.

A survey to the ISRF's member countries in 1989 identified all the now well-known factors limiting female participation in sport. Member nations (almost exclusively administered by men at the time) poured funds into staging men's and boys' championships but had no funds to support their women and girl players, who were considered to be less of a priority. Few women served in administrative roles or on governing committees. Professional women's events made up only 18 percent of the international tournaments and paid out just 8 percent of the total prize money pool. A number of founder squash nations had separate men's and women's associations managing the sport, with the inevitable duplication of resources. And the women's associations had significantly smaller player bases and limited capacity to generate financial support and development of the women's game.

In 1989 a newly elected female vice president, Susie Simcock, inherited the chairmanship of the Women's Committee, which she reshaped into a development committee that recognized that special efforts were needed to raise the awareness of issues related to women and girls in the sport.

Heather McKay of Australia (right) defending her British Open title in 1975 against Margaret Zachariah. (Stephen J. Line)

When the ISRF became the World Squash Federation (WSF) in 1992, the new constitution provided for three vice presidents, with one of the vice presidents required to be of the "other sex," rather than specifying a female as before, a subtle but important change. It also became a requirement for member nations to have a single governing body, which meant that men's and women's organizations had to merge.

The WSF also took other steps to end male control of the sport. Athletes were now referred to as "he" or "she" as appropriate, not as simply "he," as had been the practice. The rules of squash were revised to make them gender-neutral, and the content of WSF publications was made gender-neutral and gender-balanced. The WSF was one of the first international federations to pledge support for the Brighton Declaration, in a unanimous vote.

In the early days, there was resistance to these changes, some of which came from nations where it was unusual to find a woman in a management position or involved in squash. A significant event took place in 1992 when Sue Baker Finch, coordinator of the Woman and Sport Unit of the Australian Sports Commission, was invited to address the WSF general meeting on gender equity. Her audience included representatives of many of the 113 member nations, mostly men. She was hard-hitting and direct in her approach as she identified the benefits, windows of opportunity, and model gender-equity policies that she felt might be appropriate for squash. The reaction to her presentation was mixed. For some, it was perceived to be counterproductive to the Management Committee's desire for member nations to address gender-equity issues, while others greeted it with enthusiasm, as a wake-up call to things that they had not previously recognized or considered. Several years later, the Management Committee revisited the topic again. This time there were no problems, just enthusiasm, interest, and constructive debate.

In 1996 Simcock was the first woman to be elected president of the WSF, one of the few women to lead an international sports federation. In the late 1990s, the sport also became more open to women around the world. For example, in 1997 Egypt hosted a women's grand prix final in a clear-view show court situated outdoors on a resort island, a spectacular event and something that would have been unthinkable just a few years earlier in this Muslim nation. Another example is Malaysia, which initially supported women's squash because it was recognized that it might be easier for a female to achieve international recognition than a male. In 1998 Malaysia had two girls in the top eight world junior rankings, one just fourteen years old.

RULES AND PLAY

Squash is played on a court measuring 32 feet (9.8 meters) long by 21 feet (6.4 meters) wide by two players, each using a racket, approximately half the size of a tennis racket, to strike a small black ball alternately against the front wall of the court. The ball is soft and "squashes" on impact, making it slow to bounce and making the players work hard, both mentally and physically, to keep it in play. Squash has been assessed as the toughest cardiovascular sport in the world played with a ball, ahead of water polo and soccer (association football).

In the 1990s the British origin of the game remained apparent in the world rankings for women. Of the top ten players, four were from England, three were from Australia (including the number one and number two players), and one each was from New Zealand, South Africa, and Germany.

Squash has evolved from a sport designed for British public schoolboys to an international sport with strong men's and women's and junior divisions. The major issue for the sport in the late 1990s was attaining Olympic status for the 2004 Olympics, a major task on the agenda of the WSF.

Edward J. (Ted) Wallbutton
Susie Simcock

Bibliography

Internet Squash Federation: web site: <www.squash.org>. 1999.

STREICHER, MARGARETE

(1891–1985)

AUSTRIAN PHYSICAL EDUCATION TEACHER

Margarete Streicher was one of the very few female educators in German-speaking Europe to influence boys' as well as girls' physical education. Growing up in an upper-middle-class Viennese family, Streicher was fascinated by the study of biology. Her ambition was to become a biology teacher, but because students at the University of Vienna were required to have two majors, she chose gymnastics as her second major. She passed her examinations for the undergraduate degree in 1914 and received a doctorate in biology in 1916.

In 1918 she began to teach the next generation of physical education teachers. In that role, as a lecturer in Austria and abroad and as a prolific writer, she spread her ideas about the reformation of physical education. Her comrade-in-arms in the campaign for gymnastic reform was Karl Gaulhofer, an official in the Austrian Ministry of Education. Together they developed the theoretical basis and the practical methods for what they called *natürliches Turnen* (natural gymnastics). They revolted against the rigid forms and re-

MARGARETE STREICHER ON GYMNASTICS AND GENDER

The truly masculine in men's gymnastics and the truly feminine in women's gymnastics are expressions of male and female nature and cannot be willed into existence. To seek femininity consciously is to produce only a distortion of it. Everyone agrees that men's gymnastics are a matter for men. With equal justice, women's gymnastics should be a matter for women. Useful scientific information can come from a man as well from a woman, but neither men's gymnastics nor women's are simply matters of scientific information. Each is a whole, and like every whole, each must grow. Neither can be fabricated.

From Gertrud Pfister, ed., Frau und Sport. *Frankfurt: Fischer, 1980. Translated by Allen Guttman.*

quired movements that had been the norm in pre–World War I gymnastics classes. Streicher and Gaulhofer advocated a holistic approach to mind and body, an age-appropriate curriculum for children, economy of movement, functional efficiency, and a concern for the environment.

In the 1920s, these new ideas were institutionalized in Austrian curricula, and physical education was completely reformed. In Germany, however, "natural gymnastics" was not as popular because it had to compete with more traditional approaches as well as with other reformist movements in gymnastics and in sport generally.

Politically, Streicher became a member, although never a leader, in the National Socialist (Nazi) party, which seized power in Germany in 1933 and in Austria in 1938. Despite this association, she was able to resume her professional career in 1948. After her retirement as a teacher, she had more time for her other passions, such as music and nature, but she continued to write about "natural gymnastics" and her work appeared in many editions. She died, highly honored, at 94. Her ideas continue to influence Austrian and German physical education.

Gertrud Pfister

Bibliography

Größing, Stefan, ed. (1991) *Margarete Streicher: Ein Leben für die Liebeserziehung*. Salzburg, Austria: University of Salzburg.

STRESS AND STRESS MANAGEMENT

Athletes often define *stress* as the pressure to perform well or win. Hans Selye, endocrinologist and pioneer in the study of stress, broadened the definition by defining stress as the nonspecific response of the body to any demand made upon it. He looked at stress as potentially positive: "eustress" (literally "harmonious stress"), as in the case of making the starting lineup, or negative "distress," as in the case of a missed free throw in the final seconds. Selye asserted that both eustress and distress produce similar physiological reactions in the human body. Physiologist Walter B. Cannon first described this reaction as the "flight-or-fight response," the body's mobilization to fight or flee. A. T. W. Simeons, best known for his work relating human evolution to psychosomatic disease in the classic *Man's Presumptuous Brain,* argued that if stress products and by-products are not used in the physical exertion of flight or fight, they eventually flood the body, causing injury, illness, disease, and death. The key for women in sports, as for all human beings, is maintaining a reasonable stress level as well as a balance between effective stress reduction and the stresses intrinsic to sporting activity.

SOURCES OF STRESS

Sources of stress for women in sports include those for women in general: environmental stressors, such as noise and air pollution; biological stressors, such as colds and flu; physiological stressors, such as lack of sleep and poor nutrition; and psychological stressors associated with body image, social relationships, career, school, family, and so forth. Additional stressors due to being an athlete relate to training, competition, travel, preparation for peak performance, financial reward and support, and retirement. Athletes today must make decisions about alcohol and drugs as well as the use of "ergogenic aids"—shortcuts to success that might add yet another set of physiological and/or psychological stressors. Athletes cope with the effects of overtraining and the toll from the psychological stress of constant evaluation. Female athletes deal with unique stressors, such as training and competing throughout the menstrual cycle, while pregnant, or throughout menopause. Some female athletes face role conflict as they strive to be a woman while displaying the traditionally masculine traits of aggressiveness, physical strength, and competitiveness. In some cases, girls and women in sports experience even more unusual stressors, such as career-ending injury, rising from poverty to wealth, or attracting media attention.

Most experts agree that an intensely competitive (must-win) approach to sport competition can negate the stress-management benefits of exercise and create greater stress for an athlete. When athletes involve their egos and self-esteem rises or falls with the outcome of each practice or performance, they are constantly threatened by the sport experience instead of being relaxed and rejuvenated by it. As technology advances, creating more ways to train and improve, the athlete is faced with an ever-growing number of ways to pursue her goals. For example, in years past it took months for an athlete to recover from knee surgery. Now it can take weeks. Yet it might still take months to rebound psychologically, creating new psychological stressors. Advanced physical training methods place more pressure on the athlete to perform flawlessly. Mental training methods inevitably focus on how to cope with this sometimes enormous pressure.

SIGNS OF STRESS

Signs and symptoms of accumulated stress—categorized as emotional, cognitive/perceptual, and behavioral—includes:

Emotional
irritability, angry outbursts, hostility, depression, jealousy, restlessness, withdrawal, anxiety, diminished initiative, feelings of unreality or overalertness, reduction of personal involvement with others, lack of interest, tendency to cry, being critical of others, self-deprecation, nightmares, decreased perception of positive experience opportunities, narrowed focus, obsessive rumination, reduced self-esteem, weakened positive emotional response reflexes

Cognitive/Perceptual
forgetfulness, preoccupation, blurred vision, errors in judging distance, reduced creativity, lack of concentration, reduced productivity, lack of attention to detail, orientation to the past, decreased psychomotor reactivity and coordination, attention deficit, disorganization of thought, negative self-esteem, diminished sense of meaning in life, lack of control/need for too much control, negative self-statements and negative evaluation of experiences

Behavioral
increased smoking, aggressive behaviors (such as while driving), increased alcohol or drug use, carelessness, under-eating, over-eating, withdrawal, listlessness, hostility, accident-proneness, nervous laughter, compulsive behavior and impatience

SYMPTOMS OF STRESS

Physical signs and symptoms of stress include elevated heart rate, pounding heart, elevated respiration rate and blood pressure, muscle tension, and cold hands and feet. Stress symptoms relate to a long list of potential health ramifications, such as headaches, neck pain, stomach aches or nausea, backache, speech difficulties, urinary hesitancy, trembling, twitching, insomnia, weight loss or gain, diarrhea, constipation, vomiting, fatigue, susceptibility to minor illness, itching, and more. Research has explored individual response patterns and suggests that people respond in different ways to stress. Some individuals respond with heightened heart rate and blood pressure (vascular response), others with muscle tension (skeletal muscle response). Some people experience cold sweaty hands (a peripheral response). Still others respond with a combination of responses. Responses to stress also vary with the frequency, duration, and intensity of the stressor.

For athletes, prolonged stress from training and competing can develop into burnout, the human reaction to chronic stress. Early signs of burnout include any of the symptoms of stress previously described as they intensify over time. Arousal and stress responses such as fatigue eventually become chronic fatigue; depression becomes chronic depression; stress-related illnesses become chronic; social withdrawal becomes prolonged isolation; self-destructive thoughts become more frequent. The final stage of burnout is complete exhaustion and breakdown, the result of a prolonged battle between stressor and stress response. Athletes who burn out eventually lose their once very strong desire and commitment to sport. When athletes lose desire and commitment,

COMPETITIVE STRESS MANAGEMENT

Competitive stress management, sometimes called arousal control, refers to methods used in the management of anxiety experienced before, during, and after competition. These methods include the following techniques.

(1) *imagery:* using any or all senses to experience sport in the mind, seeing ourselves perform as "visualization," feeling ourselves perform as "kinesthethic" imagery; guided imagery to mentally rehearse an ideal performance.
(2) *relaxation training:* training the body to identify and modify muscle tension, e.g., progressive relaxation, deep breathing, hypnosis, autogenic training, imagery.
(3) *positive self-talk:* using inner dialogue, particularly encouragement, positive feedback and reinforcement, to manage stress, including methods such as cognitive restructuring and reframing.
(4) *selective attention:* focusing on things that reduce or manage stress, for example, focusing on the present, functional cues, and/or positive memories.
(5) *positive interpretation of physiological stress symptoms:* choosing to view stress response symptoms such as cold, clammy hands as a part of the performance process, symptoms that may actually signal a readiness to perform well.
(6) *self-acceptance:* taking inconveniences, setbacks, and criticism in stride; maintaining self-worth and positive feelings about the self despite mistakes, failures, and shortcomings, thus reducing fear of failure by allowing a performer to perform without fear of losing self-worth.
(7) *goal-setting:* identifying objectives to reduce anxiety and enhance motivation and confidence by focusing on where the athlete is going and how she is getting there.
(8) *trust:* putting motor performance on auto-pilot, allowing a person to perform without fear and without pressing, pushing, or pulling.
(9) *making it fun:* enjoying the activity to make it easier to do, turning anxious moments into challenging ones.

they often lose a sense of purpose and self-worth. In extreme cases of burnout, an athlete could choose to end her life.

STRESS MANAGEMENT

According to Jerrold Greenberg (1993), comprehensive stress management involves a variety of interventions at different levels. Greenberg presents a stress model that suggests that intervention at any level protects an individual from experiencing negative effects of stress at that level and all lower levels. Therefore, the higher on the model the intervention, the more effective it is.

GREENBERG'S LEVELS OF INTERVENTION

Life situation →

Perceived as stressful →

Emotional arousal →

Physiological arousal →

Consequences

For example, by changing a life situation (such as going to a school where the coach's philosophy is similar to your own) one can avoid perceived stress and emotional and physiological arousal. No negative health consequences are experienced. Likewise, if an athlete learns how to relax in stressful situations, physiological arousal is decreased and health consequences are lessened. Due to the potential filtering effect of each stage, individuals who experience prolonged stress symptoms recover more quickly when interventions are made as soon or as high as possible on the stress model.

Many life situations cannot be changed or eliminated, highlighting the importance of perception as a mediating factor. For one individual, a situation might be very stressful; for another individual, that same situation might not be very stressful. Athletes who experience relatively greater stress have tendencies toward perfectionism, impatience, hostility, and a low tolerance for frustration. They frequently see problems as roadblocks and adversity, not opportunities for change and improvement; even small problems become large problems; and they tend to place blame on themselves or others when things do not go as well as they think they should, which is much of the time. Athletes who experience greater stress tend to set high standards that they can seldom meet. They attach self-worth to winning and losing, level of motivation, and quality of performance. Athletes' training and competition schedules and attitudes toward commitment—such as "never give up," "more is better," and "train harder than all the rest"—can make a lethal combination.

Challenging these attitudes with the goal of finding a healthy balance is essential to good stress management. Effective stress management typically includes behavior modification, particularly learning to manage anger; fostering creative alternatives to stress-producing behaviors and attitudes; and working on self-esteem and self-acceptance. Since many people prone to perceiving life situations as stressful tend to have low self-esteem, building and maintaining self-esteem become a key outcome of intervention. Athletes who separate their egos from their sport experience and develop self-acceptance—maintaining self-worth regardless of shortcomings and setbacks—are much better equipped to handle the ups and downs experienced in sport.

Stress that "filters through" the perception stage of the model creates emotional and physiological reactions, and eventually consequences such as illness, injury, and burnout. Counseling can be obtained and/or a social support network can be used to meet emotional needs. Athletes who do not have such resources—for example, freshman athletes far away from home or athletes who are on the road a lot—are at greater risk. Athletes can learn meditation, progressive relaxation, imagery, or any number of relaxation and focus-of-attention techniques to identify and modify their body's physiological reactions. Learning simple deep-breathing techniques can short-circuit a stress response and constitute an effective intervention.

Physical exercise has been shown to be helpful in lowering anxiety, managing stress, and decreasing stress-related behaviors, although different activities yield different benefits. Used effectively, sports activity can reduce stress by-products such as high blood glucose, increased heart rate, and muscle tension. Regular physical exercise has been shown to enhance self-esteem, a sense of competence, and alertness, as well as improve sensitivity to muscle tension, allowing a person to recognize and manage it. If kept in balance, physical activity can be a very effective form of stress management for the athlete. Intervention at all levels of the stress model combine to form a complete stress-management program and the key to regaining and maintaining a healthy balance.

CONCLUSION

A healthy balance is often very difficult to achieve in sport. Athletes are faced with an ever-growing number of ways to pursue goals and attain higher levels of achievement. Intense competition and a must-win attitude can negate the stress-management benefits of exercise. Athletes are faced with decisions concerning alcohol and drugs, the physical stress of overtraining, and the psychological stress from frequent and detailed evaluation. Female athletes deal with unique stressors due to hormonal changes and potential role conflict. The female athlete's world is continually changing and continually challenging her to pursue her goals with higher standards of excellence. When female athletes meet those standards while maintaining mental and physical health and well-being, they provide an exemplary model of stress management.

Barbara T. Waite

See also Burnout

Bibliography

Borysenko, Joan. (1987) *Minding the Body, Mending the Mind.* Toronto: Bantam Books.

Cottrell, Randall. (1992) *Stress Management.* Guilford, CT: Dushkin Publishing Group.

Davis, Martha, Elizabeth Eshelman, and Matthew McKay. (1988) *The Relaxation and Stress Reduction Workbook,* 3rd ed. Oakland, CA: New Harbinger.

Gauron, Eugene. (1984) *Mental Training for Peak Performance.* Lansing, NY: Sport Science Associates.

Girdano, Daniel, George Everly, Jr., and Dorothy Dusek. (1993) *Controlling Stress and Tension: A Holistic Approach,* 4th ed. Englewood Cliffs, NJ: Prentice-Hall.

Greenberg, Jerrold. (1993) *Comprehensive Stress Management,* 4th ed. Dubuque, IA: Wm. C. Brown.

Hackfort, Dieter, and Charles Spielberger. (1989) *Anxiety in Sports: An International Perspective.* New York: Hemisphere.

Orlick, Terry, and Cal Botterill. (1975) *Every Kid Can Win.* Chicago: Nelson-Hall.

SUMMITT, PAT

(1952–)

U.S. BASKETBALL COACH

Pat Summitt is the most successful women's college basketball coach of all time and also one of the most successful basketball coaches. Between 1974 and 1999, her University of Tennessee teams amassed a record of 664 wins and only 143 loses and won six national collegiate women's titles. Her Lady Vols (Volunteers) won three consecutive national championships from 1996 through 1998 and were ranked number one again for part of the 1998–1999 season, although they did not win the championship. Only one other college coach, the legendary John Wooden of the University of California at Los Angeles, whose teams won ten titles, has won more national championships as of 1999. Summitt was also the coach of the national women's team, and by 1998 her teams had a record of 63–4.

Summit was born in Henrietta, Tennessee, on 14 June 1952, the daughter of Richard and Hazel Head. A basketball star in high school in Ashland City, Tennessee, she became a star in basketball and volleyball at the University of Tennessee–Martin in the western part of the state. At the age of only twenty-two, while rehabilitating from a severe knee injury and studying for her master's degree at the University of Tennessee in Knoxville (the major campus of the state system), she was given the job of women's basketball coach. Combining coaching with her own international playing career, she produced winning teams at Tennessee while playing for the national teams that won the gold in the 1975 Pan-American Games and the silver at the 1976 Olympics in Montreal.

Beginning with the 1976–1977 season, when Summit could give her full attention to coaching, her Tennessee team made the final round of the national collegiate women's championship. From then through 1999, her teams made the final round fifteen times in twenty-two years and won the title six times (1987, 1989, 1991, 1996, 1997, 1998). Her program produced a large number of female ath-

WOMEN COACHES TALLY CAREER VICTORIES

Only eighteen American college basketball coaches have more than 700 career victories and two of them are women. As of 6 December 1999, Jody Conradt of the University of Texas had a record of 730-224 (#11 on the list) and Pat Summitt of the University of Tennessee had a record of 700-147 (#18). In first place is Dean Smith, retired coach of the University of North Carolina, with a record of 879-254.

letes who continued to find success in basketball after graduation: as of 1999, ten had played on the U.S. Olympic teams, forty had played on other international teams, and twenty had played on professional teams in the United States and Europe. Her success as a coach is seen by experts as reflecting her dedicated approach to all aspects of coaching—recruitment, strategy, teaching, and motivation. Her teams in the late 1990s demonstrated a style of aggressive, fast, athletic play with which many opponents who followed a more traditional style simply could not compete.

Summitt became involved in international play in the mid-1970s as a player on the Pan-American team and co-captain of the Olympic team. In 1977 she began coaching internationally as coach of the U.S. junior team. Afterward, she became coach of other teams representing the United States in international play, then assistant coach of the 1980 Olympic team, and finally coach of the gold-medal 1984 Olympic team. At the international level she was also involved in running workshops and teaching other coaches.

Summitt is married to R. B. Summitt; their son, Tyler, was born in 1990. She lends her time and name to various social causes in Tennessee, including the Heart and Lung Associations, the United Way, the Easter Seal Society, and Big Brothers/Big Sisters: and she also serves on the board of directors of various basketball organizations. As a native-born athlete and successful coach of the highly visible University of Tennessee team, she is certainly one of the most well-known and admired people in her state. She is in great demand as a motivational speaker at colleges, businesses, and women's organizations.

David Levinson

Bibliography

Jenkins, Sally, Pat Head Summitt, and John Sterling, eds. (1998) *Reach for the Summitt: The Definitive Dozen System for Succeeding in Whatever You Do.* New York: Broadway Books.

Jennings, Debby, ed. (1998) *1998–1999 Tennessee Lady Vols Basketball.* Knoxville: University of Tennessee Press.

Lieberman-Cline, Nancy, Robin Roberts, Kevin Warneke, and Pat Head Summitt. *Basketball for Women:Becoming a Complete Player.* Champaign, IL: Human Kinetics.

Summit, Pat Head, and Sally Jenkins (1998) *Raise the Roof: The Inspiring Inside Story of the Tennessee Lady Vols' Undefeated 1997–1998 Season.* New York: Broadway Books.

SUMO WRESTLING

Sumo is a form of wrestling that developed in Japan. Professional matches feature many ritualistic elements. In the matches, one opponent defeats the other by forcing him out of the ring or causing any part of his body (other than the soles of his feet) to touch the ground. Sumo wrestlers generally weigh 135 to 180 kilos (300 to 400 pounds). Although sumo was and remains primarily a male activity, the first recorded use of the term in an eighth-century document refers, in fact, to women. In recent years, amateur sumo organizations have been promoting the sport for women.

HISTORY

The oldest chronicles of Japan specifically mention sumo several times, but exactly what was meant by the term remains unclear since these references neglect to describe the activity. At the same time, popular histories of sumo incorporate excerpts from these ancient texts that describe activities that are neither referred to as sumo as such nor are recognizable as sumo as we know it today—such behavior as tearing off arms, stomping one's opponent to death, and similarly brutal practices.

We do know that around the eighth-century CE sumo was performed at one of the annual court banquets by young men scouted from around the country. However, significant differences distinguished this court sumo from the modern sport. Court sumo had no ring, and matches were won only by making one's opponent touch the ground with any part of his body other than the bottom of his feet. (Judo and other bare-handed combat sports also claim court sumo in their histories.)

The annual sumo banquet had been discontinued by the twelfth century, as the emperor and his court lost their political power. Sumo at this time still had a functional association with combat, but in the following centuries it developed as a spectator sport. Performances of sumo staged to raise money for repairing temples and shrines, for bridge construction, and for other causes. Groups of men organized to perform sumo on these occasions for a cut of the take. These groups eventually began to put on performances of sumo for their own income.

By the late seventeenth century professional sumo was being performed regularly in the major cities. A boundary to the playing area was defined to separate contestants from spectators, which eventually developed into the raised earthen ring. Wrestlers assumed ring names reflecting their local affiliations or suggesting the awesome power of mountains, oceans, rivers, and other natural phenomena. Professional sumo achieved great popularity in the cities and significantly influenced art and culture. Many rituals were incorporated during this period, such as throwing salt into the ring prior to the matches, which both enhanced and legitimized the spectacle. The incorporation of ceremony and spectacle continues today.

WOMEN IN SUMO'S HISTORY

The recorded history of women in sumo begins with a story from the *Nihongi,* one of Japan's earliest historical texts, that may or may not be true. As the story goes, Emperor Yuryaku (said to have reigned in the fifth century CE), on hearing a palace carpenter claim that he never made a mistake, had some of his female attendants strip to their waistcloths and perform sumo in plain view. After watching them for a while, the carpenter resumed work, only to slip and ruin the edge of the plane on his rock work surface. The emperor was accusing the carpenter not of treason, betrayal, or violation of allegiance but of another kind of *lèse majesté*—an affront to the dignity and importance of the position of emperor.

This story illuminates the history of sumo in several ways. First, it seems that women's sumo was used for its shock value. Women performing sumo was apparently a provocative spectacle even then. Second, because of its prurient nature, this passage also presents problems for those who claim that sumo originated as a solemn religious ritual. The story is often ignored in histories of sumo, or is referred to with the salacious parts omitted. One well-known scholar, for example, merely mentions that Yuryaku had his female attendants perform sumo; he is silent on their state of undress and omits the carpenter altogether. Having removed the incident from its context, he goes on to say that it supports his thesis that sumo originated as a religious dance, since the emperor's female attendants also performed as dancers.

By the late eighteenth century, Tokyo, then called Edo, had become Japan's major city, and Edo sumo was the most prosperous and popular. As the popularity of professional men's sumo grew, unrelated groups of female wrestlers were formed. The ring names they assumed reflect the nature of the attraction: "Big Boobs" and "Deep Crevice," for example. Although these performances were periodically banned from the cities, some groups were actively touring the provinces well into the twentieth century. Women, or at least respectable women, for many years could not attend the professional men's tournaments as spectators, but from 1872 on female spectators were allowed. It was not until 1877 that women were allowed to attend on the first day of the tournament.

RULES AND PLAY

Modern men's sumo is performed on a raised earthen ring, and more than half of the matches are won by forcing one's opponent out of the ring. Wrestlers wear a cloth band that is wrapped around the waist several times and passed between the legs. The band can be gripped for lifting or throwing one's opponent. Kicking above the waist and striking with a closed fist are prohibited, but slaps and thrusts with an open palm are permitted.

A national amateur organization, the Japan Sumo Federation, was established in 1946. In 1997 the federation hosted more than fifty tournaments for a variety of age groups. Many of these tournaments incorporate weight classes and team competition, which professional sumo does not. The amateur form of the sport deletes most of the rituals associated with professional sumo. The International Sumo Association was established in 1987. The sixth World Sumo Tournament was held in Tokyo in December 1997 with wrestlers from thirty-seven countries. Japan has won the team competition every year, but wrestlers from other countries have won individual titles. National sumo federations have been started in other countries, and regional tournaments have been held in North and South America, Oceania, Africa, and Europe.

The Japan Sumo Federation holds a series of local and regional tournaments for children, culminating in the national finals at the Kokugikan, the home stadium of professional sumo in Japan. Although the participants are almost exclusively young boys, local organizers occasionally allow girls to compete. In 1978 a fifth-grade girl who had won her age division in a regional tournament was denied the opportunity to participate in the national finals. To permit her to participate would have violated the "tradition" that women are not allowed into the consecrated ring in which professional tournaments are held.

ORGANIZATION OF SUMO

The sport is governed by the Japan Sumo Association, founded in the early 1900s. Several hundred wrestlers are registered with the association at any one time. All wrestlers belong to one of around fifty stables, where they live and train. The wrestlers are ranked hierarchically, with rankings adjusted after each tournament based on performance. Each of the six official tournaments per year lasts fifteen days.

In its efforts to promote sumo, the Japan Sumo Federation has come up with a version of the sport for women called Shin Zumo—(New Sumo) the only nationally organized form of the sport in which women participate in. Matches are held on a cushioned mat, and the contestants wear leotards and specially designed trunks with a thick band around the waist for gripping. There are three weight classes and a fourth "open" class, which allows contestants of any weight to compete against one another. The first national tournament for New Sumo was held in 1997, the second in 1998. Most of the participants come from other sports, especially judo, and it remains to be seen whether the new sport will actually catch on. But the amateur sumo federation is strongly promoting women's sumo, as well as sumo overseas, with the ultimate goal of making sumo an Olympic event.

Nevertheless, tradition continues to be so integral to professional sumo that even women at the highest levels of government may not violate it. At the end of every tournament, a deputy chief cabinet secretary steps into the ring to present the champion with the Prime Minister's Cup. Before the January tournament of 1990, the newly appointed chief cabinet secretary Moriyama Mayumi expressed her intention to present the cup herself. The leadership of the Sumo Association, however, was not prepared to accept Moriyama's participation. An executive of the association paid a visit to a cabinet councilor at the prime minister's official residence to explain that it is an "unwritten rule" that women are not allowed into the ring, and he appealed for the preservation of culture and tradition. A few days after her comments, one of Moriyama's secretaries informed the Sumo Association that she would not insist on presenting the trophy herself in January after all.

CONCLUSION

Criticism is not limited to who is allowed in the ring. The Sumo Association is a foundation registered with the Ministry of Education. In 1993, the newly appointed minister of education, Matsumura Ryoko, criticized the association for discriminating against women. In particular, she singled out the composition of the Yokozuna Review Board, a committee of scholars, politicians, and businessmen appointed from outside the Sumo Association who recommend wrestlers for promotion to the highest rank, *yokozuna*. The committee continues to be an all-male institution. In the absence of any fundamental change in the sport itself and its traditions, it is likely to remain primarily a male activity.

Lee Thompson

Bibliography

Cuyler, Patricia L., revised by Doreen Simmons. (1985) *Sumo: From Rite to Sport.* New York and Tokyo: Weatherhill.

Nihongi. (1972) Translated by William G. Aston. Rutland, VT, and Tokyo: Charles E. Tuttle.

Nitta, Ichiro. (1994) *Sumo no Rekishi [The History of Sumo].* Tokyo: Yamakawa Shuppansha.

Thompson, Lee. (1998) "The Invention of the Yokozuna and the Championship System." In *Mirror of Modernity: Invented Traditions of Modern Japan.* Stephen Vlastos (ed). Berkeley: University of California Press.

Wakamori, Taro. (1963) *Sumo Ima Mukashi [Sumo: Then and Now].* Tokyo: Kawade Shobo Shinsha.

SUNN, RELL

(1950–1998)

HAWAIIAN SURFER

Rell Kapolioka'ehukai Sunn was a widely admired surfer and the undisputed best female long-boarder of all time. The ocean was her passion, befitting her Hawaiian middle name, which means "heart of the sea." She was born, lived, and died at Makaha, on the west side of Oahu, where she was known as the Queen of Makaha Beach. Of Chinese, Hawaiian, and English ancestry, Sunn embodied all of Hawaii's people.

Sunn learned to swim as a toddler and learned to surf when she was about four years old. In 1964, when she entered her first competition at the age of fourteen, she had to compete against men, since there was no category for girls. Because of her skill, her enthusiasm, and her personality, men encouraged her.

Besides being a champion surfer, Sunn was an all-round waterwoman also excelling in swimming and sailing. A fine paddler, she crewed on the *Hokulea,* the traditional double-hulled canoe that traced the route of the first Polynesians to Hawaii a millennium ago. She was one of the world's greatest free-divers and spear-fishers.

Sunn racked up many firsts. She was one of the first female lifeguards for the city and county of Honolulu. Even today, of 300 lifeguards, only 5 are women.

Sunn was one of the first women to support herself through her surfing efforts. She also worked as a surf reporter for radio and television, and was a published author. With fellow surfer Jericho Poppler, Sunn co-founded the women's professional surfing tour to parallel the men's tour. She was briefly ranked number one in 1975. She also helped establish several women's surfing associations, including the Women's Professional Surfing Association.

Sunn conceived and launched the highly successful *Menehune* (little people) Surf Meet in 1971. The Meet encourages *keiki* (children) to learn to surf, and many of Hawaii's best surfers, such as Sunny Garcia, got their start through the *Menehunes.* The inaugural meet had seventeen competitors, and "Aunty Rell" declared them all first-place winners. She initially gave away her own surfing trophies as prizes. Every year saw the contest become a little more organized. Sunn stressed the importance of *keiki* learning to share waves and surfing with *aloha.* Later, she began the unusual tradition of awarding the best prizes of surf boards and valuable equipment to the fourth- and fifth-place finishers, for having learned the lessons of life. The Menehune contest is also called the "Olympics of the Little Ones," and on the day of the finals, Makaha Beach is crowded with families and community members.

When Sunn developed breast cancer in 1984, she had a mastectomy and chemotherapy. Part of her treatment revolved around the ocean that she loved so much. When she died on 2 January 1998, her Hawaiian-style funeral was attended by 3,000 people from around the world, many of whom brought the traditional surfer's gifts of sand and water from their own beach, to symbolize how all of Earth's surfers share the same ocean.

Rell Sunn was married to Dave Parmenter; she had one daughter.

Sandra Kimberley Hall

SURFING

Surfing, also known as surfboard riding, is the art of standing up and guiding a board across the face of a breaking wave. Originating in Polynesia around 1400, it reached its highest form in Hawaii. There it became, and still is, an integral part of the culture, to a degree rarely seen with other sports. It now has many varieties—longboarding, short-boarding, and body-boarding. Its offshoots include paddling, skateboarding, sandboarding, snowboarding, and windsurfing. Women came late to surfing, but their participation is growing.

HISTORY

What took thousands of years to flourish was almost obliterated by the strict missionaries who arrived in Hawaii in the 1820s and sought to repress many indigenous activities. In the early 1900s, surfing was revived and has since spread worldwide. One of the earliest documented female surfers was Isabel Letham (1899–1995) of Sydney, Australia. In 1914, Duke Kahanamoku (1890–1968), a well-known surfer, selected fifteen-year-old Letham as his first student. Letham faced parental and community opposition for what was viewed as her inappropriate fraternizing with young men. Letham said part of surfing's allure for her in the 1920s and the 1930s was to escape this Victorian mentality. Documentation of other early women surfers is sparse, but there have always been a few progressive, risk-taking females, no matter whether they lived in England, California, or New Zealand. Today, part of the sport's attraction is still that it provides an opportunity to get away from it all and to commune with nature.

Women began surfing in significant numbers in the late 1950s. The movie *Gidget* provided some impetus. Coined from "girl-midget," Kathy Kohner's patronizing nickname conveyed the cuteness of the girl surfer. A male performed the stunts. This was followed by *Gidget Goes Hawaiian* and by a television situation comedy, starring Sally Field, during the 1965–1966 season.

Recreational surfing led to an interest in contests. Some men tried to prevent women from competing by relegating them to towel-holder roles. Sometimes women forced their way into contests; on other occasions, men invited them to compete. World-champion surfer Nat Young (1947–) wrote about the prejudices women surfers faced, devoting only 3 pages of his 200-page surfing history to women. He suggested that women's events were included in professional meets for commercial and sexist reasons and that U.S. television networks wanted women on the screen and viewed surfing as a viable form of mass entertainment. In the surfing world in the mid-1960s they were regarded as freaks in the almost totally male-dominated sport. Rell Sunn surfed in men's events because there were no women's contests. She co-founded the women's professional surfing tour to parallel the men's tour. She also helped establish the Women's Professional Surfing Association.

Changes have come largely through the efforts of women themselves. Women formed their own surfing groups because of the disparity in ability between men and women, to level the playing field, and for social reasons. The world's first amateur surfing championship was held in 1964 at Manly, Australia, and was won by Australian Phyllis O'Donnell (1937–). She later wrote one of the first surfing newspaper columns by a woman. Australia's Pam Burridge (1965–) is a role model for today's surfing champions. At age ten she committed herself to be world champion, learning how to surf at a summer school, the only girl in a class of fifty-nine boys. She won the Australian amateur championship in 1981, became her country's first female professional, and in 1990 achieved her world championship goal. Yet because of the stigma attached to women in the sport, her mother has always referred to her world champion daughter as a surfboard rider rather than as a surfer. In the United States, Title IX and the feminist movement have had some positive effect.

WOMEN AND SURFING

The International Surfing Association (ISA) reports that in 1998, in a majority of countries of the world, women were participating in organized surfing events. Generally, surfing is most popular where the weather is warm and the beaches are accessible. In Australia, blessed with 12,000 miles of shore, one in ten women enjoys recreational surfing, compared with one in five men. The Surfing Industry Manufacturers Association (SIMA) estimated that women's surfing in the late 1990s was growing twice as rapidly as men's. In 1997, SIMA estimated that there were 1.75 million surfers in the United States, of whom about 250,000 were women. A majority lived in Florida or California.

In Europe, climate and the lack of good waves both limit participation. Surfing is strongest in France. There is little surfing on the Mediterranean shore because of a lack of waves. Surfing is quite popular in Israel, but it is virtually unknown in Arab countries because of cultural restrictions.

Every country has had, or still has, barriers that women must overcome to surf. For example, because of the prevailing machismo in South America, the predominant form of surfing for females is body-boarding. Brazil is more accepting; once a woman demonstrates proficiency on a board she is welcomed in the lineup (for waves).

RULES AND PLAY

Surfing depends on many environmental factors—weather, water temperature, wave size and frequency, rip currents, and so on. Very few surfers escape injury in their lifetime. There are hazards like sunburn and stinging jellyfish, as well as the danger of drowning after wiping out. These factors have often been cited as reasons why women do not surf. Women have also had to overcome issues of modesty about clothing, about their perceived limited strength to carry a board to the water's edge, and their perceived inability to paddle long distances.

Today, most countries offer a variety of clubs for surfing enthusiasts on regional, state, and national levels. Historically, there have been two tracks. Once the amateur events became popular and attracted sponsors, then the professional track evolved. In 1975, Jericho Poppler Bartlow founded the now inactive Women's International Surfing Association. By 1976, there were sufficient numbers of women to form Women's Professional Surfing (WPS), with Rell Sunn as its first president. The next year WPS inaugurated the women's professional surfing tour, with five contests. The 1968 world amateur champion, Margo Godfrey Oberg (1953–) was named the first women's professional world champion in 1977, an amazing feat but largely unrecognized. At the same time at men's professional surfing events, a women's bikini contest attracted more interest, and the bikini winner received more prize money than the world's best woman surfer.

Pam Burridge, champion surfer. (Rick Doyle/Corbis)

The year 1978 saw the formation of the National Scholastic Surfing Association (NSSA) for young surfers of both sexes. Today, with more than 5,000 members, it provides students from sixth grade to college the opportunity to participate in national surfing competitions. It awards scholarships, promotes high school and college team competitions, and sponsors international exchange trips. For many young women, participation in an NSSA event is the first step toward a surfing career.

Australia, California, and Hawaii lead the world for summer surfing clinics for young people. Often sponsored by local governments, they were initially not exclusively for boys, but boys were most interested in attending them. By the 1980s private classes were offered exclusively for females. Equipment changes have benefited women. Boards are shorter and lighter. In the 1980s, the tri-thruster fin made a board more manageable.

THE FUTURE

The potential for women's surfing is bright. Manufacturers are aware of women's economic buying power. Sales of women's products are growing about 10 to 15 percent per year. There are now clothing lines and stores exclusively for women. The first surf shop for women, Water Girl, opened in early 1996 in California, followed by Inner Rhythms Surfer Girl in Florida. Once women were able to convince manufacturers that a woman's wet suit is not just a man's suit in pink, but needed to be constructed differently, wet suit sales quadrupled in six years.

Even when the world's best women surfers are featured in the media, they are all too frequently still portrayed differently from male athlete-surfers. Their looks, their physiques, and their families have been overemphasized. There have been some changes since Lisa Andersen (1969–) became four-time world champion. She has revolutionized the sport. Andersen is often compared to Tiger Woods or Michael Jordan. Nat Young wrote in 1987: "Boys are out to prove they can conquer the waves and demonstrate their particular ability to their peer groups. But girls are more like artists who work their choreography to the waves. . . . Women now surf with more power and daring, with attacking, dramatic, and radical moves, slashing across the wave, which throws up an enormous plume of water like a motorboat." A 1998 *Surfer* article profiling Andersen told the largely male readership, "She surfs better than you."

The Association of Surfing Professionals' world championship tour is one of the most exciting series of international sports, and Australian surfer Layne Beachley (1972–) became the world champion in 1998. She held onto her title the following year. The growing numbers of women in the media are helping young female surfers gain better and more equal news coverage. The first magazine for women surfers, *Wahine,* debuted in 1995. An Internet-based magazine, *Surfer Girl,* was launched in 1996. The late 1990s also saw women surfers as the cover story for mainstream magazines such as *Outside* and *Conde Nast Sports for Women.* The year 1997 saw the publication of the first novel with a surfing heroine: Joy Nicholson's *The Tribes of Palos Verdes.*

SURFING: HAWAII'S ROYAL SPORT OF KINGS

Anthropologists such as Ben R. Finney, believe that surfing is mankind's oldest sport. It probably originated in Tahiti, then spread throughout the Pacific. After Hawaii was settled circa 1400, the sport reached its highest form. They developed fancy maneuvers, such as head stands, tandem and backward riding, and jumping from one board to another at neck-breaking speed. Over thousands of years, surfing became more than a sport; it became a lifestyle, with religious, cultural and aesthetic overtones, still in evidence today.

He'e nalu (wave sliding) was celebrated in myth. Pele, the powerful goddess of the volcano, surfed. Contests between villages were eagerly anticipated. They were raucous occasions for betting and feasting. Often a prized canoe or a pig were staked on the outcome of a thrilling race. In the winter storms, waves might tower over thirty feet. Tales are told of chiefs riding the waves to supremacy over other chiefs. In calmer seas, a race would be judged by the distance a surfer traveled on a single wave; a ride of a mile was not unusual. Fittingly, surfing is often called "the royal sport of kings."

Surfing was woven into the very fabric of the culture. Surfing *meles* (songs) filled the air. Gifts and prayers were offered at special surfing *heiau* (temple) to thank the gods for the waves. A restored heiau can be visited near Kona on the Big Island. Spectators watched the lightning speed maneuvers from bleacher-like terraces. Sometimes a contest lasted all day and was particularly well-attended when a local champion was pitted against a champion from a neighbor island.

Women are still lagging in being inducted into regional and national surfing halls of fame. Nevertheless, they are making significant contributions to women's surfing. Some examples are Hawaii's Carol Hogan in public relations and ASP's senior writer Jodi Young in surf writing. Alisa Cairns, who participated in the world championships for thirteen years, is one of the forces behind the new world qualifying series. Nonsurfers, such as Ann Beasley, a founder of the Huntington Beach International Surfing Museum, have worked tirelessly to preserve surfing's rich heritage.

CONCLUSION

Surfing is an ideal sport—affording the opportunity to commune with nature, providing an invigorating full-body physical workout, and costing relatively little.

Sandra Kimberley Hall

Bibliography

Ambrose, Greg. (1991) *Surfer's Guide to Hawaii.* Honolulu: Bess Press.

Association of Surfing Professionals. (1998) *Pro Surfing: The Official ASP World Tour Guide.* Tampa, FL: Faircount International. www.asp-worldtour.corr.

Blake, Tom. (1983) *Hawaiian Surfriders 1935.* Redondo Beach, CA: Mountain & Sea Publishing. (Re-issue of his 1935 *Hawaiian Surfboard.*)

Hall, Sandra Kimberley, and Greg Ambrose. (1995) *Memories of Duke: The Legend Comes to Life.* Honolulu: Bess Press.

Hemmings, Fred. (1997) *The Soul of Surfing Is Hawaiian.* Maunawili, HA: Sports Enterprises.

Jenkins, Bruce. (1998) "A Beautiful Fight: Hawaii Says Goodbye to Rell Sunn." *Surfer Magazine* 39, 5: 134–140.

Lueras, Leonard. (1984) *Surfing: The Ultimate Pleasure.* New York: Workman Publishing.

MacLaren, James. (1997) *Learn to Surf.* New York: Lyons and Burford.

Margan, Frank, and Ben R. Finney. (1970) *A Pictorial History of Surfing.* Dee Why, Australia: Paul Hamlyn Pty Ltd.

Silverman, Jane. (1972) "The Young Paiea." *Hawaiian Journal of History* 6: 91–106.

Stell, Marion K. (1992) *Pam Burridge.* Pymble, Australia: Angus and Robertson.

Timmons, Grady. (1989) *Waikiki Beachboy.* Honolulu: Editions Limited.

Young, Nat. (1987) *The History of Surfing.* Tucson, AZ: The Body Press.

SURF LIFESAVING

Surf lifesaving is a sport born of necessity. What began as a way of protecting swimmers, and to test and develop those who do so, has turned into a sporting event that regularly draws huge crowds of athletes and fans. Glorifying Hollywood productions to the contrary, surf lifesaving is a very difficult and strenuous job. Turning it into a sport makes it that much more challenging.

Although women have a long history of service to surf lifesaving clubs all over Australia, it wasn't until 1980 that they were first generally admitted into full active patrol duty and allowed to participate in competition. Since then, as their number has continued to grow, the number of events for women has also increased, including women's ski races, surf boats, and beach events.

HISTORY

Surf lifesaving began because of a 1902 Australian law prohibiting the wearing of a "bathing costume" during daylight. Mr. William Gocher, a newspaper publisher in Manly Beach, decided to challenge the authorities and announced he would enter the surf at noon on various Sundays. No charges were filed, but a lifestyle was born as swimming and surfing quickly became popular pastimes.

As their popularity grew, so did the dangers. A small group of experienced surfers were concerned with the increased number of drownings in the surf, and they formed lifesaving bodies to help those who needed to be rescued. The first group to be widely recognized was the Bondi Surf Bathers Lifesaving Club, founded in 1906, although some feel the honor should go to the Life Saving Club at Bronte, formed in 1903. They were the first to use a surf boat for lifesaving. As these clubs grew in size and number, there was a need for a united front to raise money and to improve lifesaving techniques. Thus, the New South Wales Surf Bathing Association was formed in 1907. The name changed a few times over the years until it became the Surf Life Saving Australia (SLSA).

By 1909 fourteen different surf lifesaving clubs (another fourteen would join in the next few years) were represented at a meeting at which they decided to stage a state championship carnival to maintain interest and foster the education of the surf-bathing public. The first was held at Manly Beach in 1908. Among the events were rescue demonstrations as well as surf and wading races, all precursors to today's events. In 1914 the New South Wales Association decided to hold four competitions, one of which would be a championship event. The next year, the first Australian surf lifesaving championships were held at Bondi Beach.

The real importance of surf lifesavers to the safety of the public was demonstrated in 1938 on what would come to be known as "Black Sunday." A series of huge waves pounded every beach in New South Wales on 6 February. Five people drowned, but 300, many on the verge of drowning, were rescued by the lifesavers. This also demonstrated the worth and future of the lifesaving movement.

For a while, the lifesaving movement was based on a 1938 agreement between the SLSA of Australia and the Royal Life Saving Society, but it had little success due to the geographic difficulties. The Tasmanian State Centre was established in 1948 and teams from Queensland, Western Australia, and New South Wales visited the northwest coast for competition. In 1949 a national council of SLSA was founded to control and direct the affairs of the movement on a national basis.

The sport of surf lifesaving continued to grow among participants and fans. By 1998, SLSA had more than 82,000 members, about a third of whom were women, and the number increased each year. More than a fourth of the members actively patrolled Australia's most popular beaches and performed an average of 12,000 surf rescues annually. The sport of surf lifesaving has spread to wherever there is an ocean coast, and international competition features teams from the United States, Japan, New Zealand, South Africa, and the United Kingdom.

The Australia surf lifesaving championships have grown into one of the world's largest sporting competitions, with more than 5,000 competitors in more than 100 events. Age groups range from under sixteen to over seventy, and all divisions in each category include competition for women. The national event is open to all surf lifesavers representing their individual clubs. Participants wear team swimsuits and headgear.

RULES AND PLAY

To qualify for competition, athletes must first earn their bronze medallion, the core award for active surf lifesavers, from their clubs. The candidate's physical fitness is tested by a 600-meter (656-yard) run–swim–run (200 meters [218 yards] for each leg) to be completed in less than 8 minutes, a 400-meter (437-yard) pool swim to be completed in less than 9 minutes, and simulated rescues using a rescue board, using a tube, and as a crew member in an inflatable rescue boat (IRB).

There are a variety of events in surf lifesaving competitions. Belt racing is one of the oldest team competitions. The swimmer, wearing a belt with rope attached, swims 200 (218 yards) meters out to a buoy in the water, raises his or her arms, and is pulled in by his or her teammates.

Surf racing requires a 20-meter (21.9-yard) beach sprint to the ocean, an ocean swim around buoys (about 200 meters [218 yards]) and back, and another 20-meter sprint to the finish line. Surf boat racing requires a five-person team to row an 8-meter (8.7 yards) wood or fiberglass boat out through the break, around a buoy 500 meters (546.8 yards) out, and back to the beach. Surf ski racing features singles and doubles. A singles surf ski measures 5.8 meters (6.3 yards) and weighs 18 kilograms (40 pounds; a doubles surf ski is slightly bigger); it is a sleek, fast racing craft propelled with double-bladed paddles. Racers start at the water's edge and paddle out around three buoys and back, covering a distance of 700 to 750 meters.

Board racing uses a 3.2-meter (3.5 yards) surfboard. Contestants go out past the breaks, around buoys, and back, covering distances of 650 to 700 meters (710.8 to 765.5 yards). Board rescue racing involves two competitors, a swimmer and a paddler. The swimmer swims out to the buoys. The paddler then comes out for the "rescue," the swimmer mounts the board from the seaward side, and both paddle to shore.

Beach sprint relays are among the fastest competition, with times typically under 12 seconds. Four-person teams cover a 90-meter (98.4-yard) course shuttle style, with teammates passing a rubber hose baton. Beach flags require the racers to start lying in the sand. On the whistle, they leap to their feet, turn around, and sprint 20 meters (21.9 yards) to try to capture a rubber hose stuck in the sand. In each heat, there is one fewer hose than competitor, making this a knockout event and one of the most exciting because virtually every race involves a diving grab. The winner must win the last race.

Ironman requires a 250-meter (273-yard) swim, 300-meter (328-yard) surfboard paddle, 350-meter (381-yard) surf ski paddle, and 40-meter (44-yard) beach run. Junior competition requires a 200-meter (218-yard) swim, 200-meter (218-yard) surfboard paddle, and 30-meter (33-yard) run. Women's competition calls for 250-meter (273-yard) swim, 350-meter (381-yard) surfboard paddle, and 40-meter (44-yard) run.

Other events are rescue and resuscitation, which is very similar to the belt racing but includes a rescue and the application of first aid, and board riding, which is very much like typical surfing competitions. First-aid competition begins with a staged accident. The teams assess the patient, carry out appropriate first aid, determine if transport is required, and determine if on-the-spot medical aid is needed. Points are awarded for actions taken. March past is also steeped in tradition. Teams of twelve are judged on their ability to parade their colors in a set of predetermined drills. Taplin relay involves a six-person team (two swimmers, two board paddlers, and two surf ski paddlers) who race in relay fashion around buoys and back to shore.

The SLSA teams' traditional surf carnivals, with new teams and special events, also contribute to the challenging calendar of surf life-style activities. The drama and strenuousness of the sport and women's participation in it on nearly every level have made surf lifesaving one of the most popular ocean sports in Australia and around the world.

Jim Hunstein

See also Lifeguarding; Surfing

Bibliography

Galton, Barry. (1984) *Gladiators of the Surf*. Frenchs Forest, NSW, Australia: Reed.

Royal Lifesaving Society Canada Web site: <http://www.lifesaving.org>. 1999.

Surf Life Saving Australia Web site: <http://www.slsa.asn.au>. 1999.

SWEDEN

Sweden is a nation of 9 million located in northwestern Europe, on the Scandinavian peninsula. The nation was an early proponent of physical education for girls and women, and women there remain very much involved in sport.

HISTORY

Sweden became prominent in the area of physical culture in the nineteenth century when Per Henrik Ling (1776–1839) created what was to become one of the primary gymnastic systems of the time. The Royal Gymnastic Central Institute of Stockholm, founded on the initiative of Ling in 1813, became the stronghold of gymnastic pursuits in the country. The so-called Swedish gymnastics system became a nationalistic dogma, cultivated by the Central Institute and the Swedish Gymnastics Federation (founded in 1891; refounded in 1904). Men headed the federation, controlled the system, and often taught gymnastics for women as well. Women's health gymnastics was introduced privately in some towns in the 1820s; girls' physical education was introduced at schools in the mid-nineteenth century. The Central Institute did not admit women until 1865. At about the same time, Hjalmar Ling (1820–1886), the son of Per H. Ling, together with Anton B. Santesson (1825–1892) tried to make the military method practiced at the institute more suitable for women, but to little avail. The first two women's gymnastics clubs were founded in 1881 and 1882.

The most important work in developing women's gymnastics of the Lingian type was done by Elli Björkstén, a Finnish graduate at the Central Institute, and by Elin Falk (1872–1942), a Swede, who developed children's pedagogical

Ludmilla Enquist of Sweden (center) competes in the women's 100-meter hurdles at the 1996 Olympic Games. (TempSport/Corbis)

gymnastics. In the 1930s Swedish achievements in women's gymnastics were highlighted by *Sofiaflickorna* (the Sofia Girls), from the Sofia elementary school in Stockholm. The troop presented modern Swedish school gymnastics on tours in Scandinavia, Germany, and the United States, led by Maja Carlquist. This group participated in the Olympic Games in Berlin in 1936 and toured the United States in 1939. As women's gymnastics developed, Swedish men's gymnastics, still nurturing the masculine images of the nineteenth century, stagnated. The Lingian era came to a close in the 1940s. The next stage of women's gymnastics was developed by two refugees from Estonia—Ernst Idla with his famous group *Idlaflickorna,* (the Idla Girls) and Leida Leesment with her group *Malmöflickorna,* (the Malmö Girls). These two figures brought a Central European influence to Swedish gymnastics.

Gymnastics for fitness developed originally outside the gymnastics federation. What were known as housewives' gymnastics, developed in the early 1940s by Elly Löfstrand, were mostly daily gymnastic exercises, started by local female consumers' organizations in Stockholm. Later, housewives' gymnastics sections were founded in gymnastics clubs. Housewives' gymnastics was often practiced outdoors in the summer and indoors during the winter. The movements were simple, without apparatus, and performed to music. This was a form of gymnastics intended to increase the housewives' fitness, break their isolation, and give them variety in their often monotonous housework. The number of participants exceeded 65,000 in 1964 (55 percent of the total adult female gymnasts in the country). In the Swedish Gymnastics Federation there were 270,000 women (83 percent in 1974, when the number of women was at its highest. The first Swedish championships in gymnastics for men and women were held in 1945. Women remain the primary practitioners of gymnastics as a fitness sport.

WOMEN'S INVOLVEMENT IN SPORTS

Swimming—along with the more rare cross-country skiing, skating, rowing, and tennis—was one of the earliest competitive sports for Swedish women. It was practiced at clubs from the early nineteenth century, and the first competitions were held in 1890. Women also participated in figure skating competitions, and it was a Swedish initiative that led to the introduction of women's events at the world championships in the sport, beginning in 1906. Before 1918 women's national championship competitions were held in cross-country skiing, figure skating, swimming, tennis, golf, and foil fencing. In 1908 Swedish women took part in the Olympic Games for the first time: Märtha Adlerstråhle won a bronze medal in tennis. At the Olympic Games on home soil in Stockholm in 1912, Greta Johansson and Lisa Regnell won gold and silver in platform diving, and Sigrid Fick won a silver and a bronze in tennis.

Track and field was becoming ever more popular among women in the 1910s, promoted by many clubs and schools. The first women's track and field club was founded in 1913. The Swedish Sports Confederation (founded in 1903) did not include track and field events, however, when it determined in 1916 its criteria for awarding badges for athletic distinction to women. The number of women involved in track and field sports grew in the 1920s, a trend that was most apparent at schools. In 1924–1925 national school sports leaders (primarily Einar Lilie) made a failed attempt to have women's events introduced into the program of the national track and field federation. The federation did agree, however, to the foundation of a separate Women's Athletics Federation (1925), which joined the Women's International Athletic Federation and organized the women's World Games at Gothenburg in 1926. The separate women's federation was disbanded in 1927, however, and the national track and field federation incorporated a section for women. The first national track and field championships for women were held in the same year. In 1928 Swedish women were successful at the Olympic Games in Amsterdam: Ruth Svedberg and Inga Gentzel won bronze medals in the discus throw and 800-meter run, respectively. But the most famous Swedish sportswoman at that time was long-distance swimmer Sally Bauer, who won the Swedish championship for the 400-meter freestyle in 1936. In 1936–1937 Bauer set Swedish swimming records in most distances. In 1938 she started a professional career as a swimming teacher, specializing in long-distance swimming, and went on to swim the English Channel twice, in 1939 and 1951.

In addition to track and field, archery was the only other sport endorsed by the Swedish Sports Confederation for introduction into national championship competitions for women in the 1920s. Badminton, walking, and canoeing events were introduced in the 1930s. Handball was the first team sport to organize championships for women, followed by bandy in the 1940s (played for recreation by women from the turn of the century onward), basketball in the 1950s, and volleyball in the 1960s. Table tennis

LING GYMNASTICS

Since the early 1800s Sweden has been among the leaders in supporting physical education and sports for women. One of its earliest and long-lasting contributions was the so-called Ling or Swedish gymnastics. Per Henrik Ling founded the Royal Gymnastics Institute in 1814 where he taught a "scientific" form of exercise based on calisthenics which came to be called Ling gymnastics. Ling gymnastics was designed to help develop every part of the body and to provide non-competitive forms of physical education. The Ling system was taken to Britain by Martina Bergman-Österberg and later became popular in several other European nations and also in girls' schools in the eastern United States. By the end of the century it faced competition from organized sports for girls and women but remained in vogue in programs into the 1940s.

The Olympic Stadium in Stockholm, Sweden, where the 1912 Games were held. (Bettmann/Corbis)

and orienteering were other new sports that became popular among women in 1966; Sweden won the first world championship titles in the latter. In the 1970s women invaded several sports that were previously considered male prerogatives, such as soccer (the first women's national titles were decided in 1973), cycling, rugby, powerlifting, judo, and various Asian martial arts. These developments continued in the 1980s. Women took part in the modern pentathlon, and the first women's national titles were decided in ice hockey in 1988 and in boxing and wrestling in 1994. Soccer became one of the most popular women's sports; in the 1980s there were over 37,000 licensed players (players with full rights for competition activities). Sweden won the first women's European championship title in 1984.

OLYMPIC PARTICIPATION

In the 1920s and 1930s, Swedish women Olympic athletes were most successful in freestyle swimming and diving, winning a total of six bronze medals. Magda Julin-Mauroy won gold and Svea Norén silver in figure skating in 1920, and in 1936 Vivi-Ann Hultén, one of the first really popular sportswomen in the country, won the Olympic bronze medal in the sport.

Between 1932 and 1992 Swedish women won only one Olympic medal in track and field events—the bronze in the long-jump by Ann-Britt Leyman in 1948. Anna Larsson was possibly the best Swedish woman runner ever, but her short career coincided with the World War II years. She set a world record in the 800-meter race (2:13.8), but her favorite event was not in the Olympic program at that time. In women's gymnastics, Sweden peaked just before Eastern Europeans took over the sport, with an Olympic gold medal in team competition with portable apparatus in 1952 and a silver in the same event in 1956. Ann-Sofi Pettersson (later Colling) won an Olympic bronze in the horse vault in 1956 and world championship titles in the rings in 1950 (the only time this was an official event for women) and in the horse vault in 1954.

Cross-country skiing was Sweden's most successful women's winter sport in the 1950s and 1960s. Sweden was active in introducing women's skiing into the Olympic Winter Games and dominated the sport alongside the Soviet Union and Finland in the 1950s and 1960s. In Olympic relay races, Sweden won bronze in 1956, gold in 1960, and silver in 1964 and 1968. In 1968 Finnish-born Toini Gustafsson won two individual Olympic gold medals for Sweden. Sonja Edström had won a bronze medal in the 10-kilometer race in 1956.

With her silver medal in 400-meter freestyle swimming in 1960, Jane Cederquist was the only Swedish Olympic medalist at the Summer Games in the 1960s. In the next decade Ulrika Knape won three Olympic medals in diving, including the gold in the platform event in 1972. All-female Swedish teams won bronze medals in dressage both in 1972 and in 1984. In 1988 there was a silver medal in women's yachting, but the most successful medal sport for Sweden in recent Olympic Summer Games has been canoeing. Between 1984 and 1996 Swedish women won a total of seven medals in the sport, three of them gold, all involving the participation of Agneta Andersson, the most successful Swedish woman Olympic athlete of all time.

In the 1990s women were prominent in the international success of Swedish sports. At the 1996 Olympic Games in Atlanta, women won both of Sweden's two gold medals; at the Olympic Winter Games in Nagano in 1998, two of the three Swedish medals were won by women. Alpine skier

Pernilla Wiberg and golfer Annika Sörenstam were among the best-known athletes in the world in their respective sports. Other successful women's sports of the 1990s included biathlon, curling, and track and field. Russian-born Ludmilla Enquist became Sweden's first female Olympic track champion in 1996, winning the 100-meter hurdles race. In 1999, the Swedish women's soccer team was one of the sixteen national teams in the women's World Cup.

All in all, as of 1999 Swedish women had won a total of eight Olympic gold medals at Summer Games and five at Winter Games. In Summer Olympic sports there were eight Swedish medals in diving, seven in canoeing, four in swimming, four in track and field, three in gymnastics, three in tennis, two in equestrian sports, and one in yachting. In Winter Olympic sports, there were seven Swedish Olympic medals in Nordic skiing, three in Alpine skiing, three in figure skating, and one each in freestyle skiing and curling.

THE FIGHT FOR EQUALITY IN SPORTS

The debate about women's sports had quieted down by the 1930s. Women's previously low level of interest in sports increased after World War II and led to a women's sports conference, held in 1945. An interim women's committee of the Swedish Sports Confederation was founded in the same year, and the first (temporary) sports consultant for women was appointed three years later. The administration was reorganized in the early 1950s; Inga Löwdin was elected as the first woman to the Swedish Sports Confederation's Council, and women's committees were established in the central organization and in most sports federations and regional bodies. In 1952 approximately 22 percent of the members of the twenty-seven sport federations endorsed by the confederation were women. The committees did a huge amount of work to promote women's sports during the 1950s and 1960s, but without significant results. Several attempts were made to discontinue the Women's Central Committee as part of organizational reform. In the late 1960s the central committee was finally discontinued with the women's own consent; it was replaced by the office of women's councilor. This had the unintended effect of ending the committee system.

Organizational work for the promotion of women in sport was resumed after a few years in the early 1970s, although this time as equality projects, in the form of various subsidies and inquiries. A Plan for Equality between Women and Men in Sport in the 1990s was adopted by the General Sports Assembly of the Swedish Sports Confederation in 1989. One of the interim goals of the plan was that each group must be represented by at least 40 percent of either sex (i.e., at least 40 percent of the group had to be of the opposite sex) in advisory and decision-making bodies at all levels by 1995. In 1996 women constituted 42 percent of the membership of the Confederation, but only 26 percent of its central administration and 26 percent of the administrative bodies of various sports federations; the objective had clearly not yet been reached.

CONCLUSION

In 1991 there were 1.1 million active sportswomen in Sweden. The two most popular sports, gymnastics and equestrian events, together accounted for 38 percent of them. According to a survey made by the Swedish Sports Confederation in 1995, girls were in the majority among those actively involved in track and field, dancing, figure skating, swimming, and disabled sports. In basketball and volleyball, the ratio between boys and girls was evenly balanced.

Leena Laine
Translated by Vesa Tikander

See also Ling Gymnastics

Bibliography

Annerstedt, Claes. (1984) *Kvinnoidrottens utveckling i Sverige.* Malmö: Liber Förlag.

Haslum, Rolf. (1994) "Damidrotten vinner terräng." Unpublished manuscript, Institute of History, the University of Stockholm.

Kamper, Erich, and Bill Mallon. (1992) *The Golden Book of the Olympic Games.* Milan: Vallardi & Associati.

Laine, Leena. (1998) "How to Cross Borders: Women and Sports Organizations in the Nordic Countries." *The International Journal of the History of Sport* 15, 1 (April): 194–205.

Nordisk Familjeboks sportlexikon, Vol. 1–6 (1938–1946). Stockholm: Förlagsaktiebolaget A. Sohlman & Co.

Olofsson, Eva. (1989) *Har kvinnorna en sportslig chans? Den svenska idrottsrörelsen och kvinnorna under 1900-*

talet. Umeå. Pedagogiska institutionen, Umeå universitet (with an English summary).

Örner, Martin. (1941) "Kvinnoidrott. Sportens lilla jätte." *Idrottsungdoms egen uppslagsbok*. Stockholm: Natur och kultur.

Persson, Lennart K., and Thomas Pettersson. (1995) *Svensk friidrott 100*. Umeå Stockholm: Sellin & Partner.

Pihlaja, Juhani. (1994) *Urheilun käsikirja*. Lahti: Tietosportti.

Swedish Sports Federation. (1994) "Equality of Opportunity in Sport?" (A survey of attitudes on equality among senior officials. Measures taken to promote equality of opportunity in the Sports Associations). Excerpts from the Final Report (unpublished).

Von Euler, Roland. (1935) "Idrottsrörelsen för i dag." In *Svensk idrott 1903–1953*, edited by Sten Svensson. Malmö: Allhems förlag.

SWIMMING, DISTANCE

Long-distance swimming conventionally defines open-water races swum over a distance greater than 1500 meters (1640 yards). Before the 1997 World Cup organized by the Fédération Internationale de Natation Amateur (FINA), many races or individual performances took place in rivers, in lakes, or at sea. Notably, women have always been well represented in such events, although the male-to-female ratio was at times skewed toward men. During the twentieth century, because women beat men on many occasions, long-distance swimming undoubtedly contributed to modifying the general attitude of men toward women, forcing men to acknowledge women's physical capacities and symbolically shaking men's certainty of their own superiority in sports performances.

In myth and legend, however, women are portrayed both as taking an active role in their fate by swimming and as remaining passive while the man swims. The story of the virgin Coelia, who escaped from King Porsenna by swimming the Tiber to get back to Rome, is an example of the first. In the Greek myth of Hero and Leander (the subject of an 1810 poem by Byron and referred to in all early books on swimming), Leander nightly swam across the Hellespont, the strait that separates Europe and Asia, to see his beloved Hero. When Leander drowned in a storm, Hero threw herself into the sea.

HISTORY

Legend notwithstanding, long-distance swimming for women really began in the mid-nineteenth century in England, where professional female swimmers no longer hesitated to perform in long-distance races. One of the most famous, Agnes Beckwith, was known for her 1878 swim of the Thames River, a distance of 16 kilometers (9.94 miles). In the following decades, women—including Walburga de Isasescui of Austria in 1900—attempted to swim the English Channel. Before 1926 fourteen attempts had been made, although none had succeeded. After three failures, the Australian professional swimmer Annette Kellerman (1886–1975) decided to build her fame through aquatic galas, which included diving, dancing, and swimming performances rather than distance swimming.

Before 1926, only a few male swimmers had successfully crossed the English Channel, including Captain William Webb in 1875, Thomas William Burgess in 1911, and Henry Sullivan, Charles Toth, and Enrico Tiraboschi in 1923. The newspapers frequently ridiculed women who dared to compare themselves to men in such a challenge. "When will it be understood that it is ridiculous for a woman to reach such a performance and that only phenomena as Burgess are able to achieve it?" commented the French sports newspaper *La Vie au Grand Air* in 1912.

For swimmers and women's suffrage advocates such as Kellerman, however, "swimming is a graceful art and women can swim more gracefully than men. What is more they can swim with almost as much strength, and, at least in distance swims, very nearly equal men's records." Among the most serious contenders, Gertrude Ederle of the United States trained with the well-known Women's Swimming Association of New York.

A MAN IN WOMAN'S CLOTHING (1900)

An American Swimming Teacher Describes the Experience of Swimming in a Woman's Bathing Suit

Not until then did I rightly understand, what a serious matter a few feet of superfluous cloth might become in water. The suit was amply large, yet pounds of apparently dead weight seemed to be pulling me in every direction. In that gear a swim of 100 yards was as serious a task as a mile in my own suit. After that experience, I no longer wondered why so few women swim well, but rather that they are able to swim at all.

GUNDULA WOLTERS
(1994) Hosen, weiblich. *Marburg, Germany: Jonas Verlag.*

Born on 23 October 1906, daughter of a wealthy businessman, she became in 1919 the youngest female in swimming history to hold the world record on the 880-yard (804.7-meter) race. She was then only twelve years old. Over the next few years, she set nine world records and won two bronze medals for 100- and 400-meter freestyle and a gold medal in the 4 × 100-meter relay during the 1924 Olympic Games. She progressed to the professional level the following year and was unsuccessful in her first attempt to cross the English Channel. This failure, followed by journalists from all over Europe and the United States, did not prevent her from trying again a few months later. On 6 August 1926, at the age of nineteen, she started from Cape Gris-Nez in France and reached Kingston in England in 14 hours and 34 minutes, breaking the old record of 16 hours and 43 minutes held by Tiraboschi since 1923.

When she returned to the United States, Ederle received a hero's welcome. The press made much of her parents' German origins to emphasize the achievement of an immigrant, since she had announced in the *New York Times* that she had crossed the Channel for her country. In fact, she had bet her personal fortune and she later acknowledged that her father promised to buy her a roadster if she succeeded. Her achievement led to many movie contracts in the United States and Europe (in particular *Swim, Girl, Swim*), as well as shows and advertising, earning her an estimated $900,000. Sadly, she became a victim of her success, and in 1928 she experienced psychological problems that led to her withdrawal from professional swimming. She became and remained a swimming instructor for deaf children.

Ederle's achievement did not remain an exceptional feat for very long. Indeed, three weeks after her swim, another American, Mille Gade Corson, also swam the Channel—though taking an hour longer than Ederle to make the crossing—after a previous failure in 1923. Corson was twenty-seven years old, married, and wanted to earn enough money to educate her two children. Her status as a mother contributed even more to questions about the traditional representations of femininity.

Ederle's pioneering performance, however, had multiple consequences. First, she offered an extraordinary contradiction to the usual assertions on women's inferiority by demonstrating their equal physical and psychological abilities. She became the first woman to set a sporting record that had no gender distinction. Crossing the Channel added decisive elements to the debates of opposing experts on new styles of swimming (such as the crawl) and on swimming as an end or as a tool. Finally, the popularity of the American swimmer motivated a businessman to create a 21-mile (34.8-kilometer) "Channel of America" race in the Catalina Channel off California, with a prize of $25,000. This new race marked the definitive beginning of aquatic marathons in North America, which then multiplied by attracting pro-

GRACE AND STRENGTH (1918)

Annette Kellerman on the Competition Between Men and Women Swimmers

I insist that swimming is not only a splendid sport for women but that it is the sport for women, the one sport, with the possible exception of dancing, in which [they] can fully complete with men. While it is true that men hold the actual racing records in swimming for both time and distance, yet, when we consider the more limited opportunity for women to swim and the small number of women who really master the art, and consider also the element of grace in swimming as well as the mere exhibition of strength, we must concede that women outrank men as swimmers. This is seen in the endurance competitions where the women swimmers, while lacking the speed which the strength of man may give, make a better average showing and show a smaller percentage of failures and quitters.

ANNETTE KELLERMAN
(1918) Physical Beauty. How to Keep it. *New York, p. 85.*

fessionals from all over the world, including many women.

From 1926 on, the English Channel attracted an increasing number of women, who progressively represented a higher percentage of the annual achievements. Between 1926 and 1975, approximately 20 percent of the swimmers crossing the Channel were women; as of 1999, one-third of those who succeeded were women. Ederle's record was not broken until 1950. In addition, when the performances of swimmers are evaluated without gender distinction, women's performances place them at the top of the rankings. The two best performances ever were those of the English swimmer Wendy Brook, who in 1976 crossed the Channel in 8 hours and 56 minutes, and the American Penny Dean, who beat that record on 29 July 29 1978 with a time of 7 hours and 40 minutes. This time had not been bested as of 1999. In September 1977, the nineteen-year-old Canadian swimmer Cynthia Nicholas, already the world champion in aquatic marathon, became the first woman to accomplish a two-way cross of the Channel, an occasion on which she decisively bested men's performance records by swimming the distance in 19 hours and 55 seconds, compared to 30 hours by Jon Erikson of the United States. In 1982 both the ten best times for crossing the Channel and the nonstop records were held by women. By 1984 Nicholas herself had already crossed the English Channel nineteen times and was awarded the "Queen of the Channel Trophy."

RECORD CHALLENGES AND AQUATIC MARATHONS

Between World War I and World War II, women who swam long-distance races, unlike female athletes in other sports, were already winning substantial sums of money, similar to those won by men. In 1929 the American Martha Norelius, who specialized in professional aquatic marathons, won $10,000 for crossing Lake Ontario, a distance of 40 kilometers (24.9 miles). In 1953 the Canadian Marilyn Bell won $20,000 in another Lake Ontario crossing, and $25,000 was promised to the first person to swim the 56 kilometers (34.8 miles) across Lake George in New York State. Surprising all the spectators, a twenty-five-year-old woman, Diane Strubler of the United States, won the prize in 1959.

In their quest for fame, more and more women took part in marathons to challenge aquatic records. In April 1928 Mercedes Gleitze achieved the first crossing of the Strait of Gibraltar in 12 hours and 50 minutes, a time that resisted twenty years of challenges by both men and women. In 1931 Myrtle Hudleston of New York swam for 87 hours and 27 minutes, a performance that was very close to the men's record. The American professional Florence Chadwick was the first woman to successfully cross the English Channel both ways, in 1950 and in 1951, and the first woman to succeed in the most difficult direction (from England to France). In 1952 she was the first woman to achieve the Catalina Channel cross (Strait of San Pedro), in 13 hours and 47 minutes, beating the record of 15 hours and 48 minutes that George Young had held since 1927. This performance, filmed by a television crew, earned her much popularity. She was also holder of the female record for the Gibraltar crossing in 1953.

At the end of the 1950s, as aquatic marathons increased worldwide, the best woman swimmer was unquestionably the Danish-American Greta Andersen-Sonnichsen. She had won the Atlantic City marathon seven times (women); was five times the winner of the English Channel marathon (twice without gender distinctions); once won the Canadian National, one of the most difficult races; and, finally, was victorious in crossing Lac Saint-Jean in Quebec (also for both men and women). From 1958 to 1966, she held the women's record for the English Channel race, the France–England route, of 11 hours and 1 minute, and from 1964 to 1971, for the England-France way, 13 hours and 40 minutes.

Given the large number of spectators, sponsors, and participants of both genders, professional organizations began to be established. The first was the Fédération Internationale de Natation de Longue Distance (FINLD), founded in 1954, and later the World Professional Marathon Swim Federation (WPMSF), founded in 1963. The FINLD is located in Heliopolis, Egypt, where marathons have been regularly organized since World War II (for example, the Marathon of the Nile); the WPMSF is located in Fort Lauderdale, Florida. Both organizations were immediately opened to women, and the first female world championship for professional marathoners was organized in 1964, as a tour, holding several races during the year. The Dutchwoman Judith De Nijs-Van Berkel won the first five championships, through 1968. Thereafter, the best marathon swimmers came from countries with a long-distance swimming tradition, such as Egypt (Shadia El Rageb), Canada (Cynthia Nicholas), the United States (Diana Nyad), and Argentina (Angela Marchetti).

Marilyn Bell, Canadian distance swimmer who was the first person to swim the 32 miles across Lake Ontario in 1954. (Bettmann/Corbis)

From 1967 to 1977, "the 24 hours of La Tuque (Quebec)" was added to the races in the marathon world championship tour. In this new race, teams of two swimmers of either gender compete. It has been won several times by mixed teams (Judith De Nijs-Van Berkel of the Netherlands and Horaco Iglesias of Argentina in 1967, Sandra Bucha and John Kinsella of the United States in 1974). These mixed-gender races were easy to promote because women's performances were as good as, if not better than, the men's. For example, women long held the records for one-way and round-trip swims of the Catalina Channel. Finally, the races frequently did not distinguish gender in classifying swimmers' final results. Thus, in Australia, an ultramarathon race, the Sydney–Melbourne, of approximately 1000 kilometers (621.4 miles) has been established. In 1985 twenty-seven swimmers started the race; only nine finished, including all three women contestants, who finished seventh, eighth, and ninth. The following year, three women again entered the race; two finished, in fourth and ninth places. Eleanor Smith was the first woman home on both occasions.

In addition to these professional marathons, some countries have long sponsored long-distance races. In the United States, a 3-mile (4.8 kilometer) distance championship has existed since 1909 for men and since 1916 for women. A women's race team was also created in 1927. Beginning in 1921 in England—forty-four years after men's championship began—a long-distance women's championship was held annually for women at least sixteen years old. This championship disappeared after World War II and was instated in 1956, with the creation of the British Long Distance Swimming Association. Indeed, all these races at times led to the foundation of national or regional organizations, as the National Federation of Long Distance Swimming in Australia and the Association Provinciale des Nageurs Amateurs de Longue Distance in Quebec.

RULES AND PLAY

Aquatic marathons can be swum on a round (start and arrival at the same point), on a cross (lake), on a river, or along a coast. The distances are very different from one course to another. However, the rules promoted by the WPMSF must be applied in order for the race to count toward the professional world championship, which began in 1964. A certain number of races take place each year, and each one provides points toward championship—for example, 500 points for a first place, 350 for a second place, or in proportion to the time of the winner. Since 1970, only the four best performances of a year are credited to the candidate.

CONCLUSION

The success of these races has led to the recognition by FINA of long-distance swimming for women as well as men. In 1994 a race of more than 25 kilometers (15.5 miles) took place for the first time during the world championship in Rome. Among women, the Australian Melissa Cunningham beat out the Hungarian Rita Kovacs and another Australian, Shelley Taylor-Smith. In 1997, in the first FINA long-distance World Cup, Anne Chaignaud of France seized first place.

Marathon swimming, as with any extreme and grueling athletic event, is a sport for the few, not for the masses. It has, however, persisted long enough that its future seems assured.

Thierry Terret

See also Swimming, Open-Water

Bibliography

Birell, Susan, and Cheryl L. Cole, eds. (1994) *Women, Sport and Culture.* Champaign, IL: Human Kinetics.

Dyer, K. F. (1982) *Challenging the Men.* St. Lucia: University of Queensland Press.

Forsberg, Gerald. (1963) *Modern Long Distance Swimming.* London: Routledge and Kegan Paul.

George, J. J. (1995) "The Fad of North American Women's Endurance Swimming During the Post–World War I Era." *Canadian Journal of History of Sport* 26, 1 (May): 52–72.

Guttmann, Allen. (1989) *Women's Sports: A History.* New York: Columbia University Press.

Keil, Ian, and Don Wix. (1996) *In the Swim.* Loughborough, UK: Swimming Time Ltd.

Kellerman, Annette. (1918) *How to Swim.* London: William Heinemann.

Menke, Franck G. (1953) *The Encyclopedia of Sports,* new ed. New York: American Book—Stratford Press.

Oppenheim, François. (1977) *Histoire de la natation mondiale.* Paris: Chiron.

Scharenberg, Swantje. (1997) "Cross-Channel Swims: A Matter of National Pride, Gender and Money?" In *La Comune Eredità dello Sport in Europa,* edited by Arnd Krüger and Angela Teja. Rome: CONI, 286–296.

Terret, Thierry. (1994) *Naissance et diffusion de la natation sportive.* Paris: L'Harmattan.

———. (1995) "La traversée de la Manche à la nage." In *Education et politique sportives: 19ème–20ème siècles,* edited by Pierre Arnaud and Thierry Terret. Paris: CTHS, 165–182.

SWIMMING, OPEN-WATER

Modern open-water swimming or rough-water swimming traces its roots to the first recorded crossing of the English Channel (between England and France) in 1875 by Captain Matthew Webb. Open-water swimming refers to swimming competitions held in natural settings such as oceans, lakes, or rivers as opposed to competitions held in a pool. Many swims are individual in nature, where a solo swimmer swims an established course, such as the 33-kilometer (21-mile) English Channel Swim, or a point-to-point challenge in which an individual swims to set a time standard (or to beat the previously established time). Lynn Cox became well known in the 1980s for her point-to-point challenges—swimming between two landmasses where no other individual had swum previously. She was the first person to swim the Strait of Magellan in Chile and to swim around the Cape of Good Hope in South Africa. In 1987 Cox swam the Bering Strait from Little Diomede Island off the United States coast to Little Diomede in the Soviet Union, a 4.3-kilometer (2.7-mile) course in water ranging from 4.4 to 8.3 degrees Celsius (40 to 47 degrees Fahrenheit).

In contrast to these individual swim challenges, amateurs and professionals alike compete in mass open-water races such as the annual 1200-meter (1312-yard) Lorne Pier to Pub swim in Australia, which draws as many as 3,000 participants each year. Mass races across the English Channel are also held periodically. Six-person relay races are also common. In this format, one swimmer is in the water at all times, while the teammates remain on an accompanying boat. At a predetermined time (usually 30 to 60 minutes) a second swimmer enters the water, the swimmers tag and the second swimmer continues while the first swimmer gets back on the boat. This pattern is continued until the team reaches the finish. Well-known relay races include the Lake Tahoe Swim in the Sierras between California and Nevada, and the Maui Channel Swim between the islands of Lanai and Maui in Hawaii. Open-water swims are also usually the first leg of triathlon races (followed by a bike leg and then a run). Well-known triathlons include the Ironman races in Canada, New Zealand, Brazil, Austria, Switzerland, and the world championship in Hawaii. The Ironman swim distance is 3.9 kilometers (2.4 miles) but numerous other triathlons can be found worldwide with open-water swims ranging from 183 meters (200 yards) to 8 kilometers (5 miles) in length.

In pool races, the longest racing distance typically faced by competitors is the 1500-meter (1640-yard) race. In open-water swimming, 1500 meters would likely be the shortest race available and is referred to as a short-course race. Long-course open water races are from 1.5 to 25 kilometers (0.9 to 15.5 miles). Any swims over 25 kilometers or lasting more than 5 hours are considered marathon swims. Water temperatures typically range from 14 to 25 degrees Celsius (58 to 78 degrees Fahrenheit) for competitions, but temperatures for individual swim efforts can range from 9 to 32 degrees Celsius (48 to 90 degrees Fahrenheit).

Gertrude Ederle, the American swimmer who was the first woman to swim the English Channel, in 1926, at age 19. (Bettmann/Corbis)

In triathlons, participants are often allowed to wear wetsuits to aid in maintaining body temperature. In most open-water races, the wearing of wetsuits is not allowed or, if participants wear wetsuits, they are not eligible for placing or setting records.

In the open water, the swimmer must contend with many challenges, such as dangerous tides and currents, oil slicks, jellyfish, seaweed, and boats. Swimming in very cold water for long distances, however, is one of the main challenges of open-water swimming. The body loses heat more quickly in cold water than in warm water, and hypothermia is a very real danger. To protect themselves from the cold, swimmers usually wear one or more swim caps—in very cold water, a neoprene cap is typical and can prevent as much as 20 percent of the heat loss from the body. Some swimmers also use earplugs as an aid against the cold. Grease, though not proven actually to maintain warmth, is often used—lanolin (thick and messy) and petroleum jelly (wears off easily) are typical choices. The average female carries more body fat than males; this may serve to help insulate women from the cold water. Some consider this to be an advantage that women have over men, which could explain why women often beat their male competitors and even hold many of the overall records in this sport.

PIONEERS OF THE SPORT

Gertrude Ederle, in 1926, was the first woman to swim the English Channel and held the women's record of 14 hours and 39 minutes until 1950, when it was broken by Florence Chadwick; both were former Olympic swimmers. Prior to Ederle's 1926 swim, she had set nine world records in the pool and won three Olympic medals. Chadwick was the first woman to complete a double crossing of the channel—a 68-kilometer (42.3-mile) effort if it is possible to swim straight across. Due to cross-currents and changing tides, with waves fluctuating between 4 and 12 feet (1.2 and 3.7 meters), the actual distance swum is considerably longer. In 1978 Penny Lee Dean broke both the men's and women's English Channel records with a swim of 7 hours and 40 minutes. This overall record stood for seventeen years before being broken in 1995 by Chad Hundeby (who was coached by Dean in preparation for his swim). In 1999 Alison Streeter held the record for most crossings, having swum the English Channel thirty-seven times since 1982.

Many women have surpassed the performances of men in long open-water swims. Former Olympian (1948) Greta Anderson was the overall winner in two English Channel races in 1957 and 1958. Anderson also set overall records in the 25-mile (40-kilometer) Atlantic City race; in an 18-mile (29-kilometer swim in Lake St. John; and in a 42-mile (67.6-kilometer) double crossing of the San Pedro Channel between Catalina Island and the shore in southern California. In 1952 Florence Chadwick was the first female to swim from Catalina Island, breaking the male record by 2 hours. In 1999 Penny Lee Dean still held the record of 7 hours, 15 minutes, set in 1976, for the single crossing from Catalina Island.

TURNING PROFESSIONAL

Despite the number of races in North America, marathon swimming is more popular in Argentina, India, Egypt, and Australia, where the sport draws many spectators, and winners become well known in their country. The Fédération Internationale de Natation Amateur (FINA) is the international governing body for open water swimming. The first FINA world championships were held in 1991 in Perth, Australia, and in 1998 FINA began sponsoring a professional circuit with US$47,000 in prize money awarded to winners. FINA sets rules that cover all sanctioned swims. These rules include the prohibition of floatation devices (including wetsuits) and the no-drafting rule. Drafting close to another swimmer or support craft might provide a swimmer with an advantage over other competitors (less energy is required when following in the wake of a swimmer or boat). Swimmers may not be closer than 3 meters (5.7 yards) and cannot touch a support boat or support persons during a race (swimmers typically stop for 2 to 4 seconds several times during long swims to rehydrate or refuel).

The top swimmers in these competitions swim from between 3.2 to 4 kilometers (2.0 to 2.5 miles) per hour, using a modified freestyle stroke throughout. During mass races, swimmers typically need to adapt their stroke to look up at the course markings periodically. Courses are often marked by buoys and patrolled by lifeguards on paddleboards or in kayaks. In longer races, motorized craft are used and swimmers rely on the craft to set the most efficient course, with swimmers maintaining a legal distance.

Marathon swimming has its own governing body, the International Marathon Swimming Association (IMSA). Races typically bring cash awards for individuals of up to US$12,000. Peggy Büchse from Germany dominated the women's category in the 1990s, winning her fifth IMSA marathon swimming world championship in 1998. IMSA sponsors a circuit of international races in which competitors score points for each race, which are then tallied for a final world ranking. The final swim is a 25.2-mile (40.6-kilometer) race around Atlantic City. Women and men swim in separate categories; however, women often better the male winning time in many races. In 1993 and 1994, Shelley Taylor Smith of Australia finished first overall in the Atlantic City Swim. Taylor Smith also holds the overall record for the 28-mile (45.1-1 kilometer) Manhattan Swim, with a time of 5 hours, 45 minutes (set in 1995).

Linda S. Stanley

See also Swimming, Distance

Bibliography

Dean, Penny Lee. (1998) *Open Water Swimming: A Complete Guide for Distance Swimmers and Triathletes*. Champaign, IL: Human Kinetics.

Fédération Internationale de Natation Amateur. (1996) *Open Water Swimming Guidelines*. Lausanne, Switzerland: Author.

Wennerberg, Conrad. (1974) *Wind, Waves, and Sunburn: A Brief History of Marathon Swimming*. New York: A. S. Barnes.

SWIMMING, SPEED

Swimming for speed is a major international sport and one in which women draw as much—perhaps more—attention than do men. Elite competitive swimming is a sport for the young; the best are now in their teens or early twenties, although competitive swimming leagues offer masters competitions for swimmers well into their seventies. Speed swimming distinguished itself by being one of the first women's sports to develop and to be viewed favorably by men.

HISTORY

The history of female swimming is the history of women's transformation at poolside from spectators to competitors, with a stint in between as performers. In all cases, their practices developed on the fringe of men's activities.

In the first half of the nineteenth century, women were not allowed to show their bodies. In Europe, as well as North America and Australia, they were permitted to bathe in the sea or enclosed places, far away from the eyes of men. From 1830 to 1870, when swimming became more competitive and took on the characteristics of a sport, women were not among those present, either as spectators or participants. There were several reasons for their absence, particularly during sporting events. During the races, men routinely bet on the outcome, a practice viewed as unsuitable for women to witness, let alone try. In addition, male competitors did not commonly wear bathing trunks, and this posed moral problems because male nudity could not be exposed to women. Also, the competitions were organized as shows, or exhibitions, another activity in which female participation was unacceptable. Even if women had been permitted to swim in competition, they would have been greatly hampered by female bathing costumes of the day, which were particularly uncomfortable. Morality figured in here, too; women were not to be viewed in these costumes.

Seventeen-year-old Esther Williams is shown stealing the thunder at the Los Angeles Examiner competition before 10,000 fans in 1939. (Bettmann/Corbis)

Given these conditions, women's swimming developed away from the presence of men, on the fringe of competitions, and was linked to medical and hygienic concerns rather than sport. Baths for women already existed for both hygienic and/or recreational activities in most European cities at the end of the eighteenth century, although they remained novel in many places through the second half of that century. Other than at sea resorts, swimming still required the separation of the sexes, either by having two designated pools or by assigning men and women different bathing times during the week. The famous swimmer from London, Agnes Beckwith, daughter of another famous professional swimmer, was considered a phenomenon because she could swim, dive, and perform in the water like a man. Al-

WOMEN IN THE SEA (1889)

A Nineteenth-Century Glimpse into Women's Water Sports

I recommend special days, Tuesdays for example, to be reserved for ladies with competitions for them only. Women swim more quickly than men. Moreover, costumes suit them better; when they are well made. . . . There is also the diving competition—a baby made out of rubber is thrown into the water and the swimmers rush after it, dive and dive again. . . . Finally, there is the interlude. Some ladies . . . put clothes with no value on over their bathing costume. An accomplice designed as the prowler pushes them and makes them fall into the water. Everyone lets out a cry: a woman in the sea. But suddenly, the victim reappears with a smile and undresses while swimming with the applause of the gallery.

A. de Saint Albin
(1889) Le sport à Paris. *Paris: 206-208.*

though some professional women swimmers did race one another in the 1860s and 1870s, the spectators and journalists present were as uneasy as they were enthusiastic.

For competitive swimming (as opposed to hygienic bathing), women were initially allowed at pools during male races as simple spectators, after making sure that all the precautions of decency had been taken. In England, the decision of the Ilex Swimming Club to authorize women to attend its team's training session on 4 November 1861 marked one of the first steps in the diffusion of the sport of speed swimming to Englishwomen.

In the 1870s, in Australia and Great Britain, some shows by and a few races among women could be seen from time to time. The first swimming associations for women, however, did not appear until the 1880s. At times these groups were simply female sections within male clubs, a system that was intended, as with the Saint James Swimming Club, founded in London in 1888, to facilitate women's access to the pools. In other cases, the new women's clubs were indeed specific, autonomous entities, such as the Brighton Ladies' Swimming Club in the 1890s or, some years later, l'Ondine of Paris in 1906. The famous Women's Swimming Association in New York was founded during this time and went on to produce, during the 1920s, many international champions: Ethelda Bleibtrey (1907–1978), Gertrude Ederle (1906–), Helen Wainwright (1906–), Aileen Riggin (1906–) and Eleanor Holm (1913–).

This trend continued during the early years of the twentieth century. Some women's swimming organizations were established for women only from their inception, while others were part of existing male associations. In the United States, the Amateur Athletic Union (AAU) started a women's section in 1914. In Australia, however, the New South Wales Ladies Amateur Swimming Association (NSWLASA), founded in 1906, started and remained independent of any male-run associations. In other cases, as in France, the national union took control of women's swimming before it was well developed and incorporated it into an association with no special section for women. The French association was called the Union des Sociétés Françaises de Sports Athlétiques (USFSA) after 1907. After 1908 this situation changed (theoretically) with the creation of the Fédération Internationale de Natation Amateur (FINA), which recognized only one union per country.

Swimming remained limited for women, in part because most men opposed it forcefully, but an increasing number of women patronized swimming pools in spite of this opposition. Women's competitive swimming benefited by specific national championships, which male sports' authorities more or less recognized. In 1891 Scotland was the first to propose a "championship for ladies," set at 200 yards (182.9 meters). Pending the creation of a Ladies Amateur Swimming Association, which never, in fact, was established, in 1901 the Amateur Swimming Association (ASA) of England recognized the female amateur saltwater championship, which had until then been organized by the Portsmouth Swimming Club. Australia began to hold swimming championships for women in 1902, as did France in 1908.

By the beginning of the twentieth century, at times more than thirty years after male competitive swimming had been established, women's competitive swimming gradually became accepted as a sport, at least in industrialized nations. Women's swimming took place on a modest scale, but it did exist. In 1907 the ASA counted 33 women's swimming associations out of a total of 518. Australia had 900 women members within the NSWLASA in 1909. In most of the nations where speed swimming existed, however, such as in Hungary, Germany, and France, the female clubs remained very rare until the 1920s. That decade really represented the beginning of the rise of swimming for women. Before then, the small number of associations made it difficult to organize races strictly for women. Meets could be mixed male–female events, with distinct classifications and events, but training sessions had to observe women's privacy strictly.

THE MALE ATTITUDE

The first developments of female swimming were largely linked to the way men viewed the sport. In the most religiously strict societies, women's status made any show of the female body unacceptable. These same stances prohibited mixed bathing in England until 1899. In Australia, the rules of the NSWLASA prohibited women from swimming in the presence of men. Only with the 1912 Olympic Games did this last rule change when it would have prohibited swimmer Fanny Durack from taking part in the event, and so jeopardized the nation's chances for a medal. In contrast, in countries where the moral norms were less strict, the organizers of water festivals and other shows considered women's performances good investments because they drew spectators.

In all cases, however, men seemed more tolerant of women swimmers than they were of other women athletes. Their tolerance became evident in the early changes to women's swimming costumes. The first swimming costumes that were adapted more to the stroke itself than to the protection of virtue date from the 1870s. Made of cotton and revealing part of the arms and calves, they indicated that rationality was gradually beginning to prevail over moral pressure. By the beginning of the twentieth century, women's costumes resembled those of men. The swimming costume gave women a legitimate opportunity to give up wearing the corset and represented far more than a simple clothing emancipation. This early relaxation of the rules for women's athletic attire led the way toward a more positive male reaction some years later: when they were introduced, the female versions of the bicyclist's and runner's outfits were hardly criticized at all.

In countries where swimming for men was well established, medical opinion—and related to that, political opinion and public discourse—had long agreed that swimming was useful for both sexes for fitness and hygienic reasons. In this sense, men viewed swimming the female sport par excellence. This view was based on their view that swimming would make women better mothers; they would be accustomed to water and bathing for cleanliness and to putting forth the effort it required.

Speed swimming, however, was another matter, and physicians continued to denounce it. In 1925, Dr. Maurice Boigey explained that it was dangerous for women to compete in swimming events because swimming would jolt the uterus. For the same reason, he believed that women should practice the less jolting breaststroke rather than the Australian crawl. Generally, swimming gave the appearance of a restrained effort that preserved the traditional attributes of femininity without showing overexertion or tiredness. Far from the grimaces, sweating, and potential fainting provoked by bicycling or running, it offered an image of propriety and incorporated the traditionally masculine qualities of stamina, endurance, and striving for physical excellence, yet was conducted in a cool, aquatic environment. It retained a female image of gracefulness. It was, in a word, ladylike.

This male tolerance coincided with women's desire for emancipation and feminist claims, a sort of paradox considering that the acceptance came at a time when few women were swimming. At the beginning of the century, the aquatic shows of Australian Annette Kellerman (1887–1975) also displayed the physical power that a woman might have, which helped convince the male community that women might assume a larger role in society. Some swimming clubs for women, without rejecting the hygienist justifications or the image of the symbolic woman-as-mother, announced explicitly in their statutes their wish to liberate women. This project, less political than social, did not question the favorable attitude of men toward women swimmers. Men's acceptance allowed woman swimmers, at times, to represent their area or nation, as was the case in Scotland just before and during World War II. Nancy Riach made her club, the Motherwell Amateur Swimming and Water Polo Club, the symbol of success against England and the heart of the traditional qualities of the Scottish people.

RULES AND PLAY

Speed swimming is an extremely diverse sport. It is practiced at the community and school level, in colleges and universities, and in adult leagues for older swimmers. A swimming meet includes multiple events, with various strokes used alone or in sequence during the same event. The first basic event—whatever the stroke or the distance—is individual competition. Individuals also compete in the individual medley, in which they use breaststroke, backstroke, butterfly, and freestyle sequentially. Relays involve teams of swimmers. Scoring is based on speed. Swimmers frequently specialize in a particular stroke, although they must be adept enough in all to be competitive.

ELITE COMPETITION

Swimming was not the first sport in which women took part at the Olympic Games, but it was one of the first to be an exception to modern Olympic founder Pierre de Coubertin's rule affirming that "there will be no female Olympiad." Indeed, under pressure from FINA, a 100-meter freestyle, a 4 × 100-meter freestyle relay, and a diving event were added as early as 1912 in Stockholm, with a 300-meter race outside the competition intended as a testing program (exhibition only, in order to observe the reactions of people before making it an official event). In 1920 a 400-meter freestyle event was added. In 1924 there appeared a 100-meter backstroke and a 200-meter breaststroke, and the 300-meter race was dropped. The official participation of women in the Olympic Games after 1928 did not modify this program, which remained unchanged until 1956. The 100-meter butterfly was included at this time in the female program (200 meters for men). In 1960 women swam the 4 × 100-meter four-stroke relay and, in 1964, the 4 × 400-meter four-stroke relay. The women's program was brought closer to the men's in 1968 with the addition of the 200-meter backstroke, the 100-meter breaststroke, the 200-meter butterfly, and the 200-meter individual medley (all four strokes). Men had a long-distance event from 1908 on with the 1500-meter race; women received a half-measure sixty years later with the 800-meter. After 1968, however, the programs became more and more similar and, with the addition of the 4 × 200-meter freestyle relay in the women's program in 1996, the only differences that remained as of 1999 were the 800- versus the 1500-meter events. Times are recorded in minutes, seconds, tenths of seconds, and, now, hundredths of seconds.

In these elite international competitions, men's and women's teams from a particular country are not necessarily equally good. Japanese women, for example, were unsuccessful for many years, whereas Japanese men have regularly competed very well. The Netherlands, in contrast, has always had a stronger women's team than men's team.

Throughout the twentieth century, women from the United States were the most consistently victorious, winning 128 of the 363 Olympic medals presented (ahead of Germany's 83, and Australia's 35). However, other nations would, during some periods, dominate swimming competitions, shifts that reflected both the development of the sport and the status of women in these societies. Although the first woman's best performance to be ratified by FINA in 1908 was that of the German Martha Gerstrung, who swam the 100-meter freestyle in 1.35.0, the more well-known top swimmers at that time were Australians. Diver, swimmer, and water dancer Annette Kellerman was known not only for her 1902 world record of swimming 100 yards (91.4 meters) in 1.22.0, but also for the shows she gave all around the world.

Indeed, her tours had a real impact in promoting female swimming and influenced men's attitudes toward women swimmers. In 1912, another Australian, Fanny Durack, became the first woman to achieve an Olympic record. Until the last weeks before the event, she was thought ineligible to participate in the Games, since the people in charge of selection in the NSWLASA were still not in favor of letting a woman swim in front of a male public.

Within a few years, Durack had beaten all the world records in every distance from the 100 yards to the mile. But at the Antwerp Olympics in 1920, the U.S. women's team, led by Esthelda Bleibtrey, were the stars. They continued to dominate in all freestyle events until 1932 with Sybil Bauer, Albina Osipowich, Martha Norelius, and Hélène Madison. In backstroke and breaststroke, England's Lucy Morton, the Netherlands' Marie Braun, Germany's Hilde Schrader, and Australia's Claire Dennis managed, with difficulty, to retain their supremacy. In Berlin in 1936, their reign ended, however, when Willie den Ouden, Hendrika Mastenbroek, Nida Senff, and other members of the Dutch team won all but one medal. The first woman to break the 1-minute record for swimming 100 yards, den Ouden also beat the world record for the 100-meter freestyle in 1933, then again in 1936 with a time of 1.04.6. Unbeaten for twenty years, it represents the longest-held record for best performance in swimming for either men or women.

Denmark's Ragnhild Hveger and Inge Sorensen led in international events for several years. The former won all the world records in freestyle in meters and yards, except for the 100-meter event, in 1939, and beat forty-two world records during her career. After World War II, the duel between the United States and Northern European swimmers continued for a time, while new nations appeared in the records. In 1952, Hungarian women who asserted themselves in all strokes were Katalin Szoke (1935–), Valérie Gyenge (1933–), and Eva Szekely (1927–). In 1956 Dawn Fraser (1937–) and Lorraine Crapp (1936–) of Australia defeated several records.

Another champion, the American Esther Williams, won the American championship in 100-meter freestyle in 1939 before moving on to synchronized swimming. This led her to Hollywood, where she starred in several films. Her fame contributed to the development of synchronized swimming in many countries.

Chinese swimmer Liu Linin competes in the woman's 200-meter butterfly at the 1994 World Championships in Rome. (TempSport/Corbis)

In 1962, Dawn Fraser of Australia was the first woman to swim under the symbolical limit of one minute for the 100-meter freestyle. The 1960s, however, saw the return of the U.S. swimmers, particularly noteworthy for the performances of the triple Olympic champion in Mexico, Debbie Meyer, and of Donna de Varona.

From 1968 on, the East German women came closer to the Americans and dominated in 1973 at the world championship in Belgrade. Within a few years, they had beaten all world records and confirmed their supremacy at the Olympic Games of Montreal. Kornélia Ender won five medals there, including four golds. She broke four world records, including two in which she swam the events less than half an hour apart. Her time of 55.65 in the 100-meter freestyle made her the prototype of the new swimmer. Ender along with Petra Thumber (1961–), Ulrike Richter (1959–), Hannelore Anke (1957–), Andrea Pollack (1961–), and Ulrike Tauber (1958–), made up the most impressive team seen in swimming. At Montreal, they won eleven of the thirteen gold medals, beating seven world records, far in front of the American and Australian swimmers. This East German supremacy prevailed in 1980, when the U.S. boycott allowed the German Democratic

Republic (GDR) to win more than 75 percent of all medals. In 1984 the boycott of the Soviet-bloc countries allowed U.S. swimmers to win ten of the fourteen gold medals, beating any world record. In addition, the GDR was still successful in Seoul, Korea, in 1988, with Kristin Otto winning six Olympic titles.

At the time, observers attributed East Germany's twenty years of superior swimming to their training methods, which included a new program for specific muscular development that differed greatly from the traditional physical preparation of female swimmers. The supremacy of East German swimmers ended after the fall of the Berlin Wall and the reunification of Germany. This development led to strong doubts about the part played by simple differences in training methods in the team's earlier successes.

More generally, the use of illicit drugs—doping—during the 1970s and 1980s was a particular concern in regard to women's swimming. Steroids and male hormones became systematically associated with training in the GDR in order to develop muscular mass and limit the fatigue due to extensive efforts. Developed at the Research Institute of Leipzig and controlled by the secret police, called the Stasi, these banned substances were given to swimmers from the age of fourteen, as revealed in lawsuits against former coaches and the admissions of swimmers such as Petra Schneider, Christine Knacke-Sommer, and others. The athletes were strictly supervised during their journeys abroad for racing and had to wear T-shirts when at poolside to hide the traces of punctures. Toward the end of the 1980s, the Chinese began to employ systematic doping on a large scale, and notable cases existed in other countries as well (American Angel Myers in 1988, for instance).

Suspicion of this practice sprang from exceptional performances by previously undistinguished swimmers. In 1994 some previously unknown Chinese women swimmers won twelve of the sixteen races at the world championships in Rome. A few months later, during the Asian Games in Hiroshima, seven Chinese women swimmers tested positive for testosterone. In spite of the international reactions and promises of the Chinese government to cease such practices, coach Zhou Zheven and swimmer Yuan Yuan were compromised in 1994 with growth hormones suspicions. Thus, some team members were dropped and others competed without the benefit of doping-enhanced training, and Chinese swimmers performed relatively poorly at the 1996 Olympics.

These controversies triggered the establishment of international efforts to reduce the monopoly of only a few nations and to make it easier for other nations to produce elite swimmers. However, in 2000, the best female swimmers continue to come from the United States, China, Germany, and Australia.

Thierry Terret

Bibliography

Besford, Pat, ed. (1971) *Encyclopedia of Swimming.* New York: St Martin's Press.

Breuer, H., and Roland Naul. (1994) *Schwimmsport und Sportgeschichte: Zwischen Politik und Wissenschaft.* Sankt Augustin: Academia Verlag.

Colwin, Cecil. (1992) *Swimming into the Twenty-First Century.* West Point, NY: Leisure Press.

Howell, Reet, ed. (1982) *Her Story in Sport: A Historical Anthology of Women in Sports.* West Point, NY: Leisure Press.

Kellerman, Annette. (1918) *How to Swim.* London: William Heinneman.

Oppenheim, François. (1977) *Histoire de la natation mondiale et française.* Paris: Chiron-sports.

Pahnacke, W. (1979) *Schwimmen in Vergangenheit und Gegenwart.* Berlin: Sportverlag.

Rasveja, Veronica. (1992) "A Decent and Proper Exertion: The Rise of Women's Competitive Swimming in Sydney to 1912." *Australian Society for Sports History (ASSH) Studies in Sports History* 9.

Sprawson, Charles. (1992) *Haunts of the Black Masseur: The Swimmer as Hero.* London: Jonathan Cape.

Terret, Thierry. (1992) "Natation et émancipation féminine au début du siècle." *Jeux et sports dans l'histoire,* Vol. 2. Paris: CTHS.

———. (1994) *Naissance et diffusion de la natation sportive.* Paris: L'Harmattan.

———. (1995) "Professional Swimming in England Before the Rise of Amateurism, 1837–1875." *The International Journal of the History of Sport* 12, 1.

Walker, G. (1994) "Nancy Riach and the Motherwell Swimming Phenomenon." In *Scottish Sport in the Making of the Nation: Ninety Minute Patriots?,* edited by G. Jarvie and G. Walker. Leicester, UK: Leicester University Press.

SWIMMING, SYNCHRONIZED

Synchronized swimming is a water sport in which groups of swimmers perform choreographed routines synchronized to music and with each other. It is relatively young as a sport, since the first competition recognizable as synchronized swimming was held in 1939.

HISTORY

The origins of activities that resemble synchro (as it is called) extend very far back in time. Ancient woodblock prints, vases, and other items show water positions and actions that resemble synchro maneuvers. Before the turn of the twentieth century, England and Canada were experimenting with competitions in water tricks and stunts (figures), and after a few years Canada added strokes for form. Descriptions of various stunts and tricks can be found in turn-of-the-century books.

The earliest competitive activity related to synchronized swimming was probably developed from the "tricks and stunts" part of the 1891 requirements of England's all-male Royal Life Saving Society. The first record of actual competition for ornamental and scientific swimming was held in Yorkshire in 1892. Canada held a competition in stunts and strokes, for form, in Winnipeg in 1898 as a requirement for the gold medal of its (male) Royal Life Saving Society. Both competitions continued for many years. In 1924 in Montreal, Canada held a competition in tricks and water skills for women, with awards based on the perfection of stroking form and tricks such as somersaults, surface dives, and circles. No music was involved.

Annette Kellerman (1887–1975), the Australian swimming sensation of 1904, helped popularize water ballet maneuvers in tours of England and the United States, where she performed aquatic tricks in a glass tank. She appeared at New York's Hippodrome in 1907 and had made five movies displaying her aquatic talents by 1914.

Japanese synchronized swimmers Miho Takeda (right) and Miya Tachibana perform their free routine program at the 1998 Asian Games. (AFP/Corbis)

The Red Cross used music in water rehabilitation exercises it developed after World War I. In Canada, Germany, Belgium, the Netherlands, England, and France, floating formations were a popular activity for women and led to competitions in Germany. Cues for changing formations were initially made by whistle signals, but music began to be used for cues in the 1930s. Stephens College in Missouri was reported to have held the first water pageant in the United States in 1916. Both the University of Wisconsin's Dolphin Club and the Seals Club of the University of Iowa produced pageants in 1920. Water pageantry spread throughout the colleges of the United States and Canada and provided the base for later commercial aquacades.

Colleges held large water pageants in the 1920s and 1930s. Then came the large aquacades and movie productions. Busby Berkeley included an aquatic dream scene in the 1933 film *Footlights of 1933*. The aquacade of Chicago's Century of Progress World's Fair of 1934 played to audiences of more than 10,000 people. Touring aquatic show groups emerged. Then came the New York World's Fair aquacade of 1939 and San Francisco's Golden Gate International Exposition aquacade of 1940. The latter, starring Esther Williams, led to MGM movies that did much to popularize the activity throughout the world.

THE EMERGENCE OF COMPETITION

Katharine Curtis is credited for laying the foundation for the transition of collegiate water ballet into synchronized swimming, the competitive sport. While a student at the University of Wisconsin in 1915, she experimented with actions that were the basis for figures, which, along with strokes and floating formations, are the fundamental elements of synchro routines. A women's swim club was formed there in 1917 and produced a water pageant in 1920 that demonstrated the Curtis activities set to music. On becoming a teacher at the University of Chicago in 1923, she continued to develop what she called "rhythmic swimming"—strokes, stunts (figures), and floats combined into routines set to musical rhythms. In 1934 thirty of her students, called the "Modern Mermaids," performed three times a day at Chicago's Century of Progress World's Fair. Announcer Norman Ross, himself a former swimmer, applied the name "synchronized swimming" to the routines, as the best description of the action set to music.

Curtis developed a rhythmic swim group while teaching at Chicago's Wright Junior College in 1937. The following year, now teaching at Chicago Teacher's College, she developed another group that proposed having a competition with her former Wright College team. Curtis recalled, "Through their own interest and enthusiasm, the students, under the leadership of Frank Havlicek, student leader of the group, developed rules and events for a Dual Meet between the coeducational teams of the two institutions." Events in this first competition, held 27 May 1939 as part of Chicago's Teacher's Day Program, consisted of duet, team, large floating patterns, and stunts (figures).

David Clark Leach, Central Association chairman of the Amateur Athletic Union (AAU) at the time of the dual meet, had observed Curtis's work from as early as 1924. Believing that her rhythmic swimming would make an interesting competitive event to add to swimming and diving championships, he organized a committee, under Curtis, to set up rules for a competitive sport. Synchronized swimming was chosen as the name in order to distinguish the competitive activity from the water ballets being done in New York (1939–1940) and San Francisco (1940). Leach obtained acceptance for competitions in synchronized swimming team and duet events from the AAU's national governing body in December 1940. The first official national championship was not held until 1946. The solo event was added in 1950. Synchronized swimming continued under the wing of the AAU in the United States until the U.S. Amateur Sports Act of 1978, which stipulated that all Olympic sports must be administered independently. U.S. Synchronized Swimming, Inc., is established as the national governing body for the sport in the United States.

Canada's competition evolved independently from the strokes and stunts competitions to include composed sequences of strokes and stunts, as well as solos that became routines to music. The first Canadian solo championship was held in 1948. Duet and team events were added in the next two years. Worldwide interest was developing, particularly following demonstrations by both the United States and Canada at the first Pan-American Games in Buenos Aires in 1951 and at the 1952 Olympics in Helsinki. The Fédération Internationale de Natation Amateur (FINA) accepted the sport in 1952, and a technical committee was formed in 1954, under Jan Armbrust of Holland, to set rules for international competition.

International competition for solo, duet, and team events in synchronized swimming began with the second Pan-American Games in Mexico City in 1955. In 1973 the first world swimming championships at Belgrade included swimming, diving, water polo, and synchronized swimming. Only the solo and duet events were added to the Olympic Games for Los Angeles in 1984; they continued in 1988 at Seoul and in 1992 at Barcelona but were deleted in favor of the team event in 1996 at Atlanta. The duet event was restored for the 2000 Olympic Games in Sydney, to be held along with the team event.

Major international competitions held every four years include the Olympic Games, World Aquatic championships, Goodwill Games, and most regional championships, such as the Pan-American Games, Asian Games, Coman (Mediterranean), and Central and South American championships. FINA World Cups, junior world championships, European championships, Pan-

Pacifics, and the American Cup are held every two years. Numerous open international competitions are held each year, many in conjunction with each country's national championships. Longstanding events include the Swiss Open, French Open, Loano Cup, Roma Sincro, Hans Christian Andersen Cup, and Scandinavian Open Championships. Russia began its Women's Day events in Moscow in 1980. More than sixty nations are now known to conduct national championships, and the number continues to grow. The sport is practiced on all continents.

RULES AND PLAY

Solo, duet, and team (eight-member) events make up the competitive program. Present-day competition in each may include a technical program, free routine, and figure competition. Technical routines require incorporation of a set of compulsory standard actions, with almost all parts of the routine required to be performed simultaneously by members of duets and teams. The free routines allow the athletes free choice of actions, skills, and composition to best display their abilities. The figure competition involves individual performance of standardized body-action sequences, each sequence a named figure.

Routine events are judged by panels of five to seven judges, preferably assigning separate panels to determine the two awards, Technical Merit and Artistic Impression. The Technical Merit award, which includes categories of execution, synchronization, and difficulty, comprises 60 percent of the total routine score. Artistic Impression, which includes choreography, music interpretation, and manner of presentation, comprises the remaining 40 percent of the score.

In figure competition, each athlete is judged individually on four separate figures. Judgment is based on the swimmer's conformation to the action description and the demonstration of height, strength, and control. Actions include spins, twists, somersaults, verticals, and other special, described movements. Where possible, each figure is assigned to one of four separate panels of five judges.

Competitions throughout the world are held at the senior, junior (ages fifteen to eighteen), and age-group levels of twelve and under, thirteen to fifteen, and sixteen to eighteen years. Collegiate competition is held in some nations, but not internationally, and some countries now hold competitions for masters athletes, where the minimum age is twenty.

The competitive programs at the Olympic Games, world championships, and World Cups include only the technical and free routine events. Junior world championships include figure competition and free routine. All other international competitions can hold all three events, but may hold just two, which would be the free routine and either the technical routine or figure competition. When all three events are held, the free routine comprises 50 percent of the score and the technical routine and figures count 25 percent each. When two events are held, the free routine is 65 percent and the other, technical routine or figures, counts 35 percent.

While FINA rules must be applied to all international contests, countries are free to adapt rules for their own national competitions. For example, some nations, including the United States, include

BILL MAY: SYNCHRONIZED SWIMMER

The exclusion of males from the Olympic Games and World Championships may become a controversy since the U.S. National Champion duet and team include a male who will also be a member of the national team. Even after qualifying for the American national team, Bill May was excluded from the top world events (1998 World Championships) and could only participate in competitions such as the French Open, Swiss Open, and others that do not list the sport as an event for women.

trios as part of some programs. Switzerland holds a special figure event for the top twelve contenders from the regular figure competition. Some nations hold ten or fewer events.

RECREATIONAL ACTIVITIES AND COMPETITION

More swimmers are involved in recreational synchro than in the competitive programs. Most recreational activities are more like water ballet than synchronized swimming, and they are often part of preparation for performances at spring water shows in high schools and colleges or summer shows in city recreation programs. Some municipal programs hold citywide competitions at the end of the summer but usually not under the auspices of the national governing body. However, all the recreational programs have introduced large numbers of swimmers to synchronized swimming–type activities.

PROFESSIONAL ACTIVITIES

There are few professional outlets for a synchronized swimmer upon retiring from amateur competition. Even Olympic champions may have limited prospects except in a few places such as Canada, Japan, and France, where synchro champions have been asked to do endorsements and are more well known. More generally, coaching and teaching may be the only outlets. Occasional opportunities exist in large-scale professional aquacades, such as those associated with the World's Fairs in New Orleans and Australia. Throughout the 1990s, the Riviera Hotel in Las Vegas held a *Splash* water show that featured Linda Shelley, U.S. and international champion. Muriel Hermine, 1988 Olympian, developed an annual Aquacade in France that has been successful as a show and also attracted great television coverage. The fall of 1998 saw the opening of Canada's Cirque du Soleil aquacade in Las Vegas. Canada's Olympian Sylvie Frechette was both directing and performing in the show.

WOMEN'S PARTICIPATION

Although competition in water tricks and skills began as a competition for men, the featuring of feminine beauty in water shows and movies influenced the public to view water ballet, and the derivative synchronized swimming, as a women's activity. The original rules for synchro in the United States made no distinction between men and women, allowing both to be included in teams and duets. It was only the AAU's restrictions against men competing with or against women that ended the mixed groups. Even then, the AAU rules continued to list men's synchro events until 1955. A few U.S. national events for men were held in 1953 and 1954, but lack of participation ended interest in holding more. The Esther Williams movies caused girls to flock to synchro and probably helped depress male interest even more. But when U.S. synchro gained autonomy from the AAU, mixed competition once more became feasible.

Under international rules, no gender distinctions were made originally, but the women's association had taken over before the first major international competition, the Pan-American Games of 1955. The world aquatic championships program included synchro events for women only. Similarly, women were specified for the events adopted into the Olympic Games. Recently, men were excluded from the events of the FINA World Cups, which had been previously open to them.

Males are seldom excluded from most national rules, so a few men have persisted despite the predominance of women. Stephane Miermont of France became the first male to win titles in a major open international competition (the French Open) in 1990, as a member of the winning French duet and team. In 1998, Bill May rose to the top in the U.S. nationals as a member of the winning duet and team. He had won the solo and duet titles in the 1997 Swiss Open. May's performance qualified him to represent the United States in the 1998 Goodwill Games, one of the few major international competitions remaining open to men. Although these few males are impressive in their skills, they are the exceptions; the sport remains primarily a women's sport.

FACTORS HINDERING OR ENCOURAGING PARTICIPATION

In the United States, synchro's water show beginnings still haunt it in its quest to be considered a sport. It has been hard to convince swimming officials, the public, and the media that "water ballet is show, but synchronized swimming is sport." Its acceptance into the Olympic Games came only after Lord Killanin, then chair of the International Olympic Committee (IOC), saw it for himself at the third world aquatic championships. "I am very impressed. I saw synchronized swimming for the first time today. It is a very elegant sport," he said later.

In some countries, synchro is highly respected and quite popular. In Japan, Mikako Kotani, bronze medalist in solo and duet at the Olympics of 1988, was followed everywhere by television camera operators, inspiring Swiss television to televise the Swiss Open for the first time when Kotani competed there. Canadian television has a high regard for synchro and televises their national championships in 1-hour programs for each of the three events. In France, popularity surged after television airings of their Olympian Muriel Hermine in the 1984 and 1988 Olympic Games. Her subsequent series of spectacular water shows has helped boost French synchro registrations far higher than those in the United States, where almost no television coverage occurs. In Germany, television viewers were asked to vote on which two sports to cover in their entirety for the Barcelona Olympic Games. Gymnastics and synchronized swimming were chosen. For most countries, though, the show-or-sport controversy continues to hinder acceptance by the media and prevents the public from gaining a realistic concept of the sport.

Dawn Pawson Bean

Bibliography

Amateur Athletic Union. (1941–1953) *Official AAU Swimming Handbook.* New York: Author.

———. (1954–1980) *Official AAU Synchronized Swimming Handbook.* New York and Indianapolis, IN: Author.

Barry, Dave. (1996) "I Am Now a Trained Eggbeater." *Synchro Swimming USA* 4: 2–3.

Bean, Dawn. (1979–1992) *Synchro.* Santa Ana, CA: Dawn & Ross Bean.

———. (1963–1978) *Synchro-Info.* Santa Ana, CA: Dawn & Ross Bean.

———. (1991–1992) "Synchro's History—As I Know It." *Synchro* 29: 6, 30: 1–6.

Clark, Laurene. (1985) *Synchronized Swimming, 60 Years to Celebrate.* Ottawa, Canada: Canadian Amateur Synchronized Swimming Association.

Curtis, Katherine Whitney. (1941) "Competitive Synchronized Swimming." *Journal of Health and Physical Education* (January). Synchronized Swimming Scrapbook, Henning Library, International Swimming Hall of Fame, Ft. Lauderdale, FL.

———. (1942) *Rhythmic Swimming.* Minneapolis, MN: Burgess.

Dawson, Buck. (1987) *Weismuller to Spitz.* Ft. Lauderdale, FL: International Swimming Hall of Fame.

Dodson, Richard. (1952–1955) *The Synchronized Swimmer.* Chicago: Richard Dodson.

Fédération Internationale de Natation Amateur. (1946) *FINA Handbook.* Lausanne, Switzerland: FINA.

Gyarfas, Tamas. (1977) *International Swimming and Water Polo.* Belgrade: International Swimming and Water Polo.

Henning, Jean. (1988) "How It Began." *International Swimming and Water Polo* (Spring).

Kane, Donald T. (1978) *Synchro-Info* 16: 5.

LaMarca, Laura, and Brian Eaton. (1993) *Synchro Swimming USA.* Indianapolis, IN: United States Synchronized Swimming Inc.

Leach, Clark. (1973) "To Set the Record Straight." (25 July) Synchronized Swimming Scrapbook, Henning Library, International Swimming Hall of Fame, Ft. Lauderdale, FL.

Luick, Wilbur. (1958–1961) *Synchro News.* San Jose, CA: Wilbur Luick.

Lundholm, Jean. (1976) "The Story of Synchronized Swimming" *Synchro-Info* 14: 6.

Rackham, George. (1968) *Synchronized Swimming.* London: Faber and Faber.

Stoerker, Marian L. (1956) "Summary: The Historical Development of Synchronized Swimming in the United States" Unpublished. Synchronized Swimming Scrapbook, Henning Library, International Swimming Hall of Fame, Ft. Lauderdale, FL.

Strubbe, Albert B. P. (1958) "Origin and Development of Synchronized Swimming." *Synchro News* 2: 5.

Synchro Canada. (1975) *Highlights of Synchro Swim, 1925–1975, Commemorative Issue.* Ottawa, Canada: Canadian Amateur Synchronized Swimming Association.

United States Synchronized Swimming. (1981) *United States Synchronized Swimming Official Rules.* Indianapolis, IN: United States Synchronized Swimming Inc.

Van den Broeck, Gill. (1959) "AAU Sponsored Tour." *Synchro-News* 3: 1.

Zajac, Dawn. (1969) "History of Synchronized Swimming in England." *Synchro-Info* 3: 3.

Ghada Shouaa, Syrian heptathlete and first Syrian winner of an Olympic gold medal. (Eric Feferberg/Corbis)

SYRIA

The Syrian Arab Republic is a Middle Eastern nation with a population of 16 million. Because of the climate, only summer sports are practiced in Syria. Although Syria in many respects retains traditional Muslim attitudes about women, girls and women are nevertheless participating in sports and other fitness activities in increasing numbers.

HISTORY

Syrian women first became involved in sports in the 1940s, when the country gained its independence from France. At that time, the most popular sports for girls and women were basketball and track and field. In the following decade, several young Syrian women graduated from sports colleges in Egypt and returned to Syria to work as physical education teachers and coaches in the schools. Their presence provided new athletic opportunities for girls at all levels of the educational system, and championships for Syrian schoolgirls were established for track and field, basketball, and volleyball, then later for gymnastics and handball.

The interest and support of President Hafez al-Assad spurred further development of sports in Syria. The government has supported sports throughout the country by providing funds and establishing and updating sports facilities; and successful athletes, both male and female, are awarded housing, jobs, and other amenities. In addition, the money they can make in sports events outside Syria brings athletes a level of wealth and celebrity status not available to most other Syrians.

The National Sport Federation organizes various official championships for women's teams and oversees the selection of the national teams that represent Syria in the Arab, Asian, Mediterranean, and Olympic Games as well as in competitions in neighboring nations.

In the early 1970s, women began to take a more public role in some aspects of Syrian life, and both their numbers and their influence increased in the governmental, judicial, and military sectors. After the founding of a general National Sport Federation, women began to be more involved in sports as well. In the 1990s, women were members of sports clubs, sports federations, and the Syrian National Olympic Committee; they were also employed by the National Sport Federation. In addition, each individual sports federation established a special committee dedicated to women's sports. Thus, Syria became a leader among Arab and Asian nations in bringing women into leadership positions in sports organizations.

INTERNATIONAL COMPETITION

In 1987, Syria organized the tenth Mediterranean Games, with eighteen Mediterranean countries participating. Women took part in track and field, basketball, cycling, gymnastics, handball, judo, shooting, swimming, table tennis, tennis, and volleyball. At the international level, Syrian women have competed in four Olympic Games: Munich (1972)—Malak Nasser, track and field; Moscow (1980)—Dia Totonji, high jump, and Halla Moughrabi, 800-meter race; Barcelona (1992)—Ghada Shouaa, heptathlon; and Atlanta (1996)—Ghada Shouaa, heptathlon.

Shouaa has emerged as Syria's best-known athlete, male or female, with her victories in the Asian Games in 1994, the world championships in 1995 and 1996, and the Olympics in 1996. Her Olympic victory (the first by a Syrian athlete of either sex) was hailed by President Assad: "You have boosted the name of Syria and your glorious victory shows that nothing is impossible with an iron will and continuous training."

Aside from Shouaa's achievements, Syrian women have won relatively few medals in international competitions; the country sent only one woman (Shouaa) to the 1992 and 1996 Olympics. There are several reasons for this. First, despite the effort to promote sports, Syria is not a wealthy nation and there are limited resources with which to build facilities and support international training for and competition by athletes. Second, Syrian women athletes are amateurs, not professionals, and thus have limited personal resources to support their training, equipment, and travel to competitions. Third, in Syria women are to some extent defined primarily as wives and mothers, roles that do not allow for participation in sports.

THE FUTURE

The situation may improve in the future because as of 1999, Syria had four women's sports institutes that had graduated 2,000 women. Women also constituted 30 percent of the students at the coeducational college of sport education. By the late 1990s, Syria had more than 360 sports clubs, where men and women participated in track and field, basketball, cycling, equestrian events, gymnastics, handball, judo, karate, shooting, swimming, table tennis, tennis, and volleyball. Of the 7,000 members of these clubs, about 2,000 were women. In addition, women were training in the many physical fitness centers throughout the country. Those who did not live near such facilities had the option of walking and training on country and city roads and in public parks.

Nour Elhouda Karfoul

See also Shouaa, Ghada

SZEWINSKA, IRENA KIRSZENSTEIN

(1946–)

POLISH TRACK AND FIELD ATHLETE AND ADMINISTRATOR

Irena Szewinska is considered by some sport historians to be the best female track and field athlete and perhaps the best female athlete of the twentieth century. She is certainly the best Polish female athlete of all time. Szewinska specialized in the sprints and long jump, setting numerous records in both events in national, regional, and international competitions in a career that ran from the early 1960s to 1980.

Irena Kirszenstein was born in Leningrad, Russia, on 24 May 1946 but was a Polish citizen because her parents were Poles living in Russia. Her international career began with the 1964 Olympics in Tokyo, the first of five Olympics in which she competed. She won a gold medal as a member of the Polish 400-meter relay team and also took silvers in the long jump and the 200-meter. At the 1966 European championship in Budapest, she continued her dominance, taking gold in the 400-meter relay, the 200-meter sprint, and the long jump, and finishing second in the 100-meter sprint behind her countrywoman Ewa Klobukowska (who was disqualified from further competition when she failed a gender-verification test in 1967). In the same year Kirszenstein married her coach Janusz Szewinski and took his name. At the 1968 Olympics in Mexico City she moved up to take gold in the 200-meter

Irena Szewinksa winning the 200-meter dash at a competition in Augsburg, Germany, in 1974. (AP Photos)

sprint and also the bronze in the 100-meter sprint.

In 1969 she took time off from competition to give birth to a son but resumed competing in 1970. At that time, the prevailing opinion in the sports community was that a woman could never again achieve top performances in track and field following pregnancy and childbirth; and at the World University Games in Turin in 1970, some journalists labeled her "old glory." At the 1972 Olympics in Munich, Szewinska called into question this prevailing opinion as she took the bronze medal in the 200-meter sprint and became the first woman to win three straight Olympic medals in that event. By 1974 she was back at the top, winning the 100- and 200-meter races at the European championship in Rome—and beating the world record holder Renate Stecher-Meissner in the process. The victories made her the only woman athlete to win five European individual events.

In 1976 at the Montreal Olympics, at the age of thirty, she moved up to the more grueling 400-meter race—and set a world record as she won the gold. Unfortunately, her career ended in disappointment at the 1980 Olympics, when she had to drop out after pulling a leg muscle in the semifinals of the 400-meter race. After her retirement from competition in 1980, she became an official in the Polish sport federation and in 1998 was elected a member of the International Olympic Committee (IOC).

Szewinska's lifetime achievements in track and field were unequaled. She won nineteen titles in Poland in four events (100-, 200-, and 400-meter races and the long jump); five golds, one silver, and four bronzes in the European championships; and seven Olympic medals, including three golds.

Gherardo Bonini

T

TABEI JUNKO

(1939–)

JAPANESE MOUNTAIN CLIMBER

Tabei Junko was the first woman to reach the summit of Mount Everest, the highest mountain in the world, in 1975. Tabei was born in Fukushima Prefecture, Japan, on 22 September 1939. She climbed her first mountain on a school field trip when she was ten. After graduating from Tokyo's Showa Women's University in 1962, Tabei worked as an editor and formed a women's climbing club. She led a successful expedition up Annapurna III in Nepal and then applied for permission to climb Everest. During the four-year waiting period, she lined up corporate sponsorship, raised additional money by giving piano lessons, and gave birth to a daughter.

Tabei nearly did not survive Everest. At a base camp at 22,000 feet, she and her climbing companions were buried under the ice and snow of an avalanche. Tabei was buried in her sleeping bag under a jagged block of ice, completely immobilized. She lost consciousness, but Sherpa guides dug the team out, saving their lives and the expedition. Twelve days later, on 16 May 1975, Tabei, accompanied by Sherpa Ang Tsering, reached the summit at 8,848 meters (29,029 feet). Upon descending, Tabei was greeted by a parade in Katmandu and congratulatory messages from the prime minister of Japan and the king of Nepal. Thousands of supporters cheered her arrival at the Tokyo Airport.

Years later, she organized the Japanese chapter of the Himalayan Adventure Trust, an organization devoted to removing oxygen cylinders and trash left by Everest climbers. She also leads clean-up climbs in Japan, often accompanied by her husband, daughter, and son.

In 1992, at age fifty-three, Tabei completed a climb of Mount Jaya, the highest peak in Australasia. This made her the first woman to climb the highest mountains on all seven continents, also known as the Seven Summits.

Kelly Nelson

Bibliography

Bumiller, Elisabeth. (1991) "At the Peak of Her Profession." *Washington Post* (8 April): C1 Kelly Nelson.

Horn, Robert. (1996) "No Mountain Too High for Her." *Sports Illustrated* 84, 17: 5B.

Matsuoka, Tadaaki. (1993) "Record-breaking Climber Scales New Peaks with Clean-Up Drive." *Nikkei Weekly* (12 April): 16.

TABLE TENNIS

Table tennis is a sport in which women have excelled from the moment they began to participate. Initially a distinctly European sport, Chinese women have dominated international competition in the 1980s and 1990s. Despite the excellent quality of women's play at this level, the administration and promoting of the game continue to be oriented toward male players and audiences.

INTERNATIONAL COMPETITION: HARD-BAT ERA (1926–1951)

The modern-day Olympic sport of table tennis is quite unlike the genteel and gentle game of Ping-Pong (a trademarked name) devised around 1900. The transformation from game to sport can be marked from the first International Table Tennis Federation (ITTF) world championships in London in 1926. Then a small group of women perspired quietly in long dresses before an equally small and quiet crowd. Today, Olympic table tennis is a vigorously fought athletic contest, with blocks of spectators crying, "CHIN-a! CHIN-a!"

Deng Yaping of China prepares to serve during a women's singles table tennis game at the 1996 Olympic Games in Atlanta. (TempSport/Corbis)

Equipment, too, has evolved. The first blade was a "hard bat," a plain wooden paddle, covered by cork or ball-destroying sandpaper. A thin sheet of far more spin-effective "pippled rubber"—still in use—was finally adopted.

Although Hungarian Maria Mednyanszky (1901–1974) did not have fluid strokes, she was able—with an up-to-the-table, backhand chop-block, and favoring a backhand angled-off hit from the forehand side—to win every world singles match from 1926 through 1931. In 1932 and 1933 she was runner-up to her teammate Annus "Anna" Sipos (1908–1972), with whom she won six straight world doubles titles.

Following Sipos, who later retired to practice medicine, was two-time world singles champion Marie Kettnerova (1911–1998), one of the three Czech stars of the 1930s. The other two, supporting the "cluster theory" that playing with champions begets champions, were Vlasta Depetrisova (1920–) and Vera Votrubcova (1911–1981).

Ruth Aarons (1918–1980), four-time U.S. champion and the only U.S. player ever to win a world singles title, succeeded Kettnerova. Runner-up to both was Germany's five-time champion Astrid Krebsbach who, after she married a Dr. Hobhom, had to promise she would attend to wifely duties and give up international play. In contrast, the independent-minded Aarons, who came from a famous theatrical family, never married, and she startled the staid table tennis world by wearing unusual outfits of her own design.

In 1937 Aaron's women's team was the first U.S. team to win the world championship Corbillon Cup. But on defending her 1936 Prague World Singles title, she suffered time–lag trouble in the final against Austria's Gertrude "Trude" Pritzi (1920–1968)—a future world champion when she was later forced by Adolf Hitler to represent Germany. Pritzi was a notorious defender who would not, under any circumstances, attempt an aggressive shot. When, according to the rules, her match with Aarons was not over after 105 minutes, the women's title was declared "vacant," a unique historical happening.

Immediately after this event, however, Aarons was the victim of another unparalleled occurrence. She was suspended by the ITTF for failing to obtain the permission of the English Association to put on her theater and cabaret exhibitions in London; permission that would have been denied. At nineteen years of age, she retired from tournament competition to play the celebrity. Performing her well-paid table tennis act with experienced partners through the late 1930s and beyond, she shared the bill on famous vaudeville stages and at nightclubs.

Because of World War II, from 1940 to 1946 there were no world championships. Beginning with the 1947 Paris world championships and continuing on through the 1955 championships at Utrecht, the Netherlands there were only two different women's singles winners: Hungary's Gizelle Farcas (1925–1996), finalist seven years in a row, and, following her, Romania's Angelica Adelstein Rozeanu (1921–), unequaled holder of six straight singles championships. In winning her first world title when she was twenty-eight (somewhat older than most competitors), Rozeanu took full advantage of what she had learned playing with men in Bucharest. Because they had more powerful topspin strokes, she had learned how to win not by force but by "feel," placing the ball where her opponents did not want it to be placed.

Women players from the United States and Great Britain had their postwar world championship victories in the 1940s and 1950s. The Ohio-born Thall sisters—Thelma "Tybie" Sommer (1924–) and Leah "Miss Ping" Neuberger (1915–1993), for many years the USATT historian and in 1971 one of the U.S. players to enter China—took turns winning the Mixed Doubles. Sommer's 1949 Corbillon Cup-winning teammates, Peggy McLean Folke (1927–) and Mildred Shahian (?–1992), were, with Aarons, the only Americans ever to win the U.S. and English Opens. Shahian was one of the very few women who persisted in trying to run a successful, open-to-the-public table tennis club.

No woman from England has ever won a world singles title, but two of the English runners-up were also very accomplished lawn tennis players—1946 winner of the Beckenham grass courts tournament Vera Dace Thomas (1922–95) and 1969 Wimbledon champion Ann Haydon Jones (1938–). Diane Rowe Scholer and Rosalind Rowe Cornett (1933–), twin sisters from Middlesex, were twice women's doubles champions and finalists five years in a row.

INTERNATIONAL COMPETITION: SPONGE ERA (1952–1998)

In 1952 at the Bombay world championships, the Japanese, on winning the women's team championship, showed early signs of a period in which, beginning in 1956, they would win seven of the next eight women's singles. The Japanese were the first to use the disorienting "soundless" sponge-rubber racket—its blade covered by a sheet of sponge and a layer of pips-out or pips-in (inverted) rubber—that provided more speed and spin. In addition, their athleticism and their fast-attack, penholder play proved extremely effective opposite the European hard-bat, shakehands style often associated with drawn-out defensive play. ("Penholder" means blade head held downward, handle held as a pen is held. "Shakehands" means head held upward, handle held as a tennis racket is held.) Indeed, in winning the 1957 women's singles, Fujie Eguchi (1933–) actually used the old hard bat rather than the new sponge-rubber racket already adopted by most of her compatriots. Two-time singles champion Kimiyo Matsuzaki Kurimoto (1938–) was another whose crouch-and-spring fast footwork allowed her to hit devastating penhold forehand shots even from her backhand corner. In her games, Matsuzaki was always fast and aggressive, but away from the sport, using a special *fude* (brush) pen, she showed great patience studying the traditional art of sketching *waka* (32-syllable) and *haiku* (17-syllable) poetry (Boggan 1970).

In the 1950s and 1960s, Europeans were still able to contest the championships. Eva Koczian (1936–), like her brother Jozsef earlier, was a singles finalist. Romania's hot-tempered defensive star Maria Alexandru (1945–) was runner-up to Matsuzaki, and, during an indefatigable fourteen-year span, three-time women's doubles champion.

In the 1990s, age-group competitions were introduced. These encouraged the return to competitive play of former champions. The 1996 world veterans championships at Lillehammer, Norway, drew almost 2,000 men and women to compete in the forty-through-eighty age events (one Japanese female player was 87). Russia's Svetlana Grinberg Fedorova, 1969 women's doubles champion, won the over-50 singles.

During the Cultural Revolution (1966–1970), the Chinese were absent from world championships; some women were forced to give up table tennis and do manual labor on farms, losing perhaps forever their earlier promise. Others were able to maintain their skills over this period. Lin Hui-qing (1941–), who in 1965 had been the singles runner-up to Japan's Naoko Fukazu (1944–), won the 1971 championship. On their return to international competition, the Chinese introduced new techniques that made the game even more competitive. One technique, introduced by two-time world singles champion Cao Yanhua, was the 15-foot-high toss when serving: as the descending ball neared the table, she would pivot and strike with quite unpredictable effects. The look-alike sides of Cao's racket had different properties, which only intensified the confusion of her opponents. The ball came off "dead" when hit by one side of the blade, but off the other side, it would be quite "alive." This tactic was so confusing that the ITTF finally insisted that one side of the racket-covering must be colored bright red, the other black.

Cao's domination of table tennis in the 1980s has been extended by the Chinese to the 1990s. From 1991 through 1995, Liu Wei (1969–) won three straight world mixed doubles and also a women's doubles. Qiao Hong (1968–) won not only a world women's singles (and was runner-up in another) but the Olympic singles too. In 1997 Deng Yaping (1973–) was three-time world women's singles champion, three-time world women's doubles champion, two-time Olympic singles and doubles champion, and a revered national hero.

THE MODERN GAME: STATUS

Whether one speaks of high-level competitive play in the Western world from 1926 to 1951, or of the arrival and ascendancy of the Japanese, Chinese, and Koreans after 1952, the history of the International Table Tennis Federation (ITTF) shows a very clear pattern of male dominance.

Although there have been modifications in the rules of play (most notably with regard to service) and dynamic and controversial changes in speed-and-spin technology, one constant feature of the sport is that men have almost always controlled it. Since the men are acknowledged to be far better players than the women (eight to ten points a game), the assumption has been that because of their spectacular physical play, they provide more spectator appeal, and so deserve a greater reward—specifically more prize money and more vanity payments for the male officials and coaches in control.

In 1997 Diane Rowe Scholer (1933–), after serving for many years as its secretary, became the first woman president of the Swaythling Club International, a club with a membership of about 550 well-known veteran players and officials from over sixty countries. Of the top twelve officials in the ITTF at the end of the twentieth century, none were women. Of the thirty-two subordinate council members, only about 10 percent were women. Of the various committee heads, only one, the 1977 world mixed doubles champion Claude Bergeret (1954–) of France, was a woman.

Bergeret had great hopes for the proposals that emerged from the International Olympic Committee (IOC) "World Conference on Woman and Sport" in 1997 in Lausanne. These included organizing training courses for elementary school and high school teachers in all countries of the world, especially those of Africa, and encouraging Muslim countries to permit their women to participate in certain competitions wearing regular sports clothes. In October 1997, as head of the ITTF's Athlete's Commission, Bergeret traveled to Beirut, where forward-looking male officials organized not only a Women's Training Camp, in which Bergeret's administrative and coaching expertise was put to good use, but also—to offset the richest ITTF Pro Tour event, the Qatar Open, in which only men were allowed to play—a new prize-money tournament just for women, the Lebanon Open.

In an article published in *Table Tennis Digest* in 1990, Jill Hammersley-Parker (1949–), European singles and doubles champion in 1976 and captain of the English women's team at the 1997 world championships in Manchester, England, objected to the fact that there were too few women coaches and that male coaches too often adopt an authoritarian style. She noted that if the table tennis world wanted more girls involved as players and coaches, they needed as role models female coaches who would bring a more caring, sensitive approach to coaching. But such changes in the system were unlikely, and the most successful team captains and coaches continued to be men.

THE MODERN GAME: CHINESE DOMINATION

In Manchester, the women's singles drew close to 300 entries from almost eighty countries. All but one of the quarterfinalists, however, were from China. The January 1999 ITTF Rankings showed that of the top twenty-three women players in the world, the first fifteen were born and trained in China, and, except for one Croatian, one South Korean, and one German, the others were too.

The Chinese have dominated the game with excellent play since 1971. They have won every world women's singles championship, except for losses to one North Korean, Pak Yung Sun (1957–) and one South Korean, Hyun Jung Hwa (1969–).

In twenty years following 1978, they lost the women's doubles and the mixed doubles only once each. From 1975 to 1998 they won every world women's team championship, save one—in 1991, in Chiba, Japan, to a combined North/South Korea Team.

Though many found it surprising, it was the Europeans—including the 1996 champion, Nicole Struse (1971–) of Germany, and the 1994 champion, Marie Svensson (1967–) of Sweden—who were shut out during the 1980s and 1990s, not the North Koreans who were thought to be so isolated. In 1989 and 1991, Li Bun Hui (1968–) was a singles finalist; and in 1997 North Korea, having beaten the South Koreans in Manchester, ranked as the number two women's team in the world.

The Chinese women achieved such success because of systematic efforts to develop their skills. Canadian table tennis official Pierre Abran noted on his return from a China visit that at a very young age, many Chinese women attended "half-time sport schools." Students, age eight to twelve, left home with the permission of their parents and the approval of a coach, and went to live with their peers to devote half of their time to studies and the other half to training. After a demanding learning period that lasted until they were thirteen or fourteen, the best of the girls were then ready to represent their particular province. At this stage they spent less time on their studies and more time on their table tennis. If they were good enough, they continued their training at a national training center in Beijing. The better the players were (especially if they got to play in world championships and the Olympic Games, the more the perquisites (a new apart-

CHINESE IMMIGRATION—A CONTINUING PROBLEM?

Through the 1980s and 1990s, the lure of living and working outside China became more and more appealing to Chinese players. Although the Chinese media began referring to those who had immigrated as their "overseas corps," the Chinese Table Tennis Association itself did not take kindly to the fact that players still in their prime whom they had spent a great deal of time and effort training to be world-class might want to defect and play for other countries. At the same time, those other countries—Canada, for example, with the arrival of 1985 world singles runner-up Geng Lijuan (1963–) and other strong immigrant players—were becoming more and more wary of just how many Chinese ought fittingly to be on their national team.

Consequently, the ITTF over the years gradually stiffened its rules on international eligibility from a two-year *residency* requirement to *citizenship* of the new country. Despite these restrictions, Chinese women continue to fan the globe—sometimes with the calculated blessing of the Chinese Association, sometimes not.

Chen Jing (1968–), China's amply rewarded 1988 Olympic singles champion, went on to become the 1993 world singles runner-up while playing for Taiwan. He Zhili, China's 1987 world singles champion, defected to Japan and became that country's champion under the name Chire Koyama after being denied a spot on China's 1988 Olympic team. Reportedly, China's snubbing of He Zhili occurred after she disobeyed orders to throw a match to a compatriot at the 1987 world's competitions. In the 1994 Asian Games in Hiroshima, she beat the nearly invincible Chinese world champions, Qiao Hong and Deng Yaping, shouting point after triumphant point in Japanese. Branded a "traitor" by the Chinese media, she did not show for the 1995 World Championships in Tianjin, pleading illness at the last minute.

No country has felt the impact of Chinese immigration more strongly than the United States. For the last six years there, women's championships have been won by "Amy" Feng (1969–), 1986 runner-up in the Chinese nationals, and Gao Jun (1969–), 1991 world women's doubles champion. Also, of the five U.S. women who qualified to play in the most recent Manchester World Championships, one was Vietnamese-born, the others all Chinese-trained expatriates.

ment, perhaps) and the higher financial rewards. At the end of their careers (when they were in their mid- to late twenties), with wave upon wave of world-class younger players waiting to take their places, they might become table tennis coaches or administrators in China or, increasingly in the 1990s, emigrate to countries where they were highly valued (and paid) players and coaches.

As ten-time Canadian champion and current Canadian Women's National Coach Mariann Domonkos (1958–) explained in an account of her team's trip to Seoul, the South Korean system is also effective but very different. High school girls who play well are scouted and recruited by company teams (the company may be a cosmetics firm, a bank, an airlines, etc.), always headed by a male general manager. The athletes receive a salary, but their sole responsibility is to train and compete. Upon retirement, most get married, have children, and, preoccupied with family life, no longer want to be involved in playing or coaching. One athlete, however, who modified her assigned woman's "place" was Seoul's Insook Na Bhushan (1952–) who, unhappy at being selected the nominal South Korean women's team captain rather than a player at the 1973 World Championships, emigrated to the United States, where she married, had two sons, got an accounting degree, did table tennis administrative work, and won a record eleven national singles championships.

Europeans also recruit youngsters to their training centers. One big difference between European and Chinese or Korean systems is that, as the players improve with age, they have more independence than players in Asia. They may represent one of the many sport clubs in one of the various play-for-pay leagues, though not necessarily in the country in which they live or represent at world championships. Also, as Scholer (1991) points out, European women earn only enough to cover the daily expenses and continue with their education and careers, seeing those avenues as their future.

CHALLENGE IN THE TWENTY-FIRST CENTURY

Chinese domination is so complete that it threatens to reduce the potential audiences for an otherwise successful and growing sport. After sixteen years of World Cup play for men only, China's Wang Nan placed first and Li Ju placed second in the 1997 and 1998 events for women. In 1997 the ITTF's new round-the-world Pro Tour was won by Li over Wang, but Wang was able to win over Li in the 1998 Pro Tour. There was a sense that television audiences enthusiastic over the longer-point play of the women would be even more enthusiastic, with sponsors following suit, if real rivalries could be established between East and West. But, what Scholer noted thirty-five years ago remains true in 2000. The Asian players hit the ball much faster than non-Asians and so far non-Asians have not been able to catch up. Many observers believe that if the women's play is to flourish as an international, rather than regional, sport, the gap to be bridged is not only between men and women, but between Asian and non-Asian women.

Tim Boggan

Bibliography

Abran, Pierre. (1987) "Coaches' Coaching." *Table Tennis Technical/Technique Tennis de Table* (June/July): 47–48.

Barna, Victor. (1962) *Table Tennis Today.* London: Arthur Barker.

Bergeret, Claude, and Eva Jeler. (1997) "Immediate Objectives." *Table Tennis Illustrated* (February–March): 13.

Boggan, Tim. (1970) "Kimiyo Kurimoto" *Table Tennis Topics* (September–October): 1.

———. (1992) "Mildred Shahian." *Table Tennis Topics* (May–June): 36.

Cao, Jianjie. (1996) "Injury Laden Deng Yaping Vows to Fight On." *Table Tennis Illustrated* (December): 6.

Craydon, Ron. (1995) *The Story of Table Tennis: The First 100 Years.* Hastings, England: English TTA.

Domonkos, Mariann. (1990) "West Goes East." *Table Tennis Year* (Spring): 24.

Hammersley-Parker, Jill. (1990) "Women in Table Tennis." *Table Tennis Digest* (February): 41.

Lu, Xiaoming. (1991) "A Dwarf May Also Tower." *Table Tennis Topics* (June–July): 17.

Rowe, Diane. (1965) *Table Tennis.* London: Stanley Paul.

Scholer, Diane Rowe. (1991) "Closing the Gap." *Table Tennis Digest* (March): 90.

Tajima, Masaaki. (1993) "Women in Sports." *Table Tennis Today* (May/June): 38.

TAEKWONDO

Taekwondo was developed in the 1940s for Korean military and police organizations as a means of defense and physical conditioning. Since then it has become a major international sport that attracts many male and female participants including elite competitors; *do-jang* (studio) owners and teachers; and many women who participate for fun, personal growth, and physical conditioning.

The term "taekwondo" is a combination of the words *tae,* which means a system of foot techniques; *kwon,* which means a system of hand techniques; and *do,* which means the art or the way of life. But taekwondo is not a single, unified martial art system. There are many individual styles and *kwans* (associations) that teach and practice forms or variations of taekwondo. Tang Soo Do (China hand way), for example, is a major variant style, with various *kwans.* Hwarang Do (named after the Korean knights of the Silla dynasty who first studied and systematized martial arts) is another style with various *kwans.* Therefore, while the World Taekwondo Federation (WTF) has been successful in standardizing and popularizing taekwondo, it is important to remember that there are various major styles and *kwans* that do not participate in the WTF that are also vital, all of them sharing a common Korean heritage, all of them providing opportunities for women to participate. Still, it is the taekwondo that has been standardized and popularized through the WTF that emerged as a full Olympic sport in the year 2000.

South Korea's Sun-Hee Lee exchanges kicks with an opponent during the women's taekwondo lightweight final at the Asian Games in Bangkok in 1998. (AP Photos)

HISTORY

The first historical indication of unarmed self-defense or martial arts is found in ancient India around 2600 BCE. These techniques likely complemented the use of weapons and provided self-defense tools against people and animals. These unarmed self-defense techniques from India were brought to China in about 525 CE by Buddhist monks. Chinese martial arts spread to Okinawa in the 1400s, and Okinawan martial arts spread to Japan in the 1800s.

Early Koreans, the Tonkin people, also developed unique martial art forms for unarmed self-defense to complement their skills with weapons. The first recorded evidence of what was to become modern taekwondo dates back to about 2,000 years ago in the form of a mural painting from the Koguryu kingdom (37 BCE to 66 CE), which was the easternmost corner of the Chinese Han dynasty. The mural was in a tomb believed to have been built sometime between 3 and 427 CE. It shows people practicing martial arts techniques and is in accord with documents from the Koguryu period that mention the practice of martial arts techniques and tournaments. These early forms had different names, such as *kwonbak, bakhi, dangsoo, taesoo,* and *kongsoo.* From about 600 to about 1400 CE, the mainstream form was *soobak,* practiced by the Hwarang (literally "flower of youth") of the Silla dynasty (c. 670–935 CE), which further evolved into *taekyon* beginning in the late 1300s. Taekyon was the dominant Korean martial art form until the Japanese invasion in 1910, which introduced Japanese culture and martial arts.

The modern period of taekwondo began with the defeat of the Japanese and the liberation of Korea in 1945. Korean martial arts masters wanted to eliminate Japanese influences; they began to return to the traditional taekyon based Korean martial arts and attempted to standardize the various martial arts schools and styles into a single style and national sport. Although many teachers and *kwans* never joined the central organization, after several years of discussion the name "taekwondo" was chosen in April 1955 by a board of masters from several of the major *kwans*. These *kwans* began to unite into one organization, and in 1961 the Korea Taesoodo Association was created. In 1965 the association changed its name to the Korea Taekwondo Association (KTA).

The 1970s was the decade of firm establishment and worldwide dissemination. An important milestone was the establishment in 1972 of the *Kukkiwon*, or world taekwondo headquarters. The Kukkiwon, through WTF and various national organizations, certifies *dans* (black-belt holders) worldwide, promotes taekwondo, and strives for worldwide development of the sport. Kukkiwon *dan* holders were estimated at 3.2 million in 1995.

In 1973 the first men's world taekwondo championship, a biannual event, was held at the Kukkiwon. The women's world taekwondo championship was not started until 1987. Other major national, regional, and international taekwondo competitions were developed in the 1970s and 1980s. Taekwondo also became a part of most of the major multisport competitions, including the World Games, Pan-American Games, All-Africa Games, Southeast Asian Games, and Central American Games.

In both the taekwondo and the multisport competitions, the introduction of women's divisions usually trailed those of men, but by the end of the 1980s most contests were open to men and women. The Asian taekwondo championship was instituted in 1974, but women competitors were not admitted until 1986; the Asian Games saw the introduction of taekwondo in 1988, but female competitors were not admitted until 1998; and there was a fourteen-year interval between the first men's and first women's world championships sponsored by the WTF. Competitions that began more recently more often included women from the beginning. In 1991 taekwondo, with men's and women's events, was introduced into the Pan-American Games; in 1993 men and women competed in the Southeast Asian Games for the first time. Likewise, taekwondo in the Olympic Games has always been open to men and women. Taekwondo was a demonstration sport in 1988 at Seoul and 1992 at Barcelona and will be a full Olympic sport at Sydney in 2000.

THE PHILOSOPHY OF TAEKWONDO

Korean traditional martial arts reflect Chinese influence. All Korean martial arts stress spiritual as well as physical development, and they draw inspiration from Chinese Taoism and Buddhism and the works of Lao Tzu and Confucius. A taekwondoist strives to bring her physical, mental, and spiritual aspects into harmony or unity. Thus, the perfectly executed movement represents not only physical perfection but perfection on other planes as well. Two keys to this kind of integration, which are also typical of various Eastern meditative practices, are the control and unification of the breath and bodily energy known as *chi*, or *ki*, in Korean.

Korean traditional martial arts also express traditional Korean social virtues such as benevolence, righteousness, politeness, and wisdom; these have corresponding physical manifestations as well. Benevolence is the idea of respect for life and is the virtue corresponding to the lower part of body and to the earth. Righteousness and politeness are the virtues relating to trunk of the body and to humanity. And wisdom corresponds to the face and to heaven. Taekwondo practice is not, therefore, just a simple matter of blocking, thrusting, and kicking. It is a metaphysical action and a form of practical philosophy meant to assist the practitioner in reaching the world where the self corresponds with the universe beyond the world of individual existence.

RULES AND PLAY

Taekwondo practitioners can develop physical fitness and mental strength through basic techniques (kicks, punches, blocks, stances), *poomse* or *hyung* (forms), *kyukpa* (breaking), *machuo kyorugi* (arranged sparring), and *jayu kyorugi* (free sparring). Through practicing the spectrum of taekwondo skills the practitioner can prepare herself not only for competition but also for any life-threatening situations. Taekwondo is a total fitness program. If "taekwon" denotes the external form of the art, "do" connotes the internal essence. The essence of taekwondo begins from the spirit of martial arts. It is a way of improving the self through constant internal struggles between the negative self and the positive self.

Basic taekwondo training consists of first learning the stances, blocks, kicks, and punches that form taekwondo's basic elements. The student also learns how to use these techniques in response to an attack in arranged sequences of attack and defense. Another significant element is the practice of patterns (forms): a prearranged series of twenty to forty movements of different blocks, kicks, and strikes are performed in imaginary combat against a number of different assailants. Self-defense techniques are also taught as responses to real-life, "street" situations. Men and women usually train together, although sometimes there are separate classes for women. Children and adults sometimes train together, but often there are separate classes for different age groups.

In most taekwondo styles there is a ranking system that is usually marked by different-colored belts worn by the participants. Beginning students usually wear white, the most advanced before *dan* rank usually wear brown or red. *Dans* wear black or midnight-blue belts. *Dans* over the fourth degree are usually considered masters. The head of each *kwan* is acknowledged as grandmaster. Just as each taekwondo studio, or *do-jang*, is a unique combination of the general style, so also is the culture of the *kwan* and the character and objectives of the instructors, known in Korean as *sa-bom*. The value placed on ranking and testing for rank can vary widely; some taekwondo students find themselves testing for a new rank every two months, while others test only when they or their instructors feel they are ready.

Physically, taekwondo develops coordination, motor skills, agility, flexibility, muscular strength, endurance, balance, posture, cardiovascular fitness, aerobic fitness, and anaerobic fitness. Due to its physical nature, taekwondo training promotes a healthy life-style, including proper physical training, proper nutrition, proper rest, and the maintenance of a balance in life. Taekwondo promotes good character and a nonviolent attitude by teaching courtesy, humility, integrity, respect for others, self-reliance, courage, and self-control under stress. In response to conflict, taekwondo teaches calmness, avoidance, and neutralization. It features a nonconfrontational and controlled approach to aggression through the teaching of self-control, self-confidence, and violence-as-a-last-resort response to conflict. Students must respect fellow students and obey instructors. Taekwondo demands patience, perseverance, and a striving for perfection.

Psychologically, taekwondo reduces tension and anxiety by providing a socially acceptable means of physical self-expression, of controlling aggression, and of venting hostility and frustration in a healthy, beneficial manner. It requires self-respect, complete self-control, and respect for others, whether training a partner or meeting an adversary. It also provides a means of personal achievement and advancement through mastery of its curriculum, testing, and progression through belt levels. Dedication to attaining a goal and successful goal attainment improve one's self-image and sense of self-worth. Aesthetically, taekwondo involves specific skills and techniques that must be mastered, with some latitude for personal style and self-expression. It develops a set of core techniques, which the taekwondo student can master, and also emphasize those most natural to and effective for each individual. Rhythm, timing, balance, proper form, and proper breathing are all essential for correct technical execution. Mentally, taekwondo practitioners have to master focused concentration and detachment from external distractions. There is beauty and grace in the practice of the taekwondo movements and techniques, and great satisfaction in mastering and controlling one's mind and body in the execution of demanding physical exercise.

COMPETITION

Kyorugi is an actual fight between two competitors using the offensive and defensive skills acquired through the practice of taekwondo. There are two types of *kyorugi* as defined by the degree of limitation of the skills allowed. They are *machuo kyorugi* (arranged sparring) and *jayu kyorugi* (free sparring). *Jayu kyorugi* is the form of sparring that is used in taekwondo competition. Taekwondo competition is neither a specialized form of taekwondo isolated from general taekwondo nor simply a sport set apart from the tradition of taekwondo. Rather, taekwondo competition is an element of training that attempts to realistically test the viability of techniques through a system of competition. Thus, competitions are designed with both safety and technical training of the participants in mind.

Valid techniques for scoring points in sparring competition include a variety of punching and kicking skills. The punch can be used only to the trunk (areas covered by the chest guard), and kicking techniques can be executed to the face (head, in front of the ears) and trunk (areas covered by the chest guard). One point is awarded to a technique that is delivered accurately on a legal area with the proper amount of power. As an element of training in some competitions, in order to encourage and develop certain practices, more than one point may be awarded for the execution of more advanced techniques.

The winner, in WTF-sanctioned matches, is decided by points or knockout. Other *kwans* and styles rely on points exclusively and strictly regulate the force of contact permitted. Illegal techniques and behavior are penalized by a warning (*kyung-go*) or deduction of a point (*gam-jeom*). The competitor who accumulates three deduction points throughout the match is automatically disqualified.

Most of the vital points of the legal target areas are shielded by protection gear worn by the competitors. It is mandatory for all competitors to wear headgear, a chest protector, shin guards, forearm guards, and a groin protector to prevent injuries. In styles and *kwans* that do not permit full contact, some of this equipment, especially chest gear, is optional.

Taekwondo competition takes place on the 12-meter-square (13-yard-square) mat between two competitors identified by the color of their chest protectors as blue (*chung*) and red (*hong*). WTF competitors are divided by weight and gender into sixteen divisions. A standard international match consists of three rounds of 3 minutes with a 1-minute break between rounds. When a non-electronic trunk protector is used, the officials are a referee and three judges.

Other competitions involve the display of *poomse* or *hyung*. These are usually divided by gender and by rank. Forms are performed in front of a panel of judges and are rated in much the same way that gymnasts might be rated in a gymnastics event. Judging criteria include the technical execution of all the required movements in the form combined with the individual performer's display of confidence and unique style. Occasionally forms and other demonstrations are performed by teams as yet another aspect of competition.

WOMEN IN MODERN TAEKWONDO

Since the 1980s, women have figured prominently in taekwondo practice and competition. Many women are instructors or studio owners, many have achieved master rank, and many have achieved prominence in various taekwondo organizations and kwans. At the 1999 WTF world championship, 230 women (compared to 320 men) from fifty-three countries competed. Korean women dominated with three gold and three silver medals; Spain followed with two gold, one silver, and two bronze; Taiwan had two gold and two bronze; and China had one gold, one silver, and two bronze.

The United States Taekwondo Union (USTU), a WTF-affiliated organization, runs a separate women's program, which addresses the concerns of women and produces its own newsletter. USTU features as many female elite athletes at its Web site as it does male athletes.

Taekwondo in the 1990s attracted a broad range of female participants. While some competed at the elite level, the majority were women who integrated taekwondo practice into their lives to enhance their physical, emotional, and spiritual well-being. Many were mothers who, after taking their children to class for a year or more, decided to take up the sport themselves. Others were college students, or former students, who were first introduced through a college club. Others were professional women, who used taekwondo or some other form of martial art to relieve career tensions and to stay in shape.

Sarah Chung
Maarten Reilingh

Bibliography

Bain, Ron. (1999) "Ron Bain's Korean Martial Arts Page." <http://www.cyberbeach.net/~bainr/malinks.htm>.

Burdick, Dakin. (1997) "People and Events in Taekwondo's Formative Years." *Journal of Asian Mar-*

tial Arts 6, 1. Published online by the author at <http://www.indiana.edu/~iutkd/history/tkdhist.html>.

Cohen, Greta L. (1993). *Women in Sport: Issues and Controversies.* Newbury Park, CA: Sage Publications.

Kim, D. S. (1991). *Background Readings in Taekwondo and Martial Arts.* Seoul: Na Nam Publishing.

Kim, Sang H., Kuk H. Chung, and Kyung M. Lee. (1994) *Taekwondo Kyorugi: Olympic Style Sparring,* 2d rev. Hartford, CT: Turtle Press.

Segura, Daniel. (1999) "Warrior-Scholar" <http://www.warrior-scholar.com/>.

United States Taekwondo Union web site. (1999) <http://www.ustu.com/>.

World Taekwondo Federation web site. (1999) <http://www.worldsport.com/sports/taekwondo/>.

A woman does her tai chi exercises next to Hoan Kiem Lake in Hanoi, Vietnam, in 1995. (Steve Raymer/Corbis)

TAI CHI

Tai chi quan, or tai ji quan, is the most popular type of Chinese *wushu* (traditional martial arts). Literally, *tai chi* means "grand ultimate" and *quan* means "boxing" in Chinese. Originally it was called *chang quan* (long boxing) because the practice consists of many movements and takes a long time to complete. It was also called *shi san shi* (thirteen forms), as the essential movements of tai chi quan are eight basic postures and five patterns of footwork. Tai chi quan obtained its current name during the Qian Lun period (1736–1795) of the Qing Dynasty (1644–1911), when Wan Tsung Yueh, a noted tai chi master, wrote *On Tai Chi Quan* and other works that analyzed marital arts in the context of Chinese philosophic ideas such as tai chi, yin and yang, the five elements (metal, wood, water, fire, and earth), and the eight diagrams. A good tai chi quan performance is characterized by simple and graceful circular movements that are done in a continuous flow and at a slow, even pace, and also by a strict composition in which lightness is integrated with firmness and tranquility with solemnity. Women's participation was restricted until the twentieth century, but by the 1980s women were fully involved, and by the end of the century more women than men were practicing tai chi.

HISTORY

There are several theories regarding the origin of tai chi quan. The most popular view is that it was originated by Chen Wang Ting (?–1719), an army officer, who created the sport while living in retirement in his hometown of Chen Jia Gou (Chen Village, Wen County in Henan province). Proponents of this theory point to the fact that all other subschools of tai chi quan came, directly or indirectly, from the Chen style. Nonetheless, it seems unlikely that one person could have created all forms of tai chi quan, which seems to draw on so many aspects of Chinese culture. As an advanced form of Chinese *wushu,* tai chi quan integrates elements from three sources: 1) various boxing styles of the Ming Dynasty (1368–1644), especially the thirty-two postures of *chang quan* summarized by General Qi Ji Guang (1528–1587); 2) the ancient *tao yin* (an ancient fitness exercise somewhat similar to modern gymnastics) and *qi gong* (exercises mainly to cultivate internal vital energy); and 3) traditional Chinese philosophy and medicine.

Women's participation in tai chi quan experienced a dramatic increase in the twentieth century. Before then, male dominance in Chinese society and Confucianism, which frowned on female participation in martial arts, discouraged participation by women. Nonetheless, tai chi quan's elegant, slow, and smooth movements and its health benefits attracted women. Although there is little in written history, it is known that women did participate from the earliest times of the sport. In the 1920s several *wushu* schools and societies formed in various Chinese cities, and classes for women were offered for tai chi quan and other *wushu* activities and even for training female *wushu* instructors. Tai chi participation by women has gradually increased since the middle of the twentieth century, and more and more women have enjoyed the elegant physical exercises. A 1996 survey indicated that 56.5 percent of tai chi quan exercisers in China were women, and in Japan this percentage was as high as 81.3 percent.

In the 1990s tai chi quan was practiced equally by men and women. In all *wushu* tournaments, including the World Wushu/Kung Fu Championship organized by the International Wushu Federation, tai chi quan is the core event. Men and women athletes show their best skills in separate groups under the same rules. As more women participated, many began to achieve master rank. Women began to assume more important roles in tai chi quan circles, and it was not unusual to see women as instructors in physical education institutions and sports clubs, as referees at tai chi quan tournaments, as contributors to tai chi quan publications, and even as innovators of new tai chi quan routines. For instance, Sun Jian Yong, the granddaughter of the creator of the Sun style, presented a simplified routine by abstracting thirty-five forms from the original ninety-eight movements. This new routine was easier for ordinary people to learn and it further popularized the style.

RULES AND PLAY

There are five major styles that developed from the basic Chen style. They are Yang, Wu (Wu Yu Xiang), Wu (Wu Jian Quan), Sun, and Zhao Bao. The Yang style is the most popular and has even replaced the Chen Style. Yang Lu Chan (1799–1872), the creator of the Yang style, played a significant role in popularization of tai chi quan. Having learned the Chen style, he taught the arts extensively, first in his hometown and later in the capital city of Beijing. He and his descendants reformed the Chen style by eliminating difficult movements that require jumping or great strength and by smoothing out the routines, to make them more accessible to a wider range of people.

Tai chi quan routines vary in length from the simplified routine of 24 forms to complicated ones of 108. Each form is named by the vivid image created in that form, and many are named after wild animals such as "part the wild horse's mane," "grasp sparrow's tail," "white ape presents fruit," and "yellow dragon stirs water." Tai chi quan has thirteen basic postures: *peng* (warding), *lu* (diverting), *ji* (pressing), *an* (pushing), *cai* (plucking), *lie* (twisting), *zhou* (elbowing) and *kao* (leaning), which are connected with the eight diagrams, and *jin* (stepping forward), *tui* (stepping backward), *gu* (look to the left), *pan* (look to the right), and *zhong ding* (central equilibrium).

Tai chi quan has four sets of requirements for participants. The first one deals with mind and breath: one has to be calm and guide the movement with the mind, keeping the breath slow, deep, and in accordance with body movements. The second refers to body postures: the body is held erect and relaxed without leaning in any direction, with the waist as an axis to keep all parts of the body as a whole in the entire moving process. The third is about the movement: all moves are in circles, as smooth as flowing water and at the same time making clear the rhythms of empty and heavy. And the fourth deals with the nature of the arts: the movements should be light and agile; softness and hardness supplement each other so as to emit *jing* (internal strength) completely.

In addition to individual performances, tai chi quan has a pairs practice called *tui shou* (push-hand) for training as well as competition. In this practice, two players, with each of their forearms touching their opponent's opposite forearm, try to push the opponent off balance. Tai chi quan also includes routines with various weapons such as broadsword, sword, and spear. They are all played in accordance with the principles of the bare hand tai chi quan.

The emphasis on physical and mental development has made tai chi quan an excellent form of exercise, and it was frequently used in wellness programs and for rehabilitative purposes in physical therapy. However, to serious *wushu* artists, tai chi quan was also a powerful combat art designed to defeat hardness with softness. For example, Yang Lu Chan, the creator of the Yang style, was very skillful in techniques that appeared so soft that they were called *mian quan* (cotton boxing): he was never defeated and yet he never hurt his opponents. However hard he was hit, he could shake it off easily, and, as the tai chi quan proverb says, he would "use four ounces to deflect a thousand pounds." Yang's marvelous achievement earned him the nickname "Yang the Invincible."

Chi Quan's unique features and availability to a broad range of age groups and to men and women has made it popular around the world, including many western countries. Clubs appeared in the United States, Canada, United Kingdom, France, Germany, Italy, and many other nations; and tai chi documents in various languages can be found at many Websites on the Internet. With the rapid increase of the aged population and development of the new communications technology, further developments in tai chi quan around the world may be expected.

Hai Ren

Bibliography

Lu, Shaojun. (1997) "A Social Investigation and Analysis on the Tai Chi Quan Exercises in China and Japan." Master's thesis, Beijing University of Physical Education.

Ma, Xianda, ed. (1990) *Grand Dictionary of Chinese Wushu.* Beijing: People's Sport Press.

People's Sport Press. (1988) *A Complete Book of Tai Chi Quan.* Beijing: People's Sport Press.

Ren, Hai. (1990) *Ancient Chinese Wushu.* Beijing: Commerce Press.

Wan, Tsung Yueh, et al. (1991) *Book of Tai Chi Quan.* Beijing: People's Sport Press.

Xie, Shoude, and Wenying Li. (1989) *Chinese-English Wushu Glossary.* Beijing: People's Sport Press.

TEAM PLAY *see* Cooperation; Socialization

TECHNOLOGY

Women have played in the center court at Wimbledon for over a century, but only recently has their game overtaken the men's in television ratings, popularity, and style, thanks in a large part to technology. Strong and lightweight materials such as graphite, boron, and titanium have revolutionized sport and increased opportunities for female athletes to develop their athletic potential. Gone are heavy wood rackets. The space-age materials now on the courts allow women to play aggressive baseline shots, slam overheads, volley with both touch and power, and serve up to 125 miles per hour. For the men's game, these innovations have eliminated rallies and transformed men's tennis into "quick-draw showdowns between gunslingers," as someone put it. Technology has usurped the traditional feel, style, and skill of the men's game—turning the sport into a serving contest. Technology, thus, can both enhance and usurp the athletic skill a sport provides.

ATHLETIC CHALLENGE

Sport provides an athletic challenge and an arena to display athletic excellence. The javelin throw requires precise technique, optimal launch angle, and physical strength. In the 1980s aerodynamics engineers redesigned the javelin. By moving its center of gravity, the spear would soar farther than it had ever before. The drawback was, however, that to realize this increased distance, the launch had to be much more technically precise—there was less room for error. Those athletes who mastered the skill took victories and world records from previous champions. The mix of skills the new equipment demanded for javelin success required less physical strength and greater technique. After the distances athletes were achieving with the new spear proved dangerous by landing in the judges' tent at the 1984 Los Angeles Olympic Games, the governing body mandated a return to the old equipment. This return in equipment led to a return to championship status of the physically strong athletes who had lost standing

A scoreboard shows the leaders for the 1000-meter speed skating competition at the 1998 Winter Olympics in Nagano, Japan. (Wally McNamee/Corbis)

to the more technique-oriented athletes with the aerodynamic javelin.

Softball players test their eye-hand coordination, swing accuracy, and hitting power at the plate. The best expression of these talents requires optimal equipment. The distance the ball travels off the bat depends on the mass and velocity of the bat hitting the ball. Thus, an athlete wants the heaviest bat she can swing at maximum velocity and control reliably. (Without accuracy and control, the bat might not hit the ball in which case bat speed and weight become irrelevant.) Studies have found this optimum weight to be much lighter than could be achieved with wood. Thus, if softball players were required to use heavy wood bats, hitting would become solely a test of physical strength and not accuracy, quickness, and eye-hand coordination. Strong lightweight materials have complemented women's physical abilities and allowed them to optimize their athletic potential.

Hope of optimizing athletic potential and financial success has led companies to invest money and time into research and development of sport equipment. The 1960s brought an influx of money into sport and a faith in the power of science and technology. Television began to invest heavily in sport broadcasting. The thrill of victory and agony of defeat was no longer simply an emotional but a financial experience, as well. With victories bringing financial success, athletes would buy new devices that promised to increase their speed, height, and strength.

Science and technology were viewed as the victors of World War II. Promises of success through science and technology continued after the war and through the Cold War. After the 1957 launch of the Russian satellite Sputnik, increased investment in science and technology became essential for international prestige. The innovations and new materials developed during the wars were transferred into athletic arenas, among others.

The research and development in sport technology did not focus on equipment to improve opportunities for female athletes. The new materials that allowed sporting goods manufacturers to design lightweight and powerful golf clubs, large-head tennis rackets, and lighter bicycles fa-

TECHNOLOGICAL INNOVATIONS FOR WOMEN'S SPORTSWEAR

Since the late 1940s, sport performance has been greatly influenced by technological innovations in equipment and clothing. Initially, these innovations were meant for men and men's sports. Women athletes were limited to using innovations which also helped them but perhaps were less than perfect as they ignored differences between men and women in anatomy and physiology. Since the 1970s, as women's participation in sport has increased, designers have been developing technological innovations for women. These include lighter tennis rackets, sport bras and other suitable clothing, footwear designed for the female anatomy, new bicycle seats, lower nets in volleyball, and smaller basketballs.

cilitated recreational and senior participation, but the unique need of female athletes was still generally ignored. Women tended to use equipment designed for men, modified only for size: women had smaller running shoes, shorter bicycles, and smaller ski boots. Only since the 1980s have equipment manufacturers realized women are proportionally different: heels have been made more narrow in womens shoes, the space between the seat and the handle bar has been shortened for female bicyclists, and ski boots have been reshaped to accommodate the female calf muscle.

Different equipment rules for male and female athletes may seem to take us back to the days of three-zone women's basketball. However, equipment differences do enhance female participation in sport. One size does not fit all. Women tend to be smaller and shorter, and thus the skills of the game might best be contested if they had smaller basketballs and shorter volleyball nets. Spiking is an essential skill in volleyball. If the net were too high for most female athletes to spike, they would be excluded from participation in the sport.

With new technology, women have been able to excel where they were previously excluded. Equipment in a variety of sizes and weights has increased opportunities for women to participate. Women, however, are not the only ones to have benefited from new materials and designs for athletic equipment. Modern technology has to some extent eliminated the issue of female and male equipment by creating technology suited to the individual. Custom manufacturing allows athletes to purchase ski boots custom-molded to their feet. With new materials and designs, rackets, clubs, and bats can be produced to suit the individual athlete. With the athlete selecting the equipment best suited to his or her talents, the issue of separate technology for males and females vanishes.

Individualized technologies not only enhance women's participation in sports but also their training for success. Just as equipment had been designed for men and simply shrunk for women, so too had training regimens. With computerized training systems, the individual athlete's technique can be refined and the athlete's physiological traits monitored for optimal development. When a model that is modified to fit the individual is no longer necessary, females no longer become modified males.

CONCLUSION

Women are not modified males. The technology that best complements their unique abilities allows them to express their athletic talent and reach their athletic potential. Research on how technology shapes sports is essential to understanding sport history, philosophy, and sociology. Technology influences the skills a sport tests, the type of athletes who succeed, the injuries that plague the sport, and the costs of participation.

J. Nadine Gelberg

Bibliography

Bahill, Terry, and William Karnavas. (1991) "The Ideal Baseball Bat." *New Scientist* (April 6) 130: 26–32.

Betts, John Rickards. (1953) "The Technological Revolution and the Rise of Sport, 1850-1900." *Mississippi Valley Historical Review* 40: 231–256.

Bjerklie, David. (1993) "High-Tech Olympians." *Technology Review* (January) 96, 1: 22–30.

Busch, Akiko. (1998) *Design for Sports: The Cult of Performance*. New York: Princeton Architectural Press.

Cahn, Susan K. (1994) *Coming on Strong: Gender and Sexuality in Twentieth-Century Women's Sport*. Cambridge, MA: Harvard University Press.

Davies, Richard O. (1994) *America's Obsession: Sports and Society Since 1945*. Fort Worth, TX: Harcourt Brace.

Gelberg, J. Nadine. (1997) "The Big Technological Tennis Upset." *American Heritage of Invention & Technology* (Spring) 12, 4: 56–61.

Hoberman, John. (1992) *Mortal Engines: The Science of Performance and the Dehumanizing of Sport*. New York: Free Press.

Kretchmar, R. Scott. (1975) "From Test to Contest: An Analysis of Two Kinds of Counterpoint in Sport." *Journal of the Philosophy of Sport* 2: 23–30.

Post, Robert. (1994) *High Performance: The Culture and Technology of Drag Racing 1950-1990*. Baltimore: Johns Hopkins University Press.

Radar, Benjamin. (1984) *In Its Own Image: How Television Has Transformed Sports*. New York: Free Press.

Suits, Bernard. (1978) *The Grasshopper: Games, Life, and Utopia*. Toronto: University of Toronto Press.

TELEVISION & RADIO *see* Media

TENNIS

Tennis is one of the most popular sports in the world. It is played at the recreational, competitive amateur, and professional levels by men and women of all ages. It was one of the first major sports to involve women, and women remain a major force in the game. Women's participation very likely influenced women's later involvement in other sports.

HISTORY

The origin of the word *tennis* is not definitely known, but the most generally accepted belief is that it is derived from the French word *tenez.* It is thought that *tenez* was used as the word "play" is used today.

Varied forms of tennis were known in antiquity. Pictures of early ball games can be found on Greek vases and Roman coins. The ancient Greeks engaged in an activity called *Sphairistike,* which probably was derived from the Greek word *Sphairos,* meaning ball. Tennis as we know it today was almost certainly originally a French game called *jeu de paume,* or the game of the palm. References to this game appear in French manuscripts in the twelfth century. The game became a favorite pastime of the French and English monarchy. The original outdoor game consisted of hitting the ball with the bare hand, or the hand covered by a glove. Originally an activity for the privileged, it soon became a game for the masses. By the early 1800s there was a major decline of tennis due partly to the French Revolution and the Napoleonic Wars. By the end of the nineteenth century the sport again became popular and reverted back to the wealthy classes because play began to take place indoors on expensive, elaborate courts, very different from the indoor courts of today. When the indoor game became popular, players invented crude rackets to extend their reach.

Most historians agree that Major Walter Clopton Wingfield should be given the credit for inventing the modern game of lawn tennis, which he introduced to his friends at a garden party in Nantclwyd, Wales, in December 1873. Wingfield patented "A Portable Court of Playing Tennis," which included the equipment and rules. The game was an immediate success and soon became the most popular lawn game in English society, especially since men and women could play it together.

INTRODUCTION OF TENNIS TO THE UNITED STATES

A few months after the game of Sphairistike was patented, the British garrison stationed in Bermuda obtained some sets of equipment. An American visitor, Mary Ewing Outerbridge of Staten Island, New York, returned home in the spring of 1874, with a net, some balls, and several rackets that she had been given by some of the British officers. Miss Outerbridge's older brother, A. Emilius Outerbridge, was at that time a director of the Staten Island Cricket and Baseball Club. Through him she obtained permission to set up a court on the club's grounds. This court on Staten Island, which was laid out in 1874, was the first lawn tennis court in America.

The next court was set up in Nahant, Massachusetts, and soon courts were constructed at Newport, Rhode Island; Plainfield, New Jersey; and Tuxedo Park, New York. This new game of tennis was played by relatively small numbers during its first few years in America. Tennis was a sport for the wealthy people who either belonged to clubs that had grass areas or who owned estates with suitable lawns so that they could lay out a court on the premises. The game's modest popularity was limited to the eastern area of the United States. The rules developed in England affected the early game of tennis in the United States. The American players were at first completely dependent upon England, not only for the necessary equipment, but for the regulations of the game.

In July 1877 the All-England Croquet Club, now known as Wimbledon, staged the first All-England championship tournament. New rules were drawn up at that time. The hourglass court, which had not served any useful purpose, was abandoned, and the rectangular shape of the court of today was adopted. The width of the court was also altered to the modern dimension. Shortly after this tournament, the rules were revised again, to include the present system of scoring and the provision for one fault on a serve.

WOMEN'S PARTICIPATION

This novel game, tennis, was not treated with much respect at first, and many scoffed at the sport, thinking it was appropriate only for women and unathletic men. The ridicule arose both from the game's leisurely pace and from the players' attire. Nevertheless, the game gained popularity and spread quickly among members of the upper classes. In 1887, eight years after the first men's tournament, due to increased play by women, the United States Lawn Tennis Association (USLTA) established a national women's singles and doubles' tournament. Soon, tournaments for women were held with increasing frequency on the local, regional, and national level. By 1902 the USLTA reported that one of the outstanding events of the season was the increased play of women and increase in women's tournaments. The association had previously waxed enthusiastic about women's participation in the game and indicated they believed this interest was a "natural result of increasing tendency on the part of women to enter athletics."

Some men and women began to play a more energetic game and in a short time some bold women played very aggressively and developed overhead serves and smashes and rushed the net to put points away with short volleys. These same players rebelled against the traditional cumbersome skirts and petticoats and wore loose fitting garments with rolled up sleeves.

The social environment surrounding the early women's tournaments deserve mention. They were always held at the most prestigious clubs, and the social element was regularly included in the write-up of matches. The players were usually house guests of some prominent socialite in the area, and the competitions might be rescheduled if the participants had other engagements. The newspaper accounts of these matches were always detailed, colorful, and often included information extraneous to the tennis.

Many authorities believe that if it had not been for the game of tennis, the acceptance of women in the sports world would have been delayed for years. Tennis paved the way for the participation by women in other sports, including basketball and field hockey. By the 1920s tennis was no longer the exclusive pastime of the wealthy but was played by people in all social classes. Cities and towns built public courts, and players no longer had to belong to a country club to play. The growth of public court play is evidenced by the USLTA's inauguration of the National Parks men's singles championship. In 1930 the association began to sponsor a similar tournament for women. By the year 1930 there were four million tennis players, and one million were playing on public courts.

Members of the Lady All-American Tennis Players. (Bettmann/Corbis)

INTERNATIONAL SCENE

As in the United States, England's women's tennis lagged slightly behind men's. The All-England Club women's singles championship was inaugurated in 1884, seven years after the beginning of the Wimbledon singles title for men. The Davis Cup, an international competition for men, began in 1900. The Wightman Cup, inaugurated in 1923, was intended as the women's counterpart to the Davis Cub, to be competed for by women of all nations, but only England and the United States participated. Over the years it became a one-sided competition as the Americans dominated both the singles and doubles. The contest was discontinued by the end of the 1980s as women chose to focus more on the Federation Cup, a true international women's trophy similar to the Davis Cup. Inaugurated in 1963 by the International

Lawn Tennis Federation (ILTF), it annually hosts most tennis-playing nations.

No history of tennis, however brief, is complete without a brief consideration of the "open" controversy. In the beginning, the USLTA and other tennis organizations were formed primarily to regulate an amateur game for amateur players. For many years this philosophy worked and there were few problems. As more and more people took up the game, the complexities of the expansion opened the door to commercialism and professionalism. For about forty years beginning in 1928 there were petitions, proposals, and committee reports on having open tournaments. Finally, in December 1967, the British Lawn Tennis Association (BLTA), in defiance of the main governing body, the ILTF, declared that the 1968 Wimbledon tournament would be open to all tennis players, regardless of whether they were amateurs or professionals. The immediate reaction from the ILTF was that if this affair took place, the BLTA would be expelled from the international federation, and any amateur who competed would be suspended. After months of worldwide publicity, negotiations, and compromises, the ILTF backed down and approved a certain number of open tournaments throughout the world. Thus, a new era of tournament tennis began.

EARLY WOMEN TENNIS PLAYERS

In the early 1900s Eleonora Sears and May Sutton Bundy defied convention and rolled up their shirt sleeves not only to facilitate their movements but also to allow for cooler and faster play. Bundy won the U.S. singles championship in 1904 and was the first American player to win the Wimbledon title in 1905. Sears was runner-up in the U.S. singles championship in 1912, and was national doubles champion four times and mixed doubles champion in 1916.

Suzanne Lenglen is considered to be the greatest woman tennis player of her day. Her colorful antics, temperamental behavior, and disregard for traditional dress (she wore a loose fitting one-piece dress) had a major impact on the game. She won the Wimbledon title six times, 1919–1923 and 1925. In 1926 she became the first female tennis player to join a professional tour.

Helen Wills assumed complete dominance of women's tennis after the reign of Lenglen. She won the singles championship at Wimbledon eight times, the U.S. championship seven times, and was ranked as the number one player for seven years.

Maureen Connolly won at Wimbledon three times, 1952–1954, and earned the U.S. singles title three times, 1951–1953. In 1953 she became the first player since Don Budge in 1938 to win the Grand Slam title, winning the four major tournaments in a single year: Australian, French, Wimbledon, and United States. Her tennis career was cut short in 1954 when she was injured while riding her horse.

Billie Jean King was not only one of America's outstanding tennis players but also one of the most influential as she brought attention to the women's game through her insistence that men and women be paid the same prize money in tournaments. King won the U.S. singles championship four times, 1967, 1971–1972, and 1974. Six times she won the Wimbledon singles title, 1966–1968, 1972–1973, and 1975. She won the Wimbledon women's (Ladies) doubles event ten times, 1961–1962, 1965, 1967–1968, 1970–1973, and 1979. This a phenomenal record, not only for the number of wins but also for its duration over an eighteen-year period. Furthermore, King won the "Battle of the Sexes" in her famous match against Bobby Riggs in 1973. After her retirement she remained involved in the game as a commentator, president of Team Tennis, and captain of the Federation Cup team.

THE 1990s

The major development in the 1990s was the large number of talented young women players who began to dominate the tournaments with their powerful games and stylish outfits. The top players were far younger than they used to be. Of the top sixteen women players listed by *Tennis* in September 1998, six were under twenty years of age and three were ranked in the top ten (Martina Hingis (2), seventeen years old; Venus Williams (4), eighteen; and Patty Schnyder (6), nineteen). Other young players who were rising rapidly were Serena Williams, Mirjana Lucic, and Anna Kournikova.

Yet the older players were holding their own in meeting the challenge of the ambitious young stars. For the 1998 season, the French Open champion was Arantxa Sanchez-Vicario, twenty-six years old; the Wimbledon champion was Jana Novotna, twenty-nine; and the U.S. Open winner Lindsay Davenport, twenty-two years. Like Novotna, Steffi Graf was also twenty-nine, but injuries hampered her career in the late 1990s. And always a threat in any tournament were Monica Seles, twenty-four, and Mary Pierce, twenty-three. However, all of these veterans of the women's tour began their professional careers in their teens. What is notable was the absence of women over thirty in singles play. The increase in the number of players who are joining the professional ranks before they are eighteen years of age (Jennifer Capriati started at thirteen) forced the Women's Tennis Council to appoint an Age Eligibility Commission. Rules were instituted that limited the number of tournaments a young player can enter before she is sixteen years of age. Martina Navratilova retired at thirty-seven years of age from the tour, and Chris Evert did so in her thirties. There were predictions that this new young group might retire as early as twenty-two.

Another dramatic change in women's—and men's—tennis is the globalization of the game at the professional level. On the annual women's tour, events were held in seventeen different nations. Similarly, the upper ranks were no longer dominated by the United States: the top players came from Switzerland (Martina Hingis), Germany (Steffi Graf), Spain (Arantxa Sanchez-Vicario), Japan (Kimiko Date), Czechoslovakia (Jana Novatna), as well as the United States (Lindsay Davenport, Venus Williams, Monica Seles).

CHANGES IN THE OPEN ERA

Since the first open at Wimbledon in 1968, the tennis world has undergone radical changes, including changes in racquet construction and design, the color of balls, methods of scoring, dress style, and the amount of prize money that today easily makes the top players millionaires.

Most important has been the new technology of racquets. Until the early 1970s, most racquets were made of wood, were of the same design, and differed only in weight and string texture. This uniformity was replaced by many racquet designs, with none made of wood. The tennis player has to choose size of the head of the racquet (regular, mid-, or oversize), its weight, and whether the racquet is made of titanium, graphite, hypercarbon, and so forth. After choosing a racquet, players must consider type and weight of strings. The cost of a racquet can range from under $50 to $300. This new equipment has led to a game based on power centered on one or two-handed ground strokes that enables top players to blast winning shots from the baseline. The serve-and-volley game has largely disappeared from women's tennis.

In the past, all tennis balls were white. This was sometimes a problem as they were easily blemished and not always readily visible under certain conditions. Now yellow, which is easier to see in both indoor and outdoor play, is the standard color for tennis balls.

To eliminate long deuce sets, as in the 1964 Eastern Grass Courts Championships when Nancy Richey and Carole Graebner won their semifinal doubles match by the score of 31–33, 6–1, 6–4, a tie-

THE FEDERATION CUP

The Federation Cup is the annual tennis competition between teams of women representing their nations. It is the women's equivalent of the men's Davis Cup, although it began using the Davis Cup format of elimination rounds and a final event of best of five matches (four singles matches and one doubles) only in 1995. The Federation Cup has been played since 1963, and in the 1960s and 1970s it was dominated by the United States, followed by Australia. Through the 1980s several European nations have been prominent. Overall, the United States has won sixteen Cups, Australia seven, Czechoslovakia and Spain five each, Germany two, and South Africa and France one each.

Venus Williams became one of the game's premiere players at the end of the twentieth century. (AP/Wide World Photos)

breaker was introduced when the score reaches 6–6. This system not only accommodates television schedules but also makes the game more exciting for the spectators.

The dress of players, which used to be all white, has also been transformed, and astonishes many traditionalists. Except at Wimbledon, it is rare now to see a player in an all-white costume; the range of clothes runs from sloppy to sensational. The commercial aspect of the game is symbolized by the different logos and emblems worn by players on their outfits to promote manufacturers and products.

Since the open era began in 1968, prize money has increased substantially for both men and women players. The top players are all millionaires, not only from money earned from matches won but also by endorsement of equipment and products. In 1968 the prize money was $50,000 for Wimbledon and $100,000 for the U. S. Open. In 1971 Billie Jean King, the top-ranked woman player at the time, became the first woman athlete to earn $100,000 in a single year. Thanks to King's and others' efforts, beginning in 1983 the U.S. Open paid equal prize money to men and women. In 1998 each singles winner received $800,000. Note the following earnings for the top five women tennis players for 1998 (through October): Martina Hingis $2,649,771; Lindsay Davenport $2,309,793; Jana Novotna $1,990,852; Venus Williams $1,671,746; and Arantxa Sanchez-Vicario $1,467,719. Gender equity is close: number one ranked Marcelos Rios made $3,088,071 but second ranked Patrick Rafter made less than the second ranked woman. However, the top ten men all made over one million dollars while only the top five women did.

There have been other important changes in the game. Players now pay much more attention to fitness and nutrition. So few tournaments are played on grass that the word "lawn" has been removed

THE WILLIAMS SISTERS ARE TOPS IN TENNIS

The Williams sisters (Venus and Serena) made it to the top of women's tennis in September, 1999 at the U.S. Open in New York City when Serena won the women's singles title, defeating Martina Hingis 6–3, 7–6. Hingis had defeated Venus in the semi-finals, thwarting Richard William's prediction that the final would be an all-Williams affair. The sisters also won the women's doubles and both ended the year ranked in the top five. Later in the month, they helped the United States defeat Russia 4–1 for the Federation Cup, with Venus winning one of her two singles matches, and the sisters winning the doubles match. The Williams sisters grew up in Compton, California, and learned to play on public courts with their father as coach.

from the name of the U.S. national tennis organization. Tennis has been reinstated in the Olympics and the gold medal is competed for by professionals. Perhaps most important, women have brought excitement and glamor to the tour, and many spectators prefer their matches to the men's because of the long rallies and strategic play in contrast to the quick serve and volley game of the men.

Joanna Davenport

See also Evert, Chris; Lenglen, Suzanne; Navratilova, Martina; Wills, Helen

Bibliography

Cummings, Parke. (1957) *American Tennis.* Boston: Little, Brown.

Davenport, Joanna. (1966) "The History and Interpretation of Amateurism in the United States Lawn Tennis Association." Ph.D. Dissertation, Ohio State University.

Dulles, Foster Rhea. (1940) *America Learns to Play.* New York: Appleton-Century Company.

Little, Alan. (1988) *Suzanne Lenglen Tennis Idol of the Twenties.* Wimbledon, U.K.: Wimbledon Lawn Tennis Museum.

Potter, Edward C., Jr. (1963) *Kings of the Court: the Story of Lawn Tennis.* New York: A. S. Barnes.

Tunis, John. (1940) *Sport for the Fun of It.* New York: A.S. Barnes.

Umminger, Walter. (1963) *Superman, Heroes and Gods.* New York: McGraw Hill Book Company.

United States Lawn Tennis Association. (1931) *Fifty Years of Lawn Tennis in the United States.* Cambridge, MA: Plympton Press.

United States Tennis Association. (1996) *The Official United States Tennis Association Yearbook and Tennis Guide with the Official Rules 1996.* MA: H. O. Zimman.

———. (1999) <http://www.usta.com/>.

TENNIS, TABLE *see* Table Tennis

THAILAND

Thailand is a mainland Southeast Asian nation with a population of 58.3 million. The word Thailand literally means "land of the free." It is the only Southeast Asian nation that has never been colonized by a Western power. Thailand has long been involved in sponsoring sports events for the Southeast Asian region. Since 1958 the nation has hosted five Southeast Asia (SEA) Games, four Asian Games, twenty-six University Games, and thirty-one National Games. Thailand is also a regional sports power, often finishing at the top of the SEA Games. Both Thai women and men contributed to these achievements.

Thailand's involvement in staging sports events have produced excellent athletic facilities throughout the country. These facilities and the sponsored contests are open to men and women on an equal basis. Thai women compete in track and field (especially in the sprints), as well as in weight-lifting, judo, shooting, volleyball, basketball, and the traditional foot and ball game *sepak-takraw*. Still, women's participation remains less than that of men. Thailand first participated in the Olympic Games in 1952, with women first competing in 1964 and again in 1976. Women have competed in each of the Olympic Games since 1984.

PHYSICAL EDUCATION

Physical education is offered in the schools but is somewhat limited for girls. Most physical education teachers are men, and 90 percent of coaches are male. Women athletes have few female role models with whom they can identify. There are few women in sport leadership positions who understand the needs of women athletes. There is, however, an effort and a trend for more women to become qualified and eligible to enter these fields. A barrier to women becoming physical education teachers is the need for more female teachers within the educational system in general. This is especially important at the elementary level. In order to increase the number of female coaches, one avenue being pursued is to have aspiring coaches gain experience as coaches in the 'Sports for All' programs, which are very popular in Thailand.

ADMINISTRATION AND RESEARCH

The number of women sport administrators increased during the 1980s and 1990s. More women are preparing themselves for administrative roles, which, in turn, will produce more female leaders in sports. Women sport administrators are mostly located at the higher education levels.

A new avenue open to women is as researchers in the field of sport science. Theoretically, sport science offers equal opportunity for both male and female scientists. However, only about 10 percent of the research projects that are funded in Thailand have a focus on women in sports.

CONCLUSION

Even as women continue to make advances in the degree to which they are involved in sports as athletes, teachers, coaches, administrators, and researchers, there continues to be an underlying cultural belief system that restricts the placement of women into positions of authority and responsibility. This trend is reflected in Thai society in general and carries over into sports. Advocates of greater involvement by women argue that Thai women need to be more assertive and better educated (the female illiteracy rate in Thailand is twice that of the male rate) if they are to increase their participation in sports.

Supitr Samahito

Bibliography

Office of the Prime Minister, Royal Thai Government. (1995) *Thailand in the 90's*. Bangkok: Amarin Printing and Publishing Public Company.

TITLE IX

Title IX of the Education Amendments Act of 1972 is a short and simple federal law that states that "No person in the United States shall, on the basis of sex, be excluded from participation in, be denied the benefits of, or be subjected to discrimination under any educational program or activity receiving Federal financial assistance." Title IX was an extension of the Civil Rights Act of 1964 and was an effort by the federal government to end and to prevent further preferential treatment on the basis of sex in education. Support for the amendment came from the civil rights movement in general and from supporters of women's sports who had pointed out the enormous inequalities in participation and funding between men's and women's sports. For example, in 1971 in U.S. high schools, only 294,015 girls participated in sports, compared to 3,666,917 boys. Similarly, in many schools and colleges, funding for men's sports was as much as fifty times that for women's sports, and it was not unusual for colleges and universities to spend as little as 1 percent of their athletic budget on women's sports.

Title IX applies to educational institutions that receive any federal money and prohibits discrimination in all educational programs and activities, not just athletics. Athletic programs are considered educational programs and activities. Title IX gives women athletes the right to equal opportunity in sports in educational institutions that receive federal money, from elementary schools to colleges and universities. Although there are few private elementary schools, middle school, or high schools that receive federal money, almost all colleges and universities, private and public, receive such funding. The penalty for noncompliance with Title IX is withdrawal of federal money. This penalty has never been applied, although most estimates are that 80 to 90 percent of all educational institutions are not in complete compliance with Title IX as it applies to athletics. When institutions are determined to be out of compliance with the law, the U.S. Department of Education Office for Civil Rights (OCR) finds them "in compliance conditioned on remedying identified problems." This means that the institution is out of compliance but has told the government that it plans to comply within a certain time period. The OCR, however, has been very inconsistent about checking whether institutions fulfill these promises.

Title IX requires that every educational institution have a Title IX compliance coordinator. The OCR is the primary agency charged with Title IX enforcement. To date, however, this agency's enforcement efforts have been inadequate. Any person, regardless of whether they have been harmed by failure of the educational institution to comply with the law, may file a Title IX complaint with the OCR, which is then obligated to investigate such a complaint within a specified time period. The person filing the complaint may request that his or her identity be kept confidential. Individuals who have been harmed by failure of the institution to comply have an individual right to sue under the law, and almost 95 percent of such lawsuits having to do with athletic program violations have been successful.

Three parts of Title IX apply to athletic programs: (1) effective accommodation of student interests and abilities (participation), (2) athletic financial assistance (scholarships), and (3) other program components (the "laundry list" of benefits to and treatment of athletes). The laundry list includes equipment and supplies, scheduling of games and practice times, travel and daily allowances, access to tutoring, coaching, locker rooms, practice and competitive facilities, medical and training facilities and services, publicity, recruitment of student athletes, and support services.

The Office of Civil Rights or the courts assess Title IX compliance by total program comparison. In other words, the entire men's and women's programs are to be compared, not just one men's team to the women's team in the same sport. This broad comparative provision was intended to emphasize that Title IX does not require institutions to create mirror image programs. Males and females can participate in different sports according to their respective interests and abilities. Thus, the law permits broad variations in the type and number of sport opportunities offered to each gender.

Title IX does not require equal expenditure of money on male and female athletes. The only dollar-for-dollar expenditure requirement is in the athletic financial assistance area, where schools are required to spend dollars proportional to participation rates. Thus, if $200,000 is awarded in athletic scholarships and the participation ratio of male to female athletes is fifty-fifty, $100,000 must be awarded to female athletes and $100,000 must be awarded to male athletes. In other areas, the equality standard is one of equal opportunity.

For Title IX's participation requirements, a school can meet the standard through three independent tests. The first test is a mathematical safe harbor. If the school offers athletic participation opportunities (number of individual athlete participation slots, not numbers of teams) proportional to the numbers of males and females in the general student body, the school meets the participation standard. If the school does not meet this mathematical test, it may be deemed in compliance if it can either demonstrate consistent expansion of opportunities for the underrepresented gender over time or show that the athletic program fully meets the interests and abilities of the underrepresented gender. The courts have ruled that "boys are more interested in sports than girls" is not an acceptable defense to lack of equitable participation opportunities.

Under Title IX there are no sport exclusions or exceptions, so football is included under the law. Individual participation opportunities (numbers of athletes participating rather than number of sports) in all men's sports and all women's sports are counted in determining whether a school meets the Title IX participation standard. The basic philosophical underpinning of Title IX is that there cannot be an economic justification for discrimination. The school cannot maintain that

FOUR MYTHS ABOUT TITLE IX

Four myths about Title IX that have been used by critics to try to weaken its impact on female participation in sports at colleges and universities:

1. There must be proportional representation in sports based on the proportion of males and females enrolled at the college or university.
2. The number of men's sports must be reduced to increase the number of women's sports.
3. It is necessary to eliminate roster positions for male non-scholarship athletes to create more positions for female athletes.
4. It is necessary to eliminate non-glamor men's sports to increase the number of women's sports.

Girls sit on the lawn during a break in physical education class in 1994. Title IX has increased the participation of girls and women in sports since 1972. (Bob Rowan/Corbis)

revenue production or other considerations mandate that male athletes receive better treatment or participation opportunities than female athletes. A good analogy would be that a school may not say that it cannot afford to provide wheelchair access for students with physical disabilities, as required under the Americans with Disabilities Act, because the football team needs the money to maintain its current level of revenue production. Similarly, a school cannot say that it cannot afford to provide participation opportunities for an underrepresented gender.

Title IX does not require the reduction of opportunities for male athletes to increase opportunities for female athletes. Schools that choose this manner of compliance are not meeting the spirit of discrimination laws. That philosophy is to bring members of the disadvantaged group up to the participation or benefit levels of the advantaged group, rather than bringing male athletes down to female athletes' current level of poor treatment or no opportunity to play. If athletic budgets do not increase and schools want to maintain current levels of participation for male athletes and increase participation levels of female athletes, the solution is to give all teams a smaller portion of the budget pie.

Typically, athletic departments have refused to tighten the budgets of popular men's sports like football, but have cut men's sports that do not produce revenue instead and blamed it on Title IX. Three points should be made in this regard: (1) it is dysfunctional to "pit the victims against the victims"—men's nonrevenue sports against women's sports, both of which have been traditionally underfunded, (2) over 80 percent of all college football programs and almost all high school football programs lose money, and (3) nothing negative would happen to men's revenue-producing sports if their budgets were decreased across the board, with all schools and all teams lowering expenditures simultaneously so the playing field is kept level. In fact, football expenditures have continued to increase at rates higher than inflation. For example, according to National Collegiate Athletic Association (NCAA) gender equity studies comparing 1992 and 1997 budgets, average per school dollar increases to Division I-A men's sports operating budgets over the past five years were three times the increases to women's sports operating budgets: spending on men increased by $1.37 million, on women, by $400,000. Football received the largest share of this increase: 63 percent or $872,000. Further, the $872,000 increase in football budgets exceeded the total average annual operating budget, $662,000, of women's sports programs by more than $200,000.

While there are considerable misconceptions and inaccuracies surrounding the discussion of Title IX as it applies to athletic programs, it is important to understand the basic premise of the law: Title IX is an important federal civil rights act that guarantees that young men and women treated in a like manner with regard to all educational programs and activities, including sports.

Donna A. Lopiano

See also Law

Bibliography

Clement, Annie. (1998) *Law in Sport and Physical Activity.* Aurora, OH: Sport and Law Press.

Fulks, Daniel. (1994) *Revenues and Expenses of Intercollegiate Athletics Programs: Analysis of Financial Trends and Relationships, 1989–93.* Mission, KS: National Collegiate Athletic Association.

———. (1998) *Revenues and Expenses of Intercollegiate Athletics Programs: Analysis of Financial Trends and Relationships, 1993–97.* Mission, KS: National Collegiate Athletic Association.

Hargreaves, Jennifer. (1994) *Sporting Females*. London: Routledge.

Isaac, T. A. (1987) "Sports—the Final Frontier: Sex Discrimination in Sports Leadership." *Women Lawyers Journal* 73, 4:15–19.

National Collegiate Athletic Association. (1992) *Gender Equity Survey*. Mission, KS: National Collegiate Athletic Association.

———. (1997) *Gender Equity Survey*. Mission, KS: National Collegiate Athletic Association.

Nelson, Mariah B. (1991) *Are We Winning Yet? How Women Are Changing Sports and Sports Are Changing Women*. New York: Random House.

Information was also provided by the NCAA research department.

TOBOGGANING *see* Sledding–Skeleton (Cresta Run) Tobogganing

TOURISCHEVA, LUDMILLA IVANOVA

(1952–)

RUSSIAN GYMNAST

Ludmilla Ivanova Tourischeva was one of the last of the mature female gymnasts who, by virtue of their grace and strength, dominated the sport before the rise in the 1970s of quicker, more agile child athletes. One of the most famous child athletes, Olga Korbut, was Tourischeva's teammate at the 1972 Olympics in Munich. Tourischeva won the all-around gold but Korbut won the hearts of the world's little girls and drew them into gymnastics participation and competition in record numbers.

Tourischeva was born in Groznyy, Russia, on 7 October 1952. Her coach throughout her career was Vladislav Rastorotsky, whom she met as a child at the Children's Sports School in Groznyy. He recognized her talent from the start. She won the Soviet Union Cup in 1967 when she was fifteen years old, and placed in the top twenty-five in her first Olympics in 1968 in Mexico City. Though the individual events were dominated by the great Czechoslovakian gymnast Vera Caslavska, the team gold went to the Soviets (who won gold in every Olympic Games from 1952 until 1992, except the 1984 games, which they boycotted).

Ludmilla Tourischeva performs on the balance beam in 1972. (AP Wide World Photos)

Tourischeva had excellent training in dance, and this background was apparent in her exploration of the eight pure expressions of effort identified by dance pioneer Rudolph Laban. By 1970, the international gymnastics community knew her as their all-around champion surpassing everyone at the world championships in Ljubljana, Yugoslavia. In 1974, perhaps her greatest year, she medaled in all five individual events at the World Competition in Varna, Bulgaria, with gold in the all-around, balance beam, and floor exercise. In 1973, she swept the European championships with five golds and in 1975 she swept the World Cup, winning five individual gold medals.

By 1976 the limelight had shifted to another phenomenal youngster, Nadia Comaneci. Tourischeva retired after winning the bronze in the all-around at the Montreal Olympics. Despite the splash made by the young athletes just before and long after her retirement, she stood third in individual medals in world championship and Olympic competition. Only Larissa Latynina and Vera Caslavska had bested Tourischeva's record.

In 1977 she married Valerie Borzov, then the Olympic 100- and 200-meter sprint champion. Borzov was named the first Minister of Youth and Sport for the independent Ukraine in 1991. Later, he became the President of the National Olympic Committee of Ukraine. Their daughter, Tetiana, was born in 1978.

A. B. Frederick

Bibliography

Gutman, Dan. (1996) *Gymnastics*. New York: Viking.

Lessa, Christina. (1997) *Gymnastics Balancing Acts*. New York: Universe Publishing.

Marshall, Nancy Thies, and Pam Vredevelt. (1988) *Women Who Compete*. Old Tappan, NJ: F.H. Revell Co.

Moran, Lyn. (1978) *The Young Gymnasts*. New York: K.S. Giniger Co.

Simons, Minot, II. (1995) *Women's Gymnastics: A History*. Carmel, CA: Welwyn Publishing.

Straus, Hal. (1978) *Gymnastics Guide*. Mountain View, CA: World Publications.

TRACK AND FIELD—JUMPING AND THROWING

In track and field, the jumping events are the high jump, the long jump, the triple jump, and the pole vault. The shot put, the discus, the javelin, and the hammer are the throwing sports. Both events have become increasingly popular. Their appeal lies in the high level of competition and in the ever more impressive achievements of athletes who participate.

The high jump and the long jump have a long history in women's athletics and were included in the program of events for the first women's organized track and field competition. Women have also been doing the triple jump and pole vault for a considerable time, but the International Amateur Athletic Federation (IAAF) has only recently begun documenting world record marks for these events by going back in time and compiling a history of record marks.

HISTORY

In the 1928 Olympics, the first Games to include women's track and field athletes, the discus was listed on the program. The javelin and shot put made their Olympic debuts as women's events in 1932 and 1948, respectively. The pole vault and the hammer were on the program for the 1999 world games.

The first recorded mark for a women's high jump competition was on 9 November 1895 at Vassar College's first Field Day (later the competitions were referred to as American Field Days). In that event, Leslie Baker won first place in the running high jump with a mark of 46 inches (1.2 m). Initially, women high jumpers were trained to use the scissors style of jumping. This method involves pushing off with the arms to propel the lead leg higher than the crossbar and then immediately bringing up the trail leg so that the hips meet, shifting the body over the bar as if the athlete is in a sitting position on clearance. Although this position restricts the height of clearance, women athletes continued to use the scissors method well into the 1960s.

Although the high jump had been included in a number of American Field Day competitions in the 1890s, the first recognized world record for the event was on 18 June 1928, when fifteen-year-old Carolina Gisolf of the Netherlands became the youngest athlete to set a world record with her jump of 1.61 meters (5 ft. 4 in.) at Maastricht. In the 1932 Los Angeles Olympics, Americans Jean Shiley and Mildred "Babe" Didrikson tied the world record at 1.65 meters (5 ft. 5 in.) and did a jump-off for the gold medal. Didrikson cleared the bar at 1.66 meters (5 ft. 6 in.), as did Shiley, but the judges ruled that Didrikson's jump was illegal because she dove head first over the bar. Didrikson used the western roll, a method of jumping made popular by George Horine that female athletes were not permitted to use. The western roll involves an angled run-up that forces the athlete's upper body over the bar first. At this time, IAAF rules disallowed women athletes from going over the bar with their shoulders preceding their bodies because it was believed women would injure themselves jumping in this manner. By the 1950s, the rules were changed to accommodate new methods of jumping that were already accepted in male competitions.

From 1939 to 1941, the world record remained at 1.66 meters and was matched by Dorothy Odam-Tyler of Great Britain, Esther Brand of South Africa, and Ilsebill Pfenning of Switzerland. Although Pfenning broke the record in 1941, she did not receive recognition for her achievement until 1976. In 1938 Dora Ratjun of Germany set a world record mark of 1.70 meters (5 ft. 8 in.) at the European championships but was disqualified because it was later confirmed that Ratjun was a man. Although Ratjun was disqualified, the record he set was not rescinded, and in 1941, when Pfenning matched the mark of 1.66, her name did not replace his as the record holder. It was only until thirty-five years later that the IAAF resolved the matter.

From 1943 to 1950, the world record was held by Fanny Blankers-Koen of the Netherlands at 1.71 meters (5 ft. 8.4 in.). Blankers-Koen, considered to be one of the greatest Dutch athletes, held fifty-eight Dutch titles and set world records in five different events. At the 1948 Olympics, she withdrew from the jumping events because she was pregnant, but she went on to win four gold medals in the sprints and hurdles. With Blankers-Koen not competing, Alice Coachman of the United States became the first African-American woman to win an Olympic gold medal when she jumped 1.69 meters (5 ft. 7.5 in.). The final round of the high jump, held on the last day of the 1948 Games, included Coachman, Michele Ostermeyer of France, and Dorothy Tyler of Great Britain. Tyler had been the silver medalist in the 1936 Olympics, and Ostermeyer had already won two gold medals in the shot and discus. Ostermeyer did not clear the height, but Coachman and Tyler cleared 5 feet 4.5 inches and so established an Olympic record. Both athletes then, in their second attempt, cleared 5 feet 6.5 inches, but Coachman was awarded the medal because she had hit the height on the first jump. Coachman's victory was the only Olympic gold medal for the American women's track and field team.

Blankers-Koen retained her world record until Great Britain's Shelia Lerwill cleared 1.72 meters (5 ft. 8.7 in.) at the 1951 world athletics championships in London. Lerwill was the first female athlete to set a world record using the straddle technique. In the straddle technique, the athlete jumps off and up with the lead leg and, with the arms driving forward, rotates the body around the crossbar into what appears to be a forward belly roll. Although the straddle technique enabled many women to clear greater heights, taller female high jumpers had difficulty using this method because their trail leg would often hit the bar. For this reason, some women began to use modified versions of the scissors method that combined the two.

Some women created their own style of jumping. Among them was Romanian Iolanda Balas, who combined the scissors form with the Eastern cut-off approach. From 1957 to 1966 Balas was ranked number one in the world. She won over 140 competitions, two Olympic gold medals (1960, 1964), and set fourteen world records, five of them in 1958. Balas shifted the high jump marks from 1.75 meters (5 ft. 10 in.) to 1.91 meters

WORLD FIELD RECORDS RECOGNIZED BY THE INTERNATIONAL AMATEUR ATHLETIC FEDERATION, 1999

Event	Mark (in m)	Individual	Nation	Date
High Jump	2.07	Heike Henkel	Germany	1992
Pole Vault	4.56	Nicole Humbert	Germany	1999
Long Jump	7.37	Neike Drechsler	East Germany	1988
Triple Jump	15.16	Ashia Hansen	Great Britain	1998
Shot Put	22.50	Helena Fibingerova	Czechoslovakia	1977

(6 ft. 4.4 in.) and was the first woman to clear six feet, which she did in 1957. Her last record remained unbroken for ten and a half years. She remains one of the greatest high jumpers in track and field history and the most dominant female athlete in her event.

Although Balas held the field in her event, she was beaten by Mildred McDaniel of the United States in 1956 at the Olympic Games in Melbourne. McDaniel beat Balas by 9 centimeters (3.5 in.) with a jump of 1.76 meters (5 ft. 10 in.). Her victory was significant; it was only the third time an American had won a major competition in an event that had been dominated by the Europeans.

Another jumper to break into the ranks of the Europeans was Chen Feng-Jung of China, who was the first athlete from her country to set a world record in track and field. She did so by clearing 1.77 meters (5 ft. 10.8 in.) on 17 November 1957 at the Chinese national championships in Beijing. Feng-Jung made her jumps using a built-up shoe that the IAAF banned in 1958.

From 1958 to 1971, no one approached Balas' mark until Austria's Ilona Gusenbauer ended Balas' world record on 4 September 1971 by one centimeter (0.4 in.) using the straddle method. However, Gusenbauer's mark was soon broken by Ulrike Meyfarth of West Germany, who became the first female athlete to set a world record using the Fosbury Flop. The flop method involves pushing off the foot but twisting the body such that the athlete's back is presented to the bar. The athlete then clears the bar going over head and shoulders first. Even though Dick Fosbury is credited with pioneering this jumping technique, Canadian Debbie Brill developed her very own flop style known as the Brill bend, which involves an extreme back arch during clearance of the crossbar. Brill's technique was modeled by a number of women athletes, including Meyfarth, who became the youngest female individual athlete to win a gold medal with her jump of 1.92 meters (6 ft. 4.8 in.) at the 1972 Munich Games.

Impressive though it was, Meyfarth's world record did not stand very long. Yolanda Blagoyeva of Bulgaria, Sara Simeoni of Italy, Tamara Bykova of the Soviet Union, and Rosemarie Ackerman of East Germany each set a record. Ackerman and Simeoni were the last great straddlers to set world records. Like Balas, Ackerman dominated a decade of jumping, the 1970s. She amassed seven world records, an Olympic gold medal in 1976, and was heralded as being the first woman to clear 2 meters (6 ft. 6.7 in.). In 1977, at an international meet in Berlin, Ackerman broke her own world record on the first try jumping 2 meters (6 ft. 6.7 in.).

In 1978 Ackerman's long time rival Sara Simeoni established a record when she cleared 2.01 meters (6 ft. 8.4 in.). Ackerman retired, and Simeoni generated a new rivalry with Meyfarth, who in the early 1980s made a comeback. At the 1982 European championships in Athens, Meyfarth not only won the high jump but set a world record at 2.02 meters (6 ft. 8.8 in.). She improved on that mark on 21 August 1983 in London when she jumped 2.03 meters (6 ft. 9 in.).

Challenging Meyfarth was Bykova, who also made a comeback. On 21 August 1983 Bykova first tied Meyfarth's jump, but four days later she improved on it. Four weeks later on 20 July 1984, Bykova lost her world mark to Bulgaria's Lyudmila Andonova. Andonova jumped 2.07 meters (6 ft. 10.8 in.) in Berlin. Neither Bykova nor Andonova competed in the Los Angeles Olympics because of the Communist boycott.

In the late 1980s and 1990s, the leading female high jumper was Bulgaria's Stefka Kostadinov, who at the age of nineteen cleared 2 meters (6 ft. 6.7 in.). She remained undefeated in 1985 and set the world record mark of 2.09 meters (6 ft. 11.5 in.) at the world championships in Rome on 30 August 1987. In 1988 Kostadinova was beaten by American Louise Ritter. Ritter had set the American record eight times, and her world record mark of 6 feet 8 inches still stood in 1999. Kostadinova's defeat began a series of setbacks for her: she injured herself, and placed fourth at the Barcelona Olympics. She recovered to win the 1995 world championships, and in 1996 she won Olympic Gold at Atlanta. Heike Henkel (Germany) and Inga Babakova (Ukraine) were also leading high jumpers in the late 1990s. Most jumpers continued to use the flop style of jumping, which may be one reason the record has not been broken.

LONG JUMP

The long jump, too, has an extensive history in women's athletics, being listed among the field events in the 1895 Vassar American Field Day competition. In 1916 an article published by Dr. Harry Eaton Stewart described the dimensions of the long jump pit to be used for women's competitions: "a 60 × 3 foot runway dug to a depth of 4 inches and filled with first a coarse and then a fine ashes, wet down and rolled . . . edged with a heavy thick plank or log buried to the level of the ground and painted white. The pit was to be 10 × 8 with a 20 × 4 extension dug to a depth of 1 & 1/2 feet and filled with a dry sifted sand and sawdust in equal parts."

At first the long jump was referred to as the running broad jump. Women competed in the broad jump, the running broad jump, and an event called the run, hop, step, and jump (the precursor of the triple jump). In the 1920s the most popular style of jumping was referred to as the hitch kick, in which the athlete flexes the lead leg at takeoff to propel herself in a mid-air stride. The athlete then cycles the legs as if running in flight and uses the arms to propel the body forward. Another method of jumping is the hang technique. Here the athlete draws the lead leg upward and then brings the trail leg up, and with both knees apart and slightly bent (though some athletes do not bend their knees), the athlete pushes the arms upward as if hanging in mid-air and then forces the arms forward to push the legs up for landing.

In 1928 the first woman to establish a world record in the long jump was Japan's Hitomi Kinue (1908–1931). Hitomi's mark of 5.98 meters (19 ft. 11 in.) was the first world record achieved by an Asian athlete. She was also the first Asian woman to win a gold medal in the Olympics. Hitomi, who was also a remarkable sprinter, excelled in several events and won eight medals at the world games in 1930. Her long jump record stood unbroken for eleven years, and she might well have broken it again, but her career was brief: she died from tuberculosis at age twenty-three.

In 1932 the long jump was omitted from the Olympic program, but seven years later, Germany's Christel Shulz cleared 6.12 meters (20 ft. 4.8 in.) at the Berlin Games. Schulz's record did not stand for long; Fanny Blankers-Koen broke the record in 1943 by jumping 6.25 meters (20 ft. 10 in.) into the wind. Although Blankers-Koen excelled at the long jump, she chose not to compete in it as an individual event and withdrew herself from the inaugural debut of the event in the 1948 Olympics.

Blankers-Koen's decision not to compete paved the way for Olga Gyarmati of Hungary to win the event at 18 feet 8 inches, two feet behind the world record. In 1952 Gymarti was unable to defend her title and the record was shifted eight times in the next ten years. In 1960 the world record was broken by Hildrun Claus who jumped 6.4 meters (21 ft. 3.9 in.). The following year, Tatyana Shchelkanova broke Claus's record and began a four-year reign as the world's leading female high jumper. Shchelkanova managed to add 28 inches to the world record, but Great Britain's Mary Rand cleared 6.7 meters (22 ft. 3.9 in.). Rand's record stood until 14 October 1968 when it was broken by Viorica Viscopoleanu of Romania by 14 centimeters (5.5 in.).

In the 1970s the women's high jump record changed hands four times. Heide Rosendahl of West Germany, Angela Voight of East Germany, Sigrun Seigl of East Germany, and Vilma Bardauskiene of the Soviet Union moved the record to 7.09 meters (23 ft. 7.5 in.). Although it appeared that the record would remain static, Anisoara Cusmir of Romania added 11 centimeters (4.4 in.) to the world mark on 1 August 1982 at the Romanian championships. Five minutes later, Valeria Ionescu of Romania jumped 7.2 meter (24 ft.). Cusmir broke the record three more times, but Heike Haute (later competing as Heike Dreschler after her marriage) of East Germany became the new leading high jumper when she added one centimeter (0.4 in.) to Cusmir's record in 1985. In 1986, Dreschler jumped 7.45 meters (24 ft. 10 in.) twice and was considered one of the most consistent high jumpers in the world.

Although successful, Dreschler faced a formidable rival in Jackie Joyner-Kersee of the United States (1962–). Joyner-Kersee, a strong heptathlete, was also a powerful long jumper. From 1987 to 1992, the two athletes rivaled each other at the Olympics and world championships. In the 1987 and 1991 world championships, Joyner-Kersee placed first and Dreschler, second. At the 1988 Olympics, Joyner-Kersee beat Dreschler again. Dreschler's turn came in the Barcelona Olympics when she beat Joyner-Kersee and Inessa Kravets (Soviet Union). The next two years Dreschler remained on top, winning the 1993 world championships and her third European championships in 1994.

The 1999 record holder for the long jump is Galina Chistyakova of the former Soviet Union, now Russia. Chistyakova became the first woman to beat the 7.50 meter mark at 7.52 meters (25 ft. 0.7 in.). She won both of her world record marks at the Znamenskiy Memorial Meet in Leningrad. Although she was second in the 1986 European championships, she was unable to win at major competitions. Challenging Chistoyakova's record is Inessa Kravets, who has proved herself a successful triple jumper.

TRIPLE JUMP

Although as early as 1895, women athletes participated in an event called the "run, hop, step, and jump," only in 1996 was the triple jump given world record status. The triple jump involves a three-jump sequence in which the athlete pushes off on one foot, lands, then pushes off the opposite leg, and then jumps into the pit. In the early days of this event athletes with strong vaulting ability and great speed excelled. Since the advent of rubberized runways, strength and speed became more important; the runways help athletes vault. On 25 August 1990, Li Huirong of China jumped 14.54 meters (48 ft. 5.5 in.) at the Chuhei Nambu Memorial Meet in Japan. She held her record until Yolanda Chen jumped 15.03 meters (50 ft. 1.2 in.). Chen's record was soon bested by Anna Biryukova of the Ukraine, who jumped 15.09 meters (50 ft. 3.6 in.). The leading female triple jumper and world record holder is Inessa Kravets of the Ukraine. Kravets broke Huirong's record on 10 June 1991 in Moscow by adding an impressive 41 centimeters (16.4 in.), jumping 14.95 meters (49 ft. 9.9 in.). At the 1995 world championships, Kravets repeated the feat and jumped 15.50 meters (51 ft. 8 in.). At the triple jump's inaugural Olympics in Atlanta in 1996, Kravets jumped 15.33 meters (51 ft. 1.2 in.) and won the gold medal. Although Kravets continues to lead triple jumpers, Ana Biryukova of Russia at 15.09 meters (50 ft. 3.6 in.) and Rodica Mateescu of Romania at 15.03 meters (50 ft. 1.2 in.) are also strong competitors.

POLE VAULT

On 7 May 1998, IAAF President Primo Nebiolo announced that the IAAF would add the women's pole vault as an official event for the 1999 world championships and 2000 Olympics, thus giving official recognition to a sport in which women had been competing throughout the history of track and field. The first documented mark for women's pole vault was recorded for Mildred Vilas of Poughkeepsie, New York, who jumped 1.49 meters (4 ft. 11.5 in.). In the 1910 *Spalding's Official Athletic Almanac,* Ruth Spencer of Lake Erie College in Painesville, Ohio, was listed as having the pole vault record of 4 feet 9 inches. In 1916 Dr. Harry Eaton Stewart conducted a study of all the women's best performances for each event and selected the following women for the pole vault: Eva Fisk of University of Nebraska, Ruth Spencer of Lake Erie College, J. Dunlap of the New Haven Normal School of Gymnastics, N. Bergami of Sargent N. School of Physical Education, and E. Drew of Lake Erie College. Fisk's vault of 6 feet 3 inches was listed as the nation's best mark.

Documentation of other pole vaulting competitions exists, but most contests were seen as exhibitions, even into the 1970s. At the Mason-Dixon Indoor Meet in Louisville, Kentucky, Irene Spiker set a record of 10 feet 0.25 inches in 1979 at one such exhibition. In the 1980s, interest in women's participation generated other amateur competitions and on 21 May 1992 Sun Caiyun of China was listed as the first record holder in the event, with a vault of 4.05 meters (13 ft. 6 in.). In 1995 Caiyun bettered her mark by 0.25 inch, but Cai Weiyan and Zhong Guiqing, also form China, broke Caiyun's record in subsequent months. The reemergence of the pole event has brought a number of new athletes into competition. In 1995 the world record was broken eighteen times.

After 1995, the leading female vaulter was Emma George of Austria, who in 1999 maintained the indoor and outdoor records at 4.45 meters (14 ft. 9.9 in.) and 4.59 meters (15 ft. 3.6 in.), respectively. Ukrainian Anzhela Balakhonova, American Stacy Dragila, and Czech Daniela Bartova were also strong competitors in the event. Balakhonova set the indoor record with her vault of 4.45 meters (14 ft. 9.9 in.) at the 1998 European championships in Valencia. In 1996 Bartova broke the world record by jumping 4.20 meters (14 ft.) but lost it to Sun Caiyun of Germany four days later. Bartova has broken the record ten times. Dragila, the leading American vaulter, has emerged as one of George's chief rivals. At the 1997 world indoor championships in Paris, Dragila won the event, posting a vault of 4.40 meters (14 ft. 7.9 in.).

THROWING, HAMMER

Like the pole vault, the hammer was added as an event for the 1999 world championships and the 2000 Olympic Games. The weight of the women's hammer is 4 kilograms (8.8 lb.), compared to the men's, which weighs 7.26 kilograms (15.9 lb.). The first recorded mark for the hammer throw was in 1931, but the IAAF only began ratifying records in 1995. The first woman to throw more than 60 meters (61.20 m. or 204 ft.) was Japan's Aya Suzuki, but Olga Kuzenkova (Russia) was recognized as the first world record holder in 1994 with her throw of 66.84 meters (222 ft. 9.6 in.). Mihaela Melinte of Romania threw 69 meters (230 ft.) on 22 February 1997, but Kuzenkova reclaimed the world record on 22 June 1997 with a throw of 73.1 meters (243 ft. 7.9 in.). Melinte and Kuzenkova continued to reign as the leading hammer throwers.

A woman competes in the Senior Putting the Shot event at the Women's Athletic Championships in England in 1958. (Corbis)

SHOT PUT

Before the first shot putting events, women athletes competed in basketball and baseball throwing competitions. The first documented record of a women's shot put competition was at Vassar College's fourth Field Day competition in 1898. Although critics charged that this event was unfeminine, it was nevertheless included on the program as the last event of the day. The 6-pound (2.7-kg) shot put was used for beginners, but the 8-pound (3.6-kg) shot was used for competition. E. V. Jones won the event with a throw of 23 feet 5 inches. Although most competitions involved throwing the 8-pound shot put, some women also competed in 12-pound shot put competitions. The earliest documented results from a 12-pound shot competition are from the American Field Day competitions in the 1900s.

The first major competitions in the shot put were held in France in 1917. At these meets a 4-kilogram (8.8-lb.) implement was used. In 1922 American Lucile Godbold set a world record in the shot put with a distance of 66 feet 4.1 inches. She threw with two hands and beat the record by more than 6 feet. In 1934 the rules changed and women were required to throw with one hand. For this reason, the first official record approved by the IAAF was Gisela Mauermayer's (Germany) throw of 14.38 meters (47 ft. 11.2 in.). Mauermayer threw the distance at a meet between Germany and Poland. Not until 1948 did the event make its debut in the Olympics. Michele Ostermeyer (France) won the gold, throwing 13.5 meters (45 ft. 1.25 in.). In 1950 Anna Andreyeva broke Mauermayer's record with her throw of 15.02 meters (50 ft. 0.7 in.).

In the history of shot put competition, the Eastern Europeans have dominated the event, and overall, the Soviet throwers have been the most competitive. In 1952 Galina Zybina proved herself one of the great female shot putters. Zybina not only broke the world record fifteen times in a row, but she increased the distance of her throws eight times. She dominated the decade with her range of 15.28 meters (50 ft. 11.2 in.) in 1952 to 16.76 meters (55 ft. 10.4 in.) in 1956. Following Zybina's reign, Tamara Press became the preeminent thrower, excelling in the shot put and the discus. She was ranked number one in the shot put in 1960, 1962, and 1966 and set six world records in the event. Like Iolanda Balas, Press was heralded as the best female thrower (shot and discus) of her time. She moved Zybina's record from 16.76 meters to 18.59 meters (61 ft. 11.6 in.).

After Press, Nadezhda Chizhova, also of the Soviet Union, became the leading female shot putter. Chizhova was the first woman to throw more than 20 meters (66 ft. 8 in.). East Germany's Margita Gummel (1941–) also broke the record, and the two athletes became strong rivals. As Gummel and Chizhova pushed one another, they changed the world record three times. It was Chizhova who earned the final distinction with her throw of 21.20 meters (70 ft. 7.9 in.) on 23 August 1973.

In the late 1970s the shot put world record distances remained consistent until Marianne Adams of East Germany and Ivanka Kristova of Bulgaria broke the 21-meter (70-ft.) mark. Adam's best of 21.67 meters (72 ft. 2.8 in.) was thrown on 30 May 1976. Only a few months later, on 4 July 1976, Kristova threw 21.89 meters (72 ft. 11.6 in.) to better Adam's mark. At the Montreal Olympics, Kristovona beat Chizhova and won Bulgaria's first track and field gold medal with her throw of 21.16 meters (70 ft. 6.4 in.) to Chizhova's 20.96 meter (69 ft. 10.4 in.). Kristova's record did not last long; on 26 September 1976, Helena Fibingerova of Czechoslovakia set a mark at 21.99 meters (73 ft. 3.6 in.). Fibingerova was the first woman to throw more than 22 meters (73 ft. 3.9 in.).

Although there were suspicions of drug abuse among the shot putters, Illona Slupianiak was the only world record holder who was caught using steroids. Despite her guilt, she was still allowed to compete, and in 1978 she won the European championships, setting a world record at 22.45 meters (74 ft. 10 in.).

In 1999 Natala Lisovskaya of the former Soviet Union was still the only woman to throw farther than 22.50 meters (75 ft.). Her personal best of 22.63 meters (75 ft. 5.2 in.) on 1 June 1987 still stood as the world record for the shot put, but Astrid Kumbernoss and Viktoriya Pavlysh of the Ukraine were closing in on the world record mark. Kumbernoss dominated the field of throwers in the late 1990s.

DISCUS

In April 1919, Eleanor Brewer threw the discus 80 feet 4 inches and set the national discus record for the United States at the Florida State University Field Day Competition for Women. The women's discus, which weighs 2 pounds and 3 ounces (1 kg) was introduced in the 1928 Olympic Games. Germany's Gisela Mauermayer set several discus records in the 1930s before she set the first world record in the women's discus on 11 July 1936. In 1948 Nina Dumbadze of the Soviet Union won Olympic gold and went on to become the leading female thrower from 1939 to 1950. Dumbadze's throw of 53.25 meters (177 ft. 6 in.) made her the first woman to throw over 50 meters (166 ft. 8 in.).

In the early 1960s Tamara Press proved to be the most formidable Soviet thrower. As with the shot put, she excelled in the discus, breaking six world records. Altogether, Press had twelve world records in her throwing events. She won a gold medal in 1964 and raised the world record over 2.5 meters (8 ft. 4 in.). Her best throw of 59.70 meters (199 ft.) was on 11 August 1965.

The leading thrower of the 1970s was Faina Melnik of the Soviet Union. From 1972 to 1976, Melnik set eleven world records, winning a gold medal at the Munich Games and two European championships. She was the first woman to break 70 meters with her throw of 70.20 meters (234 ft.) on 20 August 1975. Melnik's greatest throw of 70.50 meters (235 ft.) remained the record for two years until it was broken by her East German rival Evelia Jahl-Schlaak. Jahl-Schlaak was the only woman to win two Olympic discus titles. Her first medal, when she beat Melnik, was considered an upset. Jahl-Schlaak won the event on her first throw of 69 meters (230 ft.). On 10 May 1980 she won her second medal when she threw 71.50 meters (238 ft. 3.9 in.), a mark that made her the second woman to throw over 70 meters.

In the 1980s the world record shifted five times with East German Gabriele Reinsch leading the group. Reinsch threw 76.80 meters (256 ft.) to set a new world record in July 1988. This record still stood in 1999, but Beatrice Faumina and Natalya Sadovas were challenging the record, both leading the group of emerging throwers in the late 1990s.

JAVELIN

The women's javelin weighs 600 grams (1 lb. 5 oz.), although in 1928, women did throw javelins weighing 800 grams. Early javelins were made of wood, but now more aerodynamic spears are being made out of fiberglass. In 1928, Babe Didrikson won Olympic Gold when she threw the javelin 43.68 meters (145 ft. 7.2 in.). The first official world record listing for the javelin, however, was given to Nan Gindele of the United States when she threw 46.74 meters (153 ft. 4.2 in.) at the Central AAU championships in Chicago. Gindele's record stood for ten years and was broken by Anneliese Steinheuer of Germany at the Eintracht Frankfurt at 47.24 meters (154 ft. 11.8 in.).

Since Germany did not participate in the European championships and the 1948 Olympics, Steinheuer did not have the opportunity to test her potential against international competition. In 1947 Austrian Herma Bauma broke the world record, and Steinheuer's absence from the Olympics gave Bauma a chance to win the gold medal. A month later, Bauma set a second world record at 48.63 meters (162 ft. 1.2 in.).

Students at Woodhouse School in Finchley, London, England, in 1937, were the first secondary pupils to receive javelin throwing as part of their physical education classes. (Corbis)

In 1947 the Soviet Union resumed its participation in the IAAF. This decision allowed several Soviet athletes to challenge records in the throwing competitions. Natalya Smirnitskaya and Nadezhda Konyayeva raised the world record five times from 1949 through 1954. Konyayeva became the first woman to break the 55-meter (183-ft.-3.4-in.) mark. Her record stood for four years until Dana Zatopkova of Czechoslovakia set a record at 55.73 meters (185 ft. 9.2 in.). Zatopkova, a three-event gold medal winner at the 1952 Olympics, went on to win the European championships in 1954 and 1958.

Zaptokova's record stood for less than a month when it was broken on 24 July 1958 by Anna Pazera of Australia with a throw of 57.40 meters (191 ft. 4 in.). The title, however, was immediately reclaimed by the Soviets. Birute Kalediene and Elvira Ozolina raised the mark four times. Kalediene, the Soviet champion from 1958 to 1960, set the record at the Soviet team championships in 1958. Ozolina broke the mark in 1960 three times. She also won the Rome Olympics and the European championships, and in 1964 she became the first woman to throw more than 60 meters when she reached 61.38 meters (204 ft. 7.2 in.). The IAAF did not ratify the distance because the Soviets failed to submit it. At the Tokyo Olympics, Ozolina was beaten by teammate Yelena

JENKINS' JAVELIN

At the 1927 National Championships in California, Margaret Jenkins attempted to use a javelin constructed for her by Johnny Myrra, the defending male Olympic champion in the event. Jenkins had been using this javelin in practice and was never confronted by an official about its weight. However, Aileen Allen, the coach of Lillian Copeland, the defending national champion, protested against the inclusion of the javelin because it was lighter than the others and said to be more aerodynamic. The officials settled the dispute by removing Jenkins' javelin and placing all other competitors' javelins in a pile and allowed Jenkins to chose one of them. Jenkins picked up a javelin that just so happened to belong to Copeland, her competitor. Angered by the decision, Jenkins picked up the javelin and threw it for a new world record.

Gorchakova, whose throw of 62.40 meters (208 ft.) also set a world record.

Gorchakova's record was soon broken, twice on the same day. The first athlete to break it was Poland's Ewa Gryziecka, who threw 62.70 meters (209 ft.). The second was East German Ruth Fuchs with a throw of 65.06 meters (216 ft. 10.3 in.). Fuchs went on to set five more world record marks and dominated the 1970s and early 1980s. One of her rivals, Kate Schmidt of the United States, managed to take the record away in 1997, but Schmidt was unable to defeat Fuchs in regular competition. She was an Olympic champion twice (1972, 1976) and also won the European championships twice. She became the first woman to throw more than 65 meters, and her final record stood at 69.96 meters (233 ft. 2.4 in.).

From 1980 to 1985, the javelin title changed hands five times. Tatyana Biryulina of the Soviet Union became the first woman to throw more than 70 meters (233 ft. 3.9 in.), and Bulgarian Antoaneta Todorova became, at age eighteen, the youngest woman to hold a record in the javelin. Ilse Liilak of Finland not only set a world record, but went on to become one of Finland's great javelin throwers. Sofia Sakorafa of Greece fouled out in several major competitions from 1975 to 1978 and developed an intense rivalry with Anna Verouli, another Greek thrower. At the 1982 European championships, the two athletes battled it out, and Verouli won the final in a fifth-round contest. Sakoraka's defeat motivated her to work harder and triumph over Verouli. On 26 September 1982, Sakorafa threw 74.20 meters (247 ft. 4 in.).

Sakorafa's record stood for three years, but Petra Felke of East Germany claimed the title on 4 June 1985 and for the next five years became the dominant women's thrower. Her first record broke the 75-meter mark, and she held the East German title for six years. In 1986, Great Britain's Fatima Whitbread took the record to 77.44 meters (258 ft. 1.6 in.), but Felke came back, throwing 78.90 meters (263 ft.). Whitbread was the world champion in 1987, beating Felke for the honor. The two athletes proved to be strong rivals in competition. At the Seoul Olympics, Felke won the gold and Whitbread took the silver. Felke held the world record in 1999 with 80.00 meters (266 ft. 7.9 in.).

Women's jumping and throwing competition remains an intensely contested event. Eventually, in each event, some contender will attain the longest distance possible. What that distance will be remains an open question; as yet, no limit has been reached.

Mary Hricko

Bibliography

Lawson, Gerald. (1997) *World Record Breakers in Track & Field Athletics.* Australia: Human Kinetics.

Matthews, Peter. (1982) *The Guinness Book of Track & Field Athletics: Facts & Feats.* London: Guinness Superlatives.

———. (1996) *Athletics 1995: The International Track and Field Annual.* Surbiton, England:

Stewart, Harry E. (1916) "A Survey of Track Athletics for Women." *American Physical Education Review.*

Tricard, Louise. (1996) *American Women's Track and Field: A History, 1895 Through 1980.* Jefferson, NC: McFarland.

TRACK AND FIELD—RUNNING AND HURDLING

Track racing takes place on a 400-meter track that often encircles an athletic field. Although most familiar as an elite sport—and the focus of much media coverage during the Olympics—track racing is also contested at secondary schools, colleges, and other less glamorous venues. Indeed, it is at these events that the elite athletes get their start. The dramas that unfold on the orange oval at the Olympics are the culmination of years of intensive effort. Women participate in ten track events and have produced some dramatic and memorable moments in their performances.

HISTORY

In ancient Greece, women had competitions of their own, racing over a distance of 500 Olympic

THE FIRST OLYMPIC 800-METER FOR WOMEN (1928)

The 1928 début of the 800 meters was besieged by controversy even before the start. The women had insisted on running the event, two laps of the track. But many Olympic officials deplored the 'dangerous' decision to let them run it, as God had intended runs of such wearying distances only for men. It was a perilous distance for women to run—more than two minutes of jiggling of the insides, you know.

The winner of that first Olympic 800 meters, Lina Radke of Germany, certainly didn't think so. Radke ran this event, which was so arduously masculine, only twenty-six seconds slower than the Frenchman who won the men's 800-meter race. Undertrained, inexperienced, with no explosive start, she nonetheless zipped to the finish in two minutes, 16.8 seconds, with Hitomi Kinue, the only Japanese woman at the Olympics, right behind her for silver. The top six women finished within ten seconds of each other, the first three bettering the world record. Some of the runners collapsed with exhaustion and/or disappointment toward the end of the race or just beyond the finish—not an unusual sight today after an Olympic middle-distance final. Nor was it anything compared to the gore witnessed in men's distance running at the time. But the sight of ladies in distress offended conventional propriety. There was uproar.

ADRIANNE BLUE
(1987) Grace Under Pressure. *London: Sidgwick and Jackson.*

feet (160.22 m). These were held at Olympia every four years but were quite separate from the men's Games. Even in Greek times, men had reservations about women taking part in track. In medieval times, it is likely that women did race in rural fairs and other festive gatherings before and certainly until the more formal developments of specialized running tracks during the late nineteenth century. It has been recorded that during the fifteenth century a race for prostitutes took place in Basel, Switzerland, over a distance of 250 paces (between 200–250 yd.). Similar races occurred in France. They were essentially rituals of degradation. Folk-like races continued during the eighteenth century at fairs and associated festivities.

A more recognizable form of track running for women, timed and recorded according to the systems of modern sport, developed during the nineteenth century. Arguably the earliest recorded time for a women's track race was the forty-eight-second effort of the winner of a race over 355 Swedish cubits (210.8 m) in Finland in March 1878. The race was held on a frozen lake at Laukaa and the time was recorded on a timepiece that predated the first stopwatch introduced to Finland. Other performances have been recorded in Scandinavia, the United States, and Britain, but the earliest organized track and field meet for women is generally associated with an 1895 event at Vassar College in Poughkeepsie, New York. By the end of the nineteenth century, women's track racing was not uncommon—but not widespread—in the United States and the industrializing nations of Europe.

The early Olympic Games did not include women athletes. Baron de Coubertin, the driving force behind the modern Olympic movement, was firmly against the idea. Nevertheless, women did compete at such events as circus sports, college field days, and various national meetings. In 1917 a momentous event occurred with the founding of the Fédération Féminine Sportive de France. This resulted from the energy and enthusiasm of Alice Milliat, but her subsequent request to have women's events included in the Olympics was rejected. Milliat's national organization led to the growth of the Fédération Sportive Féminine Internationale (FSFI) in 1921, and under its auspices the first women's world games were held at

Paris a year later. Continued pressure for women to gain parity with men resulted in women being admitted to the Olympic Games of 1928, held in Amsterdam. In track racing, only the 100-meter and the 800-meter races and the 4 × 100–meter relay were contested. The Games did not do much to encourage a more modern approach among the patriarchs of the Olympic movement. The sight of exhausted women following the 800-meter race (won by Lina Radke of Germany in a world record time) led to that event being removed from the Olympic schedule until it was restored in 1960. Negative public opinion notwithstanding, women's track racing was finally legitimated by the merger of the FSFI with the IAAF in 1936.

The list of events for women that are sanctioned by the IAAF has grown to be much the same as events for men. But equality of participation has been achieved slowly, as illustrated by attitudes toward middle distance running in 1928. For many years, most track meets for women failed to include events above 400 meters, and it was the Soviet Union, which during the 1930s was not a member of the IAAF, that had the highest standards at 800 meters. Mixed races with men were not officially sanctioned and an alleged 800-meter performance of 2 minutes 10 seconds by the Norwegian Marit Hemsted-Øisted in 1946 was not accepted as a world record. The sprint hurdles were run over a distance of only 80 meters until 1969. By 1999 parity between men and women had been nearly achieved, though men and women still did not regularly run in the same races.

Although the IAAF is a global organization, the distribution of elite track talent varies considerably between the continents of the world. The nations of Europe and North America, which have the financial resources to build the costly facilities required for training for most track events, dominate the production of superior athletes. In many countries very few women take part in track because of male prejudice and social or religious conventions. India and China produce hardly any world-class track athletes, despite the occasional emergence of world record breaking Chinese distance runners. In terms of its population potential, however, China remains well below the world norm. The same is true of many countries in Africa. South Africa, one exception, is the major African producer of female track athletes, though Nigeria has produced a number of world-class sprinters, and Kenya has done the same with long distance athletes.

PIONEERS AND LANDMARKS

The first woman to break five minutes for the mile—Diane Leather (1933–) of Britain in 1954—failed to attract the attention afforded the first man (Roger Bannister) to break four minutes for the same event in the same year. Nor is the first woman known to win a timed track race (Maria Wiinikainen, on the frozen Finnish lake) as world-renowned as some might wish.

Women's participation in sport was limited before World War II, resulting in an equivalently low number of records and legendary performances. Mildred "Babe" Didrikson Zaharias (1911–1956) displayed unique talents in track and field events. In 1931 she equaled the world's 100-yard record, running for her team, the Employer's Casualty Insurance Company of Dallas, for whom she worked as a stenographer. At the Amateur Athletic Union (AAU) championships of 1932 she competed in eight events in the space of two-and-a-half-hours. While competing at the Olympic Games in Los Angeles in 1932 she won the 80-meter hurdles with a world's record (having equaled the record in her heat) and won the silver medal in the high jump. The hurdles event was marred by controversy because many people believed that the second placer, Evelyne Hall, had actually won the race. Didrikson was the only woman to have won medals in both track and field events during the same Olympic Games. Following her career in track she became a baseball player and a golfer, and she excelled at both sports.

The world's first international woman star of track and field may be Francina (Fanny) Blankers-Koen of the Netherlands (1918–). Her first event was the 800-meter race, but she competed in the 1936 Berlin Olympics in the Dutch national 4 × 100–meter relay team, which placed fifth, and achieved the same placing in the high jump. Two years later she tied the world record for the 100-yard and in 1942 tied the world's 80-meter hurdles record (she also broke the world's record in the high jump). After the war she won two gold medals (80-meter hurdles and sprint relay) at the

1946 European championships. But it was in the first postwar Olympics in London in 1948 that she won her international renown. At that event she won four gold track medals—the 100-, 200-, and 80-meter hurdles, and was also a member of the winning 4 × 100–meter relay team at the age of thirty. Reflecting the times, she was referred to as "the female Jesse Owens," and a British newspaper headline proclaimed: "Fastest woman in the world is an expert cook."

With the growth of modern sport, it has become progressively harder for a single athlete to achieve such dominance as Blankers-Koen. Some would regard the American Wilma Rudolph (1940–) as her natural successor, but Rudolph only competed until the age of twenty-two. Rudolph was an athlete who overcame formidable odds. She was born the twentieth of twenty-two children into a poor southern home. As a child she was stricken with polio, and she was twelve years old before a brace was removed from her leg. Even so, she became the youngest member of the 1956 U.S. Olympic team. It was at the 1960 Rome Olympics that the international media took note of her; she easily won the 100- and 200-meter races and ran the final leg for the winning U.S. sprint relay team. She also held world records at 100 and 200 meters.

During the 1970s and 1980s it became increasingly apparent that women's track was becoming centered in East Germany (the German Democratic Republic) and some other eastern European nations. These nations selected talented children as future athletes and applied careful but rigorous training methods as they grew up. One star was Marlies Göhr (1958–), regarded by many as the most durable female athlete of all time. She competed in the 1976 Olympics in Montreal, winning a gold medal in the sprint relay team but placing eighth in the 100-meter race. A year later she became the first woman to break 11 seconds in the 100-meter race with automatic timing, recording 10.88 seconds. She improved to 10.81 in 1983. In the 1980 Moscow Olympics she won a silver medal in the 100-meter race. Göhr's Olympic successes were impressive, but she is better known for breaking many records. The remarkable world records at 400 meters by Marita Koch (1957–) also represented East German success. She broke the 400-meter record on seven occasions, reducing it from 49.29 to 47.60 seconds between 1976 and 1985. Her record still stood in 1999. Koch's talent was contested at 400 meters by Jarmila Kratochvílová of Czechoslovakia (1951–), who in 1983 had broken the world's record with a time of 47.99, the first woman to run under 48 seconds. However, Kratochvílová is much better remembered for her remarkable 800-meter world record of 1:53.28, set in Munich in 1983. The North Korean athlete Sin Kim Dan (1938–), with a time of 1.59.1 seconds, first broke the women's 800-meter landmark of 2 minutes in 1963. A year later she improved the record to 1 minute 58 seconds. However, North Korea was not affiliated with the IAAF, and the record was therefore not ratified officially. It was not until 1973 that Hildegard Falck (1949–) of the Federal Republic of Germany officially broke the 2-minute barrier with a time of 1 minute 58.5 seconds. She won the Olympic title the following year.

Chinese women in a hurdles race, 1933. (Christiansen/Levinson)

Doubt about a record performance also applies to the 100-meter record of the American Florence Griffith-Joyner (1959–1998). Her colleague Evelyn Ashford (1957–) had twice improved on Göhr's record and in early 1988 the record stood at 10.76. However, in the 1988 U.S. Olympic Trials in Indianapolis, Flo-Jo, as she was known, reduced Ashford's mark by an astonishing 0.27 seconds, finishing in 10.49. Such was the margin of improvement that the record remains shrouded in controversy. It is alleged that a strong wind was helping the athletes during the race but was not recorded as being over the legal limit of 2.0 meters per second. However, a wind gauge beside the triple jump approach, running parallel to the sprint course, recorded wind speeds over the legal limit as the women's 100 meters began. Joyner was also accused of taking illegal performance-enhancing substances. In short, her performance was so superior to the previous record that it was, for many, beyond belief.

The record-breaking performances of athletes from China in the long distance track races received a similar reaction. At the China National Games in Beijing in September 1993, the legendary Wang Junxia (1972–) beat the world records from 1500 meters to 10,000 meters four times in five days. The 3000-meter event at that meet is nearly legendary. In the first heat Zhang Linli (1973–) broke the world record, which had been held by Soviet athletes since the mid-1970s, setting a time of 8 minutes 22.06 seconds. In the second heat Wang Junxia improved on this by almost 10 seconds, recording 8 minutes 12.19 seconds. The next day these two world record breakers were pitted against each other in the final. Wang won in the remarkable time of 8 minutes 6.11 seconds with four other athletes breaking the world record as it had stood at the start of the previous day. Wang also broke the world 1500-meter record in finishing second to Qu Junxia (1972–). In the 10,000-meter event, the path-breaking running of the Norwegian Ingrid Kristiansen (1956–) had brought the world record to within reach of the 30-minute barrier with a performance of 30 minutes 13.74 seconds, set at Oslo in 1986. It remained unassailable until Wang's remarkable run of 29 minutes 31.78 seconds—a time that would have held the men's record until 1949. Wang's performances were met with accusations of illegal drug taking and other accusations linked to Chinese cultural beliefs—that she was consuming exotic potions and that her coach exerted an unusual degree of power over her. The Chinese athletes have not reproduced their performances in Western meets. This is not to doubt the validity of their records but to suggest that they may regard the all-

WORLD TRACK RECORDS RECOGNIZED BY THE INTERNATIONAL AMATEUR ATHLETIC FEDERATION, 1999

Event	Time	Record Holder	Nation	Year
100m	10.49	Florence Griffith Joyner	United States	1988
200m	21.34	Florence Griffith Joyner	United States	1988
400m	47.60	Marita Koch	East Germany	1985
800m	1:53.28	Jarmila Kratochvílová	Czechoslovakia	1983
1000m	2:28.98	Svetlana Masterkova	Russia	1996
1500m	3:50.46	Qu Yunxia	China	1993
1 mile	4:12.56	Svetlana Masterkova	Russia	1996
2000m	5:25.36	Sonia O'Sullivan	Ireland	1994
3000m	8:06.11	Wang Junxia	China	1993
5000m	14.28.09	Jiang Bo	China	1997
10,000m	29:31.78	Wang Junxia	China	1993
Marathon	2:20:47	Tegla Laroupe	Kenya	1984
100m hurdles	12.21	Yordanka Donkova	Bulgaria	1998
400m hurdles	52.61	Kim Batten	United States	1995
4x100m relay	41.37	East Germany	East Germany	1985
4x200m relay	1:28.15	East Germany	East Germany	1980
4x400m relay	3:15.17	USSR	USSR	1988
4x800m relay	7:50.17	USSR	USSR	1984

China championships as more important than even the Olympics.

During the 1990s the global growth of track and field has continued steadily. Western observers have noted with interest that women from the Islamic world are taking up track, given the Muslim proscription against exposing women's bodies. Some of these women have become athletes at considerable personal cost. The Algerian 1500-meter runner, Hassiba Boulmerka, won the world 1500-meter championship in 1991. Boulmerka's track triumph won the admiration of thousands of Algerians and a motorcade in her honor. At the same time, the more militant Muslims in Algeria condemned her antifundamentalist position as a track athlete. Subsequently, Boulmerka won a gold medal in the Barcelona Olympics of 1994 and dedicated her medal to the former president of Algeria, who had been assassinated, allegedly by fundamentalists. She also called on all young Algerians to suffer as she had. Boulmerka no longer lives in Algeria.

RULES AND PLAY

The regularly contested outdoor track events for women range from 100 meters to 10,000 meters (over 6 miles). Flat races (without hurdles) that lie between these extremes are the 200 meters, 400 meters, 800 meters, 1500 meters, 1 mile, and 5000 meters. The 3000-meter race is also a popular event. For indoor events, races usually range from 60 meters to 3000 meters. Track is categorized by the length of the race. The sprints are from 60 through 400 meters, the middle distances 800 through 3000 meters, and the long distances from 5000 meters up. Track running can also be categorized by aerobic capacity—the sprints, the middle and long distances, and the 800 meters between the two. Some track races include hurdles. These cover distances of 100 meters and 400 meters, each of which have ten barriers, 85 centimeters high. The 3000-meter steeplechase is a relatively new event for women. It involves clearing twenty-eight solid hurdles and seven water jumps during the course of the race. Races through 100 meters are run on a straight track; the others are run counterclockwise around the 400-meter circuit. Other events include the two relay (or team) races, the 4 × 100 meters and the 4 × 400 meters. Races of up to 400 meters in distance are run in lanes to separate athletes and to avoid accidental or deliberate collision of bodies.

CONTROVERSIES

Detailed and thorough records in track racing allow closer scrutiny of some of the issues and debates surrounding women in sports. One of these is whether women are gradually closing the gap on men in terms of running performance—and whether their performances may one day equal those of men. In addition, track is one of the major sports in which the problem of illicit drug use has been widely recognized. Finally, track provides examples of cases where athletes who were thought to be female were in fact male, at least according to the tests used.

It is generally claimed that the gap between men's and women's performances is closing. Some women clearly can run faster than most men; what remains open to question is whether a woman might one day hold the absolute best performance for a particular event. Part of the debate involves deciding what data might be used to make such predictions. The respective world records for men and women make it apparent that in general, the percent difference in men's and women's world records is getting closer. It has been suggested that if progress continues at the rate recorded from 1920 to 1980, by the year 2025 the difference will have vanished in world long/middle distance records between men and women. The equivalent dates for the sprints and short/middle distances are 2040 and 2051, respectively. Arguably, however, using world records for these calculations is misleading; a more representative picture would emerge by comparing instead the average performances of a larger number of athletes over time. The performances of men and women might still converge, but the rate of convergence might differ.

The second debate relates to drug abuse in track racing. Reports of illicit drug use are widespread in sports, but women's track and field has experienced some of the most dramatic accusations and effects. From the 1970s to the 1990s several track athletes have been disqualified after it was discovered that they had consumed drugs banned by the IAAF. Florence Griffith-Joyner was among the women athletes who have been suspected of illegal drug use. Her premature death in

The women's 800-meter race at the 1996 Olympic Games in Atlanta. (Ales Fevzer/Corbis)

1998 renewed doubt about the legality of her world record-breaking performances years earlier, but autopsy results showed no evidence of illicit drug use. The muscular build of the 800-meter world record holder, Jarmila Kratochvílová, has led to similar doubts. Skeptics would regard most elite women track athletes these days to be operating at, or beyond, the legal margins of pharmaceutical acceptability, at least according to the IAAF. Today, all top athletes compete under the cloud of suspicion. The occasional suggestion that performance-enhancing substances should be legalized, providing that they are taken voluntarily, remains muted.

Third, debates surrounding women in track have included what has been described as a "sex test," or gender verification test—a procedure to verify that a female competitor truly is female. Track athletes have featured in these controversies. One of the most well known of the athletes who took part in the third FSFI games in 1930 was Stanislava Walaciewicz (1911–1980) of Poland, known as Stella Walsh following her emigration to the United States. She won three gold medals in the 60-, 100-, and 200-meter races at the 1930 FSFI games. After her death decades later, however, an autopsy revealed that Stella Walsh had male sexual characteristics. That there is, in fact, a clear-cut distinction between all men and women is controversial. The IAAF, however, maintains that it is necessary to try to distinguish between them, although different sports have different definitions of male and female. Until 1966 athletes only required a doctor's medical certificate to prove that they were women. A full visual examination was introduced in 1966 and a chromosome test in 1967. If chromosomal tests are applied, females are defined as possessing only X chromosomes in each cell of their body. The most prominent athlete to fall foul of this rule was the Polish sprinter Eva Klobukowska (1946–), a former coholder of the world's 100-meter record in 1965. She was disqualified from women's competitions in 1967 for a chromosome defect.

CONCLUSION

In the future, world champions, Olympic medalists, and world record holders may emerge from a wider variety of cultural backgrounds than has been the case. Some long distance runners of note already come from Kenya and Ethiopia; a world champion in the 400-meter hurdles came from Morocco and a great sprinter from Sri Lanka. However, it also appears that it is becoming increasingly possible for athletes to change their nations just as participants in other sports change clubs. The most well-known example was that of the South African long distance runner Zola Budd (1966–). During the apartheid era she was unable to compete internationally because of the exclusion of South Africa from international sport. On the basis of her father's English origins she was able to rapidly obtain British citizenship and compete for Britain in the Olympics. In recent years, athletes from Africa and Eastern Europe have assumed the nationality of Western European nations. This suggests a reduced emphasis on the national allegiance of athletes and a willingness to obtain citizenship of nations where their professional careers may be enhanced.

John Bale

Bibliography

Bale, John, and Joe Sang. (1996) *Kenyan Running: Movement Culture, Geography and Global Change.* London: Frank Cass.

Brownell, Susan. (1995) *Training the Body for China: Sports in the Moral Order of the People's Republic.* Chicago, IL: University of Chicago.

Dyer, K. F. (1982) *Catching up the Men: Women in Sport.* London: Junction Books.

Guttmann, Allen. (1991) *Women's Sports: A History.* New York: Columbia University Press.

Morgan, Bill. (1998) "Hassiba Boulmerka and Islamic Green: International Sports, Cultural Differences, and their Postmodern Interpretation." In *Sport and Postmodern Times,* edited by Geneviève Rail. Albany, NY: State University of New York Press, 345–366.

Quercetani, Roberto. (1990) *Athletics: A History of Modern Track and Field Athletics.* Milan: Vallardi & Associates.

zur Megede, Ekkehard, and Richard Hymans, eds. (1995) *Progression of World Best Performances and Official IAAF Records.* Monaco: IAAF.

TRIATHLON

Triathlon is a sport combining three events—swimming, biking, and running—the winner being the athlete who completes all three in sequence in the fastest time. Triathlon evolved from two-event sports (duathlon) and has become more popular, with triathlons competed over very long and shorter distances. Women have participated in all but the very early competitions and have played an important role in increasing public interest in the sport. Women triathletes compete under the same rules as do men. The event usually follows the swim-bike-run sequence, with only brief pauses for changes of clothes or equipment. These pauses (time for transitions between events) are included in the participants' total time.

HISTORY

The beginnings of the sport of triathlon are most often coupled with the beginnings of the ultradistance Hawaiian Ironman Triathlon first held in 1978. This event is a 2.4-mile ocean swim followed by a 112-mile bike ride, and a 26.2-mile run. This, in fact, was not the first such multisport event; others that involved running, biking, and/or swimming preceded it. The Ironman is nevertheless the premier event in triathlon. Originally viewed as the ultimate endurance challenge for eccentric fitness fanatics—twelve participants, all male, completed it in 1978; fifteen, including one woman, did so in 1979—the Hawaiian Ironman has become the ultradistance world championship, with close to 1,500 competitors from more than seventy-eight countries each year. Millions watch this event on network television, and recent estimates indicate that there are over 2 million triathletes around the world, of whom more than 200,000 are in the United States.

For much of the history of the sport, this emphasis on the Ironman has meant that the sport of triathlon has been viewed as an endurance sport, with the ultimate measure of triathlete status marked by participation in that world championship. This emphasis on longer events, "gruelathons," as they have been called, continued through much of the 1980s. By the late 1980s, however, triathletes began to direct much more attention to shorter, popular "Olympic" distance events—1.5-kilometer swim, 40-kilometer cycle, 10-kilometer run—that an individual could complete with a reasonable amount of effort. This emphasis came about in an attempt to bring new participants into the sport. The establishment of the International Triathlon Union (ITU) in Stockholm in 1989 and the ensuing Olympic distance ITU World Cup Triathlon Series, which is broadcast to more than 2 billion households, has done much to transform the nature of the sport.

Nonetheless, despite these developments, the primary symbol for the triathlon, particularly by those outside the sport, remains the Ironman. Moreover, because of its very nature, because it is the Iron*man,* it is viewed as an event dominated by males. Historically, male participants in triathlons have received primary attention and emphasis. In the October 1982 Ironman race, 11 percent of the 850 competitors were women; by 1997, 290 out of 1,479 competitors, or 19.6 percent, were women. The average percentage of women competing in the Hawaiian Ironman in more recent years has fluctuated but has never been more than 20 percent of the total participants.

WOMEN AND PUBLIC PERCEPTION

Nevertheless, it has been women who have played a critical role in catapulting the sport of triathlon into the mainstream consciousness and who have made it more than a passing fitness fad. In the February 1982 Ironman, it was the inspirational crawl of Julie Moss across the finish line, (passed in the last moments by Kathleen McCartney, who won the race), captured on ABC's "Wide World of Sports," that galvanized public attention. Eight months later, entries in the October event almost doubled.

A female administrator has also helped to increase interest in the Ironman. In 1981 Valerie Silk took over as race director and organizer for the event; under her direction it grew to 1,300 competitors by 1989. She viewed the Hawaiian Ironman as something more than just a race: it was an experience that could transform each and every participant—a perception that remains at the core of the Ironman. In 1990 she sold it to veteran Ironman triathlete Dr. Jim Gills of Florida, who then formed the World Triathlon Corporation. They have aggressively promoted the race worldwide since then, making it a multibillion dollar enterprise.

More than anything, however, it has been the achievements of Paula Newby-Fraser that have brought media attention and worldwide respect to triathletes. Newby-Fraser has dominated the Hawaiian Ironman since her first win in 1986; from 1986 to 1994 she won seven out of nine times. Eight-time winner of the Hawaiian Ironman, she made her mark in 1988, coming across the finish line in 9:01.01, (eleventh overall). In 1989 she improved that to 9:00.56 (thirty-fourth overall), and in 1992 set a record of 8:55.28, becoming the first woman ever to go under 9 hours in Hawaii. The Women's Sport Foundation voted Newby-Fraser to be the Professional Sportswoman of the Year in 1990 and then in 1997 voted to include her among the five best female professional athletes of the past twenty-five years. The 1990 award represented the first time a mainstream sports award had been given to a triathlete.

Other Ironwomen age-group contenders have also made an impact. Lyn Brooks has completed more Hawaiian Ironman events than anyone else, nineteen to date; she has participated every year since 1980, when she placed third overall. Her finish time at age forty was the same as a decade earlier. Sally Edwards, another pioneer in the sport who came in second in her first Ironman in 1981, was also instrumental in bringing attention to the sport in 1982 by writing the first book on triathlons, *Triathlon: A Triple Fitness Sport.* By 1990, she was a seven-time Ironman finisher, had written five books, and played a key role in helping to launch the Danskin Women's Triathlon Series, the first all-women triathlon series in the world. Other regular age-group winners include Missy Le Strange (age 46), Lesley Cens McDonald (age 52), Judy Flannery (age 57 when she died in 1997), and Sister Madonna Buder (age 68). There have

Female participants in the Baltimore Triathlon. (Paul A. Souders/Corbis)

also been multiple triathlon and duathlon world champions throughout the 1980s and to the present. All are examples of extraordinary women who continue to defy expectations and serve as important role models for women.

These women and other women who have promoted the sport of triathlon have demonstrated superior athletic capabilities, performing at any distance, under horrendous conditions, and at the highest level. Perhaps even more significant, they have also made their mark as race directors, organizers, and key players in the emergence of the USA Triathlon Federation and, even more important, the International Triathlon Union, the organizations responsible for attaining Olympic status for the triathlon in the year 2000.

WOMEN AND TRIATHLONS IN THE 1990s

Overall the 1990s have seen a significant increase in the number of women who participate in triathlons. In 1987 women made up approximately 14 percent of all triathletes; in 1999, 23 percent of triathletes were women. The majority of these were young women. Older women who have not had the exposure to sports that Title IX brought to the United States have been slower to break with tradition. Sally Edwards has noted that "only 1.1 percent of the participants in the U.S. Triathlon Series [the premier Olympic distance triathlon series in the late 1980s, early 1990s] are women 40–44 years of age," or 11 out of 1,000 triathletes.

The overwhelming nature of the competition may explain these numbers in part. Participating in an event with well-muscled males who tower over you and literally swim over you in the water is intimidating. Even with women's separate waves (which often are sandwiched between waves of fast men), the fear and intimidation factor remains ever present. Because women are typically not as fast or strong as men, they are viewed by males as second-rate athletes. Correspondingly, the prize purse and awards for women have traditionally been considerably less than those for men. In other words, significant barriers to participation confront women. It was precisely these factors that led in 1990 to the establishment of the Women's Commission (now the Women's Committee) of the ITU and the Danskin Women's Triathlon Series in the United States.

The focus of the ITU Women's Committee was to achieve equality of opportunity, recognition, and reward for women triathletes, beginning with equal prize money for female and male winners. Flo Bryan from the United States (who ran the Bud Light U.S. Triathlon Series in the late 1980s) and Sarah Springman from Great Britain were the first cochairs. By 1994 the ITU was the first international sporting organization to adopt the Brighton Declaration for Women and Sport. Beginning in 1995 at Cancun, Mexico, the Women's Committee initiated efforts to encourage women's participation in triathlons in developing countries, especially Africa and Asia. In 1998 efforts focused on support for women's race clinics and all women's events.

In 1998 there were ITU triathlon World Cup events in Australia, Canada, Japan, Germany, Hungary, Switzerland, Mexico, New Zealand, and the United States. Australian triathletes Michellie Jones, Emma Carney, Jackie Gallagher, and Loretta Harrop had dominated the ITU World Cup rankings for two years; the top-100 ranked women came from twenty-eight countries, including thirteen from the United States, twelve from Australia, and seven from Japan. In addition to these mixed races that highlight the accomplishments of elite women, there has been considerable growth in all women's triathlons. Australia, Japan, Hong Kong, Denmark, and most recently Switzerland have all hosted women's events.

The first and most successful of all women's events, however, remains the Danskin Women's Triathlon Series. The Danskin all-women sprint triathlon (7.5-k swim, 20-k bike, 5-k run) began in three cities in 1990. The goal was to provide a supportive venue for all women to take part in a multisport event, regardless of their age, athletic background, or level of fitness. Women from ages fourteen to seventy-seven, weighing 90 to 300 pounds, amateurs and professionals, have participated; there is also a special category for breast cancer survivors. The first race had 150 competitors; by the Seattle race in 1998, 2,200 women, the maximum number the race venue could support, participated. In 1999, the Danskin Women's Triathlon Series held events in six U.S. cities with an average number of participants ranging from 1,200 to 1,400. Support to help women participate in the triathlon was also carried out through prerace regional training clinics. Between 1990 and 1999, more than 32,000 women have finished at least one Danskin women's triathlon. Over half of the participants in Danskin triathlons have never entered a triathlon before or, for that matter, any athletic event.

The numbers of women who have participated in the Danskin triathlons, along with the explosive popularity of women's triathlons internationally, speak to the significance of women's participation and involvement in the triathlon sport culture. The Olympic women's triathlon, as the first event of the Summer Games 2000 in Australia, demonstrates the positive impact of women's participation on the entire sport.

Jane Granskog

Bibliography

Carlson, Timothy. (1998) "Mainstream." *Triathlete Magazine* (August):74–80.

Edwards, Sally. (1990) "Breaking Tradition: A Fresh Look at Women in Sports." *Triathlete Magazine* (May):24–25.

Edwards, Sally, and Maggie Sullivan, eds. (1997) *Caterpillars to Butterflies: If You Can Dream It, Why Not Tri It?* Sacramento, CA: Danskin Inc. and Heart Zones Company.

Graham, Richard. (1990) "Deciding Women: Five Who Have Made Their Mark on Triathlon." *Triathlete Magazine* (May):58–60, 62, 66, 68.

Granskog, Jane. (1991) "Tri-ing for Life: The Emergence of the Triathlon Sport Sub-Culture and its Impact upon Changing Gender Roles in American Society." In *Sport: The Third Millennium, Proceedings of the Quebec City International Symposium,* edited by Fernand Landry, Marc Landry, and Magdeleine Yerles. Quebec City: Presses de L' Universite Laval.

———. (1993) "In Search of the Ultimate: Ritual Aspects of the Hawaiian Ironman Triathlon." *Journal of Ritual Studies* 7, 1: 1–23.

International Triathlon Union. (1998) *Women's Committee.* (http://www.worldsport.com/worldsport/sports/triathlon/home.html)

Plant, Mike. (1987) *Ironwill, the Heart and Soul of the Triathlon's Ultimate Challenge.* Chicago, IL: Contemporary Books.

Olivares, C. J. (1988) "Ten Years of Ironman." *Triathlete Magazine* (October):32–49.

"State of the Sport." (1987) *Triathlete Magazine* (May):61–64, 66–76, 79, 111.

World Triathlon Corporation. (1995) *Ironman Program Guide.* Competitor Publishing Co.

TUG-OF-WAR

Tug-of-war is a sport contest between two teams at opposite ends of a rope, in which each team tries to drag the other across a center line. Historically, with the exception of a few societies, tug-of-war has been a male game. Today women are equal participants in the competitive sport.

HISTORY

Tug-of-war has been one of the most common games around the world since prehistoric times. In most languages, the term used means "pulling on a rope": *tauziehen* (German), *touwtrekken* (Dutch), *tiro alla funa* (Italian), *lutte à la corde* (French) and *dragkamp* (Swedish). In China, for reasons long forgotten, the game is called *ba he,* literally meaning "pulling on a river."

Initially, tug-of-war was regarded as a symbol of various mystical powers related to health, good weather, harvest, and other fortunes, and so was practiced extensively as part of ancient rituals in many cultures. For example, in Burma a rain party and a drought party pulled against each other, and the rain party was allowed the victory to indicate the beginning of the rainy season. In Korea and Japan, tug-of-war competition was organized between villages to foretell the success of the upcoming harvest. Later, tug-of-war became less a ritual activity and more a pastime in many countries. This was the case in Egypt and Greece, followed by China, Mongolia, and Turkey, and then France and Great Britain.

RULES AND PLAY

There are various styles of tug-of-war. A wooden stick can be substituted for the rope, as in Afghanistan. Players may also participate while sitting down, as is done in the Canadian Inuit game of *sarsaaraq.*

The official style of tug-of-war is a team sport, with eight active pullers on a team. The rope should not be less than 10 centimeters or more than 12.5 centimeters in circumference, and it should be free from knots or other holdings for the hands. The minimum length of the rope must be no less than 33.5 meters.

Tug-of-war was briefly an Olympic sport, played from the 1900 Olympics to the 1920 Olympics, after which it was dropped. The sport is governed by the Tug-of-War International Federation (TWIF), founded in 1960, which in 1999 had twenty-five affiliated member countries and several candidate members. The TWIF is a member

Several Indian women compete in tug-of-war at the Pushkar Camel Fair in 1988. (Jeffrey L. Rotman/Corbis)

Several women compete in tug-of-war in Jerusalem. (Ted Spiegel/Corbis)

of the General Association of International Sports Federation and follows the Olympic principles in its activities.

Formerly, tug-of-war was predominantly a male game, but there were some exceptions. For example, to the *Iglulik* people of the Arctic area, tug-of-war was a woman's game. According to TWIF regulations, women have an equal right to participate in tug-of-war, and the women's events are listed parallel to those of men in the international tug-of-war competitions organized by the TWIF.

Hai Ren

Bibliography

TWIF. (1999) Tug-of-War International Federation Homepage. <http://www.tugofwar.org/>.

Ye, Dabing. (1990) *The Dictionary of Chinese Folklore.* Shanghai: Dictionary Press.

TURKEY

The Republic of Turkey, founded in 1923, extends from Asia Minor into Europe. It has a mainly Islamic population of 62 million. The traditional sports of the region that became modern Turkey were wrestling, archery, and a version of polo. The first modern sports—football, lawn tennis, sailing, and field hockey—were introduced around 1900 by English families and French physical education teachers living in Turkey at that time. The Besiktas Gymnastics Club was founded in 1903, the Galatasaray Football Club in 1905, and the Fenerbahçe Sports Club in 1907. All of the members of these clubs were men.

Turkish women practiced archery, wrestling, and horseback riding until the tenth century. During that time, a girl could only marry the man who defeated her in archery, wrestling, and horseback riding competition. After the Turks accepted Islam in the tenth century, women were no longer able to participate in sport because of religious beliefs. The exclusion of women lasted until Kemal Atatürk, founder of the Turkish Republic and the leader of its war of independence, established a secular democracy in 1923. After the proclamation of the republic, political and social rights were extended to women and legal reforms proclaimed equal rights for Turkish women.

Middle-class women started practicing sport in significant numbers in 1924. Among the first sports they practiced were track and field, tennis, rowing, and swimming. The first women athletes were often the sisters or wives of male athletes. In 1928–1929, a female volleyball player, Sabiha Rifat Gürayman, played on one of the men's teams because there was no women's team. The team won an international championship.

In 1936 Turkish women participated in the Olympic Games for the first time. The pioneers were Suat Fetgeri Aseni and Halet Çambel. After the 1936 games, Turkish women took part in the 1948, 1960, 1972, 1976, 1984, 1988, 1992, and 1996 Summer Games. The only medalist was Hülya Senyurt, who won a bronze medal in judo in 1992.

At the international level, female athletes like Gül Çiray Akbas, Aycan Önel, and Canel Kovur became role models and motivated Turkish women by winning gold medals at the Balkan Championships and by participating in 1960 Summer Olympic Games. In the European and world championships, Turkish women did not achieve visible success until 1987. Between 1987 and 1997, eleven Turkish women athletes won gold medals in world championships: Tennur Yerlisu (1987, tae kwon do), Arzu Tan (1991, tae kwon do), Nuray Deliktas (1993, tae kwon do), Ilknur

Kobas (1994, judo), Derya Açikgöz (1994 and 1997, weightlifting), Hamide Biçkin (1995, tae kwon do), Esma Can (1996 and 1997, weightlifting), and Aysel Özgür, Fatma Kabadayi, Döndü Ay, and Aysel Uzgüp (1997, weightlifting). At the Atlanta Olympic Games of 1996, Natalia Nasaridze Çakir became the first Turkish woman to break a world record in archery.

In the late 1990s, sport was still not an important part of daily life for most Turkish women and men. Even though half of the Turkish population was female, the number of female members of sports clubs was only 29,258, compared to 521,876 men in 1998. Tradition still plays an important role in limiting women's participation in sports, but the number of women athletes has increased every year. Development of a women's movement in Turkey has increased the number of women coaches and sport administrators. At the end of the 1990s, almost every sport federation had at least one woman member on its executive board. In 1995 Turkey's National Olympic Committee (NOC) established a Women's Committee, which is now developing projects to increase women's participation in sports.

Nese Gundogan and Cem Atabeyoglu

Bibliography

Atabeyoglu, Cem. (1981) *Ataturk and Sport.* Istanbul: Hisarbank Kultur Yaymlan.

Atabeyoglu, Cem, et al. ([1987]–1992) *Turk Spor Vakfi* (History of Turkish sports). Istanbul: Hisarbank Kultur Yaymlan.

Genclik ve Spor Genel Murduglu. (1997) *Success and Honor List of Turkish Sport.* Ankara: Genclik ve Spor Genel Mudurlugu.

U

UKRAINE

Ukraine is an independent nation of nearly 31 million people, covering an area of 603,700 square kilometers (232,046 square miles), which makes it Europe's second largest country after Russia. Its geographical position between Russia and Eastern Europe makes it central to European stability as a whole. Through the ages, Ukraine has been divided and ruled by many different powers (particularly Russia since the eighteenth century until 1991), but has always retained a sense of national identity. In 1991 some 90 percent of Ukrainians voted for independence, while remaining in a loose confederation with former Soviet republics, known as the Commonwealth of Independent States (CIS).

Under the Russian czar, Ukrainian sports development followed that of Russia and Belarus; women were mostly prevented from joining sport clubs. This did not apply, however, to commercial pursuits, such as wrestling. The redoubtable Ukrainian Masha Poddubnaya, wife of the great weightlifter Ivan Poddubny, was women's world heavyweight wrestling champion at the end of the nineteenth century and would invite all comers to wrestle her in the circus ring after she had disposed of her fellow troupers.

Oksana Baiul at the 1994 Winter Olympics. (Ales Fevzer/Corbis)

In 1896 the first physical training courses for men and women instructors were established in a number of major cities, including Odessa and Kiev, though they were closed down in 1907 for "inciting student unrest." The admission of women was certainly novel and was due to the pioneering work of the educator Pyotr Lesgaft (1837–1909). By 1913 Ukraine had 196 sports clubs with 8,000 members, an unspecified number of whom were undoubtedly women. The Pan-Slavic Sokol and Bogatyr clubs encouraged women's gymnastics, figure skating, and "therapeutic health exercises." The exclusively Jewish Maccabee sport clubs in such Jewish centers as Kiev (the capital) and the southern port of Odessa also admitted women.

After the 1917 Bolshevik Revolution, women's sports received a boost from the new revolutionary government, and Ukrainian women began to take part in a wide range of sports, including soccer (association football) and ice hockey. Sports were used for achieving a number of utilitarian functions. The Ukrainian Communist Party Central Committee issued a resolution in 1926, expressing the hope that "physical culture would become a vehicle of the new life . . .

An instructor assists gymnastics students as they dance at the Dynamo Children's Sport School in Kiev, 1957. (Jerry Cooke/Corbis)

a means of isolating young people from home-made liquor and prostitution." Sport, therefore, stood for clean living, progress, good health, and rationality.

It remained a persistent theme in Soviet writing on women's emancipation that women should be drawn more into sporting activities. All the same, only a minority of Ukrainian women took part in sport on any regular basis—15.2 percent in 1959, and 30.2 percent in 1969. Some sports were discouraged by the Soviet authorities as harmful to women, such as soccer, although the government had little success in preventing women's soccer and by the 1970s several soccer teams had sprung up mainly in the Ukraine (Kiev, Kharkov, and Dnepropetrovsk).

In accord with the government's desire to win in the Olympics and defeat the leading capitalist nations (primarily the United States), much effort was put into encouraging women's participation in every Olympic event. It is hardly surprising, therefore, that Ukrainian women represented their country in sports as diverse as gymnastics (Ludmilla Turishcheva was overall gymnastics champion at the Munich Games in 1972) and shot put (Faina Melnik was Olympic shot put champion in 1972 and 1976). Following the breakup of the Soviet Union, Ukrainian athletes competed as part of the Unified Team in the 1992 Olympics and then for Ukraine in the 1994 Winter and 1996 Summer Olympics, with eighty-four women on the Summer Games team. Ukrainian women performed well in the 400-, 800-, and 1500-meter track events, jumping events, and gymnastics. Of Ukrainian Olympic athletes, the best known internationally is figure skater Oksana Baiul, who took the gold in the 1994 Games, drawing attention away from the Nancy Kerrigan-Tonya Harding media frenzy.

James Riordan

See also Russia and Belarus

Bibliography

Riordan, James. (1978) *Sport in Soviet Society*. Cambridge, UK: Cambridge University Press.

———. (1989) *Sport, Politics and Communism*. Manchester, UK: Manchester University Press.

ULTIMATE

Ultimate flying disc began in the 1960s with a group of high school students who wanted to invent a counter-cultural game. The students designed what they believed would be the "ultimate sport": a blend of football, soccer, and basketball that emphasized respect and joyful competition. Their impulse gave birth to ultimate, a fast-paced flying disc sport.

From its inception, ultimate appealed to men and women disillusioned with the win-at-all-costs mentality that pervaded mainstream sports. Ultimate requires sportsmanship and integrity as well as disc skills, athleticism, and conditioning.

HISTORY

Women have been playing ultimate since it was created at Columbia High School in Maplewood, New Jersey. In 1971, the Columbia team had eight female players. As the high school graduates began spreading ultimate to college campuses, it was not uncommon to find a few women playing on some of the men's teams. Rutgers student Peggy Delahaunty played in the first intercollegiate ultimate game, between Rutgers and Princeton, on November 6, 1972.

In 1977, the first reported women's ultimate game was played in Irvine, California, between a group of Los Angeles and Santa Barbara women. Two years later, the Santa Barbara players started the first women's ultimate team, the Lady Condors. The Condors would later become the first women's team to win four consecutive National Championships (1984-1987). Lady Godiva, a women's team from Boston, later duplicated the feat by winning the U.S. Nationals from 1995-1998.

SPIRIT OF THE GAME

Ultimate has traditionally relied upon a principle of sportsmanship known as "Spirit of the Game."

A pick-up game of Ultimate at Simon's Rock College in Massachusetts brings together male and female athletes. (Christiansen/Levinson)

No referees are present during games, so players are responsible for calling their own fouls. The participants must make honest calls to ensure fair play. Actions such as taunting, dangerous play, or intentional fouls draw frowns of disapproval from teammates and opposition alike. The integrity of ultimate depends on each player's responsibility to uphold the Spirit of the Game. Ultimate players try to keep the Spirit alive by maintaining a high level of trust and friendliness, no matter how competitive the game gets. If people cannot resolve their differences, they usually send the disc "back to the thrower," which allows play to continue without forcing the issue one way or another.

RULES AND PLAY

Ultimate is a non-contact sport played by two seven-person teams. The object of the game is to move the disc up the field by passing it, since the thrower is not allowed to run with the disc. Any time a pass is incomplete, intercepted, knocked down, or grounded in an out-of-bounds area, a turnover occurs, resulting in an immediate change of possession of the disc. A goal is scored when a player successfully passes the disc to a teammate in the end zone that his or her team is attacking.

A regulation field is 70 yards long and 40 yards wide, with two 25-yard end zones. When holding the disc, a player has ten seconds to throw it, which is counted off by the defender guarding the offensive player. If the disc is not thrown in time, it is called a "stall" and the defense takes over. Defenders generally play either a man-to-man or zone defense in their attempt to block a throw. Picks, screens, and intentional body contact are not allowed during the game. Any move intended to prevent another player from having a fair chance at catching the disc or making an interception is considered a foul.

Some ultimate teams are affiliated with high schools and colleges; others are regional club and pickup teams. Women can compete on men's (open) teams, on women's teams, or on co-ed teams (which require that at least three women be on the field at all times). The co-ed nature of the sport is unique, with no restrictions requiring women to stay in certain zones or play limited positions. Ultimate provides a remarkable model of equality for men and women in sports.

The Ultimate Players Association (UPA) serves as the governing body of the sport of ultimate in the United States. The UPA sponsors a club competition series in the fall and a college competition series in the spring. In odd numbered years, they host the World Ultimate Club Championships, where each country is allowed to send a specified number of existing club teams to compete. In 1981, the first Women's Division National Championships took place in Austin, Texas, just two years after the open division was formed and the UPA founded. Six years later, a women's college division was formed, and by 1990 there were over 100 women's teams competing within these two divisions.

CONCLUSION

Ultimate has exploded in popularity and is now played in 42 countries. It is estimated that at least 100,000 men and women play the sport worldwide, without referees, coaches, or professional leagues. Ultimate will be a medal sport in the 2001 World Games in Japan. The game's emphasis on the basic joy of play as much as the drive to win continues to draw more women to the sport of ultimate.

Robin O'Sullivan

Bibliography

Levinson, David, and Karen Christensen. (1999). *Encyclopedia of World Sport*. New York: Oxford University Press.

Fisher, Cindy. (1999) "A Retrospective on Women's Ultimate." *UPA Newsletter*. Colorado Springs: Ultimate Players Association. July, Volume 19-20.

Kelleher, Elizabeth. (2000) "The Ultimate Disc Drive." *The Washington Post Weekend*. Friday, May 26, page 76.

The Ultimate Handbook website: <http://www.ultimatehandbook.com/index.html>.

Ultimate Players Association website: <http://www.upa.org>.

UMPIRING *see* Officiating

UNDERWATER SPORTS

Underwater sports fall into three broad categories: snorkeling, free diving, and scuba diving. Snorkeling takes place at the surface and is distinct from swimming only in that the swimmer uses a rubber or plastic tube, a snorkel, that allows her to breathe without lifting her head from the water. As in all underwater sports, a mask is generally used to allow the eyes to focus properly. The second category, free or breath-hold diving, follows when the swimmer plunges farther beneath the surface with no means of getting additional air.

To remain underwater longer or travel deeper than a single breath allows, the swimmer must use a compressed breathing gas. This third category of underwater sports is known as scuba diving, which requires some source of a compressed breathing gas, or another means of remaining below the surface for extended periods. These other means include rebreathers, sophisticated life-support devices originally developed for military and industrial tasks and increasingly used in underwater sports, and surface compres-

A diver holds a green turtle, an endangered species, off Grand Cayman in the Caribbean. (Jeffrey L. Rotman/Corbis)

sors attached to the diver via a hose. The latter configuration is quite perilous because it exposes the diver to all the hazards of scuba diving while appearing to the casual observer to be little more than a power snorkel.

In many respects, underwater sports are a unique form of human recreation. They permit people to explore and enjoy an environment incapable of sustaining human life, a weightless world filled with strange and beautiful creatures. Although relatively new, underwater sports have grown steadily since their emergence after World War II. With their growth, women have found snorkeling, free diving, and scuba diving increasingly accessible and appealing.

HISTORY

Exploration and commercial exploitation of the undersea world may be traced back to antiquity. Recreational activities pursued beneath the water's surface, however, had no significant following until after World War II. Since that time, underwater activities have become increasingly popular. They are usually identified primarily by the means used to travel beneath the surface.

Free diving, submerging without any means of receiving further air, was practiced in antiquity as a means of collecting materials and foodstuffs off the shallow ocean floor. Equally ancient, no doubt, is the use of a hollow reed or similar device to allow a swimmer to breathe while face down in the water; this led to the development of the modern snorkel. The depths attainable through either technique, however, are relatively limited.

Extending the limits of a dive beyond what is possible on a single breath requires a further source of breathing gas. SCUBA, the Self-Contained Underwater Breathing Apparatus developed in France by Jacques Cousteau and Emile Gagnan in 1943, is the device that most recreational divers use to breathe under water. The acronym describing that invention, which allows divers to breathe from a tank of pressurized gas was adopted in 1952 as the name of this new means of underwater exploration, and scuba diving was born.

Recreational scuba diving emerged shortly after World War II. Equipment was scarce, primitive, and heavy. What little training there was generally came from former military divers. Reflecting the origins of those instructors and the experimental nature of the sport, training emphasized physical fitness, emergency skills, and performance under stress in an adversarial environment. As a result, few women took part in scuba diving as it developed in the 1950s.

As the sport matured, a number of clubs and agencies began to provide divers with more sophisticated and less intimidating instruction. By the 1970s, women represented an estimated 20 percent of those attending basic scuba diving courses. Standard diving practice calls for two divers to work together as dive buddies, and anecdotal evidence suggests that many of the women trained during this period did so at the request of male partners seeking their companionship in the sport rather than from their own enthusiasm for diving.

In response, manufacturers began what critics have called the "sappy" era of scuba equipment. The scuba industry tried to appeal to the expanding female market by making male-oriented designs small and pink. Women continued to a bandon the sport at a higher rate than men do after their first year of diving, a trend that implicated the motivation of many female divers and the continued inadequacies of equipment and training.

Those who remained active in the sport, however, still represented a valuable market. In 1993 the newly organized Women's SCUBA Association, a group of predominantly American instructors and others seeking to promote female participation in underwater sports, began to work closely with leading manufacturers. As a result, equipment specifically designed to be comfortable and functional on the female frame began to appear. This entailed more than simply reshaping wetsuit patterns. Buoyancy compensators, the inflatable harnesses that carry scuba tanks and much of the weight of a diver's equipment, had evolved to suit male anatomy. Designers had to reconfigure them for the female form. The first company to market such a device soon found it to be their fastest-selling item.

The availability of scuba equipment designed for women was only one element in the steady increase in female participation in the sport. In the 1990s, women accounted for nearly half of newly trained divers. Comfortable equipment and a less adversarial training regime certainly contributed to this. So, too, did the increasing numbers of women with their own careers and a demographic shift toward later marriage, which allowed women greater social and economic freedom to pursue their interests. Those women attracted to the sport in the late 1980s and afterward frequently took up the sport out of an independent interest rather than because a spouse or male companion encouraged them to do so, as had often been the case earlier. As a result, many more women remained involved in diving.

Two other trends contributed to increased female participation. The first was the increasingly active and athletic life-style of women in many Western nations. Equally significant, scuba itself began to shed its air of danger and adventure, in part as a result of the efforts of the recreational diving industry. Resort destinations catering to scuba diving promoted those trends, as the sport ceased to be the demanding, full-time obsession of a few enthusiasts and instead became a safe and affordable vacation activity.

SNORKELING AND FREE DIVING—RULES AND PLAY

Snorkeling has enjoyed growing popularity since the mid-1970s with the growth of tropical tourism and cruise ship vacations. Almost anyone may enjoy the sport; it requires minimal equipment and training requirements and very little physical exertion. A snorkeler may passively observe the undersea environment or interact with it. Feeding and handling marine life can have unforeseen consequences, however, and is increasingly restricted by environmental regulations. The sport also facilitates other activities, including photography and exploration, and for most participants serves as an introduction to free diving.

Free diving fully subjects the participant to the forces of the undersea environment, although minimally so in the few inches of water to which divers are limited. As a sport in its own right, free diving may be a simple plunge to the bottom of a swimming pool or a crashing descent below 100 meters (330 feet) in a competitive dive. Beyond simple submergence in an alien world, free diving is often associated with underwater hunting and other activities.

One such activity, the little-known sport of underwater hockey, offers biannual world championship tournaments. "Octopush," as the sport is also called, is a contest between opposing ten-member teams using snorkeling equipment, free diving to the bottom of a shallow swimming pool (2 meters, or 6.6 feet, is preferred).

The object is to move a small metal disk into a goal using a 30-centimeter (12-inch) bat that resembles the end of a hockey stick. Women participate in female and mixed leagues and, on occasion, because the sport has few participants, have appeared on nominally male teams. This sport, while quite obscure, has a dedicated following at various universities and private clubs. The 1996 world championships, held in South Africa, included teams from Australia, the Netherlands, Great Britain, Canada, New Zealand, Zimbabwe, Columbia, France, Argentina, and the United States. Like most other underwater competitive sports, underwater hockey is organized internationally by the Confédération Mondiale des Activités Subaquatiques.

SAFETY AND RISK

Although snorkeling and even free diving, as enjoyed by most participants, are relatively benign activities, those who venture beneath the water's surface nevertheless encounter unique challenges. Water pressure increases 1 atmosphere (the pressure exerted by air at sea level) for every 10 meters (33 feet) of depth. Thus, a diver only 10 meters beneath the water is subjected to twice the external pressure she feels at sea level. That simple physical reality has physiological consequences for the diver that, if not addressed, may be life-threatening. Pressure in the inner ear must be equalized with external water pressure to

DIVERS ALERT NETWORK

Scuba diving and other underwater sports present unique health threats. Decompression sickness and other pressure-related problems present diagnosis and treatment problems that, even after a half century of recreational diving, most medical practitioners are not trained to treat. Even with a relatively mild case of decompression sickness, a diver needs immediate administration of oxygen and possibly prompt treatment in a recompression chamber. However, few emergency medical facilities have the expertise to speedily diagnose and treat diving injuries.

In response, the sport of scuba diving has fostered its own medical community. Duke University's F. G. Hall Hypo/Hyperbaric Center, in Durham, North Carolina, formally established the Dive Accident Network in 1980. Subsequently renamed the Divers Alert Network (DAN), the nonprofit organization has expanded beyond the United States to support regional networks throughout the world.

When a diving accident occurs or is suspected, a phone call to DAN places the diver or medical personnel in contact with physicians specializing in diving medicine, twenty-four hours a day, anywhere in the world. If circumstances warrant, DAN can advise in diagnosis and treatment protocols, identify the nearest available hyperbaric chamber, and arrange transportation. In addition, DAN conducts extensive research in diving medicine and the prevention of diving accidents, while also providing divers and industry professionals with instruction in oxygen administration and accident management.

Because divers are not licensed or tracked beyond their initial training, statistics about the number of active divers are guesswork at best. Diving accidents, however, are tracked by a number of organizations, including DAN. Despite the growing popularity of scuba diving those numbers are remaining level or declining slightly, ample testimony to the effectiveness of the diving community's safety efforts.

avoid pain, disorientation, nausea, and potential injury. Similarly, any mask used for deep diving must enclose the nose to facilitate equalization of the air space around the eyes with the surrounding water pressure.

Shallow water blackout is a potential hazard in all free diving, particularly deeper dives. As pressure mounts, the air within the lungs is compressed along with other air spaces in the diver. This increases the partial pressure (pressure exerted by a single gas) of oxygen within the lungs, allowing the diver to metabolize more of the total amount of oxygen present than would be possible under normal conditions. As a result, when the diver returns to the surface and the partial pressure of oxygen decreases, it may no longer be sufficient to support consciousness. The diver can black out, or lose consciousness, without warning. For that reason, the depth and duration of free dives must be increased with great caution and careful supervision.

SCUBA DIVING—RULES AND PLAY

Because of the risks and the sophisticated equipment involved in scuba diving, all divers should be properly trained. This training is provided by various agencies dedicated to that purpose or through diving clubs. Divers are initially certified in the safe use of the underwater breathing apparatus and other basic equipment, such as buoyancy compensators and wet suits and may pursue more advanced and specialized training as their skills improve. In many places, only self-regulation within the diving community requires such training; it has proved effective enough to avoid direct governmental licensing. The international diving community's capacity for self-regulation and intimate connection with the underwater environment has placed it at the forefront of many conservation movements, and environmentally sound practices are encouraged at all levels of training.

Scuba diving, like snorkeling and free diving, lends itself to the interest in ecotourism and the natural environment that surfaced in the late 1980s. This has lead to the promotion of numerous tropical and subtropical locations as travel destinations based solely on their underwater appeal, making the sport a vital part of some local economies. Underwater tourism's economic value has fostered the creation of numerous underwater parks and preserves throughout the world, in developed and undeveloped regions. That factor may increase the appeal of the sport to the environmentally conscious of both genders.

Simple sight-seeing or exploring is the basic activity for scuba divers. As with snorkeling, however, the mechanism employed to travel underwater is also the vehicle for further activities. Divers may explore beneath winter ice or deep into submerged caves. Photography, hunting, and wreck diving all have their adherents, while those seeking risk and adventure continue to push the sport into deeper waters, well beyond the 40-meter (130-foot) recreational limit that many training organizations suggest. Women are part of this trend. Named for the Roman goddess of passages and new beginnings, the organization Cardea 2000 appeared in the United States in 1996 for female divers seeking to increase women's par-

RISKY AND EXPENSIVE TYPES OF DIVING

Wreck diving, night diving, and cave diving are three forms of diving that were once practiced mainly by experts or professionals but are now popular also with recreational divers. Wreck diving is exploring sunken ships—the larger and better known, the better. This activity is expensive and dangerous. More people have died exploring the *Andrea Doria* off Nantucket than died when it sank. Night diving allows divers to see fish and other creatures which only emerge at night. It is about the same cost and risk as day diving. Cave diving allows the exploration of undersea worlds few people will ever see. It is very expensive and dangerous and requires rigorous training.

ticipation in the sport's more challenging activities.

RISKS OF SCUBA DIVING

Decompression sickness, also known as the bends, is the best-known hazard of scuba diving. It results from the inevitable absorption of nitrogen into the diver's bloodstream from breathing under pressure. As pressure on the body decreases, the nitrogen must be expelled. Unless the diver follows proper procedures for ascent rates and decompression stops, the gas will form bubbles within the body that can be harmful or even fatal. Other hazards include embolism from improper breathing technique or physical impairment, ear injuries, and oxygen poisoning. The latter is another product of breathing under pressure and can cause convulsions that lead directly to drowning. Oxygen toxicity prevents the use of pure oxygen for general scuba diving. Divers normally breath compressed air, although oxygen-enriched air or more exotic gas mixes may be used to meet the needs of particularly demanding dives.

Complicating all those risks is nitrogen narcosis, the "rapture of the deep." Nitrogen acts as a narcotic when breathed at high partial pressures, as happens during scuba diving, and is a factor that begins to affect all divers as they descend below 20 meters (66 feet). The effect is subtle and unpredictable and can become debilitating. The extremes range from euphoria to panic, but the true danger lies in the less apparent effect of narcosis. High levels of nitrogen decrease the diver's ability to perform multiple tasks or reason clearly well before other symptoms become apparent. Judgment is often the first mental function affected, so that the diver may not realize that she is impaired. When confronted by a surprise or minor difficulty in such a state, the diver may be unable to react properly or may be driven to panic. Also called the "martini effect" from a comment attributed to scuba pioneer Jacques Cousteau, narcosis is a factor that divers must never ignore.

Although the list of dangers present in scuba diving may sound daunting, proper training and equipment reduce them to a low level. As a result, scuba diving has an admirable safety record.

OBSTACLES FOR FEMALE DIVERS

While underwater sports clearly enjoy growing popularity among women, obstacles to their participation remain. Social expectations, training environments, and equipment design have improved but are not equally oriented to women.

Beyond this is the female body itself. The all-important tables that govern the depth, time, and decompression requirements of any given dive were originally derived from empirical studies of male military divers. The actual physiological consequences of diving remain poorly understood and are similarly based largely on the study of young male divers. Relatively little information is available about the differences, if any, between the tolerances of male and female bodies for the rigors of diving.

At least one myth appeared in scuba's early days as a result of this lack of knowledge. Still occasionally encountered, it holds that menstrual blood increases the likelihood of shark attack. Not only is the allegation false but the fear on which it is based is itself virtually mythical. Shark attack is an extremely rare phenomenon, virtually unheard of in recreational diving.

Nevertheless, the absence of confirmed medical fact has placed some restrictions on female diving. Women are cautioned against pushing the limits of dive tables based on male physiological responses. They are also advised not to dive during pregnancy. Research suggests that the fetus may be highly susceptible to decompression sickness, unable to escape injury from dives well within the safe range predicted by dive tables. Therapy for decompression sickness in the mother involves treatment in a hyperbaric chamber, where the high partial pressure of oxygen may induce blindness in the unborn infant. The parameters for safe diving during pregnancy remain unknown, and so caution dictates that underwater sports be abandoned during that time.

CONCLUSION

The pleasures and merits of diving greatly outweigh the risks if divers take proper care. Underwater sports may be therapeutic beyond the simple benefits of cardiovascular exercise and muscular development. In or under the water, the diver becomes weightless. Participation in scuba diving has been found effective in temporarily relieving chronic pain. The Handicapped Divers' Association and similar groups facilitate access to the sport by the disabled. Underwater sports offer a temporary escape from gravity and the toll it imposes on the human body, a great opportunity to reduce physical and psychological stress. Projecting trends, there is little reason to believe that underwater sports will not continue their progress toward truly equal participation by women and men.

Jefferey Charlston

Bibliography

Bookspan, Jolie. (1995) *Diving Physiology in Plain English*. Kensington, MD: Undersea & Hyperbaric Medical Association.

Lippmann, John. (1992) *The Essentials of Deeper Sport Diving*. Locust Valley, NY: Aqua Quest.

UNIONISM

Players who are employed by clubs and leagues to produce sporting events have, like other workers, formed unions to protect and advance their employment rights and interests. Clubs and leagues have introduced various rules which have restricted the economic freedom of players or the income-earning potential of their activities. Sometimes clubs and leagues have made decisions that have not taken account of, or ignored, the needs and interest of players. In turn, players have turned to collective action to overcome difficulties they experience as individuals when negotiating with clubs and leagues.

Unions, or player associations, have been active in most of the highly popular and commercially successful male sports such as soccer (association football), baseball, basketball, American football, Australian rules football, Canadian football, ice hockey, rugby league, rugby union, tennis, and cricket. Women's team sports have not been as popular with spectators, sponsors, and television corporations, and there are fewer unions or player associations in female team sports.

In the 1990s there were several attempts to form unions for female players. Two of those attempts were in Australia. The first occurred in 1991 when lawyers associated with the male Basketball Players' Association of Australia (formed in 1989) talked about unionizing players of the women's National Basketball League. Nothing resulted from such talk. The second and more successful attempt occurred with the formation of the Australian Netball Players' Association in 1997. A third attempt was in 1998 when players in the Women's National Basketball Association (WNBA) in the United States formed a union affiliated with the union representing the male players. Their experiences provide case studies of the issues and strategies involved in forming unions of female athletes.

AUSTRALIAN NETBALL

Netball is a derivative of basketball. Precursors of the modern game were played in the last decade of the nineteenth century. Netball is a seven-on-a-side game resembling a relatively static version of basketball. Passing from zone to zone, rather than running and dribbling with the ball, is the focus of netball, which is a fast-moving, exciting, and high-scoring game. The sport is played mainly in nations once a part of the British Empire. It is the most widely played and popular sport among girls and women in Australia. Its commercial appeal was heightened by the success of the national team in the 1991 world championships played in Australia.

Netball has traditionally been an amateur sport. Within Australia, local clubs and regional competitions were complemented by an annual interstate competition. In 1997 the All Australia Netball Association, the governing body of the sport in Australia, created the National Netball League. The league comprised eight clubs of fourteen players each—two clubs each from Sydney (New South Wales), Melbourne (Victoria), and Adelaide (South Australia); and one each from Brisbane (Queensland) and Perth (Western Australia). The season ran from April to August. The All Australia Netball Association commissioned a company to market, or obtain sponsorships, for the new league, at a rumored commission of 25 percent. What were called Membership Organisations, or state bodies, were allocated $50,000 (all dollar figures in this article are Australian) per team by the National Netball League.

Approximately four weeks prior to the start of the 1997 season the National Netball League circulated a seventeen-page contract, a twenty-two-page deed of participation and forty-six pages of competition rules in seeking to obtain the signatures, or services, of players. In essence the documents required players to forego employment rights and entitlements for the privilege of playing in the league. There were also concerns among star or national team players that the signing of contracts would compromise various sponsorships they had obtained individually.

The contract required players to acknowledge that they were not employees of the league or their team, in other words, they were contractors not entitled to benefits. Furthermore, players would receive any income from clubs for playing. Players were entitled to have their transportation and accommodation expenses met at the discretion of the league or their team, be provided with a set of playing and training uniforms, and receive a (variable) meal subsidy. Players who wanted to appeal against a decision of a disciplinary committee could be required to make a deposit of $2,000.

AUSTRALIAN NETBALL PLAYERS' ASSOCIATION

Soon after these documents were circulated, a number of players expressed their concerns to former national team coach Joyce Brown. Brown was probably the most celebrated figure in the history of Australian netball. She captained the Australian team which won the inaugural world championship in 1963, coached three world championship teams, and was a netball administrator (and life member) of the All Australian Netball Association and lectured in Sports Science at Deakin University. She had been described by her biographers as "a loyal, generous friend. She has never been motivated by money. . . . She has been inspired by a passion to get the best out of herself and from those for whom she has had responsibility" (Smithers and Appleby 1996, 176).

Following a series of discussions between Brown and leading players, a decision was made to form the Australian Netball Players' Association to negotiate a more satisfactory standard contract for players. The various administrative costs involved with establishing an association were subsidized by Brown. She received free help and advice from other persons in netball, pro bono legal work from Sydney-based solicitor John de Mestre (who had acted on behalf of the Ironmen competitions), and advice and moral support from leaders of other (male) Australian players' associations.

An interim executive committee of the Australian Netball Players' Association was formed of representatives from each of the eight teams. The association was registered under the Associations Incorporation Act 1981 (Victoria) on 16 April 1997. Keeley Devery, a retired national team player and a journalist with Foxtel Sport was elected secretary, or leader, of the association. Australian National team captain Vicki Wilson was elected president, Simone McKinnis, vice-president, and Kathryn Harby and Danni Grant, executive members. Brown continued her involvement with the association in negotiations concerning player contracts.

In 1997 the association had 111 members, a membership rate of 99 per cent. The membership fee is a mere $20—scant income for a nationally based organization. Though attempts were made to obtain sponsorship income in the form of a tipping competition for the 1998 season, the limited income of the association barely covered administrative costs. Still, officeholders devoted more than their time to the welfare of members, and club delegates were in regular contact with elected officials and with each other via phone and fax. In addition, meetings of the national team were utilized to discuss association business.

Following its formation, the Australian Netball Players' Association experienced problems in negotiating a satisfactory standard player contract with the National Netball League and clubs. A tactical decision was made for members to continue playing even though they would not sign a contract. Thus individual players did not sign away their rights to whatever sponsorship income they were able to generate. Prior to the start of the 1998 season, a more satisfactory contract was negotiated.

Major clauses in the 1998 contract concerned player obligations, sponsorship, advertising promotion, and marketing (with protections for players' rights), intellectual property (which is owned by players), player compensation, dispute resolution, and termination. Schedule A listed sponsors, and schedule B minimum compensation to players. The parties experienced the most difficulty in negotiating the terms contained in schedule B.

Under schedule B players were entitled to eight months of gym membership; up to thirty rolls of strapping tape; up to sixteen massages; reimbursement for the cost of up to thirty physiotherapy sessions not covered by health insurance; a $30-a-day meal allowance away from home; accommodation to include a cooked breakfast; loss of wages, travel and private health insurance of $1,000; $100 per game during the finals; six free tickets to all matches; $75 per game; and, for each of the Perth Orioles because of extra lost time caused by travel, $1,200. Approximately 70 to 80 percent of players were on these minima. Star or national team players were receiving incomes on the order of $5,000 to $10,000 from their clubs, as well as additional income from sponsors.

Following its formation the Australian Netball Players' Association was not well received by the National Netball League. Even with the new contract in place, at least one club had pressured young players—with the threat of not being selected—to sign worse contracts than these minima. But the cohesion of the players' association finally persevered. The relationship it had with the National Netball League became more cooperative than adversarial; its role on behalf of the players of Australian netball was finally accepted, if only begrudgingly. Thus, while the Australian Netball Players' Association ended the twentieth century with some initial triumphs, its future in Australian women's netball remained an open question.

WOMEN'S NATIONAL BASKETBALL ASSOCIATION UNION

In November 1998, women players in the WNBA, one of the two women's professional basketball leagues in the United States at the time, voted 56 to 24 to form a union and to have the union that represented the male players in the NBA represent them in collective bargaining with the league. The vote in favor of the union came despite opposition from the WNBA office and in the context of a contentious contract negotiation between the league and the men's union. In fact, at the time of the vote the start of the men's season had been delayed by a lockout by the owners and there was concern that the season might not be played at all (it was, with a shortened schedule).

The women chose to form a union so that several issues of concern to all players could be addressed through collective bargaining. These included minimum salaries, a health plan, maternity leave, and job security. At the time the union was formed, the average salary was $30,000 per season, health care insurance was provided only during the season, there was no paid maternity leave, and players could be cut from their team at any time without continuation of pay. Part of the motivation for forming a union came from a comparison with working conditions in the rival American Basketball League (ABL) where women were paid an average of $80,000 per season, received year-round health care insurance, and had the opportunity to invest in a pension plan. In addition, top women players in Europe could earn over $100,000 per year.

With the union in place, the union and league began negotiations to produce a first contract. In December, the ABL went bankrupt, creating a new major issue—job security—as players from the ABL wanting to join the WNBA threatened the positions of current WNBA players. WBNA players argued that is was an issue of loyalty and WNBA players should be afforded some job security because they chose to play in the WNBA rather than the ABL. For the league, quality of play was an issue, as they wanted the best players available to play in the league.

In April, the union and league completed negotiation of a four-year contract. Both sides sought to avoid the lockout situation that damaged the men's season and compromised on key demands. The minimum salary was raised to $30,000 for veteran players and $25,000 for first-year players, year-round health and dental insurance was provided, and other benefits including maternity leave, a pension plan, and life insurance were also provided. The players also achieved some job security as players on the roster at the mid-point of the season would retain their jobs for the remainder of the season. On other issues, the players had to do more of the compromising. The league refused to give players a percentage of the league income but did agree to give players royalties on the sale of merchandise such as clothing that use the players' names or images. In addition, the new contract allowed each existing team to hire up to three players from the ABL and new teams to hire up to five in 1999. In subsequent years, there was no limit on the number of ex-ABL players hired.

CONCLUSION

While neither the Australian netball nor the United States basketball collective bargaining agreement break new ground in labor law, they are important steps in women's sports as they show that approaches and principles used in men's sports can be successfully applied to women's sports. As Pam Wheeler, the lead negotiator for the WNBA players, stated: "It's a milestone for women's sports. We wanted to ensure whatever foundation we can lay can catapult women's professional basketball for the future." (SportsLine, April 15, 1999)

Braham Dabscheck

Bibliography

Jobling, Ian. (1994) "Netball." In *Sport in Australia : A Social History,* edited by Wray Vamplew and Brian Stoddart. Melbourne: Cambridge University Press, 154–171.

Oxford Companion to Australian Sport, The, 2d ed. (1994) Melbourne: Oxford University Press, 303–306.

Smithers, Edie, and Chris Appleby. (1996) *No Limits: Joyce Brown.* Lilydale, Australia: Varenna.

SportsLine. Sports.excite.com/wnba/news/990415/sl-sports-wnba-909461.

Additional information provided by Keeley Devery, Joyce Brown, and Danni Grant of the Australian Netball Players' Association and David Levinson.

UNITED KINGDOM

The United Kingdom (UK) is composed of England, Scotland, Wales, and Northern Ireland and has a population of 59 million. The UK, also referred to as Great Britain, has played a central role in the spread of sports around the world—probably a greater role than that of any other nation. Many of the world's most popular sports, such as soccer (association football), rugby, baseball, football, netball, and cricket, were invented in, or have origins in, Britain. Netball—a sport similar to basketball that is played almost exclusively by women—is popular, for example, throughout the former British Empire and was brought to the United States by Caribbean immigrants. In addition, the spread of sports such as tennis, golf, and track and field were due largely to their popularity among the British who served around the world in the British military, colonial government, and religious and educational organizations.

Sport today plays a key part in British cultural life, in terms of expanding media coverage and spectatorship and in terms of individual participation by men and women. But sport remains for the most part a male-dominated activity, and British women have had to battle for their share of sport resources and athletic recognition.

THE EARLY YEARS

Women's sports in Britain have had a long history, but one that is enmeshed in issues of social class. Women have not all had the same experience of, and access to, sports. In the Middle Ages, hunting and hawking by ladies of the nobility were carried out within strict hierarchical codes, which associated certain birds and kinds of quarry with status and gender. Before industrialization, working-class men and women engaged in strenuous physical labor, and recreations took the form of "wakes" or annual holidays to honor the patron saint of the parish. Vigorous activities characterized the working classes' playtime, and women ran footraces competing for the prize of a smock—and perhaps a husband, too. Women's activities during this time ranged from cricket,

Charlotte Sterry, British tennis player, competes in the 1908 Wimbledon competition. (Hulton-Deutsch Collection/Corbis)

stoolball, trapball, football, golf, rowing, swimming, and dancing to sword play and even pugilism. There is a contemporary account of a female "scratching and boxing match" (in Featherstone 1986, 72) held in London in the early eighteenth century. Neither men nor women in the audience objected to its potentially unladylike associations. However, it was exactly those concerns over the appropriate occupations of a lady that circumscribed the activities of women of the upper classes. Simultaneously, greater wealth and leisure time brought them access to recreations not available to the poor. Some ladies of rank were probably able to hunt, shoot, fish, swim, climb, walk, sail, and dance, and some, like the Marchioness of Salisbury, held national reputations as daring riders in the foxhunts.

Industrialization and the rise of the middle classes brought a general decline in sporting recreations for all, and the old ways of playing were subject to assault from a number of angles. Blood sports like bear baiting and cock fighting came to be considered cruel and were outlawed, and a movement known as "rational recreation," comprising a range of individuals and groups from the middle and aspiring working classes, endeavored to replace these practices, teaching the poor how to play in ways less disruptive of their new patterns of labor in the factories of the towns and cities. The middle classes, in compensation for their lack of inherited status, sought to justify their elevated social position by demonstrating their respectability. Clearly demarcated gender roles were a central part of this, and in the nineteenth century the middle classes reinvented sports as an arena capable of demonstrating their moral superiority and skills in social leadership.

NINETEENTH CENTURY: ORIGINS OF INSTITUTIONALIZED SPORT AS A MALE PRESERVE

During the Victorian era, modern sport became an organized activity, institutionalized in the boys' public school system. Despite the name *public,* these schools required fees and were attended by the sons of the privileged middle and upper classes. In the nineteenth century, the education to be had within these institutions changed markedly. A new wave of headmasters transformed them from harsh, undisciplined places into institutions capable of producing middle-class men fit for dominant positions in the social order. Sport, originally a device to allow the boys to let off steam, became valued for its capacity to instill masculine virtues. It is possible to argue, therefore, that one of the legacies of the nineteenth century was the establishment of sport as the central site for the construction of masculinity. Victorian images of the gentleman matched physical prowess with assumed moral superiority. The public schools offered team games developed from traditional folk games, rules for most of which were standardized in the late nineteenth century. Soccer, rugby, and cricket were established as the archetypal sports for building manly character among the future leaders of the British Empire.

Differences between men and women were couched in terms of a nature/culture divide. Men were associated with the intellect and the public sphere, and women were confined to reproduction and the home. Femininity was constructed as frail and nurturing and, within the views propounded by prominent male social commentators (Ruskin, Smiles) and the medical profession (Dr. Henry Maudsley), unfit for vigorous physical activity. Despite the contradictions presented by working-class women engaged in physical labor, sport was an arena in which the bodily differences between men and women were celebrated it was undoubtedly the " 'natural' domain of men" (Hargreaves 1994, 43), and women were effectively barred from energetic sports. Many middle-class women came to be seen (and to see themselves) as inherently weak. As a result, their poor health became an issue for the establishment. Private gymnasiums became popular, influenced by the ideas of Per Henrik Ling, the Swedish promulgator of gentle, therapeutic exercise. In 1885 the first female specialists in physical education for women were trained at the college founded by Mme. Bergman-Österberg, a disciple of Ling.

Middle-class Victorians used leisure pursuits as a sign of affluence. The cultivated gardens of suburban homes provided an arena for genteel games like croquet and tennis, in which men and women engaged, conspicuously demonstrating free time and wealth in imitation of the upper classes. Tennis parties also provided a forum for courting opportunities, where men and women could meet and display their charms without social censure. Mixed tennis, while allowing women to play sport, was a means of confirming gender hierarchy with its assumptions of men's superiority and allowances made for "delicate" females. Given this context, the triumphs of early competitive female players seem all the more astounding.

A member of a women's cricket club in London in 1932. The most British of sports, cricket in the 1900s has become more open to women. (Hulton-Deutsch Collection/Corbis)

Seven years after men had begun competing at Wimbledon, the first ladies' singles championship was held in 1877. Maud Watson, the first ladies' champion, won "wearing a bustle, hat and high-heeled shoes" (Hargreaves 1994, 99). Lottie Dod (1871–1860) became the youngest player ever to win a championship at Wimbledon, when in 1887 she took the Ladies' All-English title. Her age—she was fifteen—allowed her to break with the restrictive dress codes for female players, wearing a much shorter outfit than was normally allowed. Dod retired from tennis at the age of twenty-one, with a record of five victories in the Wimbledon singles, three in the doubles, and two in the mixed doubles, and went on to excel in golf, archery and field hockey.

INTO THE TWENTIETH CENTURY

Certain factors differentiate the history of women's sports from men's. First, whereas men's sports developed from folk games, the institutionalization and regulation of women's sports followed the pattern already established by men. Second, since the development of women's sports occurred later than men's, it had a number of institutional influences beyond that exerted by the public school system. These included the colleges of physical education, girls' schools, universities, and private clubs. By the end of the nineteenth century, women and girls were involved in a range of recreational and competitive sporting activities, for example, cricket, hockey, archery, golf, lacrosse, rounders, basketball, netball, fencing, badminton, roller skating, ice skating, and cycling. British women excelled on the international stage; for example, Kitty McKane Godfree was Wimbledon tennis singles champion in 1924 and 1926. It is significant that despite the range of sports available, they all conformed to middle-class notions of femininity—minimizing body contact, exertion, and the display of female flesh.

Nevertheless, by the beginning of the twentieth century, beliefs about the physical capacities of women were changing. During the period spanning the late 1880s and the 1920s, many national associations were formed. In 1895, the Ladies' Hockey Association, with the aim of emphasizing their seriousness of purpose, dropped the term "ladies" in favor of the new title, All England Women's Hockey Association. Since hockey had a reputation in the boys' public schools as an effeminate activity, the pioneers of the women's game, despite attracting unflattering descriptions like "unsexed Amazons," were not necessarily perceived as treading on male terrain. The history of women's cricket, however, even though its history predated the nineteenth century, is littered with disapproving comments from male observers, considering cricket to be a man's game. Nevertheless, in the early twentieth century, women's cricket had a small but devoted following, and the British Women's Cricket Association was formed in 1926. These and other organizations played a vital role in the growth of women's competitive sports.

Women's increasingly exuberant attitude to sport and competitive games was experienced by many as emancipation, but it fed widespread fears of masculinization. Adventure sports (activities like climbing, skiing, and sailing) are a striking example. These became popular among women from "privileged" backgrounds in the early 1920s. Their involvement was a direct challenge to the idea that hazardous, strenuous adventure activities were the preserve of men. The Pinnacle Club was formed in 1921 by women who believed that mountaineering without male involvement was achievable and desirable. By 1934 the club had a membership of eighty women, whose activities extended ideas about female physicality, risk, and leadership skills.

Most of the opportunities to take part in physical recreation were, however, confined to the middle classes. In the twentieth century, following the pattern laid down in the previous century, involvement in sport in adult life was greatly determined by experience at school. Concerns for national fitness had meant that gymnastics had infiltrated state school provisions in the nineteenth century. However, poor facilities and insufficient teachers gave limited opportunity for working-class girls. In 1921 the United Kingdom's board of education's chief medical officer recommended that girls in secondary schools play games. In practice, lack of space, particularly in urban areas, meant that activities were limited to games like netball.

The history of netball illustrates well the dual influences of class and gender on women's sports in the United Kingdom. Developed from basketball as a "feminized"—less physical—version of basketball, its spread to working-class schools by the pioneering physical educationalists lessened its middle-class associations and has made it, to this day, the most popular female sport in the country. In 1935 the Central Council for Physical Training and Recreation (CCPTR) was set up, with the aim of improving facilities for sport and recreation throughout the country. Phyllis Colson played a vital role in its formation and the subsequent growth and running of the council, initially without any financial support from the Physical Education Associations. In 1944 the Council changed its name and subsequently became the Central Council for Physical Recreation (CCPR). The CCPR became a powerful and influential organization that led to the establishment of the Sports Councils. The struggle for resources—particularly in mixed sex environments in which men retain power and control—continues to characterize the experiences of women from all backgrounds.

Despite the remarkable growth and range of women's sporting involvement between the world wars, the relation between the sexes was far from equal. Sportswomen had to battle against practical and ideological barriers. The advances gained were as a result of continued contestation and negotiation in the pursuit of equality of opportunity with men. Men's greater leisure time enabled them to take advantage of public sport and leisure facilities, such as municipal swimming pools. Furthermore, their stranglehold on the administration of facilities, clubs, and competitive organizations effectively restricted women's access to recreational and competitive sports. For example, while the International Olympic Committee (IOC) was less concerned to assert its ultimate control over the arrangements for the Olympic Games between 1900 and 1908, women athletes were informally admitted to the competition, and British female athletes counted among the small but growing number able to take part. In 1900 British tennis player Charlotte Sterry became the first female Olympic champion in any sport. At the Games held in London in 1908, from the thirty-six female competitors (compared to 2,020 men), British women were again among the medal winners, including Frances Clytie Rivett-Carnac, who became the first woman to win an event not restricted to women, taking gold along with her husband for the 7-meter class yachting. However, the IOC took back control of the 1912 Games and restricted women's participation to a small number of sports considered appropriate for women. The IOC's position generated international resistance, and four Women's World Games were held between 1922 and 1934 as an alternative to the Olympics, with a program of eleven track and field events. The first track and field program organized for female athletes at the 1928 Olympics in Amsterdam included only five events and led to a boycott by British female athletic teams.

Sally Gunnell, British track athlete. (S. Carmona/Corbis)

CONTEMPORARY SPORTING CULTURE

Since the 1970s there has been a huge growth in the range of sports activities available to women as recreation and competition. Contemporary statistics still put women's participation behind that of men, but the gap is narrowing. The findings of the General Household Survey, carried out between April 1996 and March 1997, indicated that 58 percent of women took part in at least one activity in the four weeks before being interviewed. Walking was the most popular physical activity for men and women, but women's participation in keepfit/yoga was more than twice that of men (17 percent), and swimming (17 percent) and cycling (8 percent) were also popular activities with women. However, participation rates are higher among nonmanual than manual workers and, despite a sustained interest in walking, activity does decrease with age.

Elite British sportswomen have made an impact on the world stage (for example, track and field athletes Sally Gunnell, Liz McColgan, and Tessa Sanderson), yet their careers tend to be characterized by personal persistence in the face of lack of institutional support. A handful of top female athletes have started to make a living from sport, for instance, Laura Davies (golfer) and Jenny Pitman (racehorse trainer), but earnings from prize money and sponsorship are still far below those of the men, particularly in those sports that are marginalized by television. For example, the English women's cricket team's victory at the Fifth World Cup at Lords in 1993 was achieved largely through self-finance, the team having struggled to find sponsorship. Pentathlete Wendy Norman won the inaugural world championships at the age of seventeen in 1982 but was forced to retire in her early twenties because of lack of financial support. When sponsorship does become available, those athletes who conform most closely to conventional standards of feminine attractiveness are most likely to be beneficiaries. There is little state financial support for athletes, but the World Class Performance Program launched in 1996 provides some subsistence awards and access to training, facilities, and resources to potential world-class athletes, including women, through the Lottery Sports Fund. University-based sport schemes are in their infancy.

The commercial sector has had an increasingly important role in providing activities (like aerobics) for women. Yet the school and, increasingly, the university systems are still the main ways in which sports are introduced into women's lives. Sports organization in Britain has a tradition of voluntarism and self-organization. The traditional route into voluntary administrative positions is from ex-player/performer. For women, additional domestic responsibilities have restricted their ability to take on these time-consuming, unpaid responsibilities. Traditional attitudes to appropriate "jobs for women" have also had the effect of steering women into junior or social committees, leaving men to dominate technical and competitive committees.

There are, however, several key organizations involved with the development of women's sports in the United Kingdom. The Women's Sport Foundation (WSF) is the only organization in the United Kingdom that is "solely committed to improving and promoting opportunities for all women and girls in sports at every level." It was founded in 1984 as a charity, although today it receives some money from the English Sports Council. The WSF grew out of the women's movement in the United Kingdom and is still closely aligned with (liberal) feminist practices, promoting equality of opportunity for all women and girls in British sports. Although it is committed to promoting elite sports, high performance is only one of its strategic aims. Other key areas include increasing the number of women in leadership positions; supporting and delivering education, training, and research; helping to generate more positive attitudes toward sports among young people; and increasing participation in a wide range of sporting activities among women and girls of all backgrounds.

The Sports Councils (restructured in 1997 to become the U.K. Sports Council and a Sports Council for England to join the already existing Councils for Wales, Scotland, and Northern Ireland) are the leading government agencies for sports. They work in partnership with local authorities, health and education agencies, youth services, commercial firms, governing bodies, sports clubs, and other voluntary associations, which potentially give them a powerful position to redress gender inequalities. In 1972 the "Sport for All" campaign was launched, which aimed at getting more people interested in sports. This campaign coincided with a reorganization of local government, which resulted in the creation of departments dedicated to the provision of leisure. Leisure facilities provided by the local authorities, such as leisure centers (incorporating swimming pools, gymnasiums, sports equipment, and playing fields) mushroomed. Simultaneously, this period saw a move of women into higher education, along with the "fitness chic" boom taking place predominantly in the commercial sphere. A combination of these developments brought sports within the reach of many more women. Yet, while participation levels among women increased dramatically, patterns remained the same: middle-class women were in the best position to take advantage of opportunities.

Consequently, in the 1980s the Sport Council followed its "Sport for All" message with a "target group approach" aiming to provide increased access to sport facilities to those women who use them least (examples include those who lack transportation, single parents, the low-waged, the overweight, the disabled, the elderly, and ethnic minorities). One example was the West Midlands Asian Women's Project established in 1990. Many initiatives were the responsibility of the newly appointed Sport Development Officers, who were employed to work in the community by local authorities and were often partly funded by the Sports Council. This approach, however, was criticized for its unwillingness to uncover the underlying reasons for women's nonparticipation, favoring a policy of simply giving women "more of the same" (Talbot 1981, 1). For example, the national campaign titled "What's Your Sport?" established in 1986–1987, focused on women aged twenty to thirty-four and generated enthusiasm and high attendance for individual events but had limited success in sustaining interest.

These initiatives were reviewed, evaluated, and replaced by a longer-lasting and more penetrating approach outlined in the Sports Council Report, *Women and Sport: Policy and Framework for Action*. Work has commenced on integrating equal-opportunity policies, principles, and practices throughout all Sports Council work rather than focusing on participation targets. All Sports Council policies are underpinned by the "sports development continuum" model, which considers that women may reach their potential at any of the four stages of the continuum: foundation (basic movement literacy); participation (for fitness, health, and social contact); performance; and excellence (the stages at which talent is identified and developed through coaching, training, and structured competition, with the result that some reach recognized standards of excellence). Sports Council activity is involved in identifying and removing gender inequity at each of the four stages of the continuum, and increasing the representation of women within the organizational and administrative structures of sports in the United Kingdom.

The Sports Councils are also responsible for distributing money derived from the National Lottery, which since its launch in 1994 has been an important development in the provision of sporting facilities. Applicants for funding from the Lottery Sports Fund must include ways of encouraging the participation of women and girls in sports, which is helping to increase that participation, particularly in traditionally male-dominated sports. Yet it has been argued that during the 1990s there was an ideological shift in government policy from "Sport for All" to promoting excellence and elitism. This was reflected in the 1995 policy document from the Department of National Heritage, *Sport: Raising the Game* (1995), produced by the previous Conservative government, and in the conception of the United Kingdom Sports Institute (UKSI), which will focus on the needs of elite athletes (including women) in a rather narrowly defined group of sports.

In May 1997, however, a new Labour government was elected that made a number of encouraging statements regarding women's sports. In 1998 the Women's Unit published *Delivering for Women: Progress So Far,* which included a commitment to improve opportunities for women at all levels in sports, whether as participants, competitors, coaches, or administrators. The Minister for Sport, Tony Banks, MP, echoed this determination in his answers to questions raised in Parliament, and the English Sports Council set as a target an increase of 20 percent in the number of women, aged sixteen and over, taking part in regular sporting activity by the year 2002 (from 36 percent in 1993 to 43 percent, including walking; and from 23 percent in 1993 to 28 percent, excluding walking).

Physical training teachers take part in a lesson during an Easter holiday course at Saint Paul's Girls' School, Hammersmith, London. (Corbis)

The Sports Councils work in partnership with numerous other organizations—local authorities, health and education agencies, youth services, commercial firms, governing bodies, sports clubs, and other voluntary associations—each of which has a part to play in encouraging and enabling women to participate in sports in the United Kingdom. Local authorities are key agents for coordinating and providing sporting opportunities for women. Their adult education programs for women's sports have been radical and popular, designed to reflect women's interests in contexts that lessen the intimidation women may feel in traditional sporting environments. Voluntary associations like the National Federation of Women's Institutes (NFWI) and the Townswomen's Guilds have begun to recognize that their members wish to adopt a healthy life-style and have responded by increasing opportunities for their members to participate in new activities. Young women and girls, who may be uncomfortable within traditional sporting structures, are also provided with opportunities to take part in sports by a range of voluntary youth organizations, including uniformed groups, the church, clubs, and agencies working with disabled young people.

In the 1990s physical activity became desirable for women. The fitness and health that got under way in the mid-1980s encouraged women to take part in a range of new "body-shaping" activities (aerobics, step-aerobics, boxercise), albeit in a context of consumer culture that, arguably, plays on women's insecurities about their bodies. Nevertheless, women have penetrated many of the traditional, as well as more recent, bastions of masculinity like boxing (Jane Crouch), ocean yacht racing (Tracy Edwards and her all-female crew), rugby, and bodybuilding. There is no doubt that, for many women, sports are an important part of their identity. But feminists have argued that, while such developments appear to transgress traditional conceptions of femininity, sportswomen still need to conform to those traditional expectations. As Judith Butler argues, "You only have permission to be this strong if you can also look this beautiful" (Butler 1987, 122). This is no more apparent than in the mass media, where female athletes are underrepresented, sexualized, and treated as marketable commodities. Recent research examining the amount of space allocated to women's sport in the British broadsheet national newspapers, indicates that women's sport constituted only 5 percent to 8 percent of total sports coverage.

Likewise, women remain vastly underrepresented in positions of power in the British sports establishment, from coaches to administrators. For example, of the thirteen members of the English Sport Council, only five are women, one of them the African-American athlete Tessa Sanderson). There are, however, some notable exceptions to this general rule. Anita White is director of development at the English Sports Council, one of the most prestigious roles in sports administration. Sue Campell has held key positions in the National Coaching Foundation and is chief executive of the Youth Sport Trust. In the media, female sports journalists are becoming more prevalent. Examples include Emma Lindsey, reporter at the *Observer*, and Sue Barker, former tennis player and now key figure in the BBC sports programming. Within academia, key thinkers on issues relating to women and sports include Jennifer Hargreaves, Celia Brackenridge, and Margaret Talbot.

Eileen Kennedy
Belinda Wheaton

See also Commonwealth Games

Bibliography

Birley, D. (1993) *Sport and the Making of Britain.* Manchester, England: Manchester University Press.

Butler, J. (1987) "Revising Femininity?" In *Looking On,* edited by R. Betterton. London: Pandora.

Department of National Heritage. (1995) *Sport: Raising the Game.* London: Department of National Heritage.

Dolo, A. (1997) Women Sports Foundation Homepage. http://www.wsf.org.uk/stumedia.htm.

English Sports Council. (1997) *England, The Sporting Nation: A Strategy.* London: English Sports Council.

Featherstone, M. (1986) "The Body in Consumer Culture." In *Sports Spectators,* edited by M. Featherstone, M. Hepworth, and Allen Guttman. New York: Columbia University Press.

Hargreaves, Jennifer. (1987) "Victorian Familism and the Formative Years of Female Sport." In *From Fair Sex to Feminism,* edited by J. Mangan and R. Parkes. London: Frank Cass.

———. (1994) *Sporting Females: Critical Issues in the History and Sociology of Women's Sports.* New York: Routledge.

Holt, Richard. (1989) *Sport and the British.* Oxford, England: Clarendon Press.

Layden, J. (1997) *Women in Sports.* Los Angeles: General Publishing Group.

Mangan, James. (1981) *Athleticism in the Victorian and Edwardian Public School: The Emergence and Consolidation of an Educational Ideal.* Cambridge, England: Cambridge University Press.

McCrone, Kathleen. (1988) *Sport and the Physical Emancipation of English Women 1870–1914.* London: Routledge.

Office for National Statistics (1999) *Social Trends 99.* London: The Stationery Office.

Sports Council. (1989) *Bringing Women into Sport.* London: Sports Council.

———. (1992) *Women and Sport Consultation Document.* London: Sports Council.

———. (1993) *Women and Sport: Policy and Frameworks for Action.* London: Sports Council.

———. (1994) *Women and Sport—A Review of Research.* London: Sports Council.

———. (1995) *Women and the Sports Media—UK Directory and Media Guide.* London: Sports Council.

Talbot, Margaret. (1981) "Managing Sport for All." Paper presented at the Panhellenic Physical Education Association Conference, Athens, Greece.

Turner, B., ed. (1991) *The Body Social Process and Social Theory.* London: Sage.

Veblen, Thorstein. (1899) *The Theory of the Leisure Class.* London.

Wimbush, E., and Margaret Talbot, eds. (1988) *Relative Freedoms: Women and Leisure.* Milton Keynes: Open University Press.

The Women's Unit. (1998) *Delivering for Women: Progress So Far.* London: Cabinet Office.

UNITED STATES

Women's sports in the United States—a nation of 268 million people—reach far beyond its borders and have had an enormous influence on women's sports around the world. Two sports that originated in the United States, basketball and volleyball, are among the world's most popular sports. In addition, the United States has become a major training center for athletes from many nations, and Title IX, the 1972 U.S. legislation that has been credited with encouraging much of the growth in women's sports in the United States, has also helped to influence thinking about women's sports elsewhere in the world. U.S. companies are major producers of sports equipment and clothing.

HISTORY

Women's experiences in the sporting life of the United States defy neat historical generalizations. In part, this is because women have never constituted a single group and their behaviors and attitudes have never conformed to a single general pattern. Women's roles have also varied over time, connected as they were to the broader ideological and economic contexts. Women have been active participants (in the modern sense) in a sport, whereas at other times they have been behind-the-scenes producers or promoters.

There were times when perceptions of women's physical and moral "natures," affected sporting values, codes of conduct, rules, and even the definition of an activity as a sport. Indeed, the perception of women as the "weaker sex" helps to account for the designation of bowling as an "amusement" when women engaged in it in the nineteenth century and the development of the divided court in basketball. Even today, fans and the press persist in requiring basketball to be preceded by "women's." Women play women's basketball; men simply play basketball.

The evolution of women's role in sport in the United States can be divided into three major periods: the colonial era, the transitional nineteenth century, and the age of modern sports.

THE COLONIAL ERA: WOMEN AND TRADITIONAL SPORTS AND GAMES

Women were far more visible in American sporting life than the portraits of them in many histories would suggest, and for no period is this statement more true than in the years before the mid-eighteenth century. About 1600, before Europeans colonized the land that would become the United States, the earliest American sportswomen were Native Americans whose style of life must be characterized as a traditional one in which sports and other displays of physical prowess were embedded in the rhythms and relations of ordinary life. Religious ceremonies, for example, called on women and men to dance for hours at a time, while rites of passage from maidenhood to womanhood included physical displays and tests. Ball games occurred in the context of women's daily tasks, and the outcomes could affect one's place in the family or the village. Even equipment and items for wagering, which women often controlled, came from the material stores of wood, corn, shells, and animal hides that were used and valued in everyday life.

The migration of colonists from Europe, especially Britain, began shortly after 1600, and these people, too, fashioned a traditional, organic style of life in which sports were interspersed with ordinary tasks and rituals. Initially, women were few among the colonists and, not surprisingly, there were few opportunities for sports other than hunting and tavern games. After mid-century, however, the gender ratio gradually evened out, and a critical mass of women were present to assume their traditional roles as workers in the fields and homes and as producers of community gatherings, fairs, and family events. Some women owned the equipment with which settlers played games, especially card games. In rural areas where harvest festivals came to be fairly common, women prepared the food that the grain-cutters would consume during the postharvest celebration. Then, too, villages and the emerging towns became the settings for diverse social practices. On warm summer days in New England, husbands and wives fished and sailed on the numerous waterways. Towns like Boston, Providence, and Hartford offered an even broader variety of sports and recreations, ranging from dances to races and fist fights. By the early eighteenth century, emerging cities were sites for public, commercial, and physical displays, including tightrope dancing by women and men.

By the middle of the eighteenth century, the sporting experiences of women of European and African ancestries, as well as recent immigrants, were far more varied than they had been earlier. Enslaved African women found some solace in their brief respites from work—on Sundays, in the evenings, or in the days of celebrating made possible by the observance of holidays—when they danced, played games, and ran races. Agricultural fairs, initiated by white farmers, planters, and traders, also included contests, especially footraces, for black women who competed for articles of clothing. White farm women also made possible, and engaged in, an array of games, contests, and dancing at their rural festivals and family events, such as weddings and funerals. Occasionally as well, women in farming communities raced horses, even against men, and they were willing to lay wagers on their skills.

Middle- and upper-class women, especially those who either lived in or visited towns and cities, had access to the broadest range of sports and other recreations. In the South, white women who lived on plantations raced horses and went fox-hunting—as did their northern contemporaries, who also attended balls, played cards, and visited the increasing array of physical culture exhibitions, which included racewalking, tumbling and acrobatic displays, and equestrian shows.

THE NINETEENTH CENTURY: DOMESTICITY AND THE AGE OF DIMINISHING RETURNS

The pursuit of active sports by women was not to persist, however. During the second half of the eighteenth century, a series of complex changes gradually altered gender roles and relations. Enlightenment ideology and the emergent capitalist economy combined to redefine women's place, to move women into the home and away from public activity, and to emphasize biological differences (from men) as grounds for keeping them there. In effect, the famous "doctrine of separate spheres" stemmed from the same movements that resulted in a new nation and a Declaration of Independence that proclaimed "all men are created equal." The phrase was not tongue-in-cheek; even before 1800, women were seen as morally superior but physically inferior to men. The characterization lasted for more than a century and a half.

The immediate impact of these changes was the movement of many women from participants to spectators, or out of public view entirely, unless accompanied by men. The trend was especially pronounced in towns and cities among middle- and upper-class people whose lives were increasingly shaped by commercial and industrial tasks and rhythms and who came to believe that women's central role was to bear and nurture children and families. Slave and free women who continued to live and work on farms and plantations, as well as the increasing number who joined in the westward migration, did not experience the full weight of these changes in roles and life-styles. Indeed, the experiences of such women in 1850 more closely resembled those of their predecessors in 1750 and even 1650 than they did their urban contemporaries. They remained visible producers and consumers of traditional sports and other displays of physical prowess.

During the first half of the nineteenth century, there was increasing concern that the health of middle- and upper-class women in urbanizing areas was declining. Educators, doctors, and writers of popular magazine articles responded with analyses and prescriptions for improving women's health, including calls for renewed physical exertion via exercises and games. The logic of the health literature was simple and straightforward: if women were to fulfill their roles as caretakers of families and national virtue, they needed to maintain their physical and mental health. Catharine Beecher, Mary Lyons, and Diocletian Lewis, among others, argued for the physical education of women, started schools, and laid out regimens of calisthenics, domestic exercises (such as sweeping), and such traditional activities as walking and riding. The movement to return women to physically active pursuits had begun, albeit in their private domestic sphere.

This would not occur overnight, however. The urban areas that were home to many of the women targeted by the likes of Beecher and Lewis, as well as the economic activities that powered such areas, had reduced the social power of traditional sports and engendered an emerging new form, modern sports. Constructed by men for men, games such as baseball were becoming popular in eastern urban centers at mid-century. Other activities such as skating, croquet, and rowing were also modernizing—acquiring rules, specialized playing spaces, and an organizational base in clubs. Only gradually did women gain access to such forms. In the 1850s they did so primarily as spectators and moral guardians. Especially at baseball games, male promoters hoped that women would bring their perceived moral superiority to bear on the crowds and thus ensure social order.

CHALLENGING GENDERED BOUNDARIES

Not all the middle- and upper-class women were content to remain on the periphery of the action, sporting or otherwise. As of 1848, a feminist movement had formalized at Seneca Falls, New York, and, especially in the North, other movements such as abolitionism encouraged women to be social agents and demonstrated that their appearance in the public domain endangered neither their health nor that of the nation. Moreover, the dynamic events of midcentury, including the War between the States (1861–1865), challenged the gender boundaries and expectations that had confined women to the domestic sphere for more than three generations.

Middle- and upper-class urban women found and made opportunities in public society during and after the Civil War that drew from their long-defined practices in their domestic sphere. Nursing and teaching were precisely such activities, but they required additional training as well as sound constitutions. Not surprisingly, then, some women demanded and received access to colleges, where they did as their brothers did: they began to participate in some of the emerging modern sports whose social power was increasing in the aftermath of the Civil War and among the technological and communication changes of the 1860s and 1870s. At private colleges, such as Vassar in New York State and Smith and Wellesley in Massachusetts, women students formed clubs to play baseball and then tennis, croquet, and archery. College administrators and faculty responded, initially to the influx of women students and their own fears about the negative impact of intellectual work on women students, with requirements for medical examinations, exercise and gymnastics regimens, and the gradual absorption of women's sports clubs.

Outside of the colleges, post-Civil War middle- and upper-class women were also moving to take advantage of the increasing array of modern

RECOGNITION FOR AMATEURS

The James E. Sullivan Memorial Award is the most prestigious award given to an amateur athlete and is awarded to the athlete who "by his or her performance, example and influence as an amateur, has done the most during the year to advance the cause of sportsmanship." Awarded annually since 1930 by the Amateur Athletic Union, twelve women have been recipients: Ann Curtis (1944, swimming), Pat McCormick (1956, diving), Wilma Rudolph (1961, track), Debbie Meyer (1968, swimming), Tracy Caulkins (1978, swimming), Mary Decker Slaney (1982, track), Joan B. Samuelson (1985, track), Jackie Joyner-Kersee (1986, track), Florence Griffith Joyner (1988, track), Janet Evans (1989, swimming), Bonnie Blair (1992, speed ice skating), and Chamique Holdsclaw (1998, basketball).

Gold-medal winning softball players carry the American flag at the 1996 Olympics in Atlanta. (Wally McNamee/Corbis)

sports. Local gymnasiums, armories turned into playing areas, and a host of clubs that formed as men and women sought new forms of community provided women in towns and cities with opportunities for a range of sports, from skating and rowing to trapshooting and tennis. Such activities continued to stretch the bounds of activity acceptable for and to women, and they also quieted some of the fears held especially by the male-dominated medical profession about the negative effects that physical movement in sports might have on women's biology and reproductive functions.

An even more significant challenge to the ideology that placed women in the home and in subservience to men came in the form of a machine, the bicycle. Invented in Europe in the early nineteenth century, various forms of the bicycle had become the objects of short-lived fads through the 1860s. Then came the invention of the "ordinary" (one large and one small wheel) and, subsequently, the "safety" cycle; the latter especially appealed to women. Bicycle riding, and even some racing, became popular, and the practice afforded women with a means of physical mobility and freedom that they had not known since the days when horse ownership was common and expected even by women. Most significant, as well, the bicycle catalyzed dress reform. Bloomers and knickerbockers went on, and corsets came off. The day of the "new woman" was about to dawn.

THE AGE OF MODERN SPORTS

Historians have labeled the period from the 1890s to World War I the Progressive Era largely because "progress" was the goal of contemporaries, especially members of the urban middle class. Achievement did not always match rhetoric, but many women did see their positions and the quality of their lives enhanced. Some urban working women, for instance, earned more pay under improved conditions. Perhaps not surprisingly, some of the industries that employed women organized, first, calisthenics or physical culture classes and then team sports to promote personal health and worker efficiency. Such programs became more widespread after the turn of the century and, by the 1920s, individual companies and regional industries sponsored multiple teams in sports, such as basketball, bowling, tennis, baseball, volleyball, and eventually softball. Among the results were good advertising for the companies and competitive opportunities and even, on occasion, additional income for the athletes.

Another group of women whose lives came to incorporate opportunities for competitive sports were upper-class women. In the 1870s and 1880s such women had joined clubs—social clubs, country clubs, and then sport-specific clubs—just as their brothers and husbands had. They also engaged in sports in colleges and, importantly, on their vacations or extended stays in Europe. By 1900 seven of these women competed in their first Olympics, in Paris, and, despite the enduring opposition of the prime mover behind the modern Olympics, Baron Pierre de Coubertin, women consistently competed in the Games thereafter, albeit in small numbers and in socially acceptable sports such as tennis, archery, and, by 1924, figure skating.

The Progressive Era history of middle-class women's sporting experiences is more complicated. Especially before the turn of the century, middle-class women did experience considerable latitude in forming sports clubs and organizing competitions, and they appeared to gain a degree of physical and personal freedom in sports similar to that enjoyed by their working and upper-class sisters. Indeed, they popularized the newly created sports of basketball and volleyball, and it was the rapid spread of such sports, as well as field hockey, cycling, and tennis, that encouraged their teachers and recreation supervisors to form associations and write rules. In men's experiences, it was precisely such associations that were critical to the promotion and expansion of modern sports.

Many of the women who came to control sports for girls and adults, especially in institutions such as schools and colleges, had accepted the warnings of the medical profession that unfettered athletic competition would harm female participants, physically and psychologically, and detract from or even diminish their femininity. Consequently, in the 1890s, women physical educators began to limit sports contests, initially by changing the rules of some games, such as basketball, and eventually by altering the very nature of contests. By 1920 school and college sports were often played not in contests between teams representing their institutions but in play days or sport days in which the convened teams were broken up and the players assigned to mixed school teams.

By the 1920s the conservative approach of women physical educators was quite distinct from—indeed, out of sync with—the attitudes and expectations of many other people. The United States was experiencing its first mature burst of popular consumerism, which was buoyed by a fun ethic and a relatively expansive economy. Clubs and teams for women proliferated, in part as more institutions and businesses, from urban governments to churches to saloons, sponsored teams or provided facilities. Improvements in, and declining prices of, sporting goods, as well as the increasing popularity of sports spectating and sports as entertainment spurred the organization of amateur and semiprofessional leagues. Beyond the pale of physical educators, the latter provided underground opportunities for middle-class athletes.

After 1929 the Great Depression disrupted this sporting boom, but it did not end it entirely. In fact, the popularity of industrial sport probably peaked in the 1930s, and sports such as softball and bowling became extremely popular among women. Women's Olympic competition also gained more popular support, in part because of great performances by athletes such as Mildred "Babe" Didrikson and in part because support continued to diminish for the mythology of the negative physical and biological consequences of athletics for women. Significantly as well, women continued to enter nontraditional roles, a trend that became more pronounced as World War II began. After 1941 more women took jobs that had once belonged to men who had entered the military. Even professional baseball opened its doors to women via the All-American Girls Baseball League financed by Philip Wrigley of chewing gum and Chicago Cubs fame.

Now famous in part because of the movie, *A League of Their Own,* the All-American Girls Baseball League began play in 1943 in midsize cities in the Great Lakes region. The athletes were not, to be sure, the first professional women athletes in the United States. In the modern era that honor is likely to belong to female distance walkers in the 1870s and 1880s and rodeo competitors in the twentieth century. Nor were they the only women professional athletes of the decade. After 1949 the

ELIZABETH CADY STANTON ON "MAN'S CLAIM TO PHYSICAL SUPERIORITY" (1850)

Elizabeth Cady Stanton, the U.S. women's suffrage leader who was one of the organizers of the first women's rights convention in Seneca Falls, New York (1848), frequently wrote under the name of "Sunflower." In April 1850, Stanton discussed the topic "man's claim to physical superiority." As had Mary Wollstonecraft before her, Stanton declared: "We cannot say what the woman might be physically, if the girl were allowed all the freedom of the boy, in romping, swimming, climbing, and playing hoop and ball. . . . Physically as well as intellectually, it is *use* that produces growth and development."

United States ice hockey goalie Sarah Tueting in the 1998 Nagano, Japan, Olympics. (Wally McNamee/Corbis)

Ladies Professional Golf Association (LPGA) organized, offering $15,000 in purse money spread over nine tournaments. Five years later, women golfers could earn $225,000 a year on the LPGA tour.

In the 1940s as well, an even more significant movement developed in African-American colleges. Track and field teams were training at places such as Tuskegee Institute and Tennessee State, and these colleges would produce the athletes that would integrate U.S. women's Olympic teams and revolutionize the contests and the records. By the early 1960s African-American athletes such as Wilma Rudolph ran record-pace after record-pace, opening doors for other black women and paving the way for Jackie Joyner Kersee and Florence Griffith-Joyner, among numerous others. Other sports such as bowling and tennis also integrated in the post–World War II years.

THE SIXTIES BOOM

A greater revolution in women's sports lay ahead. In the late 1960s the modern feminist movement, a youth culture, and other sources of social unrest unsettled the nation as a whole and the sports world in particular. Billie Jean King defied international tennis tradition and authorities at Wimbledon in 1968, when she demanded an end to under-the-table payments to players; then she defeated another symbol of patriarchy, Bobby Riggs, on the court in 1973. In between King's two strikes for honesty and women, she helped organize the first of several early 1970s professional leagues for women, the Virginia Slims tennis tour.

King symbolized the commencement of the contemporary women's revolution in sports, the realization of the attributes projected in the 1890s "new woman." Legislation, especially Title IX of the Educational Amendments Act of 1972, and the subsequent and ongoing litigation against unequal opportunities in institutions continued the revolution—and probably had a greater impact on more women. Schools and colleges that accept federal money must provide athletic opportunities for women proportional to the number of women they enroll; few women are unaffected by this.

CONCLUSION

There has been a dynamic and continuing growth of women's sports since the late 1960s. Triathlons, marathons, soccer, aerobics, weightlifting, rugby, and boxing are among the many sports available to women today that scarcely existed for them a generation or two ago. And could anyone have foreseen, even a decade ago, that 90,000 people who could have stayed home and watched the game on television, would come out to cheer on U.S. Women's team playing in the World Cup for soccer? Still unknown is the full impact of the generation of women who are maturing and who grew up with opportunities of which their mothers and grandmothers never dreamed.

The experience and involvement of U.S. women in the sporting world, and their demands for equal access to individual participation and to the financial rewards of professional sports, continue to influence the development of women's sports around the world. The U.S. Women's Sports Foundation (WSF), formed in 1974, has helped other countries—including the United Kingdom and Japan—to form their own Women's Sports Foundations; these organizations have no formal ties to one another. In addition, in May 1999 the U.S. WSF was granted consultative status to the United Nations Economic and Social Council, which makes it possible for the organization to provide input to the council relating to women's issues and women's sports participation around the world, with the goal of advancing sport "as a vehicle for addressing global issues affecting girls and women."

Nancy L. Struna

Bibliography

Berlage, Gai Ingham. (1994) *Women in Baseball: The Forgotten History.* Westport, CT: Praeger.

Birrell, Susan, and Cheryl L. Cole, eds. (1994) *Women, Sport, and Culture.* Champaign, IL: Human Kinetics.

Browne, Lois. (1992) *Girls of Summer: In Their Own League.* New York: HarperCollins.

Cahn, Susan K. (1994) *Coming on Strong: Gender and Sexuality in Twentieth-Century Women's Sport.* New York: Free Press.

Cooper, Pamela. (1998) *The American Marathon.* Ithaca, NY: Syracuse University Press.

Costa, Margaret, and Sharon Guthrie, eds. (1994) *Women and Sport: Interdisciplinary Perspectives.* Champaign, IL: Human Kinetics.

Guttmann, Allen. (1991) *Women's Sports: A History.* New York: Columbia University Press.

Hargreaves, Jennifer. (1994) *Sporting Females: Critical Issues in the History and Sociology of Women's Sports.* New York: Routledge.

Hult, Joan S., and Mariana Trekell, eds. (1991) *A Century of Women's Basketball: From Frailty to Final Four.* Reston, VA: National Association for Girls and Women in Sport.

LeCompte, Mary Lou. (1993) *Cowgirls of the Rodeo: Pioneer Professional Athletes.* Urbana: University of Illinois Press.

Struna, Nancy L. (1996) *People of Prowess: Sport, Leisure, and Labor in Early Anglo-America.* Urbana: University of Illinois Press.

Verbrugge, Martha. (1988) *Able-Bodied Womanhood.* New York: Oxford University Press.

Vertinsky, Patricia. (1990). *The Eternally Wounded Woman.* Manchester: Manchester University Press.

USHA, P. T.

(1964–)

INDIAN TRACK ATHLETE

P. T. (Pilavullakandi Thekeparampil) Usha was the best track athlete and the best female athlete to come from India. In the mid-1980s she dominated the sprint events in Asia although she never achieved the same level of success in international competitions.

Usha was born in Koothali, Kerala, on 20 May 1964 and trained by running on the beach. Early in her career she competed in the 100- and 200-meter sprints, the 400-meter run, the 400-meter hurdles, and the 4 × 100 and 4 × 400 relays. Later she dropped the shorter sprints and specialized in the 400-meter events. After finishing fourth in the 400-meter hurdles at the 1984 Olympics, she was supported and encouraged by the government and won five gold medals and one bronze at the 1985 Asian track and field championships and four gold medals and a silver at the 1985 Asian Games. These successes led to her being labeled the "Queen of Asian Track." After marrying and giving birth to a son, she came out of retirement for the Asian Games in the 1990s and took a bronze in the 400-meter run and a silver in the 4 × 400 relay.

Although she did not achieve similar results in world and Olympic competitions, Usha's achievements are especially notable because India as a nation has had very little success in producing world-class, or even regional-class, athletes in most sports. Its successes have come only in the elite sports of tennis, golf, field hockey, billiards, and cricket, which were introduced by the British in the nineteenth century. An Indian athlete has won only one Olympic medal (bronze in freestyle wrestling in 1952), and the field hockey team last won a medal in 1980. Why sport development lags in India is not clear, but factors that have been cited include a cumbersome government bureaucracy, lack of government support, widespread poverty, health problems, and an ethos that places more value on participation than on winning.

David Levinson

Bibliography

Dahlberg, John-Thor. (1994) "Populous India No Contender When it Comes to Sports." *Los Angeles Times* (15 March): 6.

Matthews, Peter. (1991) *Athletics 1990: The International Track and Field Annual.* London: Sports World.

V

VALUES AND ETHICS

Values and ethics are closely related concepts. "Values" refers to those ideas and principles that are worthy of holding, while "ethics" refers to the morally consistent application of those values. In society at large and in sport in particular, the topic of values and ethics is controversial, particularly in the context of feminist scholarship and activism as well as women's increasing participation in sports.

WOMEN'S AND MEN'S VALUES AND ETHICS IN MODERN SPORTS

As children, boys and girls share similar values about sports. Both cherish fun, skill development, social interaction, and fair competition. It appears, however, that girls and boys diverge in sport values as they reach adulthood. It has also been suggested that men are preoccupied with the result of the competition while women value the process as well as the end product. At least in the United States, some commentators argue that men's sports have embraced violence, showmanship and exhibitionism, disrespect for opponents, and, on the professional level, a selfish pursuit of wealth and an arrogant disregard for the rules of conduct and laws that govern the general public.

This situation creates a dilemna for women athletes as women begin to experience opportunities to participate in sports previously denied them. Some experts suggest that it is likely that women will begin to adopt men's sports values as they begin to have the same opportunities to play and are coached by men and women who have embraced these values. Other experts suggest that this possibility should be actively avoided—that men's sports values should not be emulated.

While it is acknowledged that some women will adopt male sports values without questioning them, one must also consider the possibility that men's sports will be positively affected and irrevocably changed by female athletes and their value system. The female athlete is bringing her own values to the playing fields, and one possible result will be value changes on both sides. Many observers agree that it is unlikely that female athletes will embrace sports violence. Most are too aware of violence against women in our society to be able to ignore the implications of such an action.

In the 1990s there was a positive public reaction to differing rules in women's sports. For instance, women's lacrosse, unlike men's, is a noncontact sport. Women's ice hockey prohibits checking. The resulting games were therefore dominated by skill and the continuous flow of play. The 1998 American and Canadian Olympic female ice hockey players demonstrated that women value not only winning and competition but also fair play, fun, and genuine respect for opponents, teammates, and fans. In contrast, following the poor showing of American and Canadian male ice hockey teams in the 1998 Winter Olympics, it was suggested by even the male-dominated press that the violence of North American hockey was a determining factor; that, ultimately, physically impeding your opponent or preventing the execution of skilled play resulted in a less skilled game. The larger rinks and absence of excessive contact in European hockey had apparently contributed to the more skilled play and faster skating of the non–North American victors.

There are also comparable differences between the audiences for men's and women's sports. Data suggest that there are two separate markets for men's and women's sports, each with a 50–50 male–female demographic composition. These two audiences have different tastes. For instance, the men's basketball audience values height, strength, contact under the boards, and muscling dunks over finesse shots. The women's basketball audience values teamwork, more passing, less contact, and more accurate shooting. In other words, the men and women who watch and appreciate women's basketball are not the same men and women who watch and appreciate men's basketball.

Male and female professional athletes also seem to relate differently to their fans. Female athletes, trying to convince fans that they should support their sports, generally do not charge for autographs, do not hesitate to spend hours making sure that every fan got a signature, and appear to be extremely committed to community outreach and participation in promotional efforts. Unlike male athletes, who frequently seem like sellers in a seller's market, female athletes seem more like sellers in a buyer's market, always hustling the next sale and befriending the prospective customer. Professional male athletes are increasingly drawing high-priced corporate audiences, while female professional athletes are wooing the family audiences with affordable prices.

Observers also point out that the women's sports fan more closely identified with the sports experience of female athletes, who play the game more like the public at large; in contrast, the athletes in men's sports appear to be superhuman specimens, and the fans are merely admirers of the extraordinary.

Men's and women's sports in the 1990s appeared to be vastly different in kind and in values. Many observers and scholars remained uncertain as to whether the female athlete of the new millennium would take on the value system of the dominant men's sports model, or whether she would be able to bring her own values into the sports arena, changing men's sports for the better.

A METHOD FOR CONSIDERATION OF VALUES AND ETHICS FOR WOMEN IN SPORT

To develop a method to consider these issues; scholars, activists, and athletes in the 1990s focused on three broad efforts: (1) the understanding of gender-related biases of previous practices and scholarship, (2) the raising of women's and men's consciousness of the reality of women's experience, and (3) the development of a philosophical and political perspective that is consistent with women's experience.

The first effort involves asking what was originally referred to as "the woman question" and is now called by some researchers "the gender-biased question." This question challenges the supposed objectivity of scientific research findings regarding the nature of women and the objectivity of the professions (e.g., sport medicine) that use this research. Underlying this question is the claim that many of the "facts" about female "nature" actually reflect values based in biased social constructions. The precepts and practices of sports can be and are skewed by gender bias. This gender bias works almost unconsciously, occurring when decision makers, physicians, and coaches treat all athletes, all human bodies, as if they were all male. From this perspective, athletes—or their bodies—are viewed as dysfunctional if they fail to function like male bodies, and physical problems unique to women are of little concern or interest.

Consciousness-raising requires that women be seriously invited to discuss personal experiences in sports, so that they can have wider meaning for all women. Women who share stories about sexual stereotyping or harassment in sports, for example, often come to realize that their feeling of having been treated as a girl (rather than a woman) or treated as a man is not unique to them but common to most women. The purpose of this consciousness-raising is to achieve fundamental changes by connecting the personal experiences of women to developments in sport. Men, of course, need to learn that their's is not the only view of the world or of sporting experience.

The third effort is to synthesize a useful perspective from which to develop thinking and action for the future. This perspective aims to balance the principles, rules, ideals, values, and virtues of sport with the realities faced in actual cases in which moral decisions that apply to women athletes must be made. It is based primarily on the works of three philosophical-moral theorists: Aristotle (*Nicomachean Ethics*, Book 8), John Stuart Mill (*Utilitarianism*, 1863, and *On Liberty*, 1859), and John Rawls (*A Theory of Justice*, 1971). Aristotelian practical reasoning involves moral choices being made by several moral agents rather than by one isolated individual. Mill's views on the importance of hearing as well as speaking in the course of a moral dialogue are also important. The practice of ethics requires communication (as opposed to mere telling), corroboration, and collaboration: women are not alone when grappling with applying ethics to sport. A Rawlsian reflective equilibrium—that is, a perspective in which principles are in accord with our own intuitions—represents the kind of balanced and realistic perspective from which to consider patterns of male domination and female subordination in the realm of sport.

Within the context of these general methodological strategies, several issues have come to the forefront: general conceptions of women, the participation of women in sport, the "nature" of women in relation to the "nature" of sports (which includes the debate over separate versus integrated sports), and the power bases upon which sport and society are built.

CONCEPTIONS OF WOMAN

It should be clear that the battles representing the ethical issues for women in sports will be fought over conceptions of women—of their bodies and their minds. The traditional ideals of woman are intimately tied to a particular view of woman's body, including its being soft, graceful, weak, and beautiful. These characteristics are tied to the roles of wife, mother, and daughter. They contrast with the traditional ideal of man as hard, powerful, strong, and rational, characteristics tied to the roles of leader, warrior, and father. But more important, if we examine the underlying characteristics of the traditional ideal athlete, we can plainly see that the ideal man and the ideal athlete are very similar, particularly in the role of warrior. (It should be noted that some exceptional counterexamples stressed physicality and a warrior nature for woman, namely, the myths of Artemis, Atalanta, and the Amazons, who all rejected the traditional role for women.)

The fundamental ethical issue in this entire discussion is who chooses which images of woman are permitted, desired, or pursued in sport, a question inextricably linked to issues of power and autonomy. At the institutional level, if it is men who decide, for example, which sport women are permitted to attempt, the standards of physical perfection to be met in specific sports, or the levels of funding to be accorded women's as opposed to men's sport, then women may legitimately complain that they are not being treated with due respect. Just as it is the responsibility of each male to decide for himself what type of body and, indeed, what type of life he wishes to pursue, it is the responsibility of each woman to deal with the challenges that face female athletes.

THE ABILITY TO PARTICIPATE

Is there any reason why women should not participate in sports that men have traditionally played? It is instructive to look at what could possibly count as a morally acceptable answer. If there were a sport played by men that was physiologically impossible for women, it would be a reason for women not to participate. But there is no such sport. To qualify, the sport would probably have to centrally involve the male genitalia—and we have no institutionally sanctioned sports of this type.

A second possibility would be if there were a sport played by men that no women in the world actually wanted to play. If such a sport existed, women would not play it because *they* chose not to play, not because someone else decided that they should not. That it would somehow be bad for women to participate or that there was not enough money to allow women to participate are both morally unacceptable answers for prohibiting women from playing sports.

CONSTRUCTING A WOMEN'S SPORTS MODEL

A basic question being discussed about modern women's sports is whether they should follow the existing model of men's sports based on competition, aggression, victory, and commercialization. The various models of women's sport set forth in the 1990s suggest other values, namely personal development, cooperation, and teamwork.

Some of the challenges women athletes face are a result of the institutional climate for women in sports (i.e., biased, resistant, "chilly") and will require changes in policy and practice. Other challenges—physical, mental, and, indeed, spiritual—occur at a personal level.

From a physical perspective these challenges may include, but are not limited to, body composition and development issues related to the health and well-being of the athlete. Some of these problems are a direct result of the demands of a particular woman's participation in her sport. The ideal of *citius, altius, fortius* (swifter, higher, stronger)—pushing the human limits (male or female)—has real consequences. For example, many elite-level sports present high risks of injuries and, generally speaking, elite-level training produces fit, but not necessarily healthy, athletes. The results of those pressures can be, and are in many cases, different for men and women, but the choice whether on not to train and compete is parallel. However, there is a special class of sports (e.g., gymnastics) for which the physical requirements and resulting risks are directly caused by decisions about what counts as excellent sport. The judging criteria for these sports should be tailored so as to minimize the health risks they impose on the athletes.

Amenorrhea and its opposite, pregnancy, are unique to women and raise issues that are tied (1) to the double-bind implications that all women have faced when reproductive aspects of their lives have been designated as illness and (2) to the tension between the two conflicting traditional ideals of woman and athlete. An essential part of the traditional ideal woman is fertility because it is necessary for childbearing. Fertility and childbearing are not only not essential to the ideal athlete, they are antithetical to the role of athlete as warrior. In many ways the Amazons were viewed as monstrosities because they rejected the biological role of woman as being primary.

The classification of these reproductive aspects of women's lives as illnesses has led to wide-scale paternalistic medical management of women under the guise of beneficence. In sports, these so-called illnesses have been part of the basis for excluding women. Indeed, some countries, including Canada, the United States, and Australia, have begun to imprison women for endangering their fetuses. Most pregnant athletes who are falsely charged with harming their fetuses face, at the very least, moral pressure that is based on the view that participating in sports while pregnant is socially unacceptable behavior. This does not mean that complications for mothers or for fetuses that are serious enough to require medical interventions cannot occur. There will be particular cases where the label of illness or disease is appropriate. But that ascription should not then lead to unfair sports policies (e.g., banning them from participation in sports rather than educating them about how to simultaneously cope with their illness and participate in sports).

THE "NATURE" OF SPORTS AND "NATURE" OF WOMEN

The female athlete also faces challenges involving the mental requirements of sports competition: aggression and violence. Male athletes also face these challenges, but it is considered "normal" for men and "abnormal" for women to engage in violence. Traditionally it has also been predominantly men who have committed sexual abuses against women (and minors) in the context of sports. The control over and moral responsibility for violence, abuse, harassment, and discrimination in and surrounding sports lie predominantly with those in the sports community, and it is a concern for both men and women. Some women, weary of not having their voices heard on these issues (and for a host of other reasons), advocate completely separate sports for women and oppose any gender integration at all.

One argument against integration is that women would have to accept not only the current selection of sports—primarily designed for and practiced by men—but also an established culture of values (e.g., viewing sports as a battleground on which one conquers one's foes) that most women do not hold; whereas separation might allow women the freedom to create sports based on the values they choose. Nevertheless, some would urge women to pay the high price of integration so that they can have the same opportunities, occupations, rights, and privileges men have had in sports. This drive for women's sameness with men has sometimes denied women's qualities and ways in which these qualities might contribute in a very positive manner to sports. The argument is that if women emphasize their differences from men, viewing these differences as biologically produced and/or culturally shaped, they will trap themselves into ghettos, while men will continue on as they always have.

To think that women athletes must either act as men (if they accept the male ideal) or must be separate (so as to generate their own ideal) is to regard the sports experience as highly gender-specific. But in fact, the two views of sport—as competing (*agon*) against others or as cooperative searching and striving for excellence—may be independent of the gender of the athlete.

However, the greatest tension arises if women have an "agonistic" view of sports and yet are inherently, or "essentially," caring and connected to others. In such a model of sports women might be required to disconnect from their own experience and thus to experience some form of alienation. It is probably the case that most athletes (male and female) find themselves torn between conflicting views, because pushing oneself to one's limits challenges even the strongest sense of self and because in their moments of agony and joy, athletes tend to experience themselves as both radically alone (no one else can really understand what they feel) and fundamentally united to their teammates, their competitors, and all of humanity.

ETHICS AND POWER

Dealing with instances of gender oppression, or neglect, in sports requires complex combinations of social, biological, political, ontological (relating to essential nature), and epistemological (relating to nature of knowing) approaches. This complex approach enables development of an ethical framework that can provide the means for discerning and solving problems surrounding women and sports. It requires the acknowledgment that there is no clear line between ethics and social/political concerns. Some of the most important moral questions to be asked in the cases of gender oppression and neglect in sports are specifically about male domination and female subordination.

A coherent understanding of the causes of women's subordination to men in sports coupled with a refined program of action designed to eliminate the systems and attitudes that oppress, or cause neglect of, women in sports, must guide this complex approach. A detailed analysis of the distribution of power in each case can often identify a particular factor as the primary cause of women's subordinate status in sport, which, for the most part, has traditionally been based on biology. However, to adequately deal with these problems, researchers must also look at economics, law, education, national boundaries, and language, because all of these factors have contributed to the current status of women's sports. Researchers can, and should, attempt to ascertain the actual status of both sexes in sports and determine how far that condition deviates from what justice prescribes.

Donna A. Lopiano and Angela Schneider

See also Aggression; Amenorrhea; Body Image; Competition; Cooperation; Medicine; Reproduction

Bibliography

Bender, D., and B. Leone, eds. (1995) *Male/Female Roles: Opposing Viewpoints.* San Diego, CA: Greenhaven Press.

Bordo, Susan. (1989) "Reading the Slender Body." In *Body/Politics: Women and the Discourses of Science,* edited by Mary Jacobus, Evelyn Fox Keller, and Sally Shuttleworth. New York: Routledge.

Butcher, R. B., and Angela J. Schneider. (1998) "Fair Play as Respect for the Game." *Journal of Philosophy of Sport* 25:

Cahn, Susan K. (1994) *Coming on Strong: Gender and Sexuality in Twentieth-Century Women's Sport.* New York: The Free Press.

Cohen, Greta L. (1993) *Women in Sport: Issues and Controversies.* Newbury Park, CA: Sage.

Creedon, Pamela J., ed. (1994) *Women, Media & Sport.* Newbury Park, CA: Sage.

Fausto-Sterling, Anne. (1992) *Myths of Gender: Biological Theories About Women and Men,* 2d ed. New York: Basic Books.

Hargreaves, Jennifer. (1995) "A Historical Look at the Changing Symbolic Meanings of the Female Body in Western Sport." In *Sport as Symbol, Symbols in Sport,* edited by F. van der Merwe. Germany: Academia Verlag, 249–259.

Lander, Louise. (1988) *Images of Bleeding: Menstruation as Ideology.* New York, Orlando Press.

Leavitt, Judith W. (1999) *Women & Health in America,* 2d ed. Madison: University of Wisconsin Press.

Lenskyj, Helen. (1984) *Sport Integration or Separation.* Ottawa: Fitness and Amateur Sport.

———. (1986) *Out of Bounds: Women, Sport and Sexuality.* Toronto: Women's Press.

MacKinnon, Catharine. (1987) *Feminism Unmodified: Discourses on Life and Law.* Cambridge: Harvard University Press.

Mahowald, Mary B. (1983) *Philosophy of Woman: An Anthology of Classic and Current Concepts,* 2d. ed. Indianapolis, IN: Hackett.

Okruhlik, K. (1995) "Gender and the Biological Sciences." *Canadian Journal of Philosophy* 20:21–42.

Postow, Betsy C, ed. (1983) *Women, Philosophy, and Sport: A Collection of New Essays.* Metuchen, NJ: Scarecrow Press.

Schiebinger, Londa. (1989) *The Mind Has No Sex? Women in the Origins of Modern Science.* Cambridge, MA: Harvard University Press.

———. (1993) *Nature's Body: Gender in the Making of Modern Science.* Boston: Beacon Press.

Schneider, A. J. (1995) "Gender, Sexuality & Sport in America." *Journal of the Philosophy of Sport* 12:136–143.

———, and R. B. Butcher. (1993) "For the Love of the Game: A Philosophical Defense of Amateurism." *Quest* 45, 4:460–469.

———, and R. B. Butcher. (1994) "Why Olympic Athletes Should Avoid the Use and Seek the Elimination of Performance-Enhancing Substances and Practices in the Olympic Games." *Journal of the Philosophy of Sport* 20/21:64–81.

Sherwin, Susan. (1992) *No Longer Patient: Feminist Ethics and Health Care.* Philadelphia: Temple University Press.

Szekely, Eva. (1988) *Never Too Thin.* Toronto: Women's Press.

Tong, R. (1995) "What's Distinctive About Feminist Bioethics?" In *Health Care Ethics in Canada,* edited by F. Baylis, J. Downie, B Freedman, B. Hoffmaster, and S. Sherwin. Toronto: Harcourt Brace Canada.

VENEZUELA

In this oil-producing nation located on the north coast of South America, women participate in all public arenas, including politics, law, education, science, and sports.

Careers as athletes, physical education instructors, and coaches are open to women, and women from all social classes participate in sports. Physical education for girls and women is mandatory in schools and colleges. In addition, special attention is given to providing sport opportunities for the disabled. For girls and women, the most popular sports are basketball, kickball, swimming, tennis, and volleyball, and these are practiced at all levels of the education system.

Maria Alejandra Vento of Venezuela competing in the Central American and Caribbean Games in 1998. She defeated Milagros Seguero to win the gold medal. (AP Photos)

HISTORY

The official organization of sports in Venezuela dates back to 1934, when a movement developed to strengthen existing sports organizations. As a result, many Venezuelan sports associations and federations were created, and they joined international federations representing those sports. Since then, some Venezuelan women, both as athletes and administrators, have been part of the international movement for women's participation in sports. In the 1930s there were several obstacles to the full development of sports, including a shortage of sports facilities and properly educated trainers and national economic problems that made competing in foreign countries difficult. These obstacles were overcome slowly as sports took on increasing importance in Venezuelan society and as more resources were devoted to sports.

Venezuelan women began to draw attention as athletes in the 1930s. Perhaps the most important was the achievement of Belen de Behrens in tennis and golf in 1930. She was followed by Cristina Eggui and Carmen Urbaneja, who were successful in the Bolivarian and Central American Games between 1932 and 1945.

In the 1990s Venezuela regularly organized national competitions in numerous sporting events, periodically held seminars and conferences on women and sports, and frequently hosted international and regional championships. The country's sport facilities were on a par with those of the leading sport nations, and there was broad media coverage of women's sports.

INTERNATIONAL COMPETITION

Venezuelan women have won several world titles and have held leadership positions in international sport organizations. Flor Isava was one of the first two women appointed to the International Olympic Committee (IOC) and, in 1999, was the longest-serving female member of the IOC. She was also the first woman to serve on the IOC Executive Committee. Lina Davonish was a member of the International Swimming Federation, and Teresita Lara served as the Latin-American representative to the Sailing Federation.

Although Venezuelan women have performed well in several sports in regional competition and some have won world championships, Olympic participation has remained limited. In the 1990s there were only five women on the team in each of the two summer Olympics.

Venezuela has produced several top-ranked tennis players—Andreina Pietri, Corina Parizca, Mónica Adler, Andrea Braun, Beatriz Raytler, and the multisport athlete Flor Isava. Tennis player Marca Alejandra Vento was the best of a number of superior tennis players in the 1990s, ranking as high as thirty-fourth in the world and winning the gold medal at the Central-American and Caribbean Games in 1998. Judo is a very popular sport in Venezuela; female martial artists include Natacha Hernández, world champion in 1984, and Adriana Carmona, runner-up in the world championships in 1998. The most successful Venezuelan woman athlete was the skeet shooter Mercedes León de García, who won several world championships in the 1950s and 1960s and retired in 1978 with more than 500 national and international titles. Athletes who have participated in other sports with regional success include Annelise Rockembash, in swimming in the 1970s; Ana María Carrasco, in water skiing; Flor Isava, Carola Reverón, and Lupita Isava in equestrian events; Gisela Vidal in track and field; and Elizabeth Pope, in table tennis in the 1990s.

Many Venezuelans see sports as positive social activities that create unity among the population and teach young people to live with one another in an atmosphere free of prejudice and distinctions based on race, religion, or political ideology.

Flor Isava

VIOLENCE *see* Aggression

VOLKSSPORT

Volkssport is the general name to describe a diverse group of sports and games whose common element is their status as "popular sport." Volkssport includes traditional, ethnic, or indigenous sports and games, as well as new ones that may arise or be invented based on traditional practices. Pub games, volkswalks (noncompetitive walking events), mass gymnastics, spontaneous sports of the working classes, and games and sports associated with festivals all fall under the term. Despite the origin of volkssport activities in the preindustrial world, the idea of volkssport is itself an invention of the industrial age; the idea of volkssport stands in opposition to the highly organized nature of modern sport and also champions the idea of recreation for the masses rather than for the elite alone. Volkssport is based on festivity and community rather than rules and competition, and women have been involved in many ways, both as organizers and participants.

HISTORY

Volkssport is neither one sport nor a well-defined group of sports, and so it has no single, linear history. It is as distinct in different countries as the words used to describe it are in different languages: *volk* (Dutch, German), *narod* (Russian), *folk*

Men and women cheer on their racers in a mid-twentieth-century mouse derby. (George Konig/Corbis)

(Danish, Swedish, English), *popolo* (Italian), and *people* (English). The concept is a European one though sports and games around the world are often termed volkssport. Volkssport may be attached to a particular ideology, whether right-wing politics (*völkischer Sport*) or left-wing ideas (*sport popolare*). They may be, in all these circumstances, men's, women's, or mixed activities.

In contrast to mainstream modern sports, volkssport reveals underlying patterns both in style and participation, including the participation of women. Volkssport is based not on discipline and rules but on festival and festivity, and this means that women play an important role in it. Volkssport is connected with different kinds of cultural activities, including music, group singing, dance, theater, and outdoor experiences. The aim of volkssport is not to produce winners but to foster togetherness and celebrate variety. In contrast to the rigid structure and rationality of modern sports, volkssport, in its past and current manifestations, highlights the variations among groups, including variations in behavior both within and across the sexes.

Women have been important in many ways, but precisely what those ways have been has depended on the cultural context. It is clear from the historical record that women did take part in volkssport in many cultures, but it is not always clear what sports and roles they played. This is because early first-hand accounts of these sports and festivals often say much about the specifics of the games and sports but little about the participants. When women are mentioned, the descriptions often cast them in a negative light.

Volkssport as a whole has undertones of gender issues, comparable to its undertones of class, mostly the lower classes. The gender characteristic is, however, difficult to describe precisely; just as nature is not "female" and technology not "male," each is nevertheless associated with a gender.

PREMODERN FOLK GAMES AND FESTIVITIES

Volkssport as a concept did not exist before the industrial age because there was neither "sport" in the modern sense nor the notion of *volk,* with its modern connotations of a collective cultural identity. In earlier times, sport meant pastimes, such as hunting, falconry, and fishing, of the upper classes, mainly the nobility and gentry, who distinguished themselves from the "folk." The aristocratic tournaments and the later noble exercises were exclusive, too, both by gender and class. Meanwhile, the common people had a recreational culture of their own. Games and competitions of strength and agility were combined with dances, music, and ritual to form a rich array of activities at festivals and celebrations. These were connected with religious and seasonal events—often Christianized forms of pagan celebrations—like Christmas (Jul), erecting the May tree, Shrovetide and carnival, Midsummer dance (Valborg, St. John), harvest festivals, local fairs, a saint's day or church festival (kermis), marriage, revel, ale, and wake. Games brought suspense and excitement into a routine world, and the flirting and physical contact allowed between men and women was an important component.

Many premodern folk games and sports were reserved for men. When they were competitions based on strength, such as wrestling, lifting stones, tossing the caber (tree trunk), and finger drawing, the "strong man" not "strong woman" was the admired image. In Scotland, for example, the "stone of manhood" (Gaelic *claich cuid fir*),

SMOCK RACING IN EIGHTEENTH-CENTURY BRITAIN

The nobility and young men of fashion of most countries are rather eccentric in their amusements; and surely this observation may safely be applied to those of England in 1717, when a set of *escape graces* subscribed for a piece of plate, which was run for in Tyburn-road by six Asses rode by Chimney-sweepers; and two boys rode two Asses at Hampstead-heath for a *wooden spoon* attended by above 500 persons on horseback. Women running for Holland smocks was not uncommon; nay, a match was talked of for a race of women in hooped petticoats; and another actually took place in consequence of a wager of 1000*l*. between the Earl of Lichfield and Esquire Gage, that Gage's Chaise and pair would outrun the Earl's Chariot and four. The ground was from Tyburn to Hayes; and Gage lost through some accident. Vast sums were betted on all these eccentric operations.

JAMES PELLER MALCOLM
(1810) Anecdotes of the Manners and Customs of London During the Eighteenth Century. *London: Longman, Hurst, Rees, and Orme.*

placed beside the house of a chieftain, was used as a test of strength by the young men who had to lift it to prove their masculinity. Similarly, games of skill such as the bat and ball game of *tsan* played in the Valle d'Aosta, in northwestern Italy, in which a batter hit a ball as far as possible into a field, where it was caught by the other team, were also traditionally reserved for men. Participation by girls in the 1990s represents the transformation of *tsan* into a modern "traditional sport."

Thus, certain sports in folk culture were exclusively male not because of differences in male and female ability but because of the social division of labor and other culturally defined social roles. Whereas women were responsible for domestic work and thus were more centered in place and also had more predictable daily lives, men were often required to adjust their work seasonally between working in the field and hunting in the forests or mountains. As society became industrialized and urban, hunting and related activities were restricted and men had more time for leisure activities, including games and sports, as well as socializing with other men apart from the work context. Thus, volkssport was the product of a number of factors, including more leisure time, the development of men's social clubs, and the social organization of activities requiring various physical skills and abilities and the use of weapons.

Even such typical male sports as wrestling, however, could, in premodern times, be practiced by women. For example, Japanese women engaged in sumo wrestling, and *onna-zumo* as early as the eighteenth century and, although women were forbidden to take part during the Meiji era, they began participating again at the end of the nineteenth century. In Brittany, women participated in belt wrestling (*gouren*), and a Breton song describes how the girl Annaïg Rouzval defeated Seigneur de Runargo, a nobleman, by pinning him on his back three times. The song bears witness to a connection between gender and class honor and apparently refers to a real event of the seventeenth or eighteenth century. This was probably not an isolated case of female participation as girls practice *gouren* as a modern volkssport.

Some folk festivities included competitions for women. Women's footraces or "smock races" were a typical feature of local events in England and Scotland from the seventeenth to the nineteenth century. Participants included young girls, young women, middle-aged women, and even old women, as well as unmarried women, married women, and widows. There were races for "respectable" women, although very few "ladies" took part, and races for women from the lower social classes, including Gypsies, immigrant Irish women, and itinerant traders. The corresponding competitions for men were usually wrestling, cudgeling, stick matches, sack racing, and others, rather than footraces. Women and girls often raced to satisfy the wagering interests of their backers, thus paralleling the contemporary (eighteenth- to nineteenth-century) sport of pedestrianism. Despite the popularity of women's races between 1790 and 1830, they disappeared and were not the forerunners of modern women's track and field. Women's folk racing has survived in Württemberg, Germany, in the form of a race among shepherdesses that dates to the fifteenth century. As a modern event, the competitors maintain the old tradition of attempting to try to prevent each other from winning, thus causing much stumbling and laughing, traits that were characteristic of European folk culture.

Certain ball and pin games were also played by, or even reserved for, women. For example, in England, Shrovetide football pitted married women against unmarried women, and Shrovetide stoolball was a women's sport that resembled modern cricket or baseball. Similarly, in Aragon, Spain, women played a special form of skittle known as *birlas de mullés*.

DIFFERENCE, TOGETHERNESS, PARODY

A fundamental feature of women's participation in volkssports was the marking of differences. Just as folk competitions and festivals marked differences in marital status by setting teams of married men against teams of bachelors, they also marked the status differences between men and women and between married and unmarried women. Among the Sorbs of Germany, men engaged in ritual riding *(Stollenreiten)* while girls competed in egg races *(Eierlaufen)* and other games of agility. Among the Inuit of Greenland, the drum dance (*qilaatersorneq*) of both women and men was an important ritual. Although men and women danced to the same music, women used different rhythms and movements.

While marking individual status differences in the community, volkssports and games and the festivals in which they took place also served the important function of creating social cohesion and a sense of togetherness among the participants. The participation of women and men side by side affirmed this sense of community as did events that brought together old and young people or people who engaged in different occupations. And sometimes games and sports also brought women and men together, whether in Breton quoit, quittles, and bowls or in the Inuit drum dance. There was, however, considerable variation across cultures in the extent to which men and women competed together. For example, in Swedish folk sports, women participated only with men and competed against women. On the island of Gotland (off the coast of Sweden), in a special type of festival, or *våg*, teams challenged each other from parish to parish, with both men's sports and competitions between boys and girls. In games in which girls and boys competed, girls were normally given certain advantages. A girl could, for instance, use both hands in the pulling competition (*dra hank*) whereas the boy used one hand only. These Swedish games and sports contrasted with the English smock races, where competitions between women and men were rare. Sometimes, sports were invented to promote togetherness. In Shrovetide races in Denmark, one boy had to compete with four, six, or up to twelve girls who used a handkerchief in a sort of relay. The result of the race was not important for the participants, as the prize (money or goods) would be given to the joint feast, regardless of whether the boy or the girls won. More important was the sexual joking that took place as the girls flirted with the boy to distract him and cause him to stumble.

Flirtation was an important element of folk festivals. Along with dances, the games and sports competitions contributed to the playful encounter between boys and girls and men and women. The events, often conducted in societies in which rigid segregation of the sexes was the norm, made flirtation possible by allowing participants to take time out from the norm and, instead, run and capture, touch, or even kiss members of the opposite sex. Many folk games and dances in northern Europe had this strong erotic component, including Shrovetide pageants, Easter fire (a festival that included dancing around a fire, jumping over a fire—often in couples, and flirtatious joking), Maypole festivals, Sankt Hans (midsummer night bonfire), and New Year's fun. Volkssport and festivities were often arranged by so-called youth guilds or "game rooms," which organized the activities in ways that placed possible marriage partners together. Such activities were not restricted to people in northern Europe. For example, in Central Asia Kazakh youths played the White Bone Game on the warm summer nights. Two teams of young people, boys and girls, tried to find a bone that a referee had thrown as far as possible into the dark steppe. While the two teams were searching and fighting for the bone, some of the players searched for other experiences and became temporarily lost—in pairs of boys and girls—in the vast steppe.

Volkssport was used not only to affirm gender identity but to mock it in the form of parody. In dance and game, mummery and scene play, men could appear as women and women as men. Wearing the clothing of the opposite sex or using body movements that fit the stereotype of the other sex appealed to the spectators' sense of humor. When the European ruling classes of the seventeenth and eighteenth centuries tried to suppress the popular games as part of their attack on folk culture in general, they used the sexual content of the games as moral arguments for their elimination. In particular, mimicking the physical activity of women and assuming their dress were regarded as not reconcilable with the rules of decency.

MODERN SPORT AS CONTRAST: SEPARATION AND SAMENESS

Modern sport, as it developed in the Western world beginning in the eighteenth and early nineteenth centuries, brought a new sense of discipline and a new set of rules for relations between men and women. Sport became highly organized and each sport became a unique discipline in an effort to systematize results and maintain records. Festivity was replaced by specialization, and volkssports were abandoned and were, for the most part, relegated to the folklore of the nations in which they had once been popular. From the beginning, men dominated modern sports, and many sports, such as gymnastics, were characterized by forms of movement taken from the military. Competition and victory became all-important and the emphasis was on *swifter, altius, fortius*: faster, higher, stronger. Women were largely excluded until the twentieth century. When women did train or compete, male and female competitions were separate, and any middle position that allowed for a mixing of the sexes was not permitted. The separation of men and women in competition, however, was paradoxically accompanied by a tendency to make the sports activities of men and women as identical as possible. With winning and setting records the primary aim, male and female sports became uniform, and the ideal for an athlete's body type tended toward an "athletic" rather than a male or female ideal.

Women's efforts to gain equal rights were aimed at ending exclusion and separation. Women sought equality in male terms, striving to be the same as men. The goal of "sports for all" often characterized mainstream efforts to promote sports, and this approach also reinforced the idea that sports could be the same for men and women. Alongside mainstream sports, however, some popular sports and games activities persisted or reappeared in different forms. The circus and side shows at fairs served as one arena for such events. Workers' sports movements was another and, in Danish workers' festivities (Fagenes Fest), for example, domestic servants raced with buckets and scrubbers, pottery workers walked with piles of plates on their heads, strong women (and men) pulled the rope in the tug-of-war, and people ran obstacle races while eating cream puffs.

NEW VOLKSSPORT—WALKING, GAMES, AND FESTIVITIES

Volkssport in its modern form emerged as a reaction against the specialization of sports and the disappearance of the festival atmosphere from sporting events. In addition, people sought to resist the anonymity of modern life by engaging in physical activities together.

Volkssport developed in three main stages. The first stage was linked to the Romantic revival that emerged in early-nineteenth-century Europe. It was based on fascination with the "volk" and "popular" culture, the idea of democracy, and the quest for national identities. Women were mostly on the fringe of these early volkssport movements, including the German *volksturnen* and the Slavic Sokol gymnastics movements. While patriotic militarism and Roman Catholicism hindered women's participation in some regions, women did become active and sometimes even constituted the majority of members in some other nations. For example, Danish *folkelig* gymnastics, which was based on Swedish or Ling gymnastics, began as both a male and female activity in the late nineteenth century. In the twentieth century, women made up a majority of *folkelig* participants, and the atmosphere of its festivities has been described as soft female nationalism.

The second stage in the modern development of volkssport began about 1900 and involved the "back to nature" and progressive youth movements, some of whose activities were labeled as "volk." For example, the Woodcraft Indians and Woodcraft Folk groups turned to nature and used the names, ceremonies, and practices of Native Americans while also advocating peace and socialism in the framework of the International Falcon Movement. Boy Scouts competed with this approach through the use of a military model, which was also used by the Girl Guides and Girl Scouts. The German Naturfreunde movement, which began as a workers' tourist movement, built many shelters for volkswalkers across the country. The German youth movement Wandervogel (Birds of Passage) developed a distinct approach to outdoor activities, and units were organized as small, self-administered groups of boys or girls or mixed groups. Members walked, sang, folk-danced, and played in the context of nature. Many of these movements were disrupted by angry discussions and generational conflicts about the advisability of mixing boys and girls.

After 1945, German and Austrian *Volkswandern* was discovered by soldiers of the occupation forces, who took it back to the United States and formed the American Volkssport Association (AVA). Since the 1970s the group has promoted noncompetitive volkswalk (*volksmaching*), volksbike, volksski, and volksswim in over 500 clubs, often as family activities. Among the participants in AVA activities, 58 percent are women, 70 percent are between the ages of thirty-five and sixty, and 72 percent have children. Internationaler Volkssport Verband (IVV; International Federation of Popular Sports) has served since 1968 as an umbrella organization for noncompetitive volkssport and volkswalks, sports for all, friends of nature activities, and popular tourism in about thirty countries, with women and families forming the core membership.

Popular horseback riding is a special case that is a favorite sport of young girls in some European and Scandinavian nations. As a noncompetitive sport with about 80 percent of participants being girls, it provides an alternative to aristocratic and military riding and to the predominant image of riding as a competitive sport.

The third stage in the modern emergence of volkssport began in the 1970s and initially was linked to the "new movement" and "new games" sport and physical activity movements. These movements began in California to promote noncompetitive play and were connected to the anti–Vietnam War movement. The new games movement appealed especially to women because it emphasized the process of play rather than the result, as well as social interaction, physical creativity, and fun.

At about the same time in several European nations, many people became interested in reviving and preserving traditional folk culture, and part of that culture was sports and games. From the 1970s on, these sports and games were played at national and regional festivals. Information from the Flemish Folk Games File and the Vlaamse Volkssport Centrale in Leuven provides a profile of male and female participation in Flanders from 1969 to 1989. Most participants are elderly, lower-class men from urban areas. Some folk games included no women at all and women participated in a ratio of one to ten in bowling games, shooting games, and animal games; women were somewhat better represented in pub games (22 percent) and throwing games (25 percent). In no sports were there more women than men, but female participation was more than 40 percent in *trou madame* (a game with bowls and arches), *struifvogel* (bird darts), *gansrijden* (goose pulling), and *sjoelbak* (shuffleboard). Clearly, the imbalance was sociocultural in origin and, as with the traditional folk culture, was the result of the strongly competitive character of the games and their association with an ideology of ethnic nationalism.

In contrast, many more women take part in the Danish traditional games movement that began in the 1980s. Women form 60 percent of young instructors of folk games and are active participants in local folk festivals. The International Sport and Culture Association was founded in 1995 and, under female leadership, serves as the umbrella organization for volkssport, popular gymnastics, and festivities in about fifty countries; it advocates joint male-female participation.

Other new developments in the spread of modern volkssports also suggest more involvement by women. For example, *capoeira*, a traditionally male Afro-Brazilian sport, has become popular among young people in European cities, such as Amsterdam and Copenhagen, especially among girls and young women. Similarly, the more competitive form of modern *wushu*—historically based on male warrior training—is now practiced by women, some of whom competed in the first world wushu championship in Beijing in 1990. Additionally, immigrant cultures have (re)invented new dance forms like the *bhangra* of the South Asians in Britain. These events give young women and men a chance to meet and contribute to the process of maintaining their ethnic identity. Conversely, Western practices also change as they spread; disco has appeared in China as *disike*, old people's disco, and is especially popular among elderly women.

The emergence of modern volkssport also has political implications as in some nations it has been a component of ethnic nationalism and statehood. For example, as the Soviet Union began to dissolve in 1989, folk games and sports that were repressed in the Soviet era were revived in the Baltic nations, in Central Asia, and among indigenous peoples in Siberia. Women played important roles in the reemergence of the popular festivals, games, and sports that provided an alternative to the male-dominated Soviet sports regime.

CONCLUSION

Volkssport in its modern forms does not have one pattern of male-female participation. Rather, the nature and extent of female participation continues, as in the past, to be determined by the nature of the sports and the political and social contexts. Whereas modern sports can be defined, at least in a theoretical sense, as existing without involvement by women, volkssport must involve women. Where volkssport emphasizes the physical experience and process over competition and victory, it is especially attractive to women or may itself even be part of the women's movement.

Henning Eichberg

See also Sokol Movement

Bibliography

Brownell, Susan. (1995) *Training the Body for China.* Chicago: The University of Chicago Press.

Eichberg, Henning. (1995) "Body Culture and Democratic Nationalism: 'Popular Gymnastics' in 19th-century Denmark." *The International Journal of the History of Sport* 12, 2: 108–124.

Guttmann, Allen. (1991) *Women's Sports: A History.* New York: Columbia University Press.

———. (1996) *The Erotic in Sports.* New York: Columbia University Press.

Hargreaves, Jennifer. (1989) "Urban Dance Styles and Self-Identities: The Specific Case of Bhangra." In *Körperkulturen und Identität,* edited by Henning Eichberg and Jørn Hansen. Münster, Germany: Lit, 149–160.

Hauser, Michael. (c. 1991) *Traditional Greenlandic Music.* Copenhagen/Sisimiut: Kragen/ULO.

Hellspong, Mats. (1989) "Traditional Sports on the Island of Gotland." *Scandinavian Journal of Sports Sciences* 11, 1: 29–34.

Møller, Jørn. (1984) "Sports and Old Village Games in Denmark." *Canadian Journal of History of Sport* 15, 2: 19–29.

Nabokov, Peter. (1987) *Indian Running: Native American History and Tradition.* Santa Barbara, CA: Capra, 1981. Reprint, Santa Fe. NM: Ancient City 1987.

Palos, Cristóbal Moreno. (1992) *Juegos y Deportes Tradicionales en Espana.* Madrid: Alianza Deporte/Consejo Superior de Deportes.

Pfister, Gertrud, ed. (1997) "Traditional Games." *Journal of Comparative Physical Education and Sport* 19, 2 (Special issue).

———, Toni Niewerth, and Gerd Steins, eds. (1996) *Spiele der Welt im Spannungsfeld von Tradition und Moderne.* 2d ISHPES Congress Games of the World. Sankt Augustin: Academia.

Radford, Peter F. (1996) "Women's Foot-Races in the 18th and 19th Centuries: A Popular and Widespread Practice." In *Welt der Spiele: Politische, Soziale und Pädagogische Aspekte* edited by André Gounot, Toni Niewerth, and Gertrud Pfister. Sankt Augustin: Academia, 58–63.

Renson, Roland, Eddy De Cramer, and Erik De Vroede. (1997) "Local Heroes: Beyond the Stereotype of the Participants in Traditional Games." *International Review for the Sociology of Sport* 32, 1: 59–68.

Springhall, John. (1977) *Youth, Empire and Society: British Youth Movements, 1883–1940*. London: Croom; and Hamden, CT: Archon.

Tatz, Colin. (1995) *Obstacle Race: Aborigines in Sport*. Sydney: University of New South Wales Press.

Veijola, Soile. (1994) "Metaphors of Mixed Team Play." *International Review for the Sociology of Sport* 29, 1: 31–49.

VOLLEYBALL

Volleyball is a team sport in which opposing players use their hands to volley a ball back and forth across a high net, with points scored when a team fails to return the ball. Created by and for males, volleyball nevertheless has become a major recreational sport with mixed-sex teams, and significant numbers of women take part in competitive volleyball at all levels. Volleyball has now evolved into two sports, both competed at the Olympic level—indoor volleyball and beach volleyball—with the former covered here and the latter in a separate article.

HISTORY

Volleyball was invented in Holyoke, Massachusetts, in 1895 by William G. Morgan, director of physical education in the Young Men's Christian Association (YMCA). Concerned that the businessmen who played basketball for leisure would overexert themselves, Morgan decided to modify basketball for an aging, less fit population. Volleyball's origins have had a strong positive influence on the sport's recreational value by encouraging a broad base of participation with less intense competition and fewer physical demands.

At the same time, in many instances, this view of volleyball has contributed to its status as a secondary sport, and one that represents weakness, frailty, and passivity. Perceived to lack the male sports' values of strength, power, and dominance, volleyball has been viewed as a female sport. This has curtailed both its acceptance and its development, particularly in North America.

The recreational game of volleyball first introduced through the YMCA was exported in the early 1900s with the start of World War I. Many of the instructors from YMCAs were recruited into the armed forces as physical training personnel. Following the war, volleyball grew in popularity across Europe, but it was not until after World War II that the sport became sufficiently organized to warrant an international governing body. In 1946 the Fédération Internationale de Volleyball (FIVB) was established. Located in Lausanne, Switzerland, this organization has become a powerful voice for volleyball, boasting a current membership of 210 national federations and representing an estimated 800 million people playing volleyball throughout the world. The responsibilities of the FIVB include organizing international championships, adopting and improving rules of play, instructing and certifying referees and coaches, and generally promoting the game worldwide.

VOLLEYBALL AS A WOMEN'S SPORT

Several characteristics of the game of volleyball make it particularly acceptable, culturally, for women. As a noncontact sport, it contains no physical violence, and tradition has instilled an aura of courtesy, cooperation, and congeniality that portrays volleyball as a gentle sport. The rules are generic, except for the net height.

Certain aspects distinguish the women's game from the men's. These differences affect decisions made about the organization, promotion, and marketing of the game. The greater size, strength, and jump height of male players generates a breathtaking game of power. Although the women's net game is also spectacular, it has developed into a contest marked by greater finesse, stronger defense, and generally longer rallies than the men's game. While the rules, strategies, and overall structure of the sport remain similar, the end product of skill development and training creates the appearance of a somewhat different game. The attack, too, is a point at which differences emerge between the women's and the more aggressive men's game.

COMPETITIVE VOLLEYBALL

Volleyball has become recognized as a highly competitive sport. Introduced to the Olympic program in Tokyo in 1964, the game continued to develop in both speed and power. It was here that volleyball received worldwide exposure and respect as a demanding sport. Competitive volleyball became known as power volleyball to distinguish it from its recreational heritage.

The Japanese women's style of play, in particular, became the impetus for the changes in volleyball that have taken place since the 1960s. The Japanese women introduced the creative offense that used a greater variety of sets and included more hitters in each offensive play. They moved the game from a static and predictable pattern of play to a dynamic and unpredictable style that added excitement and intrigue. Recognizing that controlling the powerful attack from taller opponents was essential to executing their planned offense, they also used innovative defense strategy. They introduced the skill of extending and rolling to retrieve a ball. This required that players, low to the ground, leave their feet to get their hand between the ball and the floor, allowing them to take up more space defensively. The roll was developed to allow the players to recover quickly and return to action. Defense was incorporated as a strategy that extended rallies; it demanded more of the players and required greater preparation for intense competition. Thus, a recreational game with American roots shifted its focus. The fast, powerful, and competitive Japanese women also exposed the world to a new height of female athleticism.

A women's volleyball match at the University of California at Los Angeles. In the 1990s, women's volleyball became a major recreational, intercollegiate, and international amateur and professional sport. (Phil Schermeister/Corbis)

RECENT TRENDS

Today's game loosely represents a combination of the two styles. Taller players are again beginning to dominate the sport but only when they also possess the speed, agility, and athletic prowess formerly identified with smaller players.

Success has not been without cost to the players and has a darker side. Rigorous training is necessary, but the Japanese women's team may have been subjected to training that would be considered abuse by today's standards. Coach Daimatsu Hirofumi expected players, after working a full day for the company that sponsored their team, to practice for several hours, seven days a week, 365 days a year. Daimatsu's coaching style included verbal and physical tirades to motivate players to higher levels of performance. Practices were demanding, and many criticized the coach for his treatment of his players. In spite of this, his coaching style was widely imitated internationally. This hierarchical structure for the player-coach relationship—powerless-powerful—became a model followed at all levels of play around the world.

GENDER AND CONTROL

For the women's game, this era may have provided the backdrop for sexual harassment in the sport of volleyball. Many powerful male coaches and administrators, socialized to male sport values of dominance, control, and excellence at any cost, condoned this style of coaching for their programs. When exploitation of female vulnerabilities combines with athletes' dependence on coaches, sexual harassment becomes a risk within a system that, wittingly or unwittingly, has created this risk.

As the major decision-making organization for both women's and men's volleyball, FIVB nevertheless fails to give women an equal voice in the process. The FIVB board has had no female members. Few nations provide women the opportunity to coach. The small number of exceptions have included the short-term appointments of Andrea Borys in the late 1960s and Betty Baxter in the early 1980s as the Canadian women's coach. The first female coach at the Olympics was the Hungarian coach at the 1976 Montreal Games. Another major exception is China, where Lan Ping has served as the only female head coach for a national volleyball team. In 1984 at the Los Angeles Olympics, she was declared the best power hitter in the world. When she retired as a player, Lan Ping did some coaching at New Mexico State University in the United States before returning to China as national coach. She also served as national team coach at the 1996 Atlanta Olympics.

Historically, women and men have not been equally represented in competition. The first Olympics hosted ten men's and six women's teams. At the world championships, there are twenty-four men's teams compared to sixteen women's teams; this means potentially 288 male players compared to 192 female players. Recent changes have eliminated this difference in the number of teams, but a new regulation is likely to bring a return of this discrepancy; the new rule will allow an increase in female entries for outdoor (beach) volleyball on the condition that female indoor team rosters be reduced by one. Efforts to develop equitably one female sport have been supported at the expense of opportunities for women in another sport.

SOCIAL ASPECTS

With Title IX of the 1972 Education Amendments in the United States, volleyball took a forward leap. One of the advantages of volleyball's reputation as a girls' and women's sport was that it often received priority status when there were attempts to achieve equity. Program funding, athletic scholarships, coaching expertise, and facility and equipment upgrades all represented injections into varsity programs for high school and college females in order to comply with legislation that dictated athletic equity as a component of educational equity. Since volleyball was present, albeit at a minimal level, and since it was viewed as a feminine sport, socially acceptable for females, it was one of the first to benefit from the infusion of funds. In most regions of the United States, women's volleyball was leading the development of the sport. The United States Volleyball Association (USVBA), now titled USA Volleyball, established a training center for its women's team in Texas, an expression of commitment to the game and an acknowledgment that the team could be an international contender. As the founder of the game, the United States was in the process of trying to reclaim the sport, wresting it from the grip of European and Asian dominance.

As a major female sport, volleyball would seem likely to sustain a professional league for women. Indeed, successful leagues already oper-

LEGACY OF FLO HYMAN

In the United States, 2 February is designated as National Girls and Women in Sport Day. The Day was established in honor of Flo Hyman, the volleyball player who was a member of the 1984 U.S. Olympic silver medal team. Hyman played professional volleyball in Japan where she died suddenly on 24 January 1986 of a ruptured aorta caused by Marfan Syndrome. In addition to being a world-class athlete, Hyman promoted women's participation in sports, and the Day was established for that same purpose and to provide a time to take stock each year of women's progress in gaining equality in sports. The Day is sponsored by the Girls Scouts of USA, Girls Incorporated, the National Association of Girls and Women in Sport, the Women's Sports Foundation, and the YWCA of America.

ate for both women and men in Europe and in Brazil. But similar attempts to market the sport professionally in North America have failed. This is surprising considering the explosion of attendance records in collegiate women's volleyball. In 1995 the sport's popularity was marked by record attendance, with 3.9 million spectators over the season. It was the third consecutive season for the National Collegiate Athletic Association (NCAA) Division I to surpass 1.5 million fans. The top university for attendance was the University of Hawaii, averaging over 6,000 spectators per match. The 1997 NCAA championships held in Spokane, Washington, had a crowd of 10,792 for the championship match. Yet this popularity has yet to translate into professional appeal.

Chinese women playing volleyball, 1923. (Christiansen/Levinson)

RULES AND PLAY

Six players cooperate in the task of directing an inflated ball back and forth over a net. As the skills of the game developed, the net height has been changed accordingly, with the playing height for women 2.24 meters compared to 2.43 meters for men. The official volleyball, introduced in 1900, is now used only in that sport. Made of leather, the volleyball is lighter and smaller than the original basketball bladder.

The physical playing environment has become well defined over the years. The court dimensions are 18 × 9 meters with the 18-meter length divided into two equal sides by the net. Antennae, pliable batons, have been added to the net, and an attack line has been established, drawn 3 meters away and parallel to the center court line.

As the sport developed and the offense got stronger, it was necessary to regulate the attack in a manner that allowed a balance between offense and defense. This rule change controlled the offense to make it more predictable and easier to defend against at a time when offense was beginning to overpower defense, shorten the rally, and reduce the game's appeal to spectators. Also known as the 3-meter line, the attack line serves to limit back row players by allowing them to attack the ball from a contact point above the height of the net only if their takeoff is from behind this line.

A volleyball competition is a match composed of the best of five or the best of three games (sets). Since its inception, the rules of volleyball have changed dramatically. One of the few original elements to remain is that a server, the right back player, puts the ball into play by hitting the ball over the net into the opponent's court from behind the court's end line. Play continues until one team accomplishes the objective of directing the ball to the floor on the opponent's side of the net. A team can contact the ball up to three times, exclusive of a blocking contact, to return the ball to the opponent's court.

In today's game, a server can serve from anywhere behind the 9-meter width of the court. A variety of techniques may be used: a simple underhand serve, an overhand serve, and the jump serve; the last two maximize the offensive nature of the serve.

A winner is declared when a team reaches 15 points with a 2-point advantage. In the event of a tie score such as 14–14, play continues until one team has a 2-point advantage or reaches 17 points, whichever comes first. The exception to this occurs in the deciding set of the match, when a team must win by 2 points and the 17-point cap is disregarded.

The objective of the game of volleyball is to win a rally, which in turn will win your team a side-out or a point and, what is just as important, prevent the opponent from getting points. The evolution of offense has moved from the original batting the ball over the net to very complex systems of play. The year 1916 marked the combined introduction of a set, placing the ball with a high trajectory close to the net for a teammate, and a spike, striking the set ball down into the opponent's court from a position above the height of the net. Today the offense includes many different sets placed by the setter, a very specialized and skilled player, along the net at various heights and many different locations for front court players, as well as along the attack line for back court players. In this way the setter can incorporate all five players in an offensive strategy, making an attack less predictable and harder to defend against. This offensive attack has become a vital part of the game's appeal to both players and spectators.

FUTURE RULES AND PLAY

New rules for the sport are normally introduced immediately following each Olympiad although the process of change is ongoing. Between Olympic years, the FIVB experiments with ideas to improve volleyball. Some significant rule changes went into effect at the 1998 world championships. The traditional white ball was replaced with a blue, yellow, and white-paneled ball for men and a pink ball for women. Head coaches in the past were strictly confined to the seat closest to the scorer's table. The new rules permit them to encourage or instruct players on the court while walking or standing within the free zone in front of the team bench from the extension of the attack line up to the warm-up area, provided they do not obstruct or delay the match. A player known as a Libero can be designated as a defensive specialist and included in the list of twelve players registered on the score sheet. This specialist, wearing a shirt of a different color than that of his or her teammates, is restricted to playing as a back row player, cannot attack a ball above the height of the net, may not serve, and may not block or attempt to block. The Libero may enter or leave the game at any time while the ball is out of play and before the whistle for service but may not participate in regular substitutions. Substitutions involving the Libero are unlimited and will not count among the regular substitutions.

Rule changes are often introduced to increase the spectator appeal of the game and thus improve the marketability of the sport. In addition, rule change decisions are often based on what is best for the men's game, where the rules are usually tested first. Some examples of these changes in volleyball are: the rule that was introduced to disallow blocking the serve, a skill that had a more negative impact on the men's game; the rule allowing a double hit on the first contact, necessary to guarantee some defense in the men's game that was already present in the women's game; and the rule eliminating the serving zone, to allow serving across the entire back court line. These rules are generally applied to create a better balance between offense and defense in the men's game and to extend the rallies for spectator appeal. Although some of the changes may be good for the women's game as well, others may not.

Several new competitive formats are being considered in an attempt to package volleyball matches into a two-hour block for media convenience. These proposals include: (1) a two-set format composed of the best of three 21-point games within a set. All games would be rally point. In the case of a tie in sets, a single 15-point tiebreaker is played; (2) a best of five sets of 25 rally points each, with the fifth and deciding set of 15 points; (3) existing rules with a bonus point for successfully scoring on a 3-meter line attack; and (4) existing rules with a 25-minute time limit for each set.

The 1998 championships also marked the first time that financial reward for participants became part of that competition. The sum of $500,000 was distributed in the men's and women's competitions, recognizing both team achievement and individual achievement. The highest award of $100,000 went to the best player of the competition, and the best attacker, blocker, server, receiver, setter, digger, and top scorer each received $50,000. The most successful coach and the most imaginative coach each received an award of $25,000.

Uniforms have been further standardized. New regulations mandate that shirts and shorts should not be loose or baggy but should follow the body line and that women (with no mention of men) are allowed to wear one-piece uniforms. The body-line rule is undeniably a component of the marketing strategy of female athletes in general, and specifically the female volleyball player, by emphasizing their shape. Males, in contrast, are marketed on qualities of physical athleticism.

In spite of many changes that have advanced women's worldwide participation and recognition in volleyball, limitations remain that prevent full equality. Leadership positions remain dominated by males. It is a rare occasion anywhere in the world when an onlooker will see a female referee, or even an umpire, at a significant competition. Female performance continues to be judged on male standards. Gender testing is mandatory for female athletes only, suggesting that if you are too good, your femininity is questionable or you must be a man. This acts as a strong deterrent to women who aspire to athletic excellence. While most female volleyball players never reach the level of competition where they must biologically prove their sex, they are reminded that they must socially prove their gender on a regular basis. The social contradiction between athleticism (masculinity) and femininity discourages many women from reaching their athletic potential.

In spite of this, volleyball holds promise as a potential means of opening doors for women. As the sport gains respectability and as females achieve athletic success, each can promote the other's cause and benefit both. Many obstacles remain, but the rewards for females as future volleyball players, coaches, officials, administrators, and fans make the struggle for change worthwhile.

Margery Holman

Bibliography

Bertucci, Bob. (1979) *Championship Volleyball*. West Point, NY: Leisure Press.

Bratton, Robert D. (1972) *Canadian Volleyball: A History to 1967*. Vanier, Canada: Canadian Volleyball Association.

Scates, Allen E. (1976) *Winning Volleyball*. Boston: Allyn and Bacon.

Volleyball Canada. (1993–1994) *Volleyball Canada Rule Book*. Gloucester: Volleyball Canada.

Volleyball Worldwide. (1999) <http://www.volleyball.org>.

VOLLEYBALL, BEACH

Beach volleyball, in all its many variations, is similar to indoor volleyball in its structure and rules of play. The Fédération Internationale de Volleyball (FIVB) defines the sport as competition between teams of two players each. Unlike indoor volleyball, there are no coaches to help facilitate this process and there is only one teammate to rely on.

During the 1920s, 1930s, and 1940s volleyball began to be played on the beaches of southern California and Europe. By the 1950s and 1960s there were reports of tournaments in the United States, Brazil, Canada, and France, and in other parts of Europe. The appearance of women at competitive beach volleyball events was often as "beauty contestants" and not as athletic competitors. However, by the 1970s women's beach volleyball competitions became more popular. By the 1980s the United States and Australia had begun offering national tournaments for women; and once beach volleyball became an Olympic sport in 1996, many countries began providing competitive opportunities for women.

In the 1990s the FIVB, with 214 affiliated national federations, governed international beach volleyball and volleyball. From its beginnings in 1992, the FIVB world tour—formally known as the World Championship Series—the official international tour, grew rapidly.

HISTORY

Organized women's beach volleyball has been played in southern California since the 1950s. In fact, the United States was one of the first countries to develop a women's professional tour and a women's players association—the Women's Professional Volleyball Association (WPVA). The WPVA was founded in 1986 and was led by Nina Mathies, who was also a player. The purpose of the WPVA was to administer, govern, and protect the integrity of women's professional beach volleyball in the United States.

The WPVA tour started in 1987 with ten events, almost $50,000 in total prize money, and the top player earning about $8,500. Because of this minimal earning potential, many of the athletes maintained a regular job while participating in weekend tournaments. Ten years later, in 1996, the WPVA had grown to fifteen events with over $900,000 in total prize money and a top player who earned over $88,000. In 1998 the WPVA and its tour began to struggle and, for the first time in over ten years, there was no tour sanctioned by the WPVA. The WPVA was dissolved in 1998.

American beach volleyball player Holly McPeak serves in a match at "Atlanta Beach" at the 1996 Summer Olympics, the first time the sport was included in the Olympic Games. (Wally McNamee/Corbis)

The formation of the WPVA, the competitive tour that developed as a result of the WPVA, and the popularity of the sport in the United States played a major role in the development of the sport worldwide. The United States also began organizing a national tour devoted to four-person volleyball. Four-versus-four events, nationally televised and sponsored by large corporations, helped to increase the exposure of beach volleyball. Because of the increased media exposure for the four-person game, some of the athletes who competed on this tour grew in popularity and began to promote beach volleyball outside of competitions. Gabrielle Reese is one example. Reese not only began writing magazine articles but also regularly hosted television shows for MTV (Music Television). Her popularity, as well as that of other athletes, made all the variations of beach volleyball widely recognized and watched throughout the world.

The WPVA competitions in the United States drew many international players, who came to develop their skills and gain valuable experience. For example, Jackie Silva, one of the Olympic gold medalists in Atlanta in 1996, spent four years on the WPVA tour, from 1987 to 1991.

In 1992 the FIVB recognized that providing opportunities for women as well as men was essential for global development of the sport and its acceptance by the Olympic community, and 1992–1993 became the inaugural season for international women's beach volleyball. The world tour had two stops, just over thirty athletes representing eight countries, and a total of $100,000 in prize money—with women receiving half the prize money that men received at each world tour event. Since that season, the world tour has grown spectacularly. By 1998 the tour had nine stops, more than 300 athletes representing thirty some countries, and over $1.4 million in prize money—with women and men receiving equal prize money at each world tour event.

Beach volleyball athletes, like so many others, were now earning money from advertising. Women now found it possible to make careers out of playing beach volleyball. Players were able to advertise their own sponsors on their competition suits, hats or visors, and washable tattoos.

Given the importance of the WPVA tour in the development of women's beach volleyball, it is not surprising that American women set the standards in the early years of the FIVB world tour. The first beach volleyball event for women sanctioned by the FIVB took place in 1992 at the Almería, Spain, "Olympic Year Tournament." The winners of that event were Karolyn Kirby and Nancy Reno from the United States. This same duo went on to win the second FIVB women's event held in Rio de Janeiro in February 1993, and each of them has won numerous events since then.

At both the Almería event and the Rio world championships, ten women's teams were competing for $50,000 in prize money. The United States dominated these events by finishing in the top four places. The other countries that competed during that first 1992–1993 season were

Australia, Germany, Cuba, Japan, Hungary, and Spain.

Since the beginning of the FIVB world tour, Brazilian athletes have competed at a level with the American women. From the first event in 1992 to the end of the 1998 season, the FIVB had sanctioned fifty women's world tour events. The United States took the lead for the first twenty-five events (1992–1996), winning fifteen while Brazil won the other ten. From 1996 to 1998, Brazil took the lead, winning twenty of twenty-five events, while the United States won four and Australia one.

Australia was the first country to consistently join Brazil and United States at the top of the sport. Natalie Cook and Kerri-Ann Pottharst won silver at the 1996 Rio de Janeiro event. This win paved the way for their bronze medal performance at the Atlanta Olympics. This same team went on to win the 1996 Osaka, Japan, event and became the only non-United States, non-Brazilian team to win an FIVB world tour event. Pottharst has the most top-three finishes by a player from a country other than the United States and Brazil. From 1993 to 1998, she finished in the top four places twelve times and had seven top-three appearances—one gold medal, three silver medals, and three bronze medals.

Other nations began to challenge the United States and Brazil by breaking into the top four places at an FIVB world tour event in the 1994–1995 season. The Japanese team of Sachiko Fujita and Yukiko Takahashi finished fourth at Osaka. Takahashi has finished in the top four places at an FIVB world tour event three times, including one silver medal. Germany followed in this path when Beate Bühler and Danja Müsch won the bronze medal at the Brisbane, Australia, event in 1995. Thereafter, Müsch finished in the top four at an FIVB world tour event seven times, with three silver medals and one bronze. Newer still on the international scene, the Italian team of Laura Bruschini and Anna Maria Solazzi had three fourth-place finishes at the end of the 1998 world tour season.

Only one year after the first women's beach event sanctioned by the FIVB, beach volleyball was declared an Olympic sport. On 24 September 1993, Juan Antonio Samaranch welcomed beach volleyball as an Olympic sport for the 1996 Atlanta Olympics, with eighteen women's teams and twenty-four men's teams scheduled to compete.

At the first Olympic beach volleyball match, at 8 A.M. on 23 July 1996, Brigette Lesage and Anabelle Prawerman of France played Mayra Huerta Hernandez and Velia Eguiluz Soto of Mexico. This start of the Olympic beach volleyball event at the Atlanta Olympics had over 9,000 spectators. On 27 July 1996, Jackie Silva and Sandra Pires of Brazil made history by winning the first-ever Olympic gold medal in beach volleyball, defeating fellow Brazilians Monica Rodrigues and Adriana Samuel. The gold medal won by Silva and Pires was also Brazil's first Olympic gold medal in a women's sport. Natalie Cook and Kerri-Ann Pottharst of Australia won the bronze medal by defeating the pair of Linda Hanley and Barbra Fontana from the United States.

Prior to the Olympics, beach volleyball had made its first appearance at multisport international games at the 1994 Goodwill Games in St. Petersburg, Russia. Karolyn Kirby and Liz Masakayan of the United States won the gold medal by defeating Monica Rodrigues and Adriana Samuel of Brazil. At the 1998 Goodwill Games in New York, Brazilians Adriana Behar and Shelda Bede won the gold after defeating Pottharst and Pauline Manser of Australia. Beach volleyball was also added to the roster of sports at the 1999 Pan-American Games in Winnipeg, Canada. At the 2000 Olympic Summer Games in Sydney, Australia, twenty-four women's teams were expected to take to the sand alongside twenty-four men's teams.

RULES AND PLAY

A distinct feature of beach volleyball lies in the formation of teams. Unlike other sports teams, beach volleyball teams are not contracted for a specified length of time. Players are able to switch teams as often as they like. Often these changes are due to injuries and sometimes to differences between teammates. Players can play with one teammate one week and another the next. Any team that involves only two people working together is very challenging, and beach volleyball is no exception. Keeping partnerships together is not an easy task. The relationship between the two players can become very complicated and may interfere with the ability of the individual players to communicate and work together. Beach volleyball is an interesting combination of a team and an individual sport.

Beach volleyball is played on the same size court with the same net height as indoor volleyball except that it is played in sand 35–40 centimeters deep, and it is played with a slightly bigger ball. The full playing court is 18 × 9 meters and divided by a net into two equal size courts. The top of the net is 2.24 meters (2.43 for men) from the ground. The area around the playing court is called the "free zone" and is usually 3–5 meters wide. A line, 5–8cm wide, marks the playing court. This line is part of the court and, if the ball lands on the line, it is considered in bounds. As with indoor volleyball, the boundary of the court is extended up along the net. Two antennae are placed on the net where the sideline crosses under it. The antennae identify where the court boundary is located on the net. If the ball touches the antenna, it is considered out of bounds. The ball is specifically designed for outdoor use and is slightly larger and slightly softer than the indoor volleyball.

The standard play for beach volleyball is between two teams of two players. Otherwise, it is similar, but not identical, to indoor volleyball. A rally is initiated by a serve from anywhere in the area bounded by the 9-meter end of a team's playing court (baseline) and the extensions of the two 18-meter sidelines of the court. Each player has only one attempt to serve the ball and a "net" serve is a fault. Four common types of serves are overhand float, spike, underhand sky, and standing topspin serves. The server continues to serve until the opponent wins the rally. If the serving team wins the rally, it is awarded a point; if the receiving team wins the rally, there is a "side-out" and the receiving team wins the right to serve. When a team "regains" service, the serve alternates between players from the same team.

Players are allowed to move freely within their court area, and there is no distinction between the front and back court. Since there is no centerline under the net, players can go under the net as long as they do not interfere with their opponents. Players do not "rotate" from one position to the other as in indoor volleyball. During a rally the ball can be contacted by any part of the body. The maximum number of contacts allowed on each side is three. A block counts as a contact. The usual sequence of contacts is "pass" (forearm pass or dig), "set" (volley or overhand pass), and "attack" (hit or spike) over the net. The attack cannot be completed with the use of an open-handed tip. If the ball is set, or volleyed over the net to the opponents, it must be set perpendicular to the shoulders of the player setting the ball. In beach volleyball there are no substitutions allowed. During every match, each team has two time-outs of 30 seconds. Teams also switch sides at every multiple of 5 points (4–1, 6–4, etc.), with a 30-second rest between side changes.

A variety of scoring systems are used for beach volleyball. The standard scoring system on the FIVB world tour is a one-set match played to 15 points, with at least a two-point lead required for victory, to a maximum of 17 points (victory by one point is possible at 17–16). Teams can score points only when they are serving.

WOMEN OFFICIALS, COACHES, AND ADMINISTRATORS

The first female official to be assigned by the FIVB was Patty Salvatore from the United States in 1996. That same year, at the Atlanta Olympic Games, four of the twelve officials selected to officiate were women: Mireia Carreño Goma of Spain, Sue Lemaire and Salvatore of the United States, and María Amélia Villas-Bõas of Brazil. In 1998 there were over ninety FIVB international beach volleyball officials, about twelve of them women, including two refereeing delegates.

The refereeing delegate is appointed by the FIVB and is responsible for the overall coordination of all refereeing duties at a competition, ensuring that the competition on the field of play runs smoothly and according to FIVB guidelines. This responsibility involves working with the event staff to ensure the management of referees and all court personnel. In 1998 there were 10 FIVB refereeing delegates and two of them, Salvatore and Villas-Bõas, were women.

The technical supervisor is the highest authority appointed by the FIVB for world tour events. The technical supervisor coordinates all aspects of the event and is responsible for ensuring that all the FIVB guidelines are followed and that the event runs smoothly. In 1998 there were twelve technical supervisors, and four of them were women: Rita Crockett of the United States and Switzerland, Joséfina Capote of Cuba, Roseann Kuryla of the United States, and Jackie Murdoch of Australia.

The FIVB recognizes the importance of athlete involvement in decision making. Since the first women's event, there has been a player adviser to the FIVB. The women's player adviser serves as a member of the FIVB's permanent committee and world council, the major decision-making bodies with respect to the world tour. In 1992 Karolyn Kirby of the United States was recognized as the first women's player adviser to the FIVB, and she served until 1995. She was followed by Angela Rock of the United States in 1996 and Kristine Drakich of Canada in 1997.

Coaches are not allowed to coach during competition at FIVB beach volleyball events. For this reason and because, in the 1990s, beach volleyball was a relatively new sport internationally, it was very difficult to determine the number of coaching opportunities or how many coaches of athletes and teams were female. The selection of coaches was often made by individual athletes or teams. Many teams chose women as coaches, including Adriana Behar and Shelda Bede of Brazil, the top-ranked team in 1998.

Although beach volleyball is a relatively new sport, since its inception in the 1920s, it has grown into a highly competitive sport in which women from around the world have made successful careers for themselves as professional athletes, coaches, and various types of officials.

Kristine Drakich

Bibliography

"Beach Volleyball." (1993) *VolleyWorld* 5: 2–7.

"Beach Volleyball Women." (1996) *VolleyWorld* 4: 38–48.

Beach Volleyball World Championships Program—September 10–13, 1997. (1997) CA: Design Optional.

"Beach Volleyball World Tour, An Unforgettable Year." (1997) *VolleyWorld* 5: 24–29.

Fédération Internationale de Volleyball. (1996) *Olympic Beach Volleyball Teams' Information and Media Guide*. Lausanne, Switzerland: FIVB.

———. (1996) *Beach Volleyball Official Rules: 1996–2000*. Lausanne, Switzerland: FIVB.

———. (1998) *FIVB World Tour Results 1992–1998*. Lausanne, Switzerland: FIVB.

"Great Excitement for the World Tour." (1998) *VolleyWorld* 1: 4–11.

Rizzo, Pietro. (1996) *100 Years of Global Link: Volleyball Centennial 1895–1995*. Lausanne, Switzerland: FIVB.

"Special Beach Volleyball: A Dream Just One Step from Becoming a Reality." (1993) *VolleyWorld* 1: 12–39.

Additional information was provided by Natalie Cook, Liz Masakayan, and Kerri-Ann Pottharst.

WADE, VIRGINIA

(1945–)

BRITISH TENNIS PLAYER

One of the world's most successful tennis players, Virginia Wade has won tournaments and titles around the world. On the court, she was known as much for her stormy temper as for her strong play. Ironically, the most prestigious tennis title of her homeland eluded her for many years. Victory was especially sweet, therefore, when she won at Wimbledon in 1977, the year of Queen Elizabeth's Silver Jubilee.

Sarah Virginia Wade was born in Bournemouth, England, on 7 October 1945. Less than a year later, her parents moved to South Africa. As a child, Wade participated in and demonstrated skill at many sports, but it was not until the age of nine that she found an old racket and became interested in tennis. Wade spent hours hitting a ball against the wall of her parents' house. This practice paid off and Wade played with success on her school teams. When she was fifteen, her parents returned to England, where she felt that the coaching and facilities were inferior to what was offered in South Africa. She continued to play tennis, however, and in 1962 she won the British junior championships at Wimbledon.

After she graduated from Sussex University in 1966 with a degree in mathematics and physics, her career began to gain momentum. At her first U.S. Open championship in 1968, she defeated the legendary Billie Jean King and became the first British woman in thirty-eight years to hold the U.S. championship title. Wade was a member of the Wightman Cup team from 1965 until 1971. This tournament between U.S. and British women had historically been dominated by the United States, but Wade led the 1968 British team to victory. Throughout the early 1970s, Wade continued

Virginia Wade holds up the trophy for winning the 1977 Wimbledon Women's Singles Championship. Beside her stands her opponent Betty Stove of the Netherlands, the Duke of Kent, tournament chairman Sir Brian Burnett, and Queen Elizabeth. (Bettmann/Corbis)

to add championship titles to her name. She was the Rothmans Cup winner in 1967, 1968, 1973, and 1974. In 1971 she added the Italian championship to her credits. The Australian and Argentinean titles came the following year. The only championship that seemed always to elude her was Wimbledon. Eight years after her U.S. Open title, Wade was still unable to progress beyond the semifinals at Wimbledon. It was said that she choked whenever she appeared at Wimbledon. She was also stigmatized by the nickname "wild woman," given to her by other players on the circuit. Her outward displays of temper on the court were as notorious as her strong serve, and throughout her career Wade was constantly warned against breaches of tennis etiquette.

In 1977 the much-coveted Wimbledon title went to Wade when she defeated Betty Stove of the Netherlands 4–6, 6–3, 6–1 in the finals. Queen Elizabeth, who was at the match that year, presented Wade with the Wimbledon trophy. That same year, British sports journalists named Wade

Sportswoman of the Year. Throughout her career, Wade also enjoyed success as a doubles player. She was one of the first five female tennis players to earn over a million dollars in prize money.

In 1981 Wade began to place more emphasis on her career with the British Broadcasting Corporation and less on the tennis circuit. She played in the 1983 Wimbledon "just for fun" and reached the quarterfinals.

J. P. Anderson

Bibliography

Barrett, John. (1984) *World of Tennis 1984*. London: Willow Books.

Emery, David (ed). (1983) *Who's Who in International Tennis*. London: Sphere Books.

Evans, Richard. (1988) *Open Tennis*. London: Bloomsbury.

Tingay, Lance. (1973) *History of Lawn Tennis in Pictures*. London: Tom Stacey.

United States Lawn Tennis Association. (1972) *Official Encyclopedia of Tennis*. New York: Harper and Row.

Wade, Virginia, and Mary Lou Mellace. (1978) *Courting Triumph*. London: Hodder and Stoughton.

WAITZ, GRETE

(1953–)

NORWEGIAN MARATHON RUNNER

Grete Waitz was born Grete Andersen in Oslo, Norway, on 10 October 1953. During the 1970s she was one of the international athletes who made people around the world aware of long-distance running as a sport for women. Waitz helped to initiate the annual Grete Waitz Run, first held in Oslo in 1984, the biggest women-only sporting event in the world.

Already interested in running at the age of twelve, Waitz joined the Vidar Sports Club to benefit from the formal track and field training available there. Her running career began with sprinting, and she also participated in hurdling, high and low jumping, and shot put. Her first competitive

Grete Waitz (left) and two other women running in the 1986 New York City Marathon. (Joseph Sohm/Corbis)

award came at the age of thirteen in a throwing event. Her running ability first came to notice in a 300-meter cross-country race and, at the age of fourteen, she won her first race, a 400-meter cross-country event. Her club also offered her the opportunity to train at distances of up to six miles with more experienced runners, providing the foundation for her career as a long-distance runner.

Andersen became the Norwegian junior champion in the 400-and 800-meter events when she was sixteen. She set Norwegian records in the 800- and 1500-meter races at seventeen. She participated in the 1971 European championships and the 1972 Olympic Games, but did not make her mark in international competition until the 1974 European championships, when she won a bronze medal in the metric mile (1500 meters). She ran her first world record in the 3000-meter in 1975, and then lowered it to 8:45.4 in 1976, crediting some of the improvement to her 1975 marriage to Jack Waitz, a former clubmate who had become her coach. She also won the 3000-meter event at the first World Cup competition in 1977.

In 1978 Waitz was invited to the New York City Marathon, an event with 10,000 participants whose organizers longed to give it the prestige of the more established races, such as the Boston Athletic Association Marathon. With a track woman's speed and a distance runner's ability, Waitz brought honor to the New York City Marathon by setting a world record of 2:32:30 in 1978, and following it with world records of 2:27:33 in 1979 and 2:25:42 in 1980. Waitz won the New York City Marathon nine times altogether, adding a string of victories from 1982 through 1986, and then winning New York for the last time in 1988. In that year the participants in the New York City Marathon numbered 25,000. Her fastest time was 2:24:54 in the London Marathon in 1986.

Well before her retirement from serious competition, Waitz started the Grete Waitz Project to help Norwegian girls who show talent in athletics. Since 1983 she has actively helped in organizing an annual 5000-meter race for women, the Grete Waitz Run. This event emphasizes wide participation of women of all ages and abilities rather than elite runners, although in recent years the race's prize money has increasingly attracted top-level runners. Nearly 45,000 women entered the 1997 Grete Waitz Run. Their ages ranged from the teens through the nineties. Many of the older women, as well as the thousands of women who enter marathons in the United States and throughout the world, first became aware of long-distance running for women through Grete Waitz's spectacular performances in the late 1970s at the New York City Marathon.

Pamela Cooper

See also Norway

Bibliography

Averbuch, Gloria. (1998) "Grete's Great Selskap." *New York Running News* (March/April): 46.

Giller, Norman. (1984) *The 1984 Olympics Handbook.* New York: Holt, Rinehart & Winston.

Quercetani, Roberto L. (1990) *Athletics: A History of Modern Track and Field Athletics 1860–1990.* Milan, Italy: Vilardi and Associates.

Waitz, Grete, and Gloria Averbuch. (1986) *World Class.* New York: Warner Books.

WAKEBOARDING

Wakeboarding is a modern sport that combines surfing, water skiing, skateboarding, and snowboarding and that has attracted men and women athletes from all over the world. The beginnings of wakeboarding are traceable to California surfer Tony Finn, who in 1985 designed a Skurfer™ by combining a water ski and a short surfboard. Finn's creation allowed a rider to "freeboard" or "skurf," performing surfing moves on the board while it is being towed in the wave, or wake, behind a boat. Two of Finn's friends suggested that he add footstraps to the board to allow riders more freedom of movement. Eventually, water ski company owner Herb O'Brien joined with surfboard shapers to create a wakeboard that is more like a surfboard.

Today, many companies make what has evolved into the "modern" wakeboard, which has a symmetrical front-to-back shape and a "twin tail" design—one each in the front and back underneath the board—for a more balanced position when the wakeboarder is riding forward or backward.

RULES AND PLAY

Wakeboarders, or "riders," perform a variety of turns, flips, and spins called "tricks," with some riders going as high as 25 feet into the air. Wakeboarding competitions began to take shape in 1990 when Jimmy Redmon founded the World Wakeboard Association (WWA), the sport's global governing body. In 1992, World Sports & Marketing, a sports promotion and event organizer company, began to sponsor professional wakeboarding events. Today, professional wakeboarders can compete in numerous events, including the Pro Wakeboard Series, the World Wakeboard Championships, and the X Games (which consist of various so-called extreme sports). Amateur riders can participate in pro-am and other local events, with clinics sometimes offered in conjunction with competitions. These events, combined with technologically advanced equipment and sport-specific publications, have turned wakeboarding into a popular sport for pros and amateurs: wakeboarding participation has increased 111 percent from 1996 to 1998. Wakeboarders enjoy their sport around the world at all levels.

WOMEN AND WAKEBOARDING

Women are scored and ranked separately from men although they compete in the same competitions. The professional women's wakeboarding

Wakeboarder Tara Hamilton flips upside down during the women's competition at the 1998 X Games. (AP Photos)

field has competitors ranging from teenagers to riders in their mid-twenties. Tara Hamilton of the United States, a Florida high school student, competed in gymnastics for eight years before taking up wakeboarding. Training with male wakeboarder Darin Shapiro, Hamilton was ranked among the top women wakeboarders in the world just a few months after she began the sport. Andrea Gaytan, a native of Mexico City, Mexico, and a pioneer in women's wakeboarding competitions, has been competing in professional contests since they began and is still one of the top women riders. Women wakeboard champions span the globe from the United Kingdom's Emma Jones to Argentinian Gabriela Diaz.

History was made in women's wakeboarding during the 1998 X Games in San Diego, California, when eventual silver medalist and first-time participant Dana Preble performed the first "Air Raley" done by a woman. The Air Raley consists of a rider hitting the wake, swinging the wakeboard and body head over heels to cross the wake in the air, and landing on the opposite side of the wake.

In 1998 the fifteen-event Wakeboard World Cup, sanctioned by the World Wakeboard Association, was the first worldwide professional series to determine men's and women's wakeboarding champions for the season. Rankings are earned by points from each of the fifteen events. Tara Hamilton was named champion, and Dana Preble captured second place. Hamilton also took first place in the Vans Triple Crown of Wakeboarding series, an event comprising the three premier events in wakeboarding.

Cara Joy Lockman Hall

Bibliography

Geocities <http://www.geocities.com/~wake2wake/wake/final.html>.

Launch Wakeboard Magazine (1999) <http://www.launchwake.com>.

"Wake Up Call." *Eastern Surf Magazine* 6, 43: 102–106.

Wakeboard Singapore (1999) <http://home1.pacific.net.sg/~hengsim/>.

Wakeboard UK (1999) <http://www.wakeboard.co.uk>.

Wakeworld Wakeboarding Website (1999) <http://www.wakeworld.com>.

WALES *see* United Kingdom

WALKING, FITNESS

Fitness walking is probably the longest-lived women's sport of the modern era. In general, nineteenth-century medical opinion held that women were too frail to tolerate physical exertion. Only the concern for women's child-bearing potential gained them some access to recreational activity, especially after studies demonstrated that women who participated in physical education were healthier than their inactive peers. Few Victorians could object to walking as a healthful exercise for women of all classes.

HISTORY

Working-class women had always walked; for them, walking was their only method of transportation. Women of the middle and upper classes were allowed to walk at a ladylike pace, despite the restrictive day wear and strangulating foundation garments of Victorian Britain. Furthermore, walking could be pursued in suitably refined environments, such as landscaped parks. As the number of parks increased, women of all stations in life could enjoy genteel exercise among trees, flowers, and fresh air. In the nineteenth century, walking was considered an accompaniment to spiritual renewal through the observation of nature; by the early twentieth century, walking was transformed into an end in itself. One walked for walking's sake, for the exercise. In the early twentieth century, for example, it became quite fashionable to walk briskly around the Central Park reservoir in the middle of New York City.

In the later twentieth century, fitness walking began to acquire the parameters of sport through such publications as Kenneth Cooper's *Aerobics* (first published in 1968). Walking programs appeared among the lower-level exercise programs described in Cooper's text. Participants began by walking one mile in 15 minutes, and over sixteen weeks progressed to walking four miles in 56 minutes. Walking was especially recommended for patients in cardiac rehabilitation. Of course, Cooper is best known for his jogging programs, which advocated a relatively slow type of running. But women who could not tolerate the repeated impact of jogging began to find that they could often keep pace with their high-stepping friends by walking quickly. They found that this fast walking left them agreeably breathless and had the desired effects of weight loss and increased fitness.

Women walking in Alaska. (Bob Rowan; Progressive Image/Corbis)

In 1972 Fred Lebow of the New York Road Runners Club began a women's 6-mile (9.6-kilometer) road race. This was the first running of what would become a prestigious annual competition, the women's 10-kilometer (6.2-mile) Mini-Marathon, popularly known as "the Mini." In 1976 there were 429 starters in the New York Mini-Marathon, and the race received national recognition. By the late 1970s the event drew more than 6,000 participants. Many of the women who participated were not "serious" competitors; they

WOMEN WALKERS JOIN INTERNATIONAL COMPETITION

The importance of the fitness walking movement was demonstrated in the inauguration of a new athletics program for women. From 1978 through 1984, Avon sponsored a program of long-distance races aimed at women runners who expected to compete in the marathon. A new Avon program initiated in 1998 is a series of 10,000-meter running events held in tandem with formal 5,000-meter fitness-walking competitions. The venerable Mini-Marathon has become part of this new Avon circuit which, in its first year, included events in seventeen foreign countries as well as the United States. This program finally gave the woman fitness walker an official place in international sports.

completed the race by alternately running and walking the distance. Over time, feminist solidarity became the theme of the Mini-Marathon, and women entered as an expression of their support for feminist values and achievements. These participants often walked the whole distance; their numbers increased as the Mini added such award categories as the grandmother-granddaughter pairs, which symbolized the feminist hope that today's actions will make things better for the next generations of women.

As long-distance running increased in popularity in the 1970s and 1980s, women learned that they could enter many races and finish them in an enjoyable manner by walking quickly through the course. These races attracted a large field because they provided a hospitable environment, one in which women felt safe. The first line of safety was the presence of many women in a well-patrolled event. Of equal significance was a sense that this was a place in which women would learn not to be embarrassed about their bodies. Women who would not wear shorts on the street or expose their athletic ability to public criticism would enter the accepting sisterhood of a women's race. Gradually, these races started walking categories that were quite distinct from the established Olympic sport of racewalking.

More and more women have given walking credit for weight control, a glowing complexion, and a wide network of social and athletic acquaintances. Whatever running could do for them, walking could also do: burn fat, provide cardiovascular fitness, increase muscle tone, prevent osteoporosis, encompass different levels of ability and competition. There were walking clubs with a wide range of activities and events, central organizations for the various types of walking and, finally, the Olympic Games to showcase the world's finest racewalkers.

APPEAL TO BEGINNERS

Beginning walkers often start from a base of practically no fitness; walking is one of the few physical events that can be adapted to people who are morbidly obese or have an infirmity. Beginning walkers often start their walking programs in shopping malls. Many malls have measured miles and courses. These walkers also have organized groups that walk together before the malls open. Women living in rural-areas who have to cope with unleashed dogs, no sidewalks, treacherous footing, inclement weather, and isolation might prefer the mall with its crowds, climate control, smooth floors, and security guards. The landscape there is always well lit and upbeat.

The available literature on the sport gives substantial guidance on the rules of fitness walking. The walker uses her arms to pump and her abdominal muscles to breathe. Contracting the abdominal muscles flattens the lower back, pulling the buttocks in. The walker's foot hits the ground heel first; then the walker consciously pushes off with the toe. To increase speed, the walker does not force a long stride but aims for quicker steps. It is possible to walk a 5000-meter (3.1-mile) race safely if the individual has four to six weeks of training, three days a week for 30 minutes or more.

Pamela Cooper

See also Pedestrianism; Racewalking

Bibliography

Cooper, Kenneth. (1968) *Aerobics*. New York: Bantam Books.

Ingram, Leah. (1997) "When You Have a Lot to Lose." *Walking* (January/February): 32, 34.

Rudow, Martin. (1997) *Maximum Walking* (video). Seattle, WA: Technique Productions.

Smith, Kathy, with Susanna Levin. (1994) *Walkfit for a Better Body*. New York: Warner Books.

WALSH, STELLA

(1911–1980)

POLISH TRACK AND FIELD ATHLETE

Stella Walsh ranks as one of the twentieth century's most versatile track and field athletes and also one of its most controversial. Born on 3 April 1911 in Rypin, Poland, she emigrated with her family to the United States when she was two years old, settling in Cleveland, Ohio. Originally named Stanislawa (or Stephania) Walasiewice, she became known as Stella Walsh because teachers found her Polish name too difficult to pronounce. At age nine she took up track and field with the Polish Falcon Club; after graduating from high school in 1929, she equaled the women's world record of 7.3 seconds for the 60-meter sprint at a competition in Cleveland.

From 1930 to 1938, Walsh competed internationally for Poland, although she never lived there. (She had applied for U.S. citizenship in 1932, but she did not proceed with the naturalization process after she took a job in the Polish consulate in New York.) In the 1930 Women's Track and Field Meet in Prague, Czechoslovakia, she won the 60-, 100-, and 200-meter races. At the 1932 Olympic Games in Los Angeles, California, Walsh won the 100-meter event and placed sixth in the discus throw. In the 1934 Women's Track and Field Meet in London, England, she won the 60-meter race and placed second in the 100- and 200-meter races. Walsh finished second in the 100-meter dash at the 1936 Olympic Games in Berlin, Germany. In the 1938 European Track and Field Championships, she won the 100- and 200-meter races and placed second in the long jump and 400-meter relay.

Stella Walsh (right), who finished second in the 100-meter race, congratulating winner and rival Helen Stephens at the 1936 Olympics. (Hulton-Deutsch Collection/Corbis)

In addition to winning sixteen Polish national track and field championships, Walsh won thirty-three Amateur Athletic Union (AAU) indoor and outdoor titles in the United States (though never as a United States representative). Her AAU titles (outdoor unless noted) included the 100-yard/100-meter races (1930, 1943, 1944, 1948); the 200-meter/220-yard races (outdoor: 1930, 1931, 1939, 1948; indoor: 1930, 1931, 1934, 1935, 1945, 1946); long jump (1930, 1939–1946, 1948, 1951); discus throw (1941, 1942); and pentathlon (1950–1954).

Walsh became a U.S. citizen in 1947. Nevertheless, in 1948 and 1952 U.S. Olympic officials barred Walsh from trying out for the U.S. Olympic team because she had been a member of the 1932 and 1936 Polish Olympic teams. She was finally permitted to compete as an American at the 1956 Olympic trials. By then she was 45 years old and past her athletic prime, and she failed to qualify for the 200-meter event.

During her twenty-six-year career, Walsh established twenty-four world records at distances that ranged from 50 to 1,000 meters. Five of these records were officially recognized by the International Amateur Athletic Federation (IAAF). Walsh's official world records included 7.3 seconds for the 60-meter race; 11.7 and 11.6 seconds for the 100-meter race; 23.6 seconds for the 200-meter race; and 24.3 seconds for the 220-yard race. As a measure of Walsh's greatness, her accomplishment in winning the 100-meter race, the 200-meter race, and the long jump in the U.S. national track and field championship in 1930 remained unequaled until Marion Jones accomplished this triple win in 1998. In 1930 Walsh became the first woman to run the 100-yard distance in under 11 seconds, recording an unofficial world best of 10.8 seconds.

After retiring from competitive athletics following the 1956 Olympic Trials, Walsh coached various women's sports in California through the mid-1960s before returning to Cleveland. She lived with her mother, and they subsisted on Social Security benefits. Walsh earned additional income from playing semiprofessional basketball and softball and running exhibition races. In 1979 the Cleveland Recreation Department hired Walsh as the administrator of its women's track and field programs. On 4 December 1980, she was killed in the crossfire during a robbery at a discount store.

Throughout much of her athletic career, Walsh was suspected of being a man disguised as a woman, but gender verification was not used in athletics until the 1960s. Her autopsy results, however, revealed that Walsh indeed possessed male sex organs, although nonfunctional, which resulted from mosaicism, a rare genetic disorder that produces a mixture of male and female chromosomes. What effect, if any, this anomaly had on her performance is unclear.

Adam R. Hornbuckle

See also Gender Verification

Bibliography

Hendershott, Jon. (1987) *Track's Greatest Women.* Los Altos, CA: Tafnews Press.

Menke, Frank G. (1969) *The Encyclopedia of Sports.* 4th rev. ed. Revisions edited by Roger Treat. South Brunswick, NJ: A. S. Barnes.

Quercetani, Roberto L. (1990) *Athletics: A History of Modern Track and Field Athletics, 1860–1990.* Milan, Italy.

Tricard, Louise Mead. (1996) *American Women's Track & Field: A History, 1895 through 1980.* Jefferson, NC: McFarland.

Wallechinsky, David. (1988) *The Complete Book of the Olympics.* Rev. ed. New York: Viking.

WEIGHTLIFTING

The term *weightlifting* refers to the competitive sport in which the object is to determine who can lift the most weight overhead in two specified lifts—the snatch (lifting the weight over the head in one motion) and the clean and jerk (a two-stage lift). Women's weightlifting, now practiced in many countries throughout the world, was approved for inclusion for the first time in the 2000 Olympic Games and for the Commonwealth Games in 2002.

HISTORY

Although weightlifting competitions for women are largely a phenomenon of the late twentieth century, women have been using weights for at least two centuries. In 1783 in Leipzig, Germany, an unidentified "strongwoman" gave what may have been the first professional strength performance. Thirty-five years later, in 1818, a Madame Gobert advertised herself as the "French Female Hercules" and the "Strongest Woman in Europe." Gobert appeared at the Bartholomew Fair in London, where she lifted, with her teeth, a table with several people seated on it and performed a number of other feats of strength.

In the 1860s the Frenchwoman Mademoiselle Doublier toured with an act of dumbbell and barbell work that concluded with her shouldering a small cannon, which her assistant then fired. In the United States, Angela D'Atalie, known as the "female Samson," worked for the showman P. T. Barnum in the 1870s. Barnum described D'Atalie as "not only the strongest and most thoroughly developed physically of all the strongwomen, but . . . modest and retiring and without doubt the most beautifully formed woman in the profession."

By the early 1890s dozens of professional strongwomen were working in the circuses and variety theaters of Europe and the United States.

1950s weightlifter Ivy Russell. (Hulton-Deutsch Collection/Corbis)

Although many strongwomen lifted primarily horses, people, and other objects whose weight their audiences would understand, most of the early professionals also lifted barbells and dumbbells. The Belgian strongwoman Athleta, for instance, lifted 92 kilos (204 pounds) over her head in front of reliable witnesses. Katie Brumbach Heymann, known as Sandwina, lifted 120 kilos (264.5 pounds) over her head in 1910. At times, professional strongwomen also competed against one another. The most celebrated of these early contests was the one between Minerva (Josephine Wohlford Blatt, 1865–1923) and the professional strongwoman known as Victorine. Following Minerva's victory in that 1893 contest, Richard K. Fox, publisher of the *Police Gazette,* presented her with a silver and gold championship belt, comparable to the belt Fox gave boxing champion John L. Sullivan.

PROMOTING COMPETITION

The first woman to push for organized weightlifting championships for women was an Englishwoman, Ivy Russell. Born in 1907 in Surrey, England, Russell began lifting at age fourteen to cure her tuberculosis. In 1925 Russell cleaned and jerked 79.2 kilograms (176 pounds) at a body weight of only 56.25 kilograms (125 pounds). Over the next fifteen years, she gave numerous exhibitions as an amateur, making best lifts of 86.8 kilograms (193 pounds) in the clean and jerk at a body weight of 60.3 kilograms (134 pounds) and 184.7 kilograms (410.5 pounds) in the dead lift (bending and lifting the weight to waist level). But Russell wanted to do more than give exhibitions. She wanted the right to compete against other women, and she began a letter-writing campaign to the British Amateur Weightlifting Association (BAWLA) requesting that women be allowed to compete. In 1932 the BAWLA agreed to sanction a woman's meet. Only two women competed—Russell and Tillie Tinmouth. At the end of the day, however, Russell could honestly state that she was the "Nine Stone Ladies Champion of Great Britain."

In the United States during and immediately after World War II, a number of women took up weight training. A gymnasium instructor, Jean Ansorge of Grand Rapids, Michigan, began training women in weightlifting in the early 1940s. On 17 October 1943, ten women, all trained by Ansorge, competed in the All-Girl Weightlifting Meet. The lifts contested in that first meet were the press, the deep knee bend or squat, and the dead lift. Four months later, on 13 February 1944, Ansorge and her brother, Harold, hosted the All-Girl Weightlifting Contest for the Championships of Michigan. In this contest, sixteen women competed in the three lifts then used in the Olympic Games—the press, snatch, and clean and jerk.

Several years later, in Santa Monica, California, Abbye "Pudgy" Stockton and her husband, Les, helped organize the first women's meet to carry an Amateur Athletic Union (AAU) sanction. Held at the Southwest Arena in Los Angeles on 28 February 1947, the Pacific Coast Women's Weightlifting Championships featured nine women competing in three body weight divisions. On 18 January 1948, a second meet, called the Southern California Open Women's Lifting Championships, was held in Long Beach, California. Five women competed. On 2 April 1949, Walter Marcy's Gym in Los Angeles hosted a third women's contest, and then on 6 June 1950, an official women's national championship was sanctioned by the AAU. Only seven women competed in the national championships—held in Los Angeles—and Shirley Tanny had the highest total of all contestants, with lifts of 47.2 kilograms (105 pounds) in the press, 52.6 kilograms (117 pounds) in the snatch, and 68.4 kilograms (152 pounds) in the clean and jerk. Internationally, a number of other women also began practicing the Olympic lifts during the 1940s and early 1950s, and in Singapore a woman's national championship was held in 1952.

Interest in competitive weightlifting for women gradually waned in the 1950s. Although a few women continued to practice the lifts, no organized competitions appear to have been held during the next two decades. But, on 14 February 1976, gym owner and professional baseball scout Bill Clark (1932–) decided to hold a weightlifting meet for women. Clark, who served as AAU weightlifting chairman for the Missouri Valley region, knew that a number of women, including his daughter, Kelly, had begun practicing the "Olympic lifts." Although the AAU and the International Weightlifting Federation (IWF) rule books clearly stated that lifting was for males only, Clark felt that

Chinese weightlifter Yang Xia at the 1998 Asian Games. (AFP/Corbis)

it was unfair to deny women a chance to compete against one another. For the next five years, Clark included women's divisions in the other meets he hosted. He also began keeping track of women's records. Word of Clark's advocacy of women's lifting soon spread throughout the Midwest.

One woman who heard about Clark's interest in women's lifting was Mabel Kirchner Rader (1917–), wife of *Iron Man* magazine publisher Peary Rader and the only woman in the United States to have served as a national-level referee in all three weight sports: weightlifting, powerlifting, and bodybuilding. Rader, who was also involved in the formative years of women's powerlifting, felt strongly that women should be allowed to compete in weightlifting; she raised the issue with Murray Levin, who had been elected president of the United States Weightlifting Federation (USWF) in 1975. According to Levin, Kirchner was a strong advocate for women's participation and by the late 1970s, several dozen women were involved, although there were no rules for women lifters. In a 1998 interview, Levin recalled the situation: "I was worried that if we didn't do something, we'd get sued. A lot of guys were opposed to the women lifting and so they made them weigh in while nude in front of male judges and things like that." In 1980, Levin finally put the issue of women's participation on the agenda, and after a close vote women were allowed into the USWF.

Following that meeting, Levin appointed Rader to head a committee to set up rules and procedures for the participation of women. He also appointed Judy Glenney, a lifter, to act as an athletes' representative for women. Rader's first acts were to begin a newsletter for women and to search for a sponsor for the first national championships for women.

Rader had a difficult time finding someone to host the first women's nationals. After pressure from Rader, Joe Widdell, a gym owner in Waterloo, Iowa, agreed to put on the meet. He and Rader were pleased to have thirty-five women register for the meet and to have twenty-nine of them show on 23 May 1981. Glenney, lifting in the 67.5-kilo (148-pound) class, made best lifts of 75 kilos (165 pounds) in the snatch and 97.5 kilos (214.5 pounds) in the clean and jerk and was named the best lifter, pound for pound, in the meet.

Throughout the 1980s, women's weightlifting continued to grow in popularity in the United States. The second national championships, held 4 April 1982 in St. Charles, Illinois, attracted forty-six lifters. The third nationals, held in Milwaukee, Wisconsin, on 21 May 1983, had sixty competitors. Because of the growth of the sport, Rader, Levin, and Glenney began to lobby the IWF for international recognition of women's weightlifting (Glenney had been elected by the women lifters to replace Rader as women's chairperson at the 1983 national championships). On 23 March 1986, at the Pannonia Cup Championships in Budapest, Hungary, the IWF finally permitted women weightlifters to compete internationally. Women weightlifters from China, Hungary, Canada, and Great Britain, as well as the United States, participated. Then on 8 March 1987, thirty-three women participated in the Pannonia Cup. In addition to the countries originally represented, Bulgaria and Germany also sent teams.

By the mid-1980s women's weightlifting had spread around the world, even though there had not yet been a world championship meet. In May 1985, for instance, a Wave Cup Women's Weightlifting Invitational in China showcased 140 women weightlifters and twenty-three different teams. According to the meet coverage, approximately 1,000 women were "taking regular training" in various parts of China at that time. The Norwegian Weightlifting Federation reported that women in that country began competing in their men's meets as early as 1980; by 1985, even though the number of women participating was not large, Norway recognized a full set of records for women in all weight classes. Australia had also begun allowing women to compete by the mid 1980s and had twenty-five women ranked by 1985. Twenty-nine women competed on 12 October 1985 at the British Woman's Weightlifting Championships, and India held its first women's nationals in 1986 with thirty-six competitors. Finally, in 1986, after assurances from Glenney—who had been appointed coordinator of women's weightlifting by the IWF—that at least ten nations would participate, the IWF agreed to sanction a women's world championship the next year. Levin, the past president of USA Weightlifting Incorporated (USAW), agreed to stage the meet in Florida in 1987. While Glenney and the other women were delighted with this opportunity for international participation, IWF General Secretary Tamas Ajan's letter to Glenney also included the news that her services as women's coordinator would no longer be needed.

While Glenney was no doubt disappointed about women losing their somewhat limited voice with the IWF, she was not displeased about the first Women's World Championships in Daytona. Twenty-two countries sent teams to the competition for a total of 100 lifters. The Chinese women dominated the championships, winning twenty-two gold medals, four silver, and one bronze. The United States, placing second, had four gold medals, seven silver, and seven bronze. Following the meet, on 13 November 1987, Glenney received a letter from IWF President Gottfried Schodl, commending the conduct of the women in the contest and praising her for her work on behalf of women.

Following the first meet, women's world championships have been held on an annual basis. The second meet (1988), held in Jakarta, Indonesia, attracted twenty-four countries and 100 lifters. Again, the Chinese women dominated the event, winning every weight class. Since 1988 the Chinese women weightlifters have won the team title at every subsequent woman's world championships.

RULES AND PLAY

The IWF, whose headquarters are in Budapest, Hungary, controls weightlifting for men and women. In each country belonging to the federation, the IWF recognizes one national governing body. In the United States, this is United States of America Weightlifting (USAW), in Colorado Springs, Colorado. The national governing bodies sanction competitions, raise money for international travel, select the national teams, suggest rule changes to the IWF, keep national records, and encourage the growth of the sport in their respective countries. Because of the relative newness of the sport of women's weightlifting, only a few women have been elected to leadership positions within these national governing bodies. However, some member nations have established women's subcommittees that act as advisory groups to their respective organizations and thus provide women with a limited voice in their own regulation.

In a competition, women weigh in and are then divided into seven body weight categories:

DRUGS IN WEIGHTLIFTING

The use of performance-enhancing substances and methods is a major issue in weightlifting. The International Weightlifting Federation has guidelines to control the problem. Classes of prohibited substances are stimulants, narcotics, anabolic agents, diuretics, peptide and glycoprotein hormones and analogues, and marijuana. Methods for enhancing performance that are banned by the IWF are blood doping and pharmacological, chemical, and physical manipulation. Not banned outright but restricted in use are local anaesthetics, corticosteroids, and Beta-blockers.

up to 48 kilograms (105.82 pounds), up to 53 kilograms (116.84 pounds), up to 58 kilograms (127.86 pounds), up to 63 kilograms (138.88 pounds), up to 69 kilograms (152.11 pounds), up to 75 kilograms (165.34 pounds), and more than 75 kilograms (more than 165.34 pounds). Medals are awarded in each weight class in the snatch, in the clean and jerk, and in the "total," which is calculated by adding a lifter's best attempt in the snatch to her best attempt in the clean and jerk. The lifter with the highest total in each weight class is declared the winner. If two athletes in the same weight class make the same total, the lighter woman is declared the winner. In the case of a "double tie," the women are reweighed.

In 1997 the IWF adopted a smaller bar for women's competitions. The bar is shorter and thinner than a traditional Olympic bar and weighs only 15 kilograms (33 pounds).

The snatch is always done first in competition, and the goal is to pull the bar from the floor to arm's length overhead in one movement. Using a wide hand spacing, the lifter explosively pulls the barbell upward as far as possible. Then, when the bar has reached its highest point, the lifter quickly squats down or splits her legs to lower her body under the bar so that the weight can be caught overhead in a locked-arms position. Once the bar is locked out, the lifter returns to a fully erect position and waits for the judge's signal to replace the bar on the floor. Failure to lock the weight out successfully, failure to stand fully erect, failure to wait for the judge's signal to lower the bar, and a number of other infractions may disqualify the lift.

The clean and jerk is a two-part lift whose object, again, is to lift a weight overhead. The first part of the lift, the clean, involves pulling a barbell from the floor to the top of the chest in a rapid movement. As in the snatch, the lifter will generally either squat or split underneath the weight to minimize the height that the bar needs to be pulled. Then, once the bar is "racked in" at the top of the chest, the lifter returns to an erect position, and prepares for the jerk, the second part of the lift. To perform the jerk, the lifter bends her knees and drives upward with as much power as possible. The momentum generated by this powerful thrust of the body should allow the bar to be locked out overhead without any pressing motion of the arms. As in the snatch, failure to lock the weight out successfully, failure to stand fully erect, failure to wait for the judge's signal to lower the bar, and other infractions disqualify the lift.

Once fully recognized by the IWF, participation in women's weightlifting quickly spread to all divisions of the sport. Women compete at the junior and master's levels, and participate as full members in the U.S. Olympic Festivals and the Pan American Games. The push to get women in the Olympic Games took nearly a decade and required a compromise on the part of the IWF. The International Olympic Committee (IOC), voting on 15 November 1996 at a meeting in Cancún, Mexico, agreed to admit women only on the condition that the total number of weightlifters would not exceed 250 at any given Olympics. To keep within these guidelines, the IWF restructured its weight classes in 1997 and recognizes only eight weight classes for men and seven for women. Before this decision, there were nine weight classes for women and ten for men. Women will compete for the first time in the Olympics in 2000.

Jan Todd

Bibliography

Glenney, Judy. (1989) *So You Want to Be a Female Weightlifter*. Farmington, NM: Glennco Enterprises.

Dreschler, Arthur (1998) *The Weightlifting Encyclopedia: A Guide to World Class Performance*. Whitestone, NY: A to A Communications.

WHITBREAD, FATIMA

(1961–)

BRITISH JAVELIN THROWER

Fatima Whitbread was one of the most successful British women field athletes of the 1980s. Born in 1961 in England of racially mixed parents, she was abandoned by her mother and lived in a series of orphanages. She was adopted by her coach, Margaret Whitbread, who had been a top-ranked British javelin thrower from 1957 to 1965.

Whitbread became the European junior javelin champion in 1979 and qualified to compete at the 1980 Moscow Olympics. At the world championships in Helsinki in 1983, she came in second to world record holder Tiina Lillak; at the 1984 Los Angeles Olympics, she won the bronze medal. Whitbread's medal tally continued to increase throughout the late 1980s. At the European championships in 1986, she broke the world record with a throw of 77.44 meters (254 feet 1 inch). This distance is still ranked as one of the longest throws of all time by a female javelin thrower. Whitbread added more gold when she won the world championships in Rome in 1987, the year she was named British Sports Personality of the Year.

During the 1987 championships, Whitbread damaged her shoulder and did not throw at the British Olympic trials. She was nonetheless selected on the basis of her ranking as world champion. She won a silver medal at the Seoul Olympics in 1988. Whitbread had several more operations on her shoulder, but the injury returned at the U.K. championships in 1990 and forced her into retirement. Toward the end of her competitive career, Whitbread became involved in various business enterprises; she continued with these after her retirement, as well as providing commentary for the British Broadcasting Corporation.

J. P. Anderson

Bibliography

Gammon, Clive. (1988) "Throwing Caution to the Wind." *Sports Illustrated* (12 September): 50–52.

Lawson, Gerald. (1997) *World Record Breakers in Track and Field Athletics*. Champaign, IL: Human Kinetics.

Ward, Tony. (1991) *Athletics, the Golden Decade*. London: Queen Anne Press.

Whitbread, Fatima, and Adrianne Blue. (1988) *Fatima: The Autobiography of Fatima Whitbread*. London: Pelham Books.

WILDERNESS ADVENTURE

Wilderness adventure includes activities such as camping, backpacking, hiking, whitewater rafting, rock climbing, mountaineering, bicycle touring, mountain biking, canoeing, kayaking, hunting, and fishing. A person can engage in wilderness adventure as an individual or as part of a small group traveling in the natural environment. Emphasis is placed on challenging oneself through outdoor adventure activities to achieve one's full potential in body, mind, and spirit. The perception of wilderness adventure as a male domain was perpetuated from the 1800s until the early 1970s. The challenges, consequences, and achievements were reported by men, about men, and reserved for men. Women were warned that the wilderness was a dangerous and unpredictable place; since they were perceived as too fragile for the challenges of the wilderness, women would venture out only with a male protector.

EARLY HISTORY OF WOMEN ADVENTURERS

Women were not new participants in wilderness adventure. One need only read the journals of Lewis and Clark to realize that Sacajawea, a Native American woman who acted as wilderness guide, contributed greatly to the success of this early-nineteenth-century expedition to explore and survey the western territories of the United States. Later in the nineteenth century, frontier mothers and daughters would leave the comforts of the eastern United States to have countless wilderness adventures and survival challenges as they settled the West with their families; frequently they took care of their homesteads alone without men. The renowned Calamity Jane was only one of many women on the western frontier who owned land, worked ranches, and ran family businesses.

In the mid-1800s some women also became explorers. These were usually wealthy Victorian women who planned and completed expeditions to remote corners of the world. Anne Peck and Marianne North went to South America; Fanny Bullock Workman, Mary Kingsley, and May French Sheldon, to Africa; Annie Taylor, to China and Tibet; and Isabella Bird Bishop, to Korea, Japan, China, and the Rocky Mountains. By the end of the 1800s, women had created the Ladies Alpine Club to document their wilderness travels.

ROLE OF ORGANIZED CAMPING IN WILDERNESS ADVENTURE FOR GIRLS AND WOMEN

In 1902 Laura Mattoon, a private school teacher educated at Wellesley College, founded Camp

Women take part in early morning physical education at the Outward Bound Mountain School for girls in 1951. (Hulton-Deutsch Collection/Corbis)

Kehonka to educate girls about how they could contribute to and change society. She offered a program of outdoor skills and created nonrestrictive clothing (including the bloomer design) for the girls to wear at her camp. For the first time, girls could move freely and accomplish many outdoor activities and challenges. Mattoon went on to train girls and women for future careers in organized camping and outdoor wilderness adventure. In 1910 Lord and Lady Baden-Powell founded the Canadian Girl Guides. In the same year in the United States, Charlotte Gulick and her husband, Luther, created the Campfire Girls. In 1912 Juliette Lowe created the Girls Scouts. These organizations offered many opportunities for girls to learn outdoor skills and created many jobs for women.

CLIMBERS AND GUIDES

As the camping movement gained momentum in North America, women abroad were seeking wilderness adventures as climbers and guides. Miriam O'Brien climbed the Dolomites in Italy and Gwen Moffet became one of the first women climbing guides in Europe during the 1950s. Claude Kogan was one of the first women to climb in the Himalayas (1950). Inspired by these pioneers, other women began to develop their mountaineering skills. In 1978 Arlene Blum assembled the first all-women's expedition to Annapurna, the tenth highest mountain in the world. The success of this expedition led to others in the Himalayas by Alison Chadwick, Rhonda Ruskiwecz, and Stacy Allison (the first U.S. woman to reach the summit of Mount Everest).

ACADEMIC AND SOCIAL INFLUENCES

From the 1930s on, women college professors who had been campers and counselors at girls' camps began to offer outdoor skill training and career opportunities through their college curric-

UNABASHED PRIDE (1999)

A Description of the Exhilaration Experienced After a Six-Weeks' Journey By Canoe

This profound experience was a major milestone in my life, for I discovered that I could handle the rigors of wilderness canoeing. When we paddled into the native village of Baker Lake at our journey's end, the community opened its school to us for an overnight stay. The twelve women on the trip took turns checking out new muscles in the bathroom mirror, grinning at the physical changes after six weeks of paddling, and clowning around with naked poses that profiled our wiry backs. The guys in the men's room were more restrained, we learned later, but we women were taking unabashed pride in our strong bodies.

LAURIE GULLION
(1999) Canoeing. A Ragged Mountain Press Woman's Guide. *Camden, ME: Ragged Mountain Press / McGraw Hill.*

ula. These professors in the late 1940s and 1950s included Rosland Cassidy at Mills College, Mary Ellen Joy and Marjory Camp at the University of Iowa, and Edie Klein at the University of Georgia, all of whom created training courses in camp leadership. In the 1960s and 1970s, Eleanor Ells and Judy Myers at George Williams College, Betty van der Smissen at Pennsylvania State University, and Phyllis Ford at Oregon State University created courses in camp administration and worked on National Camp Director Certification. Marcia Carlson at SUNY-Cortland and Micki Little and Camille Bunting at Texas A & M University created career training in outdoor education in the 1960s–1980s. In the 1980s and 1990s Karen Warren at Hampshire College, Margaret Lechner at Earlham College, and Rita Yerkes, first at Towson State University and later at Aurora University, created courses in outdoor experiential education and advocated representation of women outdoor leaders in national organizations.

The arrival of the women's liberation movement and the growth of the baby boomer generation in the 1970s encouraged more women to participate in wilderness adventure activities. Although camp and university programs had created wilderness training opportunities for girls and women, many women still had to overcome negative peer and societal perceptions to participate in wilderness adventure activities. They often felt more comfortable going on outdoor trips as a family member or with a male friend. But, as the women's liberation movement gained momentum, women experienced new freedom to explore and challenge themselves through wilderness adventure activities. This led not only to their increased participation but also to the development of specialized equipment for women. Women also began to assert themselves and request wilderness adventure experiences that were free from imposed gender roles. Often too, they had the ability and desire to participate in wilderness activities but lacked instructions in how to proceed. This need led to an explosion in wilderness adventure trips and programs led by women for women, through such new companies as Artemis, Woodswomen, and Maria, which were initiated in the late 1970s. Artemis and Woodswomen were founded by women who practiced the philosophy of consensus leadership on their trips. These businesses, owned and run by women, created educational and recreational trips for the women who participated. Through the 1990s, organizations such as the National Outdoor Leadership School, Outward Bound, the Wilderness Education Association, the Department of Natural Resources, the National Wildlife Federation, and the Women's Professional Group of the Association of Experiential Education offered courses designed for women and led by women. These programs have increased staff opportunities for women as well. In addition, sporting gear manufacturers (such as Orvis and Mad River Canoes) and outdoor sports magazines (such as *Bowhunter* magazine) sponsor outdoor courses for women.

CONCLUSION

The success of the women's movement and, in the United States, of Title IX legislation led more girls and women to seek wilderness adventure experiences for their personal growth and development. With the availability of specialized and lightweight outdoor equipment and with societal acceptance of wilderness adventure activities, girls and women were no longer kept from enjoying the great outdoors.

Some outdoor activities, such as archery, bicycling, bow hunting, canoeing, climbing, orienteering, shooting, and fishing, may be taken up singly and are considered sports; competitions exist for each of these. Courses are also offered in all these activities, as well as in firearm safety, winter survival, wildlife ecology, camping skills, outdoor cooking. But many women choose instead to participate in wilderness adventure (which combines these skills) to gain self-esteem, confidence, companionship, the experience of nature, and a personal challenge. Girls' camping pioneer Abbie Graham captured the essence of the experience when she wrote that "Girls want to go outdoors so that they can have an experience with a little swagger in it."

Rita Yerkes
Wilma Miranda

Bibliography

Graham, Abbie. (1933) *The Girls' Camp.* New York: The Women's Press.

LaBastille, Anne. (1980) *Women and Wilderness.* San Francisco: Sierra Club.

Middleton, Dorothy. (1965) *Victorian Lady Travellers.* Chicago: Academy Chicago.

Roberts, Nina. (1995) *A Guide to Women's Studies in the Outdoors: A Review of Literature and Research with Annotated Bibliography.* Needham Heights, MA: Simon & Schuster Custom Publishing.

Stange, Mary Zeiss. (1997) *Woman the Hunter.* Boston: Beacon Press.

Thomas, Christine L. (1997) *Becoming an Outdoor Woman.* Helena, MT: Falcon Press.

Yerkes, Rita, and Wilma Miranda. (1986) "Outdoor Adventure Programming for Women." In *High Adventure Outdoor Pursuits: Organization and Leadership.* 2d ed. Edited by Joel Meier, Talmage Morash, and George Welton. Columbus, OH: Horizon, 259–267.

———. (1986) "The Status of Women Outdoor Leaders Today." *Camping Magazine* 61 (February), 4: 16–19, 28.

———. (1986) "Working Women in the Outdoors." *Women Outdoors Journal* (August): 13–20.

———. (1996) "The History of Camping Women in the Professionalization of Women in Experiential Education." In *Women Voices in Experiential Education,* edited by K. Warren. Boulder, CO: Association of Experiential Education, 61–77.

Zepatos, T. (1994) *Adventures in Good Company.* Portland, OR: Eighth Mountain Press.

WILLS, HELEN

(1905–1988)

U.S. TENNIS PLAYER

Helen Newington Wills Moody Roark was America's best woman tennis player between 1923 and 1938, winning singles championships at Wimbledon eight times, at the United States national tournament seven times, and at the French national tournament four times. In addition, she won twelve doubles titles in major tournaments and gold medals in women's singles and doubles tennis at the 1924 Summer Olympic Games in Paris, France.

Helen Wills was born on 6 October 1905 in Centerville, California, the daughter of a surgeon. When she was eight, her father bought her a tennis racket and taught her the game. At fourteen, she became a student of William "Pop" Fuller of Berkeley, who also coached Wills's rival, Helen Jacobs. Wills also worked with Hazel Wightman, one of the finest woman players of the era, who would later be her doubles partner on occasion.

Wills won the U.S. girls' singles and doubles championships in 1921 and captured her first U.S. women's title at Forest Hills, New York, in 1923, beating Molla Mallory, then the reigning queen of U.S. women's tennis. Over the next eight years, she continued her mastery at Forest Hills, winning in 1924, 1925, 1927–1929, and 1931. In addition, she won the U.S. doubles crown in 1922 (with Marion Z. Jessup), in 1924 (with Hazel Wightman), in 1925 (with Mary K. Browne), and in 1928 (with Wightman again), and the mixed doubles in 1924 (with Vincent Richards) and in 1928 (with John B. Hawkes). Wills's eight Wimbledon championships came in 1923, 1925, 1927–1932, and 1938; this record was not broken until Martina Navratilova won her ninth Wimbledon title in 1990. Wills won the French championship in 1928–1930 and 1932.

Wills's most celebrated match came in February 1926, when she played French champion Suzanne Lenglen in an exhibition match in Cannes, France. Amid great fanfare, the older and more experienced Lenglen beat Wills, 6–3, 8–6. Later that year, Wills fell victim to appendicitis and did not compete in any of the major championships until 1927. Once she returned to competitive play, she won 180 consecutive matches. Her streak, which began in 1927, was broken only in 1933 at the finals of the U.S. national tournament. Earlier in the year, she had injured a disk in her back while lifting a tennis bag. The pain persisted throughout the year and, although she won the singles championship at Wimbledon, she lost by default to Helen Jacobs in the finals at Forest Hills. Behind 0–3 in the third set of that match, she walked off the court, claiming that her leg hurt too much for her to continue. Sportswriters criticized her for avoiding an outright defeat by defaulting, but she defended her decision, claiming that it was pointless to continue when she could not play her best game. In 1935, Wills gained a measure of revenge by beating Jacobs in a three-set final at Wimbledon after Jacobs missed what appeared to be an easy shot at match point.

A tall, rangy, strong player, Wills played a very methodical baseline game, wearing her opponents down with groundstroke after groundstroke. She committed very few unforced errors and developed a good defensive game to thwart serve-and-volley opponents who tried to take advantage of her baseline position. She had immense powers of concentration on the court, never showing emotion nor speaking to her opponent. Noting this, Ed Sullivan, a sportswriter for the *New York Evening Mail,* dubbed her "Little Poker Face"; later "Miss" was added to the nickname. At times, her lack of emotion on the court provoked criticism that she was an unfeeling player. In the 1938 finals at Wimbledon, Wills was playing Jacobs, her long-time rival. In the first set, Jacobs tore her Achilles tendon. Practically immobile, Jacobs played the match out in obvious pain. Wills never betrayed any expression of concern or sympathy for her injured opponent, even after the match ended. Sportswriters berated Wills, but her concentration during tournament play was so intense that, in all likelihood, she simply was not aware of Jacobs's physical problem.

Helen Wills in the French Open mixed doubles competition in 1931. (Bettmann/Corbis)

Along with the unconventional Lenglen, Wills was important in promoting dress emancipation for women tennis players. She departed from the customary long, heavy skirts worn by players in the early 1920s; instead, she played in a white, knee-length pleated skirt with a white eyeshade. Her dress style was widely imitated until Jacobs introduced shorts at Forest Hills in 1933. Wills, however, continued to wear her pleated skirt for the rest of her career.

Wills received a B.A. in Fine Arts from the University of California at Berkeley, where her excellent academic work resulted in her selection to Phi Beta Kappa. She painted throughout her life and often provided her own illustrations for the instructional articles she wrote for magazines. She published an instructional book, *Tennis,* in 1928; an autobiography, *Fifteen-Thirty,* in 1937; and a number of novels, including *Death Serves an Ace,* which appeared in 1939. She met her first husband, Frederick Moody, a stockbroker, at the celebrated Lenglen match and married him in 1929. They were divorced in 1937, and she married Aidan Roark, a polo player, in 1939. She retired from competitive tennis after her last Wimbledon victory in 1938 and lived quietly, almost reclusively, in southern California for the rest of her life. She was chosen the Associated Press Athlete of the Year in 1935 and elected to the International Tennis Hall of Fame in 1959. She played noncompetitive tennis until the end of her life and followed the game on television, developing great admiration for Chris Evert and Martina Navratilova. After several years of declining health, she died on 1 January 1988 in a convalescent home in Carmel, California.

John E. Findling

Bibliography

Bouchier, Nancy B., and John E. Findling. (1983) "Little Miss Poker Face." In *The Hero in Transition,* edited by Ray Browne and Marshall Fishwick. Bowling Green, OH: Popular Press.

Collins, Bud, and Zander Hollander, eds. (1980) *Bud Collins' Modern Encyclopedia of Tennis.* Garden City, NY: Dolphin Books.

Engelmann, Larry. (1988) *The Goddess and the American Girl.* New York: Oxford University Press.

Grimsley, Will. (1971) *Tennis: Its History, People, and Events.* Englewood Cliffs, NJ: Prentice-Hall.

Wills, Helen. (1928) *Tennis.* New York: Charles Scribner's Sons.

———. (1937) *Fifteen-Thirty: The Story of a Tennis Player.* New York: Charles Scribner's Sons.

Wills, Helen, and Robert Murphy. (1939) *Death Serves an Ace.* New York: Charles Scribner's Sons.

WINDHOEK CALL FOR ACTION

The Windhoek Call for Action was drafted at the Second World Conference on Women and Sport held in Windhoek, Namibia, 19–22 May 1998, which was attended by 400 delegates from 74 countries. The principal purposes of the conference were to celebrate the many successful endorsements of the Brighton Declaration (1994)—which called for the development of women's sports around the world—by government agencies and sports organizations and to initiate actions that would further the development of equal opportunities for girls and women to participate fully in sports in its broadest sense. The Call for Action was designed to build on the aims of the Brighton Declaration by moving the focus to action, going beyond the statements of principles, and raising awareness. The call reflected an overwhelming desire on the part of all delegates to seek greater cooperation and coordination among the many agencies and organizations responsible for women's issues; the call also recognized and stressed the importance that sports can and should play in the advancement of girls and women.

The conference recognized the need for linkages to existing international initiatives that have an impact on the advancement of girls and women, in particular the Beijing Platform for Action and the United Nations Convention on the Elimination of All Forms of Discrimination Against Women. The conference also celebrated the successes achieved by and for girls and women since the endorsement of the Brighton Declaration in 1994.

The Windhoek Call for Action was addressed to all men and women in national and international sports organizations, governments, public authorities, development agencies, schools, businesses, educational and research institutions, and women's organizations—specifically, the people who are responsible for (or who directly influence the conduct, development, or promotion of) sports, or those who are in any way involved in the employment, education, management, training, development, or care of girls and women in sports. In addition to reaffirming the principles of the Brighton Declaration, the Conference delegates called for action in the following areas:

1. Develop action plans with objectives and targets to implement the principles of the Brighton Declaration, and monitor and report on their implementation.
2. Reach out beyond the current boundaries of the sports sector to the global women's equality movements, and develop closer partnerships between sports and women's organizations on the one side, and representatives from sectors such as education, youth, health, human rights, and employment on the other. Develop strategies that help other sectors obtain their objectives through the medium of sports and at the same time further sports objectives.
3. Promote and share information about the positive contribution that girls' and women's involvement in sports makes to social, health, and economic issues.
4. Build the capacity of women as leaders and decision-makers, and ensure that women play meaningful and visible roles in sports at all levels. Create mechanisms that ensure that young women have a voice in the development of policies and programs that affect them.
5. Avert the "world crisis in physical education" by establishing and strengthening quality physical education programs as key means for the positive introduction to young girls of the skills and other benefits they can acquire through sports. Further, create policies and mechanisms that ensure progression from school to community-based activity.
6. Encourage the media to positively portray and significantly cover the breadth, depth, quality, and benefits of girls' and women's involvement in sports.
7. Ensure a safe and supportive environment for girls and women participating in sports at all levels by taking steps to eliminate all forms of harassment and abuse, violence and exploitation, and gender testing.
8. Ensure that policies and programs provide opportunities for all girls and women in full recognition of the differences and diversity among them—including such factors as race, ability, age, religion, sexual orientation, ethnicity, language, culture, or status as an indigenous person.
9. Recognize the importance of governments to sports development, and urge them to conduct gender impact analyses and to develop appropriate legislation, public policy, and funding that ensures gender equality in all aspects of sport.
10. Ensure that Official Development Assistance programs provide equal opportunities for girls' and women's development, and recognize the potential of sports to achieve development objectives.
11. Encourage more women to become researchers in sports, and more research to be undertaken on critical issues relating to women in sport.

The Windhoek Call for Action is being promoted by the International Working Group on Women and Sport (IWG). The IWG acts as a catalyst for governments, national, regional, and international organizations throughout the world to adopt the Windhoek Call for Action as well as the Brighton Declaration. The Call for Action is seen by delegates and others in women's sports as an important step in developing sports for girls and women, in placing female sports on an equal footing with male sports, and in developing sports around the world.

Anita White

See also Brighton Declaration; International Working Group on Women and Sport

WINDSURFING

Windsurfing, or sailboarding as it is also called, combines sailing and surfing on what is basically a large, stable surfboard with a sail operated by

Woman windsurfing in Columbia Championships. (Kevin R. Morris/Corbis)

one person. The sport originated in the late 1960s and has, like surfing, developed a distinct culture. As it is a so-called new sport, the issue of women's role in windsurfing is the subject of much discussion. Women do take part, but their numbers are disproportionately low, and the sport and its culture remain dominated by men.

HISTORY

The windsurfer craft was based on designs and technologies adapted from the sports of sailing and surfing. By the mid-1970s, companies were producing windsurf boards around the developed world, particularly in Europe, Canada, Japan, and Australia, with Europe one of the fastest-growing markets. The sport expanded rapidly during the 1980s, with more than half a million boards sold worldwide. This expansion was due largely to advances in technology, particularly the development of materials with higher strength-to-weight ratios, which resulted in much lighter, more efficient, and more durable boards and rigs (the sail, mast, and boom) that were easier to use, carry, and transport. The so-called funboard, which is shorter, lighter, and easier to maneuver, contributed to the boom in the mid-1980s, a period in which windsurfing was the fastest-growing sport in Europe.

By the early 1990s, windsurfing had matured somewhat; equipment sales in Europe, the home of the sport's biggest producers and largest consumer base, peaked in the late 1980s. Windsurfing has progressed from being a fad or craze and has established itself as a genuine sport. The overall sport encompasses several different forms, ranging from long-board racing and speed sailing to freestyle and wave sailing. Windsurfing is popular among participants in many industrialized nations, although the more popular centers are in Europe, Australia, and North America. Venues range from inland waters, such as lakes and reservoirs, to the open sea. Many developing nations—including countries in Africa, South America, and the Caribbean, as well as the Pacific islands—also have some windsurfing. But, because the specialized equipment is expensive and often unavailable in some of these areas, tourists (rather than residents) often constitute the majority of participants.

THE CULTURE OF WINDSURFING

Windsurfing, along with other new sports such as surfing, snowboarding, and skateboarding (also termed "life-style sports" or "whiz sports"), developed along with counterculture social movements in North America. These activities evolved in opposition to mainstream sports and, in particular, to the institutionalization of sports in recent years. A different culture has developed around these new sporting activities. The philosophy, if it may be called that, of windsurfing promotes fun, hedonism, individualism, self-actualization, and other internal rewards. It is less institutionalized than more traditional modern sports; it has fewer formal rules and regulations and fewer formal restrictions and exclusion policies; and it promotes the idea that anyone can participate. Only a few windsurfers are active members of sport associations or organizations. Windsurfing's "grass roots" reside with the casual weekend sailor.

COMPETITION

In 1984 windsurfing was accepted in the Olympic Games as a class in the yachting events. Initially, women and men competed together, but by 1994 separate women's and men's classes were established. Nevertheless, windsurfing competition takes multiple forms, and for many the pinnacle is the professional funboard racing circuit, which operates under the auspices of the Professional Windsurfing Association (PWA). Women have their own sailing fleets in each organization, although they have less representation in funboard racing than in other forms of competitive windsurfing.

Recreational windsurfers tend not to engage in formal competitions. For example, in the mid-1990s the largest competitive windsurfing organization in the United Kingdom, the United Kingdom Board Sailing Association (UKBSA), had only 1,200 members nationwide—a figure that has since dropped. For many windsurfers, organized competition is contrary to the freedom of the windsurfing life-style.

CULTURE AND GENDER

Windsurfing, like other new sports, promotes a philosophy of freedom and openness. Nevertheless, despite the lack of institutional influence, windsurfing and its culture are clearly dominated by men. According to the limited information available, women constitute between 13 percent and 30 percent of British regular windsurfers. Survey-based research in Germany (in 1983 and 1993) and Australia suggests that women constituted between 25 percent and 33 percent of windsurfers, although 40 percent of the windsurfers classified as beginners were women.

Demographic data from the United Kingdom in the mid-1990s also suggest class differences. This research showed that British women who windsurfed regularly tended to be able-bodied, white, middle-class women. Windsurfing is an expensive leisure activity, although less so than such other water sports as sailing. Women participants in particular had disposable incomes that enabled them to buy the windsurfing board and sail. Windsurfing is a much more time-consuming activity than many other sports; several hours (at least) are needed to get to the location, assemble the equipment, and then spend time out on the water. Women windsurfers interviewed in the United Kingdom suggested that, even for the professional women whose income did not limit their ability to participate, finding time to windsurf was difficult; this was especially problematic for women who lived a considerable distance from the water, or for those who had family commitments. Young children, in particular, limited women's windsurfing opportunities, particularly women's capacity to start windsurfing.

Although improvements in teaching equipment and methods have made the sport more accessible, the perception remains that windsurfing is a difficult sport to learn and one that requires considerable strength and power. Mainstream and counterculture media (especially magazines and videos) perpetuate this image by focusing on advanced windsurfing action, with male participants dominating action photographs and editorial writing. Thus, windsurfing is represented as a male preserve, with women often playing the symbolic role of the ornamental observer. This emphasis on the hard-core element of the subculture tends to exclude all outsiders, particularly women.

Research in the United Kingdom has suggested that women's involvement in the subculture is complicated and contradictory. Women's participation in the windsurfing subculture ranged from those women who did not windsurf but whose partners were involved (the windsurfing widows) to those women for whom windsurfing was a central part of their lives.

Other areas of participation aside, women are becoming increasingly involved in the production of windsurfing magazines, and they are represented at all levels of teaching and coaching. National bodies like the Royal Yachting Association (RYA), the governing body in the United Kingdom, have been active in supporting women in windsurfing. For example, the RYA was involved with the "women in coaching action plan" in June 1991, with the aim of helping women to train and qualify as instructors. Between 1991 and 1994 the number of women instructors increased from 286 to 405.

Women windsurfers themselves have also developed various initiatives to encourage and promote participation. In the United States, the Women's Windsurfing Association (WWA) was founded in 1982 by former competitor Rhonda Smith-Sanchez. In the United Kingdom, the separatist women's windsurfing group Windsurfing Women UK (later renamed Windsurfing Women) was founded in 1984. These initiatives have successfully brought together advanced women windsurfers and less experienced participants who lack the confidence to windsurf alone. The all-female environment helps women to develop their skills in a supportive, safe, and noncompetitive environment. In these venues, women provide role models, share experiences, and have developed their own communities.

CONCLUSION

As female windsurfers continue to bring more women into the activity, elite women are still pushing the limits of this developing sport. Women windsurfers at all levels have described the freedom, confidence, and independence they feel through windsurfing; they see the windsurfing culture as an important arena for developing a sense of self, separate from other people, and as a way to challenge what society thinks women should be or should do. Although the sport itself is individual, women have nevertheless found in it a sense of community.

Belinda Wheaton

Bibliography

British Market Research Bureau (1995) *TGI Index*. London: BMRB.

Crisp, Jessica. (1996) "The Winds of Maui." Cited in *Wahine*, vol. 2. Long Beach, CA: 14–20.

Donnelly, Peter. (1993) "Subcultures in Sport: Resilience and Transformation." In *Sport in Social Development: Traditions, Transitions, and Transformations*, edited by G. Ingham and John Loy. Champaign, IL: Human Kinetics Publishers, 119–147.

Gosselin, Lisa. (1994) "Throwing Caution to the Wind." *Women's Sport and Fitness* (July/August): 56–61.

Midol, Nancy, and Gérard Broyer. (1995) "Towards an Anthropological Analysis of New Sport Cultures: The Case of Whiz Sports in France." *Sociology of Sport Journal* 12: 204–212.

Profile Sport Consultancy. (1994) "The United Kingdom Windsurf Report." Joint publication between the Profile Sport Market Consultancy and the Royal Yachting Association. March.

Schaedle, Ulrike. (1993) Girls and Women in Windsurfing. Proceedings of the XIIth Association, Melbourne.

Turner, Steven. (1983) "Development and Organisation of Windsurfing." *Institute of Leisure and Amenity Management* 1: 13–15.

Whitson, David. (1994) "The Embodiment of Gender; Discipline, Domination, and Empowerment." In *Women, Sport, and Culture*, edited by S. Birrell and C. Cole. Champaign, IL: Human Kinetics, 353–371.

Woodward, Val. (1995) "Windsurfing Women and Change." Unpublished M. Lit. thesis in Women's Studies, University of Strathclyde, Scotland.

Wheaton, Belinda. (1997) "Consumption, Lifestyle and Gendered Identities in Post-Modern Sports: The Case of Windsurfing." Unpublished Ph.D. thesis, University of Brighton, England.

Wheaton, Belinda, and Alan Tomlinson. (1998) "The Changing Gender Order in Sport? The Case of Windsurfing." *Journal of Sport and Social Issues* (22 August): 252–274.

WITT, KATARINA

(1965–)

GERMAN FIGURE SKATER

Katarina Witt of East Germany was the dominant figure skater of the 1980s. She was also an international celebrity whose performances were favorites with crowds and judges alike. Witt has been controversial, in part because her physical beauty and feminine charm sometimes attracted more attention than her athletic technique.

Witt was born on 3 December 1965 in Karl-Marx-Stadt, East Germany. Her mother was a physical therapist, and her father directed an agricultural center. When Katarina started kindergarten, she and her mother walked by the local skating rink every day on the way to school. Witt soon wanted to be on the ice, making beautiful, graceful movements herself, but her mother wanted her to take dance lessons instead. Witt pleaded for the skating lessons, and her mother finally allowed her to take them. The children in the class Witt joined were already half a year into their lessons, and the teacher expected her to work doubly hard to finish the class at the same level as the other skaters. Witt's inherent talent and love for skating blossomed, and she learned a year's lessons in only six months.

When she was nine years old, Witt was chosen as a student by Jutta Müller, whose coaching had produced several international champion skaters, including Anett Pötzsch. By the age of ten, Witt was busy studying under Müller at the prestigious Chemnitz sports school in what was then communist East Germany. Witt believes that she would never have been able to pursue skating seriously in a capitalist nation, where families have to bear the full cost of equipment and training for a child's sport. In East Germany, however, the government totally financed Witt's study of skating, paid her expenses, and provided her family with a home.

Coach Muller was controlling and demanding, imposing strict rules on Witt on and off the ice. Although Witt sometimes felt stifled and frustrated by her coach, the arrangement produced impressive results. Witt performed the triple jump, one of skating's most difficult moves, when she was only eleven years old. As Witt developed her skills and routines, Müller began controlling Witt's appearance as well, including her performance costumes, hair, and makeup. As Witt grew to be a teenager, Müller encouraged her to display the more flirtatious aspects of her personality and to leverage these to her advantage. She taught Witt a trick: Pick out one man in the audience and skate the entire program as though she were skating just for him. Witt would later credit that as the one thing that most heightened her connection with audiences. Like Müller's technical training, these lessons in performance artistry would have a lasting impact on Witt's career.

At the age of fourteen, Witt finished a respectable tenth in the 1980 world championships. In 1982 she placed second in the world championships. In the same year, she also won her first European championship, and she claimed the European title for six consecutive years, from 1982 through 1987. The 1984 Olympics in Sarajevo provided the stage for Witt to capture not only her first Olympic gold but also the attention and admiration of the international media. Skating energetically to a routine of well-known American show tunes, Witt finished ahead of American Rosalyn Sumners. She continued to dominate skating in the years that followed, winning the 1985 European and world championships. In 1986 Debi Thomas upset Witt at the world championships, leaving her in second place. Although Witt recaptured the title in 1987, she was determined to beat Thomas in the 1988 Olympics in Calgary.

Katarina Witt, Olympic figure skater and gold medalist. (Ales Fevzer/Corbis)

Witt's performance at the 1988 Olympics was a history-making event for several reasons. She and arch-rival Thomas skated to music from the opera *Carmen,* and the media quickly seized the opportunity to promote the competition as "the dueling Carmens." Thomas had a disappointing performance, missing the landings on her first triple-toe move and several subsequent jumps. Witt's performance was outstanding, and it brought her a second Olympic gold medal. No woman since Sonja Henie, who won her gold medals in 1932 and 1936, had won two consecutive Olympic gold medals in skating. Witt's performance to *Carmen* would also spark a later project for her—a television special called *Carmen on Ice*—for which she would win an Emmy Award.

After the 1988 Olympics, Witt won her last victory at the world championships. She then became a professional skater. It was a difficult decision for Witt because, after competing for thirteen years, she was not quite sure what life in a noncompetitive atmosphere would be like. She made several television specials with fellow Olympic gold medalist Brian Boitano, including *Carmen on Ice*. In 1990 they toured the United States together, presenting a series of successful live shows to audiences around the country.

By 1992 Witt's professional status made her ineligible to compete in the Olympics, but she remained visible, providing figure skating commentary for the CBS television network. In 1994 a rule change allowed professionals to compete in the Olympics at Lillehammer, and Witt placed seventh among a field of competitors that included skaters such as Nancy Kerrigan.

Detractors have criticized Witt for the emphasis she placed on her beauty and femininity, saying that she played up her body and flirted with the judges to win. Witt has responded that skating should be full of "theater and visual appeal." She believes that enhancing the beauty of the performance through costume, makeup, and personality only adds to the sport and that skating only for technical merit lacks the artistic expression that has come to characterize the best in figure skating history.

In the 1990s, Witt pursued many new projects. She published an autobiography, *Meine Jahre zwischen Pflicht und Kür* (My Years Between Duty and Free Skating), and launched her own line of jewelry called *It's My Style*. She appeared on television shows—*Frasier*, for instance—and she starred in and coproduced television specials for HBO. She also appeared in movies, including a cameo role in *Jerry Maguire* and a small costarring role in *Ronin*. In 1998 she continued to cause controversy when she became the first major female athlete to pose nude in *Playboy*.

Wendy Painter

Bibliography

Coffey, Wayne. (1992) *Olympic Gold: Katarina Witt*. Woodbridge, CT: Blackbirch Press.

Johnson, Anne Janette. (1996) *Great Women in Sports*. Detroit: Visible Ink Press.

Markel, Robert. (1997) *The Women's Sports Encyclopedia*. New York: Henry Holt.

WOMENSPORT INTERNATIONAL

WomenSport International (WSI) is an organization that advocates the view that sport is a basic human right for women. The organization helps women to achieve this right by working toward positive change, lobbying, and, where appropriate, challenging the status quo.

WomenSport International was officially launched at the international conference on "Women and Sport: the Challenge of Change," in Brighton, England, in May 1994. However, the impetus for the new organization came much earlier, from discussions among several women's sports advocates during congresses of the International Association for Physical Education and Sport for Girls and Women (IAPESGW) in 1987 (Finland) and 1993 (Melbourne). These conferences left some participants disappointed at the slow pace of change on behalf of girls and women in sport, especially concerning such difficult issues as eating disorders, sexual discrimination and harassment, and political change. Some of those attending the Melbourne conference decided to take the initiative: they arranged a meeting outside the main congress, which was attended by women from twenty-three countries. The president of the IAPESGW, Patricia Bowen West, was also present by invitation. Following a lively debate that raised the possibility of starting up a new organization, those in attendance agreed to give the IAPESGW time to respond to their concerns.

The organization, however, did not address the issues. Soon after, Barbara Drinkwater (United States), the de facto founder of WSI and a former president of the American College of Sports Medicine (the first woman to hold this post at the college), contacted Kari Fasting (Norway) to urge her to join in a new initiative. Neither had seen any signs of movement from the IAPESGW, and both believed that something radical was needed to instigate change. The two women subsequently agreed to meet at the November 1993 conference of the North American Association of Sport Sociology. There, they and other major figures in the women's sport advocacy movement, such as Ann Hall, Helen Lenskyj, Marion Lay, and Sandi Kirby (all of Canada), and Libby Darlison (Australia), decided to set up WSI. An interim executive committee was formed, consisting of Drinkwater, Fasting, Darlison, and Lay. Celia Brackenridge was invited to join the executive committee in view of her previous efforts at establishing the Women's International Sports Coalition (WISC), and the committee began work immediately to fashion a constitution, aims, and goals for the new organization.

WOMEN'S INTERNATIONAL SPORTS COALITION (WISC)

WomenSport International was the latest effort to establish a global advocacy group for women's sports. Prior to WSI, there was the WISC, another embryonic international organization for women and sports that appeared briefly. The coalition emerged following a series of workshops on international issues relating to women and sports, held during the 1992 annual conference of the Women's Sports Foundation (United States) in Denver, Colorado. Diane Palmeson, formerly of Sport Canada and the Canadian Association for the Advancement of Women+Sport (CAAW+S) and Brackenridge, first chair of the Women's Sports Foundation (WSF) (UK) led a group from different parts of the English-speaking world in brainstorming and planning sessions. These discussions focused on raising the profile of women's sport by drawing on the work of various existing national organizations. The group's members included several prestigious individuals from the world of women and sports who brought with them extensive skills and a shared commitment to develop a working model for the advocacy of women's sport internationally. Notable among them was Bobbie Steen, from Canada's Promotion Plus, who was to die from cancer in 1996; Darlene Kluka, former president of the U.S. National Association for Girls' and Women's Sport; and Yvonne Rate, representing the Australian Sports Commission and the Australian government's Women's Sports Promotion Unit.

The idea behind WISC was to ask each national group to lend its voice, energy, and power to an international coalition while retaining each group's own national identity. In this way, in the words of Donna Lopiano, the newly appointed chief executive of the WSF (United States), WISC would be able to draw on enormous "illusory power" because of the many women represented via their organization's memberships; the organization could perhaps influence such bodies as the International Olympic Committee (IOC). At the plenary session of the Denver conference, members presented a rationale for WISC together with proposals for its working agenda. However, as Carole Oglesby (who was later elected president of the WSI) predicted at the time, the WISC would never develop beyond this stage because it lacked its own identity.

PURPOSE

Organizations dedicated to the betterment of women's sports range from those based purely on voluntary action to those based entirely in government departments. Between these extremes of the nonstatutory (public) and statutory (government) lie a number of partnership arrangements that also embrace charitable foundations and private sector interests. WSI draws support from any government agency or individual that subscribes to its aims and objectives; in so doing, WSI shares many of its basic values with other agencies working for women's sport. Crucially, WSI is demarcated by its approach, which is to transform women's sport, to work toward positive change, lobbying and, where appropriate, challenging the status quo. WSI advocates the view that sport is a basic human right of the female.

The mission statement of WSI sets out its main purpose: "WomenSport International is an organization dedicated to increasing positive opportunities and experiences for girls and women in sport and physical activity."

WSI was formed in recognition of the following:

1. Enormous global growth in participation by women in sport and physical recreation;
2. Shared problems facing women in sport across many different cultures;
3. Persistent inequalities between men's and women's sport, despite several decades of struggle for parity;

4. Failure of existing organizational mechanisms to address or resolve issues facing women in sport; and
5. A need for an international, politicized approach to women's sport that would help to transform the structures and practices of sport and improve the quality of women's experience and place women's sport within the broader context of women's lives.

AIMS AND STRATEGIES

The organization has multiple aims. These include identifying and addressing issues of importance to girls and women in sport and physical activity, as well as serving as an international contact point to provide and exchange information, expertise, and support. Beyond this, WSI aims to operate as an effective international advocacy group to increase the participation and advancement of girls and women in sport and physical activity at all levels. Basic to the above is the group's aim to make sport a more female-friendly institution.

The strategies that WSI uses to achieve these aims include forming liaisons with, and developing cooperative working relationships with, key international sports organizations, including multigame organizations, international federations, and other government and private bodies to ensure that all these groups are fair and equitable on gender issues and reflect the needs and interests of women and girls. The organization also initiates and cooperates with projects on the advancement of girls and women in sport and physical activity; produces and disseminates educational materials and other information; and advises all international organizations, conferences, forums, and the like whose agendas include issues relating to girls and women in sport and physical activity. WSI works to ensure that issues relevant to girls and women in sports are included on the programs of major international conferences, develops strong international networks between women in sport through dissemination and exchange of information, and continues to build a representative and active membership.

ACTIVITIES

WSI was established as an organization oriented toward issues and actions. In the words of President Carole Oglesby at the 1998 Windhoek Conference, the organization uses "cooperative advocacy" and "assertive advocacy." In the first three years of its existence, WSI set up several task forces to address such issues as physical activity and girls' and women's health, the female athlete triad (amenorrhea, osteoporosis, and eating disorders), master athletes, gender verification, and sexual harassment in sports. Other task forces are established as issues of concern arise. The WSI advisory board, committees, and task force members are drawn from individuals from all over the world who demonstrate expertise, experience, and commitment to WSI's agenda.

WSI members have presented many academic papers on research relevant to these task forces; they have also been active in delivering speeches, lobbying politicians, and appearing in the media to communicate the organization's work. An international database and an information exchange network have been established to facilitate the sharing of ideas, contacts, and knowledge. WSI has also worked closely with many of the major sport agencies to explore issues of concern to women and girls. Activities include: (1) sending representatives to the IOC at its Centennial Conference in Paris in 1996 and at a special conference on the place of women in Olympic sport, held in Lausanne in 1996; (2) offering significant input to the Women's Tennis Council Commission on age eligibility, which resulted in raising the minimum age for the pro tour; (3) ensuring that the issue of gender was included on the program of the First World Forum on Physical Activity and Sport in Canada; and (4) assuming a place on the International Working Group on women and sports that collated cross-government strategies on the issue between the 1994 Brighton and 1998 Windhoek Conferences.

WSI has also designed and run developmental training courses for women sports leaders in the Pacific and in Africa and was represented in 1995 at the Fourth United Nations World Conference on Women, which was held in Beijing. This conference, for the first time, adopted a set of resolutions about women's health, sports, and physical activity levels.

WSI produces a members' newsletter, *The Starting Line,* and has also published leaflets on "The Female Athlete Triad" and "Sexual Harassment in Sport." Membership in WSI is open to individuals and organizations. By January 1995 more than 30 countries were represented in the membership list.

Celia Brackenridge

WOMEN'S SPORTS FOUNDATION

The Women's Sports Foundation (WSF) is a nonprofit, educational membership organization established in 1974 by several leading women athletes in the United States to promote the participation of girls and women in sports and physical fitness. Billie Jean King, a well-known tennis professional, Donna de Varona, an Olympic swimmer, and others were frustrated over the obstacles women had to overcome to participate in sports and, once participating, the difficulties they faced in gaining media coverage, financial support, and spectator interest.

In schools, whether at the high school or college level, there were often no coaches, no recognition, and no financial aid. On the professional level, the stark disparity between support and salaries for female as opposed to male athletes made clear the need for an organized political and educational campaign for gender equality in American sports.

The passage of Title IX of the Education Amendments of 1972 opened the door to equal opportunity by requiring that females be provided the same opportunity to participate in sports as males at schools and colleges that received federal support. It also required that female athletes receive athletic scholarships proportional to their participation. For example, if there were equal numbers of male and female basketball players, the scholarship budget had to be divided equally among males and females. From its very beginning, the Women's Sports Foundation advocated rigorous enforcement of, and compliance with, Title IX.

On the professional level, by 1974 there had been increasing success for women athletes in sports such as tennis and golf; there were, however, no professional opportunities for women in sports like softball, basketball, gymnastics, and track and field. The WSF worked hard to ensure that women athletes were treated equally and to enlarge and expand their opportunities.

STRUCTURE OF THE ORGANIZATION

The WSF is governed by a board of trustees whose members are leaders in women's sports. They include athletes, coaches, administrators, businesspeople, and others who support women's sports. A national advisory board, with more than 300 members, provides expertise in marketing, media, history, research, business, public relations, sports medicine, and other areas. The collective membership of all organizations represented on the advisory board totals more than 50 million. Organizations represented include the professional sports leagues, such as the Ladies' Professional Golf Association (LPGA), Women's National Basketball Association (WNBA), and Women's Tennis Association (WTA), coaching organizations such as the National Softball Coaches Association (NSCA) and the Women's Basketball Coaches Association (WBCA), girl-serving agencies including the U.S. Girl Scouts and YWCA, and national sport-governing bodies such as U.S. Field Hockey and U.S. Gymnastics. The advisory board is divided into six councils: athletes, business, coaches, communities, research, and organizations.

MISSION OF OBJECTIVES

The Women's Sports Foundation concentrates on four major areas: education, opportunity, advocacy, and recognition. In education, the foundation works to increase public understanding of the benefits of sports and fitness for females of all ages. Its annual summit brings leading figures in sports and fitness together to share information and plan for future events and initiatives. The foundation publishes newsletters and research papers, creates public service announcements, produces video programming, and hosts an information service and website.

For example, the 1985 *Miller Lite Report on Sports & Fitness in the Lives of Working Women* surveyed the responses of 1,682 athletic women about their interest in participating in or watching specific sports, their early childhood experiences, the support of friends and family, their encounters with coeducational participation, and their attitudes and experiences with drugs, prejudice, and single sex or coed sports. The study found that "a generational shift may be occurring in American sports today, one that could transform the way children and adults encounter one another as they participate in future sports activities. Coed sports, previously found mostly among selected groups, and in specific activities, have become commonplace." According to the study, three developments have spurred this change: "the efforts of women to seek sports partners of equal skill, regardless of gender; the belief that women have something to teach men about humane competition; and abundant evidence of a strong self-confidence among athletic women."

In the area of opportunity, the foundation sponsors grants for girls and women to discover and develop their athletic and leadership potential. An internship program has offered more than 300 women an opportunity to gain experience in variety of sports careers. Former interns have gone on to work for ESPN sports television network, the New York Mets, the National Hockey League (NHL), Spalding (manufacturer of sports equipment), and Reebok (manufacturer of sports shoes).

The WSF's Community Action Program (CAP) involves cities in more than thirty-six states. The program provides awards and grants to recognize the achievements of girls and women from the age of six. The Ocean Spray Travel and Training Fund has awarded grants of more than $1 million to help more than a thousand individuals and teams since its inception in 1984. Former recipients of these grants include: Picabo Street, the Olympic gold medal skier; Kristi Yamaguchi, the 1992 Olympic figure skating champion; Mary Ellen Clark, the 1996 Olympic bronze medal diver; Kerri Strug, the 1996 Olympic gold medal gymnast; and Michelle Akers, the 1996 Olympic gold medalist in soccer.

Other grant programs of the foundation include: Leadership Development Grants for programs that train female coaches, officials, and other sports leaders; Tampax Grants for Girls for sports programs for girls nine to eighteen participating in school athletics and sports organizations; the Quaker Rice Cakes Research Grant Program for nutrition and exercise programs; the Dorothy Harris Scholarship for female graduate students in sports-related majors; and the Linda Riddle/SGMA Scholarship for financial support of young female athletes. In 1998 the foundation awarded more than $1 million to 199 individuals and 498 teams or sports programs.

The WSF advocates changes in laws, policies, programs, and social patterns that discourage female participation in sports and fitness. With four other organizations, the foundation created the first National Girls and Women in Sports Day in 1987. The foundation also organizes an annual event to educate U.S. leaders about the needs and achievements of girls and women in sports and holds events throughout the nation to provide the public with information about issues facing women in sports and fitness.

The WSF continues to advocate thorough enforcement of the provisions of Title IX and offers information and aid to women facing discrimination. An example of the foundation's advocacy efforts is the "Gender Equity Report Card 1997,"

ATHLETIC REWARDS

One important way the Women's Sports Foundation supports the growth of women's sports is through its small-grant program which each year awards more than $1 million in financial assistance to female athletes at all stages of their sports careers. The grants have helped many athletes who reached world class status, and of the 76 American women who won medals at the 1996 Olympics, 44 had received grants from the foundation. Among notable athletes who have received grants are tennis player Billie Jean King, figure skater Kristi Yamaguchi, and soccer player Michelle Akers.

prepared by Dr. Don Sabo, which graded 767 institutions from Division I-A through Division III in terms of how well they met equity standards. Sabo noted that "in 1996, male athletes were still receiving almost twice as many opportunities to play in school and college athletic programs and over $184,000,000 more in college athletic scholarships each year than their female counterparts. Plain and simple, this is not right and is in violation of federal law." The report stressed that "the Office of Civil Rights has been incredibly ineffective in executing its responsibility to make sure that federally funded educational institutions are complying with the conditions of such funding, one of which is non-discrimination on the basis of gender."

The WSF's recognition programs include honoring outstanding individuals for their achievements in athletics and their contributions to women's sports. Founded in 1980, the International Women's Sports Hall of Fame honors female coaches and athletes who have made historic contributions to women's sports. They are chosen because of their achievements, breakthroughs, innovative styles, and great commitment to women's sports in three different categories: Coach, Pioneer (pre-1960 achievements), and Contemporary (post-1960 achievements). Some of the inductees are Mildred "Babe" Didrikson-Zaharias, Althea Gibson, Billie Jean King, Wilma Rudolph, Flo Hyman, and Mary Lou Retton. Some of the honored coaches are Constance Applebee, Sharon Backus, Nell Jackson, and Pat Head Summit.

Plans are under way to build a permanent site for the Women's Sports Hall of Fame at the foundation's new International Center for Women's Sports and Fitness in East Meadow, New York. The center will house a library of Hall of Fame videos, athletes' memorabilia, photos, artwork, and interactive exhibits, as well as a library and resource center. The first facility of its kind in the United States to highlight female athletes, the center is meant to inspire a greater appreciation of the accomplishments of female athletes and encourage greater opportunity for girls and women in sports. The center will also house the foundation's extensive collection of research materials and its referral service, a primary source of information on women's sports in the nation.

The foundation accomplishes its mission by raising money. More than 10,000 members/donors contribute to programs. Fund-raising events and outings supply critical dollars. For example, the foundation's Annual Salute to Women in Sports provided more than $700,000 for programs in 1998. Corporate sponsors have also been a major element of revenue production since the foundation's inception. General Motors, Mervyn's California, Merrill Lynch, Ocean Spray, Reebok, and other corporations support events, awards, grant programs, and educational materials.

INTERNATIONAL INFLUENCE

The foundation has helped other countries—including the United Kingdom and Japan—to form their own Women's Sports Foundations. In addition, in May 1999 the WSF was granted consultative status to the United Nations Economic and Social Council, a position that makes it possible for the organization to provide input to the council on women's issues and women's sports participation around the world. The aim of the organization is to advance women's sports "as a vehicle for addressing global issues affecting girls and women," in addition to promoting and supporting girls' and women's full and equal participation in sports and fitness activities in the United States. By encouraging such participation, the WSF aims to improve the physical, emotional, and mental well-being of all females.

Mickey Friedman

Bibliography

Women's Sports Foundation. (1999) <http://www.lifetimetv.com/WoSport/index.htm>.

WORKER SPORTS

Worker sports were an outgrowth of the socialist movements that took shape between World War I and World War II. For millions of workers between the two wars, sports were an integral part of the labor movement, and worker sports clubs existed in almost every country of Europe, North

Peasants at the First International Workmen's Olympiade in Prague. (Hulton-Deutsch Collection/Corbis)

and South America, and Asia. By 1930 worker sports united well over 4 million people, making it by far the largest working-class cultural movement. Today, the residue of the movement remains; it is strongest in the *Hapoel* (meaning "The Worker") associations in Israel and in France.

The worker sport movement was important for women because it represented an opportunity to take part in activities that, at the time, were otherwise closed to most women. The aims of worker sports differed from country to country. In all nations, however, the goal was to give working people the chance to take part in healthy recreation and to do so in a socialist atmosphere. Worker sports differed from bourgeois sports in that the worker version was open to all workers, women as well as men, black as well as white. It provided a socialist alternative to bourgeois competitive sports, to commercialism, chauvinism, and obsession with stars and records. It replaced capitalist values with socialist ones and set the foundation for a true working-class culture. Worker sports, therefore, initially emphasized less competitive physical activities, such as gymnastics, acrobatics, tumbling, pyramid-forming, hiking, cycling, and swimming (often against the clock and oneself rather than opponents). Thus, no one was put at a competitive disadvantage.

IDEALS AND REALITIES

During the 1920s and 1930s, worker sports were trapped in a society where working-class women continued to be unfairly treated at work and in the home, with unequal pay, domestic drudgery, and large families. It was difficult for women to escape into sports. Despite the good intentions of the various leagues, there were obstacles to women's full participation. In Great Britain, there were complaints from women members of sport organizations that men viewed the women as getting in the way with male-sponsored initiatives. In Israel, where Hapoel is the only worker sport organization actually controlling its country's sports, there are many complaints from women that no money is specifically allocated for their sport, and that the organization largely neglects women.

Women elsewhere also made strong efforts to counteract male domination. In Norway, the Worker Sports Federation set up a Women's Central Committee, and in 1934 as many as 47 percent of the local clubs in Oslo had organized women's sport committees. The federation's general assembly of 1935 decided to make "physical age" the basis for classification in competition for young people of both sexes. The basis for calculating this was a person's height, weight, and chronological age—thus trying to obviate discrimination based on size and sex. In 1937, Norway instituted a form of sex quota whereby a women's committee had the right to attend the annual meetings of the various sports if any female member was registered in that particular sport. In some countries, women took part in almost all competitive sports. In others, however, such as Finland, women confined themselves mainly to noncompetitive gymnastics, dance, and such sports as cycling. The Finnish Worker Sports Federation (TUL) continued to play an important role in Finnish sports even after World War II and had its own periodical as well as a separate publication for women. Women's participation extended to other sports after 1945 as TUL, like worker sport federations everywhere, embraced more competitive, commercial sports.

In the United States, the Labor Sports Union of America (LSUA), formed in 1927, advocated sports-for-all activities, including women, and competed with the Young Men's Christian Association for the use of local sport facilities. In 1932 in Chicago, the LSUA held a counter-Olympics to the Games in Los Angeles, stressing that its Games were open to all truly amateur women and men. The Chicago Games illustrated the fundamental unity of all working people, regardless of sex, color, creed, or national origin (in contrast with the Olympic Games, which were mainly confined to the sons of the rich and privileged). All in all, the worker sports movement tried to provide an alternative experience based on worker culture and inspired visions of a new socialist culture.

James Riordan

Bibliography

Krüger, Arnd, and James Riordan. (1996) *The Story of Worker Sport*. Champaign, IL: Human Kinetics.

WORLD UNIVERSITY GAMES

The World University Games, or Universiades, are one of the oldest international multisport competitions. Organized in summer and winter versions, the games are open to full-time university students between seventeen and twenty-eight years of age, from any nation. Students who have graduated from a university within the previous twelve months are also eligible to participate. The World University Games have outpaced the Olympic Games in providing international competitive opportunities for women; at the same time, however, they have generally lagged behind the Olympics in making a place for women in the games' organization and administration.

HISTORY

The games were first sponsored by the Confédération Internationale d'Étudiants (CIE; International Student Confederation), a group founded in 1919; Frenchman Jean Petitjean was the first president of the CIE. A test event consisting of track and field events in Paris in 1923 is often considered to be the first of the University Games. In 1924 the CIE organized its first multisport games in Warsaw, Poland.

Originally, Petitjean promoted the games as the University Olympic Games until Baron Pierre de Coubertin, president of the International Olympic Committee (IOC), protested and convinced Petitjean to change the name so that the word *Olympic* would be used solely for the Olympic Games. Newspaper reports of the time reveal the sparsity of events for women. Women did take part in the 1937 Paris games but in a very limited schedule in track and field.

The CIE International University Games were held in the following years and locations (see Table 1).

After World War II the Union Internationale d'Étudiants (UIE; International Union of Students) was formed to continue the work of the CIE, which had dissolved because of the war. The first games held after World War II were the winter games of January 1947 in Davos, Switzerland. In August 1947 summer games were held in Paris, France. Cold War divisions and differing ideologies led to the creation of the Fédération Internationale du Sport Universitaire (FISU; Inter-

Table 1. Locations of World University Games

Summer	Winter
1923 Paris, France	1928 Cortina, Italy
1924 Warsaw, Poland	1930 Davos, Switzerland
1927 Rome, Italy	1933 Bardonecchia, Italy
1928 Paris, France	1935 St. Moritz, Switzerland
1930 Darmstadt, Germany	1937 Zell am See, Austria
1933 Turin, Italy	1939 Lillehammer, Norway
1935 Budapest, Hungary	
1937 Paris, France	
1939 Monte Carlo, Monaco	

national Federation of University Sport) in 1949, and for a time the UIE (which had become an Eastern bloc organization) and the FISU (which was created as a Western European group) sponsored separate University Games for their respective members. The FISU organized Summer Sports Weeks in Merano, Italy in 1949; Luxembourg in 1951; and San Sebastián, Spain, in 1955. The federation also organized winter sports weeks in Bad Gastein, Germany, in 1951; Saint Moritz, Switzerland, in 1953; Jahorina, Yugoslavia, in 1955; and Oberammergau, Germany, in 1957. In contrast, the UIE held summer games in Budapest in 1949, in Berlin in 1951, and again in Budapest in 1954. Winter games of the UIE Games were held in Poiana, Romania, in 1949; Semeringen and Vienna, Austria, in 1953; and Zakopane, Poland, in 1956.

Finally, in 1957, the two bodies agreed to hold competitions together, which they did later that year in Paris. The UIE still held separate games two more times, in Vienna in 1959 and in Helsinki in 1962.

The Paris 1957 games came to be known as the University Unity Games, and in 1959 the term *Universiade* was adopted. The 1959 games held in Turin, Italy, were numbered as the first Universiade. (See the table for a list of Universiades.)

Since 1959 the women athletes in the University Games have become increasingly visible. Table 2 compares the participation figures of the summer World University Games to the summer Olympic Games. A figure of 50 percent would signify an equal number of male and female competitors. (Olympic Games are in bold)

Numerous female athletes have starred at the University Games. In 1961, Olympic track and field stars such as the sisters from the Soviet Union, Irina and Tamara Press, and Romania's Lia Manoliu and Iolanda Balas were advertised as the top athletes of the games.

In 1973 Olga Korbut, fresh from her 1972 Olympic medal-winning performances in Munich, caused a stir at the 1973 Moscow University Games when she wanted to make her routines more difficult. Korbut was threatened with expulsion by the International Gymnastic Federation, which claimed her routines were too dangerous. Korbut threatened to quit the sport but eventually got her way, competing and winning more gold for the Soviet Union.

Table 2. Women Competitors in World University Games

Year	Host City	Men	Women	Total	Percentage of Women
1959	Turin	865	120	985	12.18%
1960	**Rome**	**4738**	**610**	**5348**	**11.41%**
1961	Sofia	899	371	1270	29.21%
1963	Porto Allegre	565	148	713	20.76%
1964	**Tokyo**	**4457**	**683**	**5140**	**13.29%**
1965	Budapest	1290	439	1729	25.39%
1967	Tokyo	698	240	938	25.59%
1968	**Mexico City**	**4750**	**781**	**5531**	**14.12%**
1970	Turin	1542	542	2084	26.01%
1972	**Munich**	**5848**	**1299**	**7147**	**18.18%**
1973	Moscow	1940	778	2718	28.62%
1975	Rome	336	132	468	28.21%
1976	**Montreal**	**4834**	**1251**	**6085**	**20.56%**
1977	Sofia	2071	868	2939	29.53%
1979	Mexico City	2262	712	2974	23.94%
1980	**Moscow**	**4265**	**1088**	**5353**	**20.33%**
1981	Bucharest	2071	841	2912	28.88%
1983	Edmonton	1669	731	2400	30.46%
1984	**Los Angeles**	**5458**	**1620**	**7078**	**22.89%**
1985	Kobe	2009	774	2783	27.81%
1987	Zagreb	2685	1219	3904	31.22%
1988	**Seoul**	**7218**	**2471**	**9689**	**25.50%**
1989	Duisburg	1271	514	1785	28.80%
1991	Sheffield	2134	1212	3346	36.22%
1992	**Barcelona**	**7330**	**2923**	**10253**	**28.51%**
1993	Buffalo	2407	1175	3582	32.80%
1995	Fukuoka	2636	1313	3949	33.25%
1996	**Atlanta**	**7223**	**3626**	**10849**	**33.42%**
1997	Sicily	2299	1233	3532	34.91%

At the same games, Cathy Carr, a U.S. swimmer, the world record holder and Munich Olympic gold medalist in the 100-meter breaststroke, was upset by the Russian Lubov Rusanova, who would win the silver medal in the same event in the Montreal Olympics three years later.

Other Olympic champion gymnasts have repeated their successes at the University Games. Nadia Comaneci of Romania competed at the

World University Games after her Olympic triumphs. At the 1981 games in Bucharest, Romania, Comaneci first lit the torch in the opening ceremonies and then led the Romanian team by winning five gold medals. Another Romanian, Ekaterina Szabo, won three individual gold medals at the Los Angeles Olympics and the all-around silver medal in the 1984 Olympic Games and the 1985 Kobe Universiade. Szabo won three more silver medals at the 1987 Universiade. Her primary competition at the 1987 games in Zagreb was the Soviet Union's Elena Chouchounova, who won six gold medals. Chouchounova was the all-around champion in the Seoul Olympics the following year.

Basketball stars Lynnette Woodward, Anne Myers, and Anne Donovan all represented the United States at the University Games during their respective collegiate careers. Track and field has had many star female athletes competing in the University Games, before and after their Olympic triumphs. High jumper Sara Simeoni of Italy won the gold medal at the Games of 1979 and 1981 and took the Olympic gold in 1980, between the two Universiades. Gabriella Dorio of Italy and Doina Melinta of Romania placed first and second, respectively, in the 1500-meter run at the 1981 Universidade in Bucharest and at the 1984 Olympics in Los Angeles. And in Bucharest, Melinta took the gold medal in the 800-meter run, and Dorio won the silver medal, whereas, in the Los Angeles Olympic 800-meter race, Melinta won again, and Dorio finished fourth.

Three-time Olympian Gwen Torrance of the United States first won the 100-meter dash at the Kobe games in 1985 and won the 100- and 200-meter races in the 1987 games in Zagreb. Romania's Paula Ivan won the gold medals in the 1500- and 3000-meter events at the Zagreb Universiade; she also won the gold medal for the 1500-meter race and the silver medal for the 3000-meter race at the Seoul Olympics. She returned to the University Games in 1989 in Duisburg to win the 1500- and 3000-meter races again.

The Buffalo Universiade of 1993 was historically significant as the first international multi-sport event to include women's soccer. China upset the heavily favored U.S. team and won the gold medal. Women, however, have been included in other aspects of the games as well. Diana, Princess of Wales, along with her husband, Prince Charles, opened the 1983 games in Edmonton, Canada. The 1991 games were opened by Princess Anne, a member of the International Olympic Committee. The torch for the 1989 games was lit by Heidi Rosendahl, a two-time Olympic gold medal long jumper and pentathlete (for Germany, 1972). The 1991 torch was carried into the stadium by British astronaut Helen Sharman. Kathy Scanlan was the head of the organizing committee for the 1993 games in Buffalo.

The University Games have experienced some of the problems that face other major competitions. The Sheffield Games of 1991 are significant in that they marked the first time any University Games athlete, male or female, registered a positive drug test. A female shot putter, Xinmei Sui of China, tested positive after winning her event. Also in Sheffield, controversy raged in gymnastics over the propriety of certain uniforms. Twenty-eight female athletes had points deducted because their apparel was considered too revealing.

The organizing committee for the Buffalo games broke with international sports policy by refusing to require the sometimes controversial gender testing for females at the games. The FISU first made the organizing committee get permission to waive the tests from the various international federations that normally require them. Each federation agreed and gender testing was dropped for those games.

Notwithstanding the success that women have achieved at the University Games, they are not well represented on the executive levels of the FISU. As of 1998, one woman, Yvonne Bouanga Akpa, from the Ivory Coast, held a position on the twenty-four-member executive committee. But the games continue to serve the purpose of providing young athletes with the opportunity to compete at the international level and to meet athletes from other nations.

Daniel Bell

Bibliography

Campana, Roch, ed. (1993) "1923–1993, the World University Games Celebrate Their 70th Anniversary." *FISU Magazine* (June): 17–21.

WRESTLING

Wrestling is a contact sport in which the participants aim to take down their opponent by using various holds. These holds usually involve placing both the opponent's shoulders in contact with the mat; this is called a pin or fall. The objective may seem simple; accomplishing it often requires extraordinary effort and skill. Traditionally, wrestling has been a male domain from which, to a great extent, women were excluded. Only recently have females been welcomed by the international wrestling community and by the sport in general, though women are still not on equal terms with men. Women have not yet been permitted to participate in the Olympic Games, and separate international competitions are organized for women and men. That competitions are being set up for women and men together is one sign of progress and growth in female wrestling.

HISTORY

Wrestling is one of the world's oldest sports, with a history that extends back thousands of years to the development of the first great empires of the world, around the Mediterranean and in the valleys of the Nile and Euphrates, and in India and China. Paintings from Egypt about 3000 BCE are believed to be the oldest evidence of the sport. In Greece, wrestling is known from the stories and legends handed down by the early poets and storytellers. Homer gives accounts of wrestling matches in the *Iliad*, probably in the ninth century BCE, including a story of a wrestling combat between Ajax and Odysseus with Achilles as the referee. From the Roman Empire the oldest signs of wrestling are found in wall paintings dating from the fifth century BCE.

Wrestling has developed in several forms around the world, and different countries have distinct styles. The Greco-Roman and freestyle have been dominant in Europe, and freestyle is the most common form in the United States. Among the many styles throughout Asia, sumo is the oldest form and is still very popular, as are the martial arts, which are related disciplines.

The history of women's wrestling in ancient times is largely unrecorded, but some documentation does exist. This evidence suggests that such activities were related to holy or religious ceremonies contested by girls of noble heritage, in which only virgin, unmarried females could participate. From the Greek myths, the legend of Atalanta is best known through a vase painting from the fifth or sixth century BCE, which shows her grappling with Peleus.

As wrestling developed in the twentieth century, combats were organized professionally and took place in the circus or in traveling booths, in Europe and the United States. Most participants were men, but women were also allowed to perform. Between World War I and World War II, female wrestlers became very popular in several countries, but most of the women who took part were well aware that the crowds came for the novelty, to see women wrestle. The matches were gimmicks, for the most part, including mud-wrestling.

Although participation has increased, women's wrestling remains controversial. The sport's physical requirements and high degree of body contact link it with masculinity, and so it is still often considered inappropriate for females. Therefore, as women's wrestling has developed during the 1970s through the 1990s, the athletes have experienced various barriers within the sport and in daily life.

In the 1970s, female wrestling was largely practiced in some European countries, such as France, Belgium, and Norway but, during the 1980s, the sport began to develop on other continents. In 1983 the International Federation of Associated Wrestling Styles (FILA) established the first commission for women's wrestling.

WOMEN'S WRESTLING WORLDWIDE

In the United States and Canada, women participate in professional wrestling. In other parts of the world, they are primarily involved with amateur wrestling. Major international competitions for females began in 1987, with the world championship, followed the next year by the European championship, then the African championship and the Oceania championship (both in 1996), and the Pan American championship in 1997. Discussion continues about including women in the Olympic Games, and FILA proposed their inclusion in the year 2000 Games in Sydney. FILA has suggested reducing the number of weight classes among men and replacing them with events for women.

Today, about 10,000 women wrestle worldwide in about eighty countries. World championship events generally attract more than 100 women from twenty-five to thirty countries.

RULES AND PLAY

About 200 different forms of wrestling are practiced today, with freestyle and Greco-Roman dominating amateur competition. Women's style is called female wrestling and is very close to the men's freestyle. Until 1987 some females also participated in Greco-Roman wrestling but, because so few women took part in the sport, FILA decided to concentrate on freestyle only. The main difference between the two styles is that, in Greco-Roman, wrestlers may not use holds below the hips or use their legs for gripping, pushing, or pressure—both of which are permitted in freestyle and female wrestling.

In competitions, wrestlers are divided into various classes based on sex, age, and weight. The wrestlers weigh in the day before the competition. A wrestling match for women lasts 4 minutes and is prolonged another 2 minutes when the results are a draw. The match takes place on a wrestling mat, which is 12 × 12 meters (13 × 13 yards). Three referees are needed, each with his or her separate tasks. According to the standardized value system, the wrestlers are rewarded for the holds they use to take down the opponent. The various holds are estimated as more and less difficult and are rewarded differently. Points are given for each rewarded hold. A match is terminated when one wrestler is 10 points ahead or when time runs out. The contestant with the most points wins. At least three points are needed to win the match. The rules in wrestling are continually being changed by FILA, the controlling organization.

A wrestler's personal equipment needs are simple: light, soft-soled boots and a wrestling costume, generally a sleeveless jersey. Some wrestlers also use knee pads, a mouth guard, or headgear.

POSITIVE AND NEGATIVE EFFECTS OF WRESTLING

Advocates of wrestling emphasize that it offers wholesome physical and mental exercise. It is said to be one of the best sports for developing physical fitness: it builds muscle tone, improves balance, and develops quickness, agility, flexibility, and power. It also may foster positive personality characteristics, such as courage, determination, self-confidence, and self-reliance. For girls, in particular, wrestling is considered useful in self-defense and to impart a feeling of security in daily life.

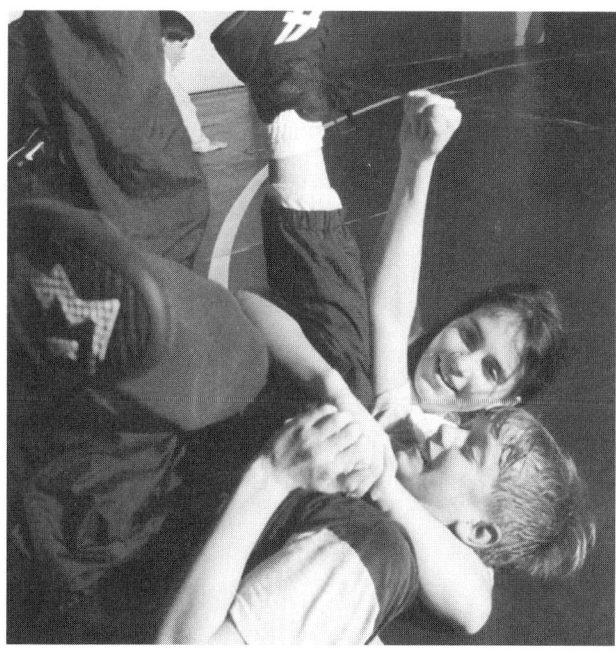

A female wrestler takes down her male teammate during a high school practice. (AP Photo)

Injuries are common in wrestling, but they are seldom serious. Use of protective equipment can reduce some injuries; for example, headgear will protect against "cauliflower ear," which refers to an ear that becomes disfigured after many falls.

That the athletes' weight is a major concern in wrestling may have implications for health. To maintain the proper weight, most wrestlers focus on nutrition and calories. This may lead to a healthy life-style, but it may also increase the risk of eating disorders. Athletes in general are more prone to developing eating disorders than non-athletes, and the highest incidence of eating disorders is among female athletes competing in sports in which leanness or specific weight are important for performance. Many wrestlers use weight-reducing strategies before competitions. Most do so only before competing, but the use of such strategies may trigger chronic eating disorders.

Two of the first women wrestlers in the early 1900s. (Underwood & Underwood/Corbis)

BARRIERS FACED BY WOMEN WRESTLERS

That women's wrestling has gained more acceptance may be due in part to the women's movement, as well as the support of some men in wrestling clubs and federations around the world. The more masculine a sport is perceived to be, the more obstacles women who take it up must face. Some countries still bar women from the sport for cultural or religious reasons. Where females do take part in the sport, they may face such barriers as differential treatment in funding and training conditions. And the public in general may view them as masculine and be suspicious of their sexual orientation.

SUMMARY

Although the history of wrestling includes female wrestlers, it is reasonable to argue that wrestling has been developed by men and for men. But during the later years of the twentieth century, the perception of women wrestling changed from a kind of curious entertainment into a legitimate sport. Nevertheless, female wrestlers still experience barriers to participation in the sport setting as well as in private life.

Mari-Kristin Sisjord

See also Sumo Wrestling

Bibliography

Camaione, D.N., and K.G. Tillman. (1980) *Teaching and Coaching Wrestling. A Scientific Approach*. New York: John Wiley.

Gundersen, O. (1996) *Atalanta . . . og de andre*. Langhus, Norway: Norsk Bryting.

Kent, G. (1968) *A Pictorial History of Wrestling*. London: Spring Books.

Additional information was provided by Institut für Angewandte Trainingswissenschaft.

WUSHU

Wushu, also known as *gong fu* and *kung fu,* means "martial arts" in Chinese. It is a broad group of Chinese traditional sports that are used for military training, self-defense, exercise, competition, entertainment, and performance. Technically, wushu consists of a variety of fighting skills based on kicking, striking, throwing, and grasping. The sport, or group of sports, can be traced back to ancient China, but modern forms emerged during the late Ming Dynasty (1368–1644) and the early Qing Dynasty (1644–1911).

HISTORY

Women have participated in wushu since ancient times but, until the revolution their involvement was rare. This lack of involvement was a result of social forces in Chinese society that restricted women's physical activities. China was a feudal society in which men had more status and power than women and in which women's roles were carefully defined. Wushu, as an expression of Chinese culture and, at times, an important leisure occupation for men, was deeply influenced by the nature of feudal society. The top priority for wushu masters was to maintain their particular wushu style by passing it from generation to generation through the male line. In following the patrilineal customs on which Chinese society was based, fathers passed their wushu skills on to their sons. At the same time, they kept these skills secret from the daughters who would marry outside the family and might divulge the secrets to competitors. In addition, women's participation was restricted by Confucianism, a philosophical system that stressed traditional values and argued against women engaging in vigorous physical activities, and especially in such activities as martial arts, which totally contradicted the expected role of women in Chinese society.

Nevertheless, women did sometimes take part in wushu, even in ancient times. Women participated during times of social change, when Confucianism lost influence, and among the lower classes, where Confucianism was less influential. In addition, in northern China, women in non-Chinese ethnic groups were quite active in all kinds of physical activities, including martial arts. Frequent contact between Chinese and non-Chinese people led to much cultural borrowing, and some Chinese women took up wushu and even became quite proficient.

The earliest known female to engage in wushu was a girl who lived in the ancient state of Yue (c. 496 BCE). She was an expert with sword, good in practical fighting and formal technique. Later she was invited to instruct her skills to the Yue army. Under her instruction the Yue state built a powerful military force, finally defeated its old foe, the state of Wu, and became a superpower. This story of the "Maiden of Yue" embodies the basic martial arts principle that one should "concentrate the spirit within and appear calm without."

The earliest literary references to female participation in wushu date back to the fifth century CE. The most popular is a long poem titled *Hua Mu Lan* (or Mulan), which describes a heroine proficient at wushu who went into military service for her old father when he was unable to serve. On the battlefield she outfought many men and led the troops to victory. The poem is popular in modern China and appears in many high school textbooks. (Her story was also the basis for a popular U.S. children's film in the 1990s.) And the poet Tu Fu (712–770) praised a swordswoman, Madame Kung Sun: "Her swinging sword flashes like the nine falling suns shot by Yi, the legendary bowman/She moves with the force of a team of dragons driven by the gods through the sky."

Two young women demonstrate the art of wushu fighting. (Hulton-Deutsch Collection/Corbis)

Another famous female wushu master was Yang Miao Cheng of the southern Sung Dynasty (1127–1279). After twenty years of continuous practice, her spear work was characterized by powerful and unpredictable flourishes in all directions. Such was her force and skill that her spear could be used for a push or pull, a plunge or parry, a cut or block. She was so good that she found it difficult to find a meritorious rival. Later, Chi Ji Kuang, a well-known wushu master in the Ming Dynasty, highly praised Yang and commented that spear skills had been developed by her alone.

Another famous female wushu practitioner was Qiu Jin (1875–1907), who was executed by the Ching court for taking part in a rebellion. Qiu Jin struggled not only against the feudal monarchy but also against the male-dominated social system. From a local wushu master she learned the skills of broadsword, sword, and staff and she was called "the knight-errant of Jian Lake."

RULES AND PLAY

The main difference between wushu and Western-style combative sports like boxing or wrestling is that all skills and training methods in wushu are based on traditional Chinese philosophical and religious systems, including Confucianism, Taoism, and Buddhism. Ideas from traditional Chinese medicine play a role as well, particularly a belief in channels of energy that run through the body. These energy channels are reflected in wushu as the three external conformities (integration of elbows and knees, integration of hands and feet, and integration of shoulders and hips) and the three internal conformities (integration of mind and will, integration of vital energy and strength, and integration of will and vital energy).

Modern wushu is classified into two basic categories: taolu (routine displays) and sanshou (full contact sparring). Hand events that comprise taolu include many forms of boxing, from chang kuan (long boxing) to tang lang kuan (mantis-style boxing) and ba kuatsang zhang (eight-diagrams palm). Taolu weapons events include short weapons (broadsword, sword), long weapons (spear, staff), and double weapons (including double broadsword, double daggers, and double battle-axes). Taolu participants also spar (with limited contact) and make team demonstrations. Sanshou events involve actual combats under controlled circumstances. Categories include free sparring, push-hand competition, and weapons competition.

Wushu has spread beyond China and gained an international following since the late 1980s. In 1990 the International Wushu Federation (IWUF) was established in Beijing, China, and in 1998 had member organizations from seventy-seven nations. The first world wushu championship was held in Beijing in 1991, with 440 athletes from forty-one countries. Since then, championships have been held every two years, in Singapore in 1993, in Baltimore in 1995, and in Rome in 1997. In Rome there were 516 athletes from fifty-nine countries who competed in the taolu (seven compulsory events for men and women) and sanshou (eleven events for men only).

Hai Ren

Bibliography

Chen, Dali. (1995) *Chinese Wushu—History and Culture.* Chendou: Si Chuan University Press.

Kuang, Wennan, ed. (1990) *Introduction to Chinese Wushu Culture.* Chendou: Si Chuan Education Press.

Ma, Xianda, ed. (1990) *Grand Dictionary of Chinese Wushu.* Beijing: People's Sport Press.

Ren, Hai. (1990) *Ancient Chinese Wushu.* Beijing: Commerce Press.

Xie, Shoude, and Li Wenying. (1989) *Chinese-English Wushu Glossary.* Beijing: People's Sport Press.

YACHTING *see Sailing*

YAMAGUCHI, KRISTI TSUYA

(1971–)

U.S. FIGURE SKATER

Kristi Yamaguchi was the most successful U.S. figure skater of the 1990s and the only one in the decade to win the national, world, and Olympic championships. She is also one in a long line of female figure skaters going back to Sonja Henie in the 1920s to use her success in the popular sport of figure skating to forge a post-competition career in entertainment and advertising.

Yamaguchi was born on 12 July 1971 in Hayward, California, with a clubfoot. Her toes turned in so severely that she required corrective shoes, physical therapy, and a night brace. After watching Dorothy Hamill win the 1976 Olympic gold medal, Yamaguchi asked for skating lessons, and her mother agreed, thinking the sport might strengthen her daughter's legs. Yamaguchi learned quickly, and competed in singles competitions and pairs skating. She and Rudi Galindo became the 1986 junior pairs national champions, and the 1989 national pairs champions. In 1989 Yamaguchi also earned a silver medal in singles, the first woman to win a medal in two nationals events since Margaret Graham in 1954.

In 1990 Yamaguchi began concentrating solely on singles. After winning the Goodwill Games in 1990 and placing second in the 1991 nationals, she became the world champion in 1991 in Munich, Germany. With Tonya Harding earning the silver and Nancy Kerrigan winning the bronze, this was the first time three women from one country had swept the medals. Yamaguchi also earned gold at the 1992 nationals.

In her gold medal performance, Kristi Yamaguchi spins on the ice during the Women's Figure Skating Competition at the 1992 Winter Olympics in Albertville, France. (Neal Preston/Corbis)

The next step was the 1992 Olympics, held in Albertville, France, and there, Yamaguchi won the gold medal—the first American woman to do so since her idol, Dorothy Hamill. Yamaguchi then won the 1992 World Figure Skating Competition, the first American woman with consecutive international wins since Peggy Fleming in 1968, and the first since Dorothy Hamill to win the triple crown of skating—the national, Olympic, and world championships. She then turned professional and toured with an ice show, profiting as well from product endorsement contracts.

Kelly Boyer Sagert

Bibliography

Donohue, Shiobhan. (1994) *Kristi Yamaguchi: Artist on Ice.* Minneapolis, MN: Lerner Publications.

Rambeck, Richard. (1998) *Kristi Yamaguchi.* Chicago: Child's World.

Savage, Jeff. (1993) *Kristi Yamaguchi: Pure Gold.* New York: Dillon Press.

YANG XIUQIONG

(1918–1982)

CHINESE SWIMMER

In the 1930s Yang Xiuqiong was widely known inside and outside China as the "Chinese mermaid." A national and international champion in several events, she was a popular role model for many women in the Nationalist Chinese republic.

Yang came from a peasant family in Yangwua village, Dongwan County, Guangdong Province on the mainland. The village was in a region of rivers and lakes, and children learned to swim as soon as they could walk. Yang was no exception. She swam when she was only two years old. When she was ten, her father was employed as a lifeguard at the swimming pool of the Nanhua Sports Association in Hong Kong. Under his supervision, Yang swam every day and her swimming improved rapidly.

In October 1930, when the Hong Kong Open Swimming Championships took place, Yang was only twelve years old. She participated in the championships and won two titles: the 50- and 100-meter freestyle. After she defended her title in 1932, Yang was invited by the Sydney Sports Association to compete there, the first Chinese female swimmer to be invited by a foreign sports association.

Yang Xiuqiong. (Christiansen/Levinson)

Yang was a member of the Hong Kong swimming team when the fifth national games took place in October 1933 at Nanjing, the capital of the Nationalist government. She broke four national records and won five gold medals. Chu Minyi, the minister of the Administration Council of the Nationalist government and the chief organizer of the games, imitated an ancient Olympic tradition by driving her around Nanjing in a chariot. Yang's pictures and stories filled newspapers, magazines, posters, and illustrations. She became a national hero.

Yang's success continued in the tenth Far-East Asian Games in Manila, Philippines, in May 1934. She won four gold medals for individual events and one for the 400-meter relay. In July, Yang was invited to perform in Nanchang, the capital city of Jiangxi province. It was reported that when she was swimming, "the whole city was empty, because everyone had gone to see her."

When the sixth national games were held at Shanghai in October 1935, Yang broke four national swimming records and won two gold medals. During her appearance, the price of a ticket increased twentyfold. If she did not appear in an event, spectators asked for a refund. As a matter of course, she was selected as a member of China's 1936 Olympic team. Yang's outstanding performances made the Chinese proud, while her beauty and her gentle demeanor caught the attention of men. Her success in sport helped to build a new femininity—no longer fragile and dependent but fit and independent—which was radically different from the past. Yang was the perfect image of a modern woman for Nationalist China. Yang was married in 1937 and she then retired from swimming.

Fan Hong
Yan Xuening

Bibliography

The Chinese Sports History Working Committee and the Chinese Swimming Association, eds. (1993) *Zhongguo youyong yundong shi (The History of Chinese Swimming)*. Wuhan: Wuhan chubanshe.

Fan Hong and Wang Daping. (1990) *Tiyu shihua (Sports History)*. Beijing: Kexue puji chubanshe, 207–210.

Qin Fen Tiyu Yuebao (Qin Fen Sports Monthly). (1933–1935). Vol. 1, no. 2 (October 1933): 32–33; vol. 1, no. 4 (August 1934): 32; vol. 3, no. 2 (November 1935): 157–158.

The Research Centre of Sports History, Chengdu Physical Education Institute, ed. (1986) Zhongguo jindai tiyushi ziliao (Modern Chinese Historical Sports Material). Sichuan: Sichuan jiaoyu chubanshe, 491 and 495.

YEGOROVA, LJUBOV

(1966–)

RUSSIAN CROSS-COUNTRY SKIER

Winning six gold and three silver medals at the 1992 and 1994 Winter Olympics, Ljubov ("love" in English) Yegorova became the most successful cross-country skier in Olympic history.

Ljubov Yegorova (center) after winning the gold medal in the 5-kilometer classic style ski race in the 1994 Winter Olympics. (AP Photos)

Yegorova was born in the Siberian town of Tomsk but moved to St. Petersburg (then known as Leningrad) to live with her aunt, Nina Balditscheva, an Olympic gold winner in 1976 as a member of the Soviet Union's 3 × 5-kilometer cross-country relay team. Yegorova came to international attention in 1984 when she finished fourteenth over the 5-kilometer at Strbske Pleso in what was then Czechoslovakia.

After skiing on the winning relay team at the 1985 junior championships, Yegorova proved herself a winner in individual competition. In 1986 she finished first in the junior championship 5-kilometer race. Two additional silver medals for the 15-kilometer race and the 3 × 5-kilometer relay underscored her enormous talent. Although she attracted considerable attention, she was not quite ready to sweep away her older rivals. In 1988 she was fourth (over the 10-kilometer course) in World Cup competition at the Russian site of Kavgolovo. Yegorova failed to qualify for the 1988 Winter Olympics in Calgary because she had done no better than twenty-ninth in World Cup competition. She was unable to improve her standing in the 1988–89 season. Ranked forty-second, she had to sit out that year's World Cup finals.

During the winter of 1990, Yegorova competed in seven World Cup races and never fell below fifteenth place. Her best results were second-place finishes in the 10-kilometer freestyle race at Val di Fiemine in Italy and in the 10-kilometer classic race at Bohinj in Yugoslavia. She finished the World Cup season in sixth place, eclipsed by her teammates Larissa Lasutina, Elena Valbe, and Raisa Smetanina.

The following winter, at Val di Fiemine, Yegorova achieved her first world championship (30-kilometer freestyle). She took a second gold medal with the Soviet relay team and was fourth in the 5-kilometer classic and eighth in the 10-kilometer freestyle races. Despite these achievements, she remained in the shadow of the triple gold medalist Valbe. In World Cup competition she managed a second and third place and was ranked third in the final classification.

In Olympic competition in 1992 in Albertville, France, Yegorova won the 15-kilometer classic race and the 10-kilometer pursuit. She earned a third gold medal with the relay team and two silver medals in the 5-kilometer classic and 30-kilometer freestyle races. These triumphs made the 5 foot 9 inch athlete "Queen of Albertville," but she was not happy to see the flag of the Unified Team (for athletes from the former Soviet Union) hoisted in her honor. She and her trainer-husband Igor Sissoyev were Russian patriots who would have preferred to see their own flag raised.

In her "world-championship winter" of 1992–1993, Yegorova won four World Cup races and was unbeatable in the rankings, but she was unable to keep up her gold medal pace. Still, in the world championships at Falun (Sweden), she managed to win bronze medals in the 10-kilometer pursuit and the 30-kilometer classic races and a gold in the relay. At the Lillehammer Olympics in 1994, she won silver over the 15-kilometer freestyle and then glided to a trio of gold medals: 5-kilometer classic, 10-kilometer freestyle, and the relay. In the first two races, Yegorova avenged her loss in the Lillehammer 15-kilometer race to Italy's Manuela de Centa. In the relay the Russians easily defeated the second-place Norwegian team.

Allen Guttmann

Bibliography

Die 100 des Jahrhunderts. (1994) *Sportler*. Reinbek bei Hamburg: Rororo, 76–77.

YOGA

Yoga is a form of physical and spiritual exercise that originated in India and has spread to other parts of the world in various forms, under the various names, and with a number of well-known exponents, including the violinist Yehudi Menuhin and, more recently, the singer Madonna.

Yoga is not, by any conventional Western standard, a sport (except in an unusual form, "artistic yoga sport," which is more like acrobatics and is practiced in Argentina, Brazil, Spain, and India). Yoga is, however, increasingly included in coverage of women's sports and fitness in magazines and the popular press, and many of its practitioners train in ways that are similar to competitive athletes. Some people take up yoga because of injury or disillusionment with competitive sports, and people who had bad experiences with sports—perhaps as a child—may come to yoga as an alternative form of physical activity. Many competitive athletes and professional dancers find yoga an effective addition to their training routine, and even professional male basketball players can be found in yoga studios working on the downward dog and cobra poses.

THE PHILOSOPHY OF YOGA

The Sanskrit term "yoga" means "to unite" or "to yoke." Yoga is a method of training designed to lead to integration or union. It includes physical exercises, but its traditional goal is the yoking of individual soul to universal spirit. As one of the six classical Indian philosophies—*darshanas*, or ways of seeing—yoga has been influential in Indian thought. It is viewed as a precise metaphysical method for developing a greater clarity of the way in which we "see" and "know" ourselves. Although yoga today is often taught and practiced as a means to health and fitness, its spiritual roots are still important to many modern practitioners.

Several ancient metaphysical or religious texts contribute to the body of yoga knowledge, among them the *Vedas*, the *Upanishads*, and the *Bhagavad Gita*, but the basic text is the *Yoga Sutras*. Most researchers agree that yoga's emergence as a full-fledged tradition did not occur until about 500 BCE. This ancient yoga was strictly taught and practiced almost exclusively by men, used for centuries as training for the warrior class in India.

The essence of yoga is "mindfulness," or the process of directing the attention toward whatever it is one is doing at the moment. Thus, to the *yogi*, or yoga practitioner, the "process" of actually doing yoga is the appropriate focus for the attention, not the "progress" on the path. Through the practice of various yoga techniques, the attention is constantly directed toward the present moment, often through the vehicle of the breath, thus uniting the mind, for a moment or two, "here and now," with the body.

Classically, yoga is defined in Patanjali's *Yoga Sutra* as "*citta vritti nirodahah*" or "the cessation of the fluctuations of the mind." In yoga, these *vritti*, or "waves" of the mind are referred to as "monkey mind". The practice of yoga is this actual effort to direct the mind toward one-pointedness, without distraction or interruption, and to calm and steady this wild monkey that jumps around in the jungle from branch to branch. It is in this state of focused mind, which takes many years of yoga practice to achieve, that a greater clarity of vision and deeper understanding of "self" develops. Resting in the present moment, the mind and body are joined and individual consciousness can then "know" its connection to universal, or "divine," consciousness. Once experienced, this state is recognized as the true nature of "self," or "self-realization"; according to classical yoga thought, it liberates the individual from the cause of human suffering, which is the illusion of isolation and separation from universal reality, or "the infinite."

While the goal of self-realization is rarely what most beginners in yoga have in mind, the slow, steady, and gradual awakening that comes from a regular and earnest practice, no matter what the method, often brings change. Many practitioners claim that they experience tangible aspects of personal transformation, such as improved health and vitality, reduced stress, an increased sense of well-being, and feelings of generosity, compassion, and understanding. What may have started, for example, as a curiosity about yoga or a purely physical pursuit of the yoga postures for increased fitness and flexibility, often becomes a vehicle for emotional growth and spiritual adventure.

Woman in Siddhasana pose. (Ronnen Eshel/Corbis)

MODERN HISTORY

Yoga first attracted popular attention in America in the 1960s when the Beatles brought transcendental meditation (TM) to the West from India. A growing interest in Eastern religions opened the gates for a small flood of male Indian yoga teachers to come to the United States. Most early yoga practices from India that followed TM were gentle and imprecise ventures into what in America is commonly, although not correctly, called *hatha* yoga. (Common usage generally depicts *hatha* yoga as simply the practice of the yoga *asanas*, or postures, the third limb of the classical astanga path. But technically, *hatha* yoga is an extremely intricate and eclectic path, of which practice of the postures is only a part).

Since yoga was first introduced as a fairly "soft" method of exercise for stretching and relaxation, it drew primarily women practitioners. It came to be regarded, particularly by men, as a somewhat boring and sleepy pursuit, and a notably soft form of physical training, if indeed it could be called "training" at all.

Through the 1970s and 1980s, however, more Westerners began to be exposed to some "new," at least to the West, yoga *systems* that introduced the full spectrum of a well-rounded yoga practice. Krishnamacharya, an Indian Brahmin from the south of India who is said to have lived to be over 100 years old and was one of the greatest yogis of the modern era, placed great emphasis on a strong practice of *asana* and *pranayama*. His primary reference point for the teaching of the classical eight-limbed, or *astanga*, path of yoga, was the *Yoga Sutra*. Krishnamacharya died in 1989, but through the teachings of three of his students, he had a great influence on the way yoga is taught today in the United States and throughout Europe, Australia, South America, and the rest of the Western world.

MAJOR BRANCHES OF YOGA

The combined methodologies of Krishnamacharya's son Desikachar, Sri K. P. Pattabhi Jois, and B. K. S. Iyengar have contributed to the introduction of strength, correct alignment, controlled breathing, and directed *prana*, or "energy," into the physical and mental discipline of yoga practice.

The first of these three teachers to have a wide impact was Iyengar, whose innovative method emphasizes standing poses that develop strength, vigor, and correct alignment; supported inversions (upside-down positions like headstands) and back bends that passively relax the nerves; props (walls, blocks, belts, bolsters, blankets, chairs, tables, benches, weights, and other devices) to facilitate ease and depth of practice; specific sequencing of postures for general and therapeutic benefits; and individualized adjustments by certified Iyengar teachers.

Iyengar's teaching set the stage for Pattabhi Jois, who, around the same time that Iyengar began to make inroads in the United States in the 1970s, introduced a method that he called astanga yoga, after the eight-limbed path. Astanga yoga, sometimes referred to as power yoga, consists of series of postures, performed in sequence with connecting movement and without interruption, and accompanied by a specific method of breathing, or *pranayama*, called *ujjayi*. This particular method brought in the factor of heat and flow, which was to be of incredible importance to the tight and injured athletic world and its ability to even do yoga.

The last of the three to gain widespread prominence in the Western world of yoga was Desikachar. One of his major contributions to the practice of the postures was the importance of an *asana* routine that took into consideration the specific limitations of the individual. These three teachers each had many students, who, in turn, have begun to teach and develop their own schools as well.

YOGA AND WOMEN

Women's involvement in yoga has changed dramatically since the 1970s or 1980s, largely because of their growing involvement in sports. In the 1990s, yoga took on new vigor in the United States, in part because women who had taken to both recreational and competitive sports began to look for new pursuits and in part because sports injuries drew attention to yoga as a system for conditioning and rehabilitation.

Initially drawn to yoga because it was gentle exercise for the mind, body, and spirit, women continue to be drawn to yoga and are the primary

YOGA IN THE WEST

Yoga is a good example of a non-Western activity that has been adopted by Western society and transformed in the process. Since the 1980s, yoga has become an increasingly popular form of exercise for women and more recently for men in the United States and Europe. In its Hindu context, yoga is an ascetic practice meant to develop one's spiritual side along with one's physical side. In the West, where Hinduism is a minority religion, the reverse is true as people more often use yoga as a form of physical relaxation, exercise, and physical conditioning.

teachers and practitioners of yoga in the West. In the 1990s increasing numbers of women were drawn to forms of yoga that emphasize strength and power, a change that corresponds to the changing attitudes toward women's sports that has taken place.

As recently as the early 1990s, women were still assumed, by both men and women, to be "naturally" more flexible than men. Many yoga teachers maintain that differences in flexibility instead arise out of differences between the sports experiences of boys and girls, and young men and women. As these differences diminish in the 1990s and beyond, the "natural" flexibility of women is changing. Formerly the only injuries in women's sports were those that came from being hit in the head by a field hockey stick or from falling down playing softball. Now injuries are a main concern of both professional and recreational women athletes. Women who train as hard as men will, for the most part, become just as tight and suffer many of the same injuries.

Women are "tighter" than they used to be in other ways, as well. As women have gone from the role of passive onlooker to that of active participant in the world of sports, politics, business, education, health care, and so forth, women have been subject to greater tension. On all levels women, like men, have developed a greater need for a strong antidote to the stresses of life.

YOGA AND SPORT

Yoga can be soft and relaxing. But traditionally a yoga *asana*, or postures, must be *sukkha* and *sthira*, or "soft" *and* "hard," "comfortable" *and* "steady," "pliable" *and* "strong." New forms of yoga, brought from India and developed for Western practitioners in the 1990s, link the hard and the soft sides of yoga practice. Women concerned about their shape—including some well-known models and actors—realized that yoga produced long lean muscles, similar to those produced by dance, and newly popular forms of yoga used intense breathing and continuous movement (*vinyasa*) to produce a sweaty, aerobic workout.

Beryl Bender Birch's *Power Yoga*, published in 1995, made yoga accessible to a broad American audience and especially to athletes, many of whom had seen yoga as a soft, passive physical activity. Birch's book came out of her work with athletes and the astanga yoga system of Pattabhi Jois. Birch, who had worked with skiers and who ran the official yoga program for the New York Road Runners Club, wrote: "Sports don't really get us in shape. In fact, sports get us out of shape. Sports develop tight muscles and uneven use of muscle groups, or the uneven use of one side of the body. Running, for instance, is great for the cardiovascular system. But it dramatically tightens the muscles at the back of the legs and does virtually nothing for the rest of the body. This intense shortening or disproportionate strengthening results in muscular and structural imbalance."

Birch's experience with runners and skiers led her to conclude that if training continues without alternative work to open the tightness and realign the imbalance, injury is inevitable. Rest may give the torn connective tissue or muscle tissue a chance to heal, but it doesn't eliminate the source of the problem. Once training starts again, the same limited range of motion or biomechanical imbalance will cause the same injury over and over again. Birch maintains that the physical discipline of yoga, especially the combined systems of Jois, Iyengar, and Desikachar, has proven to be a uniquely effective method for restoring range of motion to tight muscles and therapeutically realigning the body.

Another benefit of adding yoga to a training program, in addition to preventing and/or rehabilitating injury, is the effect it has on performance. It enables an athlete to train harder and at a higher level because range of motion is greater and the fear of injury is lessened. Yoga also develops sinewy strength, as opposed to bulky strength, and while that might not be an advantage for all athletes, it is a benefit for most endurance athletes. Yoga may also be used as a form of mental conditioning. The ability to direct energy, concentrate on the present moment, and shut out noise and distraction becomes an essential skill, and the yogic emphasis on stilling the "monkey mind" provides practical sports benefits.

YOGA PRACTICE

There is no formal competition in yoga, and no grades or belts to be won, as in the martial arts. Nonetheless, yoga is a challenging activity, where practitioners work for years, and even decades, to reach certain standards. The standards are those set by the most advanced teachers and focus on the ability to achieve certain physical postures. Many advanced yoga postures look like contortions to be achieved only by those with extraordinary flexibility, but for the practitioner they are goals to be reached through extensive stretching and muscle development. Often yoga seems extremely difficult to beginners, especially to high-level athletes who are very fit at their own sport.

A typical yoga class is an hour and a half long and consists of a series of postures: standing, seated, and what are known as "inversions"—upside-down positions including handstands and headstands. Many of the postures are done only once, but they are held for a period ranging from 20 seconds to a minute or more. Iyengar teachers sometimes have students hold positions for up to 10 minutes. *Vinyasa* yoga systems, like astanga yoga, emphasize continual movement and effort between postures, creating a vigorous aerobic workout. Yoga can be practiced anywhere in any weather, without a trainer, special equipment, or health club membership, though almost all practitioners go to classes. Most people use rubber or cloth yoga mats, but no other equipment is necessary.

In yoga, developing proficiency in concentration, focus, and breath control is part of the *asana* practice. Although *asana* refers only to the third limb of the astanga path, the other limbs come into play as the practitioner trains the mind to focus on the postures and the breath. The fourth limb of *pranyama,* or breath (energy) control, the fifth limb of *pratyahara,* or "withdrawal of the senses," the sixth limb of *dharana,* or concentration, and the seventh limb of *dhyana,* or meditation, are continuously interwoven into the practice of some forms of yoga, though there are many yoga enthusiasts who have no interest in the spiritual aspects of yoga, and most Western yoga classes have no spiritual or philosophical content.

CONCLUSION

Yoga's popularity is growing throughout the United States, in Europe, and elsewhere in the world, and its place in the world of women's sports is clear, as it demonstrates the broad range of physical activities that women enjoy. Yoga, like other individual physically challenging activities, appeals to many modern women (and men) who enjoy its unique combination of strength training and flexibility development, stress relief, and psychological or spiritual benefits.

Karen Christensen
Beryl Bender Birch

Bibliography

Bender Birch, Beryl. (1995) *Power Yoga.* New York: Simon and Schuster.

Couch, Jean. (1990) *The Runner's Yoga Book.* Berkeley, CA: Rodmell.

Desikachar, T. K. V. (1995) *The Heart of Yoga: Developing a Personal Practice.* Rochester, VT: Traditions International.

Iyengar, B. K. S. (1977) *Light on Yoga.* New York: Schocken.

Iyengar, Geeta S. (1990) *Yoga: A Gem for Women.* Palo Alto, CA: Timeless Books.

Jackson, Ian. (1975) *Yoga and the Athlete.* Mountain View, CA: World Publications.

Kogler, Aladar. (1995) *Yoga for Every Athlete: Secrets of an Olympic Coach.* St. Paul, MN: Llewellyn.

Miller, Barbara Stoler. (1995) *Yoga: Discipline of Freedom: The Yoga Sutra Attributed to Patanjali.* Berkeley: University of California Press.

Nikhilananda, Swami. (1953) *Vivekananda: The Yogas and Other Works.* New York: Ramakrishna-Vikekananda Center.

Scaravelli, Vanda. (1991) *Awakening the Spine.* San Francisco: Harper.

YOUTH SPORTS

Children in all societies participate in various forms of movement and physical activity. For the most part, these activities take place in informal settings and are characterized by freedom and spontaneity. They do not occur in social and cultural vacuums, however. In fact, the forms and dynamics of children's physical activities are connected indirectly with larger socialization processes through which participants learn how to be girls and boys and learn about the systems of social relations that exist in their families, communities, or nation-states. These processes vary from society to society and from one status group to another within particular societies.

Traditions of movement and physical activities are passed from generation to generation, and they nearly always represent the dominant ideas about gender in a particular cultural setting. This is because gender is constructed and experienced through the body. In most societies, adults are encouraged or entrusted to teach traditionally accepted forms of movement and physical activity to girls and boys. This may occur in various childcare settings or in institutionalized educational settings. Regardless of the settings in which physical activities are learned and played, they tend to reproduce in the lives of children the dominant ideas about gender and social relations.

ORGANIZED YOUTH SPORTS

While movement and physical activities exist in all cultures, organized youth sports are a luxury. They require resources and discretionary time among children and adults. They exist only when children are not required to work and only when there is a widespread belief in society that childhood experiences strongly influence a person's development and character.

Youth sports have a unique history in every society where they exist. However, they have always been constructed to emphasize experiences and teach values that are defined as important in the society as a whole. To the extent that dominant definitions of important experiences and values are grounded in forms of social relations that privilege males, youth sports are organized to teach boys the lessons they must learn to meet the demands of manhood in their society. Under these conditions, girls sometimes are excluded from participation, or they are included in ways that reproduce traditional notions of femininity and the established gender order.

The importance of girls' participation in sports increased dramatically towards the end of the twentieth century. (Richard Cummins/Corbis)

Youth sports in many societies have been organized traditionally around the notion that boys require opportunities to learn to be men in a world where conquest and domination are seen by those with power as being necessary for military security or economic expansion. To this end,

YOUTH PARTICIPATION IN SPORTS INDICATOR OF LATER PARTICIPATION

Research conducted by Linda Bunker of the University of Virginia suggests that a girl who doesn't become involved in sports is highly unlikely to do so later in life. In Bunker's survey, only 10% of girls who did not participate when they were younger than age ten were involved in sports after they were twenty-five years of age.

youth sports have been organized primarily to discipline the bodies and minds of the boys expected to be the next generation of leaders and workers. Programs have sometimes permitted or encouraged the participation of girls and, on rare occasions, boys and girls have participated together in youth sports. Gender-integrated participation takes place primarily when children are younger than about nine years old. Gender segregation at all ages has been the rule, and it has been nearly universal for young people over the age of twelve. Youth sports for girls have, for the most part, been organized around concerns about motherhood and sexuality; they have emphasized physical coordination and good health rather than conquest and domination.

TRADITIONAL CONSTRAINTS ON GIRLS' PARTICIPATION IN YOUTH SPORTS

Youth sport participation among girls in all societies has always been limited compared with participation among boys. From infancy through childhood, the range and variety of movement and physical activity among girls has been more carefully limited and monitored than it has been for their male counterparts. As infants, girls have been handled more gently and protectively, their exploration of the physical environment has been more constrained by parents and caretakers, and they have had less access to toys requiring active play and the use of motor skills. This pattern of "protectiveness" and constraint has continued through childhood in many societies and has limited girls' participation in youth sports. To the extent that this pattern has been reaffirmed through other social institutions such as religion and education, participation has been limited even further.

Girls' participation in most societies has also been limited by cultural myths about the consequences of vigorous physical exercise on their bodies, especially on their abilities to conceive and bear children. Although these myths vary from one culture to another, they have generally raised questions about the extent to which girls should take participation in sport seriously.

Even in societies where physical activities for girls and women have been encouraged in recent years, girls continue to receive mixed messages about the importance of participation and success in youth sports. Even when they receive encouragement, the encouragement is often couched in terms of conditional permission. For example, girls may be told that it is good to be physically active and to play sports *as long as* they do not stray too far from their homes, play with children unknown to parents, or do things that might be dangerous. Furthermore, encouragement may be neutralized by expectations that make girls responsible for household labor and caring for younger siblings, thus limiting or even eliminating free time for participation in sport.

Structural as well as cultural factors have inhibited girls' participation in youth sports. For example, there are no nations in which there are as many youth sports programs for girls as there are for boys. In those nations where opportunities have increased dramatically during the last third of the twentieth century, the increases have been due primarily to government legislation mandating equity. In all nations today, however, youth sports for girls receive fewer resources, including financial support, than do youth sports for boys, and participation rates reflect these inequities.

NEW OPPORTUNITIES IN GIRLS' PARTICIPATION IN YOUTH SPORTS

Youth sports have grown and changed in many ways through the twentieth century, but one of the most dramatic changes has been the increased participation among girls since the early 1970s, continuing through the end of the century. These changes have not occurred evenly nor have they occurred in all nations around the world. Girls' participation has increased most in those societies where per capita income is high, where transportation and communication technology is highly developed, and where the cultural emphasis on gender equity is strongest. This means that increases are most evident in Western nations and in nations where communist or formerly communist governments have actively promoted youth sports for girls and boys as a way of developing world-class athletes for international competition. Not surprisingly, youth sport development for girls has been much slower in developing nations, and only in the late 1990s have organized sports outside of schools been developed for girls in many African, Asian, and Latin American countries.

As the women's rights movement has spread around the globe, more people have come to realize that girls are enhanced as human beings when they have opportunities to develop their intellectual and physical abilities. Women's organizations have gradually included access to involvement in physical activities and sports as part of their overall emphasis on girls' health. The global diffusion of knowledge about health and fitness has assisted people as they challenge cultural myths about the consequences of vigorous exercise for the female body and as they promote the need for gender equity in youth sports. In connection with the diffusion of this knowledge, there has been a growth of "Sport for All" campaigns. Although these campaigns have been most common in Europe, they have inspired similar efforts in other parts of the world. These campaigns continue to emphasize gender equity and the participation by girls in physical activities and youth sports.

The slow but relatively steady growth of media images portraying women in sports has also helped to encourage participation in sports among girls because it enables them to envision sports participation as a part of their own lives. Visual media representations of strong, physically competent women athletes have challenged the notion that playing sports is somehow incompatible with what it means to be a woman.

GLOBAL TRENDS AND ISSUES IN YOUTH SPORTS

Global trends in youth sports have been fueled partly by major international efforts during the 1990s to increase sport participation opportunities for girls and women. In 1994 the first World Conference on Women in Sport was held in Brighton, England. The 280 attendees developed an international covenant known as the Brighton Declaration. One of the ten principles in the declaration concerns youth sports: "Those responsible for sport, education, recreation and physical education of young people should ensure that an equitable range of opportunities and learning experience, which accommodate the values, attitudes and aspirations of girls, is incorporated in programs to develop physical fitness and basic sport skills of young people."

The Brighton Declaration, combined with other global developments, encouraged delegates to the United Nations fourth World Conference on Women (held in Beijing in 1995) to make three specific references to the need for girls to have access to sport participation opportunities. Then in 1998 the second World Conference on Women and Sport was hosted in Windhoek, Namibia. This conference marked a continuation of global political efforts to "advance opportunities for girls and women in sport and physical activity." Furthermore, it was important that these latter two conferences were hosted in Asia and Africa. This demonstrated clearly that the cause of promoting sport participation among girls is not limited to Europe, North America, and Australia.

Specific trends and issues in youth sports have been identified in a cross-national, comparative study titled "Children, Youth and Sport," administered through the Committee on Sport and Leisure of the International Council of Sport Science and Physical Education (ICSSPE). During the mid-1990s, thirty scholars helped in the collection of data on youth sports in twenty countries. The study identified the following major trends:

GIRL SCOUTS SPORTS

GirlSports 2000 is a program of Girl Scouts of the U.S.A. designed to promote sports and to encourage physical activity for girls between the ages of five and seventeen. It focuses on teaching sports skills, promoting health and nutrition. encouraging sports participation, building self-esteem and teamwork, and fostering leadership. The program is also meant to increase interest in scouting. By the end of 1999 over 100,000 girls from all fifty states and fifteen other nations had participated in GirlSports 2000 activities.

1. Youth sport opportunities have increased substantially since the mid-1980s.
2. Youth sports have become more formally organized.
3. Youth sports are increasingly differentiated in terms of the range of sports offered and the levels of performance intensity for participants.
4. Differences between boys and girls in the type and extent of involvement in youth sports have steadily decreased since the mid-1980s.
5. First-time participation in youth sports is occurring at younger ages among girls and boys.

The major issues identified in this study include the following:

1. Youth sport dropout rates are high among adolescents, especially among girls.
2. Youth sports are often based on adult sport models without adapting them to the needs and abilities of children.
3. Youth sports have in recent years become less playful and more serious.
4. Youth sports continue to be characterized by gender inequities.
5. Youth sport funding is increasingly dependent on corporate sponsorships.

The overall findings of this study are encouraging in regards to participation by girls. As the twenty-first century begins, many girls around the world have increased access to a more varied set of youth sport participation opportunities. However, equity is far from being achieved, and in some countries it is not even recognized as an issue. Youth sports continues to require resources that are in short supply in many countries, and girls' participation depends on widespread societal recognition of the rights of girls and women.

Jay Coakley

Bibliography

The Brighton Declaration. (1994) London: The Sports Council.

DeKnop, Paul, Lars-Magnus Engstrom, Berit Skirstad, and Maureen Weiss, eds. (1996) *Worldwide Trends in Youth Sport.* Champaign, IL: Human Kinetics.

Hargreaves, Jennifer. (1994) *Sporting Females: Critical Issues in the History and Sociology of Women's Sports.* London: Routledge.

Lenskyj, Helen. (1986) *Out of Bounds: Women, Sport and Sexuality.* Toronto, Canada: The Women's Press.

Vertinsky, Patricia. (1994) *The Eternally Wounded Woman: Women, Exercise, and Doctors in the Late Nineteenth Century.* Champaign, IL: University of Illinois Press.

YUGOSLAVIA

Yugoslavia, from 1918 to 1991–1992, was a nation in the Balkan region of southern Europe. What was Yugoslavia is in 1999 the five separate nations of Slovenia, Croatia, Macedonia, Bosnia and Herzegovina, and Yugoslavia (primarily Serbia and Montenegro). The history of Yugoslavia and with it the history of the development of sports, and especially women's sports, can be divided into three chronological periods. The first is the history of the southern Slavic peoples of the region (excluding the Bulgarians), which ended with the founding of the combined Kingdom of Serbs, Croats, and Slovenes in the fall of 1918. The second is the history of the unified Yugoslavian state, which lasted until 1991–1992, interrupted only by the Italian and German occupation of 1941–1945. The third is the history of the former Yugoslavian nations since 1989.

DEVELOPMENTS UNTIL 1918

The area later called Yugoslavia contained the territories that subsequently became Slovenia and Croatia, which then partially belonged to the Habsburg monarchy. Following the Austrian occupation in 1878, it also contained Bosnia and Herzegovina, as well as the independent principalities of Montenegro and Serbia. In 1912–13 it succeeded in expanding its territory to include the Kosovo region bordering Albania and the area now known as Macedonia. These territorial units, which tended to be the home of different ethnic groups, were not unified by a common political structure, economy, or shared religion. Each region had its particular social, economic, and political characteristics.

Thus, there was little real unity, and before World War I the only unified gymnastics and sports movement was the Sokol movement of the south Slavic peoples. The movement was founded in the 1860s as a means of creating some degree of unity among the Serbs, Slovenes, and Croats across the region. The first women's gymnastics section within the Sokol movement was established in Slovenia in 1898, along with a children's gymnastics club for girls. In 1913 the Slovenian Sokol had 6,000 members in 115 clubs, including 550 active female gymnasts and 520 girls.

In the Croatian town of Zagreb, the Sokol was especially committed to bicycling, and some women were attracted by the Sokol Bicyclist Club. In 1890 the club's active members included forty-five men and ten women. But, generally, gymnastics and school sports for girls and women remained underdeveloped despite various efforts to promote them.

Yugoslavian gymnast Z. Mijatovic performs a routine on the balance beam during competition at Earl's Court in 1948. (Hulton-Deutsch/Corbis)

FROM 1918 TO 1991–1992

The Kingdom of Serbs, Croats, and Slovenes, proclaimed on 1 December 1918 (and renamed Yugoslavia in 1929), offered a wide range of new perspectives for the development of gymnastics and sports. In June 1919 the first joint Sokol Association was founded. In 1921 the association had 30,000 members with 8,200 women, though the Croats of the Zagreb district had resigned. But the percentage of women in the association decreased, and by 1929 there were only 8,300 women among the 70,000 members. Among children, however, females were represented in much better proportions; there were 4,000 young female gymnasts compared to 7,000 young men, and there were 8,000 girls as members compared to 9,000 boys.

In 1925 in Zagreb, women established their own females-only Házená Club, where they played *Ceska házená* (Czech *házená*)—a kind of handball played on a small field and originally developed by the Czechs. In 1934 the Croatian women's team even won the world championship, shortly before házená handball was replaced by the much more popular standard team handball. But the tradition survives, and the later success of the Yugoslavian women's handball team can be traced to the házená experience.

After Yugoslavia came under dictatorial rule in 1929, the Sokol became a de facto governmental organization with less involvement in gymnastics and sports. Nevertheless, the Sokol of the Yugoslavian kingdom continued to take part in international sports. After the male Yugoslavian gymnasts participated in the Olympic Games in Paris in 1924, a women's team of fifteen members competed for the first time at Olympic Games in Berlin in 1936. But sports in Yugoslavia remained dominated by men. For example, in 1940 there were 716 soccer clubs (a men's sport) out of 1,250 sports associations.

The Federal People's Republic of Yugoslavia was established after World War II. Its main focus in sports was on the development of school sports and school sports clubs. Handball became an important sport that was played by boys and girls and men and women. Emphasis was also placed on developing more visible Olympic sports, such as swimming, basketball, and skiing. These efforts paid off as Yugoslavia continued to send women's teams to the Olympics. Durdica Bjedov, a breaststroke swimmer, won gold in the 100-meter event and silver in the 200-meter event at the 1968 Olympic Games in Mexico. At the 1980 Olympic Games in Moscow, the Yugoslavian women's team won the silver medal in handball and the bronze medal in basketball. In Los Angeles in 1984, the Yugoslavian women finally won gold in handball.

Yugoslavian women were also successful at several individual sports. The 1984 Winter Olympic Games in Sarajevo were the high point in the history of Yugoslavian sports as the figure skater Sandra Dubravcic, who had finished second in the European championship in Salzburg in 1981, lit the Olympic flame. At the 1988 Winter Games in Calgary, skier Mateja Svet won the silver medal in the slalom competition. At the Summer Games in Seoul the same year, Jasna Sekaric won the gold medal in shooting, while Jasna Falic and Gordana Perkucin placed third in table tennis doubles, and the traditionally strong women's basketball team won the silver medal. The European track and field championship took place in Split in 1990 and was the last major sports event hosted by Yugoslavia. Snezana Pajkic won an unexpected first place in the 1500-meter race and Biljana Petrovic won the silver medal in the high jump. In 1990 the dissolution of Yugoslavia began, and by 1992 it was five separate nations, each with its own sports organizations, none nearly as powerful in women's sports as athletes and teams from Yugoslavia had been.

CROATIA

The Republic of Croatia declared independence in 1991, with a population of about 4.8 million. The National Olympic Committee (NOC) was organized in 1991 and accepted by the International Olympic Committee (IOC) in 1992, the same year the country was recognized by the international community. In 1992 two Croatian women participated in the Winter Olympic Games in Albertville, France, and three women went to the Summer Games in Barcelona. In the 1996 Olympics, the Croatian team had nine women members.

In Croatia, the traditional focus on handball continued, and in 1994 and 1995 Croatian women were finalists in the European championship. The female volleyball players from Mladost were cup finalists in Croatia in 1992 and 1994, and in 1995 they finished the European championship as the Croatian national team. The best-known international female athlete is the tennis player Iva Majoli, who was chosen the Croatian SportsWoman of the Year in 1995. The center of Croatian women's sports in the late 1990s is the Women's Infoteka in the capital city of Zagreb. This organization collects information about the women's movement and is interested in the issue of women's sports; it has its own library and publishes a women's magazine.

BOSNIA-HERZEGOVINA

The republic came into existence after the Dayton Peace Treaty of 1995 and has a population of about 4.4 million. The National Olympic Committee was founded in 1992; three Bosnian women participated in the 1992 Olympic Games and two in the 1996 Olympics. The nation was devastated by the civil war that followed the breakup of Yugoslavia in 1991, and little information is available about women's sports.

MACEDONIA

The Republic of Macedonia, officially called "the former Yugoslavian Republic Mazedonia" came into existence after the demise of Yugoslavia in 1992; it has a population of about 2.1 million. The National Olympic Committee of Macedonia was founded in 1992, and three Macedonian women competed in the 1996 Summer Olympics. Little is known about the status of women's sports as the nation has been consumed since independence by political crisis involving neighboring Greece and the Albanian population in Macedonia.

SLOVENIA

The Republic of Slovenia was established in 1992 and has a population of about 2 million. The National Olympic Committee of Slovenia was organized in 1991. The Slovenian women's movement dates to the nineteenth century, when the region was under the rule of the Habsburg monarchy. In 1897 the first Slovenian women's magazine, *Slovenka* ("Slovenian Woman"), was published. In 1925 twelve women's organizations demonstrated against the adoption of Serbian-based principles of family law that discriminated against women. They also fought for equality in inheritance and for the right to vote. Finally, in the spring of 1989–90, when Slovenia separated from Yugoslavia, women played an important role.

Perhaps Slovenian women's long history of fighting for their rights has had a positive effect on their relatively high level of involvement in international sports. In 1996 Slovenia sent twelve women to the Atlanta Olympics, more than any of the other former Yugoslavian nations. The hurdler Brigita Bukovec won the silver medal in the 100-meter hurdles. Skiing is the most popular sport in Slovenia, especially in the alpine Triglav area. The slalom skier Katja Koren and the downhill skier Alenka Dovzan are among the best-known personalities in the country, and both won bronze medals at the Lillehammer Winter Olympics in 1994.

Diethelm Blecking

See also Sokol Movement

Bibliography

Croatian Olympic Committee, ed. (1996) *Sports in Croatia*. Zagreb, Croatia: Croatian Olympic Committee.

Kessler, Wolfgang. (1991) "Der Sokol in den jugoslawischen Gebieten (The Sokol in the Yugoslavian Territories) 1863–1941." In *Die slawische Sokolbewegung* (*The Slavic Sokol Movement*), edited by Diethelm Blecking. Dortmund: Forschungsstelle Ostmitteleuropa Universität Dortmund, 198–218.

Prut-Pregelj, Leopoldina, and Carole Rogel, eds. (1996) *Historical Dictionary of Slovenia*. Lanham, MD: Scarecrow, 100–101, 261–262, 289–290.

Radan, Zivko. (1981) *Pregled historije tjelesnog vjezbanija i sporta* (*Historical Survey of Physical Education and Sport*). Zagreb: Skolsa Knjiga.

Slovenian Olympic Committee, ed. (1997) *Obvestila* (News). Ljubljana: Slovenian Olympic Committee, 3.

Stepisnik, Drago. (1977) "Sokol." *Enciklopedia Fizicke Kulture* (*Encyclopedia of Physical Culture*), 2. Zagreb, 277–286.

Z

ZAMBIA

Zambia, formerly Northern Rhodesia, is a landlocked south-central African nation with a population of about 9.3 million. Located in the tropics, its topography, which is primarily high plateau, results in a moderate climate permitting year-round sporting activities. Early-twentieth-century explorers and missionaries observed myriad indigenous games, which were ignored by the colonizers. Organized Western sports, however, were not introduced until the end of British rule in 1964. With independence, the new Zambian government adopted an active role, first among men and then among women, fostering sports involvement. Women's sporting associations and clubs, originating throughout the 1960s and 1970s, by 1999 consisted of over 500 members participating locally, nationally, and internationally in golf, track and field, netball, squash, bowling, and swimming.

Zambia's first international sportswomen were members of the Ladies' Golf Union, who competed in Kenya in 1966. By the 1970s Zambia's female track and field athletes regularly qualified for the East and Central African championships, the All-African Games, and the Commonwealth Games. In 1970 Loveness Kamaga captured Zambia's first international medal, a bronze in the long jump at the East and Central African championships in Nairobi, Kenya. At the same championships a year later in Dar-es-Salaam, Tanzania, Audrey Chikani earned a gold medal for her high jump as did Carol Mumbi in 1976 in Zanzibar, Tanzania. Eliminated in their first two attempts in the Commonwealth Games in 1978 and 1982, Zambia's qualifying athletes competed in the 1994 Games, with Beatrice Lungu finishing sixth out of seven in the 200-meter race and Grace Munene, eighth of eight in the 400-meter race.

In 1975 Zambia joined Kenya to become the second African country in the Third World Confederation of Netballers. A ten-member team first competed at the East and Central Africa Challenge Cup Tournament in 1976 and won in 1983 and 1985.

By 1986 the Zambia Women's Bowling Association boasted 160 members. The Zambia Bowls won the African States Tournaments at Lobatse, Botswana, in 1984 and at Bulaywayo, Zimbabwe, in 1986, and secured a bronze medal at the World Bowls in Scotland in 1992.

Two teams represented the nation at the African women's volleyball championships at Gaborone, Botswana, in 1993 and were defeated by Egypt and Nigeria. Zambia's national women's team debuted at the African Nations Confederation of African Volleyball match in 1998.

One female Zambian athlete, Ngozi Mwananwambwa, has realized Olympic status, competing in the 200- and 400-meter races in the 1992 Games in Barcelona and in 1996 at Atlanta.

Unlike their counterparts in some other African countries who get little support, Zambia's female athletes are encouraged by individual, corporate, and governmental promotional efforts. Especially important was Flo Morgan, 1980 Sports Administrator of the Year, who popularized softball and field hockey among Zambian women, dedicating over two decades to sport administration. Annually, Rothmans of Pall Mall Zambia sponsors the Sportswoman of the Year Award, selecting winners based on local and international competitive performances. In the early 1990s Zambia's national government established the Zambia Association for Women's Sports to increase and broaden the role of women in athletics and, in 1992, President Chiluba reaffirmed this commitment, unveiling his "Vision 2000 Sport for All" program. Outlining sport development until 2000, this grassroots program offered promise for future advancements in women's sports and inspiration to Zambia's female athletic hopefuls.

Susan Coopersmith
Kezia Nalweya

APPENDIX A
Female Medalists at the Summer Olympics

ARCHERY – INDIVIDUAL

1972 Munich

G	Doreen Wilber	United States
S	Irena Szydlowska	Poland
B	Emma Gapchenko	Soviet Union

1976 Montreal

G	Luann Ryon	United States
S	Valentyna Kovpan	Soviet Union
B	Zebiniso Rustamova	Soviet Union

1980 Moscow

G	Keto Losaberidze	Soviet Union
S	Natalya Butuzova	Soviet Union
B	Päivi Meriluoto	Finland

1984 Los Angeles

G	Seo Hyang-soon	South Korea
S	Li Lingjuan	China
B	Kim Jin-ho	South Korea

1988 Seoul

G	Kim Soo-nyung	South Korea
S	Wang Hee-kyung	South Korea
B	Yun Young-sook	South Korea

1992 Barcelona

G	Cho Youn-jeon	South Korea
S	Kim Soo-Nyung	South Korea
B	Natalya Valeyeva	Commonwealth of Independent States

1996 Atlanta

G	Kim Kyung-Wook	South Korea
S	He Ying	China
B	Olena Sadovnycha	Ukraine

ARCHERY – TEAM

1988 Seoul

G	South Korea
S	Indonesia
B	United States

1992 Barcelona

G	South Korea
S	China
B	Commonwealth of Independent States

1996 Atlanta

G	South Korea
S	Germany
B	Poland

ARCHERY – DOUBLE COLUMBIA ROUND

1904 St. Louis

G	Lida Howell	United States
S	Emma Cooke	United States
B	Jessie Pollock	United States

ARCHERY – DOUBLE NATIONAL ROUND

1904 St. Louis

G	Lida Howell	United States
S	Emma Cooke	United States
B	Jessie Pollock	United States

ARCHERY – NATIONAL ROUND

1908 London

G	Sybil "Queenie" Newall	Great Britain
S	Charlotte "Lottie" Dod	Great Britain
B	Beatrice Hill-Lowe	Great Britain

BADMINTON – SINGLES

1992 Barcelona

G	Susi Susanti	Indonesia
S	Bang Soo-hyun	Korea
B	Huang Hua	China

1996 Atlanta

G	Bang Soo-hyun	South Korea
S	Mia Audina	Indonesia
B	Susi Susanti	Indonesia

BADMINTON – DOUBLES

1992 Barcelona

G	Hwang Hye-young Chung So-young	South Korea
S	Guan Weizhen Nong Quinhua	China
B	Lin YanFen Yao Fen	China

1996 Atlanta

G	Ge Fei Gu Jun	China
S	Gil Young-ah Jang Hye-ock	South Korea
B	Qin Yiyuan Tang Yongshu	China

BADMINTON – MIXED DOUBLES

1996 Atlanta

G	Gil Young-ah Kim Dong-moon	South Korea
S	Ra Kyung-min Park Joo-bong	South Korea
B	Liu Jianjun Sun Man	China

BASKETBALL

1976 Montreal

G Soviet Union
S United States
B Bulgaria

1980 Moscow

G Soviet Union
S Bulgaria
B Yugoslavia

1984 Los Angeles

G United States
S Korea
B China

1988 Seoul

G United States
S Yugoslavia
B Soviet Union

1992 Barcelona

G Commonwealth of Independent States
S China
B United States

1996 Atlanta

G United States
S Brazil
B Australia

CANOEING – KAYAK SINGLES 500 METERS

1948 London

G	Karen Hoff	Denmark
S	Alida van der Anker-Doedens	Netherlands
B	Fritzi Schwingl	Austria

1952 Helsinki

G	Sylvi Saimo	Finland
S	Gertrude Liebhart	Austria
B	Nina Savina	Soviet Union

1956 Melbourne

G	Yelizaveta Dementyeva	Soviet Union
S	Therese Zenz	West Germany
B	Tove Soby	Denmark

1960 Rome

G	Antonina Seredina	Soviet Union
S	Therese Zenz	West Germany
B	Daniela Walkowiak	Poland

1964 Tokyo

G	Lyudmila Khvedosyuk	Soviet Union
S	Hilde Lauer	Romania
B	Marcia Jones	United States

1968 Mexico City

G	Lyudmila Pinayeva (Khvedosyuk)	Soviet Union
S	Renate Breuer	West Germany
B	Viorica Dumitru	Romania

1972 Munich

G	Yulia Ryabchynska	Soviet Union
S	Mieke Jaapies	Netherlands
B	Anna Pfeffer	Hungary

1976 Montreal

G	Carola Zirzow	East Germany
S	Tatiana Korshunova	Soviet Union
B	Klára Rajnai	Hungary

1980 Moscow

G	Birgit Fischer	East Germany
S	Vania Gesheva	Bulgaria
B	Antonina Melnikova	Soviet Union

1984 Los Angeles

G	Agneta Andersson	Sweden
S	Barbara Schüttpelz	West Germany
B	Annemiek Derckx	Netherlands

1988 Seoul

G	Vania Gesheva	Bulgaria
S	Birgit Schmidt (Fischer)	East Germany
B	Izabella Dylewska	Poland

1992 Barcelona

G	Birgit Schmidt (Fischer)	Germany
S	Rita Köbán	Hungary
B	Izabella Dylewska	Poland

CANOEING – FLATWATER K1 500 METERS

1996 Atlanta

G	Rita Köbán	Hungary
S	Caroline Brunet	Canada
B	Josefa Idem	Italy

CANOEING – KAYAK PAIRS 500 METERS

1960 Rome

G	Maria Chubing Antonia Seredina	Soviet Union
S	Therese Zenz Ingrid Hartmann	West Germany
B	Klára Fried-BánFalui Vilma Egresi	Hungary

1964 Tokyo

G	Roswitha Esser Annemarie Zimmermann	West Germany
S	Francine Fox Gloriane Perrier	United States
B	Hilde Lauer Cornelia Sideri	Romania

1968 Mexico City

G	Roswitha Esser Annemarie Zimmermann	West Germany
S	Anna Pfeffer Katalin Rozsnyói	Hungary
B	Lyudmila Pinayeva (Khvedosyuk) Antonina Seredina	Soviet Union

1972 Munich

G	Lyudmila Pinayeva (Khvedosyuk) Kateryna Nahirna-Kuryshko	Soviet Union
S	Ilse Kaschube Petra Grabowski	East Germany
B	Maria Nichiforov Viorica Pumitru	Romania

1976 Montreal

G	Nina Gopova Galina Kreft	Soviet Union
S	Anna Pfeffer Klára Rajnai	Hungary
B	Bärbel Köster Carola Zirzow	East Germany

1980 Moscow

G	Carsta Genäuss Martina Bischof	East Germany
S	Galina Alexeyeva (Kreft) Nina Trofimova (Gopova)	Soviet Union
B	Éva Rakusz Mária Zakariás	Hungary

1984 Los Angeles

G	Agneta Andersson Anna Olsson	Sweden
S	Alexandra Barre Susan Holloway	Canada
B	Josefa Idem Barbara Schüttpelz	West Germany

1988 Seoul

G	Birgit Schmidt (Fischer) Anke Nothnagel	East Germany
S	Vania Geshera Diana Paliiska	Bulgaria
B	Annemick Derckx Annemarie Cox	Netherlands

1992 Barcelona

G	Ramona Portwich Anke von Seck (Nothnagel)	Germany
S	Susanne Gunnarsson (Wiberg) Agneta Andersson	Sweden
B	Rita Köbán Éva Dónusz	Hungary

CANOEING – FLATWATER K2 500 METERS

1996 Atlanta

G	Agneta Andersson Susanne Gunnarsson	Sweden
S	Birgit Fischer Ramona Portwich	Germany
B	Anna Wood Katrin Borchert	Australia

CANOEING – KAYAK FOURS 500 METERS

1984 Los Angeles

G Romania
S Sweden
B Canada

1988 Seoul

G East Germany
S Hungary
B Bulgaria

1992 Barcelona

G Hungary
S Germany
B Sweden

CANOEING – FLATWATER K4 500 METERS

1996 Atlanta

G Germany
S Switzerland
B Sweden

CANOEING – KAYAK SLALOM SINGLES

1972 Munich

G	Angelika Bahmann	East Germany
S	Gisela Grothaus	West Germany
B	Magdalena Wunderlich	West Germany

1992 Barcelona

G	Elisabeth Micheler	West Germany
S	Danielle Woodward	Austria
B	Dana Chladek	United States

1996 Atlanta

G	Stepanka Hilgertova	Czech Republic
S	Dana Chladek	United States
B	Myriam Fox-Jerusalmi	France

CYCLING – 1,000-METER MATCH SPRINT

1988 Seoul

G	Erika Salumäe	Soviet Union
S	Christa Luding-Rothenburger	East Germany
B	Connie Young	United States

1992 Barcelona

G	Erika Salumäe	Commonwealth of Independent States
S	Annett Neumann	Germany
B	Ingrid Haringa	Netherlands

CYCLING – INDIVIDUAL SPRINT (3 LAPS)

1996 Atlanta

G	Felicia Ballanger	France
S	Michelle Ferris	Australia
B	Ingrid Haringa	Netherlands

CYCLING – 3,000-METER INDIVIDUAL PURSUIT

1992 Barcelona

G	Petra Rossner	Germany
S	Kathryn Watt	Australia
B	Rebecca Twigg	United States

1996 Atlanta

G	Antonella Bellutti	Italy
S	Marion Clignet	France
B	Judith Arndt	Germany

CYCLING – ROAD RACE

1984 Los Angeles

G	Connie Carpenter-Phinney	United States
S	Rebecca Twigg	United States
B	Sandra Schumacher	West Germany

1988 Seoul

G	Monique Knol	Netherlands
S	Jutta Niehaus	West Germany
B	Laima Zilporite	Soviet Union

1992 Barcelona

G	Kathryn Watt	Australia
S	Jeannie Longo-Ciprelli	France
B	Monique Knol	Netherlands

1996 Atlanta

G	Jeannie Longo	France
S	Imelda Chiappa	Italy
B	Clara Hughes	Canada

CYCLING – TRACK, INDIVIDUAL POINTS RACE

1996 Atlanta

G	Nathalie Lancien	France
S	Ingrid Haringa	Netherlands
B	Lucy Tyler Sharman	Australia

CYCLING – ROAD, INDIVIDUAL TIME TRIAL

1996 Atlanta

G	Zulfiya Zabirova	Russian Federation
S	Jeannie Longo-Ciprelli	France
B	Clara Hughes	Canada

CYCLING – MOUNTAIN BIKE, CROSS COUNTRY

1996 Atlanta

G	Paola Pezzo	Italy
S	Alison Sydor	Canada
B	Susan DeMattei	United States

DIVING – SPRINGBOARD

1920 Antwerp

G	Aileen Riggin	United States
S	Helen Wainwright	United States
B	Thelma Payne	United States

1924 Paris

G	Elizabeth Becker	United States
S	Aileen Riggin	United States
B	Caroline Fletcher	United States

1928 Amsterdam

G	Helen Meany	United States
S	Dorothy Poynton	United States
B	Georgia Coleman	United States

1932 Los Angeles

G	Georgia Coleman	United States
S	Katherine Rawls	United States
B	Jane Fauntz	United States

1936 Berlin

G	Marjorie Gestring	United States
S	Katherine Rawls	United States
B	Dorothy Poynton Hill	United States

1948 London

G	Victoria Draves	United States
S	Zoe Ann Olsen	United States
B	Patricia Elsener	United States

1952 Helsinki

G	Patricia McCormick	United States
S	Madeleine Moreau	France
B	Zoe Ann Jensen-Olsen	United States

1956 Melbourne

G	Patricia McCormick	United States
S	Jeanne Stunyo	United States
B	Irene MacDonald	Canada

1960 Rome

G	Ingrid Krämer	East Germany
S	Paula Jean Pope (Myers)	United States
B	Elizabeth Ferris	Great Britain

1964 Tokyo

G	Ingrid Engel- Krämer	East Germany
S	Jeanne Collier	United States
B	Mary "Patsy" Willard	United States

1968 Mexico City

G	Sue Gossick	United States
S	Tamara Pogosheva (Fyedosova)	Soviet Union
B	Keala O'Sullivan	United States

1972 Munich

G	Maxine "Micki" King	United States
S	Ulrika Knape	Sweden
B	Marina Janicke	East Germany

1976 Montreal

G	Jennifer Chandler	United States
S	Christa Köhler	East Germany
B	Cynthia Potter	United States

1980 Moscow

G	Irina Kalinina	Soviet Union
S	Martina Proeber	East Germany
B	Karin Guthke	East Germany

1984 Los Angeles

G	Sylvie Bernier	Canada
S	Kelly McCormick	United States
B	Christina Seufert	United States

1988 Seoul

G	Gao Min	China
S	Li Qing	China
B	Kelly McCormick	United States

1992 Barcelona

G	Gao Min	China
S	Irina Lashko	Commonwealth of Independent States
B	Brita Baldus	Germany

1996 Atlanta

G	Fu Mingxia	China
S	Irina Lashko	Russian Federation
B	Annie Pelletier	Canada

DIVING - PLATFORM

1912 Stockholm

G	Margareta Johanson	Sweden
S	Lisa Regnell	Sweden
B	Isobel White	Great Britain

1920 Antwerp

G	Stefanie Clausen	Denmark
S	B. Eileen Armstrong	Great Britain
B	Eva Olliwer	Sweden

1924 Paris

G	Caroline Smith	United States
S	Elizabeth Becker	United States
B	Hjördis Töpel	Sweden

1928 Amsterdam

G	Elizabeth Becker Pinkston	United States
S	Georgia Coleman	United States
B	Lala Sjöquist	Sweden

1932 Los Angeles

G	Dorothy Poynton	United States
S	Georgia Coleman	United States
B	Marion Roper	United States

1936 Berlin

G	Dorothy Poynton Hill	United States
S	Velma Dunn	United States
B	Käthe Köhler	Germany

1948 London

G	Victoria Draves	United States
S	Patricia Elsener	United States
B	Birte Christoffersen	Denmark

1952 Helsinki

G	Patricia McCormick	United States
S	Paula Jean Myers	United States
B	Juno Irwin (Stover)	United States

1956 Melbourne

G	Patricia McCormick	United States
S	Juno Irwin (Stover)	United States
B	Paula Jean Myers	United States

1960 Rome

G	Ingrid Krämer	East Germany
S	Paula Jean Pope (Myers)	United States
B	Ninel Krutova	Soviet Union

1964 Tokyo

G	Lesley Bush	United States
S	Ingrid Engel-Krämer	East Germany
B	Galina Alekseyeva	Soviet Union

1968 Mexico City

G	Milena Duchková	Czechoslovakia
S	Natalya Lobanova (Kuznetsova)	Soviet Union
B	Ann Peterson	United States

1972 Muncih

G	Ulrika Knape	Sweden
S	Milena Duchková	Czechoslovakia
B	Marina Janicke	East Germany

1976 Montreal

G	Elena Vaytsekhovskaya	Soviet Union
S	Ulrika Knape	Sweden
B	Deborah Wilson	United States

1980 Moscow

G	Marina Jäschke	East Germany
S	Servard Emirzyan	Soviet Union
B	Liana Tsotadze	Soviet Union

1984 Los Angeles

G	Zhou Jihong	China
S	Michele Mitchell	United States
B	Wendy Wyland	United States

1988 Seoul

G	Xu Yanmei	China
S	Michele Mitchell	United States
B	Wendy Lian Williams	United States

1992 Barcelona

G	Fu Mingxia	China
S	Yelena Miroshina	Commonwealth of Independent States
B	Mary Ellen Clark	United States

1996 Atlanta

G	Fu Mingxia	China
S	Annika Walter	Germany
B	Mary Ellen Clark	United States

EQUESTRIAN – THREE-DAY EVENT, INDIVIDUAL

1964 Tokyo

G	Mauro Checcoli	Italy
S	Carlos Moratorio	Argentina
B	Fritz Ligges	West Germany

1968 Mexico City

G	Jean-Jacques Guyon	France
S	Derek Allhusen	Great Britain
B	Michael Page	United States

1972 Munich

G	Richard Meade	Great Britain
S	Alessandro Argenton	Italy
B	Jan Jönsson	Sweden

1976 Montreal

G	Edmund Coffin	United States
S	J. Michael Plumb	United States
B	Karl Schultz	West Germany

1980 Moscow

G	Euro Federico Roman	Italy
S	Alesandr Blinov	Soviet Union
B	Yuri Salnikov	Soviet Union

1984 Los Angeles

G	Mark Todd	New Zealand
S	Karen Stives	United States
B	Virginia Holgate	Great Britain

1988 Seoul

G	Mark Todd	New Zealand
S	Ian Stark	Great Britain
B	Virginia Leng (Holgate)	Great Britain

1992 Barcelona

G	Matthew Ryan	Australia
S	Herbert Blöcker	Germany
B	Blyth Tait	New Zealand

1996 Atlanta

G	Blyth Tait	New Zealand
S	Sally Clark	New Zealand
B	Kerry Millikin	United States

EQUESTRIAN – THREE-DAY EVENT, TEAM

1964 Tokyo

G	Italy
S	United States
B	East and West Germany

1968 Mexico City

G	Great Britain
S	United States
B	Australia

1972 Munich

G	Great Britain
S	United States
B	West Germany

1976 Montreal

G	United States
S	West Germany
B	Australia

1980 Moscow

G	Soviet Union
S	Italy
B	Mexico

1984 Los Angeles

G	United States
S	Great Britain
B	West Germany

1988 Seoul

G	West Germany
S	Great Britain
B	New Zealand

1992 Barcelona

G	Australia
S	New Zealand
B	Germany

1996 Atlanta

G	Australia
S	United States
B	New Zealand

EQUESTRIAN – JUMPING, INDIVIDUAL

1964 Tokyo

G	Pierre Jonquères D'Oriola	France
S	Hermann Schridde	West Germany
B	Peter Robeson	Great Britain

1968 Mexico City

G	William Steinkraus	United States
S	Marion Coakes	Great Britain
B	David Broome	Great Britain

1972 Munich

G	Graziano Mancinelli	Italy
S	Ann Moore	Great Britain
B	Neal Shaprio	United States

1976 Montreal

G	Alwin Schockemöhle	West Germany
S	Michel Vaillancourt	Canada
B	François Mathy	Belgium

1980 Moscow

G	Jan Kowalczyk	Poland
S	Nikolai Korolkov	Soviet Union
B	Joaquin Perez Heras	Mexico

1984 Los Angeles

G	Joe Fargis	United States
S	Conrad Homfeld	United States
B	Heidi Robbiani	Switzerland

1988 Seoul

G	Pierre Durand	France
S	Greg Best	United States
B	Karsten Huck	West Germany

1992 Barcelona

G	Ludger Beerbaum	Germany
S	Piet Raymakers	Netherlands
B	Norman Dello Joio	United States

1996 Atlanta

G	Ulrich Kirchhoff	Germany
S	Willi Melliger	Switzerland
B	Alexandra Ledermann	France

EQUESTRIAN – JUMPING, TEAM

1964 Tokyo

G	West Germany
S	France
B	Italy

1968 Mexico City

G	Canada
S	France
B	West Germany

1972 Munich

G	West Germany
S	United States
B	Italy

1976 Montreal

G	France
S	West Germany
B	Belgium

1980 Moscow

G	Soviet Union
S	Poland
B	Mexico

1984 Los Angeles

G	United States
S	Great Britain
B	West Germany

1988 Seoul

G	West Germany
S	United States
B	France

1992 Barcelona

G	Netherlands
S	Austria
B	France

1996 Atlanta

G	Germany
S	United States
B	Brazil

EQUESTRIAN – DRESSAGE, INDIVIDUAL

1952 Helsinki

G	Henri Saint Cyr	Sweden
S	Lis Hartel	Denmark
B	André Jousseaume	France

1956 Stockholm

G	Henri Saint Cyr	Sweden
S	Lis Hartel	Denmark
B	Liselott Linsenhoff	West Germany

1960 Rome

G	Sergei Filatov	Soviet Union
S	Gustav Fischer	Switzerland
B	Josef Neckermann	West Germany

1964 Tokyo

G	Henri Chammartin	Switzerland
S	Harry Boldt	West Germany
B	Sergei Filatov	Soviet Union

1968 Mexico City

G	Ivan Kizimov	Soviet Union
S	Josef Neckermann	West Germany
B	Reiner Klimke	West Germany

1972 Munich

G	Liselott Linsenhoff	West Germany
S	Yelena Petushkova	Soviet Union
B	Josef Neckermann	West Germany

1976 Montreal

G	Christine Stückelberger	Switzerland
S	Harry Boldt	West Germany
B	Reiner Klimke	West Germany

1980 Moscow

G	Elizabeth Theurer	Austria
S	Yuri Kovshov	Soviet Union
B	Viktor Ugryumov	Soviet Union

1984 Los Angeles

G	Reiner Klimke	West Germany
S	Anne Grethe Jensen	Denmark
B	Ottol Hofer	Switzerland

1988 Seoul

G	Nicole Uphoff	West Germany
S	Margi Otto-Crépin	France
B	Christine Stückelberger	Switzerland

1992 Barcelona

G	Nicole Uphoff	Germany
S	Isabell Werth	Germany
B	Nikolaus "Klaus" Balkenhol	Germany

1996 Atlanta

G	Isabell Werth	Germany
S	Anky Van Grunsven	Netherlands
B	Sven Rothenberger	Netherlands

EQUESTRIAN – DRESSAGE, TEAM

1952 Helsinki

G	Sweden
S	Switzerland
B	West Germany

1956 Stockholm

G	Sweden
S	West Germany
B	Switzerland

1964 Tokyo

G	West Germany
S	Switzerland
B	Soviet Union

1968 Mexico City

G	West Germany
S	Soviet Union
B	Switzerland

1972 Munich

G	Soviet Union
S	West Germany
B	Sweden

1976 Montreal

G	West Germany
S	Switzerland
B	United States

1980 Moscow

G	Soviet Union
S	Bulgaria
B	Romania

1984 Los Angeles

G	West Germany
S	Switzerland
B	Sweden

1988 Seoul

G	West Germany
S	Switzerland
B	Canada

1992 Barcelona

G	Germany
S	Netherlands
B	United States

1996 Atlanta

G	Germany
S	Netherlands
B	United States

FENCING – FOIL, INDIVIDUAL

1924 Paris

G	Ellen Osiier	Denmark
S	Galdys Davies	Great Britain
B	Grete Heckscher	Denmark

1928 Amsterdam

G	Helene Mayer	Germany
S	Muriel Freeman	Great Britain
B	Olga Oelkers	Germany

1932 Los Angeles

G	Ellen Preis	Austria
S	Heather "Judy" Guinness	Great Britain
B	Erna Bogáthy Bogen	Hungary

1936 Berlin

G	Ilona Elek	Hungary
S	Helene Mayer	Germany
B	Ellen Preis	Austria

1948 London

G	Ilona Elek	Hungary
S	Karen Làchmann	Denmark
B	Ellen Müller-Preis	Austria

1952 Helsinki

G	Irene Camber	Italy
S	Ilona Elek	Hungary
B	Karen Lachmann	Denmark

1956 Melbourne

G	Gillian Sheen	Great Britain
S	Olga Orban	Romania
B	Renée Garihe	France

1960 Rome

G	Heidi Schmid	West Germany
S	Valentina Rastvorova	Soviet Union
B	Maria Vicol	Romania

1964 Tokyo

G	Ildikó Ujlaki-Rejtö	Hungary
S	Helga Mees	West Germany
B	Antonella Ragno	Italy

1968 Mexico City

G	Yelena Novikova	Soviet Union
S	Maria del Pilar Roldan	Mexico
B	Ildikó Ujlaki-Rejtö	Hungary

1972 Munich

G	Antonella Ragno-Lonzi	Italy
S	Ildikó Bóbis	Hungary
B	Galina Gorokhova	Soviet Union

1976 Montreal

G	Ildikó Schwarczenberger	Hungary
S	Maria Consolata Collino	Italy
B	Yelena Belova (Novikova)	Soviet Union

1980 Moscow

G	Pascale Trinquet	France
S	Magda Maros	Hungary
B	Barbara Wysoczańska	Poland

1984 Los Angeles

G	Luan Jujie	China
S	Cornelia Hanisch	West Germany
B	Dorina Vaccaroni	Italy

1988 Seoul

G	Anja Fichtel	West Germany
S	Sabine Bau	West Germany
B	Zita-Eva Funkenhauser	West Germany

1992 Barcelona

G	Giovanna Trillini	Italy
S	Wang Huifeng	China
B	Tatyana Sadovskaya	Commonwealth of Independent States

1996 Atlanta

G	Laura Badea	Romania
S	Valentina Vezzali	Italy
B	Giovanna Trillini	Italy

FENCING – FOIL, TEAM

1960 Rome

G Soviet Union
S Hungary
B Italy

1964 Tokyo

G Hungary
S Soviet Union
B West Germany

1968 Mexico City

G Soviet Union
S Hungary
B Romania

1972 Munich

G Soviet Union
S Hungary
B Romania

1976 Montreal

G Soviet Union
S France
B Hungary

1980 Moscow

G France
S Soviet Union
B Hungary

1984 Los Angeles

G West Germany
S Romania
B France

1988 Seoul

G West Germany
S Italy
B Hungary

1992 Barcelona

G Italy
S Germany
B Romania

1996 Atlanta

G Italy
S Romania
B Germany

FENCING – ÉPÉE, INDIVIDUAL

1996 Atlanta

G	Laura Flessel	France
S	Valerie Barlois	France
B	Gyoengyi Szalay Horvathne	Hungary

FENCING – ÉPÉE, TEAM

1996 Atlanta

G France
S Italy
B Russian Federation

FIELD HOCKEY

1980 Moscow

G Zimbabwe
S Czechoslovakia
B Soviet Union

1984 Los Angeles

G Netherlands
S West Germany
B United States

1988 Seoul

G Australia
S South Korea
B Netherlands

1992 Barcelona

G Spain
S Germany
B Great Britain

1996 Atlanta

G Australia
S South Korea
B Netherlands

FOOTBALL (SOCCER)

1996 Atlanta

G United States
S China
B Norway

GOLF

1900 Paris

G	Margaret Abbott	United States
S	Pauline "Polly" Whittier	United States
B	Daria Pratt	United States

GYMNASTICS – ALL-AROUND

1952 Helsinki

G	Maria Horokhovska	Soviet Union
S	Nina Bocharova	Soviet Union
B	Margit Korondi	Hungary

1956 Melbourne

G	Larysa Latynina	Soviet Union
S	Ágnes Keleti	Hungary
B	Sofia Muratova	Soviet Union

1960 Rome

G	Larysa Latynina	Soviet Union
S	Sofia Muratova	Soviet Union
B	Polina Astakhova	Soviet Union

1964 Tokyo

G	Vera Cásalavská	Czechoslovakia
S	Larysa Latynina	Soviet Union
B	Polina Astakhova	Soviet Union

1968 Mexico City

G	Vera Cásalavská	Czechoslovakia
S	Zinaida Voronina	Soviet Union
B	Natalya Kuchinskaya	Soviet Union

1972 Munich

G	Lyudmila Turischeva	Soviet Union
S	Karin Janz	East Germany
B	Tamara Lazakovich	Soviet Union

1976 Montreal

G	Nadia Comaneci	Romania
S	Nelli Kim	Soviet Union
B	Lyudmila Turischeva	Soviet Union

1980 Moscow

G	Yelena Davydova	Soviet Union
S	Nadia Comaneci	Romania
B	Maxi Gnauck	East Germany

1984 Los Angeles

G	Mary Lou Retton	United States
S	Ecaterina Szabó	Romania
B	Simona Pauca	Romania

1988 Seoul

G	Yelena Shushunova	Soviet Union
S	Daniela Silivas	Romania
B	Svetlana Boginskaya	Soviet Union

1992 Barcelona

G	Tatyana Gutsu	Commonwealth of Independent States
S	Shannon Miller	United States
B	Lavinia Milosovici	Romania

GYMNASTICS – ARTISTIC INDIVIDUAL ALL-ROUND COMPETITION

1996 Atlanta

G	Lilia Podkopayeva	Ukraine
S	Gina Gogean	Romania
B	Simona Amanar	Romania
	Lavinia Milosovici	Romania

GYMNASTICS – SIDE HORSE VAULT

1952 Helsinki

G	Yekaterina Kalinchuk	Soviet Union
S	Maria Horokhovska	Soviet Union
B	Galina Minaicheva	Soviet Union

1956 Melbourne

G	Larysa Latynina	Soviet Union
S	Tamara Manina	Soviet Union
B	Ann-Sofi Colling-Pettersson	Sweden

1960 Rome

G	Marharyta Nikolayeva	Soviet Union
S	Sofia Muratova	Soviet Union
B	Larysa Latynina	Soviet Union

1964 Tokyo

G	Vera Cáslavská	Czechoslovakia
S	Larysa Latynina	Soviet Union
B	Birgit Radochla	East Germany

1968 Mexico City

G	Vera Cáslavská	Czechoslovakia
S	Erika Zuchold	East Germany
B	Zinaida Voronina	Soviet Union

1972 Munich

G	Karin Janz	East Germany
S	Erika Zuchold	East Germany
B	Lyudmila Turischeva	Soviet Union

1976 Montreal

G	Nelli Kim	Soviet Union
S	Carola Dombeck	East Germany
B	Lyudmila Turischeva	Soviet Union

1980 Moscow

G	Natalya Shaposhnikova	Soviet Union
S	Steffi Kräker	East Germany
B	Melita Rühn	Romania

1984 Los Angeles

G	Ecaterina Szabó	Romania
S	Mary Lou Retton	United States
B	Lavinia Agache	Romania

1988 Seoul

G	Svetlana Boginskaya	Soviet Union
S	Gabriela Potorac	Romania
B	Daniela Silvas	Romania

1992 Baracelona

G	Lavinia Milosovici	Romania
S	Henrietta Ónodi	Hungary
B	Tatyana Lysenko	Commonwealth of Independent States

1996 Atlanta

G	Simona Amanar	Romania
S	Mo Huilan	China
B	Gina Gogean	Romania

GYMNASTICS – ASYMMETRICAL (UNEVEN) BARS

1952 Helsinki

G	Margit Korondi	Hungary
S	Maria Horokhovska	Soviet Union
B	Ágnes Keleti	Hungary

1956 Melbourne

G	Ágnes Keleti	Hungary
S	Larysa Latynina	Soviet Union
B	Sofia Muratova	Soviet Union

1960 Rome

G	Polina Astakhova	Soviet Union
S	Larysa Latynina	Soviet Union
B	Tamara Lyukhina	Soviet Union

1964 Tokyo

G	Polina Astakhova	Soviet Union
S	Katalin Makray	Hungary
B	Larysa Latynina	Soviet Union

1968 Mexico City

G	Vera Cáslavská	Czechoslovakia
S	Karin Janz	East Germany
B	Zinaida Voronina	Soviet Union

1972 Munich

G	Karin Janz	East Germany
S	Olga Korbut	Soviet Union
B	Erika Zuchold	East Germany

1976 Montreal

G	Nadia Comaneci	Romania
S	Teodroa Ungureanu	Romania
B	Márta Egervári	Hungary

1980 Moscow

G	Maxi Gnauck	East Germany
S	Emilia Eberle	Romania
B	Marcia Filatova	Soviet Union

1984 Los Angeles

G	Ma Yanhong	China
S	Julianne McNamara	United States
B	Mary Lou Retton	United States

1988 Seoul

G	Daniela Silivas	Romania
S	Dagmar Kersten	East Germany
B	Yelena Shushunova	Soviet Union

1992 Barcelona

G	Lu Li	China
S	Tatyana Gutsu	Ukraine
B	Shannon Miller	United States

1996 Atlanta

G	Svetlana Chorkina	Russian Federation
S	Bi Wenjiing	China
	Amy Chow	United States
B	None awarded	

GYMNASTICS – BALANCE BEAM

1952 Helsinki

G	Nina Bocharova	Soviet Union
S	Maria Horokhovska	Soviet Union
B	Margit Korondi	Hungary

1956 Melbourne

G	Ágnes Keleti	Hungary
S	Eva Bosáková (Vechtová)	Czechoslovakia
B	Tamara Manina	Soviet Union

1960 Rome

G	Eva Bosáková (Vechtová)	Czechoslovakia
S	Larysa Latynina	Soviet Union
B	Sofia Muratova	Soviet Union

1964 Tokyo

G	Vera Cáslavská	Czechoslovakia
S	Tamara Manina	Soviet Union
B	Larysa Latynina	Soviet Union

1968 Mexico City

G	Natalya Kuchinskaya	Soviet Union
S	Vera Cáslavská	Czechoslovakia
B	Larissa Petrik	Soviet Union

1972 Munich

G	Olga Korbut	Soviet Union
S	Tamara Lazakovich	Soviet Union
B	Karin Janz	East Germany

1976 Montreal

G	Nadia Comaneci	Romania
S	Olga Korbut	Soviet Union
B	Teodora Ungureanu	Romania

1980 Moscow

G	Nadia Comaneci	Romania
S	Yelena Davydova	Soviet Union
B	Natalya Shaposhnikova	Soviet Union

1984 Los Angeles

G	Simona Pauca	Romania
S	Ecaterina Szabó	Romania
B	Kathy Johnson	United States

1988 Seoul

G	Daniela Silivas	Romania
S	Yelena Shushunova	Soviet Union
B	Phoebe Mills	United States

1992 Barcelona

G	Tatyana Lysenko	Commonwealth of Independent States
S	Lu Li	China
B	Shannon Miller	United States

1996 Atlanta

G	Shannon Miller	United States
S	Lilia Podkopayeva	Ukraine
B	Gina Gogean	Romania

GYMNASTICS – FLOOR EXERCISES

1952 Helsinki

G	Ágnes Keleti	Hungary
S	Maria Horokhovska	Soviet Union
B	Margit Korondi	Hungary

1956 Melbourne

G	Ágnes Keleti	Hungary
S	Larysa Latynina	Soviet Union
B	Elena Leustean	Romania

1960 Rome

G	Larysa Latynina	Soviet Union
S	Polina Astakhova	Soviet Union
B	Tamara Lyukhina	Soviet Union

1964 Tokyo

G	Larysa Latynina	Soviet Union
S	Polina Astakhova	Soviet Union
B	Anikó Jánosi-Ducza	Hungary

1968 Mexico City

G	Vera Cáslavská	Czechoslovakia
S	Larissa Petrik	Soviet Union
B	Natalya Kuchinskaya	Soviet Union

1972 Munich

G	Olga Korbut	Soviet Union
S	Lyudmila Turischeva	Soviet Union
B	Tamara Lazakovich	Soviet Union

1976 Montreal

G	Nelli Kim	Soviet Union
S	Lyudmila Turischeva	Soviet Union
B	Nadia Comaneci	Romania

1980 Moscow

G	Nadia Comaneci	Romania
S	Nelli Kim	Soviet Union
B	Maxi Gnauck	East Germany

1984 Los Angeles

G	Ecaterina Szabó	Romania
S	Julianne McNamara	United States
B	Mary Lou Retton	United States

1988 Seoul

G	Daniela Silvas	Romania
S	Svetlana Boginskaya	Soviet Union
B	Diana Dudeva	Bulgaria

1992 Barcelona

G	Lavinia Milosovici	Romania
S	Henrietta Ónodi	Hungary
B	Cristina BontaIl	Romania

1996 Atlanta

G	Lilia Podkopayeva	Ukraine
S	Simona Amanar	Romania
B	Dominique Dawes	United States

GYMNASTICS – TEAM COMBINED EXERCISES

1928 Amsterdam

G	Netherlands
S	Italy
B	Great Britain

1936 Berlin

G	Germany
S	Czechoslovakia
B	Hungary

1948 London

G	Czechoslovakia
S	Hungary
B	United States

1952 Helsinki

G	Soviet Union
S	Hungary
B	Czechoslovakia

1956 Melbourne
G Soviet Union
S Hungary
B Romania

1960 Rome
G Soviet Union
S Czechoslovakia
B Romania

1964 Tokyo
G Soviet Union
S Czechoslovakia
B Japan

1968 Mexico City
G Soviet Union
S Czechoslovakia
B East Germany

1972 Munich
G Soviet Union
S East Germany
B Hungary

1976 Montreal
G Soviet Union
S Romania
B East Germany

1980 Moscow
G Soviet Union
S Romania
B East Germany

1984 Los Angeles
G Romania
S United States
B China

1988 Seoul
G Soviet Union
S Romania
B East Germany

1992 Barcelona
G Commonwealth of Independent States
S Romania
B United States

ARTISTIC TEAM COMPETITION

1996 Atlanta
G United States
S Russian Federation
B Romania

GYMNASTICS – RHYTHMIC ALL-AROUND

1984 Los Angeles
G	Lori Fung	Canada
S	Doina Staiculescu	Romania
B	Regina Weber	West Germany

1988 Seoul
G	Marina Lobach	Soviet Union
S	Adriana Dunavska	Bulgaria
B	Oleksandra Tymoshenko	Soviet Union

1992 Barcelona
G	Oleksandra Tymoshenko	Commonwealth of Independent States
S	Carolina Pascual Gracia	Spain
B	Oksana Skaldina	Commonwealth of Independent States

1996 Atlanta
G	Ykaterina Serebryanskaya	Ukraine
S	Ianina Batyrchinta	Russian Federation
B	Ylena Vitrichenko	Ukraine

GYMNASTICS – TEAM EXERCISE WITH PORTABLE APPARATUS

1952 Helsinki
G Sweden
S Soviet Union
B Hungary

1956 Melbourne
G Hungary
S Sweden
B Poland

GYMNASTICS – RHYTHMIC ALL-AROUND COMPETITION

1996 Atlanta
G Spain
S Bulgaria
B Russian Federation

HANDBALL–TEAM

1976 Montreal

G Soviet Union
S East Germany
B Hungary

1980 Moscow

G Soviet Union
S Yugoslavia
B East Germany

1984 Los Angeles

G Yugoslavia
S South Korea
B China

1988 Seoul

G South Korea
S Norway
B Soviet Union

1992 Barcelona

G South Korea
S Norway
B Commonwealth of Independent States

1996 Atlanta

G Denmark
S South Korea
B Hungary

JUDO – EXTRA LIGHTWEIGHT

1992 Barcelona

G	Cécile Nowak	France
S	Ryoko Tamura	Japan
B	Amarilis Savón Carmenaty	Cuba

1996 Atlanta

G	Kye Sun-Hi	Democratic People's Republic of Korea
S	Ryoko Tamura	Japan
B	Yolanda Soler	Spain
	Amarilis Savon	Cuba

JUDO – HALF-LIGHTWEIGHT

1992 Barcelona

G	Almudena Muñoz Martinez	Spain
S	Noriko Mizoguchi	Japan
B	Li Zhongyun	China

1996 Atlanta

G	Marie-Claire Restoux	France
S	Hyun Sook-hee	South Korea
B	Legna Verdecia	Cuba
	Noriko Sagawara	Japan

JUDO – LIGHTWEIGHT

1992 Barcelona

G	Miriam Blasco Soto	Spain
S	Nicola Fairbrother	Great Britain
B	Driulis González Morales	Cuba

1996 Atlanta

G	Driulis Gonzalez	Cuba
S	Jung Sun-yong	South Korea
B	Marisabel Lomba	Belgium
	Isabel Fernandez	Spain

JUDO – HALF-MIDDLEWEIGHT

1992 Barcelona

G	Catherine Fleury	France
S	Yael Arad	Israel
B	Yelena Petrova	Commonwealth of Independent States

1996 Atlanta

G	Yuko Emoto	Japan
S	Gella Van de Caveye	Belgium
B	Jenny Gal	Netherlands
	Jung Sung-sook	South Korea

JUDO – MIDDLEWEIGHT

1992 Barcelona

G	Odalys Reve Jiménez	Cuba
S	Emanuela Pierantozzi	Italy
B	Kate Howey	Great Britain

1996 Atlanta

G	Cho Min-sun	Korea
S	Aneta Szczepanska	Poland
B	Wang Xianbo	China
	Claudia Zwiers	Netherlands

JUDO – HALF-HEAVYWEIGHT

1992 Barcelona

G	Kim Mi-jung	South Korea
S	Yoko Tanabe	Japan
B	Irene de Kok	Netherlands

1996 Atlanta

G	Ulla Werbrouck	Belgium
S	Yoko Tanabe	Japan
B	Ylenia Scapin	Italy
	Diadenis Lung	Cuba

JUDO – HEAVYWEIGHT

1992 Barcelona

G	Zhuang Xiaoyan	China
S	Estela Rodriguez Villanueva	Cuba
B	Natalina Lupino	France

1996 Atlanta

G	Sun Fuming	China
S	Estela Rodriguez	Cuba
B	Johanna Hagn	Germany
	Christine Cicot	France

ROWING – SINGLE SCULLS

1976 Montreal

G	Christine Scheiblich	East Germany
S	Joan Lind	United States
B	Yelena Antonova	Soviet Union

1980 Moscow

G	Sanda Toma	Romania
S	Antonina Makhina	Soviet Union
B	Martina Schröter	East Germany

1984 Los Angeles

G	Valeria Racila	Romania
S	Charlotte Geer	United States
B	Ann Haesebrouck	Belgium

1988 Seoul

G	Jutta Behrendt	East Germany
S	Anne Marden	United States
B	Magdalena Georgieva	Bulgaria

1992 Barcelona

G	Elisabeta Lipa (Oleniuc)	Romania
S	Annelies Bredael	Belgium
B	Silken Laumann	Canada

1996 Atlanta

G	Yekaterina Khodotovich	Belarus
S	Silken Laumann	Canada
B	Trine Hansen	Denmark

ROWING – DOUBLE SCULLS

1976 Montreal

G	Svetla Otsetova	Bulgaria
	Zdravka Yordanova	
S	Sabine Jahn	East Germany
	Petra Boesler	
B	Leonora Kaminskaite	Soviet Union
	Genovaite Ramoskiene	

1980 Moscow

G	Yelena Khloptseva	Soviet Union
	Larissa Popova (Aleksandrova)	
S	Cornelia Linse	East Germany
	Heidi Westphal	
B	Olga Homeghi	Romania
	Valeria Răcilă-Rosca	

1984 Los Angeles

G	Marioara Popescu	Romania
	Elisabeta Oleniuc	
S	Greet Hellemans	Netherlands
	Nicolette Hellemans	
B	Daniele Laumann	Canada
	Silken Laumann	

1988 Seoul

G	Birgit Peter	East Germany
	Martina Schröter	
S	Elisabeta Lipa (Oleniuc)	Romania
	Veronica Cogeanu	
B	Violeta Ninova	Bulgaria
	Stefka Madina	

1992 Barcelona

G	Kerstin Köppen	Germany
	Kathrin Boron	
S	Veronica Cochelea (Cogeanu)	Romania
	Elisabeta Lipa (Oleniuc)	
B	Gu Xiaoli	China
	Lu Huali	

1996 Atlanta

G	Marnie McBean	Canada
	Kathleen Heddle	
S	Cao Mianying	China
	Zhang Xiuyun	
B	Irene Eljs	Netherlands
	Eeke van Nes	

ROWING – QUADRUPLE SCULLS WITHOUT COXSWAIN

1988 Seoul

G East Germany
S Soviet Union
B Romania

1992 Barcelona

G Germany
S Romania
B Commonwealth of Independent States

1996 Atlanta

G Germany
S Ukraine
B Canada

ROWING – FOUR-OARED SHELL WITHOUT COXSWAIN

1992 Barcelona

G Canada
S United States
B Germany

ROWING – PAIR OARS WITHOUT COXSWAIN

1996 Atlanta

G	Megan Still Kate Slatter	Australia
S	Missy Schwen Karen Kraft	United States
B	Christine Gosse Helene Cortin	France

ROWING – EIGHT-OARED SHELL WITH COXSWAIN

1976 Montreal

G East Germany
S Soviet Union
B United States

1980 Moscow

G East Germany
S Soviet Union
B Romania

1984 Los Angeles

G United States
S Romania
B Netherlands

1988 Seoul

G East Germany
S Romania
B China

1992 Barcelona

G Canada
S Romania
B Germany

1996 Atlanta

G Romania
S Canada
B Belarus

ROWING – LIGHT WEIGHT FOUR OARS WITHOUT COXSWAIN

1996 Atlanta

G	Constantina Burcica Camelia Macoviciuc	Romania
S	Teresa Z. Bell Lindsay Burns	United States
B	Rebecca Joyce Virginia Lee	Australia

ROWING – QUADRUPLE SCULLS WITH COXSWAIN

1976 Montreal

G East Germany
S Soviet Union
B Romania

1980 Moscow

G East Germany
S Soviet Union
B Bulgaria

1984 Los Angeles

G Romania
S United States
B Denmark

ROWING – PAIR-OARED SHELL WITHOUT COXSWAIN

1976 Montreal

G	Siika Kelbecheva Stoyanka Gruicheva	Bulgaria
S	Angelika Noack Sabine Dähne	East Germany
B	Edith Eckbauer Thea Einöder	West Germany

1980 Moscow

G	Ute Steindorf Cornelia Klier	East Germany
S	Malgorzata Dlużewska Czeslawa Kościańska	Poland
B	Siika Barbulova (Kelbecheva) Stoyanka Kurbatova (Gruicheva)	Bulgaria

1984 Los Angeles

G	Rodica Arba (Puscata) Elena Horvat	Romania
S	Elizabeth Craig Tricia Smith	Canada
B	Ellen Becker Iris Völkner	West Germany

1988 Seoul

G	Rodica Arba (Puscata) Olga Homeghi	Romania
S	Radka Stoyanova Lalka Berberova	Bulgaria
B	Nicola Payne Lynley Hannen	New Zealand

1992 Barcelona

G	Marnie McBean Kathleen Heddle	Canada
S	Stefani Werremeier Ingeburg Schwerzmann	Germany
B	Anna Seaton Stephanie Pierson	United States

ROWING – FOUR-OARED SHELL WITH COXSWAIN

1976 Montreal

G East Germany
S Bulgaria
B Soviet Union

1980 Moscow

G East Germany
S Bulgaria
B Soviet Union

1984 Los Angeles

G Romania
S Canada
B Australia

1988 Seoul

G East Germany
S China
B Romania

SHOOTING – SPORT PISTOL

1984 Los Angeles

G	Linda Thom	Canada
S	Ruby Fox	United States
B	Patricia Dench	Australia

1988 Seoul

G	Nino Salukvadze	Soviet Union
S	Tomoko Hasegawa	Japan
B	Jasna Šekarić	Yugoslavia

1992 Barcelona

G	Marina Logvinenko (Dobranchev)	Commonwealth of Independent States
S	Li Duihong	China
B	Dorzhsuren Munkhbayar	Mongolia

1996 Atlanta

G	Li Duihong	China
S	Diana Yorgova	Bulgaria
B	Marina Logvinenko	Russian Federation

SHOOTING – AIR PISTOL

1988 Seoul

G	Jasna Šekarić	Yugoslavia
S	Nino Salukvadze	Soviet Union
B	Marina Dobrancheva	Soviet Union

1992 Barcelona

G	Marina Logvinenko (Dobrancheva)	Commonwealth of Independent States
S	Jasna Šekarić	Yugoslavia
B	Maria Grozdeva	Bulgaria

1996 Atlanta

G	Olga Klochneva	Russian Federation
S	Marina Logvinenko	Russian Federation
B	Mariya Grozdeva	Bulgaria

SHOOTING – SMALL-BORE RIFLE, THREE POSITIONS

1984 Los Angeles

G	Wu Xiaoxuan	China
S	Ulrike Holmer	West Germany
B	Wanda Jewell	United States

1988 Seoul

G	Sylvia Sperber	West Germany
S	Vessela Lecheva	Bulgaria
B	Valentina Cherkasova	Soviet Union

1992 Barcelona

G	Launi Meili	United States
S	Nonka Matova	Bulgaria
B	Malgorzata Ksiazkiewicz	Poland

1996 Atlanta

G	Aleksandra Ivosev	Yugoslavia
S	Irina Gerasimenok	Russian Federation
B	Renata Mauer	Poland

SHOOTING – AIR RIFLE

1984 Los Angeles

G	Pat Spurgin	United States
S	Edith Gufler	Italy
B	Wu Xiaoxuan	China

1988 Seoul

G	Irina Shilova	Soviet Union
S	Sylvia Sperber	West Germany
B	Anna Malukhina	Soviet Union

1992 Barcelona

G	Yeo Kab-soon	South Korea
S	Vessela Lecheva	Bulgaria
B	Aranka Binder	Yugoslavia

1996 Atlanta

G	Renata Mauer	Poland
S	Petra Horneber	Germany
B	Aleksandra Ivosev	Yugoslavia

SHOOTING – DOUBLE TRAP

1996 Atlanta

G	Kim Rhode	United States
S	Susanne Kiermayer	Germany
B	Deserie Huddleston	Australia

SOFTBALL

1996 Atlanta

G	United States
S	China
B	Australia

SWIMMING – 50-METER FREESTYLE

1988 Seoul

G	Kristin Otto	East Germany
S	Yang Wenyi	China
B	Katrin Meissner	East Germany

1992 Barcelona

G	Yang Wenyi	China
S	Zhuang Yong	China
B	Angelina Martino	United States

1996 Atlanta

G	Amy Van Dyken	United States
S	Le Jingyi	China
B	Sandra Volker	Germany

SWIMMING – 100-METER FREESTYLE

1912 Stockholm

G	Sarah "Fanny" Durack	Australia
S	Wilhelmina Wylie	Australia
B	Jennie Fletcher	Great Britain

1920 Antwerp

G	Ethelda Bleibtrey	United States
S	Irene Guest	United States
B	Frances Schroth	United States

1924 Paris

G	Ethel Lackie	United States
S	Mariechen Wehselau	United States
B	Gertrude Ederle	United States

1928 Amsterdam

G	Albina Osipowich	United States
S	Eleanor Garatti	United States
B	Margaret Joyce Cooper	Great Britain

1932 Los Angeles

G	Helene Madison	United States
S	Willemijntje den Ouden	Netherlands
B	Eleanor Saville (Garatti)	United States

1936 Berlin

G	Hendrika "Rie" Mastenbroek	Netherlands
S	Jeannette Campbell	Argentina
B	Gisela Arendt	Germany

1948 London

G	Greta Andersen	Denmark
S	Ann Curtis	United States
B	Marie-Louise Vaessen	Netherlands

1952 Helsinki

G	Katalin Szöke	Hungary
S	Johanna Termeulen	Netherlands
B	Judit Temes	Hungary

1956 Melbourne

G	Dawn Fraser	Australia
S	Lorraine Crapp	Australia
B	Faith Leech	Australia

1960 Rome

G	Dawn Fraser	Australia
S	S. Christine Von Saltza	United States
B	Natalie Steward	Great Britain

1964 Tokyo

G	Dawn Fraser	Australia
S	Sharon Stouder	United States
B	Kathleen Ellis	United States

1968 Mexico City

G	Jan Henne	United States
S	Susan Pedersen	United States
B	Linda Gustavson	United States

1972 Munich

G	Sandra Neilson	United States
S	Shirley Babashoff	United States
B	Shane Gould	Australia

1976 Montreal

G	Kornelia Ender	East Germany
S	Petra Priemer	East Germany
B	Enith Brigitha	Netherlands

1980 Moscow

G	Barbara Krause	East Germany
S	Caren Metschuck	East Germany
B	Ines Diers	East Germany

1984 Los Angeles

G	Nancy Hogshead	United States
S	Carrie Steinseifer	United States
B	Annemarie Verstappen	Netherlands

1988 Seoul

G	Kristin Otto	East Germany
S	Zhuang Yong	China
B	Catherine Plewinski	France

1992 Barcelona

G	Zhuang Yong	China
S	Jennifer Thompson	United States
B	Franziska van Almsick	Germany

1996 Atlanta

G	Le Jingyi	China
S	Sandra Volker	Germany
B	Angel Martino	United States

SWIMMING - 200-METER FREESTYLE

1968 Mexico City

G	Deborah Meyer	United States
S	Jan Henne	United States
B	Jane Barkman	United States

1972 Munich

G	Shane Gould	Australia
S	Shirley Babashoff	United States
B	Keena Rothhammer	United States

1976 Montreal

G	Kornelia Ender	East Germany
S	Shirley Babashoff	United States
B	Enith Brigitha	Netherlands

1980 Moscow

G	Barbara Krause	East Germany
S	Ines Diers	East Germany
B	Carmela Schmidt	East Germany

1984 Los Angeles

G	Mary Wayte	United States
S	Cynthia Woodhead	United States
B	Annemarie Verstappen	Netherlands

1988 Seoul

G	Heike Friedrich	East Germany
S	Silvia Poll Ahrens	Costa Rica
B	Manuela Stellmach	East Germany

1992 Barcelona

G	Nicole Haislett	United States
S	Franziska van Almsick	Germany
B	Kerstin Kielgass	Germany

1996 Atlanta

G	Claudia Poll	Costa Rica
S	Franziska van Almsick	Germany
B	Dagmar Hase	Germany

SWIMMING – 400-METER FREESYTLE

1920 Antwerp

G	Ethelda Bleibtrey	United States
S	Margaret Woodbridge	United States
B	Frances Schroth	United States

1924 Paris

G	Martha Norelius	United States
S	Helen Wainwright	United States
B	Gertrude Ederle	United States

1928 Amsterdam

G	Martha Norelius	United States
S	Maria Braun	Netherlands
B	Josephine McKim	United States

1932 Los Angeles

G	Helene Madison	United States
S	Lenore Kight	United States
B	Jennie Maakal	South Africa

1936 Berlin

G	Hendrika "Rie" Mastenbroek	Netherlands
S	Ragnhild Hveger	Denmark
B	Lenore Wingard (Kight)	United States

1948 London

G	Ann Curtis	United States
S	Karen-Margrete Harup	Denmark
B	Catherine Gibson	Great Britain

1952 Helsinki

G	Valérie Gyenge	Hungary
S	Éva Novák	Hungary
B	Evelyn Kawamoto	United States

1956 Melbourne

G	Lorraine Crapp	Australia
S	Dawn Fraser	Australia
B	Sylvia Ruuska	United States

1960 Rome

G	S. Christine Von Saltza	United States
S	Jane Cederqvist	Sweden
B	Catharina Lagerberg	Netherlands

1964 Tokyo

G	Virginia Duenkel	United States
S	Marilyn Ramenofsky	United States
B	Terri Stickles	United States

1968 Mexico City

G	Debbie Meyer	United States
S	Linda Gustavson	United States
B	Karen Moras	Australia

1972 Munich

G	Shane Gould	Australia
S	Novella Calligaris	Italy
B	Gudrun Wegner	East Germany

1976 Montreal

G	Petra Thümer	East Germany
S	Shirley Babashoff	United States
B	Shannon Smith	Canada

1980 Moscow

G	Ines Diers	East Germany
S	Petra Schneider	East Germany
B	Carmela Schmidt	East Germany

1984 Los Angeles

G	Tiffany Cohen	United States
S	Sarah Hardcastle	Great Britian
B	June Croft	Great Britain

1988 Seoul

G	Janet Evans	United States
S	Heike Friedrich	East Germany
B	Anke Möhring	East Germany

1992 Barcelona

G	Dagmar Hase	Germany
S	Janet Evans	United States
B	Hayley Lewis	Australia

1996 Atlanta

G	Michelle Smith	Ireland
S	Dagmar Hase	Germany
B	Kirsten Vlieghuis	Netherlands

SWIMMING – 800-METER FREESTYLE

1968 Mexico City

G	Deborah Meyer	United States
S	Pamela Kruse	United States
B	Maria Teresa Ramirez	Mexico

1972 Munich

G	Keena Rothhammer	United States
S	Shane Gould	Australia
B	Novella Calligaris	Italy

1976 Montreal

G	Petra Thümer	East Germany
S	Shirley Babashoff	United States
B	Wendy Weinberg	United States

1980 Moscow

G	Michelle Ford	Australia
S	Ines Diers	East Germany
B	Heike Dähne	East German

1984 Los Angeles

G	Tiffany Cohen	United States
S	Michele Richardson	United States
B	Sarah Hardcastle	Great Britain

1988 Seoul

G	Janet Evans	United States
S	Astrid Strauss	East Germany
B	Julie McDonald	Australia

1992 Barcelona

G	Janet Evans	United States
S	Hayley Lewis	Australia
B	Jana Henke	Germany

1996 Atlanta

G	Brooke Bennett	United States
S	Dagmar Hase	Germany
B	Kirsten Vlieghuis	Netherlands

SWIMMING – 100-METER BACKSTROKE

1924 Paris

G	Sybil Bauer	United States
S	Phyllis Harding	Great Britain
B	Aileen Riggin	United States

1928 Amsterdam

G	Maria Braun	Netherlands
S	Ellen King	Great Britain
B	Margaret Joyce Cooper	Great Britain

1932 Los Angeles

G	Eleanor Holm	United States
S	Philomena "Bonny" Mealing	Australia
B	Elizabeth Valerie Davies	Great Britain

1936 Berlin

G	Dina "Nida" Senff	Netherlands
S	Hendrika "Rie" Mastenbroek	Netherlands
B	Alice Bridges	United States

1948 London

G	Karen-Margrete Harup	Denmark
S	Suzanne Zimmerman	United States
B	Judith Davies	Australia

1952 Helsinki

G	Joan Harrison	South Africa
S	Geertje Wielema	Netherlands
B	Jean Stewart	New Zealand

1956 Melbourne

G	Judith Grinham	Great Britain
S	Carin Cone	United States
B	Margaret Edwards	Great Britain

1960 Rome

G	Lynn Burke	United States
S	Natalie Steward	Great Britain
B	Satoko Tanaka	Japan

1964 Tokyo

G	Cathy Ferguson	United States
S	Christine Caron	France
B	Virginia Duenkel	United States

1968 Mexico City

G	Kaye Hall	United States
S	Elaine Tanner	Canada
B	Jane Swagerty	United States

1972 Munich

G	Melissa Belote	United States
S	Andrea Gyarmati	Hungary
B	Susan Atwood	United States

1976 Montreal

G	Ulrike Richter	East Germany
S	Birgit Treiber	East Germany
B	Nancy Garapick	Canada

1980 Moscow

G	Rica Reinisch	East Germany
S	Ina Kleber	East Germany
B	Petra Riedel	East Germany

1984 Los Angeles

G	Theresa Andrews	United States
S	Betsy Mitchell	United States
B	Jolanda de Rover	Netherlands

1988 Seoul

G	Kristin Otto	East Germany
S	Krisztina Egerszegi	Hungary
B	Cornelia Sirch	East Germany

1992 Barcelona

G	Krisztina Egerszegi	Hungary
S	Tünde Szabó	Hungary
B	Lea Loveless	United States

1996 Atlanta

G	Beth Botsford	United States
S	Whitney Hedgepeth	United States
B	Marianne Kriel	South Africa

SWIMMING – 200-METER BACKSTROKE

1968 Mexico City

G	Lillian "Pokey" Watson	United States
S	Elaine Tanner	Canada
B	Kaye Hall	United States

1972 Munich

G	Melissa Belote	United States
S	Susan Atwood	United States
B	Donna Gurr	Canada

1976 Montreal

G	Ulrike Richter	East Germany
S	Birgit Treiber	East Germany
B	Nancy Garapick	Canada

1980 Moscow

G	Rica Reinisch	East Germany
S	Cornelia Polit	East Germany
B	Birgit Treier	East Germany

1984 Los Angeles

G	Jolanda de Rover	Netherlands
S	Amy White	United States
B	Aneta Patrascoiu	Romania

1988 Seoul

G	Krisztina Egerszegi	Hungary
S	Kathrin Zimmerman	East Germany
B	Cornelia Sirch	East Germany

1992 Barcelona

G	Krisztina Egerszegi	Hungary
S	Dagmar Hase	Germany
B	Nicole Stevenson (Livingstone)	Australia

1996 Atlanta

G	Krisztina Egerszegi	Hungary
S	Whitney Hedgepeth	United States
B	Cathleen Rund	Germany

SWIMMING – 100-METER BREASTSTROKE

1968 Mexico City

G	Djurdjica Bjedov	Yugoslavia
S	Halina Prozumenshchykova	Soviet Union
B	Sharon Wichman	United States

1972 Munich

G	Catherine Carr	United States
S	Halina Stepanova (Prozumenshchykova)	Soviet Union
B	Beverly Whitfield	Australia

1976 Montreal

G	Hannelore Anke	East Germany
S	Lyubov Rusanova	Soviet Union
B	Marina Koshevaia	Soviet Union

1980 Moscow

G	Ute Geweniger	East Germany
S	Elvira Vasilkova	Soviet Union
B	Susanne Nielsson	Denmark

1984 Los Angeles

G	Petra van Staveren	Netherlands
S	Anne Ottenbrite	Canada
B	Cathérine Poirot	France

1988 Seoul

G	Tania Dangalakova (Bogomilova)	Bulgaria
S	Antoaneta Frenkeva	Bulgaria
B	Silke Hörner	East Germany

1992 Barcelona

G	Yelena Rudkovskaya	Commonwealth of Independent States
S	N. Anita Nall	United States
B	Samantha Riley	Australia

1996 Atlanta

G	Penny Heyns	South Africa
S	Amanda Beard	United States
B	Samantha Riley	Australia

SWIMMING – 200-METER BREASTSTROKE

1924 Paris

G	Lucy Morton	Great Britain
S	Agnes Geraghty	United States
B	Gladys Carson	Great Britain

1928 Amsterdam

G	Hildegard Schrader	Germany
S	Miejte "Marie" Baron	Netherlands
B	Lotte Mühe	Germany

1932 Los Angeles

G	Clare Dennis	Australia
S	Hideko Maehata	Japan
B	Else Jacobsen	Denmark

1936 Berlin

G	Hideko Maehata	Japan
S	Martha Geneger	Germany
B	Inge Sörensen	Denmark

1948 London

G	Petronella van Vliet	Netherlands
S	Beatrice Lyons	Australia
B	Éva Novák	Hungary

1952 Helsinki

G	Éva Székely	Hungary
S	Éva Novák	Hungary
B	Helen "Elenor" Gordon	Great Britain

1956 Melbourne

G	Ursula Happe	West Germany
S	Éva Székely	Hungary
B	Eva-Maria ten Elsen	East Germany

1960 Rome

G	Anita Lonsbrough	Great Britain
S	Wiltrud Urselmann	West Germany
B	Barbara Göbel	East Germany

1964 Tokyo

G	Halyna Prozumenshchykova	Soviet Union
S	Claudia Kolb	United States
B	Svetlana Babanina	Soviet Union

1968 Mexico City

G	Sharon Wichman	United States
S	Djurdjica Bjedov	Yugoslavia
B	Halyna Prozumenshchykova	Soviet Union

1972 Munich

G	Beverly Whitfield	Australia
S	Dana Schoenfield	United States
B	Halyna Stepanova (Prozumenshchykova)	Soviet Union

1976 Montreal

G	Marina Koshevaia	Soviet Union
S	Maryna Yurchenya	Soviet Union
B	Lyubov Rusanova	Soviet Union

1980 Moscow

G	Lina Kaciušyte	Soviet Union
S	Svetlana Varganova	Soviet Union
B	Yulia Bogdanova	Soviet Union

1984 Los Angeles

G	Anne Ottenbrite	Canada
S	Susan Rapp	United States
B	Ingrid Lempereur	Belgium

1988 Seoul

G	Silke Hörner	East Germany
S	Huang Xiaomin	China
B	Antoaneta Frenkeva	Bulgaria

1992 Barcelona

G	Kyoko Iwasaki	Japan
S	Lin Li	China
B	N. Anital Nall	United States

1996 Atlanta

G	Penny Heyns	South Africa
S	Amanda Beard	United States
B	Agnes Kovacs	Hungary

SWIMMING – 100-METER BUTTERFLY

1956 Melbourne

G	Shelly Mann	United States
S	Nancy Ramey	United States
B	Mary Sears	United States

1960 Rome

G	Carolyn Schuler	United States
S	Marianne Heemskerk	Netherlands
B	Janice Andrew	Australia

1964 Tokyo

G	Sharon Stouder	United States
S	Ada Kok	Netherlands
B	Kathleen Ellis	United States

1968 Mexico City

G	Lynette McClements	Australia
S	Ellie Daniel	United States
B	Susan Shields	United States

1972 Munich

G	Mayumi Aoki	Japan
S	Roswitha Beier	East Germany
B	Andréa Gyarmati	Hungary

1976 Montreal

G	Kornelia Ender	East Germany
S	Andrea Pollack	East Germany
B	Wendy Boglioli	United States

1980 Moscow

G	Caren Metschuck	East Germany
S	Andrea Pollack	East Germany
B	Christiane Knacke	East Germany

1984 Los Angeles

G	Mary T. Meagher	United States
S	Jenna Johnson	United States
B	Karin Seick	West Germany

1988 Seoul

G	Kristin Otto	East Germany
S	Birte Weigang	East Germany
B	Qian Hong	China

1992 Barcelona

G	Qian Hong	China
S	Christine Ahmann-Leighton	United States
B	Catherine Plewinski	France

1996 Atlanta

G	Amy van Dyken	United States
S	Liu Limin	China
B	Angel Martino	United States

SWIMMING – 200-METER BUTTERFLY

1968 Mexico City

G	Ada Kok	Netherlands
S	Helga Linder	East Germany
B	Ellie Daniel	United States

1972 Munich

G	Karen Moe	United States
S	Lynn Colella	United States
B	Ellie Daniel	United States

1976 Montreal

G	Andrea Pollack	East Germany
S	Ulrike Tauber	East Germany
B	Rosemarie Gabriel (Kother)	East Germany

1980 Moscow

G	Ines Geissler	East Germany
S	Sybille Schönrock	East Germany
B	Michelle Ford	Australia

1984 Los Angeles

G	Mary T. Meagher	United States
S	Karen Phillips	Australia
B	Ina Beyermann	West Germany

1988 Seoul

G	Kathleen Nord	East Germany
S	Birte Weigang	East Germany
B	Mary T. Meagher	United States

1992 Barcelona

G	Summer Sanders	United States
S	Wang Xiaohong	China
B	Susan O'Neill	Australia

1996 Atlanta

G	Susan O'Neill	Australia
S	Petria Thomas	Australia
B	Michelle Smith	Ireland

SWIMMING – 200-METER INDIVIDUAL MEDLEY

1968 Mexico City

G	Claudia Kolb	United States
S	Susan Pedersen	United States
B	Jan Henne	United States

1972 Munich

G	Shane Gould	Australia
S	Kornelia Ender	East Germany
B	Lynn Vidali	United States

1984 Los Angeles

G	Tracy Caulkins	United States
S	Nancy Hogshead	United States
B	Michele Pearson	Australia

1988 Seoul

G	Daniela Hunger	East Germany
S	Yelena Dendeberova	Soviet Union
B	Noemi Lung	Romania

1992 Barcelona

G	Lin Li	China
S	Summer Sanders	United States
B	Daniela Hunger	Germany

1996 Atlanta

G	Michelle Smith	Ireland
S	Marianne Limpert	Canada
B	Lin Li	China

SWIMMING – 400-METER INDIVIDUAL MEDLEY

1964 Tokyo

G	Donna De Varona	United States
S	Sharon Finneran	United States
B	Martha Randall	United States

1968 Mexico City

G	Claudia Kolb	United States
S	Lynn Vidali	United States
B	Sabine Steinbach	East Germany

1972 Munich

G	Gail Neall	Australia
S	Leslie Cliff	Canada
B	Novella Calligaris	Italy

1976 Montreal

G	Ulrike Tauber	East Germany
S	Cheryl Gibson	Canada
B	Becky Smith	Canada

1980 Moscow

G	Petra Schneider	East Germany
S	Sharron Davies	East Germany
B	Agnieszka Czopek	Poland

1984 Los Angeles

G	Tracy Caulkins	United States
S	Suzanne Landells	Australia
B	Petra Zindler	West Germany

1988 Seoul

G	Janet Evans	United States
S	Noemi Lung	Romania
B	Daniela Hunger	East Germany

1992 Barcelona

G	Krisztina Egerszegi	Hungary
S	Lin Li	China
B	Summer Sanders	United States

1996 Atlanta

G	Michelle Smith	Ireland
S	Allison Wagner	United States
B	Krisztina Egerszegi	Hungary

SWIMMING – 400 X 100-METER FREESTYLE RELAY

1912 Stockholm

G	Great Britain
S	Germany
B	Austria

1920 Antwerp

G	United States
S	Great Britain
B	Sweden

1924 Paris

G	United States
S	Great Britain
B	Sweden

1928 Amsterdam

G	United States
S	Great Britain
B	South Africa

1932 Los Angeles

G	United States
S	Netherlands
B	Great Britain

1936 Berlin

G	Netherlands
S	Germany
B	United States

1948 London

G	United States
S	Denmark
B	Netherlands

1952 Helsinki
G Hungary
S Netherlands
B United States

1956 Melbourne
G Australia
S United States
B South Africa

1960 Rome
G United States
S Australia
B East and West Germany

1964 Tokyo
G United States
S Australia
B Netherlands

1968 Mexico City
G United States
S East Germany
B Canada

1972 Munich
G United States
S East Germany
B West Germany

1976 Montreal
G United States
S East Germany
B Canada

1980 Moscow
G East Germany
S Sweden
B Netherlands

1984 Los Angeles
G United States
S Netherlands
B West Germany

1988 Seoul
G East Germany
S Netherlands
B United States

1992 Barcelona
G United States
S China
B Germany

1996 Atlanta
G United States
S China
B Germany

SWIMMING – 4 X 200-METER FREESTYLE RELAY

1996 Atlanta
G United States
S Germany
B Australia

SWIMMING – 4 X 100-METER MEDLEY RELAY

1960 Rome
G United States
S Australia
B East and West Germany

1964 Tokyo
G United States
S Netherlands
B Soviet Union

1968 Mexico
G United States
S Australia
B West Germany

1972 Munich
G United States
S East Germany
B West Germany

1976 Montreal
G East Germany
S United States
B Canada

1980 Moscow
G East Germany
S Great Britain
B Soviet Union

1984 Los Angeles

G	United States
S	West Germany
B	Canada

1988 Seoul

G	East Germany
S	United States
B	Canada

1992 Barcelona

G	United States
S	Germany
B	Commonwealth of Independent States

1996 Atlanta

G	United States
S	Australia
B	China

SYNCHRONIZED SWIMMING – TEAM

1996 Atlanta

G	United States
S	Canada
B	Japan

SYNCHRONIZED SWIMMING – SOLO

1984 Los Angeles

G	Tracie Ruiz	United States
S	Carolyn Waldo	Canada
B	Miwako Motoyoshi	Japan

1988 Seoul

G	Carolyn Waldo	Canada
S	Tracie Ruiz-Conforto	United States
B	Mikako Kotani	Japan

1992 Barcelona

G	Kristen Babb-Sprague	United States
S	Sylvie Fréchette	Canada
B	Fumiko Okuno	Japan

SYNCHRONIZED SWIMMING – DUET

1984 Los Angeles

G	Candy Costie Tracie Ruiz	United States
S	Sharon Hambrook Kelly Kryczka	Canada
B	Saeko Simora Miwako Motoyoshi	Japan

1988 Seoul

G	Michelle Cameron Carolyn Waldo	Canada
S	Sarah Josephson Karen Josephson	United States
B	Miyako Tanaka Mikako Kotani	Japan

1992 Barcelona

G	Karen Josephson Sarah Josephson	United States
S	Penny Vilagos Vicky Vilagos	Canada
B	Fumiko Okuno Aki Takayama	Japan

TABLE TENNIS – SINGLES

1988 Seoul

G	Chen Jing	China
S	Li Huifen	China
B	Jiao Zhimin	China

1992 Barcelona

G	Deng Yaping	China
S	Qiao Hong	China
B	Hyun Jung-hwa	South Korea

1996 Atlanta

G	Deng Yaping	China
S	Chen Jing	Taiwan
B	Qiao Hong	China

TABLE TENNIS – DOUBLES

1988 Seoul

G	Hyun Jung-hwa Yang Young-ja	South Korea
S	Chen Jing Jiao Zhimin	China
B	Jasna Fazlič Gordana Perkucin	Yugoslavia

1992 Barcelona

G	Deng Yaping Qiao Hong	China
S	Chen Zihe Gao Jun	China
B	Hong Cha-ok Hyun Jung-Hwa	North Korea

1996 Atlanta

G	Deng Yaping Qiao Yunping	China
S	Liu Wei Qiao Yunping	China
B	Park Hae-jung Ryu Ji-hae	South Korea

TENNIS – SINGLES

1900 Paris

G	Charlotte Cooper	Great Britain
S	Hélène Prévost	France
B	Marion Jones	United States

1906 Athens

G	Esmee Simiriotou	Greece
S	Sophia Marinou	Greece
B	Euphrosine Paspati	Greece

1908 London

G	Dorothea Lambert Chambers	Great Britain
S	P. Dora Boothby	Great Britain
B	R. Joan Winch	Great Britain

1908 London (Indoor Court)

G	Gladys Eastlake-Smith	Great Britain
S	Alice Greene	Great Britain
B	Märtha Alderstråhle	Sweden

1912 Stockholm

G	Marguerite Broquedis	France
S	Dora Köring	Germany
B	Anna "Molla" Bjurstedt	Norway

1912 Stockholm (Indoor Courts)

G	Edith Hannam	Great Britain
S	Thora Castenschiold	Denmark
B	Mabel Parton	Great Britain

1920 Antwerp

G	Suzanne Lenglen	France
S	E. Dorothy Holman	Great Britain
B	Kathleen "Kitty" McKane	Great Britain

1924 Paris

G	Helen Wills	United States
S	Julie "Diddie" Vlasto	France
B	Kathleen "Kitty" McKane	Great Britain

1988 Seoul

G	Stefanie "Steffi" Graf	West Germany
S	Gabriela Sabatini	Argentina
B	Zina Garrison	United States

1992 Barcelona

G	Jennifer Capriati	United States
S	Stefanie "Steffi" Graf	Germany
B	Mary Joe Fernandez	United States

1996 Atlanta

G	Lindsay Davenport	United States
S	Arantxa Sanchez Vicario	Spain
B	Jana Novotna	Czech Republic

TENNIS – DOUBLES

1920 Antwerp

G	Winifred McNair Kathleen "Kitty" McKane	Great Britain
S	W. Geraldine Beamish E. Dorothy Holman	Great Britain
B	Suzanne Lenglen Elisabeth d'Ayen	France

1924 Paris

G	Hazel Wightman Helen Wills	United States
S	Phyllis Covell Kathleen "Kitty" McKane	Great Britain
B	Dorothy Shepherd-Barron Evelyn Colyer	Great Britain

1988 Seoul

G	Pam Shriver Zina Garrison	United States
S	Jana Novotná Helena Soková	Czechoslovakia
B	Elizabeth Smylie Wendy Turnbull	Australia

1992 Barcelona

G	Beatriz "Gigi" Fernandez Mary Joe Fernandez	United States
S	Conchita Martínez Arantxa Sánchez-Vicario	Spain
B	Rachel McQuillan Nicole Provis	Australia

1996 Atlanta

G	Gigi Fernandez Mary Joe Fernandez	United States
S	Jana Novotná Helena Soková	Czechoslovakia
B	Arantxa Sánchez-Vicario Conchita Martínez	Spain

TENNIS – MIXED DOUBLES

1900 Paris

G	Charlotte Cooper Reginald Doherty	Great Britain
S	Hélène Prévost Harold Mahoney	France and Great Britain
B	Hedwig Rosenbaum Archibald Warden	Czechoslovakia and Great Britain

1906 Athens

G	Marie Decugis Max Decugis	France
S	Sophia Marinou Georgios Simiriotis	Greece
B	Aspasia Matsa Xenophon Kasdaglis	Greece

1912 Stockholm

G	Dora Köring Heinrich Schomburgk	Germany
S	Sigrid Fick Gunnar Setterwall	Sweden
B	Marguerite Broquedis Albert Canet	France

1912 Stockholm (Indoor Courts)

G	Edith Hannam Charles Dixon	Great Britain
S	F. Helen Aitchison Herbert Roper Barrett	Great Britain
B	Sigrid Fick Gunnar Setterwall	Sweden

1920 Antwerp

G	Suzanne Lenglen Max Decugis	France
S	Kathleen "Kitty" McKane Maxwell Woosnam	Great Britain
B	Milada Skrbková Ladislav "Rázný" Žemla	Czechoslovakia

1924 Paris

G	Hazel Wightman Richard Norris Williams	United States
S	Marion Jessup Vincent Richards	United States
B	Cornelia Bouman Hendrik Timmer	Netherlands

TRACK AND FIELD – 100 METERS

1928 Amsterdam

G	Elizabeth Robinson	United States
S	Fanny Rosenfeld	Canada
B	Ethel Smith	Canada

1932 Los Angeles

G	Stanislawa Walasiewicz	Poland
S	Hilda Strike	Canada
B	Wilhelmina Von Bremen	United States

1936 Berlin

G	Helen Stephens	United States
S	Stanislawa Walasiewicz	Poland
B	Käthe Krauss	Germany

1948 London

G	Francina "Fanny" Blankers-Koen	Netherlands
S	Dorothy Manley	Great Britain
B	Shirley Strickland	Australia

1952 Helsinki

G	Marjorie Jackson	Australia
S	Daphne Hasenjager (Robb)	South Africa
B	Shirley Strickland de la Hunty	Australia

1956 Melbourne

G	Elizabeth Cuthbert	Australia
S	Christa Stubnick	East Germany
B	Marlene Matthews	Australia

1960 Rome

G	Wilma Rudolph	United States
S	Dorothy Hyman	Great Britain
B	Giuseppina Leone	Italy

1964 Tokyo

G	Wyomia Tyus	United States
S	Edith McGuire	United States
B	Ewa Klobukowska	Poland

1968 Mexico City

G	Wyomia Tyus	United States
S	Barbara Ferrell	United States
B	Irena Szewinska (Kirszenstein)	Poland

1972 Munich

G	Renate Stecher	East Germany
S	Raelene Boyle	Australia
B	Silvia Chivás	Cuba

1976 Montreal

G	Annegret Richter	West Germany
S	Renate Stecher	East Germany
B	Inge Helten	West Germany

1980 Moscow

G	Lyudmila Kondratyeva	Soviet Union
S	Marlies Göhr (Oelsner)	East Germany
B	Ingrid Auerswald	East Germany

1984 Los Angeles

G	Evelyn Ashford	United States
S	Alice Brown	United States
B	Merlene Ottey-Page	Jamaica

1988 Seoul

G	D. Florence Griffith-Joyner	United States
S	Evelyn Ashford	United States
B	Heike Drehsler (Daute)	East Germany

1992 Barcelona

G	Gail Devers	United States
S	Juliet Cuthbert	Jamaica
B	Irina Privalova	Commonwealth of Independent States

1996 Atlanta

G	Gail Devers	United States
S	Merlene Ottey	Jamaica
B	Gwen Torrence	United States

TRACK AND FIELD – 200 METERS

1948 London

G	Francina "Fanny" Blankers-Koen	Netherlands
S	Audrey Williamson	Great Britain
B	Audrey Patterson	United States

1952 Helsinki

G	Marjorie Jackson	Australia
S	Bertha Brouwer	Netherlands
B	Nadezhda Khnykina	Soviet Union

1956 Melbourne

G	Elizabeth Cuthbert	Australia
S	Christa Stubnick	East Germany
B	Marlene Matthews	Australia

1960 Rome

G	Wilma Rudolph	United States
S	Jutta Heine	West Germany
B	Dorothy Hyman	Great Britain

1964 Tokyo

G	Edith McGuire	United States
S	Irena Kirszenstein	Poland
B	Marilyn Black	Australia

1968 Mexico City

G	Irena Szewinska (Kirszenstein)	Poland
S	Raelene Boyle	Australia
B	Jennifer Lamy	Australia

1972 Munich

G	Renate Stecher	East Germany
S	Raelene Boyle	Australia
B	Irena Szewinska (Kirszenstein)	Poland

1976 Montreal

G	Bärbel Eckert	East Germany
S	Annegret Richter	West Germany
B	Renate Stecher	East Germany

1980 Moscow

G	Bärbel Wöckel (Eckert)	East Germany
S	Natalya Bochina	Soviet Union
B	Merlene Ottey	Jamaica

1984 Los Angeles

G	Valerie Brisco-Hooks	United States
S	D. Florence Griffith	United States
B	Merlene Ottey-Page	Jamaica

1988 Seoul

G	D. Florence Griffith-Joyner	United States
S	Grace Jackson	Jamaica
B	Heike Drechsler (Daute)	East Germany

1992 Barcelona

G	Gwendolyn Torrence	United States
S	Juliet Cuthbert	Jamaica
B	Merlene Ottey	Jamaica

1996 Atlanta

G	Marie-José Perec	France
S	Merlene Ottey	Jamaica
B	Mary Onyali	Nigeria

TRACK AND FIELD – 400 METERS

1964 Tokyo

G	Elizabeth Cuthbert	Australia
S	Ann Packer	Great Britain
B	Judith Amoore	Australia

1968 Mexico City

G	Colette Besson	France
S	Lillian Board	East Germany
B	Natalya Pechenkina	Soviet Union

1972 Munich

G	Monika Zehrt	East Germany
S	Rita Wilden (Jahn)	West Germany
B	Kathy Hammond	United States

1976 Montreal

G	Irena Szewinska (Kirszenstein)	Poland
S	Christina Brehmer	East Germany
B	Ellen Streidt (Stropahl)	East Germany

1980 Moscow

G	Marita Koch	East Germany
S	Jarmila Kratochvilová	Czechoslovakia
B	Christina Lathan (Brehmer)	East Germany

1984 Los Angeles

G	Valerie Brisco-Hooks	United States
S	Chandra Cheeseborough	United States
B	Kathryn Cook (Smallwood)	Great Britain

1988 Seoul

G	Olha Bryzhina	Soviet Union
S	Petra Müller	East Germany
B	Olga Nazarova	Soviet Union

1992 Barcelona

G	Marie-José Pérec	France
S	Olha Bryzhina	Commonwealth of Independent States
B	Ximena Restrepo Gaviria	Columbia

1996 Atlanta

G	Marie-José Pérec	France
S	Cathy Freeman	Australia
B	Falilat Ogunkoya	Nigeria

TRACK AND FIELD – 800 METERS

1928 Amsterdam

G	Karoline "Lina" Radke	Germany
S	Kinue Hitomi	Japan
B	Inga Gentzel	Sweden

1960 Rome

G	Lyudmyla Shevtsova	Soviet Union
S	Brenda Jones	Australia
B	Ursula Donath	East Germany

1964 Tokyo

G	Ann Packer	Great Britain
S	Maryvonne Dupureur	France
B	M. Ann Marise Chamberlain	New Zealand

1968 Mexico City

G	Madeline Manning	United States
S	Ileana Silai	Romania
B	Maria Gommers	Netherlands

1972 Munich

G	Hildegard Falck	West Germany
S	Nijole Sabaite	Soviet Union
B	Gunhild Hoffmeister	East Germany

1976 Montreal

G	Tatyana Kazankina	Soviet Union
S	Nikolina Shtereva	Bulgaria
B	Elfi Zinn	East Germany

1980 Moscow

G	Nadiya Olizarenko	Soviet Union
S	Olga Mineyeva	Soviet Union
B	Tatyana Providokhina	Soviet Union

1984 Los Angeles

G	Doina Melinte	Romania
S	Kimberly Gallagher	United States
B	Rafira Fita Lovin	Romania

1988 Seoul

G	Sigrun Wodars	East Germany
S	Christine Wachtel	East Germany
B	Kimberly Gallagher	United States

1992 Barcelona

G	Ellen van Langren	Netherlands
S	Lilia Nurutdinova	Russia
B	Ana Fidelia Quirot Moret	Cuba

1996 Atlanta

G	Svetlana Masterkova	Russian Federation
S	Ana Fidelia Quirot	Cuba
B	Maria Lurdes Mutola	Mozambique

TRACK AND FIELD – 1,500 METERS

1972 Munich

G	Lyudmila Bragina	Soviet Union
S	Gunhild Hoffmeister	East Germany
B	Paola Cacchi	Italy

1976 Montreal

G	Tatyana Kazankina	Soviet Union
S	Gunhild Hoffmeister	East Germany
B	Ulrike Klapezynski	East Germany

1980 Moscow

G	Tatyana Kazankina	Soviet Union
S	Christiane Wartenberg	East Germany
B	Nadiya Olizarenko	Soviet Union

1984 Los Angeles

G	Gabriella Dorio	Italy
S	Doina Melinte	Romania
B	Maricica Puică	Romania

1988 Seoul

G	Paula Ivan	Romania
S	Laimute Baikauskaite	Soviet Union
B	Tetyana Samolenko	Soviet Union

1992 Barcelona

G	Hassiba Boulmerka	Algeria
S	Lyudmila Rogacheva	Commonwealth of Independent States
B	Qu Yunxia	China

1996 Atlanta

G	Svetlana Masterkova	Russian Federation
S	Gabriela Szabo	Romania
B	Theresia Kiesl	Austria

TRACK AND FIELD – 3,000-METERS

1984 Los Angeles

G	Maricica Puica	Romania
S	Wendy Sly	Great Britain
B	Lynn Williams	Canada

1988 Seoul

G	Tetyana Samolenko	Soviet Union
S	Paula Ivan	Romania
B	Yvonne Murray	Great Britain

1992 Barcelona

G	Yelena Romanova	Commonwealth of Independent States
S	Tetyana Dorovskikh (Samolenko)	Ukraine
B	Angela Chalmers	Canada

TRACK AND FIELD – 5,000 METERS

1996 Atlanta

G	Wang Junxia	China
S	Pauline Konga	Kenya
B	Roberta Bruney	Italy

TRACK AND FIELD – 10,000 METERS

1988 Seoul

G	Olga Bondarenko	Soviet Union
S	Elizabeth McColgan	Great Britain
B	Olena Zhupiyova	Soviet Union

1992 Barcelona

G	Derartu Tulu	Ethiopia
S	Elana Meyer	South Africa
B	Lynn Jennings	United States

1996 Atlanta

G	Fernanda Ribeiro	Portugal
S	Wang Junxia	China
B	Gete Wami	Ethiopia

TRACK AND FIELD MARATHON

1984 Los Angeles

G	Joan Benoit	United States
S	Grete Waitz	Norway
B	Rosa Mota	Portugal

1988 Seoul

G	Rosa Mota	Portugal
S	Lisa Martin	Australia
B	Kathrin Dörre	East Germany

1992 Barcelona

G	Valentina Yegorova	Russia
S	Yuko Arimori	Japan
B	Lorraine Moller	New Zealand

1996 Atlanta

G	Fatuma Roba	Ethiopia
S	Valentina Yegorova	Russian Federation
B	Yuko Arimori	Japan

TRACK AND FIELD – 100-METER HURDLES

1932 Los Angeles

G	Mildred "Babe" Didriksen	United States
S	Evelyne Hall	United States
B	Marjorie Clark	South Africa

1936 Berlin

G	Trebisonda Valla	Italy
S	Anni Steuer	Germany
B	Elizabeth Taylor	Canada

1948 London

G	Francina "Fanny" Blankers-Koen	Netherlands
S	Maureen Gardner	Great Britain
B	Shirley Strickland	Australia

1952 Helsinki

G	Shirley Strickland de la Hunty	Australia
S	Maria Golubnichaya	Soviet Union
B	Maria Sander	West Germany

1956 Melbourne

G	Shirley Strickland de la Hunty	Australia
S	Gisela Köhler	East Germany
B	Norma Thrower	Australia

1960 Rome

G	Iryna Press	Soviet Union
S	Carole Quinton	Great Britain
B	Gisela Birkemeyer (Köhler)	East Germany

1964 Tokyo

G	Karin Balzer	East Germany
S	Teresa Ciepla-Wieczorek	Poland
B	Pamela Kilborn	Australia

1968 Mexico City

G	Maureen Caird	Australia
S	Pamela Kilborn	Australia
B	Chi Cheng	Taiwan

1972 Munich

G	Anneliese Ehrhardt	East Germany
S	Valeria Bufanu	Romania
B	Karin Balzer	East Germany

1976 Montreal

G	Johanna Schaller	East Germany
S	Tatiana Anisimova	Soviet Union
B	Natalya Lebedeva	Soviet Union

1980 Moscow

G	Vera Komisova	Soviet Union
S	Johanna Klier (Schaller)	East Germany
B	Lucyna Langer	Poland

1984 Los Angeles

G	Benita Fitzgerald-Brown	United States
S	Shirley Strong	Great Britain
B	Michele Chardonnet	France

1988 Seoul

G	Yordanka Donkova	Bulgaria
S	Gloria Siebert	East Germany
B	Claudia Zackiewicz	West Germany

1992 Barcelona

G	Paraskevi "Voula" Patoulidou	Greece
S	LaVonna Martin	United States
B	Yordanka Donkova	Bulgaria

1996 Atlanta

G	Ludmila Engquist	Sweden
S	Brigita Bukovec	Slovenia
B	Patricia Girard-Léno	France

TRACK AND FIELD – 400-METER HURDLES

1984 Los Angeles

G	Nawal El Moutawakel	Morocco
S	Judi Brown	United States
B	Cristina Cojocaru	Romania

1988 Seoul

G	Debra Flintoff-King	Australia
S	Tatyana Ledovskaya	Soviet Union
B	Ellen Fiedler	East Germany

1992 Barcelona

G	Sally Gunnell	Great Britain
S	Sandra Farmer-Patrick	United States
B	Janeene Vickers	United States

1996 Atlanta

G	Deon Hemmings	Jamaica
S	Kim Batten	United States
B	Tonja Buford-Bailey	United States

TRACK AND FIELD – 4x100-METER RELAY

1928 Amsterdam

G	Canada
S	United States
B	Germany

1932 Los Angeles

G	United States
S	Canada
B	Great Britain

1936 Berlin
G United States
S Great Britain
B Canada

1948 London
G Netherlands
S Australia
B Canada

1952 Helsinki
G United States
S West Germany
B Great Britain

1956 Melbourne
G Australia
S Great Britain
B United States

1960 Rome
G United States
S West Germany
B Poland

1964 Tokyo
G Poland
S United States
B Great Britain

1968 Mexico City
G United States
S Cuba
B Soviet Union

1972 Munich
G West Germany
S East Germany
B Cuba

1976 Montreal
G East Germany
S West Germany
B Soviet Union

1980 Moscow
G East Germany
S Soviet Union
B Great Britain

1984 Los Angeles
G United States
S Canada
B Great Britain

1988 Seoul
G United States
S East Germany
B Soviet Union

1992 Barcelona
G United States
S Commonwealth of Independent States
B Nigeria

1996 Atlanta
G United States
S Bahamas
B Jamaica

TRACK AND FIELD – 4x400-METER RELAY

1972 Munich
G East Germany
S United States
B West Germany

1976 Montreal
G East Germany
S United States
B Soviet Union

1980 Moscow
G Soviet Union
S East Germany
B Great Britain

1984 Los Angeles
G United States
S Canada
B West Germany

1988 Seoul
G Soviet Union
S United States
B East Germany

1992 Barcelona
G Commonwealth of Independent States
S United States
B Great Britain

1996 Atlanta

G	United States
S	Nigeria
B	Germany

TRACK AND FIELD – 10,000-METER WALK

1992 Barcelona

G	Chen Yueling	China
S	Yelena Nikolayeva	Commonwealth of Independent States
B	Li Chunxiu	China

1996 Atlanta

G	Yelena Nikolayeva	Russian Federation
S	Elisabetta Perrone	Italy
B	Wang Yan	China

TRACK AND FIELD – HIGH JUMP

1928 Amsterdam

G	Ethel Catherwood	Canada
S	Carolina Gisolf	Netherlands
B	Mildred Wiley	United States

1932 Los Angeles

G	Jean Shiley	United States
S	Mildred "Babe" Didriksen	United States
B	Eva Dawes	Canada

1936 Berlin

G	Ibolya Csák	Hungary
S	Dorothy Odam	Great Britain
B	Elfriede Kaun	Germany

1948 London

G	Alice Coachman	United States
S	Dorothy Tyler (Odam)	Great Britain
B	Micheline Ostermeyer	France

1952 Helsinki

G	Esther Brand	South Africa
S	Sheila Lerwill	Great Britain
B	Aleksandra Chudina	Soviet Union

1956 Melbourne

G	Mildred McDaniel	United States
S	Thelma Hopkins	Great Britain
B	Maria Pissaryeva	Soviet Union

1960 Rome

G	Iolanda Balas	Romania
S	Jaroslawa Józwiakowska	Poland
B	Dorothy Shirley	Great Britain

1964 Tokyo

G	Iolanda Balas	Romania
S	Michele Brown (Mason)	Australia
B	Taisa Chenchyk	Soviet Union

1968 Mexico City

G	Miloslava Režková	Czechoslovakia
S	Antonina Okorokova	Soviet Union
B	Valentyna Kozyr	Soviet Union

1972 Munich

G	Ulrike Meyfarth	West Germany
S	Yordanka Blagoyeva	Bulgaria
B	Ilona Gusenbauer	Austria

1976 Montreal

G	Rosemarie Ackermann (Witschas)	East Germany
S	Sara Simeoni	Italy
B	Yordanka Blagoyeva	Bulgaria

1980 Moscow

G	Sara Simeoni	Italy
S	Urszula Kielan	Poland
B	Jutta Kirst	East Germany

1984 Los Angeles

G	Ulrike Meyfarth	West Germany
S	Sara Simeoni	Italy
B	Joni Huntley	United States

1988 Seoul

G	D. Louise Ritter	United States
S	Stefka Kostadinova	Bulgaria
B	Tamara Bykova	Soviet Union

1992 Barcelona

G	Heike Henkel	Germany
S	Galina Astafei	Romania
B	Ioamnet Quintero Alvarez	Cuba

1996 Atlanta

G	Stefka Kostadinova	Bulgaria
S	Niki Bakoyianni	Greece
B	Inga Babakova	Ukraine

TRACK AND FIELD – LONG JUMP

1948 London

G	Olga Gyarmati	Hungary
S	Noëmi Simonetto De Portela	Argentina
B	Ann-Britt Leyman	Sweden

1952 Helsinki

G	Yvette Williams	New Zealand
S	Aleksandra Chudina	Soviet Union
B	Shirley Cawley	Great Britain

1956 Melbourne

G	Elzbieta Krzesinska	Poland
S	Willye White	United States
B	Nadezhda Dvalischvili (Khnykina)	Soviet Union

1960 Rome

G	Vira Krepkina	Soviet Union
S	Elzbieta Krzesinska	Poland
B	Hildrun Claus	East Germany

1964 Tokyo

G	Mary Rand (Bignal)	Great Britain
S	Irena Kirszenstein	Poland
B	Tatyana Schelkanova	Soviet Union

1968 Mexico City

G	Viorica Viscopoleanu	Romania
S	Sheila Sherwood	Great Britain
B	Tatyana Talisheva	Soviet Union

1972 Munich

G	Heidemarie Rosendahl	West Germany
S	Diana Yorgova	Bulgaria
B	Eva Šuranová	Czechoslovakia

1976 Montreal

G	Angela Voigt	East Germany
S	Kathy McMillan	United States
B	Lidiya Alfeyeva	Soviet Union

1980 Moscow

G	Tatyana Kolpakova	Soviet Union
S	Brigitte Wujak	East Germany
B	Tetyana Skachko	Soviet Union

1984 Los Angeles

G	Anisoara Cusmir-Stanciu	Romania
S	Valeria Ionescu	Romania
B	Susan Hearnshaw	Great Britain

1988 Seoul

G	Jacqueline Joyner-Kersee	United States
S	Heike Drechsler (Daute)	East Germany
B	Regina Cistjakova	Soviet Union

1992 Barcelona

G	Heike Drechsler	Germany
S	Inessa Kravets	Commonwealth of Independent States
B	Jacqueline Joyner-Kersee	United States

1996 Atlanta

G	Chioma Ajunwa	Nigeria
S	Fiona May	Italy
B	Jacqueline Joyner-Kersee	United States

TRACK AND FIELD – TRIPLE JUMP

1996 Atlanta

G	Inessa Kravets	Ukraine
S	Inna Lasovskaya	Russian Federation
B	Sarka Kasparkova	Czech Republic

TRACK AND FIELD – SHOT PUT

1948 London

G	Micheline Ostermeyer	France
S	Amelia Piccinini	Italy
B	Ine Schäffer	Austria

1952 Helsinki

G	Galina Zybina	Soviet Union
S	Marianne Werner	West Germany
B	Klavdia Tochenova	Soviet Union

1956 Melbourne

G	Tamara Tyshkevich	Soviet Union
S	Galina Zybina	Soviet Union
B	Marianne Werner	West Germany

1960 Rome

G	Tamara Press	Soviet Union
S	Johanna Lüttge	East Germany
B	Earlene Brown	United States

1964 Tokyo

G	Tamara Press	Soviet Union
S	Renate Garisch-Culmberger	East Germany
B	Galina Zybina	Soviet Union

1968 Mexico City

G	Margitta Gummel (Helmboldt)	East Germany
S	Marita Lange	East Germany
B	Nadezhda Chizhova	Soviet Union

1972 Munich

G	Nadezhda Chizhova	Soviet Union
S	Margitta Gummel (Helmboldt)	East Germany
B	Ivanka Hristova	Bulgaria

1976 Montreal

G	Ivanka Hristova	Bulgaria
S	Nadezhda Chizhova	Soviet Union
B	Helena Fibingerová	Czechoslovakia

1980 Moscow

G	Ilona Slupianek (Schoknecht)	East Germany
S	Svetlana Krachevskaya (Esfir Dolzhenko)	Soviet Union
B	Margitta Pufe (Droese)	East Germany

1984 Los Angeles

G	Claudia Losch	West Germany
S	Mihaela Loghin	Romania
B	Gael Martin	Australia

1988 Seoul

G	Natalya Lisovskaya	Soviet Union
S	Kathrin Neimke	East Germany
B	Li Meisu	China

1992 Barcelona

G	Svetlana Krivelyova	Commonwealth of Independent States
S	Huang Zhihong	China
B	Kathrin Meimke	Germany

1996 Atlanta

G	Astrid Kumbernuss	Germany
S	Sui Xinmei	China
B	Irina Khudorozhkina	Russian Federation

TRACK AND FIELD – DISCUS THROW

1928 Amsterdam

G	Halina Konopacka	Poland
S	Lillian Copeland	United States
B	Ruth Svedberg	Sweden

1932 Los Angeles

G	Lillian Copeland	United States
S	Ruth Osburn	United States
B	Jadwiga Wajs	Poland

1936 Berlin

G	Gisela Mauermayer	Germany
S	Jadwiga Wajs	Poland
B	Paula Mollenhauer	Germany

1948 London

G	Micheline Ostermeyer	France
S	Edera Cordiale Gentile	Italy
B	Jacqueline Mazéas	France

1952 Helsinki

G	Nina Romaschkova	Soviet Union
S	Yelisaveta Bagryantseva	Soviet Union
B	Nina Dumbadze	Soviet Union

1956 Melbourne

G	Olga Fikotová	Czechoslovakia
S	Irina Beglyakova	Soviet Union
B	Nina Ponomaryeva (Romaschkova)	Soviet Union

1960 Rome

G	Nina Ponomaryeva (Romaschkova)	Soviet Union
S	Tamara Press	Soviet Union
B	Lia Manoliu	Romania

1964 Tokyo

G	Tamara Press	Soviet Union
S	Ingrid Lotz	East Germany
B	Lia Manoliu	Romania

1968 Mexico City

G	Lia Manoliu	Romania
S	Liesel Westermann	West Germany
B	Jolán Kleiber	Hungary

1972 Munich

G	Faina Melnik	Soviet Union
S	Argentina Menis	Romania
B	Vassilka Stoyeva	Bulgaria

1976 Montreal

G	Evelin Schlaak	East Germany
S	Maria Vergova	Bulgaria
B	Gabriele Hinzmann	East Germany

1980 Moscow

G	Evelin Jahl (Schlaak)	East Germany
S	Maria Petkova (Vergova)	Bulgaria
B	Tatyana Lesovaya	Soviet Union

1984 Los Angeles

G	Ria Stalman	Netherlands
S	Leslie Deniz	United States
B	Florenta Craciunescu (Tacu)	Romania

1988 Seoul

G	Martina Hellmann	East Germany
S	Diana Gansky	East Germany
B	Tzvetanka Hristova	Bulgaria

1992 Barcelona

G	Maritza Marten Carcia	Cuba
S	Tzvetanka Hristova	Bulgaria
B	Daniela Costian	Australia

1996 Atlanta

G	Ilke Wyludda	Germany
S	Natalya Sadova	Russian Federation
B	Elya Zvereva	Belarus

TRACK AND FIELD – JAVELIN THROW

1932 Los Angeles

G	Mildred "Babe" Didriksen	United States
S	Ellen Braumüller	Germany
B	Ottilie "Tilly" Fleischer	Germany

1936 Berlin

G	Ottilie "Tilly" Fleischer	Germany
S	Luise Krüger	Germany
B	Maria Kwasniewska	Poland

1948 London

G	Hermine "Herma" Bauma	Austria
S	Kaisas Parviainen	Finland
B	Lily Carlstedt	Denmark

1952 Helsinki

G	Dana Zátopková (Ingrova)	Czechoslovakia
S	Aleksandra Chudina	Soviet Union
B	Yelena Gorchakova	Soviet Union

1956 Melbourne

G	Inese Jaunzeme	Soviet Union
S	Marlene Ahrens	Chile
B	Nadiya Konyayeva	Soviet Union

1960 Rome

G	Elvira Ozolina	Soviet Union
S	Dana Zátopková (Ingrova)	Czechoslovakia
B	Birute Kalediene	Soviet Union

1964 Tokyo

G	Mihaela Penes	Romania
S	Márta Rudas	Hungary
B	Yelena Gorchakova	Soviet Union

1968 Mexico City

G	Angéla Németh	Hungary
S	Mihaela Penes	Romania
B	Eva Janko	Austria

1972 Munich

G	Ruth Fuchs	East Germany
S	Jacqueline Todten	East Germany
B	Kathryn Schmidt	United States

1976 Montreal

G	Ruth Fuchs	East Germany
S	Marion Becker	West Germany
B	Kathryn Schmidt	United States

1980 Moscow

G	María Colón Rueñes	Cuba
S	Saida Gunba	Soviet Union
B	Ute Hommola	East Germany

1984 Los Angeles

G	Theresa "Tessa" Sanderson	East Germany
S	Ilse "Tiina" Lillak	Finland
B	Fatima Whitbread	Great Britain

1988 Seoul

G	Petra Felke	East Germany
S	Fatima Whitbread	Great Britain
B	Beate Koch	East Germany

1992 Barcelona

G	Silke Renk	Germany
S	Natalya Shikolenko	Belarus
B	Karen Forkel	Germany

1996 Atlanta

G	Heli Rantanen	Finland
S	Louise McPaul	Australia
B	Trine Hattestad	Norway

TRACK AND FIELD – HEPTATHLON/PENTATHLON

1964 Tokyo

G	Iryna Press	Soviet Union
S	Mary Rand (Bignal)	Great Britain
B	Galina Bystrova	Soviet Union

1968 Mexico City

G	Ingrid Becker	West Germany
S	Elisabeth "Liese" Prokop	Austria
B	Annamária Tóth	Hungary

1972 Munich

G	Mary Peters	Great Britain
S	Heidemarie Rosendahl	West Germany
B	Burglinde Pollak	East Germany

1976 Montreal

G	Sigrun Siegl	East Germany
S	Christine Laser (Bodner)	East Germany
B	Burglinde Pollak	East Germany

1980 Moscow

G	Nadiya Tkachenko	Soviet Union
S	Olga Rukavishnikova	Soviet Union
B	Olga Kuragina	Soviet Union

1984 Los Angeles

G	Glynis Nunn	Australia
S	Jacqueline Joyner	United States
B	Sabine Everts	West Germany

1988 Seoul

G	Jacqueline Joyner-Kersee	United States
S	Sabine John (Paetz)	East Germany
B	Anke Behmer	East Germany

1992 Barcelona

G	Jacqueline Joyner-Kersee	United States
S	Irina Belova	Commonwealth of Independent States
B	Sabine Braun	Germany

1996 Atlanta

G	Ghada Shouaa	Syria
S	Natasha Sazanovich	Belarus
B	Denise Lewis	Great Britain

VOLLEYBALL

1964 Tokyo

G Japan
S Soviet Union
B Poland

1968 Mexico City

G Soviet Union
S Japan
B Poland

1972 Munich

G Soviet Union
S Japan
B North Korea

1976 Montreal

G Japan
S Soviet Union
B South Korea

1980 Moscow

G Soviet Union
S East Germany
B Bulgaria

1984 Los Angeles

G China
S United States
B Japan

1988 Seoul

G Soviet Union
S Peru
B China

1992 Barcelona

G Cuba
S Soviet Union
B United States

1996 Atlanta

G Cuba
S China
B Brazil

VOLLEYBALL – BEACH

1996 Atlanta

G Brazil
S Brazil
B Australia

YACHTING – EUROPE

1992 Barcelona

G	Linda Andersen	Norway
S	Natalia Via Dufresne Pereña	Spain
B	Julia Trotman	United States

1996 Atlanta

G	Kristine Roug	Denmark
S	Margriet Matthijsse	Netherlands
B	Courtenay Becker-Dey	United States

YACHTING – 470

1988 Seoul

G	Allison Jolly Lynne Jewell	United States
S	Marit Söderström Birgitta Bengtsson	Sweden
B	Larysa Moskalenko Iryna Chunykhorska	Soviet Union

1992 Barcelona

G	Theresa Zabell Lucas Patricia Guerra Cabrera	Spain
S	Leslie Egnot Jan Shearer	New Zealand
B	Jennifer "JJ" Isler Pamela Healy	United States

1996 Atlanta

G	Theresa Zabel Begona Via DuFresne	Spain
S	Yumiko Shige Alicia Kinoshita	Japan
B	Rusiana Taran Olena Pakholchik	Ukraine

YACHTING – LASER, MIXED

1996 Atlanta

G Spain
S Australia
B Brazil

YACHTING – SAILBOARD

1992 Barcelona

G	Barbara Kendall	New Zealand
S	Zhang Xiaodong	China
B	Dorien de Vries	Netherlands

1996 Atlanta

G	Shan Lee Lai	Hong Kong, China
S	Barbara Kendall	New Zealand
B	Alessandra Sensini	Italy

YACHTING – SOLING, MIXED

1972 Munich

G United States
S Sweden
B Canada

1976 Montreal

G Denmark
S United States
B East Germany

1980 Moscow

G Denmark
S Soviet Union
B Greece

1984 Los Angeles

G United States
S Brazil
B Canada

1988 Seoul

G East Germany
S United States
B Denmark

1992 Barcelona

G Denmark
S United States
B Great Britain

1996 Atlanta

G Germany
S Russian Federation
B United States

YACHTING – STAR, MIXED

1932 Los Angeles

G United States
S Great Britain
B Sweden

1936 Berlin

G Germany
S Sweden
B Netherlands

1948 London

G United States
S Cuba
B Netherlands

1952 Helsinki

G Italy
S United States
B Portugal

1956 Melbourne

G United States
S Italy
B Bahamas

1960 Rome
G Soviet Union
S Portugal
B United States

1964 Tokyo
G Bahamas
S United States
B Sweden

1968 Mexico City
G United States
S Norway
B Italy

1972 Munich
G Australia
S Sweden
B West Germany

1980 Moscow
G Soviet Union
S Austria
B Italy

1984 Los Angeles
G United States
S West Germany
B Italy

1988 Seoul
G Great Britain
S United States
B Brazil

1992 Barcelona
G United States
S New Zealand
B Canada

1996 Atlanta
G Brazil
S Sweden
B Australia

YACHTING – TORNADO, MIXED

1976 Montreal
G Great Britain
S United States
B West Germany

1980 Moscow
G Brazil
S Denmark
B Sweden

1984 Los Angeles
G New Zealand
S United States
B Australia

1988 Seoul
G France
S New Zealand
B Brazil

1992 Barcelona
G France
S United States
B Australia

1996 Atlanta
G Spain
S Australia
B Brazil

APPENDIX B
Female Medalists at the Winter Olympics

BIATHLON – 7.5 KILOMETERS

1992 Albertville

G	Anfisa Reztsova	Commonwealth of Independent States
S	Antje Miserky	Germany
B	Yelena Belova	Commonwealth of Independent States

1994 Lillehammer

G	Myriam Bédard	Canada
S	Svetlana Paramygina	Belarus
B	Valentyna Tserbe	Ukraine

1998 Nagano

G	Galina Koukleva	Russian Federation
S	Ursula Disl	Germany
B	Katrin Apel	Germany

BIATHLON – 15 KILOMETERS

1992 Albertville

G	Antje Misersky	Germany
S	Svetlana Pecherskaya	Commonwealth of Independent States
B	Myriam Bédard	Canada

1994 Lillehammer

G	Myriam Bédard	Canada
S	Anne Briand	France
B	Ursula Disl	Germany

1998 Nagano

G	Ekaterina Dafovska	Bulgaria
S	Elena Petrova	Ukraine
B	Ursula Disl	Germany

BIATHLON – 4 X 7.5 KILOMETER RELAY

1992 Albertville

G	France
S	Germany
B	Commonwealth of Independent States

1994 Lillehammer

G	Russia
S	Germany
B	France

1998 Nagano

G	Germany
S	Russian Federation
B	Norway

CURLING

G	Canada
S	Denmark
B	Sweden

ICE HOCKEY

1998 Nagano

G	United States
S	Canada
B	Finland

LUGE – SINGLE

1964 Innsbruck

G	Ortrun Enderlein	East Germany
S	Ilse Geisler	East Germany
B	Helene Thurner	Austria

1968 Grenoble

G	Erica Lechner	Italy
S	Christa Schmuck	West Germany
B	Angelika Dünhaupt	West Germany

1972 Sapporo

G	Anna-Maria Müller	East Germany
S	Ute Rührold	East Germany
B	Margit Schumann	East Germany

1976 Innsbruck

G	Margit Schumann	East Germany
S	Ute Rührold	East Germany
B	Elisabeth Demleitner	West Germany

1980 Lake Placid

G	Vera Zozulya	Soviet Union
S	Melitta Sollmann	East Germany
B	Ingrida Amantova	Soviet Union

1984 Sarajevo

G	Steffi Martin	East Germany
S	Bettina Schmidt	East Germany
B	Ute Weiss	East Germany

1988 Calgary

G	Steffi Martin	East Germany
S	Ute Oberhoffner Weiss	East Germany
B	Cerstin Schmidt	East Germany

1992 Albertville

G	Doris Neuner	Austria
S	Angelika Neuner	Austria
B	Susi Erdmann	Germany

1994 Lillehammer

G	Gerda Weissensteiner	Italy
S	Susi Erdmann	Germany
B	Andrea Tagwerker	Austria

1998 Nagano

G	Silke Kraushaar	Germany
S	Barbara Niedernhuber	Germany
B	Angelika Neuner	Austria

FIGURE SKATING

1908 London

G	Florence "Madge" Syers	Great Britain and Northern Ireland
S	Elsa Rendschmidt	Germany
B	Dorothy Greenhough-Smith	Great Britain and Northern Ireland

1920 Antwerp

G	Magda Julin-Mauroy	Sweden
S	Svea Norén	Sweden
B	Theresa Weld	United States

1924 Chamonix

G	Herma Planck-Szabó	Austria
S	Beatrix Loughran	United States
B	Ethel Muckelt	Great Britain and Northern Ireland

1928 St. Moritz

G	Sonja Henie	Norway
S	Fritzi Burger	Austria
B	Beatrix Loughran	United States

1932 Lake Placid

G	Sonja Henie	Norway
S	Fritzi Burger	Austria
B	Maribel Vinson	United States

1936 Garmisch

G	Sonja Henie	Norway
S	M. Cecilia Colledge	Great Britain and Northern Ireland
B	Vivi-Anne Hultén	Sweden

1948 St. Moritz

G	Barbara Ann Scott	Canada
S	Eva Pawlik	Austria
B	Jeanette Altwegg	Great Britain and Northern Ireland

1952 Oslo

G	Jeanette Altwegg	Great Britain and Northern Ireland
S	Tenley Albright	United States
B	Jacqueline du Bief	France

1956 Cortina

G	Tenley Albright	United States
S	Carol Heiss	United States
B	Ingrid Wendl	Austria

1960 Squaw Valley

G	Carol Heiss	United States
S	Sjoukje Dijkstra	Netherlands
B	Barbara Roles	United States

1964 Innsbruck

G	Sjoukje Dijkstra	Netherlands
S	Regine Heitzer	Austria
B	Petra Burka	Canada

1968 Grenoble

G	Peggy Fleming	United States
S	Gabriele Seyfert	East Germany
B	Hana Mašková	Czechoslovakia

1972 Sapporo

G	Beatrix Schuba	Austria
S	Karen Magnussen	Canada
B	Janet Lynn	United States

1976 Innsbruck

G	Dorothy Hamill	United States
S	Dianne de Leeuw	Netherlands
B	Christine Errath	East Germany

1980 Lake Placid

G	Anett Pötzsch	East Germany
S	Linda Fratianne	United States
B	Dagmar Lurz	West Germany

1984 Sarajevo

G	Katarina Witt	East Germany
S	Rosalynn Sumners	United States
B	Kira Ivanova	Soviet Union

1988 Calgary

G	Katarina Witt	East Germany
S	Elizabeth Manley	Canada
B	Debra Thomas	United States

1992 Albertville

G	Kristi Yamaguchi	United States
S	Midori Ito	Japan
B	Nancy Kerrigan	United States

1994 Lillehammer

G	Oksana Baiul	Ukraine
S	Nancy Kerrigan	United States
B	Chen Lu	China

1998 Nagano

G	Tara Lipinski	United States
S	Michelle Kwan	United States
B	Chen Lu	China

FIGURE SKATING PAIRS

1908 London

G	Anna Hübler Heinrich Burger	Germany
S	Phyllis Johnson James Johnson	Great Britain and Northern Ireland
B	Florence "Madge" Syers Edgar Syers	Great Britain and Northern Ireland

1920 Antwerp

G	Ludovika Jakobsson-Eilers Walter Jakobsson	Finland
S	Alexia Bryn-Schøien Yngvar Bryn	Norway
B	Phyllis Johnson Basil Williams	Great Britain and Northern Ireland

1924 Chamonix

G	Helene Engelmann Alfred Berger	Austria
S	Ludovika Jakobsson-Eilers Walter Jakobsson	Finland
B	Andrée Joly Pierre Brunet	France

1928 St. Moritz

G	Andrée Joly Pierre Brunet	France
S	Lilly Scholz Otto Kaiser	Austria
B	Melitta Brunner Ludwig Wrede	Austria

1932 Lake Placid

G	Andrée Brunet Pierre Brunet	France
S	Beatrix Loughran Sherwin Badger	United States
B	Emília Rotter Lásló Szollás	Hungary

1936 Garmisch

G	Maxi Herber Ernst Baier	Germany
S	Ilse Pausin Erik Pausin	Austria
B	Emília Rotter Lásló Szollás	Hungary

1948 St. Moritz

G	Micheline Lannoy Pierre Baugniet	Belgium
S	Andrea Kékessey Ede Király	Hungary
B	Suzanne Morrow Wallace Diestelmeyer	Canada

1952 Oslo

G	Ria Falk Paul Falk	West Germany
S	Karol Kennedy Michael Kennedy	United States
B	Marianna Nagy László Nagy	Hungary

1956 Cortina

G	Elisabeth Schwartz Kurt Oppelt	Austria
S	Frances Dafoe Norris Bowden	Canada
B	Marianna Nagy Lászlό Nagy	Hungary

1960 Squaw Valley

G	Barbara Wagner Robert Paul	Canada
S	Marika Kilius Hans-Jürgen Bäumler	West Germany
B	Nancy Ludington Ronald Ludington	United States

1964 Innsbruck

G	Lyudmila Belousova Oleg Protopopov	Soviet Union
S	Marika Kilius Hans-Jürgen Bäumler	West Germany
B	Debbi Wilkes Guy Revell	Canada

1968 Grenoble

G	Lyudmila Belousova Oleg Protopopov	Soviet Union
S	Tatyana Zhuk Aleksandr Gorelik	Soviet Union
B	Margot Glockshuber Wolfgang Danne	West Germany

1972 Sapporo

G	Irina Rodnina Aleksei Ulanov	Soviet Union
S	Lyudmila Smirnova Andrei Suraikin	Soviet Union
B	Manuela Gross Uwe Kagelmann	East Germany

1976 Innsbruck

G	Irina Rodnina Aleksandr Zaitsev	Soviet Union
S	Romy Kermer Rolf Österreich	East Germany
B	Manuela Gross Uwe Kagelmann	East Germany

1980 Lake Placid

G	Irina Rodnina Aleksandr Zaitsev	Soviet Union
S	Marina Cherkosova Sergei Shakrai	Soviet Union
B	Manuela Mager Uwe Bewersdorff	East Germany

1984 Sarajevo

G	Yelena Valova Oleg Vasilyev	Soviet Union
S	Caitlin "Kitty" Carruthers Peter Carruthers	United States
B	Larissa Selezneva Oleg Makarov	Soviet Union

1988 Calgary

G	Yekaterina Gordeyeva Sergei Grinkov	Soviet Union
S	Yelena Valova Oleg Vasilyev	Soviet Union
B	Jill Watson Peter Oppegard	United States

1992 Albertville

G	Natalya Mishkutenok Artur Dmitriev	Commonwealth of Independent States
S	Yelena Bechke Denis Petrov	Commonwealth of Independent States
B	Isabelle Brasseur Lloyd Eisler	Canada

1994 Lillehammer

G	Yekaterina Gordeyeva Sergei Grinkov	Russia
S	Natalya Mishkutenok Artur Dmitriev	Russia
B	Isabelle Brasseur Lloyd Eisler	Canada

1998 Nagano

G	Oksana Kazakova Artur Dmitriev	Russian Federation
S	Yelena Berezhnaya Anton Sikharulidze	Russian Federation
B	Mandy Woetzel Ingo Steuer	Germany

FIGURE SKATING ICE DANCE

1976 Innsbruck

G	Lyudmila Pakhomova Aleksandr Gorshkov	Soviet Union
S	Irina Moiseyeva Andrei Minenkov	Soviet Union
B	Colleen O'Conner James Millns	United States

1980 Lake Placid

G	Natalya Linichuk Gennady Karponosov	Soviet Union
S	Krisztina Regöczy András Sallay	Hungary
B	Irina Moiseyeva Andrei Minenkov	Soviet Union

1984 Sarajevo

G	Jayne Torvill Christopher Dean	Great Britain and Northern Ireland
S	Natalya Bestemianova Andrei Bukin	Soviet Union
B	Marina Klimova Sergei Ponomarenko	Soviet Union

1988 Calgary

G	Natalya Bestemianova Andrei Bukin	Soviet Union
S	Marina Klimova Sergei Ponomarenko	Soviet Union
B	Tracy Wilson Robert McCall	Canada

1992 Albertville

G	Marina Klimova Sergei Ponomarenko	Commonwealth of Independent States
S	Isabelle Duchesnay-Dean Paul Duchesnay	France
B	Maia Usova Aleksandr Zhulin	Commonwealth of Independent States

1994 Lillehammer

G	Oksana Grischuk Yevgeny Platov	Russia
S	Maia Usova Aleksandr Zhulin	Russia
B	Jayne Torvill Christopher Dean	Great Britain and Northern Ireland

1998 Nagano

G	Pasha Grishuk Evgeny Platov	Russian Federation
S	Angelika Krylova Oleg Ovsyannikov	Russian Federation
B	Marina Anissina Gwendal Peizerat	France

SPEED SKATING – 500 METERS

1960 Squaw Valley

G	Helga Haase	East Germany
S	Natalya Donchenko	Soviet Union
B	Jeanne Ashworth	United States

1964 Innsbruck

G	Lydia Skoblikova	Soviet Union
S	Irina Yegorova	Soviet Union
B	Tatyana Sidorova	Soviet Union

1968 Grenoble

G	Lyudmila Titova	Soviet Union
S	Jennifer Fish Dianne Holum Mary Meyers	United States United States United States

1972 Sapporo

G	Anne Henning	United States
S	Vera Krasnova	Soviet Union
B	Lyudmila Titova	Soviet Union

1976 Innsbruck

G	Sheila Young	United States
S	Cathy Priestner	Canada
B	Tatyana Averina	Soviet Union

1980 Lake Placid

G	Karin Enke	East Germany
S	Leah Mueller Poulos	United States
B	Natalya Petruseva	Soviet Union

1984 Sarajevo

G	Christa Rothenburger	East Germany
S	Karin Enke	East Germany
B	Natalya Chive	Soviet Union

1988 Calgary

G	Bonnie Blair	United States
S	Christa Rothenburger	East Germany
B	Karin Kania Enke	East Germany

1992 Albertville

G	Bonnie Blair	United States
S	Ye Qiaobo	China
B	Christa Luding Rothenburger	East Germany

1994 Lillehammer

G	Bonnie Blair	United States
S	Susan Auch	Canada
B	Fanziska Schenk	Germany

1998 Nagano

G	Catriona Lemay-Doan	Canada
S	Susan Auch	Canada
B	Tomomi Okazaki	Japan

SPEED SKATING – 1,000 METERS

1960 Squaw Valley

G	Klara Guseva	Soviet Union
S	Helga Haase	East Germany
B	Tamara Rylova	Soviet Union

1964 Innsbruck

G	Lydia Skoblikova	Soviet Union
S	Irina Yegorova	Soviet Union
B	Kaija Mustonen	Finland

1968 Grenoble

G	Carolina Geijssen	Netherlands
S	Lyudmila Titova	Soviet Union
B	Dianne Holum	United States

1972 Sapporo

G	Monika Pflug	West Germany
S	Atje Keulen-Deelstra	Netherlands
B	Anne Henning	United States

1976 Innsbruck

G	Tatyana Averina	Soviet Union
S	Leah Poulos	United States
B	Sheila Young	United States

1980 Lake Placid

G	Natalya Petruseva	Soviet Union
S	Leah Mueller	United States
B	Silvia Albrecht	East Germany

1984 Sarajevo

G	Karin Enke	East Germany
S	Andrea Schöne	East Germany
B	Natalya Petruseva	Soviet Union

1988 Calgary

G	Christa Rothenburger	East Germany
S	Karin Kania	East Germany
B	Bonnie Blair	United States

1992 Albertville

G	Bonnie Blair	United States
S	Ye Qiaobo	China
B	Monique Garbrecht	Germany

1994 Lillehammer

G	Bonnie Blair	United States
S	Anke Baier	Germany
B	Ye Qiaobo	China

1998 Nagano

G	Marianne Timmer	Netherlands
S	Christine Witty	United States
B	Catriona Lemay Doan	Canada

SPEED SKATING – 1,500 METERS

1960 Squaw Valley

G	Lydia Skoblikova	Soviet Union
S	Elwira Seroczyńska	Poland
B	Helena Pilejczyk	Poland

1964 Innsbruck

G	Lydia Skoblikova	Soviet Union
S	Kaija Mustonen	Finland
B	Berta Kolokoltseva	Soviet Union

1968 Grenoble

G	Kaije Mustonen	Finland
S	Carolina Geijssen	Netherlands
B	Christina Kaiser	Netherlands

1972 Sapporo

G	Dianne Holum	United States
S	Christina Baas-Kaiser	Netherlands
B	Atje Keulen-Deelstra	Netherlands

1976 Innsbruck

G	Galina Stepanskaya	Soviet Union
S	Sheila Young	United States
B	Tatyana Averina	Soviet Union

1980 Lake Placid

G	Annie Borckink	Netherlands
S	Ria Visser	Netherlands
B	Sabine Becker	East Germany

1984 Sarajevo

G	Karin Enke	East Germany
S	Andrea Schöne	East Germany
B	Natalya Petruseva	Soviet Union

1988 Calgary

G	Yvonne van Gennip	Netherlands
S	Karin Kania	East Germany
B	Andrea Ehrig	East Germany

1992 Albertville

G	Jacqueline Börner	Germany
S	Gunda Niemann	Germany
B	Seiko Hashimoto	Japan

1994 Lillehammer

G	Emese Hunyady	Austria
S	Svetlana Fedotkina	Russia
B	Gunda Niemann	Germany

1998 Nagano

G	Marianne Timmer	Netherlands
S	Gunda Niemann-Stirnemann	Germany
B	Christine Witty	United States

SPEED SKATING – 3,000 METERS

1960 Squaw Valley

G	Lydia Skoblikova	Soviet Union
S	Valentina Stenina	Soviet Union
B	Eevi Huttunen	Finland

1964 Innsbruck

G	Lydia Skoblikova	Soviet Union
S	Han Pil-hwa	North Korea
B	Valentina Stenina	Soviet Union

1968 Grenoble

G	Johanna Schut	Netherlands
S	Kaija Mustonen	Finland
B	Christina Kaiser	Netherlands

1972 Sapporo

G	Christina Baas-Kaiser	Netherlands
S	Dianne Holum	United States
B	Atje Keulen-Deelstra	Netherlands

1976 Innsbruck

G	Tatyana Averina	Soviet Union
S	Andrea Mitscherlich	East Germany
B	Lisbeth Korsmo	Norway

1980 Lake Placid

G	Bjørg Eva Jensen	Norway
S	Sabine Becker	East Germany
B	Beth Heiden	United States

1984 Sarajevo

G	Andrea Schöne	East Germany
S	Karin Enke	East Germany
B	Gabi Schönbrunn	East Germany

1988 Calgary

G	Yvonne van Gennip	Netherlands
S	Andrea Ehrig	East Germany
B	Gabi Zange	East Germany

1992 Albertville

G	Gunda Niemann	Germany
S	Heike Warnicke	Germany
B	Emese Hunyady	Austria

1994 Lillehammer

G	Svetlana Bazhanova	Russia
S	Emese Hunyady	Austria
B	Claudia Pechstein	Germany

1998 Nagano

G	Gunda Niemann-Stirnemann	Germany
S	Claudia Pechstein	Germany
B	Anna Friesinger	Germany

SPEED SKATING – 5,000 METERS

1988 Calgary

G	Yvonne van Gennip	Netherlands
S	Andrea Ehrig	East Germany
B	Gabi Zange	East Germany

1992 Albertville

G	Gunda Niemann	Germany
S	Heike Warnicke	Germany
B	Claudia Pechstein	Germany

1994 Lillehammer

G	Claudia Pechstein	Germany
S	Gunda Niemann	Germany
B	Hiromi Yamamoto	Japan

1998 Nagano

G	Claudia Pechstein	Germany
S	Gunda Niemann-Stirnemann	Germany
B	Lyudmila Prokasheva	Kazakhstan

SHORT TRACK SPEED SKATING – 500 METERS

1992 Albertville

G	Cathy Turner	United States
S	Li Yan	China
B	Hwang Ok-sil	North Korea

1994 Lillehammer

G	Cathy Turner	United States
S	Zhang Yanmei	China
B	Amy Peterson	United States

1998 Nagano

G	Annie Perreault	Canada
S	Yang Yang	China
B	Chun Lee-kyung	South Korea

SHORT TRACK SPEED SKATING – 1,000 METERS

1994 Lillehammer

G	Chun Lee-kyung	South Korea
S	Nathalie Lambert	Canada
B	Kim So-hee	South Korea

1998 Nagano

G	Chun Lee-kyung	South Korea
S	Yang Yang	China
B	Won Hye-kyung	South Korea

SHORT TRACK SPEED SKATING – 3,000 METER RELAY

1992 Albertville

G	Canada
S	United States
B	Commonwealth of Independent States

1994 Lillehammer

G	South Korea
S	Canada
B	United States

1998 Nagano

G	South Korea
S	China
B	Canada

ALPINE SKIING – DOWNHILL

1948 St. Moritz

G	Hedy Schlunegger	Switzerland
S	Trude Beiser	Austria
B	Resi Hammer	Austria

1952 Oslo

G	Trude Jochum-Beiser	Austria
S	Annemarie Buchner	West Germany
B	Guiliana Minuzzo	Italy

1956 Cortina

G	Madeleine Berthod	Switzerland
S	Frieda Dänzer	Switzerland
B	Lucile Wheeler	Canada

1960 Squaw Valley

G	Heidi Biebl	West Germany
S	Penelope Pitou	United States
B	Traudl Hecher	Austria

1964 Innsbruck

G	Christl Haas	Austria
S	Edith Zimmermann	Austria
B	Traudl Hecher	Austria

1968 Grenoble

G	Olga Pall	Austria
S	Isabelle Mir	France
B	Christl Haas	Austria

1972 Sapporo

G	Marie-Theres Nadig	Switzerland
S	Annemarie Pröll	Austria
B	Susan Corrock	United States

1976 Innsbruck

G	Rosi Mittermaier	West Germany
S	Brigitte Totschnigg	Austria
B	Cynthia Nelson	United States

1980 Lake Placid

G	Annemarie Moser-Pröll	Austria
S	Hanni Wenzel	Liechtenstein
B	Marie-Theres Nadig	Switzerland

1984 Sarajevo

G	Michela Figini	Switzerland
S	Maria Walliser	Switzerland
B	Olga Charvátová	Czechoslovakia

1988 Calgary

G	Marina Kiehl	West Germany
S	Brigitte Oertli	Switzerland
B	Karen Percy	Canada

1992 Albertville

G	Kerrin Lee-Gartner	Canada
S	Hilary Lindh	United States
B	Veronika Wallinger	Austria

1994 Lillehammer

G	Katja Seizinger	Germany
S	Picabo Street	United States
B	Isolde Kostner	Italy

1998 Nagano

G	Katja Seizinger	Germany
S	Pernilla Wiberg	Sweden
B	Florence Masnada	France

ALPINE SKIING – SLALOM

1948 St. Moritz

G	Gretchen Fraser	United States
S	Antoinette Meyer	Switzerland
B	Erika Mahringer	Austria

1952 Olso

G	Andrea Mead Lawrence	United States
S	Ossi Reichert	West Germany
B	Annemarie Buchner	West Germany

1956 Cortina

G	Renée Colliard	Switzerland
S	Regina Schöpf	Austria
B	Yevgenya Sidorova	Soviet Union

1960 Squaw Valley

G	Anne Heggtveit	Canada
S	Betsy Snite	United States
B	Barbara Henneberger	West Germany

1964 Innsbruck

G	Christine Goitschel	France
S	Marielle Goitschel	France
B	Jean Saubert	United States

1968 Grenoble

G	Marielle Goitschel	France
S	Nancy Greene	Canada
B	Annie Famose	France

1972 Sapporo

G	Barbara Cochran	United States
S	Danièlle Debernard	France
B	Florence Steurer	France

1976 Innsbruck

G	Rosi Mittermaier	West Germany
S	Claudia Giordani	Italy
B	Hanni Wenzel	Liechtenstein

1980 Lake Placid

G	Hanni Wenzel	Liechtenstein
S	Christa Kinshofer	West Germany
B	Erika Hess	Switzerland

1984 Sarajevo

G	Paoletta Magoni	Italy
S	Perrine Pelen	France
B	Ursula Konzett	Liechtenstein

1988 Calgary

G	Vreni Schneider	Switzerland
S	Mateja Svet	Yugoslavia
B	Christa Kinshofer-Güthlein	West Germany

1992 Albertville

G	Petra Kronberger	Austria
S	Annelise Coberger	New Zealand
B	Blanca Fernández Ochoa	Spain

1994 Lillehammer

G	Vreni Schneider	Switzerland
S	Elfriede Eder	Austria
B	Katja Koren	Slovenia

1998 Nagano

G	Hilde Gerg	Germany
S	Deborah Compagnoni	Italy
B	Zali Steggall	Australia

ALPINE SKIING – GIANT SLALOM

1952 Oslo

G	Andrea Mead Lawrence	United States
S	Dagmar Rom	Austria
B	Annemarie Buchner	West Germany

1956 Cortina

G	Ossi Reichert	West Germany
S	Josefine Frandl	Austria
B	Dorothea Hochleitner	Austria

1960 Squaw Valley

G	Yvonne Rügg	Switzerland
S	Penelope Pitou	United States
B	Guiliana Chenal-Minuzzo	Italy

1964 Innsbruck

G	Marielle Goitschel	France
S	Christine Goitschel	France
B	Jean Saubert	United States

1968 Grenoble

G	Nancy Greene	Canada
S	Annie Famose	France
B	Fernande Bochatay	Switzerland

1972 Sapporo

G	Marie-Theres Nadig	Switzerland
S	Annemarie Pröll	Austria
B	Wiltrud Drexel	Austria

1976 Innsbruck

G	Kathy Kreiner	Canada
S	Rosi Mittermaier	West Germany
B	Danièlle Debernard	France

1980 Lake Placid

G	Hanni Wenzel	Liechtenstein
S	Irene Epple	West Germany
B	Perrine Pelen	France

1984 Sarajevo

G	Debbie Armstrong	United States
S	Christin Cooper	United States
B	Perrine Pelen	France

1988 Calgary

G	Vreni Schneider	Switzerland
S	Christa Kinshofer-Güthlein	West Germany
B	Maria Walliser	Switzerland

1992 Albertville

G	Pernilla Wiberg	Sweden
S	Diann Roffe	United States
B	Anita Wachter	Austria

1994 Lillehammer

G	Deborah Compagnoni	Italy
S	Martina Ertl	Germany
B	Vreni Schneider	Switzerland

1998 Nagano

G	Deborah Compagnoni	Italy
S	Alexandra Meissnitzer	Austria
B	Katja Seizinger	Germany

ALPINE SKIING – SUPER GIANT SLALOM

1988 Calgary

G	Sigrid Wolf	Austria
S	Michela Figini	Switzerland
B	Karen Percy	Canada

1992 Albertville

G	Deborah Compagnoni	Italy
S	Carole Merle	France
B	Katja Seizinger	Germany

1994 Lillehammer

G	Diann Roffe	United States
S	Svetlana Gladisheva	Russia
B	Isolde Kostner	Italy

1998 Nagano

G	Picabo Street	United States
S	Michaela Dorfmeister	Austria
B	Alexandra Meissnitzer	Austria

ALPINE SKIING – COMBINED

1936 Garmisch

G	Christl Cranz	Germany
S	Käthe Grasegger	Germany
B	Laila Schou Nilsen	Norway

1948 St. Moritz

G	Trude Beiser	Austria
S	Gretchen Fraser	United States
B	Erika Mahringer	Austria

1988 Calgary

G	Anita Wachter	Austria
S	Brigitte Oertli	Switzerland
B	Maria Walliser	Switzerland

1992 Albertville

G	Petra Kronberger	Austria
S	Anita Wachter	Austria
B	Florence Masnada	France

1994 Lillehammer

G	Pernilla Wiberg	Sweden
S	Vreni Schneider	Switzerland
B	Alenka Dovžan	Slovenia

1998 Nagano

G	Katja Seizinger	Germany
S	Martina Ertl	Germany
B	Hilde Gerg	Germany

FREESTYLE SKIING – AERIALS

1994 Lillehammer

G	Lina Cheryazova	Uzbekistan
S	Marie Lindgren	Sweden
B	Hilde Synnøve Lid	Norway

1998 Nagano

G	Nikki Stone	United States
S	Nannan Xu	China
B	Colette Brand	Switzerland

FREESTYLE SKIING – MOGULS

1992 Albertville

G	Donna Weinbrecht	United States
S	Yelizaveta Kozhevnikova	Russia
B	Stine Lise Hattestad	Norway

1994 Lillehammer

G	Stine Lise Hattestad	Norway
S	Elizabeth McIntrye	United States
B	Yelizaveta Kozhevnikova	Russia

1998 Nagano

G	Tae Satoya	Japan
S	Tatjana Mittermayer	Germany
B	Kari Traa	Norway

NORDIC SKIING – 5 KILOMETERS (CLASSICAL)

1964 Innsbruck

G	Klavdia Boyarskikh	Soviet Union
S	Mirja Lehtonen	Finland
B	Alevtina Kolchina	Soviet Union

1968 Grenoble

G	Toini Gustafsson	Sweden
S	Galina Kulakova	Soviet Union
B	Alevtina Kolchina	Soviet Union

1972 Sapporo

G	Galina Kulakova	Soviet Union
S	Marjatta Kajosmaa	Finland
B	Helena Šikolová	Czechoslovakia

1976 Innsbruck

G	Helena Takalo	Finland
S	Raisa Smetanina	Soviet Union
B	Nina Baldycheva	Soviet Union

1980 Lake Placid

G	Raisa Smetanina	Soviet Union
S	Hilkka Riihivuori	Finland
B	Květoslava Jeriová	Czechoslovakia

1984 Sarajevo

G	Marja-Liisa Hämäläinen	Finland
S	Berit Aunli	Norway
B	Květoslava Jeriová	Czechoslovakia

1988 Calgary

G	Marjo Matikainen	Finland
S	Tamara Tikhonova	Soviet Union
B	Vida Venciené	Soviet Union

1992 Albertville

G	Marjut Lukkarinen	Finland
S	Lyubov Yegorova	Commonwealth of Independent States
B	Yelena Välbe	Commonwealth of Independent States

1994 Lillehammer (Freestyle)

G	Lyubov Yegorova	Russia
S	Manuela Di Centa	Italy
B	Marja-Liisa Kirvesniemi	Finland

1998 Nagano

G	Larissa Lazutina	Russian Federation
S	Katerina Neumannova	Czech Republic
B	Bente Martinsen	Norway

NORDIC SKIING – COMBINED PURSUIT

1992 Albertville

G	Lyubov Yegorova	Commonwealth of Independent States
S	Stefania Belmondo	Italy
B	Yelena Välbe	Commonwealth of Independent States

1994 Lillehammer

G	Lyubov Yegorova	Russia
S	Manuela Di Centa	Italy
B	Stefania Belmondo	Italy

NORDIC SKIING – 10 KILOMETERS PURSUIT/FREE

1998 Nagano

G	Larissa Lazutina	Russian Federation
S	Olga Danilova	Russian Federation
B	Katerina Neumannova	Czech Republic

NORDIC SKIING – 15 KILOMETERS (CLASSICAL)

1992 Albertville

G	Lyubov Yegorova	Commonwealth of Independent States
S	Marjut Lukkarinen	Finland
B	Yelena Välbe	Commonwealth of Independent States

1994 Lillehammer (Freestyle)

G	Manuela Di Centa	Italy
S	Lyubov Yegorova	Russia
B	Nina Gavrilyuk	Russia

1998 Nagano

G	Olga Danilova	Russian Federation
S	Larissa Lazutina	Russian Federation
B	Anita Moen-Guidon	Norway

NORDIC SKIING – 30 KILOMETERS (FREESTYLE)

1992 Albertville

G	Stefania Belmondo	Italy
S	Lyubov Yegorova	Commonwealth of Independent States
B	Yelena Välbe	Commonwealth of Independent States

1994 Lillehammer (Classical)

G	Manuela DiCenta	Italy
S	Marit Wold	Norway
B	Marja-Liisa Kirvesniemi	Finland

1998 Nagano

G	Julija Tchepalova	Russian Federation
S	Stefania Belmondo	Italy
B	Larissa Lazutina	Russian Federation

NORDIC SKIING – 4 x 5-KILOMETER RELAY

1956 Cortina (3 x 5-Kilometer)

G Finland
S Soviet Union
B Sweden

1960 Squaw Valley (3 x 5-Kilometer)

G Sweden
S Soviet Union
B Finland

1964 Innsbruck (3 x 5-Kilometer)

G Soviet Union
S Sweden
B Finland

1968 Grenoble (3 x 5-Kilometer)

G Norway
S Sweden
B Soviet Union

1972 Sapporo (3 x 5-Kilometer)

G Soviet Union
S Finland
B Norway

1976 Innsbruck

G Soviet Union
S Finland
B East Germany

1980 Lake Placid

G East Germany
S Soviet Union
B Norway

1984 Sarajevo

G Norway
S Czechoslovakia
B Finland

1988 Calgary

G Soviet Union
S Norway
B Finland

1992 Albertville

G Commonwealth of Independent States
S Norway
B Italy

1994 Lillehammer

G Russia
S Norway
B Italy

1998 Nagano

G Russian Federation
S Norway
B Italy

NORDIC SKIING – 10 KILOMETERS (CLASSICAL)

1952 Oslo

G	Lydia Wideman	Finland
S	Mirja Hietamies	Finland
B	Siiri Rantanen	Finland

1956 Cortina

G	Lyubov Kozyreva	Soviet Union
S	Radya Yeroshina	Soviet Union
B	Sonja Edström	Sweden

1960 Squaw Valley

G	Maria Gusakova	Soviet Union
S	Lyubov Baranova	Soviet Union
B	Radya Yeroshina	Soviet Union

1964 Innsbruck

G	Klavdia Boyarskikh	Soviet Union
S	Yevdoyka Mekshilo	Soviet Union
B	Maria Gusakova	Soviet Union

1968 Grenoble

G	Toini Gustafsson	Sweden
S	Berit Mördre	Norway
B	Inger Aufles	Norway

1972 Sapporo

G	Galina Kulakova	Soviet Union
S	Alevtina Olunina	Soviet Union
B	Marjatta Kajosmaa	Finland

1976 Innsbruck

G	Raisa Smetanina	Soviet Union
S	Helena Takalo	Finland
B	Galina Kulakova	Soviet Union

1980 Lake Placid

G	Barbara Petzold	East Germany
S	Hilkka Riihivuori	Finland
B	Helena Takalo	Finland

1984 Sarajevo

G	Marja-Liisa Hämäläinen	Finland
S	Raisa Smetanina	Soviet Union
B	Brit Pettersen	Norway

1988 Calgary

G	Vida Venciené	Soviet Union
S	Raisa Smetanina	Soviet Union
B	Marjo Matikainen	Finland

NORDIC SKIING – 20 KILOMETERS (FREESTYLE)

1984 Sarajevo

G	Marja-Liisa Hämäläinen	Finland
S	Raisa Smetanina	Soviet Union
B	Anne Jahren	Norway

1988 Calgary

G	Tamara Tikhonova	Soviet Union
S	Anfisa Reztsova	Soviet Union
B	Raisa Smetanina	Soviet Union

SNOWBOARDING – GIANT SLALOM

1998 Nagano

G	Karine Ruby	France
S	Heidi Renoth	Germany
B	Brigitte Koeck	Austria

SNOWBOARDING – HALFPIPE

1998 Nagano

G	Nicola Thost	Germany
S	Stine Brun Kjeldaas	Norway
B	Shannon Dunn	United States

APPENDIX C
Women's Participation in the Summer Olympics by Sport, Nation, and Continent

1900, PARIS

Total Women Participants: 22

Sport	Number of Participants
Croquet	3
Equestrian	1
Golf	10
Tennis	7
Yachting	1

Nation	Number of Participants
Bohemia	1
France	12
Great Britain	1
Switzerland	1
United States	7

Continent	Number of Participants
Europe	15
America	7

1904, ST. LOUIS

Total Women Participants: 6

Sport	Number of Participants
Archery	6

Nation	Number of Participants
United States	6

Continent	Number of Participants
America	6

1908, LONDON

Total Women Participants: 37

Sport	Number of Participants
Archery	25
Motorboating	1
Tennis	10
Yachting	1

Nation	Number of Participants
Great Britain	35
Sweden	2

Continent	Number of Participants
Europe	37

1912, STOCKHOLM

Total Women Participants: 54

Sport	Number of Participants
Swimming	40
Tennis	14

Nation	Number of Participants
Australia	2
Belgium	1
Denmark	1
Finland	2
France	1
Germany	5
Great Britain	10
Norway	3
Sweden	23

Continent	Number of Participants
Europe	52
Oceania	2

1920, ANTWERP

Total Women Participants: 65

Sport	Number of Participants
Swimming	41
Tennis	23
Yachting	1

Nation	Number of Participants
Australia	1
Belgium	9
Czechoslovakia	1
Denmark	4
France	6
Great Britain	13
Italy	1
The Netherlands	1
New Zealand	1
Norway	3

Nation	Number of Participants
South Africa	1
Sweden	11
United States	13

Continent	Number of Participants
Europe	49
America	13
Africa	1
Oceania	2

1924, PARIS

Total Women Participants: 135

Sport	Number of Participants
Fencing	25
Swimming	74
Tennis	35
Yachting	1

Nation	Number of Participants
Austria	3
Belgium	5
Czechoslovakia	4
Denmark	10
France	20
Great Britain	26
Greece	1
Hungary	3
India	1
Ireland	2
Italy	3
Luxembourg	2
The Netherlands	9
New Zealand	1
Norway	2
Poland	1
Spain	2
Sweden	13
Switzerland	4
United States	23

Continent	Number of Participants
Europe	110
America	23
Asia	1
Oceania	1

1928, AMSTERDAM

Total Women Participants: 277

Sport	Number of Participants
Athletics	96
Fencing	27
Gymnastics	58
Swimming	94
Yachting	2

Nation	Number of Participants
Australia	4
Austria	5
Belgium	12
Canada	7
Czechoslovakia	1
Denmark	9
Finland	2
France	32
Germany	31
Great Britain	29
Hungary	18
Ireland	1
Italy	18
Japan	1
Latvia	2
Lithuania	1
Luxembourg	2
The Netherlands	35
New Zealand	3
Poland	5
Romania	2
South Africa	6
Sweden	13
Switzerland	1
United States	37

Continent	Number of Participants
Europe	219
America	44
Asia	1
Africa	6
Oceania	7

1932, LOS ANGELES

Total Women Participants: 126

Sport	Number of Participants
Athletics	54
Fencing	17
Swimming	55

Nation	Number of Participants
Australia	4
Austria	2
Belgium	1
Brazil	1
Canada	17
Denmark	6
France	2
Germany	7
Great Britain	14
Hungary	2
Japan	16
Mexico	2

The Netherlands	11
New Zealand	1
Poland	3
South Africa	2
Sweden	1
United States	34

Continent	Number of Participants
Europe	49
America	54
Asia	16
Africa	2
Oceania	5

1936, BERLIN

Total Women Participants: 331

Sport	Number of Participants
Athletics	98
Fencing	41
Gymnastics	64
Swimming	125
Yachting	3

Nation	Number of Participants
Argentina	1
Australia	4
Austria	18
Belgium	5
Brazil	6
Canada	18
Chile	1
China	2
Czechoslovakia	13
Denmark	15
Finland	5
France	11
Germany	42
Great Britain	37
Greece	1
Hungary	18
Italy	13
Japan	17
The Netherlands	19
Norway	2
Poland	11
Romania	2
Sweden	7
Switzerland	5
Turkey	2
United States	41
Yugoslavia	15

Continent	Number of Participants
Europe	241
America	67
Asia	19
Africa	0
Oceania	4

1948, LONDON

Total Women Participants: 390

Sport	Number of Participants
Athletics	141
Canoeing	10
Fencing	39
Gymnastics	88
Swimming	112

Nation	Number of Participants
Argentina	11
Australia	9
Austria	26
Belgium	19
Bermuda	2
Brazil	11
Canada	15
Chile	4
Czechoslovakia	13
Denmark	18
Finland	5
France	36
Great Britain	47
Greece	1
Hungary	20
Iceland	3
Ireland	1
Italy	16
Jamaica	4
Korea, South	1
Luxembourg	3
Mexico	7
The Netherlands	34
New Zealand	1
Norway	3
Poland	4
South Africa	1
Sweden	19
Switzerland	6
Turkey	1
United States	38
Yugoslavia	11

Continent	Number of Participants
Europe	282
America	92
Asia	5
Africa	1
Oceania	10

1952, HELSINKI

Total Women Participants: 519

Sport	Number of Participants
Athletics	186
Canoeing	13
Equestrian	4
Fencing	37
Gymnastics	134
Swimming	142
Yachting	3

Nation	Number of Participants
Argentina	8
Australia	10
Austria	20
Belgium	5
Bermuda	2
Brazil	5
Bulgaria	9
Canada	10
Chile	3
Czechoslovakia	13
Denmark	14
Finland	30
France	31
Germany	32
Great Britain	44
Guatemala	1
Hong Kong	2
Hungary	27
India	4
Israel	3
Italy	23
Jamaica	2
Japan	11
Korea, South	1
Mexico	3
The Netherlands	26
New Zealand	2
Norway	6
Poland	22
Portugal	3
Romania	11
Saar	5
Singapore	1
South Africa	4
Soviet Union	40
Sweden	23
Switzerland	9
United States	41
Uruguay	1
Venezuela	2
Yugoslavia	10

Continent	Number of Participants
Europe	406
America	78
Asia	19
Africa	4
Oceania	12

1956, STOCKHOLM

Total Women Participants: 377

Sport	Number of Participants
Athletics	141
Canoeing	10
Equestrian	13
Fencing	23
Gymnastics	65
Swimming	125

Nation	Number of Participants
Argentina	1
Australia	44
Austria	5
Belgium	4
Brazil	1
Bulgaria	3
Canada	15
Chile	1
Cuba	1
Czechoslovakia	12
Denmark	6
Finland	1
France	18
Germany *	22
Great Britain	29
Hungary	20
India	1
Indonesia	2
Ireland	1
Israel	1
Italy	15
Japan	15
Kenya	1
Luxembourg	1
Malaysia	1
Mexico	3
New Zealand	8
Norway	3
Philippines	4
Poland	15
Romania	11
Singapore	2

* The German team was composed of 3 athletes from East Germany (German Democratic Republic) and 19 from West Germany (Federal Republic of Germany).

South Africa	6
Soviet Union	39
Sweden	14
United States	47
Yugoslavia	3

Continent	Number of Participants
Europe	225
America	68
Asia	25
Africa	7
Oceania	52

1960, ROME

Total Women Participants: 611

Sport	Number of Participants
Athletics	203
Canoeing	28
Equestrian	8
Fencing	78
Gymnastics	124
Swimming	170

Nation	Number of Participants
Australia	29
Austria	21
Belgium	8
Brazil	1
Bulgaria	9
Canada	11
Chile	1
Cuba	3
Czechoslovakia	17
Denmark	12
Finland	10
France	28
Germany*	56
Great Britain	46
Guyana, British	1
Hungary	27
Iceland	1
Indonesia	2
Ireland	2
Israel	6
Italy	34
Japan	20
Korea, South	1
Luxembourg	5
Mexico	6
The Netherlands	30
New Zealand	4
Norway	1
Panama	4
Philippines	4
Poland	29
Portugal	5
Puerto Rico	1
Rhodesia	5
Romania	16
South Africa	2
Soviet Union	50
Spain	11
Sweden	19
Switzerland	2
Taiwan	3
Turkey	3
United States	51
Venezuela	5
Yugoslavia	9

* The German team was composed of 30 athletes from East Germany (German Democratic Republic) and 26 from West Germany (Federal Republic of Germany).

Continent	Number of Participants
Europe	457
America	84
Asia	30
Africa	7
Oceania	33

1964, TOKYO

Total Women Participants: 678

Sport	Number of Participants
Athletics	237
Canoeing	27
Equestrian	13
Fencing	56
Gymnastics	83
Swimming	195
Volleyball	66
Yachting	1

Nation	Number of Participants
Argentina	6
Australia	39
Austria	11
Belgium	1
Brazil	1
Bulgaria	7
Canada	20
Cuba	2
Czechoslovakia	9
Denmark	7
Finland	5
France	20
Germany*	63
Ghana	3

* The German team was composed of 37 athletes from East Germany (German Democratic Republic) and 26 from West Germany (Federal Republic of Germany).

Great Britain	44
Hong Kong	1
Hungary	32
Iceland	1
India	1
Iran	4
Ireland	1
Israel	2
Italy	11
Jamaica	4
Japan	56
Korea, South	26
Luxembourg	2
Malaysia	4
Mexico	4
Mongolia	4
The Netherlands	20
New Zealand	8
Nigeria	2
Norway	2
Panama	4
Peru	1
Philippines	7
Poland	25
Portugal	1
Puerto Rico	2
Rhodesia	4
Rhodesia, North	1
Romania	30
Soviet Union	63
Spain	3
Sweden	18
Switzerland	1
Taiwan	3
Thailand	7
Uganda	2
United States	79
Venezuela	1
Yugoslavia	3

Continent	Number of Participants
Europe	382
America	124
Asia	113
Africa	12
Oceania	47

1968, MEXICO CITY

Total Women Participants: 781

Sport	Number of Participants
Athletics	241
Canoeing	29
Equestrian	21
Fencing	58
Gymnastics	102
Shooting	3
Swimming	239
Volleyball	88

Nation	Number of Participants
Argentina	5
Australia	24
Austria	8
Belgium	5
Brazil	3
Bulgaria	10
Canada	28
Chile	2
Colombia	5
Costa Rica	1
Cuba	14
Czechoslovakia	27
Denmark	4
Ecuador	1
El Salvador	8
Finland	6
France	31
Germany, East	40
Germany, West	43
Ghana	1
Great Britain	50
Hungary	32
Iceland	2
Ireland	5
Israel	3
Italy	15
Jamaica	4
Japan	25
Kenya	2
Korea, South	13
Luxembourg	2
Mexico	42
Mongolia	4
The Netherlands	25
Netherlands Antilles	2
New Zealand	5
Nigeria	5
Norway	8
Peru	13
Philippines	4
Poland	37
Portugal	1
Puerto Rico	4
Romania	16
Soviet Union	66
Spain	2
Sweden	14
Switzerland	5
Taiwan	8

United States	82
Uruguay	6
Vietnam	2
Yugoslavia	10

Continent	Number of Participants
Europe	468
America	220
Asia	56
Africa	8
Oceania	29

1972, MUNICH

Total Women Participants: 1059

Sport	Number of Participants
Archery	40
Athletics	369
Canoeing	56
Equestrian	31
Fencing	65
Gymnastics	118
Shooting	3
Swimming	284
Volleyball	93

Nation	Number of Participants
Argentina	4
Australia	29
Austria	14
Bahamas	1
Barbados	5
Belgium	6
Brazil	3
Bulgaria	23
Canada	50
Chile	2
Colombia	4
Cuba	28
Czechoslovakia	36
Denmark	12
Finland	7
France	30
Germany, East	66
Germany, West	83
Ghana	2
Great Britain	74
Greece	2
Haiti	1
Hungary	45
Iceland	1
India	1
Indonesia	3
Ireland	7
Israel	2
Italy	27
Jamaica	12
Japan	36
Kampuchea	3
Kenya	2
Korea, North	14
Korea, South	12
Lebanon	2
Luxembourg	1
Malawi	3
Malaysia	3
Mexico	22
Mongolia	2
Morocco	2
The Netherlands	28
New Zealand	7
Nicaragua	1
Nigeria	5
Norway	11
Peru	3
Philippines	5
Poland	38
Romania	27
Singapore	2
Soviet Union	73
Spain	5
Sweden	27
Switzerland	29
Taiwan	6
Trinidad and Tobago	1
Turkey	1
Uganda	2
United States	84
Uruguay	3
Venezuela	3
Yugoslavia	13
Zambia	3

Continent	Number of Participants
Europe	688
America	227
Asia	89
Africa	19
Oceania	36

1976, MONTREAL

Total Women Participants: 1260

Sport	Number of Participants
Archery	27
Athletics	303
Basketball	72
Canoeing	39
Equestrian	24
Fencing	71
Gymnastics	86

Handball	82
Rowing	204
Shooting	8
Swimming	247
Volleyball	96
Yachting	1

Nation	Number of Participants
Argentina	4
Australia	34
Austria	6
Bahamas	1
Barbados	2
Belgium	26
Bermuda	1
Brazil	7
Bulgaria	53
Canada	123
Colombia	3
Costa Rica	1
Cuba	25
Czechoslovakia	38
Denmark	10
Dominican Republic	1
Fiji	1
Finland	6
France	29
Germany, East	113
Germany, West	57
Great Britain	66
Greece	2
Guatemala	2
Haiti	3
Hong Kong	2
Hungary	54
Iceland	4
Indonesia	2
Iran	4
Ireland	3
Israel	2
Italy	27
Ivory Coast	1
Jamaica	9
Japan	60
Korea, North	2
Korea, South	12
Liechtenstein	2
Mexico	5
Mongolia	2
The Netherlands	36
New Zealand	9
Norway	6
Panama	1
Peru	13
Philippines	1
Poland	27
Puerto Rico	7
Romania	54
San Marino	3
Senegal	2
Singapore	1
Soviet Union	125
Spain	10
Sweden	17
Switzerland	3
Thailand	3
Tunisia	1
United States	118
Uruguay	2
Venezuela	9
Virgin Islands, U.S.	2
Yugoslavia	5

Continent	Number of Participants
Europe	784
America	339
Asia	89
Africa	4
Oceania	44

1980, MOSCOW

Total Women Participants: 1113

Sport	Number of Participants
Archery	29
Athletics	266
Basketball	72
Canoeing	32
Equestrian	9
Fencing	51
Gymnastics	62
Handball	83
Hockey	92
Rowing	148
Shooting	5
Swimming	175
Volleyball	88
Yachting	1

Nation	Number of Participants
Angola	1
Australia	28
Austria	19
Belgium	15
Benin	1
Brazil	15
Bulgaria	88
Cameroon	3
Congo	14

Nation	Number of Participants
Costa Rica	1
Cuba	32
Cypress	2
Czechoslovakia	47
Denmark	3
Dominican Republic	1
Ecuador	1
Ethiopia	2
Finland	6
France	23
Germany, East	124
Great Britain	70
Greece	3
Guinea	1
Hungary	81
India	16
Ireland	3
Italy	38
Jamaica	7
Korea, North	8
Laos	2
Libya	2
Madagascar	3
Mali	1
Malta	1
Mexico	10
Mongolia	4
Mozambique	2
The Netherlands	18
Nicaragua	2
Nigeria	6
Peru	14
Poland	75
Portugal	1
Romania	62
Senegal	2
Seychelles	2
Sierra Leone	2
Soviet Union	150
Spain	9
Sweden	23
Switzerland	8
Syria	2
Tanzania	5
Vietnam	8
Yugoslavia	28
Zimbabwe	20

Continent	Number of Participants
Europe	895
America	84
Asia	40
Africa	66
Oceania	28

1984, LOS ANGELES

Total Women Participants: 1566

Sport	Number of Participants
Archery	47
Athletics	386
Basketball	71
Canoeing	37
Cycling	45
Equestrian	47
Fencing	60
Gymnastics	98
Handball	82
Hockey	96
Rowing	161
Shooting	77
Swimming	261
Volleyball	96
Yachting	2

Nation	Number of Participants
Antigua	4
Argentina	10
Australia	73
Austria	31
Bahamas	5
Barbados	3
Belgium	16
Bermuda	1
Bhutan	3
Bolivia	1
Brazil	21
Cameroon	4
Canada	151
Cayman Islands	1
Chile	2
China	86
Colombia	3
Congo	1
Costa Rica	1
Denmark	11
Dominican Republic	4
Ecuador	1
Egypt	5
El Salvador	1
Fiji	3
Finland	13
France	48
Gabon	2
The Gambia	4
Germany, West	123
Ghana	7
Great Britain	106
Greece	4

Grenada	1
Guatemala	4
Guyana	2
Haiti	2
Honduras	3
Hong Kong	11
Iceland	3
India	6
Indonesia	3
Ireland	14
Israel	8
Italy	46
Ivory Coast	1
Jamaica	14
Japan	51
Jordan	1
Kenya	5
Korea, South	61
Lebanon	1
Liberia	1
Liechtenstein	2
Luxembourg	1
Malaysia	1
Malta	2
Mauritius	1
Mexico	21
Morocco	1
Mozambique	1
The Netherlands	53
Netherlands Antilles	5
New Zealand	32
Nigeria	2
Norway	19
Panama	1
Papua New Guinea	3
Peru	17
Philippines	4
Portugal	9
Puerto Rico	7
Romania	53
Rwanda	1
San Marino	1
Senegal	1
Seychelles	1
Sierra Leone	2
Spain	16
Sweden	43
Switzerland	26
Taiwan	7
Tanzania	2
Thailand	10
Trinidad and Tobago	5
Tunisia	1
Turkey	1
Uganda	2
United States	182
Uruguay	1
Venezuela	1
Virgin Islands, U.S.	3
Yugoslavia	34
Zaire	1
Zimbabwe	3

Continent	Number of Participants
Europe	683
America	478
Asia	246
Africa	48
Oceania	111

1988, SEOUL

Total Women Participants: 2194

Sport	Number of Participants
Archery	62
Athletics	554
Basketball	95
Canoeing	64
Cycling	65
Equestrian	53
Fencing	69
Gymnastics	129
Handball	111
Hockey	124
Rowing	193
Shooting	111
Swimming	330
Table Tennis	49
Tennis	48
Volleyball	93
Yachting	44

Nation	Number of Participants
Algeria	2
Angola	5
Antigua	3
Argentina	25
Aruba	4
Australia	72
Austria	7
Bahamas	4
Barbados	1
Belgium	24
Benin	1
Bermuda	1
Bolivia	1
Brazil	33
Bulgaria	67
Burkina Faso	1
Cameroon	2

Canada	105
Cayman Islands	1
Chile	1
China	125
Colombia	6
Congo	2
Cook Islands	1
Costa Rica	7
Cyprus	2
Czechoslovakia	53
Denmark	21
Dominican Republic	1
Ecuador	3
Egypt	1
El Salvador	1
Fiji	4
Finland	19
France	74
Gabon	1
The Gambia	1
Germany, East	103
Germany, West	103
Ghana	6
Great Britain	126
Greece	12
Grenada	2
Guam	5
Guatemala	3
Guinea, Equatorial	2
Guyana	1
Haiti	1
Honduras	1
Hong Kong	10
Hungary	36
Iceland	4
India	7
Indonesia	6
Ireland	9
Israel	4
Italy	41
Ivory Coast	17
Jamaica	11
Japan	68
Jordan	2
Kenya	4
Korea, South	133
Laos	1
Lebanon	2
Liberia	1
Liechtenstein	3
Luxembourg	3
Malaysia	4
Mali	1
Malta	1
Mauritius	2
Mexico	11
Monaco	1
Mongolia	4
Morocco	3
Mozambique	2
Myanmar	2
Nepal	3
The Netherlands	53
Netherlands Antilles	1
New Zealand	16
Nigeria	8
Norway	25
Papua New Guinea	2
Peru	14
Philippines	5
Poland	33
Portugal	9
Puerto Rico	3
Romania	36
Rwanda	3
Senegal	1
Sierra Leone	1
Singapore	1
Soviet Union	162
Spain	30
Sri Lanka	2
St. Vincent and Grenadines	1
Suriname	2
Sweden	37
Switzerland	27
Taiwan	18
Thailand	2
Tonga	1
Trinidad and Tobago	1
Tunisia	2
Turkey	5
Uganda	4
United States	192
Uruguay	1
Vanuatu	1
Venezuela	2
Vietnam	1
Virgin Islands, U.S.	3
Yugoslavia	38
Zaire	2
Zimbabwe	6

Continent	Number of Participants
Europe	1168
America	447
Asia	396
Africa	81
Oceania	102

1992, BARCELONA

Total Women Participants: 2705

Sport	Number of Participants
Archery	61
Athletics	621
Badminton	84
Basketball	94
Canoeing	105
Cycling	75
Equestrian	66
Fencing	71
Gymnastics	134
Handball	113
Hockey	124
Judo	165
Rowing	187
Shooting	117
Swimming	349
Table Tennis	79
Tennis	87
Volleyball	89
Yachting	84

Nation	Number of Participants
Albania	2
Algeria	2
Andorra	1
Angola	3
Antigua	4
Argentina	17
Aruba	1
Australia	92
Austria	31
Bahamas	2
Bangladesh	1
Barbados	1
Belgium	24
Belize	1
Benin	2
Bermuda	6
Bhutan	3
Bolivia	5
Bosnia-Herzegovina	3
Brazil	50
Bulgaria	47
Cameroon	5
Canada	115
Chad	1
Chile	3
China	128
Colombia	3
Com. Ind. States	64
Congo	1
Costa Rica	5
Croatia	3
Cuba	50
Cyprus	4
Czechoslovakia	65
Denmark	33
Dominican Republic	2
Ecuador	6
Egypt	3
El Salvador	1
Estonia	4
Ethiopia	6
Fiji	4
Finland	28
France	96
Gabon	1
Germany	163
Ghana	2
Great Britain	141
Greece	14
Grenada	1
Guam	6
Guatemala	2
Guinea	2
Guinea, Equatorial	2
Guyana	1
Honduras	3
Hong Kong	11
Hungary	58
Iceland	3
Indep. Olymp. Partic.	20
India	4
Indonesia	15
Ireland	9
Israel	5
Italy	76
Ivory Coast	5
Jamaica	14
Japan	79
Jordan	1
Kenya	9
Korea, North	28
Korea, South	72
Latvia	9
Lesotho	1
Liechtenstein	3
Lithuania	11
Luxembourg	1
Madagascar	5
Malawi	1
Mali	2
Malta	3
Mauritius	7
Mexico	24
Monaco	1

Mongolia	6
Morocco	1
Mozambique	3
Myanmar	3
Namibia	1
Nepal	1
The Netherlands	83
Netherlands Antilles	1
New Zealand	42
Nicaragua	1
Nigeria	23
Norway	32
Papua New Guinea	1
Paraguay	3
Peru	4
Philippines	2
Poland	52
Portugal	22
Puerto Rico	6
Romania	67
Rwanda	3
San Marino	1
Senegal	2
Seychelles	1
Sierra Leone	2
Singapore	4
Slovenia	6
South Africa	24
Spain	122
Sri Lanka	6
St. Vincent and Grenadines	4
Suriname	1
Sweden	44
Switzerland	28
Syria	1
Taiwan	8
Thailand	23
Tunisia	2
Turkey	5
Uganda	2
United States	188
Vanuatu	2
Venezuela	5
Vietnam	3
Virgin Islands, U.S.	5
Zaire	2
Zambia	1
Zimbabwe	9

Continent	Number of Participants
Europe	1484
America	535
Asia	401
Africa	138
Oceania	147

1996, ATLANTA

Total Women Participants: 3512

Sport	Number of Participants
Archery	64
Athletics	752
Badminton	96
Basketball	143
Beach Volleyball	36
Canoeing	121
Cycling	110
Diving	56
Equestrian	66
Fencing	88
Football	122
Gymnastics	193
Handball	119
Hockey	128
Judo	151
Rowing	204
Shooting	125
Softball	120
Swimming	346
Synchronized Swimming	71
Table Tennis	81
Tennis	83
Volleyball	137
Yachting	100

Nation	Number of Participants
Albania	4
Algeria	6
Andorra	2
Angola	15
Antigua	5
Argentina	47
Armenia	2
Australia	166
Austria	16
Azerbaijan	3
Bahamas	7
Bangladesh	1
Barbados	2
Belarus	65
Belgium	20
Belize	3
Benin	1
Bermuda	2
Bhutan	1
Bolivia	2
Bosnia-Herzegovina	2
Brazil	65
Bulgaria	37
Burkina Faso	2
Burundi	1

Cameroon	4
Canada	151
Cape Verde	1
Cayman Islands	1
Chad	1
Chile	5
China	187
Colombia	9
Comoros	1
Congo	2
Cook Islands	1
Costa Rica	5
Croatia	9
Cuba	53
Cyprus	2
Czech Republic	39
Denmark	65
Dominica	2
Dominican Republic	4
Ecuador	2
Egypt	2
El Salvador	2
Estonia	8
Ethiopia	8
Fiji	3
Finland	29
France	101
Gabon	1
The Gambia	1
Georgia	7
Germany	189
Ghana	2
Great Britain	116
Greece	34
Guam	2
Guatemala	1
Guinea	1
Guinea, Equatorial	1
Guyana	1
Honduras	3
Hong Kong	9
Hungary	66
Iceland	4
India	9
Indonesia	17
Iran	1
Ireland	16
Israel	7
Italy	104
Ivory Coast	1
Jamaica	19
Japan	149
Jordan	2
Kampuchea	2
Kazakhstan	24
Kenya	10
Kirgizstan	7
Korea, North	9
Korea, South	113
Laos	1
Latvia	13
Lebanon	1
Lesotho	4
Liberia	1
Liechtenstein	2
Lithuania	16
Luxembourg	4
Macedonia	3
Madagascar	7
Malaysia	3
Maldives	1
Mali	2
Malta	3
Mauritius	5
Mexico	27
Mongolia	4
Monaco	1
Morocco	2
Mozambique	1
Myanmar	1
Namibia	2
Nepal	3
The Netherlands	102
New Zealand	29
Nicaragua	1
Niger	1
Nigeria	15
Norway	54
Pakistan	1
Panama	2
Paraguay	1
Peru	14
Philippines	4
Poland	39
Portugal	24
Puerto Rico	22
Romania	67
Russian Federation	157
Saint Lucia	1
Samoa, American	1
Samoa, Western	1
San Marino	1
Seychelles	1
Sierra Leone	4
Singapore	5
Slovakia	13
Slovenia	12
Solomon Islands	1

Spain	94
Sri Lanka	4
St. Vincent and Grenadines	1
Suriname	2
Swaziland	1
Sweden	66
Switzerland	43
Syria	1
Tajikistan	2
Taiwan	42
Tanzania	1
Thailand	12
Tonga	1
Trinidad and Tobago	4
Tunisia	6
Turkey	9
Turkmenistan	3
Uganda	3
Ukraine	84
United States	270
Uruguay	2
Uzbekistan	8
Vanuatu	1
Venezuela	5
Vietnam	3
Virgin Islands, U.S.	6
Yugoslavia	9
Zaire	12
Zambia	1
Zimbabwe	1

Continent	Number of Participants
Europe	1772
America	753
Asia	628
Africa	154
Oceania	205

Compiled by Wolf Lyberg and the Olympic Museum of the International Olympic Committee

APPENDIX D
Women's Summer Olympic Participation by Nation

	1900	1904	1908	1912	1920	1924	1928	1932	1936	1948	1952	1956	1960	1964	1968	1972	1976	1980	1984	1988	1992	1996
AFRICA																						
Algeria	-	-	-	-	-	-	-	-	-	-	-	-	-	-	-	-	-	-	-	2	2	6
Angola	-	-	-	-	-	-	-	-	-	-	-	-	-	-	-	-	-	1	-	5	3	15
Benin	-	-	-	-	-	-	-	-	-	-	-	-	-	-	-	-	-	1	-	1	2	1
Burkina Faso	-	-	-	-	-	-	-	-	-	-	-	-	-	-	-	-	-	-	-	1	-	2
Burundi	-	-	-	-	-	-	-	-	-	-	-	-	-	-	-	-	-	-	-	-	-	1
Cameroon	-	-	-	-	-	-	-	-	-	-	-	-	-	-	-	-	-	3	4	2	5	4
Cape Verde	-	-	-	-	-	-	-	-	-	-	-	-	-	-	-	-	-	-	-	-	-	1
Central African Rep	-	-	-	-	-	-	-	-	-	-	-	-	-	-	-	-	-	-	-	-	2	1
Chad	-	-	-	-	-	-	-	-	-	-	-	-	-	-	-	-	-	-	-	-	1	1
Comoros	-	-	-	-	-	-	-	-	-	-	-	-	-	-	-	-	-	-	-	-	-	1
Congo	-	-	-	-	-	-	-	-	-	-	-	-	-	-	-	-	-	14	1	2	1	2
Egypt	-	-	-	-	-	-	-	-	-	-	-	-	-	-	-	-	-	-	5	1	3	2
Equatorial Guinea	-	-	-	-	-	-	-	-	-	-	-	-	-	-	-	-	-	-	-	2	2	1
Ethiopia	-	-	-	-	-	-	-	-	-	-	-	-	-	-	-	-	-	2	-	-	6	8
Gabon	-	-	-	-	-	-	-	-	-	-	-	-	-	-	-	-	-	-	2	1	1	1
Gambia, The	-	-	-	-	-	-	-	-	-	-	-	-	-	-	-	-	-	-	4	1	-	1
Ghana	-	-	-	-	-	-	-	-	-	-	-	-	-	3	1	2	-	-	7	6	2	2
Guinea	-	-	-	-	-	-	-	-	-	-	-	-	-	-	-	-	-	1	-	-	2	1
Ivory Coast	-	-	-	-	-	-	-	-	-	-	-	-	-	-	-	-	1	-	1	17	5	1
Kenya	-	-	-	-	-	-	-	-	-	-	-	1	-	-	2	2	-	-	5	4	9	10
Lesotho	-	-	-	-	-	-	-	-	-	-	-	-	-	-	-	-	-	-	-	-	1	4
Liberia	-	-	-	-	-	-	-	-	-	-	-	-	-	-	-	-	-	-	1	1	-	1
Libya	-	-	-	-	-	-	-	-	-	-	-	-	-	-	-	-	-	2	-	-	-	-
Madagascar	-	-	-	-	-	-	-	-	-	-	-	-	-	-	-	-	-	3	-	-	5	7
Malawi	-	-	-	-	-	-	-	-	-	-	-	-	-	-	-	3	-	-	-	-	1	-
Mali	-	-	-	-	-	-	-	-	-	-	-	-	-	-	-	-	-	1	-	1	2	2
Mauritius	-	-	-	-	-	-	-	-	-	-	-	-	-	-	-	-	-	-	1	2	7	5
Morocco	-	-	-	-	-	-	-	-	-	-	-	-	-	-	-	2	-	-	1	3	1	2
Mozambique	-	-	-	-	-	-	-	-	-	-	-	-	-	-	-	-	-	2	1	2	3	1
Namibia	-	-	-	-	-	-	-	-	-	-	-	-	-	-	-	-	-	-	-	-	1	2
Niger	-	-	-	-	-	-	-	-	-	-	-	-	-	-	-	-	-	-	-	-	-	1
Nigeria	-	-	-	-	-	-	-	-	-	-	-	-	-	2	5	5	-	6	2	8	23	15
Rhodesia	-	-	-	-	-	-	-	-	-	-	-	-	5	4	-	-	-	-	-	-	-	-
Rhodesia, North	-	-	-	-	-	-	-	-	-	-	-	-	-	1	-	-	-	-	-	-	-	-

	1900	1904	1908	1912	1920	1924	1928	1932	1936	1948	1952	1956	1960	1964	1968	1972	1976	1980	1984	1988	1992	1996
Rwanda	-	-	-	-	-	-	-	-	-	-	-	-	-	-	-	-	-	-	1	3	3	-
Sao Tome & Principe	-	-	-	-	-	-	-	-	-	-	-	-	-	-	-	-	-	-	-	-	-	1
Senegal	-	-	-	-	-	-	-	-	-	-	-	-	-	-	-	-	2	2	1	1	2	-
Seychelles	-	-	-	-	-	-	-	-	-	-	-	-	-	-	-	-	-	2	1	-	1	1
Sierra Leone	-	-	-	-	-	-	-	-	-	-	-	-	-	-	-	-	-	2	2	1	2	4
South Africa	-	-	-	-	1	-	6	2	-	1	4	6	2	-	-	-	-	-	-	-	24	20
Swaziland	-	-	-	-	-	-	-	-	-	-	-	-	-	-	-	-	-	-	-	-	-	1
Tanzania	-	-	-	-	-	-	-	-	-	-	-	-	-	-	-	-	-	5	2	-	-	1
Tunisia	-	-	-	-	-	-	-	-	-	-	-	-	-	-	-	-	1	-	1	2	2	6
Uganda	-	-	-	-	-	-	-	-	-	-	-	-	-	2	-	2	-	-	2	4	2	3
Zaire	-	-	-	-	-	-	-	-	-	-	-	-	-	-	-	-	-	-	1	2	2	12
Zambia	-	-	-	-	-	-	-	-	-	-	-	-	-	-	-	3	-	-	-	-	1	1
Zimbabwe	-	-	-	-	-	-	-	-	-	-	-	-	-	-	-	-	-	20	3	6	9	1
AMERICAS																						
Antigua	-	-	-	-	-	-	-	-	-	-	-	-	-	-	-	-	-	-	4	3	4	5
Argentina	-	-	-	-	-	-	-	-	1	11	8	1	-	6	5	4	4	-	10	25	17	47
Aruba	-	-	-	-	-	-	-	-	-	-	-	-	-	-	-	-	-	-	-	4	1	-
Bahamas	-	-	-	-	-	-	-	-	-	-	-	-	-	-	-	1	1	-	5	4	2	7
Barbados	-	-	-	-	-	-	-	-	-	-	-	-	-	-	-	5	2	-	3	1	1	2
Belize	-	-	-	-	-	-	-	-	-	-	-	-	-	-	-	-	-	-	-	-	1	3
Bermuda	-	-	-	-	-	-	-	-	-	2	2	-	-	-	-	-	1	-	1	1	6	2
Bolivia	-	-	-	-	-	-	-	-	-	-	-	-	-	-	-	-	-	-	1	1	5	2
Brazil	-	-	-	-	-	-	-	1	6	11	5	1	1	1	3	3	7	15	21	33	50	65
Canada	-	-	-	-	-	-	7	17	18	15	10	15	11	20	28	50	123	-	151	105	115	151
Cayman Islands	-	-	-	-	-	-	-	-	-	-	-	-	-	-	-	-	-	-	1	1	-	1
Chile	-	-	-	-	-	-	-	-	1	4	3	1	1	-	2	2	-	-	2	1	3	5
Colombia	-	-	-	-	-	-	-	-	-	-	-	-	-	-	5	4	3	-	3	6	3	9
Costa Rica	-	-	-	-	-	-	-	-	-	-	-	-	-	-	1	-	1	1	1	7	5	5
Cuba	-	-	-	-	-	-	-	-	-	-	-	1	3	2	14	28	25	32	-	-	50	53
Dominica	-	-	-	-	-	-	-	-	-	-	-	-	-	-	-	-	-	-	-	-	-	2
Dominican Republic	-	-	-	-	-	-	-	-	-	-	-	-	-	-	-	-	1	1	4	1	2	4
Ecuador	-	-	-	-	-	-	-	-	-	-	-	-	-	-	1	-	-	1	1	3	6	2
El Salvador	-	-	-	-	-	-	-	-	-	-	-	-	-	-	8	-	-	-	1	1	1	2
Grenada	-	-	-	-	-	-	-	-	-	-	-	-	-	-	-	-	-	-	1	2	1	-
Guatemala	-	-	-	-	-	-	-	-	-	-	1	-	-	-	1	-	2	-	4	3	2	1
Guyana	-	-	-	-	-	-	-	-	-	-	-	-	-	-	-	-	-	-	2	1	1	1
Guyana, British	-	-	-	-	-	-	-	-	-	-	-	-	1	-	-	-	-	-	-	-	-	-
Haiti	-	-	-	-	-	-	-	-	-	-	-	-	-	-	-	1	3	-	2	1	-	-
Honduras	-	-	-	-	-	-	-	-	-	-	-	-	-	-	-	-	-	-	3	1	3	3

	1900	1904	1908	1912	1920	1924	1928	1932	1936	1948	1952	1956	1960	1964	1968	1972	1976	1980	1984	1988	1992	1996
Jamaica	-	-	-	-	-	-	-	-	-	4	2	-	-	4	4	12	9	7	14	11	14	19
Mexico	-	-	-	-	-	-	-	2	-	7	3	3	6	4	42	22	5	10	21	11	24	27
Netherlands Antilles	-	-	-	-	-	-	-	-	-	-	-	-	-	-	2	-	-	-	5	1	1	-
Nicaragua	-	-	-	-	-	-	-	-	-	-	-	-	-	-	-	1	-	2	-	-	1	1
Panama	-	-	-	-	-	-	-	-	-	-	-	-	4	4	-	-	1	-	1	-	-	2
Paraguay	-	-	-	-	-	-	-	-	-	-	-	-	-	-	-	-	-	-	-	-	3	1
Peru	-	-	-	-	-	-	-	-	-	-	-	-	-	1	13	3	13	14	17	14	4	14
Puerto Rico	-	-	-	-	-	-	-	-	-	-	-	-	1	2	4	-	7	-	7	3	6	22
Saint Lucia	-	-	-	-	-	-	-	-	-	-	-	-	-	-	-	-	-	-	-	-	-	1
St. Kitts & Nevis	-	-	-	-	-	-	-	-	-	-	-	-	-	-	-	-	-	-	-	-	-	7
St. Vincent & Grenadines	-	-	-	-	-	-	-	-	-	-	-	-	-	-	-	-	-	-	-	1	4	1
Suriname	-	-	-	-	-	-	-	-	-	-	-	-	-	-	-	-	-	-	-	2	1	2
Trinidad & Tobago	-	-	-	-	-	-	-	-	-	-	-	-	-	-	-	1	-	-	5	1	-	4
United States	7	6	-	-	13	23	37	34	41	38	41	47	51	79	82	84	118	-	182	192	188	270
Uruguay	-	-	-	-	-	-	-	-	-	-	1	-	-	-	6	3	2	-	1	1	-	2
Venezuela	-	-	-	-	-	-	-	-	-	-	2	-	5	1	-	3	9	-	1	2	5	5
Virgin Islands, U.S.	-	-	-	-	-	-	-	-	-	-	-	-	-	-	-	-	2	-	3	3	5	6
ASIA																						
Bangladesh	-	-	-	-	-	-	-	-	-	-	-	-	-	-	-	-	-	-	-	-	1	1
Bhutan	-	-	-	-	-	-	-	-	-	-	-	-	-	-	-	-	-	-	3	-	3	1
China	-	-	-	-	-	-	-	-	2	-	-	-	-	-	-	-	-	-	86	125	128	187
Hong Kong	-	-	-	-	-	-	-	-	-	-	2	-	-	1	-	-	2	-	11	10	11	9
India	-	-	-	-	-	1	-	-	-	-	4	1	-	1	-	1	-	16	6	7	4	9
Indonesia	-	-	-	-	-	-	-	-	-	-	-	2	2	-	-	3	2	-	3	6	15	17
Iran	-	-	-	-	-	-	-	-	-	-	-	-	-	4	-	-	4	-	-	-	-	1
Israel	-	-	-	-	-	-	-	-	-	-	3	1	6	2	3	2	2	-	8	4	5	7
Japan	-	-	-	-	-	-	1	16	17	-	11	15	20	56	25	36	60	-	51	68	79	149
Jordan	-	-	-	-	-	-	-	-	-	-	-	-	-	-	-	-	-	-	1	2	1	2
Kampuchea	-	-	-	-	-	-	-	-	-	-	-	-	-	-	-	3	-	-	-	-	-	2
Kazakhstan	-	-	-	-	-	-	-	-	-	-	-	-	-	-	-	-	-	-	-	-	-	24
Kirghizstan	-	-	-	-	-	-	-	-	-	-	-	-	-	-	-	-	-	-	-	-	-	7
Korea, North	-	-	-	-	-	-	-	-	-	-	-	-	-	-	-	14	2	8	-	-	28	9
Korea, South	-	-	-	-	-	-	-	-	-	1	1	-	1	26	13	12	12	-	61	133	72	113
Laos	-	-	-	-	-	-	-	-	-	-	-	-	-	-	-	-	-	2	-	1	-	1
Lebanon	-	-	-	-	-	-	-	-	-	-	-	-	-	-	-	2	-	-	1	2	-	1
Malaysia	-	-	-	-	-	-	-	-	-	-	-	1	-	4	-	3	-	-	1	4	-	3
Maldives	-	-	-	-	-	-	-	-	-	-	-	-	-	-	-	-	-	-	-	-	1	1
Mongolia	-	-	-	-	-	-	-	-	-	-	-	-	-	4	4	2	2	4	-	4	6	4

	1900	1904	1908	1912	1920	1924	1928	1932	1936	1948	1952	1956	1960	1964	1968	1972	1976	1980	1984	1988	1992	1996
Myanmar	-	-	-	-	-	-	-	-	-	-	-	-	-	-	-	-	-	-	-	2	3	1
Nepal	-	-	-	-	-	-	-	-	-	-	-	-	-	-	-	-	-	-	-	3	1	3
Pakistan	-	-	-	-	-	-	-	-	-	-	-	-	-	-	-	-	-	-	-	-	-	1
Philippines	-	-	-	-	-	-	-	-	-	-	-	4	4	7	4	5	1	-	4	5	2	4
Singapore	-	-	-	-	-	-	-	-	-	-	1	2	-	-	-	2	1	-	-	1	4	5
Sri Lanka	-	-	-	-	-	-	-	-	-	-	-	-	-	-	-	-	-	-	-	2	6	4
Syria	-	-	-	-	-	-	-	-	-	-	-	-	-	-	-	-	-	2	-	-	1	1
Taiwan	-	-	-	-	-	-	-	-	-	-	-	-	3	3	8	6	-	-	7	18	8	42
Tajikistan	-	-	-	-	-	-	-	-	-	-	-	-	-	-	-	-	-	-	-	-	-	2
Thailand	-	-	-	-	-	-	-	-	-	-	-	-	-	7	-	-	3	-	10	2	23	12
Turkmenistan	-	-	-	-	-	-	-	-	-	-	-	-	-	-	-	-	-	-	-	-	-	3
Uzbekistan	-	-	-	-	-	-	-	-	-	-	-	-	-	-	-	-	-	-	-	-	-	8
Vietnam	-	-	-	-	-	-	-	-	-	-	-	-	-	-	2	-	-	8	-	1	3	3
EUROPE																						
Albania	-	-	-	-	-	-	-	-	-	-	-	-	-	-	-	-	-	-	-	-	2	4
Andorra	-	-	-	-	-	-	-	-	-	-	-	-	-	-	-	-	-	-	-	-	1	2
Armenia	-	-	-	-	-	-	-	-	-	-	-	-	-	-	-	-	-	-	-	-	-	2
Austria	-	-	-	-	-	3	5	2	18	26	20	5	21	11	8	14	6	19	31	7	31	16
Azerbaijan	-	-	-	-	-	-	-	-	-	-	-	-	-	-	-	-	-	-	-	-	-	3
Belarus	-	-	-	-	-	-	-	-	-	-	-	-	-	-	-	-	-	-	-	-	-	65
Belgium	-	-	-	1	9	5	12	1	5	19	5	4	8	1	5	6	26	15	16	24	24	20
Bohemia	1	-	-	-	-	-	-	-	-	-	-	-	-	-	-	-	-	-	-	-	-	-
Bosnia & Herzegovina	-	-	-	-	-	-	-	-	-	-	-	-	-	-	-	-	-	-	-	-	3	2
Bulgaria	-	-	-	-	-	-	-	-	-	-	9	3	9	7	10	23	53	88	-	67	47	37
Croatia	-	-	-	-	-	-	-	-	-	-	-	-	-	-	-	-	-	-	-	-	3	9
Cyprus	-	-	-	-	-	-	-	-	-	-	-	-	-	-	-	-	-	2	-	2	4	2
Czechoslovakia	-	-	-	-	1	4	1	-	13	13	13	12	17	9	27	36	38	47	-	53	65	-
Czech Republic	-	-	-	-	-	-	-	-	-	-	-	-	-	-	-	-	-	-	-	-	-	39
Denmark	-	-	-	1	4	10	9	6	15	18	14	6	12	7	4	12	10	3	11	21	33	65
Estonia	-	-	-	-	-	-	-	-	-	-	-	-	-	-	-	-	-	-	-	-	4	8
Finland	-	-	-	2	-	-	2	-	5	5	30	1	10	5	6	7	6	6	13	19	28	29
France	12	-	-	1	6	20	32	2	11	36	31	18	28	20	31	30	29	23	48	74	96	101
Georgia	-	-	-	-	-	-	-	-	-	-	-	-	-	-	-	-	-	-	-	-	-	7
Germany	-	-	-	5	-	-	31	7	42	-	32	22	56	63	-	-	57	-	-	-	163	189
German, East	-	-	-	-	-	-	-	-	-	-	-	-	-	-	40	66	113	124	-	103	-	-
Germany, West	-	-	-	-	-	-	-	-	-	-	-	-	-	-	43	83	-	-	123	103	-	-

	1900	1904	1908	1912	1920	1924	1928	1932	1936	1948	1952	1956	1960	1964	1968	1972	1976	1980	1984	1988	1992	1996
Great Britain	1	-	35	10	13	26	29	14	37	47	44	29	46	44	50	74	66	70	106	126	141	116
Greece	-	-	-	-	-	1	-	-	1	1	-	-	-	-	-	2	2	3	4	12	14	34
Hungary	-	-	-	-	-	3	18	2	18	20	27	20	27	32	32	45	54	81	-	36	58	66
Iceland	-	-	-	-	-	-	-	-	-	3	-	-	1	1	2	1	4	-	3	4	3	4
Ireland	-	-	-	-	-	2	1	-	-	1	-	1	2	1	5	7	3	3	14	9	9	16
Italy	-	-	-	-	1	3	18	-	13	16	23	15	34	11	15	27	27	38	46	41	76	104
Latvia	-	-	-	-	-	-	2	-	-	-	-	-	-	-	-	-	-	-	-	-	9	13
Liechtenstein	-	-	-	-	-	-	-	-	-	-	-	-	-	-	-	-	2	-	2	3	3	2
Lithuania	-	-	-	-	-	-	1	-	-	-	-	-	-	-	-	-	-	-	-	-	11	16
Luxembourg	-	-	-	-	-	2	2	-	-	3	-	1	5	2	2	1	-	-	1	3	1	4
Macedonia	-	-	-	-	-	-	-	-	-	-	-	-	-	-	-	-	-	-	-	-	-	3
Malta	-	-	-	-	-	-	-	-	-	-	-	-	-	-	-	-	-	1	2	1	3	3
Moldova	-	-	-	-	-	-	-	-	-	-	-	-	-	-	-	-	-	-	-	-	-	4
Monaco	-	-	-	-	-	-	-	-	-	-	-	-	-	-	-	-	-	-	-	1	1	1
The Netherlands	-	-	-	-	1	9	35	11	19	34	26	-	30	20	25	28	36	18	53	53	83	102
Norway	-	-	-	3	3	2	-	-	2	3	6	3	1	2	8	11	6	-	19	25	32	54
Poland	-	-	-	-	-	1	5	3	11	4	22	15	29	25	37	38	27	75	-	33	52	39
Portugal	-	-	-	-	-	-	-	-	-	-	3	-	5	1	1	-	-	1	9	9	22	24
Romania	-	-	-	-	-	-	2	-	2	-	11	11	16	30	16	27	54	62	53	36	67	67
Russia	-	-	-	-	-	-	-	-	-	-	-	-	-	-	-	-	-	-	-	-	-	157
Saar	-	-	-	-	-	-	-	-	-	-	5	-	-	-	-	-	-	-	-	-	-	-
San Marino	-	-	-	-	-	-	-	-	-	-	-	-	-	-	-	-	3	-	1	-	1	1
Slovakia	-	-	-	-	-	-	-	-	-	-	-	-	-	-	-	-	-	-	-	-	-	13
Slovenia	-	-	-	-	-	-	-	-	-	-	-	-	-	-	-	-	-	-	-	-	6	12
Soviet Union	-	-	-	-	-	-	-	-	-	-	40	39	50	63	66	73	125	150	-	162	-	-
Spain	-	-	-	-	-	2	-	-	-	-	-	-	11	3	2	5	10	9	16	30	122	94
Sweden	-	-	2	23	11	13	13	1	7	19	23	14	19	18	14	27	17	23	43	37	44	66
Switzerland	1	-	-	-	-	4	1	-	5	6	9	-	2	1	5	29	3	8	26	27	28	43
Turkey	-	-	-	-	-	-	-	-	2	1	-	-	3	-	-	1	-	-	1	5	5	9
Ukraine	-	-	-	-	-	-	-	-	-	-	-	-	-	-	-	-	-	-	-	-	-	84
Unified Team (CIS)	-	-	-	-	-	-	-	-	-	-	-	-	-	-	-	-	-	-	-	-	164	-
Yugoslavia	-	-	-	-	-	-	-	-	15	11	10	3	9	3	10	13	5	28	34	38	-	9
OCEANIA																						
Australia	-	-	-	2	1	-	4	4	4	9	10	44	29	39	24	29	34	28	73	72	92	166
Cook Islands	-	-	-	-	-	-	-	-	-	-	-	-	-	-	-	-	-	-	-	1	-	1
Fiji	-	-	-	-	-	-	-	-	-	-	-	-	-	-	-	-	1	-	3	4	4	3
Guam	-	-	-	-	-	-	-	-	-	-	-	-	-	-	-	-	-	-	-	5	6	2
New Zealand	-	-	-	-	1	1	3	1	-	1	2	8	4	8	5	7	9	-	32	16	42	29
Papua New Guinea	-	-	-	-	-	-	-	-	-	-	-	-	-	-	-	-	-	-	3	2	1	-

	1900	1904	1908	1912	1920	1924	1928	1932	1936	1948	1952	1956	1960	1964	1968	1972	1976	1980	1984	1988	1992	1996
Samoa, American	-	-	-	-	-	-	-	-	-	-	-	-	-	-	-	-	-	-	-	-	-	1
Samoa, Western	-	-	-	-	-	-	-	-	-	-	-	-	-	-	-	-	-	-	-	-	-	1
Solomon Islands	-	-	-	-	-	-	-	-	-	-	-	-	-	-	-	-	-	-	-	-	-	1
Tonga	-	-	-	-	-	-	-	-	-	-	-	-	-	-	-	-	-	-	-	1	-	1
Vanuatu	-	-	-	-	-	-	-	-	-	-	-	-	-	-	-	-	-	-	-	1	2	1

Compiled from information supplied by Wolf Lyberg and the Olympic Museum of the International Olympic Committee

APPENDIX E
Major Women's Sports Organizations

International Working Group on Women and Sport
1. The Sports Council International Affairs Unit
Walkden House
3–10 Melton Street
London, NW1 2EB
United Kingdom
Secretariat: Andreas Hansen
Tel: +44 171 383 3896
Fax: +44 171 383 3147
URL: http://www.iwg.women-and-sport.org

2. Department of Canadian Heritage (Sport Canada)
15 Eddy Street, 8th Floor
Hull, Quebec K1A OM5
Canada
Tel: 819 956 8036
Fax: 819 956 8019
Secretariat: Trice Cameron

Women's Sports Foundation (U.S.)
Eisenhower Park
East Meadow, NY 11554
Tel: 800 227 3988
Fax: 516 542 4716
URL: http://www.womenssportsfoundation.org

Women's Sports Foundation (U.K.)
305–15 Hither Green Lane
Lewisham
London, SE13 6TJ
United Kingdom
Tel/Fax: +44 181 697 5370
URL: http://www.wsf.org.uk

Islamic Countries' Women's Sports Solidarity Council
No. 10, Simin Alley, Asef St. Vali Asr Ave.
Zafaranieh, Tehran 19879 Iran
Tel: +98 21 2409932 5
Fax: +98 21 2409906 7
Contact: President, Ms. Faezeh Hashemi

International Olympic Committee/ International Working Group on Women and Sport
Chateau de Vidy, Case Postale 356
1001 Lausanne, Switzerland
Tel: +41 21 621 61 11
Fax: +41 21 621 63 54
URL: http://www.ioc.com

National Association for Girls and Women in Sport
1906 Association Drive
Reston, VA 20191-1599
Tel: 703 476 3450
Fax: 703 476 4566
URL: http://www.aahperd.org/nagws/nagws.html

International Council for Health, Physical Education, Recreation, Sport and Dance (ICHPER-SD)
1900 Association Drive
Reston, VA 20191-1599
Tel: 703 476 3462 or 703 476 3486
Fax: 703 476 9527
URL: http://www.ichpersd99.org

International Association of Physical Education and Sport for Girls and Women (IAPESGW)
Leeds Metropolitan University
Becket Park
Leeds LS6 3QS
United Kingdom
Tel: +44 113 283 7431
Fax: +44 113 283 7430
URL: http://www.udel.edu/PhysEd/bkelly/iapesgw.html

INDEX

Page numbers in **boldface** type are main entries.

D

E

G

H

J

L

Q

S

T

X

Y

Z

Date Due

SEP 2 2 2005

PRINTED IN U.S.A. CAT. NO. 24 161 BRODART